The Latin American Spirit:
Art and Artists in the United States, 1920–1970

DATE DUE

The Latin American Spirit: Art and Artists in the United States, 1920–1970

Essays by Luis R. Cancel, Jacinto Quirarte, Marimar Benítez, Nelly Perazzo, Lowery S. Sims, Eva Cockcroft, Félix Angel, and Carla Stellweg

The Bronx Museum of the Arts in association with Harry N. Abrams, Inc., Publishers, New York

This book is dedicated to Dr. Stanton L. Catlin in recognition of his continuing and vital contributions to Latin American scholarship over the past fifty years.

Published in connection with a traveling exhibition: sponsored by The Bronx Museum of the Arts.
Exhibition venues:
The Bronx Museum of the Arts, September 29, 1988–January 29,1989
El Paso Museum of Art, February 27, 1989– April 23, 1989
San Diego Museum of Art, May 22, 1989– July 16, 1989
Instituto de Cultura Puertorriqueña, San Juan, August 14, 1989–October 8, 1989
Center for the Arts, Vero Beach, Florida, January 28, 1990–March 31, 1990

This exhibition was made possible by the generous support of Philip Morris Companies Inc.

Additional support for the exhibition and catalog were provided by:
The Rockefeller Foundation
The Ford Foundation
National Endowment for the Humanities
National Endowment for the Arts
New York State Council on the Arts
New York Council on the Humanities
The Altman Foundation
Integrated Resources, Inc.
Reliance Group Holdings

This exhibition is supported by an indemnity from the Federal Council on the Arts.

The Bronx Museum of the Arts receives general operating support from the Department of Cultural Affairs of the City of New York with the cooperation of Bronx Borough President Fernando Ferrer.

On the Title Page: Candido Portinari. *Prospecting. Sketch for "Discovery of the Americas" (mural at The Hispanic Foundation, The Library of Congress, Washington, D.C.).* 1941. Gouache on paper, 11⅝ x 11⅜. Prints and Photographs Division, The Library of Congress, Washington, D.C. Photo: courtesy The Library of Congress

Library of Congress Cataloging-in-Publication Data

The Latin American spirit.
 Bibliography: p.
 Includes index.
 1. Art, Latin American—United States. 2. Art, Modern—20th century—United States. 3. Artists— Latin America. 4. Artists—United States. I. Quirarte, Jacinto, 1931–
N6538.L3L38 1988   704'.0368073   88-6267
ISBN 0-8109-1271-6
ISBN 0-8109-2406-4 (pbk.)

Copyright ©1988 The Bronx Museum of the Arts
Published in 1988 by Harry N. Abrams, Incorporated, New York
All rights reserved. No parts of the contents of this book may be reproduced without the written permission of the publisher
A Times Mirror Company
Printed and bound in Japan

The Latin American Spirit is also available in a Spanish-language edition

Editor: Charles Miers
Designer: Franchini & Cabana, Inc., New York City

Contents

Exhibition Sponsor's Statement

The Latin American Spirit: Art and Artists in the United States, 1920–1970 recognizes the vital contributions of Latin Americans to world cultures and is a valuable statement in the cultural dialogue between Latin America and the United States.

Philip Morris has a long-standing commitment to Latin Americans as customers and employees. We support a broad range of Hispanic cultural and civic activities on the simple premise that if companies are to prosper, all segments of society must be kept strong.

We are proud to help bring this art to the widest possible audience and hope you enjoy this part of our priceless Latin American heritage.

Hamish Maxwell
Chairman and Chief Executive Officer
Philip Morris Companies Inc.

Introduction

by Luis R. Cancel

At the outset of this publication I want to state what the goals of the The Bronx Museum of the Arts have been in organizing the exhibition and publication *The Latin American Spirit: Art and Artists in the United States, 1920-1970:*

I. To document and examine the participation of Latin American artists in the cultural life of the United States over a fifty-year period.

II. To demonstrate how broadly based the Latin American participation has been, including the contributions by artists not generally mentioned by U.S. critics and art historians.

III. To record and evince the cultural activity of Puerto Rican artists, as Latin Americans, both on the island and in the continental United States.

Despite the ambitious scale of this project it is not intended to be definitive, but rather to stimulate the organization of other exhibitions and to indicate directions for more detailed research along the lines of the thematic issues touched upon here. Although much new material is brought forth here, there still exists a substantial history worthy of continued investigation. From the outset, this exhibition was designed to examine a very specific slice of American art history as it was played out by Latin American and Hispanic American artists. Artistic "presence" in the United States is the central tenet; but during the course of the fifty years under review, there have been literally thousands of Latin American artists who have exhibited in the United States. This fact necessitated the establishment of certain criteria for the inclusion of an artist in the book and exhibition. The six art historical categories that constitute the project—Constructivism and geometric art, socially concerned Latin American art, New World Surrealism, abstraction, figuration and Realism, and the multifaceted art of the 1960s—share the same basic premise: each of the selected artists had a prolonged and substantive professional career as an artist in the United States, including numerous exhibitions, the receipt of commissions, grants and fellowships, reviews by the critical media, etc. One or two group shows or undergraduate study alone was not sufficient for inclusion. This clearly removed from consideration many talented and, in some cases, significant artists from south of the border who never were directly involved with this country or who were present here before 1920 or after 1970. Important artists such as Anita Malfati (Brazil), who was active in New York in 1917, and Claudio Bravo (Chile), who first showed at Marlborough Gallery in 1971, have therefore been omitted. This still left a very sizable group, larger than would be realistically possible to include in one exhibition, outside of the final selection. This is one of the reasons why this exhibition and publication are not definitive. It would be presumptuous to suggest that there is a "short list" of artists worthy of attention: the pool of talented artists in this period is vast and worthy of additional review. The Bronx Museum hopes that by providing this broad "road map," scholars will make their own ancillary investigations. It is through the cumulative effect of these various independent research efforts that "definitiveness" emerges.

The decisions to organize the exhibition into six stylistic groups and to limit it to the period from 1920 to 1970 emerged after holding a series of long and stimulating planning meetings at The Bronx Museum involving many scholars. Through these conversations, a consensus slowly emerged that recognized Latin American artists had usually been presented and discussed by North American critics and curators in ways that placed undue emphasis either on national boundaries or on the notion that there exists some globally unifying style called "Latin American art." Some of the elements that supposedly constitute that art are brash colors, violent or energetically gestural brushwork, and "nativist" or folklorist references. In the quest to establish this unifying aesthetic, those artists whose styles did not conform to these preconceived notions were considered problems and therefore often ignored. Artists such as Amilcar de Castro, whose minimal sculptures emerged from the Brazilian Concrete and Neo-Concrete movements of the 1950s and 1960s, were considered "derivative" of American and Western European artists who were working contemporaneously. During his short stay in New York in the 1960s, his sculptures were not once shown to derive from a vigorous intellectual movement in his native Brazil, which also included architects and poets.

One can cite dozens of similar examples in the experiences of Latin artists. They were typecast as members of the "Bold and Colorful" movement, or their work was dismissed as derivative of prevalent art movements. In either case, the contributions of these artists have been undervalued, and their personal histories have been overlooked by art historians. They are the "Invisible Men" (and women) of twentieth-century art history. Part of the goal of this exhibition and publication, therefore, is to challenge the standing premise under which Latin American art is discussed in this country. The stylistic structure of the exhibition is our attempt to encourage art historians and critics to include the works of Latin American artists when they are discussing formalist topics and to break with the earlier notion that Latin American art is monolithic in nature.

Furthermore, the essays have been written to convey historical data on the activities of these artists in the United States as a way of providing a context for further scholarly research on these artists. Where did the artist come from? What personal and cultural forces have a bearing on the art that he or she produced? This book will serve as the starting point in the quest to answer such questions about most of these artists.

The fifty years the exhibition embraces covers a complex period in art history, but from the exhibition organizers' point of view, the activities of the Latin American artists could be discussed within the formal categories already described. After 1970 the numbers of artists and the variety of movements increases to such an extent that the exhibition would have become unwieldy, obscuring the earlier histories that are being resurrected.

In our efforts to facilitate a deeper understanding of the issue of context, additional essays were included to provide social and historical information on the two largest Hispanic population groups in the United States. Jacinto Quirarte, who has already written two books on the activities of Mexican American artists, has contributed a useful overview of the interrelationship between Mexican, Mexican American, and American artists. Marimar Benítez accepted the challenging task of providing both a historical framework for understanding the relationship that exists between the United States and Puerto Rico and conveying a synoptic art history course on the activities of Puerto Rican artists—most of whom are totally unknown to audiences outside of the island.

The origins of this exhibition date back to my undergraduate days in the early 1970s, when I first wanted to learn more about my Puerto Rican heritage and Latin American art in general. What started out as simple undergraduate curiosity evolved into a passionate mission—perhaps a bit too evangelical at times—to eliminate some of the basic obstacles that confronted me. I share the following personal experience in order to illustrate a broader general condition that still exists and that this exhibition and publication attempt to redress in part. Both as an undergraduate (Pratt Institute) and graduate student (Columbia University and New York University) I was unable to find any art history courses at the schools I attended that addressed my interest in twentieth-century Latin American or Puerto Rican art. If I had been interested in the history, literature, or pre-Columbian cultures of this region, I would have fared considerably better, and as a consolation I did take several courses in those areas. But in my field of choice, in the area of knowledge I truly thirsted for, I had to resort to self-education, independent research, and the marshaling of a diverse group of resources, including fellowships and special exhibition grants, to satisfy my intellectual interest in the Latin American art of our century.

What does this illustrate? At some of the most prestigious and influential art history departments in the country—where past, present, and future curators, museum directors, and art critics interact—there is virtually no exposure to the rich and complex art history that exists south of the Rio Grande. Eighty-five to ninety percent of the course offerings at the Institute of Fine Arts at N.Y.U., for example, concern European and other Western cultural history. I am sure the institute is not unique in this regard. Since it helps to form the movers and shakers of the American art world—the very group that is responsible for the organization of museum exhibitions and publications on Western material culture—its graduates will have had little or no exposure to the postcolonial cultures of most of the Western Hemisphere. It should not be surprising, therefore, that there is a paucity of exhibitions or publications on this subject. What exists are mostly monographs on individual artists who, for a combination of reasons, are viewed as having "risen above" their cultural context and therefore worthy of study.

The implications of this are significant when you consider what is at stake: the ability of U.S. citizens to understand Latin American culture and society and to promote hemispheric cooperation. The "Latin" stereotypes that exist in the minds of most North Americans are generally shaped by what sources are available to them: newspaper stories or popular films and television shows that almost never discuss cultural issues: on the rare occasion when they do, they will invariably cover either the pre-Columbian or the colonial period. In the popular imagination then, Latin American cultural history has yet to enter the twentieth century. Only art history doctoral students, whose theses are specifically focused on a Latin American artist, or private collectors will deviate from this perceptual mold of contemporary life south of the border.

I don't think I belie the truth when I say that most Americans have no idea what Latin American movements or artists have been important to twentieth-century art. This lack of knowledge also applies to most undergraduate and graduates of American art history departments who possess at best a superficial knowledge of a handful of artists from that region. One of the central goals of this exhibition then is to go beyond the seven or eight names that come to mind when one discusses Latin American art: first, *los tres grandes*, Rivera, Siqueiros, Orozco (who are very often thought of as one persona with little differentiation between their individual histories); then Torres-García, Matta, Lam, Tamayo, Botero, and, since the feminist movement, Frida Kahlo. This exhibition attempts to broaden that limited perspective and to document an aspect of American art history that has been buried in archives, filing cabinets, and fine-art storage areas.

One of the important insights one can glean from this exhibition is the cyclical nature of the American fascination with Latin America. The essays by Eva Cockcroft, Jacinto Quirarte, and Félix Angel in the present volume give an overview of periodic waves of exhibitions in American museums. These museum exhibitions represent the peaks of a broader social and political interest in specific regions at various times in American history. During the 1930s and 1940s there were a number of major exhibitions organized by numerous American museums that focused on the artists and culture of Mexico. This was at a time when Washington was concerned with the rising tide of fascism in Europe and wanted to bolster hemispheric solidarity. To cite a few exhibition examples: the Metropolitan Museum of Art, *New York Mexican Arts* (1930–31); The Museum of Modern Art, New York, *Diego Rivera* (1931–32) and *Twenty Centuries of Mexican Art* (1940); Detroit Institute of Arts, *Diego Rivera* (1931); and the Institute of Modern Art, Boston, *Modern Mexican Painters* (1941). Similar exhibitions were held in major museums in Philadelphia (1939, 1943), San Francisco (1939), and many other cities. Often, these exhibitions, sometimes consisting of thousands of objects, would travel to five or six American venues, thus providing tremendous exposure.

Likewise, after the Cuban Missile Crisis of 1962 and the formation of the Alliance for Progress in 1961, a similar wave of Latin American exhibitions materialized both in American museums and galleries. At that time it was Washington's concern with Communist movements in Latin America that momentarily focused our attention south. That upsurge was short-lived and was not as broadly based as that of the late 1930s and 1940s. Within the last two years another upswing in the organization of Latin American exhibitions has begun, and South and Central America are once again the focus of the U.S. media and popular attention. The Detroit Institute of Arts organized a major retrospective on Diego Rivera, the Houston Museum of Fine Arts and the Corcoran Gallery collaborated on the exhibition *Hispanics in the United States*, which is circulating widely, and every monthly art publication brings us news of one-person shows by both mature and younger Latin American artists. Will the current wave survive long? If history repeats itself the wave will probably crest within a year or so. And yet there is an opportunity to gain some lasting beneficial effects from the current crop of activity. If serious efforts are made to enlist educators to follow up with activities in the public schools and in art history departments, then the knowledge base with respect to Latin American art and culture can be broadened. What is disheartening, though, is the manner in which the art historical data from the earlier peak periods of interest were treated during the nadir years: Latin America just dropped off the art historical map. Later, new generations of curators and audiences had to "discover" Latin American art all over again.

This brings me to what may be the most controversial of the three goals I mentioned at the outset: the elucidation of the cultural activity of Puerto Rican artists. Why should a straightforward exposition of historical data be so emotionally charged? Because it goes to the root of the legal and political question of the status of Puerto Rico as a body politic. Puerto Rican art and artists are unknown in this country due in large measure to the fact that their cultural activity is not considered part of American art history by North American scholars—they uniformly say it is part of Latin America—and Latin American art historians consider Puerto Rico a part of the United States and therefore none of their concern. Only the Colombian critic Marta Traba attempted to situate Puerto Rican art in a Latin American context. Most critics and art historians from both continents, however, have ignored whatever took place in the visual arts on the island.

Additionally, Puerto Rican artists collectively tend to have strong views on the issue of the commonwealth's status. The vast majority favor independence for the island. Their sympathies for that political position gave birth in the 1950s to an influential school of artists centered in San Juan who identified with the independence movement and embraced a very populist and social role for their art. Three role models: Lorenzo Homar, Rafael Tufiño, and Carlos Raquel Rivera, although acutely aware of international art movements, spurned any identification with the "metropolis" and pursued their creative activities in defiance of mainstream art. They were important artists who would exhibit and achieve recognition in international exhibitions in Europe and Central and South America, especially through their graphic work, but they would not pursue exhibition opportunities in the United States. This posture was prevalent among their generation and continues to be so among Puerto Rican artists today.

Two powerful factors—the ambiguous role of Puerto Rico among nations and the artists' objections to being identified with the metropolis—have contributed to the lack of critical literature on Puerto Rican art. Several of the Puerto Rican artists who will be discussed in the thematic sections and in Ms. Benítez's essay may initially react with concern at seeing themselves placed in a North American art historical context. But the premise of this exhibition—to document the activity of Latin American artists in the United States—is not conditioned to mean only "mainland" United States but also to include Puerto Rico. Therefore, Puerto Rican artists on the island, *as Latin Americans*, have contributed to this history, irrespective of whether they were setting their sights on the continental United States or embracing the rest of the world. In historical and humanistic terms, Puerto Rico is part of Latin America, and its literature, poetry, and music have found ready acceptance as such. Only in the visual arts, where the language is universal and therefore not obviously Hispanic, is this issue of categorization such an obstacle to the diffusion of their culture.

One can argue the political and moral issues of whether or not Puerto Rico should be part of the United States, but for all intents and purposes, since the Treaty of Paris in 1898 Puerto Rico has been linked to this country, and since the Jones Act of 1917 every Puerto Rican is born a citizen of the United States. The organizers therefore felt that the Commonwealth of Puerto Rico should not be excluded when examining the

(left to right) Antonio Torres-Martino, Lorenzo Homar, Rafael Tufiño, Julio Rosado del Valle. Centro Cultural Puertorriqueño, 1950

role of Latin American artists in the United States.

This exhibition may not succeed in convincing Puerto Rican artists and American art historians to reevaluate their positions with respect to the inclusion of Puerto Rican artists in general art history texts; but for those who are willing, it does help to point the way toward a rich and exciting culture that has received very little critical attention.

The Latin American Spirit has from its inception been viewed by its organizers as an ambitious, high-stakes venture aiming to redefine the way Latin American art is viewed and discussed in this country, opening up the playing field so that many other Latin American artists could be reexamined—a venture that goes beyond the accumulation of pretty pictures, an exhibition that will ask more from its viewers than just a passing visit. For the curatorial team and myself, it has been an instructive and exciting journey. I hope some of that excitement will be conveyed to you.

Acknowledgments

As I retrace the evolution of this project, two trustees of The Bronx Museum of the Arts stand out for playing particularly important roles in securing the early and generous support of Philip Morris Companies Inc. They are Jane Lee Garcia, past president of the board of trustees, and Frank Saunders, who until 1985 was vice-president of Cultural Affairs at Philip Morris and is currently president of the museum's board of trustees. Their enthusiastic endorsement of the *The Latin American Spirit* enticed George Weissman and Hamish Maxwell, chief executive officers of Philip Morris in 1978 and 1984 respectively, to lend major support to the exhibition and this publication.

The first grant in support of the exhibition came in 1984 from the Museum Program of the National Endowment for the Arts. Drew Oliver, director of the Museum Program, the program's staff, and the Special Exhibitions Panel are to be commended for having had the vision to support a project that in form and content was still evolving. Additionally, the chairman of the NEA, Frank Hodsoll, provided a Chairman's Grant and a Museum Fellowship that permitted me to meet private collectors, museum colleagues, and artists in Argentina, Brazil, France, Mexico, Puerto Rico, Uruguay, and Venezuela. Thanks to his support, The Bronx Museum has been able to forge strong links with museums and individuals involved in Latin American art.

The early substantive support enabled the museum to bring together an international group of scholars, who met in New York on five occasions over a three-year research period. Three scholars in particular deserve special recognition for having survived this marathon: Jacinto Quirarte, director of the Research Center for Arts and Humanities at the University of Texas at San Antonio; Marimar Benítez, art critic and art historian (formerly of the Museo de Arte de Ponce); and Laurence Hurlburt, art historian, who was one of several Latin American specialists brought in to challenge and refine the theoretical premise of the exhibition. Also joining us at an early stage was Stanton L. Catlin, professor emeritus of the History of Art at Syracuse University. Dr. Catlin always asked the toughest questions, provided valuable insights, and helped to mold a more rational basis for the selection of artists and topics. He was the project's intellectual mentor, and he helped open many doors for the museum both in Latin America, where he is revered, and in the United States. Jacqueline Barnitz, lecturer in Art History at the University of Texas at Austin, joined Dr. Catlin in making valuable suggestions to the final text. Donald Goodall, a Latin American art specialist, who gave much of his time in the early stages of the project, was also part of the original consulting team.

I want to thank the contributing essayists: Félix Angel, curator for Temporary Exhibitions at the Museum of Modern Art of Latin America, Washington, D.C.; Eva Cockcroft, adjunct associate professor at the Center for Latin American and Caribbean Studies, New York University; Nelly Perazzo, professor of the History of Art at . Salvador University in Buenos Aires; Lowery S. Sims, associate curator of Twentieth-Century Art at the Metropolitan Museum of Art; and Carla Stellweg, curator at the Museum of Contemporary Hispanic Art in New York. All of the contributors came into the project when it was already at an advanced stage and worked under extraordinary time limitations.

Armando Colina and Victor Acuña of the Galería Arvil in Mexico City, Clara Diament Sujo of the C.D.S. Gallery in New York, and Thomas M. Messer, director of the Solomon R. Guggenheim Museum in New York, each played a significant role in helping to secure loans of important works of art. The quality and variety of works in the exhibition is due in large measure to the personal intervention of these three individuals and their institutions. The viewing public and the curatorial staff of the museum are deeply in their debt.

The Bronx Museum is extremely grateful to the funders of this exhibition. Ruth Mayleas of the Ford Foundation offered early support that helped ensure this publication would appear in separate English and Spanish editions. At the National Endowment for the Humanities, Donald Gibson, director of the Division of General Programs, provided important advice about the proposal. Alberta Arthurs, director for Arts and Humanities of the Rockefeller Foundation, and Steve Lavine, associate director of the foundation, provided support for the catalog and have long been leading supporters of discussions fostering a deeper examination of African, Latin American, and Asian cultures. I also thank the museum's trustee Jack Berger for his assistance with South American contacts, and Jack E. Bronston, who helped to secure additional support for this exhibition from Selig Jay and Seymour Zises of Integrated Resources, Inc., and from Saul Steinberg of Reliance Group Holdings. Jay Kaplan, director of the New York Council on the Humanities, assisted the museum in overcoming a number of technical obstacles. Ward Mintz, former director of the Museum Program of the New York State Council on the Arts was also very encouraging. Karen Rosa, program officer with the Altman Foundation, has been an enthusiastic supporter of the educational potential of the exhibition. Finally, I want to thank Bronx Borough President Fernando Ferrer and the Department of Cultural Affairs of the City of New York for the important general operating support The Bronx Museum receives each year.

The staff of The Bronx Museum has worked very diligently on this project since its inception. My primary aide-de-camp on this and many other projects has been the chief curator of the museum, Philip Verre. Assisting him have been Margaret Rennie, the museum's registrar, and Laura Hoptman, assistant curator, both of whom have given invaluable service. Jeffrey Ramirez and Carmen Ruíz de Fischler worked on the educational component of the exhibition, as did Carlos de Jesús. Anna Rank has worked long and hard on various phases of this project, and Rosemary O'Neil, Maria Fernández, Laura Hoptman, and Cynthia Fusillo spent many hours doing research for the extensive biographies that accompany this volume.

My special thanks go to those responsible for the publication of this book: Paul Gottlieb, president and publisher, and Charles Miers, editor, at Harry N. Abrams, Inc., for their expertise, patience, and dedication to this project; and to Alessandro Franchini of Franchini & Cabana who designed the book. For their work on the Spanish edition of the book, my thanks to Ralph Dimick and particularly to Nicolás Kanellos of Arte Publico Press in Houston, who along with his expert team of Julián Olivares and Edith Pross translated the text. Lucian Leone was responsible for the exhibition design at The Bronx Museum.

Numerous other individuals assisted us and deserve special mention. In the United States: Franklin Robinson, director of the Museum of Art at the Rhode Island School of Design; Marifé Hernandez, president of the Cultural Communications Group; Mary-Anne Martin of Mary-Anne Martin Fine Arts; David de la Torre, director of the Mexican Museum in San Francisco; Petra Barreras, director, and Rafael Colón-Morales, curator of El Museo del Barrio in New York; Eric McCready, director of the Huntington Art Gallery of the University of Texas at Austin; William Luers, president, Richard Mülberger, vice-director of Education Services, and William Lieberman, curator of Twentieth-Century Art at the Metropolitan Museum of Art; John Stringer, former visual arts director for the Americas Society; Fernanda Bonino of the Bonino Gallery; Jaime Davidovich; Juan Downey; and Irving MacManus.

In Argentina: Marcos Curi, director of the Museo de Arte Contemporáneo in Buenos Aires; Adriana Bianco; Guillermo Whitelow; Roberto del Villano, director of the Museo de Arte Moderno; Blanca Carusillo; and Hernán Dompé; Jorge Helft, president of the Fundación San Telmo; Julia Lublin of the Galería del Retiro; Jacques Martínez of the Galería Jacques Martínez; Ruth Benzacar of Galería Ruth Benzacar; Jorge Glusberg, director of the Centro de Arte y Comunicación; Laura Bucellato; Daniel Martínez, director of the Museo Nacional de Bellas Artes; Nelida Secreto; Silvia de Ambrosini; Helena Stern; and Cultural Attaché Merrie Blocker of the U.S. embassy in Buenos Aires, who provided much needed logistical support.

In Rio de Janeiro, Brazil: Luciano Figueiredo and Thomas Valentin of Projecto HO; Paolo Herkenhoff, director of the Museu de Arte Moderna; Gilberto Chateaubriand; Christina Scarabôtolo Penna, adjunct director of the Projecto Portinari; Alcidio Mafra de Souza, director of the Museu Nacional de Belas Artes; Gloria Ferreira of Funarte; and Rubens Gerchman. In São Paulo: Aracy Amaral; Pietro Maria Bardi, director of the Museu do Arte de São Paulo; Denise Mattar, director Museu do Arte Moderna; Ivo Mesquita of the Fundação Bienal de São Paulo; Paulina Nemirovsky of the Fundação José e Paulina Nemirovsky; Francis Switt and Maria Estela Segatto Corrêa of the U.S. embassy; Maria Elvira Iriarte; Eduardo Ramírez Villamizar; Manabu Mabe; Marcelo and Sonia Grassmann; Aurea Pereira da Silva; and Noêmia Vasconcelos.

In France: Ms. Denise René of Denise René Gallery; Enrique Zañartu; Frank Spath, assistant to Carlos Cruz-Diez; Mrs. Jesús Soto; Marie Odell Briot.

In Mexico: Ambassador Jorge Alberto Lozoya of the Ministry of Foreign Affairs; Lic. Manuel de la Cera, director of the Instituto Nacional de Bellas Artes; Lic. Jorge Bribiesca, director of Artes Plasticas, INBA; Dr. Luz del Amo, director, Relaciones Exteriores of the Ministry of Foreign Affairs; Jorge Alberto Manrique, former director of Museo de Arte Moderno; F. Javier Martínez, director of Museo de Monterrey; Lic. Cristina Galvez, director of the Museo Rufino Tamayo; Silvia Pandolfi, director of the Museo Carrillo Gil; Patricia Feria and photographer Gerardo Suter of Galería Arvil; Jorge Thompson; Francisco and Laura Osio; Elva Podesta de Holm; Mr. and Mrs. Marcos Micha; Angel Cristóbal; Dr. Alma Elizabeth del Rio; Enrique Beraha; Ing. Joaquín Zendejas and Rosa Maria Quijano Méndez; and Ignacio Duran Loera, minister for Cultural Affairs at the Mexican embassy in Washington, D.C. We also appreciate the help in New York of the Mexican Consulate, ambassador Joaquín Bernal, Mireya Teran, and Theodore Maus.

In Puerto Rico: Antonio Martorell; Myrna Báez; Osiris Delgado; Eliaz Lopez Sobá, director of the Instituto de Cultura Puertorriqueña; Ricardo Alegria, director of Centro de Estudios Avanzados de Puerto Rico y el Caribe; Ernesto Ruiz de la Matta; and Johnny Betancourt, who assisted us in many ways, including photography.

In Uruguay: Angel Kalemberg, director of the Museo Nacional de Artes Plásticas; Anne V. Stenzel of the U.S. embassy in Montevideo; Sra. Elena Faget Figari de la Force; Mario César Tempone, director of the Museo Blanes; Alicia Haber de Porxecanski; Ing. Gustavo Lorieto Díaz; and Augusto Torres.

In Venezuela: Don Alfredo Boulton; Mr. and Mrs. Pedro Perez Lazo; Miguel Angel and Magaly Capriles; Sofia Imber, director, and Susan Benito, Beatriz Hernández, and Rita Savetrini of the Museo de Arte Contemporáneo de Caracas; Nelson Bocaranda; Graziana la Rocca; Ivan Lansberg Henriques; Roger Boulton; Stephanie Smith Kinney, Laura Celis, Guy W. Farmer, Beatrice Friere of the U.S. embassy; Axel Stein, director of the Fundación Mendoza; Luisa Palacios, artist and director of TAGA; Leopoldo Sucre Figarella, president of EDELCA; Alejandro Otero; Carlos Cruz Delgado, Francisco Ramírez, and José García from the studio of Carlos Cruz-Diez; and my good friends Hugo and Helena Brillembourg, who helped me to meet Caracas society.

Finally, I wish to thank my wife, Rose, and my son, John, for accepting my long absences while I worked on this exhibition.

Luis R. Cancel
Director,
The Bronx Museum of the Arts

Mexican and Mexican American Artists in the United States: 1920–1970

by Jacinto Quirarte

Nineteen twenty marks the beginning of the modern period of Mexican art. It was a time in Mexico when efforts were being made to create a truly Mexican art, an art that would reflect the national character and culture. The birth of that art, which was initially seen in mural paintings and later in the graphic arts as well, can be attributed to the Mexican Revolution of 1910 and the desire of the artists and their supporters in the government to create an art that would serve the needs of the people. The revolution had led to the destruction of the thirty-year dictatorship of Porfirio Díaz and the creation of a constitutional government whose primary aim was to give the vast majority of the Mexican people hitherto inaccessible opportunities in the economic, political, and educational spheres of the nation. The purpose and function of the new art was to educate the Mexican people and to create a Mexican national identity. The motifs and themes used by the artists in their murals, drawings, and prints revolved mainly around the history of Mexico, although other areas of Mexican life were eventually included in these works. The practitioners of this art became known as the Mexican School.

The new art, which led to a new Mexican "style," was also informed by developments in Europe, where African and Oceanic art, the art of the untrained (naive or self-taught artists), children's drawings, and even images made by the insane were being "legitimized" and elevated to the status of high art. The nationalistic tendencies in Mexico combined with the new orientation of the art world aroused interest in Indian arts and crafts, pre-Columbian art, and the work of earlier "authentic" Mexican talents, such as the *retablo* (votive or ex-voto) painters and the printmaker José Guadalupe Posada (1851–1913). These were the thematic and formal sources used by the Mexican School to create a distinctive Mexican style. The new artists made a conscious break with their immediate predecessors, who had simply echoed European Neoclassicism, Romanticism, Impressionism, Fauvism, or Cubism, albeit occasionally focusing on "Mexican" subjects in their works. Ultimately, the aim of the new Mexican artists was to create an art that was based on Mexican reality and experience.

The mural was selected by the Mexican School artists as the medium best suited to achieve an art that represented the national identity. Among those who championed muralist art at an early date was Gerardo Murillo Cornadó, known as Dr. Atl. As early as 1910 he spoke of the need for an artistic center that would promote the painting of murals.[1] As a result of the chaos caused by the revolution, however, efforts to organize the new Mexican artists splintered until 1920. In the summer of that year a number of events signaled the changes that would take place in Mexico in the early 1920s. José Vasconcelos was appointed president of the National University of Mexico (in June 1920), and Alfredo Ramos Martínez was elected head of the Academy of San Carlos (in July 1920).[2] Both men acted as catalysts for the new art: the former was the official patron of the muralists, and the latter advocated a more open approach to the creation of art, exemplified by the open-air schools he introduced in Santa Anita Iztapalapa in 1913.[3]

Indicative of the new spirit was the exhibition of Carlos Mérida's paintings at the Academy of Fine Arts in 1920.[4] His work represented the earliest effort to create a modern aesthetic based on native art and native subjects. Among the subjects he chose for his pictures were the Tribute to Maize ritual and the Feast of the Dead. These and other themes related to the beliefs and customs of the Mexican people became

1

2

Diego Rivera
1. *Mother and Child.* 1926
Oil on canvas, 22½ x 14⅔″
Collection Elva Podesta de Holm. Courtesy Galería
Arvil, Mexico City
Photo: Gerardo Suter

Diego Rivera
2. *The Laborers.* 1944
Oil on Masonite, 9 x 11½″
Collection Francisco and Laura Osio. Courtesy
Galería Arvil, Mexico City
Photo: Gerardo Suter

central to the new art.

Another important event took place in Europe in May 1921. David Alfaro Siqueiros, one of the early Mexican muralists, published *"Manifiesto a los Plásticos de América"* in the first (and only) issue of the magazine *Vida Americana.*[5] Siqueiros called for "a monumental and heroic art, a human art, a public art, with the direct and alive example of our great and extraordinary pre-Hispanic cultures of America."[6] Specifically, he made "Three Appeals of Timely Orientation to Painters and Sculptors of the New American Generation."[7] The second appeal was of particular interest to the new artists. Siqueiros referred them to the use of "Negro" and primitive arts by contemporary European artists and urged his fellow painters to use pre-Columbian art as an inspiration for their work. At the same time, he cautioned against the use of "lamentable archaeological reconstructions so fashionable among us, 'Indianism,' 'primitivism,' 'Americanism.'"[8] Siqueiros was referring to the use of pre-Columbian and other Indian sources to create images in paintings and sculptures in which the motifs were simply transcribed and their real artistic qualities and inherent meanings ignored.

The publication was extremely timely because its appearance coincided with the first mural commission awarded by Vasconcelos (the recipient was Roberto Montenegro).[9] Within a short time other commissions were given by Vasconcelos to paint the walls of the National Preparatory School and the Ministry of Education. Among the artists who worked on the mural programs were Jean Charlot, Ramón Alva de la Canal, Amado de la Cueva, Fernando Leal, Mérida, José Clemente Orozco, Fermín Revueltas, Diego Rivera, and Siqueiros.[10]

In 1923 the artists formalized their views on public mural art with the creation of the *Sindicato de Obreros Técnicos, Pintores y Escultores* (Syndicate of Technical Workers, Painters, and Sculptors) of Mexico and its official publication, *El Machete.*[11] Their manifesto called for artists to identify with the Mexican people and their struggle against imperialism and the class structure. It also called for a revolutionary art that would reflect the social conditions, the native land (the "geography") of the Mexican people, and the Amerindian heritage, as well as the international currents of modern art. In part, this was to be achieved by a collective effort modeled on the workshops of ancient times.[12] The artists believed that the great ideological art of the past had been created by the collective effort of those affiliated with workshops run by master craftsmen or artists.

The Mexican muralists soon became known as the artists responsible for a renaissance in Mexican art.[13] The new art was considered to be the successor to an authentic Mexican tradition. Thus, there were numerous references to a resurgence or rebirth of art. The new art, however, actually represents an amalgamation of Indian and Hispanic strands in Mexican life and culture; it was not the rebirth of pre-Columbian ideas or of a purely indigenous sensibility or spirit as so often emphasized in the contemporary articles, books, and reviews of exhibitions.[14]

The actual experience of painting murals proved to be difficult because the artists did not know how to use the fresco technique, and the encaustic method (used by Rivera in his first mural for the Simón Bolívar Amphitheater at the National Preparatory School) turned out to be a very laborious process.[15] Nor did they know exactly which formal and thematic programs they should use. Both problems were eventually solved by the artists—by trial and error—after they had painted a number of panels in the National Preparatory School, the building selected for the first murals commissioned by the Mexican government. Orozco and Rivera, who had the most experience as artists, used classical and Christian references in their first murals, which were undoubtedly the result of their traditional art training at the Academy of San Carlos in Mexico City.[16] They may well have been inspired too by Vasconcelos, who as a philosopher was interested in the classical world.

Images of the Spanish conquest of Mexico and other themes related to the history of Mexico and the trials of the white-clad *peón*, symbol of the Mexican peasantry, became identified with the mural movement soon after they were first painted by some of the younger artists (plates 1 and 20). Charlot used a confrontation between the Aztecs and the Spaniards as the subject for his mural *Massacre in the Main Temple* (1922–23) in the National Preparatory School.[17] The *peón* and women wrapped in *rebozos* (shawls) were first used by Revueltas in his mural *Homage to the Virgin of Guadalupe* (1922–23), also in the National Preparatory School.[18]

Unfortunately, students of the National Preparatory School, as well as visitors to the school and Mexican newspapermen, did not like the murals, which were considered bad art and inappropriate for the walls of a public building. This eventually led to their defacement during a student riot. Those painted by Orozco and Siqueiros in the school's courtyard were particular targets (Rivera's mural was in the auditorium of the school and therefore out of public view).[19] Orozco and Siqueiros were dismissed as a result of the public pressure; only Rivera survived the public outcry and continued to paint murals even after the conservative Elías Plutarco Calles was elected president of Mexico and J. M. Puig Casauranc was appointed minister of Education in 1924.[20]

Regardless of the changed conditions under which Rivera and Orozco thereafter worked as muralists, both turned to the Mexican Revolution as a source of ideas for the murals they painted during the remainder of the 1920s in Mexico City, Orizaba, and Cuernavaca.[21] Some of the themes they chose were presented within the context of Christian iconography.[22] They also used events from the conquest and from pre-Columbian history in the murals they painted in Mexico and the United States.[23]

Orozco, Rivera, Siqueiros, and other mural artists also revered Emiliano Zapata, who was the foremost hero of the revolution because of his radical position on land reform and related issues, and they included his portrait in a number of images.[24] Ultimately, Zapata became the icon of the revolution most often used by the Mexican artists during this early period. The Zapata motif and some of the themes of the revolution, presented within a Christian iconographic program, were later used by Rivera, Orozco, and Siqueiros for panel and easel paintings and lithographs made in the United States.[25]

Although the goal of the Mexican muralists remained essentially consistent, to create a truly Mexican art, the conditions that had led to the development of the muralist movement had changed by the mid- to late 1920s. The government no longer sponsored major mural programs (except for those carried out by Rivera at the Ministry of Education, the National Palace, and the National Agricultural School at Chapingo). As a result, Orozco left Mexico for the United States in 1927, where he remained until 1934. He and the other Mexican muralists and their followers who concentrated on easel painting and printmaking (woodcuts, linoleum cuts, engravings, and lithographs) moved in various directions in the 1930s (plates 3, 4, and 6). They are still generally grouped under the label of the Mexican School because they all focused on Mexican subject matter in their work, but they can be separated into distinct coalitions according to their various intentions. Some were interested primarily in furthering their political points of view, while others displayed little or no interest in matters of state and could more accurately be described as artists of the "Mexican scene," because their main interest was the folklore and customs of the Mexican people.

Nevertheless, from the 1920s to the 1960s the Mexican School was perceived by art critics in the United States as a homogeneous group of artists.[26] Organizers of exhibitions of Mexican art in the United States ignored the distinctions between the political and nonpolitical artists in Mexico. The works of the leading muralists and others identified with the Mexican School were exhibited in the United States alongside the works of Tamayo and Mérida, who were primarily interested in formal rather than ideological problems. Also ignored were the disagreements within the ranks of the political artists, who splintered into groups that each claimed to have the "true revolutionary artists."

The internal dissension was best exemplified by a famous confrontation between Siqueiros and Rivera that took place over a period of months in 1934-35. It began with Siqueiros leveling a long list of particulars against Rivera in an article that appeared in the *New Masses* (May 1934) and continued during a discussion following a public lecture presented by Rivera at the Palace of Fine Arts in Mexico City (August 1935).[27] Siqueiros charged Rivera with using folklore and archaeological sources to create an art that was false and the opposite of what true revolutionary art should be. He even characterized Rivera's art as the result of a "Mexican curio" frame of mind. In addition, he opposed Rivera's use of anachronistic methods, such as fresco painting and his series of static images. He considered his own dynamic compositions far more appropriate to the present-day activity of the revolution. Rivera responded to these attacks, which he attributed to personal as well as political differences with Siqueiros, in a brochure he published in December 1935.[28] Rivera, who considered himself a Leninist, characterized Siqueiros's attacks as part of a concerted effort by Stalinists in the Communist party to discredit him. He also saw Siqueiros as an artist who used these attacks to make himself better known.

In subsequent decades the battle shifted from within the ranks of the Mexican School to its perceived enemy—the formalists or nonpolitical artists.[29] The latter, led by Rufino Tamayo, considered the art of the Mexican School artists propagandistic, nationalistic, and false. The former vehemently attacked the formalists for creating an art that simply echoed the Paris School and did not serve the needs of the Mexican people.

The Mexican School had control of government patronage for the arts from the very beginning of the new art movement in the 1920s. This was evident in the support provided by the government for a number of touring exhibitions of Mexican art sent to Europe, South America, and the United States. From the first exhibition, *Mexican Arts*, which opened at the Metropolitan Museum of Art in New York in 1930 and traveled to seven other cities in the United States, the focus was on the new painting, and was dominated by muralists and other members of the Mexican School.[30]

The emphasis on the Mexican School continued unabated through the 1930s and was particularly evident in the momentous exhibition *Twenty Centuries of Mexican Art* held at The Museum of Modern Art in New York in 1940.[31] In this exhibition and subsequent shows held in the 1940s and 1950s, emphasis was placed on the modern Mexican painters and the related arts of the pre-Columbian, colonial, or nineteenth-century epochs, as well as on the arts and crafts of the Indians, the art of children, and the art of self-taught or naive painters.[32]

The Mexican government continued to support exhibitions in which the Mexican School was the primary focus in the 1950s and 1960s, but the situation began to change in the 1960s with the rising importance of the abstract movements.[33] No longer did the Mexican School have the upper hand in aesthetic matters. By the end of the 1960s, government support for murals (the key index for funding given to the Mexican School) had dwindled considerably, and exhibitions under the patronage of the government began to be taken over by abstract artists.[34] The watershed was a series of debates that revolved around the government-sponsored international biennials (*Bienal Interamericano de Pintura y Grabado*) held in Mexico in 1958 and 1960.[35] In 1958 the Mexican School maintained the preeminent position it had held for over thirty years; but by 1960 the abstract artists had gained the upper hand. For the rest of the 1960s exhibitions favored the abstract artists and the New Figurative artists.[36]

The Mexican Presence in the United States
The Literature: 1920–1929

Mexican artists and the new Mexican art did not reach the U.S. consciousness until the middle of the 1920s, when a number of articles and books on the art and artists were published in English and exhibitions of Mexican art were presented in the United States. The actual presence of the artists in the United States, which also began in the late 1920s, did not become universally known until the 1930s.

Articles and books on Mexican art and artists published in the United States in the 1920s were few in number compared to those published in the following decade— a statistic that reflects the growing interest in the new Mexican art in the United States. However, the various publications created an audience for Mexican art, and a number of U.S. artists, among them Pablo O'Higgins and Philip Goldstein (who later changed his name to Philip Guston), went to Mexico to study with the artists and to paint murals after they had read about the new art.[37]

Diego Rivera and José Clemente Orozco received most of the attention in the publications of the 1920s. Indeed, only two other artists—Carlos Mérida and Jean Charlot—were discussed in articles published during this period.[38] And most of the articles were written by a relatively limited number of authors from Mexico, the United States, and Europe. The articles appeared in art publications, newspapers (including

The New York Times), and other national magazines in the United States.

José Juan Tablada, a Mexican poet and newspaperman who wrote on art and resided in the United States at the time, wrote extensively on the artists up to the time the modern movement began in Mexico.[39] Among the artists he discussed were Saturnino Herrán, Rivera, Orozco, Adolfo Best Maugard, and Mérida. He also wrote about contemporary events, including Rivera's Paris work and his new murals at the National Preparatory School as well as Orozco's early drawings and watercolors of prostitutes (which he compared to Goya's work).[40] Toward the end of the decade he wrote about the use of Indian sources by the muralists.[41]

Anita Brenner, an energetic supporter of Mexican art in the United States and Mexico, her native country, wrote on the work of Mérida, Orozco, and the Mexican muralist movement.[42] She discussed all aspects of Mexican art as an expression of the Mexican spirit in her book *Idols Behind Altars*, in which she also included chapters on the beginnings of the modern muralist movement and the work of Siqueiros, Orozco, and Rivera.[43]

Walter Pach, a well-known American art critic and historian, included Rivera in a book he wrote on modern art.[44] He also wrote about the early Mexican movement, focusing on an exhibition of children's art and the work of Charlot in one article and on the French and Mexican influences on Rivera's development in another.[45] Some authors, among them Ernest Gruening, an American, and Eileen Dwyer, an Englishwoman, wrote on the new movement only.[46]

Rafael Vera de Córdova, a Mexican, discussed the fine and applied arts of Mexico in a review of an exhibition at the Gallery of Modern Art in Mexico City.[47] In his view, the time was right for the establishment of the gallery, given the advent "of a renaissance in Mexican art." He mentioned the work of Rivera, Revueltas, Montenegro, Dr. Atl, Charlot, and artists from the United States influenced by the Mexicans, including the photographers Edward Weston and Tina Modotti and the painter Pablo O'Higgins. He also mentioned the "ceramics, lacquers, sarapes, embroideries" included in the exhibition. "All the gems in the gamut of our exceptional national art."

Other authors concentrated on the work of one artist, with the movement serving as a backdrop for their critiques. Rivera received the most attention. Bertram Wolfe typically described the new movement in its early days by focusing on Rivera.[48] The artist's work at the Ministry of Education and the mural in the National Preparatory School were reviewed by Frederick Leighton, and his Ministry of Education murals were also discussed by Ernestine Evans and John Dos Passos.[49] The articles published in national magazines by well-known American authors indicate the level of attention and importance given to the work of Rivera. Other Mexican artists, like Orozco, were largely ignored. When they were mentioned, they were relegated to the status of a follower of Rivera. Evans, for example, focused on Rivera's use of the Indian as a primary motif in her article and identified Orozco as one of the young painters who benefited from Rivera's example. (Orozco was three years older than Rivera!) She also discussed Rivera's artistic career in the introduction to her book *The Frescos of Diego Rivera*, which includes reproductions of the murals in the Ministry of Education, the National Preparatory School, and Chapingo, as well as a number of his easel paintings and sketches.[50] Aside from articles by Tablada and Brenner on the work of Orozco, only a short note on his murals was published by Emily S. Hamblen.[51]

Rivera and Orozco also published their views on art in several articles. Katherine Anne Porter reported on Rivera's goals in one article, and Rivera himself wrote another piece on the same subject.[52] In other articles, Rivera dealt with the meaning of revolutionary art in Mexico and Orozco called for a new art based on the experience of the "new races" in the Americas and defended the mural as the appropriate vehicle for this art.[53]

Exhibitions of Mexican Art: 1920–1970

Group exhibitions of Mexican artists, organized by Americans in collaboration with representatives of the Mexican government, began in the late 1920s and invariably contained evidence of the new developments in Mexican art. The exhibition held at the Gallery of Modern Art in Mexico City in 1926 set the pattern for the exhibitions of

3

Diego Rivera
3. *Roots.* 1937
Watercolor on linen, 19 x 24″
Courtesy Galería Arvil, Mexico City
Photo: courtesy Galería Arvil

4

José Clemente Orozco
4. *The Beggars. c.* 1940
Oil on canvas, 16½ x 18¾"
Collection Francisco and Laura Osio. Courtesy
Galería Arvil, Mexico City
Photo: Gerardo Suter

Mexican art that were sent abroad in the 1930s and 1940s.[54] Exhibitions sponsored by the Mexican government always displayed Mexican arts and crafts of the colonial and modern periods alongside the work of modern Mexican artists. Eventually, the work of pre-Columbian peoples was also included in the vast surveys of Mexican art that the government sponsored to travel outside of Mexico from the 1940s to the 1960s. Exhibitions with an exclusive focus on modern art, which began to appear in the late 1930s, were organized by Americans with the assistance of Mexican specialists in Mexico.

Frances Flynn Paine, an American, and René d'Harnoncourt, an Austrian who resided in Mexico and later in the United States, were the first to organize large group exhibitions of Mexican artists shown in the United States.[55] Other Americans, among them MacKinley Helm, Henry Clifford, and John Leeper, organized exhibitions that focused exclusively on modern Mexican art.[56] Miguel Covarrubias, a Mexican artist living in the United States, selected works for the modern section of an exhibition that covered all three epochs of Mexican art (pre-Columbian, colonial, and modern) plus folk art.[57] Inés Amor, the director of the Galería de Arte Mexicano in Mexico City, was responsible for at least three exhibitions of modern Mexican art, two of which were coupled with exhibitions of arts and crafts.[58]

Most of the reviews of the exhibitions of Mexican art that appeared in the late 1920s through the 1930s were positive. This was particularly true of the articles written by organizers of other Mexican art exhibitions. (See the appendix to this essay for more information.) Occasionally there were critical reviews. Charlot criticized the modern section of the exhibition *Twenty Centuries of Mexican Art*, held at The Museum of Modern Art in 1940, because works by the early Mexican muralists were not included in it.[59] James S. Plaut, who reviewed the exhibition of modern Mexican art at the Boston Institute of Modern Art in 1941, expressed the predictable American prejudices against "national" and "political" art that did not relate to the formalist tendencies seen in European and American art of the time.[60] By the 1950s and 1960s the modern sections of the large exhibitions of Mexican art were overshadowed by the sections devoted to pre-Columbian art, colonial art, and modern folk arts and crafts. In spite of this, the best-known artists, notably Rivera, Orozco, Siqueiros, Tamayo, Charlot, and Mérida, continued to be singled out by most reviewers for positive comments. The evaluations of the works of Rivera and Orozco changed the most from the 1920s to the 1950s. Rivera, the most discussed and valued artist at the beginning of the Mexican muralist movement, was faulted by Jules Langsner (in his review of the exhibition *Art of Mexico* held at the Pasadena Art Institute in 1953) for exhibiting works that were "weak" in comparison to those by Orozco, Siqueiros, and Tamayo.[61]

The actual presence of Mexican artists in the United States during the 1920s and early 1930s remained largely unnoticed by the general public. Indeed, their presence became widely known only when controversies erupted in places where the best-known artists were painting murals: Rivera in San Francisco, Detroit, and New York (1930–33); Siqueiros in Los Angeles (1932); and Orozco in Hanover, New Hampshire (1933).[62] Other indices of presence, such as lectures, commissions for theater and ballet productions, and illustrations for books and other publications, added to the overall presence of the artists but did not receive the attention of the press. Art exhibitions provided more tangible evidence of their presence (to which artists, students, and the general public could react), and reviews of the exhibitions and articles and books on the artists added appreciably to this presence.

The Mural Controversies

Americans reacted most of all to the murals painted by Rivera, Siqueiros, and Orozco in various parts of the country. The response was often violently critical, reflecting U.S. xenophobia and its attendant paranoia that U.S. institutions would be contaminated by outsiders. Individuals as well as groups objected in principle to foreigners being awarded commissions to paint murals in the United States. Other objections focused on the subjects of the murals, which many Americans considered offensive for a variety of reasons. A few individuals—artists, art critics, and patrons— fought these attacks. Mild as well as acrimonious debates were aired in articles published

5

Diego Rivera
5. *Industry*. 1933
   Fresco, South Wall, Detroit Institute of Arts
   Photo: courtesy Detroit Institute of Arts

6

Diego Rivera
6. *In Vinum Veritas.* 1945
Oil on canvas, 44 x 160''
Courtesy Galería Arvil, Mexico City
Photo: Gerardo Suter

in national magazines and in letters written to the editors of newspapers in the towns where the artists painted murals. The controversies polarized entire communities and led to demands that the murals in Detroit and Hanover, New Hampshire, be whitewashed and to the actual destruction of murals in Los Angeles and New York.

The controversy surrounding the murals Rivera painted seemed to grow with each successive commission. The negative reactions began in San Francisco even before he arrived in the city to paint murals.[63] Protesting artists, who felt that they had been slighted when the commissions were awarded to Rivera, contended that his "Communist ideas" placed him out of sympathy with his subject. These initial concerns were soon forgotten when Rivera arrived in San Francisco at the end of 1930. However, objections were raised shortly after the artist completed his first mural in 1931 at the San Francisco Stock Exchange, entitled *Allegory of California*.[64] A number of people objected to the artist's selection of Helen Wills Moody, a tennis champion, for the mural's large central figure, which they thought should have been a generalized icon rather than a portrait of a specific individual. *The Making of a Fresco Showing the Building of a City*, painted at the California School of Fine Arts (now the San Francisco Institute of Art) in 1931, created a stir among some of the locals because the artist included a portrait of himself in the act of painting on a scaffold with his back to the public.[65] Many considered it a premeditated insult. Rivera had merely intended to portray himself as a worker along with the many others he portrayed in the mural. This was the first of many misunderstandings that occurred largely due to differences in background and ideology between Mexican artists and their hosts in the United States (plates 9 and 10).

There was an uproar in Detroit over a small panel as well as over an entire mural program—*Portrait of Detroit*—painted by Rivera at the Detroit Institute of Arts in 1932–33 (plate 5).[66] An editorial in *The Detroit News* voiced the most frequently heard criticisms: "The whole work and conception is un-American, incongruous, and unsympathetic; it bears no relation to the soul of the community, to the room, to the building, or to the general purpose of Detroit's Institute of Arts." Finding no clear-cut solution to the problem, the editorial called for the entire mural to be whitewashed. In addition, religious groups reacted violently to the panel entitled *Biological Research*, which they thought was a veiled representation of the birth of Christ in the manger ("a caricature of the Holy Family"), and therefore sacrilegious. Dr. Valentiner, who awarded the commission to Rivera to paint the murals, defended the work against all the critics. He believed that it was as out of place for him to ask the artist to change the murals to please the critics "as it would be…to remove the many crucifixes, religious paintings, and church relics from our collections because they give offense to Jews, unorthodox Christians, and the thousands who have no interest in any church." Walter Pach sent a wire in support of the murals and stated that he found "no allusion whatever to the Holy Family" in them. He further stated that "if these paintings are whitewashed, nothing can ever be done to whitewash America." Given Rivera's combative personality, it is very likely that he fully intended to make a reference to the Holy Family in the controversial panel in the same way that he made similar allusions to the Temptation of Saint Anthony in another panel of the Detroit murals, entitled *Pharmaceutics*.[67] The murals were saved in spite of the many calls for their destruction because Edsel Ford, who paid for them, gave his support to the artist and his work.

The Detroit problem was minor compared to the controversy Rivera created in New York when he began work in 1933 on a mural entitled *Man at the Crossroads* for the newly completed Rockefeller Center.[68] The work was never finished because Rivera refused to remove a portrait of Lenin he included in the mural despite the protests of Nelson Rockefeller, who had commissioned the work. Numerous articles as well as editorials appeared in *The New York Times* during the controversy, which began in the spring of 1933 and continued through the winter of 1934, when the mural was destroyed. The controversy was also given extensive coverage in the major art publications of the United States.

Because of its subject matter, controversy also surrounded Siqueiros's mural *Tropical America*, which he painted in Los Angeles.[69] The artist represented a crucified Indian in front of a pyramid along with a woman bound with rope. On one side of the mural were two menacing guerrillas (one Peruvian, the other Mexican) on top of a building. The whole scene was dominated by an American eagle perched on top of a cross. The obvious references to U.S. imperialism and the implied call for armed struggle caused an uproar in the community, and the mural was whitewashed soon after it was completed in 1932.

Orozco's mural *The Epic of American Civilization*, painted at the Baker Library of Dartmouth College in 1932–34 (plate 7), created a controversy that embroiled the Dartmouth faculty, administrators, students, and alumni.[70] Orozco and his patrons were criticized by individuals as well as organizations within and beyond the college. The National Committee to Advance American Art indicted Dartmouth College simply for giving a major commission to a foreign artist.[71] The committee opposed foreign artists in general and proposed that such commissions in future be awarded by competition. On the other hand, John Sloan, president of the Society of Independent Artists, condemned the committee's stand because it would "throw the result into the arena of art politics, which has had such miserable results in the past."

Of far greater seriousness was an attack on the murals by Harvey M. Watts, an editorial writer who published a review of an illustrated booklet on the murals in the September 1, 1934, issue of *The Art Digest*.[72] Watts objected to the subject matter of the murals, "which deals with the hideous divinities of Mexico before the conquest." He also faulted the artist for not focusing on a story, which in his view was always a necessary component in a great work of art, and he reproached Dartmouth for allowing the artist "to satirize the English-speaking traditions, spiritual and educational, and academic, while forcing on the college the extremely tiresome tradition of an absent and somewhat abhorred civilization of the Toltec-Aztec cults."

A number of prominent figures in the art world immediately came to the defense of Dartmouth and Orozco. The art critic E. M. Benson, Frederic Hynd, director of the Hartford School of Art, and Hugh R. O'Neill, a newspaperman from New York, responded to Watts's indictment of the Orozco murals.[73] By contrast, Edward Alden Jewell, the art critic of *The New York Times*, reported the Watts review but without any editorial comment. In separate articles, Benson and O'Neill responded to Watts's criticism of the murals' pre-Columbian subject matter by pointing out that they dealt with the contributions of the Indians to America's civilizations as well as those of the "white man" to the New World. Watts's characterization of the divinities as "hideous" made no sense to Benson, unless Watts was applying "magazine-cover or National Academy standards" of beauty to them. In any case, Benson pointed out that Huitzilopochtli, the Aztec war god, was supposed to look "bloodthirsty," and Quetzalcoatl, the cult hero and god who brought civilization to the Indians, was "much more Western European in conception than Mexican." Benson and O'Neill also responded to the charge that Orozco had focused on the "tiresome" and "somewhat abhorred civilization of the Aztec-Toltec cults," by pointing out that Dartmouth was founded to convert American Indians, and it was therefore appropriate for Orozco to focus on this subject in his mural program. It is interesting to note that Benson thought it ironic that a college founded to convert the American Indian should now be converted by one. This was typical of the many misconceptions American critics had concerning the racial and cultural backgrounds of the Mexican artists. Orozco was not an Indian; although he was born in Mexico, his parents were Spanish. Indeed, as a Hispanist he also consistently criticized Rivera and all those who championed the Indian of the past and present in their efforts to forge a Mexican identity.

Watts's critics also evaluated Orozco's murals at the expense of U.S. art. In Hynd's view, Orozco had "attained a technical ability which places him well above the run of American painters." According to O'Neill, Orozco "handled his mural legitimately and brilliantly" from the traditional point of view; and "from the artistic, no less." Regarding the issue of whether a foreign artist should be given a commission to paint a mural in the United States, O'Neill stated that "it is better to have one powerful painting on this continent by a Mexican, Spaniard, Oriental or African than a thousand American mediocrities."

Watts, in his rejoinder to the criticisms by Benson, Hynd, and O'Neill in the October 15, 1934, issue of *The Art Digest*, steadfastly refused to believe that Orozco was capable of making a statement about "European-American" civilization in

7

8

José Clemente Orozco
7. *The Epic of American Civilization: The Machine.*
1932-34
Fresco, 120 x 118"
Courtesy the Trustees of Dartmouth College,
Hanover, New Hampshire
Photo: courtesy Hood Museum of Art, Dartmouth
College

José Clemente Orozco
8. *The Requiem.* 1928
Lithograph on paper, 12 x 16"
San Francisco Museum of Modern Art. Albert M.
Bender Collection
Gift of Albert M. Bender
Photo: courtesy San Francisco Museum of Modern
Art

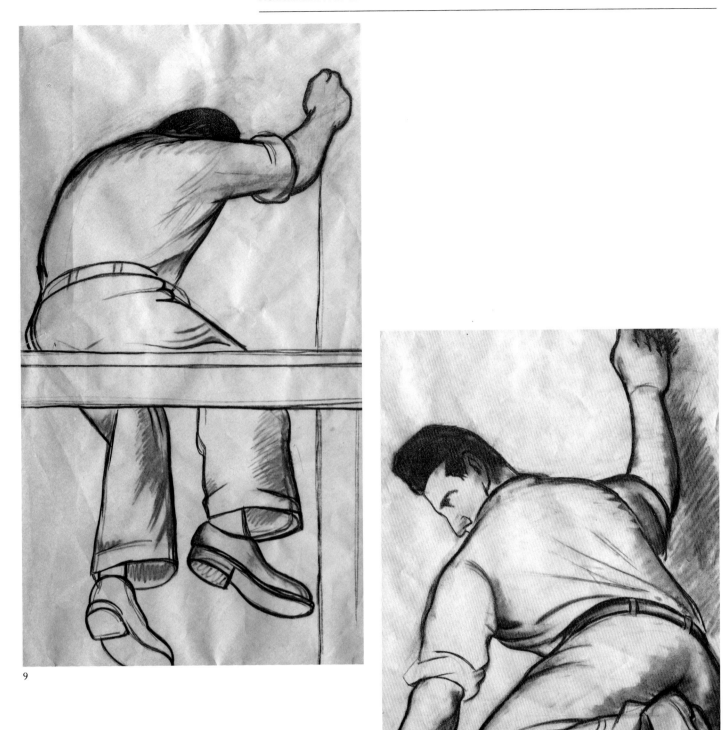

9

10

Diego Rivera
9. *John Viscount Hastings Sitting on a Beam, Dropping a Plumb Line.*
Sketch for "The Making of a Fresco Showing the Building of a City" (mural at The San Francisco Art Institute). 1931
Charcoal on paper, 35¾ x 20"
Courtesy Galería Arvil, Mexico City
Photo: Crispin Vazquez

Diego Rivera
10. *Clifford Wight Measuring.*
Sketch for "The Making of a Fresco Showing the Building of a City" (mural at The San Francisco Art Institute). 1931
Charcoal on paper, 23¾ x 18"
Courtesy Galerías Cristóbal, Mexico City
Photo: Gerardo Suter

11

12

José Clemente Orozco
11. *Vaudeville in Harlem.* 1928
Lithograph on paper, 11⅞ x 15⅞"
San Francisco Museum of Modern Art. Albert M.
Bender Collection.
Gift of Albert M. Bender
Photo: courtesy San Francisco Museum of Modern
Art

José Clemente Orozco
12. *Rear Guard.* 1929
Lithograph on paper, 14 x 18¾"
The Phillips Collection, Washington, D.C.
Photo: courtesy The Phillips Collection

30

the Dartmouth murals, given his Mexican background and his espousal of "the radical provinciality of the Rand School of thought."[74] More important, he was "concerned that art in America shall not be an art by proxy through imported helots." He simply did not believe that outsiders should be commissioned to paint murals at the expense of native-born artists. In his view, a little "xenophobia" was needed to help Americans realize their "artistic destiny." He pointed to the example of the ancient Greeks who created great works of art without bringing in outsiders. His narrow definition of Americanism was brought out when he referred to "Kipling, who once said that American literature was suffering from too much Ellis Island; and a little later Cortissoz [who] indicted the Ellis Island element in American art as deleterious." His final diatribe was specifically aimed at Mexico. He accused D. H. Lawrence of glorifying "the dull peon and his duller divinities," and he condemned the tourist bureaus for showing "us the infinite possibilities for mischief, artistic and otherwise, of the open border on the Rio Grande!"

Orozco, Rivera, and Siqueiros in the United States

The direction, if not the full development, of Orozco's painting style was established by the time he arrived in New York in 1927. Orozco had tentatively explored using the theme of the Mexican Revolution in a mural for an industrial school in Orizaba, Veracruz, in 1926, and he expanded on the same theme later that year at the National Preparatory School.[75] Orozco continued to focus on the Mexican Revolution and also used New York subjects in drawings, prints, and easel paintings he did in the United States. He introduced new motifs and themes, based on the worlds of classical antiquity and ancient American civilizations, in murals he painted at Pomona College in 1930 and Dartmouth College in 1932–34.[76] The image of fire associated with Prometheus and Quetzalcoatl—and identified with the Old and New Worlds respectively—was later used by the artist as a primary focus in murals he painted in Mexico City at the Palace of Fine Arts in 1934, and in Guadalajara at the University of Guadalajara (lecture hall), the Government Palace (stairway), and the orphanage, or *Hospicio Cabañas* (dome), in 1936–39. These major works can only be fully understood and appreciated by studying the earlier murals painted by the artist in the United States.

When Rivera arrived in San Francisco in 1930 to begin work on his first mural there, he had been working continuously as a muralist for seven years. The many commissions he received to paint murals in Mexico had enabled him to develop his painting style and to disseminate his ideas regarding the purpose and function of muralist art.[77] He eventually painted what many consider his best mural at the Detroit Institute of Arts in 1932–33.[78] It exemplifies the period of his greatest maturity as an artist, and his work thereafter is generally not as well considered.

Siqueiros initiated the second and most important phase of his mural career in the United States. He began to use new materials and techniques as well as to formulate and implement his ideas regarding the treatment of the painted wall as a dynamic surface in several murals he painted in Los Angeles in 1932 and in Argentina in 1933.[79] He further developed these ideas in New York in the Siqueiros Experimental Art Workshop, which he established in 1936, and in the murals he later painted in Mexico. Siqueiros's work in the United States was seminal in the development of his later work in Mexico.

Soon after his arrival in New York, Orozco began a series of ink and gouache drawings based on the Mexican Revolution.[80] Among the lithographs based on the drawings are *The Requiem* (1928) and *Rear Guard* (1929).[81] The stark whites and the varying shades of gray and black used to define the figures—seen facing away from the observer and presented in simple compositional arrangements—convey the quiet dignity of the religious observance in *The Requiem* as well as the dramatic movements of the combatants in *Rear Guard* (plates 8 and 12).

In 1928 Orozco also began to use scenes of New York as subjects for his prints and paintings (plates 13–15). In the oil painting *The Subway*, the artist expressed the anonymity of the urban dweller riding the subway in an almost reportorial manner, without his usual dramatization of structures and stark contrasts of dark and light areas.[82] The highly textured surface of the painting is all that remains of the artist's

13

José Clemente Orozco
13. *Los Muertos (Skyscrapers).* 1931
   Oil on canvas, 43 x 36"
   Instituto Nacional de Bellas Artes, Museo Carrillo
   Gil, Mexico City
   Photo: Gerardo Suter

14

15

José Clemente Orozco
14. *Coney Island*. n.d.
    Oil on canvas, 9⅝ x 8⅛"
    Collection Miss Claudia Thompson. Courtesy
    Galería Arvil, Mexico City
    Photo: Gerardo Suter

José Clemente Orozco
15. *New York Factory, Williamsburg*. 1928
    Oil on canvas, 28¼ x 19¾"
    Collection Elva Podesta de Holm. Courtesy Galería
    Arvil, Mexico City
    Photo: Gerardo Suter

expressive vocabulary. *Vaudeville in Harlem* (plate 11) is appropriately lighter in mood. The viewer is invited to witness the acts on stage, barely discernible in the central part of the image, as seen from the back of the auditorium. The sets of heads in the audience rise above the backs of the theater seats, and the semblance of a festive mood is created by the repetitive patterns set against the light background.

Immediately following the completion of the Pomona College mural (1930), Orozco painted *The Caudillo Zapata* (also known as *Zapata Entering a Peasant's Hut*).[83] This large painting, over six feet high and almost four feet wide, has the intensity of some of the panels he painted on the first floor of the National Preparatory School, in particular *Barricade* (1926) and *Trinity* (1926). The large figure of Zapata, which looms over the anonymous figures in the hut and fills the doorway opening, is seemingly oblivious to the suffering people before him. The artist used the figures inside the hut to create a cruciform arrangement, made up of a series of interlocking diagonals, which contrasts with the vertical figure of Zapata. The arms, legs, and hats of the figures inside the hut convey a feeling of despair and hopelessness, and there is the threat of impending violence, signaled by the sword placed directly in front of Zapata's face.

Among the works Orozco painted in 1931 in the United States is *The Barricade*, which is based on his mural panel at the National Preparatory School. The oil painting has two extra figures in it (to the right of the three main figures) and a number of new additions (a rope around the feet of the central figure and a long knife held by the figure on the lower right). More important, the artist changed the pose of the central figure (no longer seen in the crucified pose of the original) and the pose of the figure on the immediate right. The area occupied by the latter was filled by three bodies heaped on top of one another, and the diagonals which give the original such emotive power were modified in the oil painting.

From 1932 to 1934 Orozco painted the walls of Baker Library at Dartmouth College. He focused on the history of the Americas for the first time and created a series of jarring scenes, each corresponding to one aspect of the hemisphere's history. Among the preparatory sketches the artist made for this mural program are two for the panel entitled *The Departure of Quetzalcoatl*.[84] One is a crayon drawing of the head of Quetzalcoatl, which in a few strokes conveys the legendary figure's clear-eyed stare.[85] The other, a composition sketch for the right half of the fresco panel, shows the powerful figure of the departing Quetzalcoatl pointing to the viewer's right, to indicate his destination is to the east. He is surrounded by writhing serpents, which are his standard iconographic accompaniments.[86]

Among the many works made by Rivera during the four years he resided in the United States (1930–33) are portable murals, lithographs, and drawings based on the murals he painted in Mexico and the United States. Two of the portable murals he painted for his 1931 exhibition at The Museum of Modern Art in New York are *Liberation of the Peón*, based on the mural panel of the same title in the Ministry of Education, and *Agrarian Leader Zapata*, based on one of the panels of the Cuernavaca murals.[87] Rivera used the latter subject again in 1932 in a lithograph entitled *Zapata*.

The *Liberation of the Peón* is Rivera's variation on the Descent from the Cross, a subject frequently portrayed by European Renaissance and Baroque artists. Rivera's panel, which portrays the Mexican *peón* as a martyr, has all the drama of traditional religious paintings. The result is a very moving and tender image. The Zapata lithograph is based on the original mural in Cuernavaca, but the pose of the leader and the toylike appearance of his horse offer a less than dynamic presence. The artist presented Zapata as a passive figure, even though evidence of the violence associated with his leadership is part of the image.

Rivera's *Self-Portrait*, a lithograph of 1930, shows the artist with an expression that suggests vulnerability but appropriately provides a glimpse of his mischievous character. His technical brilliance is seen in this print and in the beautiful painting *Flower Festival* of 1931. The composition study for the Rockefeller Center mural, a pencil drawing on brown paper (1932), demonstrates the artist's very orderly approach to the arrangement of the various parts of his ill-fated mural.[88]

The work of David Alfaro Siqueiros during the 1930s typifies the art of the Mexican School at that time. Siqueiros often chose Indians as his subjects for genre paintings and prints, presenting them with great compassion and tenderness and always demonstrating their victimization.[89] He used Zapata as a subject for a painting (1931) and two lithographs (1930). The painting and one of the lithographs (plates 17 and 18) are portrait busts rather than the usual full-length presentations by other artists. The other lithograph shows Zapata on horseback against a backdrop of mountains. Some of the charisma of Zapata is evident in the portrait bust done in oil. Siqueiros partially accomplished this by capturing the squinting eyes of the leader; but what adds to the tension of the image is the representation of Zapata within an enclosed space, defined by converging walls made of large blocks of stone. The walled-in figure becomes too large for the composition to contain him comfortably. Siqueiros's lithograph of Zapata on horseback also exhibits the kind of power seen in the portrait bust. In sharp contrast to Rivera's elevation of Zapata into an icon and Orozco's portrayal of him as a catalyst for violence, Siqueiros saw him more personally, as a powerful leader of people.

The well-known portable panel paintings by Siqueiros in the collection of The Museum of Modern Art in New York were preceded by mural work he carried out in Los Angeles during a six-month period in 1932. It was at this time that he began to use plastic paints with airbrushes on a cement surface. He also began to consider the painted wall as a dynamic, rather than a static, two-dimensional surface after his experiments with a mural he painted in Argentina (1933). Following the trip to Argentina, he traveled to New York in 1934 and again in 1936, when he established his experimental workshop.[90] Not only did he continue to use new tools (airbrushes, still and movie projectors, plastic paints, and cement), which he felt reflected the times in which he lived, but he also developed new approaches to art in which chance played an important part. In spite of his interest in using these tools and techniques to create a "new" art, he thought of them as means rather than as ends in themselves. The important thing still was to express his views about society. For *Collective Suicide* (1936), he made an elaborate surface with new materials and procedures, but he used it only as the background to a narrative picture in which Europeans clash with the Indians of the New World.

From 1937 to 1939 Siqueiros fought in the Spanish Civil War. He returned to Mexico thereafter to continue his experiments in mural painting. Among the works the artist painted in 1939 are *Ethnography* and *El Sollozo*.[91] The former represents a white-clad Mexican Indian shown wearing a pre-Columbian mask made of wood, which is generally identified as Olmecoid in style. The latter focuses on the suffering of the victims of war.

Mexican School Artists in the United States

The Mexican School, initially represented by a group of muralists working under government patronage and later by independent muralists, eventually included other artists whose primary medium was either easel painting, drawing, or printmaking. Those who believed in the tenets of the Mexican muralist movement organized into two groups to carry on the traditions: they established LEAR (League of Revolutionary Writers and Artists), founded in 1934 and dissolved in 1938, and the Taller de Gráfica Popular (TGP: Workshop of Popular Graphic Arts), founded in 1937.[92] Others, who did not have a particular ideology, still used the everyday lives and customs of the Mexican people as subjects for their art. Most of these artists, who can be generically categorized as part of the Mexican School, made trips to the United States in the 1920s and 1930s to carry out commissions, to exhibit their work, and in some cases to establish permanent residence. Such travel afforded them additional opportunities to continue their work as artists. (The artists are discussed below according to their birth dates rather than by the dates of their arrival in the United States.)

Alfredo Ramos Martínez

Alfredo Ramos Martínez left Mexico for the United States in 1929 and settled in Los Angeles, where he resided until his death in 1946.[93] He painted murals in San Diego, La Jolla, Claremont, and San Francisco. The Mexican subjects used by the artist are presented in essentially static terms. His pictures are associated with pre-Columbian imagery (relief sculptures and paintings) due to his focus on symbolic accoutrements rather than personalities.[94]

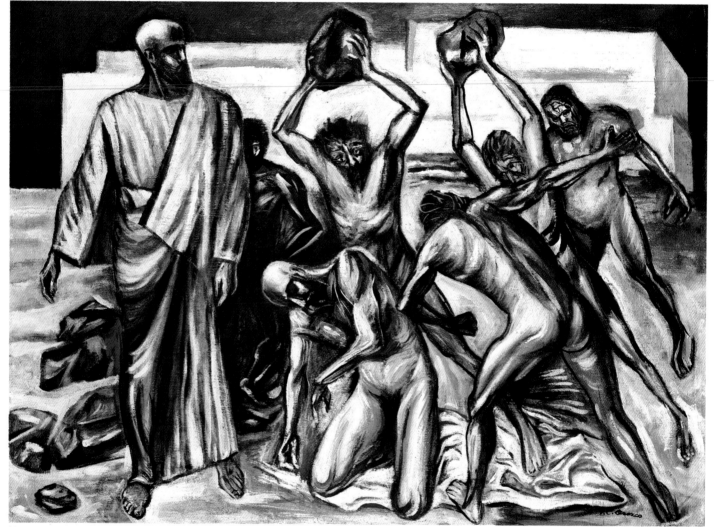

16

José Clemente Orozco
16. *The Martyrdom of St. Stephen.* 1943
Oil on canvas, 39 x 52″
Collection Zendejas Family. Courtesy Galería Arvil,
Mexico City
Photo: Gerardo Suter

17

18

David Alfaro Siqueiros
17. *Zapata.* 1930
Lithograph on paper, 21 1/16 x 15 5/8″
Cleveland Museum of Art. Mr. and Mrs. Charles G.
Prasse Collection
Photo: courtesy Cleveland Museum of Art

David Alfaro Siqueiros
18. *Zapata.* 1931
Oil on canvas, 53 1/4 x 41 1/2″
Hirshhorn Museum and Sculpture Garden,
Smithsonian Institution, Washington, D.C. Gift of
Joseph H. Hirshhorn, 1966
Photo: courtesy Hirshhorn Museum and Sculpture
Garden

19

20

Jean Charlot
19. *Tina Modotti.* 1924
Crayon on paper, 15 x 11⅛"
Collection The Museum of Modern Art, New York.
Gift of Miss Dorothy M. Hoskins
Photo: courtesy The Museum of Modern Art

Antonio Ruiz
20. *Bicycle Race in Texcoco.* 1938
Oil on canvas, 12⅝ x 16⅝"
Philadelphia Museum of Art. Purchase Nebinger Fund
Photo: courtesy Philadelphia Museum of Art

Roberto Montenegro

Roberto Montenegro was a key figure in the efforts to present Mexican folk art as one of the sources for the new art. He participated in several exhibitions of Mexican art in the United States.[95] He was the author of a number of books on the subject, founder of the Museum of Folk Art at the Palace of Fine Arts in 1934 and the Museum of Folk Art in Toluca in 1946, and curator of the folk art section of The Museum of Modern Art's exhibition *Twenty Centuries of Mexican Art*.[96] His interest in folklore and religious and folk art frequently inspired his art.

Jean Charlot

Jean Charlot left Mexico in 1929 and eventually taught at a number of schools, colleges, and universities in the United States. He also painted murals in the state of Georgia (one in the McDonough Post Office and two at the University of Georgia in Athens).[97] Earlier in his career, when he was a participant in the muralist movement, Charlot made a number of traditional drawings and prints, including a portrait of Tina Modotti (plate 19), which exemplifies the spare style of drawing that characterized works of the Mexican School of this period.[98]

Antonio Ruiz

Antonio Ruiz went to Hollywood (1926–29) to study set design.[99] Later he worked as an assistant to Miguel Covarrubias, painting murals in San Francisco's Pacific House in 1940.[100] Ruiz portrayed lively everyday Mexican scenes in his paintings. A characteristic work is the *Bicycle Race*, painted after a scene in a small Mexican town (plate 20). The bicycle riders are seen head-on, dwarfed by the enormous trees overhead and hemmed in by the reviewing stands and a high wall. The entire scene is full of onlookers, along the sides of the street, perched on the wall, and even balanced on the tree branches.

Julio Castellanos

Julio Castellanos, who is best known for paintings of nudes, traveled to the United States as early as 1920.[101] The compositions of his paintings are classical; his figures appear serene and introspective. *Three Nudes* (1930) and *The Dialogue* (c.1936) exemplify the quality of his compositions, which are based on a rigorous arrangement of verticals, slight diagonals, and horizontals. *The Angel Kidnappers* (plate 21) is a more complex work. The artist's affinity for classical arrangements, complete with shallow spaces, is demonstrated in this work. The severe vertical axes of the earlier works are supplanted by the dramatic portrayal of the figures arrested in motion.

Leopoldo Méndez

Leopoldo Méndez traveled to the United States in 1930 and exhibited his work in Los Angeles. He cofounded the Taller de Gráfica Popular with Pablo O'Higgins, Luis Arenal, and Alfredo Zalce in 1937.[102] Two years later he traveled throughout the United States on a Guggenheim Fellowship.[103] Portfolios of prints (linoleum cuts, woodcuts, and lithographs) were published by TGP from the date of its founding until the late 1960s.[104]

Vision (plate 22), a woodcut by Méndez, is typical of the prints produced by the members of TGP. Its subject is Mexico, expressed through the use of well-known emblems, motifs, and themes found in Mexican art. The Mexican national emblem is composed of an eagle perched on a cactus with a serpent in its beak. Méndez took the eagle, cactus, and serpent from their rightful places in the emblem and represented the eagle nailed to the cross with knives. The eagle's carcass forms the shape of the Nazi swastika. Marchers with their banners and priests (both typical subjects in Mexican art since the muralists) parade before the open jaws of the monstrous serpent. The death and destruction wrought by the Catholic Church in Mexico and by Nazism is vividly implied by the image. This is one of many such statements against fascism made in Mexico during the 1940s. *Deportation to Death* (also known as *Expatriation to Death*; 1942), a linocut, provides another glimpse of the expressive and narrative powers of Méndez's work. It deals with the excesses of fascism during World War II, exemplified by the deportation of Jews to Nazi extermination camps.

21

Julio Castellanos
21. *The Angel Kidnappers.* 1943
Oil on canvas, 22⅝ x 37⅜″
Collection The Museum of Modern Art, New York.
Inter-American Fund
Photo: courtesy The Museum of Modern Art

22

Leopoldo Méndez
22. *Vision.* 1945
   Woodcut on paper, 23½ x 19″
   The Art Institute of Chicago. Gift of the Print and
   Drawing Club, 1945
   Photo: courtesy Art Institute of Chicago

José Chávez Morado

José Chávez Morado worked in the citrus orchards of California and the fishing industry in Alaska from 1925 to 1931. In 1930 he studied at the Chouinard School of Art in Los Angeles.[105] Chávez Morado later represented Mexican scenes in prints as well as paintings. Religious observances and celebrations are the subjects of his oil paintings *Day of the Dead* (date unknown) and *Carnival* (plate 23).

Jesús Guerrero Galván

Jesús Guerrero Galván, who studied art in San Antonio in the early 1920s, was artist-in-residence at the University of New Mexico in Albuquerque in 1942.[106] Guerrero Galván's mature style of painting is evident in *Images of Mexico* (plate 24). The artist's sensitivity is represented by this study of a mother flanked by sleeping children. The close-knit group of idealized figures is enveloped in a soft light. The wide-eyed expression of the mother figure seems to emphasize her vulnerability.

Raul Anguiano

Raul Anguiano traveled to Cuba and then to the United States in 1940–41, where he studied at The Art Students League for three months.[107] Like other members of TGP, Anguiano worked in oils and also did prints, especially lithographs. He also used the life of the Mexican people as subject matter for his art. *La Llorona* (The Weeping Woman; plate 25) is a representation of the Mexican equivalent of the bogeyman summoned by parents whenever children misbehave. In Mexican folklore. La Llorona, who went insane when she lost her own child, went about looking for children, whom she then killed with the help of the evil one. The artist has captured the absolute terror experienced by one of her victims.

Francisco Dosamantes

Francisco Dosamantes, a member of TGP, is known in the United States primarily for his lithographs and linocuts.[108] He also painted in oils and carried out a number of mural commissions as well. He lived in New York for several years after the end of World War II. Like the other artists of the Mexican School, Dosamantes used scenes of everyday life as subjects for his paintings and graphic works. On occasion, he also dealt with political subjects. The powerful lithograph *Dead Soldier* (plate 26), for example, shows the mangled body of a lone corpse seen from above. The greatly foreshortened figure inspires the observer to ponder the severity of the crime caused by warfare.

Miguel Covarrubias

Miguel Covarrubias, initially an outsider to the developments in Mexican art of the 1920s, arrived in New York in 1923 and made a name for himself producing caricatures of famous people and drawings and watercolors of blacks in Harlem. From the early 1920s to 1936, many of his drawings were published by *Vanity Fair* and reproduced in the books *The Prince of Wales and Other Famous Americans* (1926) and *Negro Drawings* (1929).[109] In 1940 he painted *Two Mural Maps of the American Continent* in tempera at the San Francisco World's Fair. He also selected the works for the modern section of the exhibition *Twenty Centuries of Mexican Art*, which opened at The Museum of Modern Art in New York in the same year. Thereafter he devoted himself entirely to the study of the pre-Columbian arts of Mexico, but the drawings he made for his books continued to give him a high profile in the United States.

In the lithograph *The Lindy Hop* (plate 27), the artist admirably captured the rhythmic movement of the black American dancers. Other Mexican artists shared Covarrubias's fascination with Harlem. Orozco, who first visited New York in 1917, referred to Harlem "where Negroes and Spanish Americans live" as one of the "nicest and most diverting scenes."[110] He was even more laudatory in his description of the men and women he saw ten years later in the theaters, cabarets, and dancing halls of Harlem: "All of them tall and well set up. Girls of vibrant features, strong, firm bodies, and an incredible beauty. Actresses and dancers like no others in the world."

23

24

José Chávez Morado
23. *Carnival.* 1939
Oil on canvas, 28 x 38"
Phoenix Art Museum. Gift of Dr. and Mrs. Loyal Davis, 58/92
Photo: courtesy Phoenix Art Museum

Jesús Guerrero Galván
24. *Images of Mexico.* 1950
Oil on canvas, 39½ x 49½"
Dallas Museum of Art. Dallas Art Association Purchase
Photo: courtesy Dallas Museum of Art

25

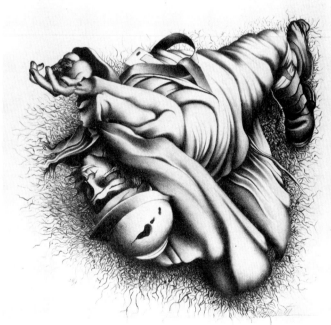

26

27

Raul Anguiano
25. *La Llorona (The Weeping Woman).* 1942
Oil on canvas, 23⅝ x 29⅝''
Collection The Museum of Modern Art, New York.
Inter-American Fund
Photo: courtesy The Museum of Modern Art

Francisco Dosamantes
26. *Dead Soldier.* 1940
Lithograph on paper, 16⅜ x 16½''
Philadelphia Museum of Art. Gift of R. Sturgis
Ingersoll
Photo: Joan Broderick

Miguel Covarrubias
27. *The Lindy Hop.* 1936
Lithograph on paper, 12⅞ x 9½''
Philadelphia Museum of Art. Purchased by
Thomas Skelton Harrison Fund
Photo: courtesy Philadelphia Museum of Art

The Mexican Influence on U.S. Art

The Mexican presence in the United States was so pervasive in the early 1930s that it dominated a good portion of all discussions on art in art periodicals and the general press.[111] The interest in the work of the Mexican artists and the furor created by it on occasion had a lasting impact on the budding U.S. muralists. The presence of the Mexican muralists also contributed directly to the development of U.S. art in the 1930s. Rivera gave lectures in conjunction with the public showing of the New Workers School panels in December 1934, and Siqueiros conducted art experiments in his workshop from April 1936 to early 1937.[112] Siqueiros, Orozco, and Tamayo had earlier participated with seven other artists from Latin America in the first American Artists Congress held in New York on February 14, 1936.[113] The involvement of the federal government as a patron of U.S. artists was a direct consequence of the Mexican example. George Biddle, a U.S. artist who was a close friend of President Roosevelt, became interested in setting up a government-sponsored project based on the Mexican model of the early 1920s. In a letter to the president outlining his plan, he referred to the success of the Mexican experience of the early 1920s and suggested a similar program of mural painting be established in the United States.[114] As a result, the federal government sponsored four art programs from 1933 to 1943.[115] The fourth program, under which most of the murals were funded (more than twenty-five hundred murals), was the Works Progress Administration's Federal Art Project (WPA/FAP), which commissioned mural paintings from August 1935 to June 1943.

The Mexican presence had been felt in a number of cities in the United States before the federally funded projects were started. In 1930 Jackson Pollock and Phillip Guston visited Orozco at Pomona College, where he was working on the *Prometheus* mural, and in 1932 Reuben Kadish worked as an assistant with Siqueiros on the *Tropical America* mural in Los Angeles.[116]

Pollock had earlier expressed an interest in Rivera's work in a letter to his brothers, Charles and Frank, dated October 22, 1929.[117] He referred to a Rivera painting he had seen in the Los Angeles museum and an article by Rivera: "I found the *Creative Art* January 1929 article on Rivera," he wrote. "I certainly admire his work." By the time Rivera began work on the New Workers School murals Pollock was in New York, too. He was studying art at the New School for Social Research when he watched Rivera paint murals there. By the mid-1930s Pollock had become aware of the work being done at the Siqueiros Experimental Art Workshop. According to Joseph Solman, Pollock witnessed the experiments Siqueiros was then conducting in his workshop with a spray gun filled with different colors. Solman supported this claim by retelling a story he had heard from Axel Horn, a member of the WPA/FAP and an early friend of Pollock's: "Axel claims this was the determining factor in the development of the famous drip style."[118]

Among the other U.S. artists who were influenced by the Mexican muralists were Thomas Hart Benton, Ben Shahn, and many New Deal muralists.[119] Edward Laning, one of the muralists, wrote about his experiences as a muralist while working for the New Deal mural projects.[120] He recalled that he and friends often visited Rivera and his wife, Frida Kahlo, in their apartment in 1933 at the time that Rivera was working on the Rockefeller Center mural. The young artists then accompanied Rivera on his trips to the center, where he worked every evening from around four or five in the afternoon to one or two in the morning. Laning watched him night after night work on the mural. After Rivera was barred from working on the mural he went on to paint other murals at the New Workers School. Laning recalled that he "followed him there and learned a lot more about fresco at close quarters than [I] had been able to gather in the vast spaces of the RCA Building."[121]

No firmer document of the Mexican influence is afforded us than the responses given by former New Deal artists to a questionnaire they filled out in the early 1970s.[122] Audrey McMahon, director of the College Art Association and regional director for one of the early New Deal mural projects, studied the completed questionnaires:

Many artists were enormously influenced by the Mexicans. They felt that art in Mexico had made so much progress that art in America should do likewise. They speak of the

Mexicans as "giants" and feel themselves "pygmies" in comparison. All this comes through as rather naive. Yet it is true that all the major Mexicans—Orozco, Rivera, Siqueiros—painted murals here during the early 1930s.

American artists had become interested in Mexican muralist art at the very beginning of the movement. Pablo (Paul) O'Higgins, an American who became a Mexican citizen in 1968, first saw reproductions of Rivera's work in a magazine he was leafing through in 1924 in Guaymas, Mexico.[123] He was so impressed with Rivera's work that he wrote to him and later received an invitation to Mexico City. O'Higgins accepted and ended up working as an assistant to Rivera on the Chapingo murals from 1925 to 1927. O'Higgins was thereafter part of the Mexican movement as a muralist and graphic artist. He traveled to New York in 1931, where he stayed for six months and had an exhibition of his work. He also had other exhibitions in New York in 1939 and 1942.[124] O'Higgins was a founding member of TGP, and he painted murals in Mexico and the United States in Seattle (1945) and Honolulu (1951).

Between 1934 and 1935, O'Higgins, Marion and Grace Greenwood, Isamu Noguchi, and a number of Mexican artists painted murals in one of the markets of Mexico City.[125] In 1933 Marion Greenwood chose the Tarascan Indians as her theme for a series of fresco panels she painted at the State University in Michoacán.[126] She later painted murals under the federally funded program in the United States.[127]

Philip Guston and Reuben Kadish, two other U.S. artists who had seen the Mexican muralists' work in Los Angeles, also went to Mexico to paint murals in 1934.[128] Kadish, who had worked as an assistant to Siqueiros in Los Angeles, wrote to him to ask about the possibility of painting murals in Mexico. Siqueiros invited them to Mexico with the promise that a project would be found for them. He and Rivera arranged for them to paint a mural in the Morelia Museum (formerly Emperor Maximilian's summer palace). Kadish, Guston, and Jules Langsner, a poet, left for Mexico City in 1934. Guston, who saw the murals in Mexico City, was disappointed in the "much-heralded Mexican Renaissance," disliked Rivera's work, and was not enthusiastic about Orozco, who "is an expressionist and dominated by emotion but at least is plastic now and then." However, he was enthusiastic about the work Siqueiros had recently carried out in Argentina, which he saw in photographs. They showed that "he is experimenting with Kinetics!"

Guston and Kadish were given four months to complete the mural program (in fresco) in Morelia. By the October deadline, the mural was half finished. In a letter to a friend, Guston wrote: "We are trying many new things and although much is more or less unsuccessful I feel it to be a great experience and have profited greatly." Guston also carried out portrait commissions and created woodcuts and linoleum cuts during his stay in Morelia. Following the completion of the mural, the artists returned to California.[129]

Guston's experience with the Mexican muralists did not have a lasting effect on his work, because his own concerns in the arts changed in subsequent decades, as did the conditions of art making in the United States. The Mexican presence of the 1930s was soon overshadowed by the advent of World War II and the emergence of Abstract Expressionism as the dominant art style in the United States. Moreover, the arrival of leading European artists in New York at the beginning of World War II had an impact on U.S. artists and the subsequent development of Abstract Expressionism in the 1940s and 1950s. Abstract Expressionism had an overwhelming influence on most U.S. artists during that period. Guston was no exception. His interest in using socially relevant subjects in his paintings of the 1930s gave way in subsequent decades to a focus on abstraction.

Pollock's relationship to the Mexican muralists is not as easily explained. Pollock's early interest in Rivera's work does not seem to have had any influence on his work, but his reaction to Orozco's work in the mid-1930s may have had greater impact on him.[130] It is generally reported that the expressive qualities of Orozco's work deeply impressed Pollock, but how these specifically influenced his later development as an artist is not easily measured. His interest in Siqueiros's experiments with new materials and techniques in the mid-1930s is perhaps easier to document, as it may have been a source for his drip style of the following decade.

Mexican American Artists and the Mexican School

Mexican American artists, who matured as artists from the 1920s to the 1950s, were keenly aware of their Mexican background and were inspired by the works of the Mexican School. Some of the artists were born in Mexico and raised in the United States. They too felt strong ties to Mexico and traveled there to study, work, and establish residences. By the 1960s the pull of the Mexican School had waned and the influence of U.S. art movements became stronger. But Mexican American artists of the late 1960s and early 1970s, who identified themselves as Chicanos, turned to Mexico for inspiration, and they began to travel there to study the murals, particularly those by Siqueiros. In spite of the varying influences of Mexican art, the Mexican American and Chicano artists were still affected by U.S. art during the period from 1920 to 1970. They must, therefore, be considered part of U.S. as well as Mexican art movements.

The paintings of the late 1920s, 1930s, and 1940s by Antonio García of Corpus Christi, and the sculptures by Octavio Medellín of Dallas (now a resident of Bandera, Texas) of the same period, were inspired by the Mexican School as well as by American Regionalism. Their contemporary, Chelo González Amézcua of Del Rio, Texas, created a fantasy world in her work, most of which dates from the 1960s. The murals by José Aceves of El Paso and Eduardo Chavez of New Mexico (now a resident of Woodstock, New York), who painted under the auspices of the Works Progress Administration (WPA/FAP), are essentially part of the American Regionalist movement.[131] The drawings dating from the 1960s by Eugenio Quesada of Phoenix, on the other hand, fit into the Mexican School, due to their subject matter as well as their style. Most of the Mexican American artists who came of age in the 1960s reflect U.S. tendencies in the arts of the 1950s and 1960s (abstraction, figurative art, Neo-Dada, Pop, etc.).[132] By the late 1960s Chicano art fists began to reflect the influence of the Mexican School muralists as they began to paint murals of their own in the barrios of the Southwest, Pacific Coast, and the Great Lakes.

Antonio García

Antonio García's work became well known in Texas when one of his paintings, *Woman Before a Mirror* (plate 29), was exhibited during the Texas centennial celebrations of 1939.[133] An earlier work, *Aztec Advance* (1929), demonstrated his interest in portraying a famous battle between the Aztecs and the Spaniards in a way that is sympathetic to the indigenous people. The Aztecs are shown moving in close formation against the unseen Spaniards, who suffered many casualties in their retreat from the Aztec city of Tenochtitlán (present-day Mexico City). The artist created dynamic compositions in both paintings by using slightly unusual perspectives.

Octavio Medellín

Octavio Medellín traveled to the Gulf Coast of Mexico and later to the Yucatán peninsula in 1939. While there, he studied the works of the pre-Columbian artists, which left a lasting impression on him. He considered pre-Columbian art an important part of his heritage, although he was also influenced by the works of U.S. sculptors John Flanagan and William Zorach and the Russian Alexander Archipenko.[134]

An early work entitled *The Struggle* (1938), a sculpture of rose sandstone, exemplifies the artists's use of direct carving to create works of strength and expressiveness. Even more direct and indicative of the artist's interest in Social Realism is *The Hanged* (plate 28), a black walnut sculpture. Another sculpture, *History of Mexico* (1949), is carved on all four sides of a square column. Each register shows one of the three epochs of Mexican history (pre-Columbian, colonial, and modern) and the fourth register depicts the future. The ancient past is at the bottom; the future on top. In most cases, the figures are half-immersed in the nucleus of the column: some figures appear to lunge forward, others are barely suggested in low relief.

Chelo González Amézcua

Chelo González Amézcua used ballpoint pens on cardboard to create highly intricate

28

29

Octavio Medellín
28. *The Hanged.* c. 1942
Black walnut, 42 x 10½ x 10″
Dallas Museum of Art. Kiest Memorial Purchase
Prize, Fourteenth Annual Dallas Allied Arts
Exhibition, 1943
Photo: courtesy Dallas Museum of Art

Antonio García
29. *Woman Before a Mirror.* 1939
Oil on canvas, 73½ x 41½″
Collection the artist
Photo: Ronald Randolf

work she called "filigree art, a new Texas culture." This was a reference to the intricate designs she made almost exclusively with an undifferentiated line and some color. She used Aztec, Egyptian, and biblical personages as sources for the themes she incorporated into extremely complex images. She made no preparatory drawings, preferring to work directly on cardboard. She started her drawings in one corner of the sheet and then proceeded to fill the surface from one end to the other.

Examples of the intricate paintings by González Amézcua are *The Magnificent Poet Netzalhualcoyotl, King and Lover of Arts* (1969) and *Hidden Treasures* (1969).[135] In the first, the ruler is shown seated on a throne, and a fantastic pyramid, topped by multicolored feathers, is seen in the background. The second has fantastic architecture, palm trees, muses, and numerous birds interspersed throughout a multilevel spatial arrangement.

Eduardo Chavez

Eduardo Chavez focused on regional American subjects in his murals. He painted murals in Glenwood Springs and Denver, Colorado; Geneva, Nebraska; Center, Texas; and Fort Warren, Wyoming. All of the Chavez murals deal with regional subjects and are painted in oils except for the one in Wyoming, which was painted with egg tempera on plywood. Among the murals painted by Chavez are two panels placed on opposite walls of the entrance to West High School, Denver. The images for this mural, commissioned by the WPA, are made up of a series of curving diagonals created by the poses of figures on the wagon trail tending to oxen and chopping down trees (plates 30 and 31). Chavez only began to paint in an abstract manner in the 1950s and 1960s.[136] *Xochimilco* (1965) and *Ocate I* (1965) are characteristic of his abstract work. The artist used a Cubist grid in both works for the displacement of the forms on the visual surface.

Eugenio Quesada

Eugenio Quesada of Phoenix, who studied and worked in Guadalajara for six years in the 1960s, paints small-scale works.[137] Fairly typical of the small works is *Bullring* (plate 32), in which he used the barest essentials to define the subject. Everything in the work is governed by the needs of the painting rather than by faithful representation of the motifs. It is an abstract painting in spirit. On a more immediate and direct level are a number of drawings he made of children and their activities, including *Mischievous Girl* (1964), a charcoal drawing in which the child's intense concentration is admirably portrayed.

Abstract, Surrealist, and Fantastic Art: 1926–1970

Rufino Tamayo

Although Surrealism did not have an impact on Mexican art until the 1940s, and abstract art did not take hold in Mexico until the 1950s, it is appropriate to begin this analysis in 1927, the year Rufino Tamayo arrived in New York for the first time.[138] His interest in the formal aspects of a work of art above all other considerations became evident in the early works he produced in New York: portraits, still lifes, nudes, and landscapes. In addition, his rejection of political art was discussed in an article published in 1929.[139] He was touted as the leader of a new Mexican school of painting in which form took precedence over the subject matter of a work of art. This initial stance, which clearly pitted him against the dominant Mexican School, prefigured the confrontations several decades later between abstract artists and followers of the Mexican School.[140] By then Tamayo was back in Mexico taking an active part in these battles. He had become the best-known Mexican abstract painter in the United States and Mexico. Young Mexican abstract painters of the 1950s identified with him and saw him as an alternative to the Mexican School.

Although Tamayo painted a number of murals early in his career and later as a well-known easel painter, he was not very interested in the programmatic purposes of muralism expounded by the early Mexican muralists. His arena was easel painting in oil and to a lesser extent the graphic arts. *Self-Portrait* (plate 33), a gouache over black chalk, demonstrates Tamayo's interest in using texture to create illusions of masses and

30

31

33

32

Eduardo Chavez
31. *Study for "The Longhorn Trail" (detail; proposed mural, Federal Arts Project).* 1938
Egg tempera on composition board, 6 x 24¾″
Collection the artist
Photo: courtesy the artist

Eugenio Quesada
32. *Bullring.* 1969
Oil on canvas, 19½ x 25½″
Collection Donna and Earle Florence, Tempe, Arizona
Photo: Sodari-Smith

Eduardo Chavez
30. *Study for "The Longhorn Trail" (detail; proposed mural, Federal Arts Project).* 1938
Egg tempera on composition board, 6 x 24¾″
Collection the artist
Photo: courtesy the artist

34

Rufino Tamayo
33. *Self-Portrait.* 1927
    Gouache over black chalk on paper, 9⁵/₁₆ x 7″
    Cleveland Museum of Art. Gift of Mrs. Malcom L.
    McBride
    Photo: courtesy Cleveland Museum of Art

Rufino Tamayo
34. *Mandolins and Pineapples.* 1930
    Oil on canvas, 19³/₄ x 27¹/₂″
    The Phillips Collection, Washington, D.C.
    Photo: courtesy The Phillips Collection

color applied in very subtle ways. The self-appraisal is rare in Tamayo's work. The intense, introspective portrait is emphasized by the crowded visual field, and the pose is unlike the traditional three-quarter views of self-portraits that are the result of an artist looking at his reflection in the mirror.

Tamayo exhibited the work he produced from 1927 to 1928 in New York in 1928, and he was back in Mexico City in 1929.[141] He returned to New York in 1930, where he had another exhibition of his work. An example of his canvases from this period is *Mandolins and Pineapples* (plate 34). The light diagonals and rounded shapes of the musical instruments, interspersed with the pineapples in front of an open window, create a beautifully orchestrated painting.

Back in Mexico City in 1932, Tamayo served on the Council for the Fine Arts and became head of the fine arts department of the Ministry of Education. He returned to New York in 1936 as a Mexican delegate to the Art Congress and established residence in Manhattan for the next fifteen years. In 1955 he returned to Mexico for good. For most of the 1930s, Tamayo concentrated on painting still lifes and portraits. The portraits are stiffly posed and come across like snapshot photographs. His works of this period are characterized by a palette of rich earth tones and by consciously simplified formal and thematic configurations (plate 35).

The direction of Tamayo's work was changed by an exhibition of Picasso's work at The Museum of Modern Art in New York City in 1939.[142] His experiments with new ways of representing figures and objects point directly to Picasso's influence. He began to use combinations of hemispherical and crescent shapes to represent the human figure. An example of this type of work is the painting entitled *The Carnival* (plate 38). He continued to explore positive and negative space with these motifs during this period in works such as *Animals* (1941). What is particularly distinctive is the new violence expressed in his painting—in sharp contrast to the calmer work of the previous decade. A more specific reference to Picasso's work is seen in the painting entitled *Women Reaching for the Moon* (1946). The greatly foreshortened women, presented as diagonal units within a shallow space, recall Picasso's seaside paintings of the early 1920s. Tamayo's paintings of the 1950s and 1960s became increasingly abstract, though his subjects ranged from self-portraits to portrayals of men and women shown under various emotional stresses. *Man Pouring out His Heart* (1955), *Woman in Gray* (plate 36), and *Woman Facing a Mirror* (1970) are representative works from his later years. Although the relationship of figure to ground altered—from the foreshortened figures in deeply recessed spaces in his paintings of the 1940s to the flattened-out visual fields of his later work—his focus remained constant: to use color and texture to create carefully arranged visual fields. This was an end in itself—and quite contrary to the expressions of his ideological countrymen.

Carlos Mérida

Rufino Tamayo was preceded in New York by another artist who also eventually developed into an abstract painter. The Guatemalan-born Carlos Mérida lived in New York from 1917 to 1919 and then established residence in Mexico. He had an exhibition of his work in New York in 1926.[143] The paintings in the exhibition were based on themes from folklore, which he had been using since the early 1920s. During a stay of two years in Paris (1927–29), Mérida became interested in the Surrealist works of Klee, Miró, and Picasso, and the expressionistic abstract paintings of Kandinsky. Using the newly discovered vocabulary he began to explore abstraction, which he also found in ancient Mayan art forms: "The feeling for abstraction mastered by my ancestors took form in me."[144]

Mérida exhibited his work in New York for the second time in 1930. He also had shows in Los Angeles in 1933 and San Francisco in 1934.[145] *Deer Dance* (1935), an oil on canvas depicting a Mexican Indian dance ritual, exemplifies the artist's interest in folklore during this period. From 1941 to 1942, he was a visiting professor of art at North Texas State Teachers College in Denton, Texas. *The Blue Apple* (plate 39), a representative work of Mérida's later period, is directly related to the many outdoor mosaics he made in Guatemala City, Mexico City, and San Antonio, Texas. The motifs are presented within a geometric framework but nevertheless remain recognizable forms from nature. The interpenetration of the rectilinear shapes is contrasted with a few crescent forms, relating this work to the two-dimensional Cubist grid.

Surrealism and Fantasy Art

A number of Mexican artists were influenced by Surrealist ideas in the 1940s, but only Lenora Carrington, who arrived in Mexico in the early 1940s from Europe via New York, consistently used Surrealism and fantasy in her work. Guillermo Meza was a Surrealist who should also be considered a follower of the Mexican School because his work ultimately reflected his Mexican identity. Frida Kahlo never considered herself a Surrealist, though she created an intensely personal iconography of fantasy that has been closely associated with Surrealist tendencies. Pedro Friedeberg, a European-born artist who was raised in Mexico, incorporated Surrealist ideas into his highly controlled, almost detached images and sculptures. Francisco Toledo, an Oaxacan-born and largely self-taught artist, created naive worlds of fantasy in which people and animals cavort.

Frida Kahlo

Frida Kahlo created a very personal autobiographical style that was deeply influenced by the Mexican votive (ex-voto) painters and other folk artists. In 1926 she suffered a serious accident when a bus in which she was riding collided with a trolley car. During her long convalescence in hospital, she devoted herself to painting. She later came in contact with Diego Rivera in the Ministry of Education, where he was painting murals, and in 1928 they were married. She traveled to the United States with Rivera (1930–34) and in 1938 visited New York on her own to exhibit her work.[146]

One of the earliest works that Kahlo made in the United States is *Frida and Diego Rivera* (1931). The work is similar to the traditional wedding portraits of nineteenth-century Mexico. A pink bird holds a long ribbon in its beak over Kahlo's head with an inscription that provides information about the occasion.[147] The style, technique, and the use of inscriptions are deliberately related to the work of nineteenth-century Mexican provincial painting.

Self-Portrait on the Borderline Between Mexico and the United States (plate 40) was painted during Kahlo's and Rivera's stay in Detroit.[148] The artist is shown standing on a pedestal holding a cigarette in her right hand and a small Mexican flag in her left. The inscription on the pedestal reads: "Carmen Rivera painted her portrait in the year 1932." (Carmen was one of Kahlo's given names, which she used occasionally during this period.) The left side of the painting refers to Mexico (with the emblematic sun and moon, a pre-Columbian temple and figurines on the ground, and flowers and their roots); the right side refers to the United States (with the American flag, skyscrapers, smokestacks, and electrical appliances and their wires below ground). A wire from an electrical generator is plugged into the pedestal, and two others go underground, where they are connected to the plant roots on the left side of the painting. The motifs are obvious references to the two countries and reflect the artist's view of each one. Her ambiguous relationship is emphasized by the placement of her self-portrait straddling the border. The generator wires and the plant roots are also indirectly fed into the pedestal on which the artist stands. Her Indo-European heritage was expressed in a number of other ways. The sun and the moon in the sky (usually found in Mexican religious art of the colonial period) are framed by billowy clouds, which produce lightning at their point of contact in the center of the painting. (The darker cloud around the moon is in the shape of a hand, paraphrasing Michelangelo's famous Creation panel in the Sistine Chapel.) The lightning striking the Aztec temple of Malinalco (built in 1476) symbolically connects the European and Indian components. The letters on the factory smokestacks spell out the name "Ford," a reference to the Ford Motor Company plant Kahlo and Rivera saw during their stay in Detroit. Although the motifs, signs, and symbols refer to the two countries, the conception of the work is in fact related to colonial and traditional Mexican painting, evidenced by the use of registers, a device common to ex-voto panel paintings, the emblematic sun and moon motifs borrowed from colonial-period religious art, as well as the inscription on the pedestal, also from colonial-period painting.

My Dress Hangs There (1933), which was painted by Kahlo in New York when

35

36

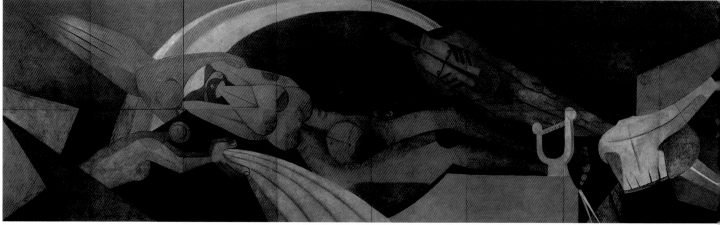

37

Rufino Tamayo
35. *The Family.* 1936
    Oil on canvas, 31½ x 47⅝″
    Minneapolis Institute of Arts. Gift of William and
    Noma Copley
    Photo: courtesy Minneapolis Institute of Arts

Rufino Tamayo
36. *Woman in Gray.* 1959
    Oil on canvas, 76¾ x 51″
    Solomon R. Guggenheim Museum, New York
    Photo: Robert E. Mates

38

Rufino Tamayo
37. *Nature and the Artist: The Work of Art and the*
   Spectator. 1943
   Fresco, 116 x 531″
   Smith College Museum of Art, Northampton,
   Massachusetts
   Photo: courtesy Smith College

Rufino Tamayo
38. *The Carnival.* 1941
   Oil on canvas, 43 x 33″
   The Phillips Collection, Washington, D.C.
   Photo: courtesy The Phillips Collection

39

Carlos Mérida
39. *The Blue Apple*. 1962
Petro plastic on parchment, 30 x 23⅝"
Phoenix Art Museum. Gift of the Friends of
Mexican Art
Photo: courtesy Phoenix Art Museum

Rivera was working on the Rockefeller Center mural, also has several levels of symbols.[149] Each of the various settings in the painting has its own spatial references, and the numerous motifs and symbols are represented in different scales. The upper part of the painting includes an aerial view of Manhattan on one side and a view of Ellis Island and the Statue of Liberty in the center and an ocean liner between them. The large central portion of the painting includes a foreshortened view of the city and its environs. A dress of the artist is seen floating above a mass of people represented along the lowermost portion of the work. The empty Tehuana dress (one of the artist's favorite costumes) refers to Mexico and her longing to be there. Other details in the picture, including a toilet on a pedestal (American efficiency), a portrait of Mae West (false values), a telephone on top of a building (connecting the financial district with American industry with its wires), and the view of the masses (suffering people), comment on American society and the severe economic conditions of the times.

Pedro Friedeberg
Friedeberg first exhibited his work in New York in 1962 and in Washington, D.C., in 1963.[150] He had other exhibitions in New York, from 1964 to 1969, and in Houston, Texas, in 1968. He also painted two murals for the Mexican pavilion of the Hemisfair in San Antonio in 1968. Although he is an architect as well as a sculptor, he is primarily known for his paintings and his furniture designs. Both fit into the category of fantasy art. Particularly well known is a chair he made of wood in the form of a large hand resting on a large foot. The palm of the hand forms the seat, the extended fingers form the back of the chair, and the thumb functions as an armrest. The foot forms the base of the chair. Friedeberg's paintings are full of architectural motifs and references to other manufactured items presented in bizarre and fantastic contexts. His works are known for their meticulous detail and his sense of humor.

Francisco Toledo
Francisco Toledo exhibited his work in Fort Worth, Texas, in 1959, and in New York in 1964, as well as in numerous galleries throughout Europe.[151] He exhibited in a number of group shows in New York in the late 1960s. Toledo's works represent fantastic scenes in which people and animals (ducks, cats, wolves, horses, and rabbits) are included. Many of his images are based on myths and legends he heard as a child in Juchitán, Oaxaca, where he was raised. Animals are used symbolically (rabbits and fish are often used in erotic contexts). His works have a strong formal network. Positive and negative spaces are given equal treatment, and the overall pattern often allows them to be seen from any angle.

The Mexican School and the Abstract Artists
A second phase of abstraction in Mexican art began in the 1950s with the advent of works by Mathias Goeritz, Gunther Gerzso, Rogier Von Gunten, Manuel Felguérez, Vicente Rojo, Luis López-Loza, Fernando García Ponce, and others. A number of these artists were not born in Mexico. Goeritz, Rojo, and Von Gunten arrived in the country in the 1950s; while others, such as Gerzso, spent many years abroad.[152] The exposure to international art movements provided by these European artists, as well as Tamayo's return to Mexico at about the same time, led to the development of abstract art in Mexico.

Unlike the Mexican School artists who received the support of the Mexican government, first in their capacities as muralists and later as participants in major exhibitions of art sent abroad, the abstract artists did not receive immediate official recognition for their work. The first steps taken to rectify this situation came in 1952 and 1953 when Tamayo was commissioned by the government to paint two separate murals for the Palace of Fine Arts.[153] A more general recognition of abstraction occurred when the prestigious first prize in the second Mexican biennial exhibition, held in 1960, was awarded to an abstract work by García Ponce.[154] This was an unprecedented move and caused an uproar. The followers of the Mexican School had been well represented in the 1958 biennial exhibition, whereas Tamayo and the other abstractionists had been excluded altogether.[155] The situation grew so tense in the following years that the third biennial exhibition never materialized.

40

Frida Kahlo
40. *Self-Portrait on the Borderline Between Mexico and the United States.* 1932
Oil on metal, 11¾ x 13½"
Collection Mr. and Mrs. Manuel Rayero, New York
Photo: courtesy Mr. Manuel Rayero

The old battle between the Mexican School artists and the abstractionists for preeminence in the arts in Mexico was renewed during the biennial exhibitions of 1958 and 1960. The Mexican School artists sought to maintain control of the support system for the arts so that they could create an art for the people, a public art, a truly revolutionary art that would serve the needs of the nation. In contrast, the abstractionists sought to rid the country of false art, riddled with unnecessary programmatic content, an art that they felt no longer served any purpose.

The Abstractionists
Mathias Goeritz
Mathias Goeritz, born in Poland and raised in Berlin, where he studied art and art history, traveled throughout Europe in the late 1930s and went to Spanish Morocco at the beginning of World War II. He stayed there several years teaching foreign languages and art history.[156] He then went to Spain, living in several cities—Granada, Madrid, and Santillana del Mar (near the caves of Altamira)—for almost five years. He exhibited his work, lectured, and taught. He arrived in Mexico in 1948 and began an active life in the arts as a teacher, artist (painter and sculptor), and founder of several galleries of art. His environments and sculpture-monuments of the 1950s, which he built and displayed in Mexico, have had an influence on Mexican and U.S. sculptors, especially the Minimalists.[157] He exhibited his work in New York in 1956, 1960, and 1962.[158]

The best-known works by Goeritz are his experimental museum, El Eco (The Echo), and the *Five Towers*, constructed in Mexico City in 1953 and 1957 respectively.[159] Both had repercussions in the United States in the 1960s in the works of U.S. sculptors such as David Smith, Robert Grosvenor, Ronald Bladen, Tony Smith, and Mark Di Suvero.[160] In both works the artist exhibited his "emotional architecture." It was an art form opposed to functionalism, formalism, and other "isms," which he felt ignored spiritual concerns.

The most impressive aspect of the experimental museum was the inclusion of a large metal sculpture known as *The Serpent*. Made up of geometric shapes painted black, it was placed directly on the floor (with no base or pedestal), actively engaging the room's walls in the aesthetic of the work. The total space environment prefigured similar experiments carried out in the United States by at least ten years.[161]

The *Five Towers*, located in a suburb of Mexico City known as Ciudad Satélite, is a work of five painted towers made of concrete. They are each 180 feet high.[162] Goeritz had originally envisioned seven towers, each between 500 and 700 feet in height. The project represents painting, sculpture, and emotional (that is, nonfunctional) architecture. It grew out of experiments the artist carried out as part of his emotional architecture series, which included *Here and There* (1955), a polychromed wood sculpture inspired by the skyline of Manhattan. When he received the commission for the Ciudad Satélite project, he tried to create a replica of Manhattan that would elicit the emotions he had experienced when he saw the play of spaces created by the overlapping skyscrapers for the first time.

In March 1960 Goeritz entered the polemics of the New York art world by making a protest in front of The Museum of Modern Art against the *Homage to New York* piece by Jean Tinguely (a sculpture programmed to self-destruct within twenty-four hours).[163] Tinguely was a neo-Dadaist who introduced chance into his mechanized machines of the mid-1950s and early 1960s. Goeritz's printed manifesto, "Please Stop," was an example of his call for spiritual values in art and his opposition to the notions of impermanence and instability exemplified by the Tinguely machine. The Abstract Expressionists, among them Franz Kline, Mark Rothko, Ad Reinhardt, and Guston, applauded his protest. The formalists, and particularly the Minimalists, among them Gregory Battcock, did not accept his calls for absolute values and permanence in art as valid.[164] As artists who made primary structures and large-scale constructions, they were interested in challenging accepted notions of scale and proportion rather than in the "timelessness of the ancient Egyptians," as Goeritz put it.

Gunther Gerzso
Gunther Gerzso, who worked in the United States in theater set design and

cinematography from 1936 to 1942, began painting in 1939. From 1942 to 1965 he worked as an art director with Mexican film companies.[165] His work was influenced by the Surrealists in the 1940s and by the Geometric Abstractionists in the 1950s. His work has remained primarily abstract. He uses overlapping geometric shapes to create illusions of shallow depth. The carefully modulated surfaces of each of the shapes are given sharp contours by the inclusion of darker or shadowed shapes underneath. The results are finely orchestrated patterns based on a Cubist grid.

Manuel Felguérez

Manuel Felguérez exhibited his work in New York in 1959 and 1960, and at the Hemisfair in San Antonio, Texas, in 1968.[166] He taught art at Cornell University in 1966, and he was a founding member of the Salón Independiente de México in 1968 with Francisco Icaza and Kazuya Sakai.[167] Felguérez has been one of the leading Mexican formalists. He has focused on welded steel sculpture and on easel painting, in which he used a vocabulary based on Abstract Expressionism in the 1960s and computer-derived geometric configurations in the 1970s. A good example of his 1960s work is *Eight and a Half* (1966), in which texture, basic shapes, and color are arranged within Cubist-derived space.

Vicente Rojo

Vicente Rojo, who was born in Spain, moved to Mexico in 1949. He exhibited his work in a number of American cities beginning in 1966 and in New York in 1968 and 1970.[168] Rojo, like other artists of the 1960s, used Abstract Expressionist motifs but tried to rid his painting of its emotional content, focusing on signs and similar elements. His textured surfaces are applied to self-referential objects made up of basic shapes, such as hexagons, circles, squares, and trapezoids.

Luis López-Loza

Luis López-Loza traveled to New York in 1963, where he worked at the Pratt Graphic Arts Center. He exhibited his work in a number of American cities beginning in 1963 and in New York from 1963 to 1970. López-Loza has used pre-Columbian sources for paintings made up of interlocking forms arranged within a Cubist grid format. His early work, exemplified by *Children's Dream* (1955), is suggestive of the biomorphic shapes used by Gorky and Miró, but unlike these artists, who always focused on the distinctions between figure and ground, López-Loza emphasized the overall patterns of the image.

The New Figurative Artists

In spite of the success of the abstractionists in the 1960 biennial, the focus of the Mexican art world shifted from the confrontation between the Mexican School and the abstractionists to the work of a new group of artists who identified themselves as the Nueva Presencia. Their art was based on figurative trends that had their sources in Mexican art. The leading practitioners were José Luis Cuevas, Arnold Belkin, Francisco Icaza, Francisco Corzas, and Rafael Coronel. Most of them rejected mural painting because of its political content and the nationalistic bent of the muralists. However, Belkin and Icaza, who founded the movement and the magazine *Nueva Presencia* in 1961, continued to focus on what they called a New Humanism.

The crucial event led to this new development in Mexican art took place in 1960. Siqueiros was imprisoned by the government for "internal dissolution" in May of that year.[169] In 1959 he had organized a committee and then a national congress to help free striking railroad workers who had been imprisoned by the government. In Caracas, where the president of Mexico was scheduled to visit, and later in Havana, Siqueiros strongly criticized the government. Finding a hostile reception upon his return to Mexico, Siqueiros held a press conference to explain his position but was severely criticized in the newspapers. He was imprisoned on April 9, 1960, for an eight-year term. He was released four years later, at the end of the six-year term of office of the Mexican president who had imprisoned him. Belkin and Icaza thought of keeping Siqueiros informed of events on the outside with a newsletter, which later developed into the publication *Nueva Presencia*.[170] This activity coincided with an exhibition of works by Belkin, Icaza, Cuevas, and others, and the appearance of Selden Rodman's book on art, *The Insiders*.[171] Rodman singled out the work of Cuevas as a prime example of "Insider" art. The artists were impressed enough with the book to use its title for their exhibition, which they translated as *Los Interioristas*. By the second exhibition, it was apparent that the title was inappropriate, given the various disparate tendencies of the artists included in it. By then, Cuevas had broken with the group. He felt that a number of younger artists who were imitating his style should not be included in the exhibition. The group survived under the name of Nueva Presencia until 1963.

Cuevas, along with Goeritz and Friedeberg, founded the group Los Hartos (Those Who Are Fed Up) as a reaction to the humanists of the Nueva Presencia group.[172] But Goeritz and Friedeberg had their own agendas outside the concerns of Cuevas, who has always been a figurative artist. Goeritz was more interested in nonfigurative art and Friedeberg in Surrealist-related sculptures and paintings.

Arnold Belkin

Arnold Belkin, a Canadian by birth, went to Mexico in 1947 to study art, and from 1949 to 1950 he worked as an assistant to Siqueiros.[173] He exhibited his work in Los Angeles and New York in 1962 and in other American cities in the 1960s, and he was a visiting professor in painting and advanced techniques at the Pratt Institute in 1967. The painting *The Dream* (1964) exemplifies the work of Belkin at the height of the Nueva Presencia period. The focus is on the emotional features of a contorted human figure. Although the emphasis is on building up the illusion of masses, the artist still consciously arranged the various parts of the image to conform to a Cubist grid in relation to the frame.

Francisco Icaza

Francisco Icaza exhibited his paintings in a number of American cities beginning in 1964, and his work was selected for a Guggenheim International Award exhibition.[174] *Los Juanes* (1961) is one of a series of paintings by Icaza in which the artist emphasized the anonymity of the figures he represented. The heavily built-up canvas of "somber earth colors," is broken up into simplified figural shapes, which nonetheless retain a semblance of identification as soldiers.

José Luis Cuevas

José Luis Cuevas, who first exhibited his work in Washington, D.C., in 1954, has received awards for his work throughout Latin America, the United States, Europe, and India, and has worked as a visiting artist in art schools in the United States.[175] He has illustrated and written a number of books and has been the subject of a number of film documentaries in Mexico and the United States.[176]

Cuevas is interested in portraying himself in various circumstances and contexts. The artist developed from a student of the work of Orozco, then of Picasso, and finally of Goya before creating his own unique calligraphic style. His early subjects—prostitutes, fortune-tellers, peddlers, beggars, and dwarfs—appeared for the first time in the United States in an exhibition held at OAS headquarters in Washington, D.C., in 1954. He also focused on victims of fights or accidents, the dying, and the insane as subjects for his drawings. He moved on to portray a world of freaks, monsters, and other bizarre creatures, inspired by the writings of Franz Kafka and the Marquis de Sade. He also based a number of self-portraits on the work of Rembrandt and Goya (plate 41).

Mexican Artists in the United States: II

From the 1930s through the 1960s, Mexican artists continued to receive attention in the national magazines and newspapers for their mural commissions and solo exhibitions in the United States and Mexico. Numerous books on the Mexican School and on individual artists were published, and Rivera, Orozco, Siqueiros, and Tamayo were so well known that even their exhibitions in Mexico were reported in the art periodicals and in *Time* and *Newsweek*.[177] However, the artist who received the most attention

41

José Luis Cuevas
41. *The Printmaker Désandré Working on a
Self-Portrait.* 1965
Ink and watercolor on paper, 18¼ x 22¾″
Solomon R. Guggenheim Museum, New York
Photo: Robert E. Mates

during this period was Tamayo. His work was reviewed almost every year and sometimes several times a year from the 1940s through the 1960s.[178] He received reviews as favorable as those of the other Mexican artists. In the late 1950s and 1960s, however, the best-known Mexican artists were evaluated by a new generation of critics, and U.S. artists were no longer paying as much attention to Mexico. Even the works of the younger Mexican artists, among them José Luis Cuevas, who was the best known, were treated more harshly. The reviewers were no longer in awe of Mexican artists.

Sam Hunter was one of the first to give Tamayo's work, exhibited at the Knoedler Gallery in 1954, a negative review.[179] In his view, there had always been a conflict in Tamayo's art "between a genuine primitive quality—something native and in the blood—and the worldling's sophisticated taste." He saw these two tendencies resolved in Tamayo's *Wounded Beast* of 1941, but not necessarily so in his recent work: "All that is left of Tamayo's earlier manner are his fine, seductive colors." Tamayo's exhibitions at the Knoedler Gallery in January 1957 and November 1959 and at the New Art Center Galleries were not well received. According to one reviewer of the 1957 show, "something is required to lift this artist from the professional trivia into which his South-of-the-Border Parisianism has slipped."[180] The reviewer of the 1959 show was also not impressed.

There is not much new or different in these stylized, chic, and pseudo-archaic paintings. He has roughed up the texture a bit, but no matter how thin Tamayo slices it, it's still the same old slice of watermelon.[181]

Although Tamayo was still given some positive reviews, misconceptions about his racial background came up in a review of his exhibition at the Far Gallery in May 1969. According to one reviewer, "Tamayo's structure adheres to an admixture of Picassoid Cubism and Mayan symbolism, a blend he has turned into a personal trademark."[182] Tamayo is Zapotecan, yet the reference to Tamayo as a Mayan Indian also appeared in a review of his exhibition at the Valentine Gallery in 1942.[183] The Mayan reference appeared repeatedly in articles by Henry McBride starting in 1943 and continuing through 1951, and was particularly evident in a review of his works at the Knoedler Gallery.[184] Even though he considered Tamayo to be far from his source material, McBride still thought his Mayan background was important:

Just how Mayan his bringing up was I do not seem to know, but I am sure he doesn't have to go into trances in the effort to recapture the ancient way of looking at things. I am sure it's in his blood.

The Mayan reference appeared one more time in a review of another exhibition of his work at the Knoedler Gallery in September 1962.[185] According to the reviewer, the "curious figures may have stemmed from ancient Mayan gods, but it would seem rather more likely that they were inspired by primordial nightmares of the painter himself."

Cuevas was initially given favorable reviews of his work in the 1950s and early 1960s. A reviewer of his first New York exhibition, at the Herbert Gallery in 1960, considered his style "strikingly original."[186] He saw the strength of his work, not in his subjects, but "in the nervous ebb and flow of his scratchy lines, and in the composition of the figures." The continuing reference to a Mexican sensibility was brought up by Langsner in his review of Cuevas's 1960 exhibition of drawings in Los Angeles.[187] "Cuevas's preoccupation with the cruelty of the human predicament embodies a peculiarly Mexican sensibility." His 1962 exhibition at the Grace Borgenicht Gallery was not well received by another reviewer:

Cuevas comes on like a lyrical poet of the pen, ink, and brush. But his sweetly mellow, gluey, wishy-washy color, and faces and figures influenced by Shahn and Picasso of the Rose and Blue phases are merely a thin disguise.[188]

Following a discussion of the artist's development, the reviewer further stated: "In one or two instances Cuevas's drawings seem almost good, but they are about as substantial as cotton candy or charlotte russe."

Mexican American and Chicano Artists

The art of Mexican Americans and, to some extent, Chicanos began to receive attention in the late 1960s and early 1970s in the United States. Artists of Mexican ancestry began to think of themselves as members of a distinct group whose ethnic antecedents had a bearing on their work. Although artists with close ties to Mexico had been working in the southwestern United States for generations, awareness of kinship among Mexican Americans, Spanish Americans, and Chicanos essentially began in the late 1960s. (It should be noted that all of these designations refer to the same people and represent a difference in self-identification over a period of almost four hundred years.) The people in the area which now forms the American Southwest and Pacific Southwest have traditionally referred to themselves as *Hispanos* (Spanish Americans), *Mexicanos* (Mexican Americans), and *Chicanos*. The people of Mexican descent who emigrated to the Pacific Northwest and Great Lakes region also refer to themselves as Mexicans and Chicanos. Spanish Americans have emphasized their Spanish background, while Mexican Americans have embraced their Mexican heritage. Chicanos discard both traditions as inappropriate because they do not reflect the true reality of a people distinct from the Spanish, the Mexican, and the American.

The first efforts to exhibit the works of Mexican American or Chicano artists were not made until about 1970. One exhibition, entitled *Tlacuilo* ("artist" in the Aztec language) was held at the Guadalupe Cultural Arts Center in San Antonio in the spring of 1970, and another, entitled *Chicano Artists*, opened at the Pasadena Art Museum in November.[189] Another exhibition, entitled *Arte de la Gente* (Art of the People), opened at the Sacramento State College Art Gallery in June 1970. Esteban Villa, who organized the exhibition, expressed the feelings of the artists who were involved in the efforts to create a Chicano art: "We are lost right now. We are stumbling around trying to find an identity. We're not trying to make a racial thing. We're trying to establish a relevance as painters."[190]

The artists who came to maturity in the 1960s were influenced by U.S. art initially and, in some cases, by Mexican art by the end of the decade. Those who were attempting to create a socially relevant art, based on their own background and unique experience in the United States, used the life of the people—folklore, superstition, religion, customs—and their history as subjects for their paintings, sculptures, and prints.[191] Eventually these same subjects and others related to the community were used in murals painted in the barrios of the Southwest, Pacific Southwest and Northwest, and the Great Lakes region.[192] Their search for antecedents and models for their work led the Chicano muralists to the early Mexican muralists and Siqueiros, in particular, the only surviving member of the *tres grandes* at this time.

Among the leaders of the Chicano art movement who were instrumental in establishing community cultural centers, organizing groups of artists and art exhibitions, and working as artists were Salvador Roberto Torres of San Diego, Leonard Castellanos of Los Angeles, Esteban Villa and José Montoya of Sacramento, Ernesto Palomino of Fresno, and Melesio Casas of San Antonio. Among the artists who were not actively involved in the movement but were later included in exhibitions and publications with a focus on Mexican American and Chicano art in the 1970s and Hispanic art in the 1980s were Manuel Neri of San Francisco and Luis Jiménez of El Paso.[193]

Although both artists used pre-Columbian art as a point of reference for their works of the 1960s, Neri (plate 42) always remained interested in the formal and expressive qualities of sculpture, while Jiménez was more interested in the subject matter. Jiménez focused on modern Mexican art and the social and political conditions in the United States to make forceful statements about American society.

Many other artists began their careers in the 1960s and by the end of the decade were fully involved in the Chicano art movement. Malaquías Montoya and Rupert García of San Francisco were among the best of the graphic and poster artists of the movement. Judy Baca of Los Angeles, who painted her first mural in Los Angeles in 1969 (*La Abuelita*), gained national recognition for her work as a muralist in the 1970s and 1980s.[194] Among the others who painted the first murals identified with the movement were Mario Castillo in Chicago in 1968 (*Metafísica*), Leonard Castellanos in Los Angeles in 1968–69 (Mechicano Art Center), Manuel Martínez in Denver in 1970, Eduardo Carrillo (plate 44) in Los Angeles in 1970, Raymond Patlán in Chicago in 1970–71 (*From My Father and Yours*), Gerónimo Garduño and others in Santa Fe in 1971 (*Clínica de la Gente*), Ernesto Palomino in Fresno in 1971, and Leo Tanguma in Houston in the early 1970s (*The Rebirth of Our Nationality*). Carmen Lomas Garza, a printmaker as well as a painter, focused on the customs and folklore of the barrio in her work. An example of her early work is the print *La Vida es Perra* (Life Is a Bitch; 1970).

Melesio Casas and Luis Jiménez

Works by Casas and Jiménez exemplify the critical views of U.S. society often expressed by Chicano artists, as well as the relationship to U.S. and Mexican arts shared by their colleagues in the movement.

Casas incorporated television and movie screens in a series of images he began painting in the 1960s, which he called "Humanscapes." Initially, he used erotic subjects as treated by the media, and later, he became more involved with social, political, and economic problems experienced by Chicano people. He began to pay particular attention to the Mexican American as migrant worker, youth, and "outsider." An example of these works is *New Horizons* (No. 65 in the series; 1970), which shows farm workers in the field with a Huelga eagle of the Farm Workers Union of California in the background.

Jiménez's sculptures, made of fiberglass from molds, painted, and then coated with epoxy, which gives them a glossy surface, are the result of extensive study and numerous sketches with colored pencils. *The American Dream* (1967–69) exemplifies the artist's interest in attracting the viewer's attention by unusual subject matter. The sculpture represents the coupling of a human female with an automobile— a contemporary variation on a common mythological motif. In this case, the artist referred to the pre-Columbian myth in which a jaguar copulates with a human female to create a supernatural being. Jiménez substituted the automobile for the jaguar and the blond, blue-eyed woman for the Indian to make a statement about U.S. society and its love affair with the automobile.

In the sculpture *The Man of Fire* (plate 43) Jiménez paraphrased Orozco's dome painting in the orphanage in Guadalajara, Mexico, and also made reference to the stories he had heard as a child regarding the torture by flames of Cuauhtemoc, the last Aztec warrior to fight the invading Spaniards in the sixteenth century. The work also refers to the Buddhist monks who set themselves on fire to protest the war in Vietnam.

42

43

Manuel Neri
42. *Figure.* 1958
Plaster, enamel, wood, and wire armature,
61 x 22 x 16½"
Private collection. Courtesy Charles Cowles Gallery,
San Francisco
Photo: courtesy Anne Kohs & Associates, Inc.

Luis Jiménez
43. *Man on Fire.* 1969–70
Fiberglass and epoxy resin coating, 89 x 60 x 16"
Collection Dug McIntyre, El Paso, Texas
Photo: Bruce Berman

44

Eduardo Carrillo
44. *Cabin in the Sky.* 1963
Oil on plywood, 72 x 52″
Collection Anthony Berlant, Santa Monica,
California
Photo: Lee Varis

Appendix

The following group exhibitions of Mexican artists seen in the United States are the most tangible evidence of the Mexican presence in the United States from the late 1920s through the 1960s. These exhibitions gave Americans opportunities to see the works of the Mexican School artists within the context of the "authentic" Mexican arts that had inspired them: namely, Indian arts and crafts, pre-Columbian art, votive paintings, and the prints of José Guadalupe Posada. The Mexican government used the exhibitions to further its national policies abroad, and the exhibiting artists enjoyed greater exposure to foreign audiences as well as economic benefits. The reviews of the exhibitions by the Mexican artists themselves, by the organizers of the exhibitions, and by the art critics for the major art periodicals demonstrate how the art was viewed and appreciated during this period. Although the reviewers often did not entirely understand the complexities of Mexican art and its antecedents, not to mention the many forces in Mexico and elsewhere that were affecting its development, they nonetheless generally responded to Mexico's art with insightful comments and appreciation.

The Art Center Gallery (1928)

The first large group exhibition of Mexican artists seen in the United States was organized by Frances Flynn Paine under the auspices of the Rockefeller Foundation and in cooperation with Mexico's Ministry of Education and the National University of Mexico. The exhibition, which presented work by twenty-two artists, was shown at the Art Center Gallery in New York City in January 1928. It formed part of a series of exhibitions of Mexican arts and crafts.

Anita Brenner, in her review of the exhibition, characterized it as the first truly significant demonstration of the new Mexican art outside Mexico.[1] Orozco, who was one of the exhibitors, attacked the show in a letter to Charlot: "The gallery is bad, just amateurs and beginners, the room dark, the director an imbecile, complete chaos, after one week there wasn't even a catalogue."[2] He complained about the hanging of the show and the public's reaction to it. "The very few people who came just laughed and joked or felt disappointed." He also noted that the "serious art press, like *The Arts*, *Art News*, etc., didn't say a word, neither did the critics…the newspapers and some magazines just ridiculed it too and a number of them had some very harsh words to say."

An American reviewer who discussed the works in the exhibition by Orozco, Rivera, and Charlot also made reference to Orozco's murals in the National Preparatory School, among them the *Maternity* panel, which he considered "fat and repulsive."[3] The other artists were categorized according to their respective styles, goals, and background. Among them were Francisco Goitia, deemed a "realist"; Siqueiros, "who seeks to fit modern murals to a machine age"; Mérida, "A Mayan, stylist, decorator, colorist"; Revueltas, "aims at pure decoration with mechanics"; Castellanos, "colorist"; Montenegro and Ruiz, "stylists and decorators"; Pablo O'Higgins, "an American amalgamated to the Mexican School"; and Tamayo, "colorist."

Metropolitan Museum of Art (1930–1931)

Mexican Arts, which opened in New York at the Metropolitan Museum of Art on October 13, 1930, traveled to seven other American cities from late November 1930 to September 1931. René d'Harnoncourt, with the cooperation of the Mexican government and the support of the American sponsors, selected the pieces, organized the exhibition, and wrote the catalog for it.[4] The exhibition of 509 items included modern Mexican paintings as well as hundreds of pieces of applied arts dating from the colonial period to the time of the exhibition. D'Harnoncourt wanted to demonstrate that there was a continuous Mexican tradition in the arts, reflecting a true Mexican spirit.

Numerous articles appeared in museum bulletins and major art magazines as well as in the newspapers of the cities where the exhibition was shown.[5] Most of them were descriptive rather than critical and were based on d'Harnoncourt's catalog.

Ralph Flint, one of the few reviewers of the exhibition, characterized the works by Orozco as "stark, turbulent and Goya-like in the macabre intensity of their mood." He lamented the fact that murals by Rivera were not on view, with the exception of a small fragment (lent by Dwight W. Morrow).[6]

Philadelphia Arts Alliance (1939)

An exhibition of Mexican paintings, prints, drawings, and crafts was held at the Philadelphia Art Alliance with the cooperation of the Mexican government in 1939. A large painting of Zapata by Orozco and a plaster intaglio by Siqueiros were exhibited along with prints by members of the Taller de Gráfica Popular, including Leopoldo Méndez, Francisco Dosamantes, Raul Anguiano, and Alfredo Zalce. A reviewer emphasized the importance of the exhibition as "a further step toward a cultural fraternity between the United States and Latin America."[7] Orozco and Siqueiros were singled out as artists who were well known and admired in the United States. Méndez was considered "the best of the Mexican lithographers" represented in the exhibition.

Golden Gate Exhibition (1939)

The first exhibition to focus entirely on modern Mexican art was organized by Ines Amor, director of the Galería de Arte Méxicano, for the *Golden Gate* exhibition held in San Francisco in 1939. Twenty-four paintings by twenty artists were included in the exhibition. A reviewer, who reproduced a painting by Federico Cantú in his article, rated the exhibition "excellent."[8] According to the reviewer, "social protest…provides the underlying theme of most of Mexico's art production." The artists mentioned as being well represented in the exhibition were Rivera, Orozco, Montenegro, Mérida, Siqueiros, Tamayo, and Cantú.

The Museum of Modern Art (1940)

The exhibition *Twenty Centuries of Mexican Art* opened at The Museum of Modern Art in the summer of 1940.[9] Some three thousand items were displayed in the show, which was organized in collaboration with the Mexican government under the supervision of Alfonso Caso. A curator was selected for each of the four sections to choose the items for the show. They were Caso (pre-Columbian art), Manuel Toussaint (colonial art), Montenegro (folk art), and Covarrubias (modern art).

In Charlot's view, the modern section was limited in scope because works from the 1920s were not included:

Even though murals cannot be transported for exhibition purposes, there exists a body of work closely related to them….Even the painters that opposed in style the school of muralists would have increased in significance against this historic background. The oversight of a bare five years [1921–1926] punches a gigantic hole into the close-knit trend of those two thousand years of Mexican art.[10]

Jeannette Lowe, who reproduced works by Siqueiros and Tamayo in her review, considered the exhibition a "brilliant survey" of Mexican art.[11] The works of Siqueiros, Tamayo, Rivera, Orozco, Best-Maugard, and Charlot are discussed in the final part of her review, which she devoted to the modern section. She made the point that not all the artists in the show "have been active radicals":

[There is] the enchanting Pretty Girl *by Tamayo, the keen sense and fine draftsmanship of Castellanos in* Day of San Juan, *Frida Kahlo's Surrealistic* The Two Fridas, *and Covarrubias's* The Bone. *Roberto Montenegro… is represented by* Maya Women, *the repeating profiles reflecting the sense of pattern and line of its original.*

The five works singled out for discussion were reproduced in the exhibition catalog.

Institute of Modern Art (1941)

An exhibition of modern Mexican art, organized by MacKinley Helm, was shown at the Institute of Modern Art in Boston in 1941, and it was toured to five other U.S. cities. The exhibition grew out of research carried out by Helm in Mexico for a book on modern Mexican painters.[12]

James S. Plaut, who reproduced works by Antonio Ruiz, Tamayo, Meza, and Carlos Orozco Romero in his review, did not count himself among the aficionados of Mexican art, and he indicated why he and many Americans were not enthusiastic about it:[13] "Since our own art is fundamentally an international mélange, we cannot instantly relish the flavor of a national art which is essentially homogeneous." He also believed there were differences in the way Americans and Mexicans had absorbed foreign influences. "In the case of the latter, [it] is usually short-lived, as native background and tradition seemingly constitute a potent antidote." According to Plaut, Mexicans made no effort to assimilate European influence in the subtle ways that Americans attempted to do. Nor did they paint their country as Americans Scene painters did. Furthermore, the focus on political matters in Mexican painting put Americans off. Nonetheless, Plaut sought to describe the broad assets of the exhibition as well as its limitations. In his view, Orozco was not well represented by the small easel paintings included in the exhibition. He was more pleased with the *Flower Vendor* and a recent self-portrait by Rivera and with *The Sob* and *La Patrona* by Siqueiros. He also praised Dr. Atl, Abraham Angel, and "the brilliant women," Maria Izquierdo and Frida Kahlo. Montenegro was singled out for his several competent portraits and "a rich still life reminiscent of the Spanish painters of the seventeenth century."

However, in Plaut's view, there were six other painters who gave the Mexican movement "current validity and [raised] it to an exalted contemporaneous position." They were Tamayo and Orozco Romero, whose works in the show "are endowed with evocative mysticism"; Ruiz, "a whimsical, urbane primitivist"; and three painters all under thirty-five years of age. These three were Jesús Guerrero Galván, "a reverent interpreter of the classicism of the Italian Renaissance and the strong plastic forms of his native past"; Cantú, "an incisive draftsman and a finished painter"; and Meza, "the most spectacular of the three…a 'natural' Surrealist…a technical prodigy [who] possesses both the natural visions and the inherent restraint shared by the better painters of his country."

Philadelphia Museum of Art (1943)

The exhibition *Mexican Painting Today* was shown at the Philadelphia Museum of Art from March 27 to May 9, 1943. The exhibition was organized by Henry Clifford, the curator of paintings at the museum. He included 100 oils, 50 watercolors and drawings, 140 prints, and 50 photographs. Clifford reproduced works by Tamayo, Chávez Morado, Siqueiros, Castellanos, Soriano, Ruiz, and Goitia in his descriptive article of the exhibition.[14] He described his visits to the studios of Orozco and Rivera, and he characterized all of the artists represented in the exhibition as being preoccupied with the theme of death. In his view, this reflected an acceptance of death that was part of Mexican culture and even celebrated on All Souls Day, or The Day of the Dead.

According to Dorothy Grafly, who reproduced works by Castellanos and Rivera in her review, the exhibition "sweeps [the observer] on a wave of emotionalism that is deeply national."[15] In addition, the works "have a unity of feeling that stamps them as indigenous." An exception, she noted, was Rivera's Cubist work *The Sailor*. Orozco painted with religious fervor and intense emotionalism in works like *Golgotha 1942, Raising of Lazarus*, and *Prometheus*. She saw a strain of El Greco in these works and "in the color and long lines of *St. Veronica* by Cantú."

Grafly contrasted the works of Orozco and Cantú with Rivera's *Liberation of a Péon* and *Sugar Cane*, in which "composition dominates feeling; in the work of [Orozco], feelings create composition." Like Clifford, she also focused on the theme of death. Among the examples she cited were Rivera's *Liberation of a Péon*; Goitia's *Tata Jesús*; and *Angel Kidnappers* by Castellanos. She considered the "innate morbidity of the people…fertile soil for such Surrealism as it appears in *What I Saw in My Bath*, the life story of Frida Kahlo." Finally, she saw Mexico as "a modern summation of the art feeling of the ages. Not only does it partake of the Renaissance, it goes beyond it to the statuesque dignity of the Egyptians, strongly sensed in *La Patrona* by Siqueiros." She saw other Egyptian echoes in the works *National Holiday* by Ruiz and *Dark Mexico* by Chávez Morado.

According to another reviewer, who reproduced works by Orozco, Juan O'Gorman, Jesús Escobedo, Guerrero Galván, Meza, Tamayo, Castellanos, and Ruiz, no other exhibition of Mexican art "has equaled in quality and completeness the show which Henry Clifford has organized for the Philadelphia Museum."[16]

New York Gallery Exhibitions (1945)

Three different but related exhibitions of Mexican art went on view in three galleries in New York City (all within one block of one another) in 1945. Henry Kleeman, Karl Nierendorf, and Knoedler Gallery organized the exhibition with the assistance of Ines Amor, director of the Galería de Arte Méxicano. Eighty works were exhibited at the Knoedler Gallery; a smaller number of works went on display at the Kleeman Gallery; and Mérida's work was exhibited at the Nierendorf Gallery.

According to a reviewer, who reproduced one work each by Mérida, Chávez Morado, and Tamayo, "U.S. painting dwindles into something literal, cautious, even a trifle pedestrian" when compared to the Mexican art seen in the three shows as well as in the earlier show in Philadelphia (1943–44).[17]

Among the artists singled out for comment in the Knoedler show were Siqueiros, for three large paintings; Tamayo, who used "primitive shapes and crude clayey colors"; Meza, the worst offender of "a rather dubious sentimental-romantic trend"; Chávez Morado, the "Bosch of the school"; and Olga Costa, whose work is "fresh and vigorous."

Among the works considered notable in the Kleeman show were four by Charlot, "three in his familiar block-hewn style [and one] in a more realistic vein [that] illustrates admirably [his] ability to combine mountains of physical forms with an almost Oriental refinement of feeling." There were also three "admirable" works by Rivera, who was "the acclaimed leader and prophet of the school." Some Tamayo works in a "quieter mood" and "some stunning brush drawings" by Alfredo Zalce, "an outstanding graphic artist," were also applauded. Mérida, "Mexico's most distinguished semi-abstractionist," exhibited his work at Nierendorf "in conjunction with the ancient potteries of Tarascon [sic] and Guerrero." According to the reviewer, Mérida "fused the Maya tradition of his people with the modern language, establishing Mexico's participation in the contemporary movement."

Grand Central Galleries (1946)

In May 1946 *From Market Place to Museum* opened at the Grand Central Galleries in New York City.[18] The items in this exhibition were selected by Montenegro (folk art), Ines Amor (painting), and Leonard G. Field (crafts). Many of the works came from the IBM collection, loaned through the courtesy of Thomas J. Watson, president of the company. Thirteen paintings, many of them exhibited earlier at Knoedler's, formed the core of the exhibition along with twenty-two watercolors and the prints by thirty artists. Collections of arts and crafts and *retablos* were also included in the exhibition.

Judith Kaye Reed considered Tamayo's *Flute Player*, "one of the magical colorist's finest paintings"; Siqueiros's *Sunrise of Mexico*, "symbolic"; Guerrero Galván's *Children Playing*, "charming but static"; and Meza's *El Mezquital*, "strange."[19] According to Reed, the works by the graphic arts group was one of the largest and most comprehensive Mexican selections ever shown in New York, and one of the highlights of the exhibition was "the brilliant folk art displays."

Pasadena Art Institute (1953)

The exhibition *Art of Mexico* arranged by John Palmer Leeper, director of the Pasadena Art Institute, went on view in early 1953. The show included fifty paintings and drawings from The Museum of Modern Art, the Philadelphia Museum of Art, and the Institute of Contemporary Art in Boston, and from the collections of a number of private collectors and dealers in the Los Angeles area. It complemented part of an intercultural conference sponsored by Occidental College with the assistance of the Rockefeller Foundation. The three-day conference on the subject of "Mexican–United States Intellectual Cooperation," took place in late March, and the exhibition ran through the middle of April.

Jules Langsner, who praised the works by Orozco, Siqueiros, and Tamayo, considered Rivera "a decorative illustrator without plastic convictions."[20] He described Orozco's *Barricade* as "a powerful expressionist statement" and Siqueiros's *War* as having "an overwhelming impact on the spectator by its plasticity of form, compelling rhythms, and monumental scale." In his view, Tamayo's earlier work *The Family* was "a kind of primitivist fantasy, its stiffly postured figures, the toy bird, the suspended hoop adding up to a dignity and reserve that are quite charming." Another reviewer also considered Rivera's works "less imposing" when compared to the work of Orozco, Siqueiros, and Tamayo.[21] According to the reviewer, Orozco and Siqueiros "displayed magnificent power."

Los Angeles County Museum of Art (1963–1964)

Masterworks of Mexican Art: From Pre-Columbian Times to the Present, an exhibition of over two thousand objects, opened in Los Angeles on October 12, 1963, following a tour that included fifteen European cities. The exhibition, directed by Fernando Gamboa, was shown in Los Angeles largely through the efforts of Richard F. Brown, director of the Los Angeles County Museum. A supplementary exhibition of works by the *Nueva Presencia* artists was shown at the Zora Gallery.

Henry J. Seldis devoted most of his review to the pre-Columbian section, essentially ignoring the colonial section and barely mentioning the modern artists.[22] In his view, Orozco, Rivera, Siqueiros, and Tamayo were responsible for the renewed interest in the pre-Columbian materials. Their own works, "starting with Posada...demonstrate that Mexican art has not lost its ability to deal with material and spiritual matters with equal vigor and incisiveness." Finally, according to Seldis, the spirit and even some of the techniques of the ancients were carried on by the contemporary folk artists.

Rosalind Wholden considered the selection of the modern paintings "skimpy" and their quality "poor and insignificant."[23] She faulted the directors of the show for failing to assemble "a larger and more representative show of prints and drawings," which would have maintained the quality of the show. She also reviewed the *Nueva Presencia* exhibition at the Zora Gallery. She considered the work promising; however, in her view, they all seemed "to confuse bulk with profundity." Among the works singled out for comment were those by Arnold Belkin, "dull, academic skull-and-muscle heaps"; Francisco Icaza; "clumsy handling of his own esoteric legends"; and Leonél Góngora, "expressive compositions."

Peter Yates, in his review of the Los Angeles exhibition, focused on the pre-Columbian section.[24] In passing, he mentioned having seen the first large exhibition of Mexican art at the Corcoran Gallery, *Mexican Arts*, in 1931. He remembered admiring the work of Rivera and Orozco. The Los Angeles show, he said, "is replete with [Rivera's] charm and has also a few of the Cubist paintings" but "contains only work of [Orozco's] last years."

The Special Case of Puerto Rico

by Marimar Benítez

Both Puerto Rico and the American Southwest came under United States jurisdiction as spoils of war: their situations, however, are not similar. In Texas and New Mexico two parallel societies exist: the dominant group is composed of "Anglos," and the other stratum is composed of Indians and Chicanos and is constantly renewed by immigration from Mexico. In the case of Puerto Rico, geographical separation has not favored an appreciable influx of people from the continental United States. The U.S. colony in the island has always been small and is almost entirely concentrated in the capital. Furthermore, Anglos have generally been assimilated into Puerto Rican society. Their children marry Puerto Ricans and their descendants wind up speaking Spanish. In short, they become Puerto Ricans. After eighty-nine years of U.S. rule, Puerto Rico has shown a surprising resistance to Anglo-Saxon culture. The resistance is conscious and manifests a serious conflict of identity that is often expressed in the visual arts.

A large segment of the population of Puerto Rico has emigrated to the continental United States. Today an estimated 40 percent of Puerto Ricans live there. These two groups—islanders and mainlanders—are now quite different. The second generation of mainlanders speaks Spanish with difficulty, and their assimilation into the American way of life takes place much more readily—although the process of incorporation into the mainstream is greatly hindered by inequality and racial prejudice. This is not to suggest that their connections with Puerto Rico are completely severed. On the contrary, there is constant movement back and forth between the mainland and the island. New generations of immigrants keep the mainland colony very much alive, and strong family bonds prevent mainland residents from forgetting their roots. Puerto Rican artists have participated in this process. Personal and professional relationships between those in the island and those in the United States, particularly during the 1960s, were important in the latter's artistic development.

There are two dimensions to the Puerto Rican artistic presence in the U.S. One is derived from historical and political considerations, the other from the impact that Puerto Ricans active in the United States, particularly Rafael Montañez-Ortiz (Ralph Ortiz) and Rafael Ferrer, have had on art in this country. The contribution of these two artists to American and international avant-garde movements in the 1960s is undeniable. For the most part, however, art produced in Puerto Rico is all but unknown and has aroused little interest in the continental United States. As is the case with the Chicanos in the Southwest, the historical process of territorial annexation has created an invisible "presence," which as a rule only comes to public attention in the form of acts of violence. The cultural and political tensions between Puerto Rico and the United States have yet to be resolved, and Puerto Rican artists have symbolized these tensions in their work.

The representation of these tensions was most apparent in the 1950s when a regional school of artists was formulated in Puerto Rico specifically to assert and exalt Puerto Rican nationality. In those same years the New York School was spawning many imitators abroad. Puerto Rican artists were torn between their desire to achieve a national form of expression and an overwhelming attraction to the fashions of the metropolis. Their easy access to the stimulating environment of New York offered a tempting way to escape provincialism. But they faced the dilemma that had also confronted Francisco Oller (1833–1917), the first Puerto Rican artist to operate on the international art stage: can the demands of the avant-garde be harmonized with the need to give visual expression to island realities?

For artists of Puerto Rican descent in the United States, the problem of roots has been central to their aesthetic. Their racial identity disadvantages them, which in turn reinforces their cultural links with their community and leads them to search for their heritage. Yet from all sides comes the pressure to create big-city art, void of immediate context and with its aspirations to universality. There is no single or final solution for the conflict between the regional and the metropolitan, the specific and the universal. Puerto Rican artists have responded to this conflict with a broad range of visual expressions.

1920–1932

By the second decade of the twentieth century changes in the economic, social, and political order that resulted from the implementation of U.S. rule had been fully effected. Ever since, Puerto Rico's destiny has been determined by the U.S. Congress. The policy for governing Puerto Rico was different from the mandates for Cuba and the Philippines, the other territories that fell under the jurisdiction of the U.S. Congress as a consequence of the Spanish-American War. In 1917, with the entrance of the United States into World War I, Congress unilaterally imposed citizenship on Puerto Ricans. It was no coincidence that until 1934 the Bureau of Insular Affairs of the War Department was the agency charged with the island's administration.

Congress provided for the separation of executive, legislative, and judicial powers in Puerto Rico. However, until 1948 it was the president of the United States who appointed the governor and the members of the Puerto Rican Supreme Court. Decisions of the Puerto Rican courts were—and continue to be—subject to review by the justices of the U.S. Supreme Court. There is also a U.S. territorial district court in the island. The administrative and political structures were established entirely in accordance with mainland interests. The legislative branch, elected by popular vote, engaged in a struggle for power with the executive branch, but the system was well designed to keep elected officials in check.[1]

By 1920 Puerto Rico had been transformed into a vast sugar and tobacco plantation, financed by U.S. capital.[2] The first sugar companies were set up in Boston about 1899, and in a very few years they gained control of vast properties on the island. Their intentions to make Puerto Rico one great sugar plantation were so obvious that the U.S. Congress passed the "law of five hundred acres," setting limits on the amount of land any one individual or company could own. The law was a dead letter. Even when the government successfully brought suit against Central Guánica, one of the biggest sugar companies in Puerto Rico, the judgment was never carried out.[3]

The transformation of Puerto Rico into a sugar and tobacco plantation had profound ramifications: land holdings and factories were concentrated in the hands of a few (generally absentee) U.S. entrepreneurs, economic stratification increased, and a huge working class was created that served the agricultural and processing needs of the two staple industries.[4] In response, unions were organized and class consciousness of a radical nature developed. In the 1920s there was a series of strikes for better working conditions.[5] The Socialist party became the electoral arm of the Puerto Rican working classes; its enormous growth in the 1920s was evidence of the militant sentiments in Puerto Rico. The descriptions U.S. officials themselves gave of the terrible conditions in which most of the population lived provide ample justification for the workers' struggle.[6]

In the 1920s the Nationalist party was founded. Its program was radically different from that of the Socialists, who emphasized class struggle and international solidarity. The Nationalists attributed the sorry state of the island to the 1898 usurpation by the U.S. of political powers granted to the Puerto Rican people by the Spanish crown. The political identity and future of Puerto Rico, not such fundamental issues as employment, health, and social justice, was the main—and indeed almost exclusive-debating point as far as the Nationalists (and all other parties except the Socialists) were concerned.

The Creole society, which had developed during the four hundred years of Spanish rule, suddenly found itself adrift. The first years of U.S. domination were a period of readjustment and also of hope. The abundant wealth of the United States and its democratic institutions created expectations that their benefits might be extended to Puerto Rico. Save for a few farsighted individuals, such as the abolitionist Ramón E. Betances and the educator Eugenio María de Hostos, Puerto Rican intellectuals awaited a more just and prosperous society. The imperialistic airs of the new rulers and their racial prejudices soon dispelled this illusion.

Still, the U.S. regime did firmly implant the democratic principle of education for all people, long advocated by many Puerto Rican educators, including de Hostos. The concept had not prospered under Spanish rule, given its conservatism and European, elitist philosophy of education. The new government, with full support from the elected officials in the legislature, gave great impetus to mass education. That the effort did not meet with success was due to the fact that until 1949 instruction was given in English.

The social climate, the adjustments to the new regime, and the opportunism of the dominant powers were clearly and eloquently depicted in Manuel Zeno Gandía's novel *Redentores* (Redeemers). Zeno wrote in the naturalistic style of Emile Zola, and his novel reflected the conflicts brought about by the new regime—conflicts between all-out opportunists, corrupt officeholders, U.S. liberals who came to the island filled with zeal for reform, and the victims of these opposing forces. The tone of the novel is decidedly pessimistic: there was no way the characters could win a game whose rules they were powerless to change.

Pessimism was prevalent at that time in artistic circles in Puerto Rico. It was clearly evident in the paintings of Ramón Frade (1875–1954). Frade, who received most of his training in the Dominican Republic, returned to his native Puerto Rico only after a varied career as a painter, illustrator, and stage designer in several Caribbean countries.[7] In the Dominican Republic and in Haiti, where he lived for a number of years, he received commissions for historical works and portraits, which he executed in the officially approved academic manner.

In 1905 he applied for a fellowship to study in Europe, and as part of his overtures to the Puerto Rican legislature he painted *Our Daily Bread* (plate 45), the most ambitious and successful of all his compositions. While the painting is modeled on the work of the nineteenth-century artists Mariano Fortuny and J. L. E. Meissonier, its Creole theme, its monumental character, and its implicit social criticism reflect the influence of Francisco Oller.[8] Oller was the leading figure in Puerto Rican art in the nineteenth century. Trained in Madrid and Paris, where he was a friend of Pissarro's and Cézanne's, Oller was part of the avant-garde during his residence in the French capital, and he introduced Impressionism to both Madrid and San Juan. Back home in Puerto Rico, however, Oller's most significant work was painted in a manner similar to the realism of Courbet. Oller, in fact, declared himself to be a disciple of Courbet's. It is the social implications of a work such as Oller's *The Wake* that can be detected in Frade's *Our Daily Bread*.

Frade's efforts to obtain a fellowship eventually met with success, and in 1907 he left for Europe. Upon his return to Puerto Rico, however, there was a marked falling-off in both the quality and quantity of his production. Frade developed a number of interests, working as an architect (he studied architecture by correspondence), a photographer, and a surveyor, all but abandoning painting. The little work he did do was unambitious and provincial in character. He painted landscapes and the people of Cayey, his hometown. Unlike Oller, he isolated himself from the little art activity that existed in San Juan.

There is no evidence, moreover, that Frade made any attempt to participate in the cultural activities of his neighbors. Cayey lies in the center of one of the principal tobacco-growing and processing regions of the island, and workers in the industry were known for their cultural interests: they even hired a man to read literary works to them while they went about their tasks.[9] Frade refused invitations to exhibit his work. Although he denounced the poverty of the artistic milieu, he made no attempt to improve the situation. His nostalgic drawings and paintings of peasants instead reflect an attitude that pervaded the artistic and cultural environment of Puerto Rico in the first four decades of this century: "Since all that is Puerto Rican is being swept away by the wind...I seek to perpetuate it in paint."[10] Whereas Zeno Gandía had succeeded in capturing in his novel the divisions in Puerto Rican society, no visual artist achieved

45

46

Ramón Frade
45. *Our Daily Bread.* c.1905
   Oil on canvas, 60 x 38¾"
   Instituto de Cultura Puertorriqueña, San Juan
   Photo: courtesy Squibb Galleries, New Jersey

Miguel Pou
46. *Ciquí.* 1938
   Oil on canvas, 34¼ x 28"
   Museo de Arte de Ponce, Puerto Rico. Fundación
   Luis A. Ferré
   Photo: John Betancourt, San Juan

anything of comparable impact. Given Frade's pessimism and withdrawal, the death of Oller in 1917 left a large vacuum.

The limited artistic activity that did take place in San Juan centered on two institutions, the Ateneo Puertorriqueño and the University of Puerto Rico. In both cases key roles were played by outsiders—Spaniards at the Ateneo and mainland Americans at the university. Fernando Díaz McKenna and Alejandro Sánchez Felipe were the principal personalities involved at the Ateneo. Though a minor painter, Díaz McKenna had a number of admirers who looked to him as a teacher, including Juan A. Rosado, who was to become active as an artist in the 1930s. Sánchez Felipe practiced an academic realism, and he was a competent draftsman: Rafael Tufiño and Augusto Marín, artists of the Generation of 1950, received their training from him. Díaz McKenna and Sánchez Felipe perpetuated a provincial artistic tradition, thereby contributing to the conservatism of the art-viewing public.

In 1929 the American artist Walt Dehner inaugurated a program of exhibitions at the university, including shows brought in from overseas.[11] Most of the exhibitions were composed of works by amateurs, however. This was also the case with shows organized by the local Art Students League.[12] The university did display Franciso Oller's masterpiece *The Wake,* and the Ateneo had a gallery of portraits executed by Oller, as well as his astonishing *Royal Palm Landscape,* but these were exhibited alongside paintings by Díaz McKenna and his disciples. The lack of aesthetic discrimination shown by these institutions lessened the impact of Oller's paintings, which could have served as important models.

The situation in Ponce was similar. The most active painter there was Miguel Pou (1880–1968). Pou had studied with the Dominican artist Luis Desangles (1861–1940) and the Spaniard Santiago Meana. During his formative years Ponce was a center of considerable theatrical and musical activity. Due to its economic importance, Ponce rivaled San Juan in cultural events. Operas and zarzuelas were performed at the La Perla Theater, and the works of the best Puerto Rican composers were premiered by the conductor and composer Juan Morel Campos. The models in the visual arts, however, were once again lesser painters, from whom Pou absorbed a realistic, academic style typical of provincial art.

Like Frade, Pou grew up under the Spanish colonial regime. Despite the atmosphere of uncertainty after the Spanish-American War, Pou persisted in painting. He traveled to the United States on a number of occasions, exhibiting there regularly after 1901, the year of his participation in the Pan American Exposition held in Buffalo.[13] He was again in the United States in 1904, 1906, and 1907. Unquestionably, however, the most significant visit he made to the United States was his 1919 trip to study at The Art Students League in New York. Although Robert Henri and Robert Sterne were his teachers, Pou's style reflects the secondhand Impressionism that was in currency in the United States at the time. This is clear from his *Landscape near Chester Springs,* which he painted while studying at the Pennsylvania Academy of the Fine Arts. Thus Pou was the first Puerto Rican artist to study in the United States, but the artistic lessons he absorbed were those of a provincial school. Paris was then the capital of modern art. His U.S. contacts led to no new directions in his art, only to a continuation of the stylistic conservatism of the artists from whom he had received his first lessons.

Pou painted landscapes, portraits, genre scenes, and the occasional still life. For forty years (1910–50) he ran an art academy in Ponce in addition to teaching in the Puerto Rican public schools. His portraits of members of Ponce's upper-class society have the prettified look characteristic of such commissions. A notable exception is *Ciquí* (plate 46), in which Pou captured both the elegant physique of the ballplayer and his likable personality. This is also his best painting of a black person, a racial type that does not figure often in Puerto Rican painting.

Pou's subjects were usually "white." In genre painting his preference ran to the poor farmer known as the *jíbaro,* who was seen as the typical Puerto Rican.[14] Pou himself emphasized the stereotype in his writings: "The true *jíbaro* is our white hill dweller, the direct descendant of the colonists, with all their virtues and vices."[15] It is symptomatic of the conflicting views of race in the island that the "white" *jíbaro* of the hills has been chosen as the authentic incarnation of simple Puerto Rican reality, not the black man of the coast, who is associated with sugar and slavery. The image of the white *jíbaro* crops up constantly in literature and conveys a distorted view of the island's population, which has in fact undergone considerable racial intermarriage.[16]

Pou's work reflects an incurable nostalgia and a rejection of contemporary society that were common to the island's artists and intellectuals of his day. In the same text from which the previous quotation was taken, Pou admitted as much. "I am a man of yesterday and today, for I have lived in another epoch and now live in the present.... I long for a past which cannot return; I persist in my search for subjects which show the genuine *jíbaro*—now ever more difficult to encounter—as I knew him in the days of my youth....That affable and hospitable man who is gradually changing....And because I realize this, my desire as an artist is to capture on canvas the *jíbaro* of my youth, or what remains of him, because he stands for what is really our own."

The portrait of Ciquí is therefore an exception in an output that, aside from commissions, was dedicated to preserving images of a vanishing past. Pou's aim was to preserve in paint a way of life whose continued existence seemed to him precarious. Turning his back on a difficult and uncertain present, Pou found his mission as a painter in documenting the past. In the presentation of an overall view of society, personal expression played a secondary role. Pou's calm manner and the lack of evolution in his passionless, workmanlike paintings are altogether appropriate for an individual who conceived of his oeuvre in terms of a social encyclopedia of human types. His landscapes reflect his romantic view that respect for nature's beauty equals love of country, a view that had literary origins in the poetry of José Gautier Benítez (1851–1880).

In the course of his long teaching career, Pou trained a considerable number of younger artists, chief among them José R. Alicea of the Generation of 1960 who also followed his regionalist style. Moreover, Pou's concern for the disappearance of Puerto Rican culture was often manifested in different guises in the work of later generations of artists.

1933–1945

Early in the 1930s Puerto Rico entered into a prolonged period of political, economic, and cultural change. Reacting to the extreme poverty, exploitation, and social injustice that characterized the first three decades of U.S. rule, Washington carried the New Deal's spirit of reform to Puerto Rico. The monopoly absentee owners exercised over the sugar industry, the substitution of the modern sugar mill for the paternalistic plantation, and the establishment of great tobacco factories had spawned an agricultural and industrial proletariat. When the workers organized to demand social justice, the United States government considered the situation in Puerto Rico potentially explosive.[17] In addition, Nationalists under the charismatic leadership of Pedro Albizu Campos were preaching armed insurrection and independence as the solution to the island's problems. Faced with the possibility of an uprising, Washington extended some New Deal programs to Puerto Rico and named U.S. and Puerto Rican liberals to high posts in the local administration. These New Deal reformers introduced a series of measures known as the Chardón Plan, which was carried out in the 1940s under the aegis of the Popular Democratic party.[18] The power of the sugar monopolies was reduced, agriculture was diversified, cooperatives were established, and industrialization under government auspices was attempted.

The desperate situation of Puerto Rico in the 1930s also inspired a series of bold social measures implemented under the leadership of Luis Muñoz Marín, founder of the reformist Popular Democratic party. The most dramatic successes were achieved in the fields of health and education. At the same time the government encouraged mass emigration to the mainland and instituted a birth-control program based on sterilization. In just a few years there was a dramatic rise in income levels, which was accompanied by a fall in the birth rate. The government's health programs brought diseases such as tuberculosis and malaria under control and effectively combated malnutrition.[19]

Artistic activity improved in quality and quantity during the 1930s. The exhibitions the University of Puerto Rico brought in from overseas introduced the public to avant-garde painting in Mexico, Peru, Spain, and the United States. These shows encouraged the development of an art-going public and inspired the beginnings of art criticism in the island. In 1938 a chapter of the American Artists Professional League was established; it sponsored an annual art week in Puerto Rico. Among the artists who distinguished themselves at exhibits were Luis Quero Chiesa and Rafael Palacios. Quero Chiesa explored black topics, most probably inspired by the Negro poetry of Luis Palés Matos, which had caused a great stir in Puerto Rican literary circles at that time. Palacios avoided the paternalism that had previously been attached to campesino themes. He did not idealize scenes of daily life, as others did to the detriment of that genre. By 1940 both of these artists had emigrated to New York, joining the growing Puerto Rican colony there.

Of critical importance during the decade was a fellowship program that allowed a number of young people to study art abroad. Félix Bonilla-Norat went to Boston in 1931 and thereafter to Madrid and Paris. In 1936 Osiris Delgado also went to Madrid, where Narciso Dobal had preceded him in 1933, and Rufino Silva went to the Art Institute of Chicago in 1938. In the 1940s the fellowship program was continued. Its recipients included José Torres Martinó (1946), Julio Rosado del Valle (1946), and José Meléndez Contreras (1947). With few exceptions, the recipients went to the United States and to Europe, especially to the San Fernando Academy in Madrid, the Grande Chaumière in Paris, and the Academy of San Marco in Florence. A few artists, including Rafael Tufiño and Antonio Maldonado, studied at the Academy of San Carlos in Mexico.

In the late 1930s the triumph of the fascists in the Spanish Civil War led to the emigration of Spanish artists and intellectuals to the Western Hemisphere. Unlike their predecessors in the colonial era, these were Spain's leading creative figures, and their presence brought new life to intellectual and artistic circles in the Americas. The University of Puerto Rico extended a warm welcome, and a number of artists took up teaching at the Edna Coll Academy of Art.[20] The new curriculum they instituted provided clear evidence of the academy's highly professional character. The lack of an institution of such quality had been keenly felt since the death of Oller, who had dedicated much of his efforts toward the establishment of a number of art schools.[21]

The Postwar Years

The postwar years saw a mass exodus of Puerto Rican workers to New York. The migration was sponsored by the ruling Popular Democratic party as one of several solutions to the problems of poverty, unemployment, and inequality. At the same time there was an internal migration as campesinos moved from the hill country to the capital in search of better living conditions. From the slums of San Juan they then moved on to Manhattan. In *La Carreta* (The Wagon) playwright René Marqués dramatized the heartbreak of this two-stage uprooting. In New York the new arrivals found a home in a community previously established by immigrants of the Depression era in upper Manhattan, a district that came to be known as "El Barrio" (The Neighborhood). The first stirrings of artistic creation by Puerto Ricans resident in America—both trained and folk artists—happened at this time.

The walls of Puerto Rican business places, particularly those of La Marketa, a huge market area that stretched from 103rd Street to 116th Street under the elevated subway tracks, began to blossom with murals painted by folk artists, a form of artistic expression that had acquired great popularity in the island.[22] Self-taught artists such as Johnny Vázquez and Millito López painted the rural scenes they had left behind. Their naively idealized landscapes breathe the beauties of the world the emigrants had been forced to abandon. This type of painting still persists in the work of self-taught artists such as Pedro Villarini, whose depictions of rural life in Puerto Rico have been quite consistent from the 1950s to the present.[23]

Another self-taught artist, Juan de Prey, took up a different direction. De Prey started painting full-time in the 1940s and participated in shows held in New York.[24] Unlike the art of the primitives, his work possesses real pictorial qualities. De Prey must have had some acquaintance with the painting of Diego Rivera and Jean Charlot, for their influence is readily apparent in his compositions.

There were also trained artists among the Puerto Ricans in New York, but the careers of Eloy Blanco and Lorenzo Homar in the 1940s exemplify the complete lack of interaction between trained artists and the working-class Puerto Rican community. Blanco came to art somewhat by chance. He was enrolled in an institution for children suffering from problems of speech development when, at the age of fourteen, he received a scholarship to study at the Brooklyn Museum Art School.[25] Lorenzo Homar and José Torres Martinó had also studied there, but there does not appear to have been any contact between the three artists.

Blanco went on to study with Max Beckman and William Baziotes. Once considered "retarded," he quickly came to be viewed as a prodigy. He had a one-man show at the Brooklyn Museum in 1949 and another the following year; both were favorably reviewed in the New York press. His early work consisted chiefly of portraits whose subjects' searchingly expressive faces have a powerful effect on the viewer. Despite the favorable reception he met with at first, Blanco did not succeed in making his way into the professional mainstream. He kept on painting but had to resort to taking various jobs to earn a living.[26] He had no association with the Puerto Rican community or with the attempts Quero Chiesa and others were making to establish a circle of Puerto Rican or Hispanic artists. At the time of his 1978 show at the Cayman Gallery, Blanco was astonished to learn of the existence of a colony of Puerto Rican artists in New York.[27] Typical of the Puerto Rican artists seeking entrance to the mainstream, he was totally estranged from the island community in Manhattan.

Homar provides another example of a trained artist's separation from the cultural activity of the Puerto Rican colony in New York. Homar had come to New York in 1928 as part of the first wave of immigrants of the Depression era. He studied at the Pratt Graphics Center and the Brooklyn Museum Art School and received on-the-job training at Cartier, where he worked as a jewelry designer.[28] He did not reestablish his connections with Puerto Rico until an exhibition at the ACA Gallery in 1949 in which nine island artists participated. Homar returned to the island in 1950 to take up residence, and it is there that his career subsequently developed. Neither Homar nor Blanco developed any links to the Puerto Rican colony in Manhattan, and the same has been true of other artists from the island who have studied in New York. This separation, due perhaps to class differences, meant that trained artists played no role in developing ghetto talent. The barriers were broken only briefly in the 1960s.

On the island, encouragement of education and the arts was one of the aims of the Popular Democratic party under Muñoz Marín. Mass literacy programs were instituted in rural areas, and special schools in the arts were created to give young people of limited resources the opportunity to pursue advanced studies.[29] The visual arts were part of the government's attempt to instill social values and attitudes that would enable the population to adapt to Puerto Rico's new industrial society.

The Department of Health was the first to make use of the arts in campaigns for social change: silk-screen posters became vehicles to promote health, education, and social consciousness. From 1946 to 1949 the Commission of Public Parks and Recreation's Motion-Picture and Graphic Arts Workshop, established and directed by Jack and Irene Delano, turned out educational materials for these campaigns. In 1949 the workshop became the Division of Community Education, attached to the Department of Public Education, and production was thereafter oriented toward works of a cultural and educational nature.[30] The division made an important contribution to the development of graphic arts and poster production, and it had a decided impact on the formation of the Generation of 1950.

First under the direction of Edwin Roskam and later under Fred Wales, the division hired and trained artists, writers, photographers, and movie technicians to produce educational materials for use in rural areas. In order to stimulate reading, it published illustrated books and leaflets for free distribution. It turned out films that dramatized social problems, whose solutions could become models for the improvement of living conditions.[31] In this endeavor a group of talented artists and writers, inspired by goals of reform and social justice, were employed.

The division resorted to silk screen, previously employed only in commercial art, to produce the posters that advertised its films.[32] The versatility of the medium and the ease and low cost of running off large printings led Irene Delano to adopt the technique for the workshops she set up in Puerto Rico. First at the Commission of Public Parks and Recreation's workshop and then at the Division of Community Education (where she was aided by Félix Bonilla-Norat), Irene Delano trained a whole generation of artists who made the poster one of the most popular art forms in Puerto Rico.

Irene Delano's posters reflect the influence of Ben Shahn and Robert Gwathmey (plate 47). Gwathmey spent some time in Puerto Rico and designed a few posters for the division.[33] The works are simple and dramatic, colors are few in number and are spread broadly over flat areas. A certain number of the division's early posters resulted from the joint efforts of Irene Delano and one or another of the artists working with her, including Juan Díaz, Lorenzo Homar, and Francisco Palacios.[34] With few exceptions, artists of the Generation of 1950 worked for the Division of Community Education, and it was there that they were trained in silk-screen techniques. The division provided many of them with their first jobs. Some even executed their first paintings under Irene Delano's direction. Artists and writers collaborated in the production of books, leaflets, and films, leading to close friendships and the development of an important body of graphics inspired by literary themes.[35] (In keeping with the spirit of the division, two posters were done each year with Christmas topics, mostly inspired by *santos*, wood carvings of saints, one of the most widespread forms of Puerto Rican folk art.)

The 1950s

The reforms undertaken by the Popular Democratic party bore their most dramatic fruits in the 1950s and brought about radical improvements in Puerto Rico's standard of living.[36] The economic transformation paved the way for the political changes that came about in 1952 with the development of commonwealth status. In his youth Luis Muñoz Marín had been a militant advocate of independence, but on assuming control of the government and faced with the problems of World War II, Muñoz Marín and most of the leadership of his party agreed, as a matter of tactics, to accept limited autonomy as a solution to the relationship between Puerto Rico and the United States.[37] Pressure from the United Nations for decolonization led the U.S. Congress to authorize a constitutional convention in 1950. The constitution that the convention produced was ratified by referendum in 1952 and approved by the U.S. Congress, with the omission of some of its more liberal provisions.[38] Commonwealth status has given the elected government of Puerto Rico a certain degree of autonomy, but attempts to expand the limits of that autonomy have not been allowed by Congress. Thus, despite the criticisms and discontent voiced by advocates of independence and statehood, the commonwealth arrangement continues in force.

At the same time that the island's status was being worked out, there were uprisings on the part of followers of Pedro Albizu Campos. In 1950 they took up arms in fifteen localities and launched an attack on La Fortaleza, the governor's palace in San Juan. In Washington there was an attack on Blair House, where President Truman was then residing. Four years later there were shootings from the gallery of the U.S. House of Representatives.[39] The political violence of the Nationalists and the repressive measures taken against them aroused fear in the population. The Independence party, which had received the second-largest number of votes in the 1952 elections, rapidly began to lose supporters, entering into a decline that has continued to the present day. Despite the fears awakened by the personality and teachings of Albizu Campos, his passionate defense of Puerto Rican independence left a very deep imprint on the artists of the time.

The nationalistic ethos permeated the artistic production of the Generation of 1950. These artists assumed the role of developing an art of national identity that would assert and exalt Puerto Rican values. The Generation of 1950 was comprised of a number of artists who had studied abroad and others trained locally who united to establish the Center for Puerto Rican Art (CAP), formally inaugurated in 1950. It served as a collective workshop, gathering place, art school, and exhibition space. Indeed it was the first gallery in Puerto Rico.[40] In 1951 the center published a portfolio of prints under the title *La Estampa Puertorriqueña* (The Puerto Rican Print). It contained a manifesto in which the artists set forth their objectives:

48

47

49

Irene Delano
47. *Defiéndalos (Defend Them)*. 1946-47
Silk-screen on paper, 26¾ x 18″
Collection Smith, Kline and French, Puerto Rico
Photo: John Betancourt, San Juan

Carlos Raquel Rivera
48. *Hurricane from the North*. 1955
Linocut on paper, 12⅛ x 16″
Museo de la Universidad de Puerto Rico
Photo: John Betancourt, San Juan

Carlos Raquel Rivera
49. *The Massacre at Ponce*. 1956
Linocut on paper, 12 x 9″
Instituto de Cultura Puertorriqueña, San Juan
Photo: Victor Vasquez

50

51

Rafael Tufiño
50. *Cane Cutter*. 1951–52
Linocut on paper, 11½ x 18½″
Instituto de Cultura Puertorriqueña, San Juan
Photo: John Betancourt, San Juan

Rafael Tufiño
51. *Storm*. 1954-55
Linocut on paper, 11½ x 18½″
Collection Luis R. Cancel, New York
Photo: John Betancourt, San Juan

This portfolio… is the fruit of the collective labor of a group of artists interested in the development of Puerto Rican art. They are of the view that the print permits the artist to reach a broader public; that in Puerto Rico art should spring from a complete identification of the artist with the people; and that only by working together and engaging in collective discussion of their work and problems, with views to self-improvement, will artists be able to bring new life to Puerto Rican art.[41]

Puerto Rican customs and folk festivals provided the subject matter for the Generation of 1950. A second portfolio, *Estampas de San Juan* (Prints of San Juan), which appeared in 1953, consisted almost entirely of scenes of working-class neighborhoods. Subjects reflecting the difficult life of the Puerto Rican working class cropped up frequently in the graphics of the Generation of 1950.

In consonance with the preachings of the Nationalists, these artists attributed social inequality to the U.S. colonial regime. Indignation and anger were their primary reactions, expressed in outright denunciations or in caricatures and satires. The center's stand was quite similar to the ideology of the Taller de Gráfica Popular in Mexico City. Rafael Tufiño and Antonio Maldonado, both members of the Generation of 1950, had studied in Mexico. Mexican art, which enjoyed great prestige throughout the Americas, was a point of departure for many regional schools, and this was certainly the case in Puerto Rico. The influence of the Mexican School artist Leopoldo Méndez, particularly his use of linoleum blocks, is readily apparent in Puerto Rican graphics. The preferred medium among members of the Generation of 1950 was the linoleum block; its strong contrasts between black and white lent themselves to images of powerful visual impact, such as Tufiño's *Cane Cutter* (plate 50).

Folk festivals, working-class neighborhoods, traditions, and genre scenes had been the subject matter of Pou, Frade, and their followers, including Osiris Delgado and José R. Oliver, who painted Creole scenes. But their message was nostalgic and paternalistic. By contrast, the Generation of 1950 identified with the difficult life of the population, bringing the audience face to face with the poverty, ugliness, heroism, and stoicism of the exploited. As artist Antonio Martorell put it, in the 1950s these artists presented their society with "unpleasant, threatening images of a world it did not wish to see."[42]

The prints of Carlos Raquel Rivera are among the best examples of the art of social content of the Generation of 1950. Some emphasize the everyday life of the people, others identify the deplorable social conditions under the colonial regime. Works such as *Cloudless Night* (1953) and *House in the Country* (1954) evoke the poetry of childhood amid poverty. *Hurricane from the North* (plate 48), an allegory of the evil effects of the U.S. presence in Puerto Rico, shows people in desperate pursuit of a will-o'-the-wisp, symbolized by a bag of money. A great eagle, the emblem of the United States, presides over *The Massacre at Ponce* (1956) and *Colonial Elections* (1955). *The Massacre* (plate 49) depicts the tragic events of March 22, 1936, when the police killed participants and spectators at a Nationalist parade in Ponce. *Colonial Elections* is a satire of the electoral process in Puerto Rico. A carnival crowd of voters propels itself forward over the edge of a precipice, while overhead U.S. soldiers dangle from the wings of an otherwise invisible eagle.

The twelve linoleum-block prints by Lorenzo Homar and Rafael Tufiño that make up the *Portafolio de Plenas* (Portfolio of *Plenas*) constitute one of the best depictions of folk customs. The *plena* is a picaresque musical commentary on local happenings. Irene Delano had had the idea for the portfolio and was responsible for its design. The format is similar throughout: the title of the *plena* appears in large letters, and the words and music of three or four verses are accompanied by an illustration of the event narrated, as in *Storm* (plate 51) by Rafael Tufiño. The *Portafolio de Plenas* epitomizes the center's principles of collective effort, identification with the daily life of the masses, and the use of prints to reach a broad public.

On Irene Delano's retirement in 1952 Homar took over the directorship of the Division of Community Education's print workshop. He remained in this job until 1957, when he was asked to organize the Graphic Arts Workshop of the recently established Institute of Puerto Rican Culture. In both establishments he trained

52

Julio Rosado del Valle
52. *Saro and Aita.* 1949
Oil on cardboard, 46¼ x 42⅞″
Collection Dr. F. Monserrate, Puerto Rico
Photo: John Betancourt, San Juan

many young people—indeed almost all of the next two generations of graphic artists—laying the groundwork for development of the contemporary movement of Puerto Rican graphics. Homar was noted for his insistence on quality in design, including the design of the letters that make up the poster captions. Poster production constitutes his most substantial contribution to contemporary Puerto Rican art, and his example in this medium was extended to the Puerto Rican colony in New York, where the art form was taken up by young artists.

At the division, artists created illustrations for publications, often using linoleum blocks.[43] This technique was used by Tufiño for a series of illustrations he and Meléndez Contreras made for the book *Los Casos de Ignacio y Santiago* (The Affairs of Ignacio and Santiago). An album of the twelve prints was run off later and was one of the first of many portfolios of prints and poems (or prints alone) inspired by literature or oral narratives to appear in Puerto Rico.

Although the Generation of 1950 loudly proclaimed its preference for graphics, painting was of no less importance at that time. The outstanding figure in painting in the 1940s and 1950s was Julio Rosado del Valle. He received his first instruction from the Spaniard Cristóbal Ruiz, who taught at the University of Puerto Rico; Ruiz's influence was slight, however. Rosado del Valle's earliest canvases, such as *The Child* in the collection of the Institute of Puerto Rican Culture, are somber-colored protest statements. His identification with the people and his condemnation of social injustice are evidence of the goals he shared with the Mexican muralists.

In 1946 a fellowship from the University of Puerto Rico enabled Rosado del Valle to study at the New School for Social Research in New York with Mario Carreño and Camilo Egas. He went on to the Academy of San Marco in Florence and then to Paris. When he returned to Puerto Rico in 1949, he worked for the Division of Community Education, creating posters and book illustrations. A still life he painted in 1948 reveals a strong interest in experimenting with forms, and the rich surface textures are evidence of his great skill in handling paint.

Rosado del Valle's gifts as a draftsman are readily apparent in this early composition and in *Saro and Aita* (plate 52). Although he was one of the founders of the Center for Puerto Rican Art, he was not altogether in agreement with his colleagues. Evidence of social protest exists in his early work, but questions of form later became his principal concern—a factor that facilitated his transition to abstraction following a stay in New York in 1957, the year in which he held a Guggenheim Fellowship. Contact with Abstract Expressionism freed Rosado del Valle's creative energies. He showed his brilliance in handling surfaces. His abstract works bubble with invention. The mastery of technique he had acquired during his formative years enabled him to be vigorously expressive without losing anything in the way of control. In the 1960s Rosado del Valle became an estimable exponent of expressionism, but only occasionally were his compositions completely abstract, since he tended to use the human figure as his point of departure. However, he completely abandoned art with a social message, placing his emphasis on formal investigations.

Foremost among the artists who trained at the Division of Community Education is Manuel Hernández Acevedo. Originally a shoemaker, Hernández Acevedo began as an apprentice printer at the division. Unlike self-taught street artists, he not only had the opportunity to be in touch with writers and trained artists but was also allowed to develop his innate talent. Hernández Acevedo stuck consistently to religious themes. He created a whole series of paintings and prints of saints and altars, including *La Capilla* (The Chapel; 1950). Hernández Acevedo's images evoke a simple world of popular faith. Sympathetic treatment of everyday scenes can also be found in paintings by Rubén Rivera Aponte and Luis Germán Cajiga, both graduates of the division's workshops.

Painting was also used by artists whose primary message was social protest. In Lorenzo Homar's *Le Lo Lai* (plate 53), three children are dressed up as the Three Wise Men, in accordance with a folk custom, but their skinny figures call attention to the malnutrition from which they suffer. La Perla, a poor district outside the walls of San Juan, was often depicted by Puerto Rican painters and graphic artists. Many genre scenes place special emphasis on the dilapidated state of slum dwellings or the sad mien of children and adults.

The strongest paintings of the social protest movement are to be found in the œuvre of Carlos Raquel Rivera. In *Playing Ball* (1951), which is in the Institute of Puerto Rican Culture collection, everyday slum life is treated with tender compassion. The quiet scene has an air of classic monumentality. *The Mother Country* satirizes Spain's colonial rule. Elements of horror are combined with a picaresque note; a touch of humor offsets the atmosphere of doom and renders the picture less threatening. Rivera's work is notable for its careful finish, which is often in tense counterpoint with the drama of the subject.

While artists associated with the Center for Puerto Rican Art and the Division of Community Education were engaged in asserting their Puerto Rican identity, at the University of Puerto Rico the Spanish Surrealist Eugenio Fernández Granell was practicing and preaching a radically different approach, quite opposed to *art engagé*. Whereas members of the Center for Puerto Rican Art had identified with life in the island and made their agenda the creation of a distinctly Puerto Rican art, artists at the university sought to create art that was "universal" in character. Félix Bonilla-Norat, for example, engaged in a kind of Surrealism. His *Four Beasts, Pegasus, and a Woman* is peopled with symbols and figures derived from classical mythology. Bonilla-Norat had worked for the Division of Community Education, but he did not share the nationalistic approach to art of his colleagues, and so he joined the faculty of the university, where the atmosphere was more receptive to his personal mode of expression. Artists in training at the university, Rafael Ferrer and Luis Hernández Cruz among others, were to find themselves on a collision course with the Generation of 1950.

While the Puerto Rican Generation of 1950 was engaging in social protest, Abstract Expressionism had become the dominant international style, and New York had replaced Paris as the capital of Western art. Critics turned against the politically and socially oriented *art engagé* that had been fashionable in the 1930s and the 1940s, and politically inspired art acquired negative connotations in the McCarthy era. Controversy broke out in Puerto Rico between engagés and "universalists"—a dispute heightened by its bearing on the local political situation.

Polemical debates were also aroused by the establishment of the Institute of Puerto Rican Culture in 1955. There was great argument in the press and in the legislature about the creation of the institute, whose stated purposes were to preserve, promote, enrich, and disseminate the cultural values of the people of Puerto Rico.[44] The University of Puerto Rico was the center of opposition to the institute, which was attacked both by the island's intellectuals and by advocates of assimilation into Anglo-American civilization. The cultural debate took a political turn not only due to appeals made by the advocates of statehood, who were interested in seeing Puerto Rico abandon its Hispanic attachments, but also due to the fear aroused by the radical endorsements of the Nationalists.

Toward the end of the 1950s, Puerto Rican visual arts entered into a long period of crisis. Disputes over assimilation and the loss of a Puerto Rican cultural identity were frequent. In *Juan Bobo y la Dama de Occidente* (Simple John and the Lady of the West) the playwright René Marqués satirized the struggle between engagés and universalists. The Generation of 1950's search for a distinctly Puerto Rican type of expression ran parallel to the rise of the New York School and its attempt to dominate the entire world of art. Thus, the relationship between Puerto Rican artists and the New York School was a difficult one. Puerto Ricans could easily get to Manhattan, and Guggenheim fellowships awarded during the 1950s facilitated communications with the new avant-garde. However, the "universal" character attributed to Abstract Expressionism was completely at odds with the postulates of the nationalist school that had emerged in Puerto Rico. The island's leading artists and intellectuals were actively resisting the influence of U.S. art as "cultural imperialism." Works of art became part of the struggle for cultural survival and took on a transcendent social importance. The problem of national identity reached acute proportions at the end of the 1950s, becoming the be-all and end-all of Puerto Rican art. As an artistic theme, it replaced social protest, which had dominated the work of the Generation of 1950.

53

Lorenzo Homar
53. *Le Lo Lai*. 1953
   Tempera and oil on Masonite, 25 x 33″
   Museo de Antropología, Arte y Historia,
   Universidad de Puerto Rico, Recinto de Río Piedras
   Photo: Tony Velez

54

55

Rufino Silva
54. *The Wake*. 1967
Oil on canvas, 56 x 76″
Collection the artist
Photo: courtesy the artist

Pedro Villarini
55. *Landscape ("La Fortaleza")*. 1968
Oil on canvas, 18 x 24″
El Museo del Barrio, New York
Photo: Tony Velez

In 1957 an exhibition was organized by the Institute of Puerto Rican Culture for presentation at the Riverside Museum in Manhattan that demonstrated the difficulties island artists would face in New York. Some critics viewed their work as exotic, owing to the artists' stress on color, while the writer for *Art News* castigated the participants for their lack of academic draftsmanship.[45] Due to the excessive number of participants—thirty-five—the low quality of some work tended to detract from the merits of the talented. Moreover, as far as the critics were concerned, abstraction was the standard of the day, and while they found things to admire in the work of Lorenzo Homar, Rafael Tufiño, Carlos Raquel Rivera, Olga Albizu, and Julio Rosado del Valle, in general they viewed the Puerto Ricans' approach as passé. Robert M. Coates, critic for *The New Yorker*, compared developments in Puerto Rico to the work done for "the late, regretted" WPA.

During the 1950s the Puerto Rican population in New York increased dramatically. The two schools of folk and trained artists that appeared in the 1940s were now represented by Pedro Villarini and Olga Albizu. A University of Puerto Rico fellowship for postgraduate study took Albizu to New York in 1948. At home she had studied with the abstract Spanish painter Esteban Vicente. In New York Hans Hofmann became her teacher, and she began to paint expressionistically. She had her first show in 1956; a brief review in *The New York Times* called attention to her potential.[46] In 1959 and 1960 she also showed at the Roland de Aenlle Gallery, receiving some coverage in leading art magazines.[47] Albizu kept up her connections with Puerto Rico, exhibiting and making sales there, but she had no contact with other Puerto Rican artists in New York and no involvement with the Puerto Rican colony there. However, she did participate in the exhibition at the Riverside Museum in 1957 and in other Puerto Rican group shows held there up to 1961. Like the self-taught artists who had decorated market stands, Villarini as a rule painted scenes of the island (plate 55). Though he lived in New York, he took inspiration from an idyllic vision of Puerto Rico. Villarini painted pictures of working-class neighborhoods with a tenderness that hardly reflected the extreme poverty from which the Puerto Rican colony of New York had fled.[48]

The arrival in New York of Rafael Tufiño, Victor Linares, and Carlos Osorio lent new vigor to the attempts to establish a stable nucleus of painters there. Their efforts coincided with those of Luis Quero Chiesa's at the Institute of Puerto Rico. All these initiatives converged in the activities of the Friends of Puerto Rico. Beginning in 1959, the association held annual art exhibitions in New York in addition to the book and record fairs it had regularly sponsored. The promotional campaign Amalia Guerrero carried out through the Friends of Puerto Rico was complemented by the activities of the Office of Puerto Rico in New York, headed by José Monserrate. In the following decade Amalia Guerrero and José Monserrate succeed in creating a center of support for young Puerto Ricans interested in pursuing a career in art.

Puerto Rican artists resident in New York also made attempts to present their work to the city at open-air group shows. Among the early participants in this activity were Pedro Villarini, Rafael Tufiño, and Carlos Irizarry.[49] They were later joined by Victor Linares and Carlos Osorio, who had previously exhibited at the Riverside show. By the end of the decade, the enterprise had gained considerable momentum and gave stimulus to young members of the burgeoning Puerto Rican community who were beginning to show an interest in art.

Although New York and the northeastern seaboard states were the locus of the most important Puerto Rican nucleus in the United States, during the 1950s island emigrants began to establish themselves in other parts of the country. The second largest concentration of Puerto Ricans took up residence in Chicago, where there was already a large Chicano population. In 1938 Rufino Silva came to Chicago on a fellowship from the Puerto Rican government for study at the School of the Art Institute of Chicago. He taught in Milwaukee in 1946 and 1947 and then spent four years in Europe and South America on grants from the Art Institute. After studying at the Stamperia Nazionale in Rome and the Grande Chaumière in Paris, he returned to Chicago and in 1952 joined the faculty of the Art Institute. He remained there until his retirement in the 1970s.[50]

In the 1950s his painting offered an interesting combination of Surrealist elements and comments of social protest that recall the subject matter and imagism of the Chicago School. Impeccably dressed, Silva's masculine figures appear to be business executives. But Silva strived to capture the inner life of his refined personages and their most scabrous and despicable traits. In many of his paintings groups of men are staring with obvious lasciviousness at female nudes. Although his work has occasionally been compared to Jack Levine's, Silva avoids the caricatures and scatological aspects of Levine's style of figurative painting. The artist himself has compared his work with Spanish art in light of his restrained use of color and his preference for earth tones (plate 54).[51] A work such as *He Who Eats Meat* renders the act of ingestion primitive and disgusting; but the formal dress of the subject provides a disconcerting touch that heightens the shock effect in this contemporary version of Goya's *Saturn*. The Surrealistic elements are particularly evident in Silva's work of the 1960s. These powerful creations fuse Spanish pictorial sensitivity and emphasis on careful finish with a spirit of aggression and social protest. Despite great stylistic differences, Silva's work and that of Carlos Raquel Rivera show certain affinities.

Silva kept up his connections with the art world in Puerto Rico. He exhibited at the Institute of Puerto Rican Culture in 1963 and 1967 and took part regularly in the biennials of Latin American graphics in San Juan.[52] He also developed a relationship with the Hispanic community of Chicago largely as a result of his contact with Chicano students at the Art Institute's school.

Other Puerto Rican painters who were active in Chicago included Félix Cordero and Rubén Cruz. Both embraced abstraction during the course of the 1960s. Their abstract compositions were, however, completely incomprehensible to the Latin community in which they lived and with which they identified. Cordero's work later evolved into realism of Creole inspiration, while Cruz gave up painting completely.

The 1960s

In the 1960s a new generation of artists renewed the graphic tradition established in the previous decade. The majority of the graphic artists of the Generation of 1960 began to work in the populist, social-protest vein of the preceding generation. They turned out silk-screen posters, linoleum-block prints, and woodcuts. The prosperity generally experienced during this decade permitted many of them to acquire presses, and some began to take up intaglio and collograph. That same prosperity also provided new opportunities for study: many artists found their way to the Pratt Institute in New York, and some began to take part in major international exhibitions, such as the Tokyo and Ljubljana biennials. The San Juan biennials of Latin American graphics, held for the first time in 1970, provided graphic artists with a world-class forum.

The 1960s marked the zenith of Lorenzo Homar's work in silk-screen posters. Never had he turned out more or better designs than those he made in his workshop at the Institute of Puerto Rican Culture. Refinement of design and astuteness in the handling of formal elements characterize his work of these years. His interest in all aspects of poster design led him to study in depth the history of letters and typography. In so doing, he was fortunate to avail himself of the resources of a very valuable library in San Juan, the Casa del Libro. In his poster designs the text came to form an important part of the composition, while the style of the posters was varied to suit the subject. In some cases the composition is mostly based on the letters, as in *5to Festival de Teatro*. About 1960 Homar gave up painting, dedicating himself completely to printmaking. He did however continue to create caricatures for various opposition publications.[53] He also produced posters of a political nature, among them *102 Aniversario del Grito de Lares* (102nd Anniversary of the Lares Uprising).

Homar's interest in letter design was complemented by his close friendship with literary figures. The artist made a number of illustrations for the journal *Revista del Instituto de Cultura Puertorriqueña*. He also designed books, record jackets, and Christmas cards. During the 1960s he became very involved in stage design, making sets and costumes for a number of productions of the San Juan Ballet and other theater groups. His interest in working in a variety of media was passed on to the artists who studied under him. The range of his enthusiasms made him an excellent instructor for aspiring artists.

Homar's ties to the literary world led to the creation of a series of prints based on texts, in which he dealt with the formal integration of image and words. In 1965 he undertook a number of large-scale woodcuts, of which *Unicorn of the Island* (plate 56) is the most ambitious and successful. Homar illustrated the poem by Tomás Blanco, creating a powerful image of the sea, the beach, and the flora of the island with Blanco's text placed at the bottom of the sheet. This woodcut won a prize at the Leipzig Book Festival in 1966. Homar's interest in overall design was shared by some of his colleagues at the print workshop. Tufiño, for example, used a similar approach in his poster *El Museo de la Familia Puertorriqueña*.

The interest in letters and calligraphy Homar cultivated took on new directions in the work of his disciples. José R. Alicea, who also studied with Miguel Pou, was a prolific printmaker of scenes representing daily life and of images inspired by poetry or oral tradition. Alicea also made prints of a political nature, as in his powerful *Pedro Albizu Campos,* in which the text of the leader's speech is the ground for the sad likeness. The use of writing in visual images became prevalent in Puerto Rican graphics and can also be found in painting and sculpture.[54]

Antonio Martorell worked on themes and genres he inherited from the preceding generation, but he added a profound sense of irony to their meanings. It was in satire that Martorell showed himself to best advantage, as can be seen from the card decks and prints made after the 1968 elections, including the large-scale playing cards *Barajas Alacrán* (Scorpion Playing Cards). His approach has a certain resemblance to that taken by Rivera in his *Colonial Elections.* Martorell produced these at his workshop, the Taller Alacrán, which he set up in the late 1960s. Like the Center for Puerto Rican Art, the Taller Alacrán aimed to produce graphic work at prices that would facilitate wide distribution.

The Taller Alacrán not only provided training for a number of graphic artists but also led to the establishment of similar workshops in the late 1960s. As there was considerable political agitation for Puerto Rican independence in that decade, the popularity of political posters reached new heights. Rafael Rivera Rosa, another graduate of Homar's workshop, made many lively posters advocating independence. *Atleta, Puerto Rico Es Tuyo. Libéralo* (Athlete, Puerto Rico Is Yours. Free It) is a good example of his work (plate 57).

Another pupil of Homar's at the institute's print workshop was José Rosa, who took over from Homar upon his retirement. In his early years Rosa studied painting at the Campeche Gallery Workshop, where he was a student of Domingo García's. Silk-screen prints, however, constitute the bulk of his mature production. His early posters are primitivistic; in later works Rosa combined images with graffitilike captions, which constitute an essential part of the overall design. Unlike Martorell, who drew on literature for his inspiration, Rosa resorted to street idioms in his novel creations.

Myrna Báez was active in printmaking and painting, handling both media with masterly skill. Her early prints, such as *Walls of San Cristóbal,* show her creation of an iconography based on everyday Puerto Rico. Her graphic work varied widely, both in its subject matter and in the materials she used—linoleum blocks, woodcuts, Plexiglas, silk screen, and collograph. The use of media in uncombined form was characteristic of Puerto Rican graphics; artists prefered to explore an individual medium's possibilities. Báez's work exemplifies still another constant in Puerto Rican graphics: impeccable technique. Both at the Center for Puerto Rican Art and the Division of Community Education, artists placed great stress on technical virtuosity. The artists themselves printed their designs (or in large-scale editions of silk-screen posters they closely supervised production). Consequently, the artists became master printers and were proficient in every phase of graphic design and production.

Báez began her career by following the examples of the previous generation. She depicted scenes from the life of the people, but then she went on to portray the new middle class that had sprung up as a result of the radical economic and social changes that had come about in the island. Her renditions of solitude and isolation in prints such as *Judge* testify to the character of the new Puerto Rico.

Abstract art made its appearance in graphics in the 1960s. Luis Hernández Cruz was the first Puerto Rican artist to make abstract prints, followed by Domingo García, Domingo López, Marcos Irizarry, and Jaime Romano. Marcos Irizarry's work is

56

57

Lorenzo Homar
56. *Unicorn of the Island.* 1965-66
   Woodcut on paper, 20 x 48"
   Instituto de Cultura Puertorriqueña, San Juan
   Photo: John Betancourt, San Juan

Rafael Rivera Rosa
57. *Atleta Puerto Rico es tuyo. Libéralo (Athlete, Puerto Rico is Yours. Free It).* c.1970
   Silk-screen poster, 22 x 28¾"
   Collection Smith, Kline and French, Puerto Rico
   Photo: John Betancourt, San Juan

outstanding for the zeal with which he explored the possibilities of form. If his early figurative work revealed the influence of the Spanish school from which he had received his training, his mature graphics, such as the *Hummingbird Portfolio,* demonstrated that he had achieved a language of his own, totally free from references to objective reality.

Carlos Irizarry, a painter and graphic artist trained in New York, was the first to use the photo silk-screen process. For Puerto Rican graphic artists this technique represented a break with the workshop tradition of the Center for Puerto Rican Art, the Division of Community Education, and the Institute of Puerto Rican Culture. Although this and other means of mechanical reproduction have since been used by some of the island's graphic artists, there is still resistance to accepting these works on an equal basis with hand-printed graphics.

The introduction of new techniques, greater receptiveness to outside influences, and contact with the best in Latin American graphics at the San Juan biennials have insured the continuing importance of graphics in Puerto Rican art. Another factor contributing to their success is the market they encounter in the island. Affordable prices have made it possible for an appreciable number of Puerto Ricans to acquire original prints. This aim, first expounded by the Center for Puerto Rican Art, has certainly been achieved.

Although the graphic arts in Puerto Rico were still the dominant art form during the 1960s, painting became the main vehicle in the search for identity and the struggle between universalists and engagés. It was in the 1960s that Carlos Raquel Rivera made his most powerful paintings. He personalized social criticism. In *La Enchapada*, a repulsive allegory on the phenomenon of assimilation, and other paintings, he presented telling images of the corrupting effect privilege and money had on Puerto Rico. Riveras's work of this decade obliges the Puerto Rican viewer to realize his own degree of complicity in the tempestuous assimilation process. At the same time, Rivera began to give his political allegories another dimension, not unrelated to the subconscious. *Paroxysm* is a fantastic depiction of fears and anxieties. The viewer is immersed in an absurd and menacing world. While the influence of Surrealism on his work is apparent, what is most striking is the power of the artist's imagination and his ability to come up with the totally unexpected. The force of Rivera's work is paradoxically enhanced by the perfection of execution. The artist is a master craftsman; his paintings and prints reveal a high degree of sophistication and meticulous attention to detail. The inner direction of his work, his exploration of individual and collective psyches, is symptomatic of the identity crisis of those years—a crisis to which the artist gave expression in images that are both fantastic and dramatic.

If the adherence of Olga Albizu and Rosado del Valle to Abstract Expressionism evoked criticism from their peers, the exhibition Rafael Ferrer and Rafael ("Chefo") Villamil staged at the University of Puerto Rico in 1961 created a perfect scandal. The aggressiveness of Ferrer's images and the spontaneity of his creations broke with one of the most firmly entrenched traditions in Puerto Rican art: emphasis on careful execution. Ferrer's compositions were not only visually aggressive, they were also full of allusions to sex. As another artist remarked, never before had anyone exhibited such shocking works.[55] Reaction was not long in coming: the exhibit was picketed and cries for censorship arose—cries which the university ignored.

Three years later Ferrer presented another show, this time of sculptures. Once again it met with rejection in art circles. The sculptures, composed of old shoes, automobile parts, bits of lumber, and other pieces of refuse, were an open challenge to the elegant designs of Homar and Tufiño and to the careful finish of Rivera's paintings. Even in his most impassioned work, Rosado del Valle had demonstrated careful treatment of surfaces and was mindful that he was creating a work of art, to be treated and contemplated with reverence. Ferrer broke sharply with that tradition and the craftsmanlike approach to art that had prevailed in Puerto Rico ever since the time of José Campeche (1751–1809). His sculptures were mature works, marked by the expressiveness that has characterized his output ever since. Even today his crudely dramatic "environment" entitled *Tableau* (plate 58) has a provocative effect to which the viewer cannot remain indifferent. In works such as *The Inheritance,* or *Family Tree,* moreover, Ferrer made reference to the mixed racial background of Puerto Ricans, a subject which is taboo in Caribbean society.

In Ferrer's work one can see the influence of the Surrealist doctrines imparted by his teacher at the University of Puerto Rico, Eugenio Fernández Granell, and the effects of the contact he had in the 1950s with European Surrealists, including André Breton.[56] The artist's acts had as much importance as his creations. This was also the view of Roberto Alberty, another of Fernández Granell's pupils. Through public statements and letters to newspapers, as well as through his work, Ferrer established himself as a harsh, dissonant figure on the Puerto Rican art scene. As a promoter of avant-garde tendencies and as an irreverent iconoclast, Ferrer represented a constant challenge to the insecure artistic and intellectual establishment that existed in Puerto Rico. The University of Puerto Rico alone lent support to Ferrer, who was in constant disagreement with other artists and with the Institute of Puerto Rican Culture.

Under the auspices of the College of Agriculture and Mechanical Arts, a branch of the University of Puerto Rico, Ferrer traveled first to Europe and then to the United States, where he met Robert Morris. The school's role as a promoter of avant-garde art was strengthened by an invitation to Morris and Ferrer to execute environmental sculptures in 1967.[57]

Ferrer's adherence to the international avant-garde and the provocative character of his spontaneous, unpolished compositions caused great commotion in nationalist circles in Puerto Rico. He opened the way to other young Puerto Ricans, who found the new international fashions both stimulating and helpful to their revolt against the Generation of 1950. Experimentation with form became a battlefield for the engagés and the universalists; both, however, were rejected by the public, which disliked the politically oriented compositions of the former and found the work of the latter utterly incomprehensible—predictable reactions, given the artistic underdevelopment of Puerto Rico. Hostility on the part of the public and lack of stimulus caused Ferrer to move to the United States in 1967, and other members of the avant-garde followed in his steps. In the United States, Ferrer would make a place for himself in the international vanguard.

By the middle of the decade, a number of artists on the island were working in styles then in vogue in the United States. Domingo García, who had won distinction as a figurative painter and as a teacher at the Campeche Gallery Workshop, began to turn out Minimalist-like prints. Domingo López also embraced Minimalism, creating elegantly simple compositions such as *Orange Energy*. These achieved a certain degree of success among the more sophisticated public. Interest in this universal type of art was furthered to some extent by efforts of the artist Carlos Irizarry, who opened Gallery 63, named for the year of his return to Puerto Rico. His own work took the form of environments and constructions in acrylic and Plexiglas. Luigi Marrozzini, owner of the Colibrí Gallery, was another promoter of the avant-garde. He succeeded in creating a modest public for his stable and performed a valuable educational function by presenting print exhibitions that were international in scope. Luis Hernández Cruz was seduced for a while by Minimalism. He abandoned the lyrical abstraction of his early paintings such as *The Undersoil* to dedicate himself to the construction of assemblages of fiberglass and acrylic.

A rage for novelty overcame the next generations of artists. In his formative years Rafael Colón-Morales created hard-edge geometric abstract paintings. Later he abandoned this for a style that owes much to Surrealism and Wifredo Lam, evident in *Stinker* (plate 60). Colón-Morales was one of the members of Borinquen 12, a cooperative established by a group of artists seeking an outlet for their works. The group embraced followers of widely differing tendencies, ranging from the Creole theme paintings of Osiris Delgado to the abstractions of Colón-Morales. Borinquen 12 had a short life and little impact, since its members were not united in pursuit of a common goal but were merely seeking to promote their individual interests.[58] Limited support for the avant-garde led López, García, and Colón-Morales to follow the example of Ferrer and set themselves up in New York.[59]

Irizarry returned to New York in 1969 and found employment in the workshops of the Friends of Puerto Rico. He tried to open a Puerto Rican art gallery in New York but met with strong opposition from the gallery's neighbors. After this

58

59

60

Carlos Irizarry
59. *Biafra.* 1970
Photo silk-screen on paper, 28¾ x 34¾"
Museo de Antropología, Arte y Historia,
Universidad de Puerto Rico, Recinto de Río Piedras
Photo: John Betancourt, San Juan

Rafael Colón-Morales
60. *Apestosito (Stinker).* 1969
Oil on canvas, 52 x 60"
Collection Haydee Venegas,
Photo: Tony Velez

Rafael Ferrer
58. *Installation of Tableau.* 1964, Museo de Arte y
Antropología, Universidad de Puerto Rico, San Juan
Photo: courtesy Dr. César Reyes

experience, Irizarry turned to art of a figurative nature, political in content. His mural *Biafra*, executed for the College of Agriculture and Mechanical Arts of the University of Puerto Rico, was the basis for later photo silk-screens (plate 59). He used reticulation and line screening to refer to the mechanical reproduction process and to the relation between original and copy. From this new beginning, Irizarry went on to pursue a career in both painting and graphics, emphasizing art with a political message.

Irizarry's transformation from avant-garde artist to engagé was symptomatic of a new attitude to styles developed in New York. The New York avant-garde's position represented the artists' reaction to the capitalist co-option of art for purposes of speculation and corporate public relations. The situation in Puerto Rico was altogether different: there was no real art market, few serious collectors, and no public sufficiently educated to respond to new artistic challenges. Marta Traba's description of the feeble establishment in San Juan contrasted dramatically with the situation in New York.[60] This realization led some artists, such as Irizarry, to become disenchanted with the avant-garde.

There were also the new movements of Ecological Art, Conceptual Art, and art that advocated the total abolition of the plastic object (a position strongly supported by Rafael Ferrer). Ferrer's Surrealist training and approach made him something of an exception; other Puerto Rican artists were not disposed to abandon traditional media. Thus the pronouncements of the vanguard artists ceased to be considered as having universal application. Disenchantment led adepts of the avant-garde in Puerto Rico to view the new movements as the consequences of, and responses to, situations entirely peculiar to the New York art scene.

The Search for a New Expression

The identity crisis in Puerto Rican art lasted throughout the 1960s. It was reflected in the limited production of Julio Rosado del Valle. The exaltation of abstraction conflicted both with his early populist leanings and with his interest in capturing the forms of nature, which he manifested in his drawings. *Black and White* demonstrated not only the boldness of Rosado del Valle's line and his great creative energy but also the distance that separated him from abstraction. In this work, as in others done during the course of the decade, Rosado del Valle never traveled far from figuration. The titles of his works also made clear their basis in reality.[61] In the latter half of the 1960s the artist concentrated his energies on drawing, a medium that brought out the tectonic character of his line. At the end of the period he executed his monumental *Mural of the Snails*. Restricted use of color and carefully controlled brushwork marked a new approach to painting by the artist, who in this work turned his back on the gestural, expansive strokes of the years in which he practiced Abstract Expressionism (plate 61).

Myrna Báez's long process of experimentation in form bore the best results in her painting of the middle 1970s—a period that falls beyond the limits of this essay. Her early work, such as *Tokyo Quarter* (plate 62), reflects the thinking of the Generation of 1950. But both in painting and in graphics Báez departed from that heritage to undertake topics more in keeping with new Puerto Rican realities. Influenced by the New York School's stress on formal elements, Báez engaged in fruitful experimentation and developed a highly personal manner of painting. Having rejected art that was merely illustration, she began to investigate themes relating to modern, industrialized Puerto Rico. A work such as *In the Bar* conveys the feeling of isolation and solitude experienced by members of the new society that was then coming into being. In her later work she explored this material still more deeply, renewing the tradition of social criticism in art through the adoption of new themes and forms of expression.[62]

At the same time, Rafael Tufiño's art reiterated his love for and celebration of Puerto Rican life in works such as *The Bottle*. His output represented the continuation into the 1960s of his generation's concern with creating a body of works that would be representative of their historical moment (plate 63).

Seeking to escape from the identity crisis that was evident in the art of his formative years, Francisco Rodón stuck to figurative painting in oil, turning his back on "modernity." Perhaps this was an act of resistance on his part to the increasing cultural pressures from the United States to which many young artists had ingenuously yielded

61

62

Julio Rosado del Valle
61. *Black and White*. 1961
    Oil on panel, 64¾ x 78¼"
    Museo de Arte de Ponce, Puerto Rico, Fundación
    Luis A. Ferré
    Photo: Museo de Arte de Ponce

Myrna Báez
62. *Barrio Tokyo*. 1962
    Acrylic on panel, 39½ x 48"
    Museo de Arte de Ponce, Puerto Rico, Fundación
    Luis A. Ferré
    Photo: John Betancourt, San Juan

in the 1960s. In Rodón's case, the identity crisis is reflected in an extremely scanty pictorial production, resulting, it would seem, from a pitched battle between the artist and his medium.[63] Ródón's painting has the paradoxical effect of escaping from the viewer's sight—an effect that became increasingly evident as his work matured.[64] The artist divided his enormous forms into color areas that at times separate themselves from the overall composition and take on an existence of their own; the whole of the image is reassembled later in the viewer's eye. Portraiture is the genre Rodón has cultivated most consistently, but he converts his subjects into archetypes—personifications of myths and demons. In *Watchful Gaze* (plate 64), for example, what at first appears to be the likeness of a little girl becomes a suggestion of a precociously perverse sexuality.

Other artists avoided choosing between being an engagé or a universalist by seeking to synthesize the conflicting currents. Augusto Marín and others all but eliminated reference to context. Marín exploits subjects from history and mythology in an attempt to produce figurative work of universal significance. Julio Micheli, another member of the Generation of 1960, resorts to semifigurative abstraction in exploring nature and the world of imagination. In a work such as *Apparition*, Micheli came close to the New Figuration artists' aim of synthesizing the disparate tendencies of the time.

After experimenting with Minimalist art, Luis Hernández Cruz returned to lyrical abstractions, recreating the forms of landscape. In *Seascape* (plate 65), Hernández Cruz conveys in abstract terms the color and tensions of tropical nature. Jaime Romano, active in Puerto Rico at the end of the decade, took a similar path. A graduate of Washington University and the University of Puerto Rico, Romano tried to invent an abstract language to depict tropical reality and tensions in Puerto Rico without recourse to narrative devices.

New York

The presence of Puerto Rican artists in the United States was quite evident in the 1960s. Reviews of Olga Albizu's shows and references to her participation in the exhibit at the Riverside Museum indicate that by the 1960s she had established a discrete presence on the New York art scene.[65] She became vastly better known when reproductions of her works began to appear on record jackets. Albizu worked for a record company, and her work was on display in the offices of RCA. There it attracted the attention of Stan Getz, which led RCA to commission her work for reproduction on the covers of Getz's and Gilberto's immensely popular bossa nova albums. Enthusiasm for bossa nova was then at its height, and this meant that Albizu's paintings came before the eyes of a very large public. Jackets featuring compositions such as *Growth* were on display in the windows of leading record shops not only in New York but throughout the United States. During this period of maximum dissemination of her work, Albizu had a solo exhibition in the gallery at the headquarters of the Organization of American States in Washington, D.C.[66] Albizu provided an important role model for young Puerto Ricans: she was a famous artist with whom they could identify—albeit at a very considerable distance (plate 66).

While Albizu was establishing a presence on her own, the Friends of Puerto Rico were increasingly active on behalf of island artists in general. In addition to the exhibits organized directly by Amalia Guerrero, the association helped arrange shows at private galleries such as Caravan House, Galería Hoy, and the Galería Sudamericana. With aid from philanthropists and the government of Puerto Rico, the Friends of Puerto Rico secured premises of its own, where exhibits could be given and where workshops for young artists were set up. The Brooklyn Museum, the Grand Street Settlement House, the IBM Gallery, and the Tibor de Nagy Gallery presented shows in which various Puerto Rican artists participated. This provided those in training with an opening to the art world. For the Puerto Rican community, however, it was undoubtedly the Friends of Puerto Rico that constituted the most visible and concrete symbol of that world. It was there that young would-be artists went for their first workshop experience.

During the 1960s Juan Maldonado, Victor Linares, Rafael Tufiño, Carlos Osorio, Domingo López, Domingo García, Rafael Colón-Morales, and Carlos Irizarry were active at the workshops of the Friends of Puerto Rico.[67] Osorio, who in all

64

63

Rafael Tufiño
63. *Museum of the Puerto Rican Family.* 1964
Silk-screen on paper, 29¾ x 19¼″
Instituto de Cultura Puertorriqueña, San Juan
Photo: John Bentancourt, San Juan

Francisco Rodón
64. *Watchful Gaze.* 1968
Oil on canvas, 60 x 48″
Collection Dr. and Mrs. Arsenio Comas
Photo: courtesy the artist

probability took the leading role, was a member of the Generation of 1950. He was originally trained in New York, but returned to Puerto Rico in 1956 and worked for a while at the Division of Community Education. In the following decades he shuttled constantly between San Juan and New York but spent most of his time on the mainland (plate 67). Tufiño had similar experiences except that he spent most of his time in San Juan.

Osorio, Linares, and Tufiño formed a group of instructors that initiated new artists into workshop practices. Their involvement in the Friends of Puerto Rico had an effect that was quite different from what had been achieved by the exhibits sporadically staged in the city in previous decades or by the highly visible art of Olga Albizu. For one thing, unlike Blanco, Homar, and Albizu, these artists identified themselves with the Puerto Rican community. The new generation was exposed not merely to their work but also to their life-style and the mystique associated with being an artist. Their affirmation of the Puerto Rican heritage and the nationalism that inspired them filled a vacuum for a generation born in and acclimated to New York but nonetheless in search of its roots. The Friends of Puerto Rico and shortly thereafter the Taller Boricua (Puerto Rican Workshop) provided training by experienced artists who—and this was still more important—imparted a certain feeling for life and a sense of mission to be accomplished in the community. As in Puerto Rico—but in still more dramatic fashion in New York—the identity conflict transformed the artist into the creator of symbols for the community. Upon the shoulders of this shaman and prophet fell the burden of caring for the wounds of a community that had been torn apart. This almost religious mission was clearly preached by Ralph Ortiz.

The impact of Ortiz on the world of art was dramatic and convulsive. His Theater of Destruction—performances at which he destroyed pianos and sacrificed animals—won him international fame (plate 68). He played a leading role at the first Destruction in Art symposium held in London in 1966. (BBC Television even transmitted a number of works, including those of Ortiz.) In 1968 a second Destruction in Art symposium was held in New York, and on this occasion the artist performed *The Life and Death of Henny Penny*, in which he resorted to violence and ritual in symbolizing the conflicts of race and identity experienced by Puerto Ricans adjusting to white society. Ortiz put on other performances in the United States, Europe, and Canada.[68]

Ortiz also created works based on pre-Columbian myths. He used pieces of broken furniture to create dramatic sculptures such as *Tlazolteotl* that allude both to Christian iconography and to Aztec creation and destruction rites.[69] In works such as *Burnt Mattress*, Ortiz made successful use of avant-garde idioms to confront the artistic establishment with the conditions of decay in minority communities. The plastic covering the mattress preserves for posterity a symbol of the blighted life of the ghetto. Although his Theater of Destruction underscores the racial stereotype of Latin violence, its complacent reception in the world of art was evidence of the blindness of an establishment that can see only what confirms its chauvinistic preconceptions.

Ortiz was concerned with more than the advancement of his individual career, and toward the end of the decade he began to devote his energies to the creation of El Museo del Barrio. Ortiz thought of the museum as having a social mission. Rather than serving as a repository for "cultural treasures," it was to be an open institution to which the community would come to discover its roots and understand its past.[70] Ortiz the artist gradually became Ortiz the educator. Just as in the ancient creation-destruction myths, after exorcising demons the artist-shaman set about healing wounds and showing the community the path it must follow. This activity was complemented by Ortiz's active participation in the Art Workers' Coalition, a protest movement aimed at overcoming museum prejudices against art produced by women and ethnic and racial minorities.[71]

Rafael Ferrer launched a new wave of attack by stacking up leaves in a number of New York galleries in 1968. The artist himself described this action in military terms, as a carefully planned and executed tactic.[72] It got him invitations to participate in a number of exhibitions in the United States and Europe. Other confrontational works followed in rapid succession: there was a sculpture made of blocks of ice at The

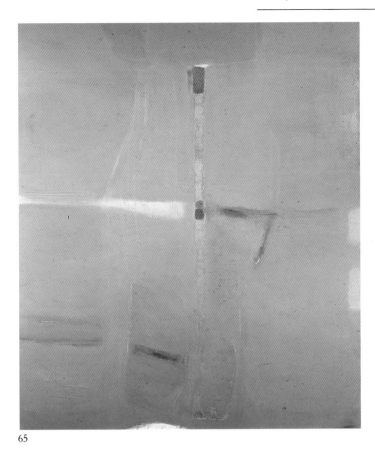

65

66

Luis Hernández Cruz
65. *Seascape.* 1970
   Oil on canvas, 60 x 70¼"
   Museo de Arte de Ponce, Puerto Rico, Fundación
   Luis A. Ferré
   Photo: John Betancourt, San Juan

Olga Albizu
66. *Growth.* 1960
   Oil on canvas, 50 x 42⅛"
   Lowe Art Museum, University of Miami. Gift, Esso
   Inter-America, Inc.
   Photo: Roland I. Unruh

67

68

Carlos Osorio
67. *Coast.* 1970
   Oil on canvas, 38 x 34″
   Collection Tola Osorio, New York
   Photo: Tony Velez

Rafael Montañez-Ortiz
68. *Performance of Henny Penny Piano Destruction*
   January 1967, New York City
   Photo: courtesy Kristine Stiles

Museum of Modern Art, and the installation of *Hay, Grease, Steel* at the Whitney Biennial, where Ferrer covered the walls of a room with grease and filled the intervening space with hay weighed down with steel bars. Outside the museum Ferrer made another stack of leaves, which he topped off with blocks of ice; when this melted Ferrer handed the last piece to Max Kozloff during his lecture in the museum auditorium.[73]

Ferrer's desecration of the walls of the museum and the creation of ephemeral works were acts of violent rebellion. Like those of Ralph Ortiz, they fitted the stereotype of the greasy, menacing Latin. In his autobiography Ferrer refers to this stereotype and tells how he used it to force Leo Castelli to honor his promise of an exhibition in 1970.[74] The show lasted only a few hours, but its expressive power and the gesture of building up a complex installation only to destroy it in a matter of minutes captured the attention of influential Manhattan art critics.[75] In *Deflected Fountain, for Marcel Duchamp*, presented in the fountain of the Philadelphia Museum of Art, Ferrer established his formal relationship with the French artist, whose famous work was to be found in that museum. The museum authorities asked Ferrer to coordinate his act with the visit of Duchamp's widow, but Ferrer refused. From his position, it was a matter of the precise execution of a task; not a performance to be put on at the request of a patron. These extreme stands on matters of artistic principle and the fecundity of Ferrer's imagination helped establish his reputation.[76]

In the late 1960s Ferrer had several one-man shows in the United States and Europe and took part in a number of group exhibitions. Aggressiveness and confrontation of the establishment are fundamental aspects of his art. His sense of humor and his references to the Caribbean, particularly in his use of percussion instruments, appeared for the first time in an installation he did at the Whitney Museum in 1970. In his later work Ferrer has returned to his Caribbean roots for the topics and imagery that now characterize his powerful expression.

Ortiz and Ferrer are the sole Puerto Ricans to have gained a certain degree of acceptance in the mainstream. The image of the artist as a cultural guerrilla, which both artists helped to establish, is what gained them entrance into the mainstream. However, in addition to conjuring up racial myths in visual form, both artists contributed to the advance of art at the time. Ortiz carried the physical, gestural aspect of Abstract Expressionism to its most dramatic extremes. His "theaters" represent a violent development of the "happening," which under other names is one of the richest manifestations of contemporary art. Ferrer, for his part, is the initiator of "process art," the instigator of the ephemeral work, of the conceptual. *Deflected Fountain* marked the beginning of "body art"—a whole series of manifestations for which his works and acts have served as a point of departure.

The force of the works of Ferrer and Ortiz tore down the gates of the art world. They remained closed, however, to other Puerto Ricans. Despite the quality of the works of Domingo López and Domingo García and the efforts they made to find an outlet for them, they were always shunted to the side. The only avenues open to them were those provided by the OAS General Secretariat in Washington, the Friends of Puerto Rico, or galleries dedicated exclusively to Latin American art.

In 1969 the Taller Boricua (Puerto Rican Workshop) was established in the Barrio, and to it moved many of the artists who had been active in the workshops of the Friends of Puerto Rico. The Taller Boricua pursued objectives similar to those of the silk-screen workshops that had proliferated in Puerto Rico during the 1960s—for which the Center for Puerto Rican Art had provided the original model. The Taller Boricua was populist in its aims and its members maintained a close relationship with the group of political activists known as the Young Lords.[77]

The outstanding artist working at the Taller Boricua was Jorge Soto. Though exposed to a variety of influences, Soto is essentially an intuitive, self-taught artist. His search for his Puerto Rican roots in the life and environment of the emigrant colony is reflected in his compositions. He reinterprets Puerto Rican art history, reworking the paintings of Campeche and Oller to produce dramatic images expressive of the hard life of the ghetto.[78] The deep religious meaning of this experience and its roots in magic are clearly conveyed by *Untitled* (plate 69); its dramatic, primitivistic effects are achieved with lines both elegant and eloquent. Like Ortiz before him, Soto draws on Western

69

Jorge Soto
69. *Untitled.* 1969
  Acrylic and ink on canvas, 36 x 24″
  El Museo del Barrio, New York
  Photo: Tony Velez

tradition to express the violence of ghetto life.

Perhaps the most complex of the artists to appear in the Puerto Rican colony during these years was José Morales. Racial prejudice and the disdain with which his creative work was received in the schools of his native New York led him to emigrate to Europe, where he was able to develop as an artist, freed of the burden of being a Puerto Rican in New York.[79] He lived for a while in Spain and then went on to Paris. He learned both from the academies he frequented and from street experiences, for it was on the sidewalk that he worked, earning a living by painting pictures to sell to tourists. He gradually developed a visual idiom that permitted him to express the inner conflict he experienced as a result of his background and the times in which he was living. The war in Vietnam and the spirit of protest prevalent in the decade provided the basis for his powerful collages, in which he combined images resulting from chance encounter, letters of the alphabet, and articles of daily life. In Sweden, far from the asphyxiating atmosphere of the ghetto and the closed world of New York galleries and museums, he succeeded in creating significant, monumental art. It is in Europe that he discovered the liberty denied to even the most thoroughly assimilated of Puerto Ricans in the Land of the Free.

One of the outcomes of the conflicting demands on Puerto Rican artists is that they have escaped the great pitfall of the art of the provinces: the trivialization of the metropolis's monumental tradition. The work of Puerto Rican artists, in the island and in the United States, is conceived as part of a fierce struggle to survive as an independent culture. But that conflict goes beyond Puerto Rico's particular circumstances. Assimilation of spurious consumer values and traditions is displacing traditional cultures worldwide, and the conflict of identity has become a truly universal one. Puerto Rican artists have been dealing with this problem, giving visual expression to the great dilemma. Their expressions—dramatic, satiric, ambiguous, at times brilliant—is a contribution to one of the basic problems of man: what are we? where are we heading? Their search for identity ends up being universal.

Constructivism and Geometric Abstraction

by Nelly Perazzo

Constructivism is an expression loosely applied in Latin American art to describe virtually all geometric art (planar or three-dimensional) from the time of Torres-García in the 1920s onward. It has been of major significance not only as an alternative to the predominantly figurative bias in regional art but also for its association with the progressive, the intellectual, and the international.[1]

This statement defines not just the basic term but also the spirit that informs the Latin American Constructivist aesthetic. Geometric Abstraction originally came into being in countries with highly developed economies. It was an attempt at synthesis, symbolic of the search for balance in a large-scale technological society. In Latin America the tendency was taken up most quickly by outward-looking societies possessed of a certain degree of cultural development and imbued with a progressive attitude. It first appeared in Buenos Aires, Caracas, São Paulo, and Montevideo.[2] However, as the Colombian critic Marta Traba has observed, there is a difference between importing a fashion wholesale and adopting a language.[3] As regards the latter, elements of a vocabulary can be manipulated for altogether different and personal purposes. Latin American artists have demonstrated this quite clearly. Joaquín Torres-García, our point of departure, provides the best example of how developments of a personal nature can give rise to new possibilities. Indeed, his work inspired one critic to write: "In societies like ours, where everything remains to be done, art that incorporates an effort to define a national or continental perspective provides a feeling of organizing existence, of transforming it, of building a new society."[4]

Conversely, it has been argued that we "see what a given work means within a determined ideological, historical, and socioeconomic context," and in this respect "the geometric trend in Latin America can be seen as a healthy corrective to the whole tradition of individualism and emotionalism in art and culture."[5] Latin American Constructivism represented a change of direction from social and historical precedents. For one thing, the societies in which it appeared, unlike those of Europe, were in the early stages of industrialization. For another, it served as "a healthy corrective" not only to excesses of irrationalism and emotionalism but also to the regionalist, picture-book art that foreigners tended to expect of the area.

In studying Latin American Constructivism, it is important to distinguish between the generation of artists born in the last decades of the nineteenth century, who are no longer living, and the generation born in the second decade of the present century and thereafter, most of whose members are still alive and active. With regard to the first generation, represented by Torres-García and Emilio Pettoruti, the perspective of time permits us to draw certain conclusions and to see certain relationships that are less readily established for the younger generation.

There are a number of differences between the two generations. The earlier artists received their training in Europe; the younger ones grew up in groups and movements thoroughly Latin American in character. For the former, Paris was the center of the art world, whereas after World War II artists shifted their attention to New York. In addition, not only did Geometric Abstractionists fleeing the war in Europe come to play an important role in the United States, but changes in the artistic infrastructure of the Latin American countries led to a marked growth of interest in this art.

What factors drew Latin American artists to the United States? The reasons varied. Some may have wished to test their talents abroad; others to establish contact with their artistic sources; still others may have sought a more stimulating environment, greater recognition, a market, the company of colleagues, interchange of ideas with critics, and the support of collectors. I believe it is premature to define "presence" in terms of the significance Latin American artists assumed or the influence they exerted in the United States. All that can be done for now is to provide a certain amount of information concerning the length of time they spent in the country, the exhibits they had, the coverage they received in the press, the degree to which they supplemented creative activity with writing or teaching, and the extent to which they are represented in museums or private art collections. In this respect, the present exhibition represents a challenge: it provides the opportunity for a fresh look at a number of problems and for an updated view of Latin American Constructivism and its relation to U.S. art. One may presume that it will lead to renewed efforts to fill in the historical record, greater interchange among those who are struggling for a better appreciation of Latin American art, and recognition of Latin America's highly individual contribution to Constructivist art worldwide.

Torres-García in the United States

It is peculiarly appropriate that 1920 should mark the beginning of the half century covered by this study, since that is the year that Joaquín Torres-García, "the sole member of this generation of Latin American artists to leave a durable mark on contemporary art," set himself up in the United States.[6] On January 23, 1920, he wrote to his fellow countryman and painter Rafael Pérez Barradas:

And now for my really big news; in April we're all going to New York! It's a sure thing unless some major problem comes up. I ought to have made this decision at least ten years ago. The reason for my going now is the unbelievable dirty trick my partner in the toy business has played on me. So I'm grateful to him for it. The United States is the country for me, Barradas! Gigantic, dynamic, free, with an abundance of activity and machines![7]

This letter was written from Spain, where Torres-García had lived ever since his father, a Catalan by birth, decided in 1891 to return to his home in Mataró after being disillusioned by a number of business failures in Uruguay. Dazzled by the cultural life of nearby Barcelona, Joaquín moved there soon after. The city's school provided him with good training; he had access to libraries; he made contact with the local artistic circle. It was there too that he had his first opportunities to show his talent for poster design and illustration. The culmination of this early period of activity came in 1901 when the most forward-looking magazine in Barcelona, *Pel e Ploma*, established Torres-García's reputation in an issue that carried a color reproduction of one of his works on its cover, more reproductions of his art inside, a charcoal portrait of the artist by Ramón Casas, samples of his writings, a note on his work by Miguel Utrillo, and an editorial in which the publication congratulated itself on numbering Torres-García among its collaborators.

During those same early years, Torres-García worked with Antonio Gaudí on the Sagrada Familia in Barcelona, engaged in his first teaching activities, and evidenced an early need to explain his artistic approach in writing.[8] By the time he decided to embark for New York he had already produced a large body of mural paintings (in the Church of San Agustín in Barcelona, in the apse of the Divina Pastora in Sarriá, and in the Hall of St. George of the Diputación in Barcelona); he had published a number of books; he had had a number of one-man shows; and he had begun a commercial venture, manufacturing wooden toys.[9]

Misfortune came in 1917, however. August of that year brought the death of Enrique Prat de la Riva, president of the city council of Barcelona, who had given Torres-García much moral support. About the same time the artist began to experience business troubles. In addition, owing to the combative character of his efforts at artistic renewal, his new work was misunderstood. Though there were a number of avant-garde groups in Barcelona and heated discussion of art matters went on at the Dalmau Gallery, Torres-García felt that he needed a broader horizon than Barcelona offered for

70

Joaquín Torres-García
70. *New York City—Bird's Eye View.* c.1920
    Gouache and watercolor on board, 13 1/4 x 19 1/8"
    Yale University Art Gallery. Gift of Collection
    Société Anonyme
    Photo: Regina Monfort

his works, and he prepared to leave.[10]

There was nothing strange about his moving. He had already visited a number of cities in Spain and had spent time in Brussels, Paris, Rome, Florence, and Geneva in search of experiences that would help him to define his artistic position. Torres-García may have thought that New York would give him a greater degree of recognition and economic support, in addition to providing a broader artistic environment that was more international in character. At first he was enthusiastic about New York. He liked his contacts with Catalan friends, with gallery owners, artists, musicians, and writers, and he enjoyed a city so teeming with life.

He made a great many friends, among them the painters Marcel Duchamp, Joseph Stella, Max Weber, Abraham Walkowitz, and Morris Kantor; the prominent businessman Charles Logasa; Hamilton Easter Field, the editor of Arts *magazine; Edgar Varèse, the well-known composer; Dr. Riefstahl of the Anderson Gallery; and Juan Agell, an engineer and part-time filmmaker. He became good friends with John Xceron, whose philosophical and artistic ideas were influenced by Greek art.*[11]

He wrote of his relationships with Americans:

People don't go in for plotting or politicking, or take roundabout ways to their goals. Why should they? There's no need to. They get right down to business. A deal's a deal or it isn't. There's no point to wasting any more time over the matter.[12]

But New York is not easily won over, and Torres-García, in part because of language problems, did not allow himself enough time. He soon found himself facing difficulties again. To earn a living he did advertising work and painted stage scenery. Gertrude Vanderbilt Whitney extended moral and financial support. She gave him a monthly allowance in exchange for pictures, provided him with a place to work (the Whitney Studio Club on West Fourth Street), and helped him get his art exhibited. In April and May 1921 he showed some of his pictures at the Studio Club alongside works by Stuart Davis and Stanislaw Szukalski. Finally, in July 1922, Mrs. Whitney purchased enough of his works so that he was able to buy a passage to Italy for himself and his family.[13]

Torres-García's presence in America was well documented. The May 5, 1921, issue of *Arts* magazine carried a note signed by Hamilton Field concerning the Studio Club show. Torres-García also received considerable support from the collector Katherine Dreier, who bought a number of his works for the Société Anonyme.[14] (These are now to be found at Yale University.) In 1927 Dreier invited him to exhibit at the Société. Two additional newspaper references to the painter are known from his New York years.[15] One is an article by Joseph Krause, which appeared in *Art Home News* of September 1, 1920; the other, which includes a reproduction, came out in *Art Review* in 1922. The latter appeared after the Torres-García family's departure for Genoa on July 17. It refers to one-man exhibits of his work at the Times Building in September 1922 and at the Hanfstaengel Gallery that same year.

Aside from the impact that Torres-García may or may not have had on New York at that time (his work had yet to achieve the qualities that made his reputation), there are a number of important facts to note about the episode. For one thing, he was able to continue his much-dreamed-of project for manufacturing wooden toys, taking it up first with the Anderson Gallery and then with Juliana Force, an assistant to Gertrude Vanderbilt Whitney. This has led some writers to say that in returning to Italy he was looking for cheap labor, with the idea of exporting toys to the United States.[16] In fact, a short time later he did send a shipment of toys to be exhibited at the Studio Club. The most significant achievement of his New York years, however, was "an album of ink and watercolor sketches, entitled *New York Sketchbook*, presenting street scenes and everyday things that seemed to him typically American, such as a fire truck, tall buildings, an open crate of eggs, milk bottles, matches, and a tin of tobacco. Each drawing was numbered, and stenciled above at an angle are the words 'New York'" (plate 71).[17] Torres-García began a second notebook, called *Good-bye New York*, in

71

72

Joaquín Torres-García
71. *New York Sketchbook.* c.1920
Watercolor on paper, 8½ x 6″ (one of ninety-two pages)
Courtesy Cecilia Torres, New York
Photo: D. James Dee

Joaquín Torres-García
72. *Cider Vinegar.* 1921
Watercolor on paper, 20 x 16″
Courtesy estate of the artist
Photo: D. James Dee

73

Joaquín Torres-García
73. *Hoy.* 1921
Watercolor and collage, 20¾ x 14¾"
Courtesy Cecilia Torres, New York
Photo: D. James Dee

74

Joaquín Torres-García
74. *Fourteenth Street.* 1924
Oil on board, 22 x 18″
Courtesy C.D.S. Gallery, New York
Photo: courtesy C.D.S. Gallery

colored crayon; but this remained unfinished.

Significant also were a series of works he made related to the life of the city—paintings of billboards, means of transportation, clocks, and scribblings on walls. He had explored this kind of subject matter in Barcelona as early as 1917, just when he began to adapt Futurist devices for his own ends. At that time he used street scenes as the basis for compartmentalized structures. It is obvious that the dynamic character of New York life and the city's bold vistas stimulated him to go farther in this direction, even after he left the United States (plates 70 and 74).

When Torres-García eventually moved to Paris in 1926, it was the center of the international avant-garde and was enhanced by the presence of several colonies of foreigners: Russians, Poles, Hungarians, Romanians, and Scandinavians. What really gave life to the Paris art scene in those years, however, was the presence of such key figures as Mondrian, Robert and Sonia Delaunay, and a throng of lesser lights— including Goncharova, Larionov, Pevsner, Pougny, Janco, Kassak, Seuphor, Prampolini, Vantongerloo, Van Doesburg, Hans Arp, and Sophie Taeuber-Arp.

In 1928 Torres-García took part in the show *Five Artists Rejected by the Autumn Salon* held at the March Gallery. There he met Theo Van Doesburg, who put him in contact with the creators of Neo-Plasticism. At a show of Vordemberge-Gildewart's works he met Michel Seuphor and, shortly thereafter, Piet Mondrian. This last encounter was to be of decisive importance. Michel Seuphor notes that "the visit the Uruguayan Torres-García paid [Mondrian] in Vannes early in 1929 was one of the events leading to the creation of the association known as *Cercle et Carré* [Circle and Square]."[18]

The association soon numbered eighty members. In March 1930 they began publication of a review that ran for three issues, and they had an important show at Gallery 23. The nucleus of the group was constituted by Mondrian, Kandinsky, Arp, Schwitters, Vantongerloo, Sophie Taeuber, Vordemberge-Gildewart, Gorin, and Pevsner. Other members included Léger, Le Corbusier, Baumeister, Russolo, Prampolini, and the American Joseph Stella. Torres-García was responsible for the administration of the group's review, the first number of which carried an article by him entitled *"Vouloir Construire"* (Wanting to Construct).[19]

The significance of this participation in the art life of Paris did not stop there, for it was the stimulus it provided that led him to give definite form to his Constructivist ideas. Torres-García had always been fascinated by the idea of structure. From the time of his earliest creations, the orderliness of his mind and his need for a system superior to the requirements of figuration are notable. Another important characteristic was his esteem for two-dimensional form: for Torres-García the reversion to flatness signified a return to real painting. He felt it was only a small step from the abolition of the traditional relationship between figure and background—volumes placed in a space with a deceptive illusion of depth—to the attempt to sustain the equipotential of the pictorial field.

However, his encounter with Mondrian caused him to realize his lack of accord with a movement whose principles failed to take into account certain aspects of humanity that he considered of fundamental importance. He needed to synthesize concepts that apparently were opposed to one another: on the one hand, an ideal order, based on geometry, which would acquire a universal dimension by expressing the unity of nature; on the other, the presence of forces that may be derived from instinct, the unconscious, and magic. It was a very ambitious undertaking that required him to call on his earlier investigations, on elements of his Parisian experience—his close relationships with the great creative figures of Geometric Abstraction—on a study of the history of man he made with his son Augusto, and on research into esoteric doctrines.

Noting the coincidence between the appearance of Constructivism and Torres-García's arrival in Paris, where he was confronted with Geometric Abstraction on the one hand and Surrealism on the other, the art historian Margit Rowell has written of them as "two movements which appeared antithetical, but which were inspired by similar responses to the state of the world. Both groups of artists were reacting against what they saw as the rampant materialism and overriding rationalism of society."[20] However, many abstract artists were also abandoning "the philosophical and religious

75

Joaquín Torres-García
75. *Composition No. 548.* 1932
Oil on carton, 41½ x 30½"
Museum of Art, Rhode Island School of Design,
Providence. Nancy Sayles Day Collection of Latin
American Art
Photo: courtesy Museum of Art, Rhode Island
School of Design

bases of art. The theosophy that had imbued the older generation had given way to materialism. The work of art no longer responded to divine principles, to universal laws; it reflected the requirements of science, technology, and the laws of optics."[21]

Not surprisingly, this approach did not satisfy Torres-García's all-embracing ambition. It should be noted that the confrontation between geometric art and Surrealism had also generated—or was generating—a trend, led by Arp, that might be termed "organic abstraction." This trend was to be taken up by notable artists whose firm support of abstraction did not presuppose a total divorce from nature. Likewise, Torres-García gradually developed his own aesthetic to reconcile opposing forces. He used symbols to establish the connection between immediate reality and the universal. "The singular invention of Universal Constructivism fused modern abstraction with the great mathematical traditions of the past," the art historian and collector Barbara Duncan has noted. "Torres-García created a highly suggestive and individual vocabulary of form, aiming to embrace eras of symbols stretching from prehistoric times to the twentieth century."[22] His philosophical idea of totality implied unity between the artist/constructor and the cosmic order of the universe—a joining of the mental, emotional, and physical realms. Torres-García, himself, wrote:

Reason is our measure, our balance.
A sign carved on a stone is something separate from nature. It is the sign of man,
the mark of Reason. Reason is Man. The tradition of Reason is an impersonal tradition
which departs from nature. It looks toward what is general: the idea. Instinct looks
inward and delves into the unconscious and ancestral memory; it is nature that must be
transformed and ordered in thought, within an intellectual framework.[23]

In Torres-García's numerous writings from that time the development of his thought and work can be traced. Reason, the golden rule, the law, the norm, organization, structure, measure, geometry, numerical series—these are the factors that determine his compartmentalization of a painting's surface.[24] He once said: "A picture should remain on the surface, since a third dimension is not real." The other basis for his expression was a symbolic language in which ideas are transformed into graphic marks that fill the basic grid; a reminder that intellect, the emotions, and instinct are integral parts of the cosmic plan.[25] Universal Constructivism is an ideal, since it is based on geometry. It is concrete, since forms are not represented in imitation of nature but in terms of their real intrinsic significance. It is metaphysical, since the images that fill the flat spaces within the grid have magic meaning and symbolize the unconscious. It is universal, since the harmonious order of the work as a whole expresses the unity of creation.[26]

There were other forces too that enriched Torres-García's art. He was interested in medieval symbolism and its deep spiritual significance and in primitive cultures, whose importance for contemporary art has been repeatedly pointed out.[27] Torres-García's son Augusto, who was a passionate student of primitive art, took his father to the Musée de l'Homme in Paris, introducing him to African and pre-Columbian art, to the Nazca pottery of ancient Peru, and to American Indian motifs. The inclusion of these forces in his aesthetic may serve to explain the influence he came to exert not only in the United States and Europe but also in the River Plate area.

In 1933 Torres-García's second New York period began. Although he did not actually visit New York, his work was included in a group show at the Museum of Living Art. The show was organized by Albert Eugene Gallatin, who had met Torres-García in Paris and had bought works from him. The selection included two of his 1929 oils, another dating from 1930, and a 1931 work painted on wood. The Gallatin collection was on display at New York University until 1943, when it was transferred to the Philadelphia Museum of Art; thus Torres-García's work was seen by a substantial number of people.

In 1943 Torres-García was included in a show at The Museum of Modern Art entitled *The Latin American Collection.*[28] In 1950 there was an exhibit of his work at the Sidney Janis Gallery and soon after one at the headquarters of the Organization of American States (OAS) in Washington, D.C. In an article published in the April

1950 issue of *Art News*, Thomas Hess recognized Torres-García as one of the few Latin American artists of real stature.[29] Other articles about him appeared that same year—one by A. Chanin in *The Sunday Compass*[30] and one by Dorothy Adlow entitled "Artist Who Sought a Universal Picture Language," which appeared in *The Christian Science Monitor*.[31] The Uruguayan master was also represented in a group show held in Washington at OAS headquarters in 1955, *Highlights of Latin American Art*. The *Boletín de Música y Artes Visuales*, published by the OAS General Secretariat, had a note on him in its February–March 1956 issue. The General Secretariat also organized a 1961 traveling exhibition; this occasioned further notes on Torres-García in the bulletin's issues of January–June 1961 and January–June 1962.[32]

There were Torres-García shows at the Rose Fried Gallery in 1960 and 1965. In March 1960 Dore Ashton wrote an article about him in *The New York Times*. The Royal Marks Gallery showed his work in 1962 and 1969. The latter event inspired a commentary by Robert Pincus Witten in the summer 1969 issue of *Artforum* and one by John Baker in the May 1969 *Arts* magazine. Baker emphasized that Torres-García was one of the few Latin American artists to develop a mode of expression that was neither a copy of European abstraction nor a vehicle for social propaganda. He pointed out the valuable contributions Torres-García had made to Geometric Abstraction and the radical differences between his art and Mexican mural painting.[33]

In 1970 there was a major retrospective, *Joaquín Torres-García 1874–1949*, at the National Gallery of Canada in Ottawa, the Solomon R. Guggenheim Museum in New York, and the Rhode Island School of Design in Providence. The accompanying catalog carried an article by Daniel Robbins.[34]

Torres-García's influence in art circles was also directly recognized. The Center for Inter-American Relations included him in the 1970 show *Forerunners of American Modernism: 1860–1930*, recognizing the important contributions he had made.[35] In the catalog of the exhibition the statement was made that "time has shown that he was the most influential South American artist of the twentieth century." Robert Pincus Witten made a detailed analysis of the relationship between Torres-García's paintings and those of Jean Xceron and Adolph Gottlieb. He declared: "Clearly, Torres-García had made one of the major contributions to painting in the twentieth century, similar to those of Mondrian and Klee, not only by the clarity of his development but by its deeply pedagogical character."[36] (The relationship between Torres-García's work and Gottlieb's pictographs has also been discussed by Barbara Rose,[37] H. H. Arnason, and Thomas Hess.[38] The approach that several of Gottlieb's contemporaries were taking at that time, incorporating symbolic and mystical elements into their painting, unquestionably was influenced by the Torres-García works in the Gallatin collection.)

Thus Torres-García's presence in the United States first meant to him a step forward in the process toward a definition of his language. While he did not achieve the definitive image and the personal and unique synthesis that so characterizes his later art, he did succeed in holding exhibitions and making contacts that opened doors in New York. As his work achieved—first in Paris and Spain and then in Montevideo—a universal dimension, so the United States became interested in him again. Numerous exhibitions and studies of his work were produced, and his influence was registered on important American artists, including Adolph Gottlieb and Louise Nevelson.

Torres-García's writings did not deal solely with his own aesthetic but also with the work of other artists. Shortly after the National Commission of Fine Arts and the Fine Arts Circle of Montevideo invited the Argentinian Emilio Pettoruti to exhibit a selection of his works at the commission's headquarters, Torres-García wrote:

Unlike some others, [Pettoruti] did not advance timidly along the new paths to true art, nor did he fear the battles he would have to wage in his own country when he returned home. He was the first to introduce the new plastic concept to South America. We were under obligation to demonstrate his firm belief in the new concept, his fortitude in keeping up the struggle, his steadfastness, and the pioneer effort for which he must always be recognized. And to think this all began ten or fifteen years ago, when the new trends in art were utterly unknown in River Plate circles.[39]

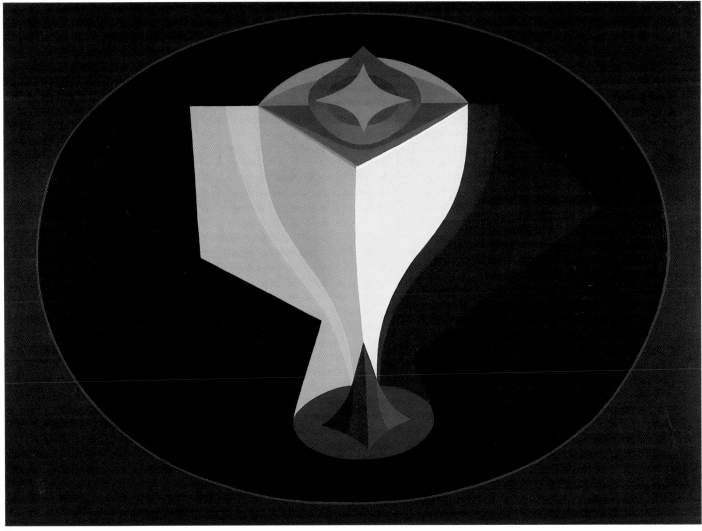

76

Emilio Pettoruti
76. *Coparmonica.* 1937
Oil on canvas, 28⅞ x 39⅜″
San Francisco Museum of Modern Art. Purchase
Photo: courtesy San Francisco Museum of
Modern Art

Thus Torres-García himself stressed the revolutionary effect Pettoruti's show had had in Buenos Aires. Pettoruti had waged a campaign to update art in Argentina through his efforts as a teacher and a writer and as the director of the provincial art museum in La Plata.[40] It is not surprising therefore that Jorge Romero Brest, one of Argentina's outstanding art critics, emphatically calls Pettoruti "the real pioneer of artistic renewal in our country" in an article he wrote for the catalog to Pettoruti's first exhibit in the United States at the San Francisco Museum of Art in 1942.[41] That exhibit covered Pettoruti's work from 1917, the moment at which he was beginning to show signs of maturity, until 1941.

Pettoruti had gone to Europe in 1913, and there had assimilated not only the lessons offered by the great masters of the past but also the latest advances of Cubism and Futurism. Futurism freed him from the bonds of literal representation of reality and incited him to suggest movement and velocity in his work. Cubism, to which he had been attracted primarily as a result of his friendship with Juan Gris, led him to organize compositions on the basis of the dissections of form and space. When Pettoruti arrived in the United States in 1942, however, he had advanced far beyond this early, exploratory state: he had successfully assimilated the European styles; he had been flattered by his associations with the avant-garde in Paris and in Italy; his work had been exhibited in a number of individual and group shows in various Italian cities; he had been invited by Herwarth Walden to exhibit at the Berlin gallery Der Sturm; and Léonce Rosenberg had offered to become his agent. All this seemed to indicate the beginning of a brilliant international career. However, Pettoruti lost this advantage as the result of his return to Argentina and the lack of understanding with which he was received there.[42]

He did, however, receive recognition in the United States. In his autobiography, *Un Pintor frente al Espejo* (A Painter Faces the Mirror), Pettoruti devoted a whole chapter to his first visit to the U.S., which concluded with a successful exhibit. In fact, he did not come as an artist with a firmly established reputation whose purpose was to exhibit his works. Instead he had been invited in his capacity as director of the Provincial Museum of Fine Arts in La Plata, an institution to which he had imparted a decidedly modern direction. In the course of his visit he met Archipenko, Zadkine, René d'Harnoncourt, Francis Henry Taylor (the director of the Metropolitan Museum of Art), Edgar Varèse, Fernand Léger, Lionello Venturi, Alfred Barr, Nelson Rockefeller, Edward W. Forbes (the director of Harvard University's Fogg Museum), Richard Fieller (the director of the Seattle Art Museum), and Grace Morley.

Morley wrote a note on the artist and his work, which was published in the bulletin of the San Francisco Museum of Art on the occasion of his 1942 exhibition there. After observing that his works from 1917 to 1920 reflected Cubist work of that period, she stated:

A sufficient number of the characteristic and important works of the twenties and mid-thirties are included [in the exhibition] to indicate clearly his development during those two active and significant periods. The group serves to present fairly, and in something approximating his full stature, the dominant figure in one aspect of contemporary Argentine art development that Emilio Pettoruti indisputably is.

She then analyzed his iconographic and formal aspects:

For him the Harlequin is a useful device for representing the human figure, but as an anonymous, remote, generalized form, not as an individual. It has for him also the value of a symbol a sort of allegory of modern man, with subtle and complex associations.[43]

And she also made reference to his still lifes, mentioning their solid structural basis, the quality of the drawing, and the increasing complexity of the compositions.[44]

When the exhibit was presented at the National Academy of Design in New York, the Metropolitan Museum's director, Francis Henry Taylor, observed: "Pettoruti's painting is vigorous yet highly controlled, his point of view that of the searching laboratory scientist." and *The New York Herald Tribune* published a review in January

1943 declaring: "The art of Pettoruti, who is one of the masters of abstract painting, evidences a clear and well-defined taste, and his forty canvases have met with real success." A number of other newspaper articles about Pettoruti were published during the course of his visit and a movie was filmed about his work. Many of his paintings were sold.[45] However, Pettoruti noted in his autobiography, "it was a very difficult moment for Argentines on diplomatic mission in the United States, since at that time Argentina was the only Latin American country that had not yet broken with the Axis."[46]

Pettoruti had other occasions to exhibit in the United States after this visit. In 1947, he had a show at the Pan American Union (which later became the General Secretariat of the Organization of American States) in Washington, D.C. In 1955 he participated in *Art of the Americas*, held at the same institution in celebration of Pan American Week. He was included in an exhibition of Latin American art sent on loan from OAS to Western College for Women in Oxford, Ohio, in February 1955, and in an exhibition of paintings, drawings, and prints sent to the Wichita Pan American Club and Wichita Art Association in Kansas. In 1959 he was in the *South American Art Today* show at the Dallas Museum of Fine Arts (a selection of artists from ten countries made by José Gómez Sicre). In 1956 he won the Guggenheim Continental Award. He was also included in the 1967 exhibit *Forerunners of American Modernism: 1860–1930*, held at the Center for Inter-American Relations in New York. Pettoruti's composition *The Quintet*, then the property of the San Francisco Museum of Art, was displayed alongside works by Orozco, Rivera, Torres-García, Maurice Prendergast, and Winslow Homer.[47] Stanton Catlin wrote on Pettoruti's art in the introduction to the catalog of the exhibition:

It begins at a time when the dominant traditions of artistic activity in all three divisions of the hemisphere were European-based Neo-Classicism and Romanticism, with the former, Latin America, highly institutionalized through its state-supported academies and art schools. It ends with the general breakthrough into radically new forms of art which followed quickly on the revolutionary developments in Europe.[48]

The choice of Pettoruti as one of the proponents of modernism in the Americas is accurate testimony to the historic significance of the role he played.

Geometric Abstraction: 1950–1970

The second part of this essay focuses on Latin American artists who were active in the United States during the 1950s and 1960s. All the artists in question were born during the second decade of the century or thereafter and could not be expected to have established any sort of presence in the United States prior to 1950. These are artists who grew out of the avant-garde geometric art that appeared in Latin America in the 1940s and continued into the 1950s. In this respect they are notably different from Torres-García and Pettoruti, who had close bonds with the European avant-garde in the 1920s and 1930s. Thus we are now dealing not only with younger artists but with members of an avant-garde that despite its roots in Europe was local in development. This generation of artists arrived at a time when a new artistic phenomenon, namely Concrete Art, was being initiated by Max Bill.

Whereas the European avant-garde of the 1930s had been very concerned with the social mission of art, Max Bill concentrated on man's visual environment. Fine art, architecture, objects of daily use, and graphics were to be united. He also emphasized that the work of art has a reality of its own and plays an active role in defining the environment, and he viewed objects of daily use as serving more than utilitarian purposes, thanks to their structural intelligibility and inner coherence.[49]

In the years following World War II the world experienced a moment of expansion, marked by the triumph of functionalism, the development of the information network, and the appearance of new materials and new methods of analysis in intellectual inquiry. It was a world in which the quantitative characteristics of a mass society called for new models in all areas. Geometric artists also wished to capitalize on the climate of reconstruction engendered by the building of a new world upon the ruins of the old. A variety of geometric styles succeeded one another from 1945 on. They are in themselves signs of searching.[50]

As a consequence of World War II the United States received a great influx of European artists, who became cynosures of influence in their new country. As regards Geometric Abstraction, one may note the arrival of the painters Joseph Albers, László Moholy-Nagy, Naum Gabo, Lyonel Feininger (an American who had been active in Germany), and Piet Mondrian, as well as the architects Walter Gropius, Marcel Breuer, and Mies van der Rohe. Upon Mondrian's arrival in the United States in 1940 he was at once surrounded by fervent disciples who reinforced the presence of Geometric Abstraction.

However, Geometric Abstraction's increased encouragement in U.S. art circles had less bearing on its appearance in Latin America than certain changes that took place in Uruguay and Argentina, which became the focus points of Latin American artistic attention. After World War II industrial and corporate patronage of the arts reached new levels in Latin America.[51] Museums of modern art were established in São Paulo in 1946 and in Rio de Janeiro and Buenos Aires in 1948. The establishment of the São Paulo Bienal in 1951 was followed by similar events elsewhere: the Kaiser Industries Biennial in Córdoba, Argentina, which began in 1962; and the Medellín Biennial in Colombia, which commenced in 1968. All these forums served not merely to promote contemporary art at home but also to stimulate U.S. interest in Latin American art. This led to interchanges, a steady series of exhibits, and a strengthening of the awareness of Latin American Constructivists in the United States.

In the catalog for *Latin America: New Departures*, an exhibition at the Institute of Contemporary Art in Boston in 1961, Thomas Messer noted that while certain pioneers had found full acceptance in the United States, it was only late in the 1950s that there was an awareness of new Latin American art as "active, creative, intelligent, and notable in its major achievements."[52] The introduction to the catalog of the *Esso Salon of Young Artists*, presented under the auspices of the OAS General Secretariat and the Standard Oil Company in 1964 and 1965, speaks of the 1960s as the decade of the revelation of Latin American art. Indeed, a great number of Latin American artists achieved a presence on the U.S. scene at this time.

Edgar Negret

Edgar Negret is a Colombian sculptor of world renown. His presence in the United States dates from 1949, when he was only twenty-nine years old. By 1969 his work had been exhibited in this country on thirty-five occasions, including twenty-two shows in New York.[53] He had a noteworthy one-man show at OAS headquarters in February 1956,[54] and in 1966 he was included in *Art of the Americas*, also at OAS. The OAS General Secretariat collaborated on certain other shows in which he was included: *From Latin America*, an exhibition of paintings and sculptures selected by José Gómez-Sicre and exhibited at the Corcoran Gallery of Art in Washington, D.C., under the auspices of the Institute of Contemporary Arts, from 1956 to 1957; *South American Art Today*, at the Dallas Museum of Fine Arts in 1959; *3500 Years of Colombian Art*, at the Lowe Art Museum, Coral Gables, in 1960; and *Selections of Latin American Art—New Personalities*, assembled by José Gómez Sicre and presented at the Pepsi-Cola Gallery in New York in 1964. In 1955 he showed in the *New Acquisitions* exhibit at The Museum of Modern Art; in 1967 he took part in the *Guggenheim International Exhibition*, and that same year he was included in a show of works from the Nelson Rockefeller collection. The commercial galleries that most frequently displayed his work during these years were Peridot, David Herbert, Graham, and Bonino after 1969. His sculpture was the subject of many articles in *The New York Times*, *The New York Herald Tribune*, *The Washington Post*, *The Arts Review*, *Art News*, *Américas*, and other publications.[55]

Negret lived in New York from 1955 to 1963, and it was there that he began to make use of unconventional techniques. The city aroused in him an interest in new materials (notably aluminum) and led him to abandon the traditional techniques he had employed during his years of apprenticeship in Colombia. Thus the two sources that inspired his highly original compositions were his contact with advanced American technology and his deep attachments to his heritage. His relationship to modern technology is readily evident. He uses mass-produced industrial materials, bends metals to form unlikely angles, and makes no attempt to disguise the bolts that hold one piece to another. His technological idiom is also revealed in his economy of means and the precision with which his pieces are handled. But the importance of Negret's work does not lie merely in his use of new techniques and materials, it derives instead from the exuberance and aggressiveness of the cultural and physical environment of Latin America.

Well versed in primitive art and myth, Negret bends sheets of aluminum into myth-charged biomorphic creations that confound the false antinomy between naturalism and abstraction (plate 79). This is high-tech art, marked by great purity of form, but it does not reflect a preconceived, rationalistic approach. The works are charged with suggestions of the culture from which they spring.[56] Indeed some of his works of the early 1960s allude to pre-Hispanic gold masks that have been found in Colombia.[57]

Eduardo Ramírez Villamizar

Ramírez Villamizar was one of the first Colombian artists to take up abstraction: "He started out as a painter. Increasing emphasis on spatial qualities and precision led him first to relief, then to sculpture, and finally to a sort of nonutilitarian architecture, severe in appearance and powerful in impact.[58] His activities in the United States from 1949 to 1970 include his participation in individual and group shows of painting and sculpture, teaching, appointments, a fellowship-financed study, and a stay in New York from 1967 to 1973.

Like his compatriot Negret, Ramírez Villamizar was a constant presence in the postwar U.S. art world. He was first presented in a group show, together with Negret and Enrique Grau, at the New School for Social Research in 1949. At that time he was still a figurative artist, although he did have a tendency to simplify forms. By the time of his 1954 show at OAS headquarters in Washington—a show that was also seen at the Roland de Aenlle Gallery in New York—his work reflected his contact with Geometric Abstractionists in Paris, the theories of his friend the French artist Jean Dewasne, and Torres-García's Universal Constructivism. In the same year Alfred Barr, director of The Museum of Modern Art in New York, bought Ramírez Villamizar's *Black and White* for the museum.

In 1957 Ramírez Villamizar exhibited in Houston and Washington. In 1958 his work was on display in Pittsburgh, and he was awarded a Guggenheim Fellowship. By that time his strong interest in three-dimensional effects was clearly apparent in his paintings, as was his search for the essence of form, expressed in part by his abandonment of color in favor of strictly black-and-white paintings. In 1960 he had a show at the David Herbert Gallery in New York, which featured reliefs executed in either white, black and white, or red.[59] With few exceptions he has limited himself to those three colors ever since, "completely occupied with reliefs on wood and the process of stripping away nonessentials."[60]

In 1963 The Museum of Modern Art acquired his *Project for a Horizontal Mural*, and in 1964 he was one of several artists selected for *Sculpture for the Wall*, an exhibition organized by the Guggenheim Museum and presented at the American Federation of Arts headquarters and elsewhere. His reliefs continued to evolve (plate 77). As one critic has noted:

The first reliefs stand out no more than a few centimeters. Then they grow increasingly thick through the application of additional coatings. Overcoming timidity, the artist openly avails himself of space. He tends more and more to free his work from the wall, creating real inner spaces in his forms. A good example is provided by his six 1967 reliefs for the American Bank of New York.[61]

Abstraction possessed absolute values for Ramírez Villamizar, and his surrender to it was based on his conviction of its superiority. This conviction is responsible for the severity of his work and the extreme refinement of craftsmanship. Félix Angel has also reflected on the purity of his art:

In many of Ramírez Villamizar's compositions, particularly those executed during the

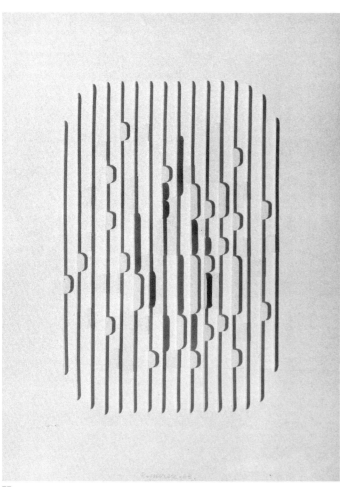

77

78

Eduardo Ramírez Villamizar
77. *Homage to Vivaldi.* 1963
Cardboard, 26¾ x 20″
Collection CIBA-GEIGY Corporation, Ardsley,
New York
Photo: courtesy CIBA-GEIGY Corporation

Alicia Peñalba
78. *The Sparkler.* 1957
Bronze on carved stone base, 68⅞ x 28¾ x 22¾″
Hirshhorn Museum and Sculpture Garden,
Smithsonian Institution, Washington, D.C. Gift of
Joseph H. Hirshhorn, 1966
Photo: courtesy Hirshhorn Museum and Sculpture
Garden

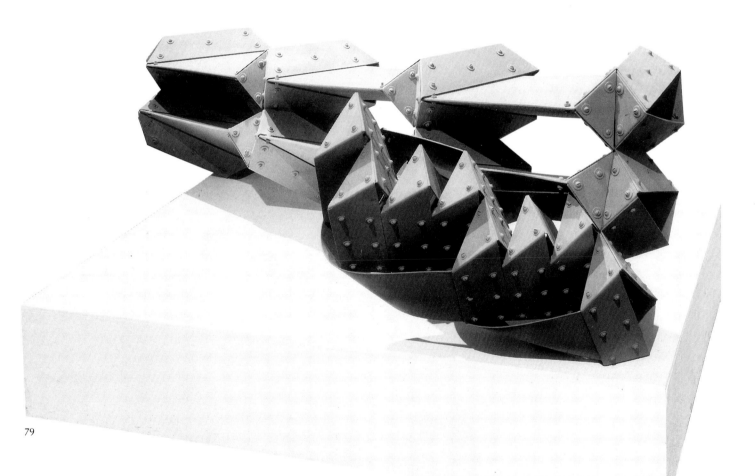

79

Edward Negret
79. *The Bridge (Homage to Paul Foster).* 1968
Painted aluminum, 45¼ x 79 x 26″
Museum of Art, Rhode Island School of Design,
Providence. Nancy Sayles Day Collection of Latin
American Art
Photo: courtesy Museum of Art, Rhode Island
School of Design

1970s, the artist has made a rhythmically progressive use of repeated elements; this may be associated with the idea of growth. Negret, once he had fixed on a basic module, developed and refined it in many ways or permitted it to expand around the axis which controls the "movement" of the piece. In Ramírez Villamizar's case, there is nothing emotional about the development process. It is worked out along rigidly mathematical lines, in arithmetic or geometric progressions, within clearly established limits indicative of the artist's controlling will. [62]

Alicia Peñalba

The Argentine sculptor Alicia Peñalba has been based in Paris since her early youth, but she has been a forceful presence in the U.S. for thirty years. She first exhibited in New York in 1958 at the Guggenheim Museum, where she was in a group show with six other sculptors, including Chillida, Hadju, and Etienne Martin, who also had a morphological approach to sculpture. In 1959 she exhibited again in New York at the Fine Arts Associates Gallery.[63] For several years she had been producing highly personal pieces based on natural forms (plate 78). They consisted of homogeneous elements, such as open or closed petals, rhythmically ordered:

This period of my work, which has been called "totemic," was inspired by a need to spiritualize the symbols of eroticism, the source of all creation, the purest and most sacred state in the life of man. All these evocations of the mystery of procreation rose toward heaven in solid forms mingled one with another, protecting the delicate fruit which lay within, suggesting both the idealization of the flesh and the birth process. [64]

In 1960 Peñalba appeared in four shows in the United States: *Paths of Abstract Art* at the Cleveland Museum of Art;[65] *Collecting in the Granite State* at the Currier Gallery of Art in Manchester, New Hampshire; *19th- and 20th-Century Painting and Sculpture* at the Otto Gerson Gallery in New York; and an exhibit at the Fine Arts Associates Gallery, which was accompanied by a text written by Michel Seuphor.[66]

In 1962 her work was presented in the show of *Modern Sculpture from the Joseph H. Hirshhorn Collection* held at the Guggenheim Museum in New York, and she had an individual exhibit at the Devorah Sherman Gallery in Chicago. Her works grew ever bolder:

My sculptures began to become airier; they were pierced by light; they reached in all directions for plastic equilibrium. I feel that equilibrium is the only thing that can bring a work to perfection. [67]

In 1964 the Carnegie Institute in Pittsburgh invited her to participate in the *Pittsburgh International Exhibition*, and she was represented at the inaugural show of the Aldrich Museum of Contemporary Art in Ridgefield, Connecticut, entitled *Selections from the Larry Aldrich Collection*. In 1966 her work was included in the show *Birds in Contemporary Art* at the Phillips Collection in Washington, D.C.,[68] and she had two individual exhibitions, one at the Bonino Gallery in New York, at which twenty-two bronzes cast in Paris were on display, and another at the Phillips Collection. In 1967 and 1970 she was again invited to participate in the *Pittsburgh International Exhibition*.[69]

In her works of the mid-1960s she made frequent use of modular elements, which she grouped in constellations and aerial structures. Like Calder and Arp, Peñalba created a language of highly individual forms derived from nature and then reduced these forms to their essentials. Owing to its organic character and freely developed rhythms, her work has the properties Herbert Read summarized as "the vital image." This characteristic vitality epitomizes a certain branch of Latin American abstraction. By the end of the period that concerns us, Peñalba's works were to be found in the collections of the Cleveland Museum of Art, the Carnegie Institute, the Isaac Delgado Museum in New Orleans, the Dallas Museum of Fine Arts, the Phillips Collection, and the Albright-Knox Art Gallery in Buffalo, New York.

80

81

Julio Alpuy
80. *The Couple from the Valley*. 1969
Painted wood, 47 x 63½ x 3½"
Collection the artist
Photo: Tony Velez

Gonzalo Fonseca
81. *Agriope's Room*. 1968
Marble and leather, 12½ x 13⅞ x 10⅞
Lumber base, 48 x 19¾ x 20¼"
The Brooklyn Museum, New York. Purchased with
funds given anonymously
Photo: courtesy The Brooklyn Museum

The Disciples of Torres-García: Augusto Torres, Julio Alpuy, and Gonzalo Fonseca
When Torres-García returned to Montevideo in 1934, he and a group of artists founded the Constructivist Art Association. Its membership included Rose Aele, Carmelo de Azardum, Sergio de Castro, Gonzalo Fonseca, Francisco Matto Vilaró, Héctor Ragni, and Augusto and Horacio Torres. García-Torres then embarked on a teaching program, publishing numerous books and giving more than six hundred lectures. Thus he became the "teacher of youths who wanted to become fully identified with contemporary art. This youthful aspiration became a mystique and ultimately an ideology; Constructivism took on the character of a creed."[70]

As the principal supporter of a new artistic concept in South America, Torres-García was a teacher who imparted a highly important message for aspiring artists. Among the earliest disciples to gather at his workshop were his sons Augusto and Horacio, José Gurvich, Manuel Pailos, Gonzalo Fonseca, and Julio Alpuy. They kept his teachings alive after his death in 1949. In an article entitled "Torres-García's Symbols," published in *Art News*, Gonzalo Fonseca stressed his teacher's importance as the originator of a wave of abstract art that due to his prodigious efforts swept through South America. Julio Alpuy has stated that Torres-García influenced him not so much by propounding a dogmatic theory of art as by appealing to his intuition and stimulating his thought, while also acquainting him with certain rules that meant liberation for his art rather than restriction.[71] There was nothing rigid about the instruction this exceptional teacher imparted; this was made clear by the diverse styles represented in the exhibition *Torres-García and His Workshop*, which was put on at OAS headquarters in Washington in February and March 1950. Artists included in the exhibition were Julio Alpuy, Elsa Andrada, Gonzalo Fonseca, José Gurvich, Angelo Hernández Ríos, Jonio Montiel, María Olga Piria, Lily Salvo, Augusto Torres, and María Vasconcellos.

In addition to learning from his father, Augusto Torres profited from his family's peregrinations by studying at the Ozenfant workshop in Paris and practicing ironwork with the sculptor Julio González. His studies of anthropology were significant for his father's artistic development,[72] but Augusto clearly had an artistic personality of his own too, evidenced in his work in such diverse media as carved and polychromed wood, painting on cardboard, and embroidered cloth. In 1960 the New School for Social Research in New York granted him a two-year fellowship.

Julio Alpuy, who began to work with Torres-García in 1942, consistently referred to his conversations with the master and the fruitful effects of his teaching. Yet in an interview with Ronald Christ he noted what a change it had made to him to come to live in New York.

R.C.—But I take it that the real change didn't manifest itself until you came to New York?
J.A.—That's right. It took place here in New York.
R.C.—What brought about the change?
J.A.—That's very difficult to say. I don't know if I even know the answer myself. The only thing I can say is the situation was like this: I had already made some changes while I was still in Uruguay. I was working on them, little by little, and people would say, "That is wonderful! You are really growing out from the school." But I always answered: "No, you're wrong. I am still in the school because the concept of my work is still the same." But, little by little, I tried to break out. You can see my worry about the problem in some of those early pictures. When I came here, I was exhausted from making constructions during all the past years of my artistic life, so I tried to make something else—I don't know what—because I was so impressed with New York. I did a lot of paintings—maybe thirty or forty—but I said, "Stop, stop," because they were all the same, just like the same thing I had been doing for years. At any rate, I don't know how it is for you, but for the person arriving in New York for the first time, the city is a terrible shock. It is an enormous city—it is too much of a city. And this effect, which works on everybody, overpowered me, and I was in a bad way for a few months—very depressed—and I tried all sorts of things, including lots of small sketches unlike anything I'd ever done before. Here, look: you see all the images are from the inside, as in a dream; all the images are natural and not things that come from this enormous, unnatural

city. All this is internal—the reality I had inside myself, the beginnings of things, about the philosophy of our epoch, the feeling you have about your origins.[73]

Alpuy's mature works expressed his splendid abilities to blend together the primitive and the organic with his knowledge of structure and symbols, and at times even his humor or ingenuousness. Unlimited freedom and inner energy characterize compositions that are uniquely his own; only the thinnest of threads link them with Torres-García's cosmic visions (plate 80).

In 1964 Julio Alpuy had a one-man show at the offices of the J. Walter Thompson Company in New York and another at the University of Massachusetts. In 1969 he had an exhibit at the Zegri Gallery in Manhattan. Of particular significance among the numerous group shows in which he participated were *Magnet: New York. A Selection of Paintings by Latin American Artists Living in New York*, held at the Bonino Gallery in 1964, and *Five Latin American Artists at Work in New York*, held at the Center for Inter-American Relations in 1968. Works by him may be found in the collections of the University of Texas at Austin, Nelson Rockefeller, and John and Barbara Duncan. A selection of works from the Duncan collection, in which Alpuy's work was represented, was on view in July and August of 1970 in New York.

Victor Hugo's aphorism "Blessed are our disciples, for their defects will be ours" could never have been made by Torres-García because his disciples had such independent personalities that they could never be considered simply followers. If there is something that unites Julio Alpuy and Gonzalo Fonseca, it is the depth of their investigations and the rigor with which they practice their art. No concessions are made in their investigations; they explore with equal intensity private, interior worlds as well as the collective consciousness of the history of man. Fonseca uses primitive motifs to link modernity with man's origins. He spans the continuum of man's creative spirit. "Fonseca's dialogue with stone is a journey through time," the critic Michael Brenson noted.[74] The revelation that art was an overpowering and genuine necessity came to Fonseca through Torres-García and his experience of pre-Columbian, ancient Greek, and Egyptian art; art which expresses universal themes and finds its roots in humanity. This led Fonseca to realize projects that were monumental in concept if not in scale. His *Torres* of 1967–68 has an architectural character that brings to mind Le Corbusier's chapel at Ronchamp in its rugged originality of form and frank expressiveness. Fonseca's ink drawings are not only valuable for the light they shed on his other projects but are also valuable works of art in their own right. The drawings sometimes suggest the conjunction of the poetic and the delirious. In his sculptures too there is a strange mixture of Constructivism and the enigmatic. Like Marcelo Bonevardi, Fonseca creates inviting hollows that promise adventure. What begins as a structural grid might be transformed into a compartmentalized wooden box filled with strange shapes, as in his *Columbarium* of 1966. Fonseca's imagination and the variety of materials he uses are infinite. He creates rigorously defined concrete murals that have lodgings for esoteric, perhaps astrological objects. The surfaces of his blocks of marble or other stone— whether smooth, textured, or left in the rough—are suddenly enlivened by staircases, hollows, or truncated pyramids that suggest ancient labyrinths. All his works bespeak a world inhabited by poetry in its purest sense (plate 81).

From 1959 to 1961 he created a wall out of Venetian mosaic for the New School for Social Research. In 1960 he made a mural of enameled brick for a medical center in Queens, New York. In 1964 and 1965 he carried out three projects in Reston, Virginia—one in wood entitled *The Building*, a playground in cast concrete called *The Sun Boat*, and fifteen pieces of cast concrete for an ensemble called *Underpass*. In 1968 he created a wooden monument for the Experimental Park Program in the Bronx, New York, and in 1970 he made a seven-piece assembly in marble for the Alza Laboratory in Palo Alto, California.

Argentine Constructivism: Ary Brizzi and Rogelio Polesello

The art historian Jacqueline Barnitz has written that in the 1960s "artists from several Latin American countries, particularly Argentina, came to the United States in great numbers, actively participating in its countless cultural opportunities, and made

82

Augusto Torres
82. *The Abstract World and the Real World.* 1962
Oil on cardboard, 20⅛ x 22″
Collection the artist
Photo: courtesy Elizabeth Fonseca

international reputations." Barnitz also noted: "During that decade, numerous exhibitions devoted to Argentine art took place: *Nine Painters of Argentina* [Widger Gallery of Modern Art, Washington, D.C., 1961], *Recent Argentinians* [The Museum of Modern Art, New York, 1964], *New Art of Argentina* [Walker Art Center, Minneapolis, 1964], and *Argentina 64* [Pepsi-Cola Building, New York, 1964]. In addition, the Bonino, Bianchini, Howard Wise, and A.M. Sachs galleries featured their work."[75] In his introduction to the catalog of *The Emergent Decade* exhibition at the Guggenheim Museum, Thomas Messer, the museum's director, also noted the importance of Argentine painting during this decade. Two artists in particular merit attention here: Ary Brizzi and Rogelio Polesello.

Brizzi is one of the outstanding figures in Argentine Geometric Abstraction. He played a leading role in the second wave of geometric artists to appear in the United States: Manuel Alvarez, Gabriel Messil, María Martorell, Puente, Torroja, Paternosto, Magariños D., and Carlos Silva were also part of this movement. Separately and collectively, these artists became aware of the possibilities Concrete Art offered. They continued to explore plastic space, sometimes stressing the contrast between figure and background, sometimes exploiting the effects of color or serial motifs based on modifications of a theme.

Brizzi first came to the United States in 1959 for the construction of the Argentine pavilion at the U.S. World Trade Fair. He had a one-man show at OAS headquarters in February 1970, but otherwise his work appeared only in group shows, several of which fall within the period under study. In 1964 he was included in *Argentina 64* at the Pepsi-Cola Building in New York; the following year he participated in the *Esso Salon of Young Artists*, sponsored by the OAS General Secretariat and the Standard Oil Company. In 1968 the Bonino Gallery in New York put on a show entitled *Four New Argentinian Artists* in which Brizzi exhibited along with Eduardo Mac Entyre, Rogelio Polesello, and Miguel Angel Vidal. That same year he also exhibited in a major exhibition, entitled *Beyond Geometry*, which was organized by the Center for Inter-American Relations and the Torcuato di Tella Institute of Buenos Aires. The idea behind the show was expressed by the Argentine critic Basilio Uribe when he referred to "an art of geometric character which nonetheless struggles against geometric constrictions." In 1969 Brizzi was represented in the traveling exhibition *Contemporary Latin American Painting*[76] and in 1970 in the exhibition of *Latin American Paintings and Drawings from the Collection of John and Barbara Duncan*, put on at the Center for Inter-American Relations. Brizzi has expressed his artistic aims succinctly:

To enhance the energy inherent within a given material, to transform it into energy which exceeds what is inherent in stone, metal, pigment, or light; appeal being made to the best in man, with hope placed in his creative power rather than his destructive instincts. Such convenient adjectives as Geometric, Optic, Kinetic, and Luminist lose meaning when all is undertaken with a view to one single, enormous change. The risky part lies in sustaining this change and carrying it forward until it becomes a culture — a culture which, viewed in retrospect, should provide satisfaction to those who have contributed to its enrichment.[77]

The conceptual basis for Brizzi's work is expressed in his intention to "enrich the spirit, to stimulate the positive forces to be found in the human being, to accept science and technology as reflections of contemporary consciousness — all of which implies a search for operative rationality in all areas of culture."[78]

Sculpture and painting are two sides of the same coin as far as Brizzi is concerned. They interact and enhance one another; they offer the spectator different but mutually supportive points of view. Brizzi's 1969 acrylic on canvas *Activated Surface No. 2*, which was exhibited in the Duncan collection, provides an excellent example of a geometric series in which fine lines of color appear in parallel bands. The angles produced by occasional crossovers impart a rhythmic pulse to the composition. Chromatic and formal relations, severely controlled, are splendidly dynamic in effect. Works by Brizzi may be found not only in the Duncan collection but also in the Museum of Modern Art of Latin America in Washington, D.C., at the University

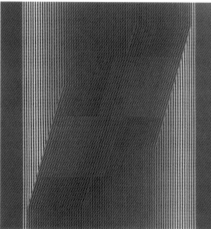

83   84

Ary Brizzi
83. *Diamante No. 6.* 1969
Oil on canvas, 12¼ x 12¼″
Courtesy C.D.S. Gallery, New York
Photo: Pollitzer, Strong & Meyer

Rogelio Polesello
84. *Phase A.* 1965
Oil on canvas, 63¾ x 51″
Lowe Art Museum, University of Miami. Gift, Esso
Inter-America, Inc.
Photo: Roland I. Unruh

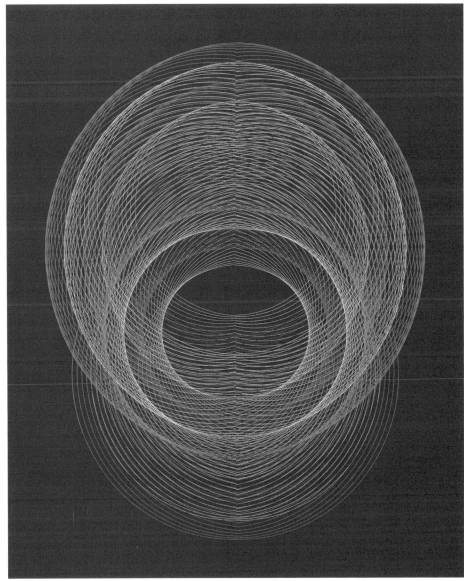

85

Eduardo Mac Entyre
85. *Discontinuous Vertical on Red.* 1969
   Acrylic on canvas, 47¼ x 39½"
   Chase Manhattan Art Collection, New York
   Photo: D. James Dee

of Texas at Austin, in the IBM and Esso collections of Latin American art, in the Nelson Rockefeller collection, and in the Albright-Knox Art Gallery (plate 83).

Rogelio Polesello is one of the best-known Argentine Geometric Abstractionists. He made an early appearance not only on the local art scene but also in other countries, and was particularly active in the United States, Venezuela, and Colombia. He was only twenty when he took part for the first time in a group show in the United States (*Paintings and Drawings from Latin America* at the art gallery of the University of Nebraska) and only twenty-two when he had his first one-man show at OAS headquarters in Washington. In the years up to 1970 Polesello took part in more than forty exhibitions; in 1965 he won first prize for painting at the *Esso Salon of Young Artists* in Washington, and his work was acquired by numerous institutions throughout the United States, including The Museum of Modern Art in New York, the Guggenheim Museum, the Indianapolis Museum, the Rhode Island School of Design, the Lowe Art Museum of the University of Miami, and the Florida State Museum in Gainesville. His works found their way into all the important collections of private institutions and into such significant private hands as those of Nelson Rockefeller and John and Barbara Duncan. In the latter half of the 1960s Polesello took part in at least four exhibits a year in the United States; in 1969 the number reached seven. He was represented in all the most important shows held from 1964 to 1970, a period in which the presence of Latin America in the United States was particularly strong—shows such as *New Art of Argentina* at the Walker Art Center in Minneapolis in 1964,[79] *Art of Latin America since Independence*[80] at the Yale University Art Gallery and the University of Texas at Austin in 1966, *The Emergent Decade*[81] at Cornell University and the Guggenheim also in 1966, and *Latin American Art: 1931–1966* at The Museum of Modern Art in New York in 1967.[82]

The artist's primary concern is with effects of reflection, refraction, and translucence. Without much justification, he has been linked with Kinetic art, unless his preoccupation with visual dynamics is taken as the point of connection. Polesello does not deal with real movement, save in the case of his carved acrylics, where a change in the position of the spectator can produce an additional visual effect. He concentrates instead on having the picture speak for itself. The works Polesello exhibited in the United States during the period of our concern represent several stages in his development. At first he experimented briefly with black-and-white grids. He went on to organize basic planes in strata and compartments, supplying a note of expressiveness by one of two devices. The first device produced what has been called Polesello's "Surrealist" phase.[83] While preserving basic structural elements, the artist applied paint with rhythmically expressive brush strokes; sometimes he engaged in rubbing the paint on the canvas or resorted to dramatic drippings. His emphasis was on accident, on brushwork, on personal imprint; the effect is one of fundamental freedom. The second device was to apply a kind of stencil onto a compartmentalized base. The design for the stencil was occasionally taken from curved, decorative elements, but generally the interwoven lines were straight, varying in size, form, and density. The patterns were executed with an airbrush. Related or contrasting colors were used to create zones of greater or lesser luminosity and to provide glimpses of geometric forms in the background. At times, the luminous zones became lines that crisscross the canvas.

Polesello has a great capacity for experimentation within a single theme. At times he plays with contrasting zones of darkness, with asymmetrical balances, with an opposition between clearly defined geometric forms and fields of diffuse color, or with violent planes of interwoven lines superimposed on a background of planes of regular geometric forms and harmonious colors. By the 1960s (plate 84) Polesello was already displaying the imagination and creativity that was to characterize his multifaceted work of the 1970s. The 1960s was also the period of his highly original sculptures in acrylic and his equally interesting prints.

Generative Art: Eduardo Mac Entyre and Miguel Angel Vidal

In 1960 the Argentine critic Ignacio Pirovano, a collector with great interest in contemporary art, suggested to Eduardo Mac Entyre and Miguel Angel Vidal that they give the name Generative Art to the work they were producing. "Generative" implies the ability to engender, and it was applied in this case to effects of movement in either two- or three-dimensional works. Mac Entyre has said:

Generative painting engenders a series of optical sequences created by shifting forms in circular, vertical, or horizontal fashion. I adopted the circle, because I think that this is the purest manner of expressing movement. It is a dominant form charged with meaning; it has movement of its own; it vibrates and turns, without beginning or end. By composing a series of circles set against a plane I achieve what I call a splendor of forms.[84]

In an article published in the Buenos Aires daily *La Nación*, Romualdo Brughetti quoted further thoughts by Mac Entyre on his artistic goals:

All the forms and structures I use have their origin in the simplicity of geometric figures, giving rise to a true poetry of drawing—poetry that seeks to express itself in pure visual language. These simple, regular, symmetrical figures, traced with precision, become dynamic in effect thanks to their disposition along certain axes of development. Geometry possesses something of the divine.[85]

Eduardo Mac Entyre began to exhibit in the United States in 1964. In that year he was included in *New Art of Argentina* exhibition at the Walker Art Center. In 1964 he was also included in *Twenty South American Artists*, which was shown in Mexico City, Oakland, Portland, and New York. Among the important exhibitions in which he participated were *Art of Latin America since Independence*[86] and *The Emergent Decade*.[87]

His activities in the United States in 1968 were particularly significant. He was in this country for the *Four New Argentinian Artists* exhibit at the Bonino Gallery in New York and *Beyond Geometry* at the Center for Inter-American Relations. Along with other artists he took part in a colloquium on Argentine art at OAS headquarters in Washington. The OAS Visual Arts Unit selected him for inclusion in the OAS pavilion at the San Antonio *Hemisfair*. Some of his compositions were also found in the *Made of Plastic* exhibition that traveled to a number of museums and other institutions throughout the United States.

His participation—along with Miguel Angel Vidal, Ary Brizzi, Rafael Squirru, and Rogelio Polesello—in a roundtable discussion of geometric art demonstrated that he was not limited to artistic production but was also keen to express his ideas. In the previous year in the U.S. he had taken part in a colloquium with students on the "New Tendencies in Argentina," an event staged at the Corcoran Gallery in conjunction with his one-man show at OAS headquarters.

At the time of his second one-man show at the Bonino Gallery he traveled to the U.S. and participated in two exhibitions in Washington, D.C., one that featured works from the OAS permanent collection and another at the Pyramid Gallery in the same city. He also participated in *The Painting and Sculpture of Today* exhibition at Kent State University.

Several U.S. critics took note of his works. In *The New York Times* of February 28, 1970, John Canaday wrote:

Up to a certain point, these paintings executed in threads with a hand compass might be merely (although fascinatingly) a group of exceptionally nicely performed exercises in geometrical patterns. Perhaps of the kind produced lately with the aid of computers, but Mac Entyre is also a colorist, and it must be his use of color that makes these mechanical patterns so personal. The execution is staggering in its precision, yet one is always aware of the artist behind the compass. All other considerations aside, this show is a vivid display.

That same year, Jean Reeves wrote in *The Buffalo Evening News:*

His acrylic painting in The Generative Painting: 1969 *at the Albright-Knox Gallery reflects training in meticulous precision, but also it has a lightness, an air, and a quality*

86

87

Miguel Angel Vidal
86. *Displacement on an Axis.* 1966
    Oil on canvas, 31 x 31″
    Archer M. Huntington Art Gallery, University of
    Texas at Austin. Gift of John and Barbara Duncan,
    1971
    Photo: courtesy Archer M. Huntington Art Gallery

Jesús Rafael Soto
87. *Blue With Silver.* 1969
    Metal and wood, 54 x 42″
    Collection the artist
    Photo: André Morain

88

Jesús Rafael Soto
88. *Vibration.* 1965
   Metal and wood, 62½ x 42½ x 5¾"
   Solomon R. Guggenheim Museum, New York. Gift,
   Eve Clendenin, New York, 1967
   Photo: Robert E. Mates

which keeps it from being something mechanical. Mac Entyre has woven small, subtle threads of paint in a design of superimposed circles and squares. The design is so intricate and ingenious that it constantly reveals new forms, new colors, and spatial relationships.

In *The Washington Evening Star* of May 19, 1967, Benjamin Forgey wrote:

Because Mac Entyre also has an idea of the painting as a beautiful object, because of his finesse in working out complex, weaving designs and in executing them impeccably in complicated color schemes and because his basic material is the endless rhythmic possibilities of the curve, his paintings are the kind of personal statement that tends to make one a believer in Op with all its limitations.

Works by Mac Entyre are to be found in numerous private collections, banks, and public institutions in the United States, including The Museum of Modern Art in New York, the Guggenheim Museum, the Museum of Modern Art of Latin America, and the Albright-Knox Art Gallery.

Generative Art implies an artist has analytically sought out basic units and organized them in accordance with relationships and inner dependencies governed by constant rules. In Vidal's case the basic element is the straight line. The fundamental process for him consists of shifting the line in a rigorously ordered manner. The syntax of form thus established has characteristics entirely of its own. His approach is ascetic: all that is unnecessary has been stripped away. The construction is systematic. But Vidal's variety is inexhaustible. His Dynamic Structures, Shifts, Integrations, Radiations, Fugues, and Reflections present images that are consistent but at the same time ever-changing. His work gives an illusion of perpetual movement, both centrifugal and centripetal. The convergence of lines at a point creates luminous focus points from which color radiates. Superimposed networks produce fleeting geometric figures and permit multiple readings. Vidal's geometry has also taken on such concentration and depth that the line-generated energy of light bears a close relationship to mysticism (plate 86).

Vidal made his first appearance in the U.S. at the *New Art of Argentina* show in 1964. In 1968 he exhibited with Brizzi, Mac Entyre, and Polesello in the *Four New Argentinian Artists* at the Bonino Gallery, in *Beyond Geometry* at the Center for Inter-American Relations, and in the *Made of Plastic* show. References to his work appeared in the February 1968 issue of *Américas* magazine, and works by him are to be found in The Museum of Modern Art, the Guggenheim Museum, the Albright-Knox Art Gallery, and the Museum of Modern Art of Latin America.

Two Venezuelan Kinetic Artists: Soto and Carlos Cruz-Diez

The Venezuelan artist Soto was also active in the international art world; however, he was more of a presence in Europe than the United States, and from a quantitative point of view his presence in the U.S. is not to be compared with the careers of Alejandro Otero, Rogelio Polesello, or Omar Rayo. *Vibrations by Soto*, the artist's first one-man show in New York, took place at the Kootz Gallery in March 1965. It was reviewed in *Arts* magazine and *Art in America*. He had another exhibit the following year at the same gallery, which was reviewed in both publications and in *Art News* as well. He also took part in two highly important Latin American group shows: *Art of Latin America since Independence* and *The Emergent Decade*.[88]

By 1966 Soto had abandoned serial compositions and works in which elements were repeated and was wholly concerned researching optical vibrations. He sought to make time and movement perceptible features in his works of art. In front of a background of black-and-white stripes of equal width he set up different types of rods so that when the spectator changed positions a striking optical impression of movement occurred. Variations on this theme included his *Incorporeal Curves*, *Vibrating Squares*, and *Hanging Parallel Rods*.

At a 1969 exhibit at the Marborough-Gerson Gallery in New York he presented still-newer concepts: a series entitled Progressions on the Floor, consisting of fields of red and orange vertical rods of varying heights, and the famous *Penetrables—*

works that the spectator can enter—in which he abandoned the frontal approach taken in his earlier compositions. The Guggenheim Museum owns a *Penetrable* of slightly later date (1974) as well as his 1965 *Vibration* (plate 88).

The critic Claude Louis Renard has made interesting observations on Soto's works of the years 1968 and 1969.[89] In his view they were important to Soto for three reasons: first, the bigger materials at his command gave him freedom to carry out works on a much larger scale; second, the relationship between the viewer and the work of art is rendered more complete; third—and this underscores the dimension assumed by Soto's creations—his works are no longer confined to the specialized world of art but become a part of daily life through their integration with architecture.

Cruz-Diez constitutes an unusual case in Venezuelan painting.[90] He belongs to the generation of Soto and the Dissidents, but it took him almost ten years to join the movement they began in the 1950s. Up to 1955 he was still a figurative painter. While he was always interested in what he called "vibrations," only in the years 1956 to 1959 did he explore the problems of consecutive movement and the persistence of vision, later carrying his research into the area of color and Polaroid effects. This led him to investigate the action of light in space and the evocation of colored forms radiating from colored strips of cardboard place at right angles to the picture. In 1959 he presented his first *Physiochrome* (plate 89); in the series that followed he developed with increasing subtlety his theory of additive colors. Basically Cruz-Diez sought to find a "personal way of codifying chromatic phenomena in a state of instability."

Thereafter his work became ever more complex. Rods were modified by changes in the materials of which they were made and in their forms and by variations in their height above the base. He experimented with the distance between them, the thickness, depth, and transparency of the perpendicular sheets, and the effects of the spread of color over nearby surfaces. His work in color mutation gave the artist an opportunity to experiment with aleatory and unpredictable effects of light.

Although he had been in the United States before 1950, studying advanced painting techniques on his own in New York in the 1940s, his work attained this state of maturity precisely during the period of its presentation in the United States from 1961 to 1970. He participated in the following group exhibits: the *Pittsburgh International Exhibition* sponsored by the Carnegie Institute in 1961; an exhibit of seventeen Venezuelan painters presented in New York, Haifa, and Tel-Aviv in 1962; an exhibit of twenty South American artists sponsored by the Kaiser Foundation, which was presented in Mexico City, Oakland, and New York in 1964; *The Responsive Eye* at The Museum of Modern Art, the City Art Museum of St. Louis, and the Baltimore Museum of Art in 1965; *Venezuelan Painting of Today* in Nashville, Tennessee, in 1965; *Latin American Art: 1931–1966* at The Museum of Modern Art in 1967; and *Constructivist Tendencies: George Rickey's Collection*, an exhibit that traveled throughout the United States in 1970.

Beyond Geometry
Marcelo Bonevardi

A Guggenheim Fellowship first brought the Argentine artist Marcelo Bonevardi to New York in 1958. Ever since, his reputation has continued to grow in the United States. His easily recognizable, highly personal imagery has been unaffected by changing fashion. His works are to be found in some of the most important collections in the country, including The Museum of Modern Art, the Philadelphia Museum of Art, the Rhode Island School of Design, the Massachusetts Institute of Technology, the University of Texas at Austin, and the Guggenheim Museum.[91] Bonevardi was twice awarded a Guggenheim Fellowship, and held fellowships from the New School for Social Research in 1963–64 and 1964–65.

Dore Ashton, who has written extensively on Bonevardi, noted that "his use of numbers and geometric symbols has nothing in common with the trivial formal inventions of modern tradition. His numbers and letters lead to the Pythagorean mysteries and even evoke the surprise of those who come upon an immeasurable number."[92] In Bonevardi's work, mathematics, astronomy, and geography become magical, irrational agents of revelation (plate 90).

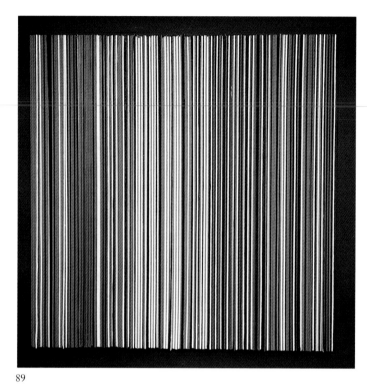

89

90

Carlos Cruz-Diez
89. *Physiochrome No. I.* 1959
Oil on cardboard, 19¾ x 19¾"
Collection the artist/Atelier Cruz-Diez
Photo: courtesy the artist

Marcelo Bonevardi
90. *The Architect.* 1964.
Oil on canvas and wood, 70 x 50"
The Aldrich Museum of Contemporary Art,
Ridgefield, Connecticut
Photo: Brian Gaumer

Fragile though his shelters may be, Bonevardi always seems to be in search of an inner recess, a secret refuge in which rationality can lead to a curious coexistence with mystery. On first introduction to Bonevardi's work, the viewer glides through waves of fright and curiosity inspired to explore dark, hidden, and forgotten fears. The magic charge seems to come from far off in time. The images suggest strange connections with the primitive and the mystic, but there is an equally strong connection with subterranean currents of our subconscious and with that intimate and personal experience of things that each of us possesses and that cannot be transferred to another. There are some artists who speak directly to our senses and whose images have an immediate, permanent impact. There are others who inspire us to peel off layer after layer of our innermost being—layers whose existence we often did not suspect existed. Bonevardi is of the latter group. His works, in which painting and sculptural relief are combined, suggest sacred elements and ancient rituals.

In the mid-1960s, Dore Ashton called attention to "the appearance of new images, which make direct reference to the mask and the talisman. Forms which previously seemed buried at the site of ancient ruins begin to assume the look of a frieze....It would take considerable imagination to introduce the age-old tradition of the frieze into a modern context." Ashton later relates Bonevardi's aesthetic of the late 1960s to the methods by which Picasso suggested themes and compared his palette of grays and greenish earth tones to synthetic Cubism.[93] New features had appeared in his drawings. The perfect order and frontal presentation of his pigeonholes gave way to foreshortenings, backward-leaning planes, surfaces covered with graphic marks and drippings, and disconcerting external spaces. The ineffable order that he previously established seemed to shift toward contingency, toward a consciousness that life is a process man cannot halt. Bonevardi has been expressing his singular artistic personality since 1958 and today enjoys a place of distinction in the art world of the United States.

Gunther Gerzso

Gunther Gerzso has been called "the only great hard-line Mexican abstractionist." Although Gerzso was born in Mexico, he received his artistic training in Germany. His European background, combined with what one critic has called "the Mexican context, which, from the plastic viewpoint, ranks among the most extravagant, luxuriant, rich in color and materials," may be responsible for his combinations of the rational and the intuitive and for his creation of exclusively personal realms.[94]

Jorge Alberto Manrique, a great student of Mexican geometric art, has attributed Mexico's late entry into the area of geometric art—late not merely by world standards but also by those of Latin America—to the sort of dictatorship that the Mexican muralists exercised in the country's art circles. Thus, despite the examples of geometric art forms provided by the ancient Olmec sites of La Venta and Teotihuacán, any attempt at contact with contemporary Constructivist tendencies was considered out of the question for most students.[95]

Well before Gunther Gerzso took up geometric art he lived in the United States, working for five years as a draftsman and stage designer for the Cleveland Playhouse. Only when he returned to Mexico in 1942 did he turn to painting. He went initially through a brief Surrealist phase, a development easily attributable to the impact on Mexican artists of the *International Exhibition of Surrealist Art*, which was held in Mexico City in 1939, as well as to Gerzso's contacts with Surrealist friends. Shortly thereafter he turned to compositions based on large, irregularly shaped planes, in which his Constructivist and chromatic concerns were clearly represented. Yet in a 1966 interview he declared: "I do not consider myself an abstract painter. I see my paintings as realistic, based on Mexican landscapes and pre-Hispanic culture. Friends of mine who travel through Chiapas tell me what they see there is what I paint."[96] He continued to develop his aesthetic of stripped-down forms, refined colors, and subtle, but severely structured planes, which caused the Mexican critic Luis Cardoza y Aragón to speak of the "afflicting nudity of Gerzso's latest pictures."[97]

These were the characteristics of the works Gerzso sent to the United States, beginning with a group show at the Houston Museum of Fine Arts in 1956. He went on to exhibit in *Contemporary Mexican Painting* at the Fort Worth Art Center in 1959; in

Contemporary Mexican Artists at the Phoenix Art Museum in 1965; in *Mexico Past and Present* at the Birmingham Museum of Art and the Dallas Museum of Fine Arts in 1965; and in *Art of Latin America since Independence* in 1966.[98]

Alejandro Otero

Nineteen forty-five was an important year in Alejandro Otero's life. He finished his education, he organized and participated in exhibitions, he won three significant prizes, and he brought the purely local phase of his career to a close by making contact with the international art scene through visits to Paris and New York.

His first exhibit in the United States took place in 1948 at the Pan American Union in Washington, D.C. The show was entitled *Alejandro Otero—Still Life, Themes, and Variations.* With his customary acuteness, José Gómez Sicre called attention to the debt Otero's still lifes owed to the work of Picasso during World War II. In 1955 and 1958 Otero participated in the *Pittsburgh International Exhibition* organized by the Carnegie Institute. In 1959 he was included in the show *The United States Collects Pan American Art* held at the Art Institute of Chicago, and in *South American Art Today* at the Dallas Museum of Fine Arts.

In the 1950s his painting changed completely. Abstraction gradually dominated his work. In the early part of the decade he started on his series Colored Lines on a White Background. Instead of representing objects he made schematized lines whose directional dynamics suggest the existence of space. This series was followed by another entitled Orthogonal Collages—which were meshes of intertwined colors reflecting Otero's admiration for Mondrian's Boogie Woogie paintings. Then came a series of polychromes and murals he did for the city of Caracas.

The most important series of the period from 1955 to 1960 were the Color Rhythms (plate 91). On long white wooden planks Otero painted darkly colored vertical lines in Duco, which provide the viewer with a glimpse of the background's vivid geometric figures. Juan Acha wrote in their regard: "The Color Rhythms are important in Venezuelan and Latin American art because they formulate the problems of color and geometric form from within, and thus constitute a bridge between the emotional conception of art and the frigidity of Constructivism."[99] A work from this series was purchased for the collection of The Museum of Modern Art.

In 1960 Otero was included in an exhibition of works from the permanent collection of contemporary art at OAS headquarters in Washington. The following year his presence in the United States became increasingly evident: he was included in *Latin America: New Departures* at the Institute of Contemporary Art in Boston (a show that later traveled to the University of Michigan at Ann Arbor and the Norton Gallery in West Palm Beach) and in an exhibit of Spanish and Latin American artists at the David Herbert Gallery in New York.

However, in 1960 he turned to assemblies and collages in reaction to the rigorous rationalism of his Color Rhythms. He wrote about the impact Tinguely's machines had on him, and how they led him to experiment with fragments of scrap materials. In the resulting creations the objects exist precariously. Tragically, they are at the mercy of time and chance. These works, which may be related to the French New Realism or to the work of Robert Rauschenberg, preoccupied Otero for the first half of the 1960s. Also before 1970, Otero made a series of collages of pieces of newspaper cut evenly into rather large geometric forms, then tinted them with various shades of acrylic so that the print could still be read. Thus he united the textural qualities of his previous collages with the lively color and Constructivist aspects of his Color Rhythms.

By 1970 Otero was on the threshold of one of his most dazzlingly inventive periods, that of his Civic Structures. The first of these was inaugurated in 1968 in the city of Maracay. Their interest lies in permitting greater public contact with his constructions. Owing to their projection into real and social space, these monuments aim for closer relations with contemporary science and technology.

Omar Rayo

Marta Traba asserts that Omar Rayo, who lived in New York from 1960 to 1971, is the

91

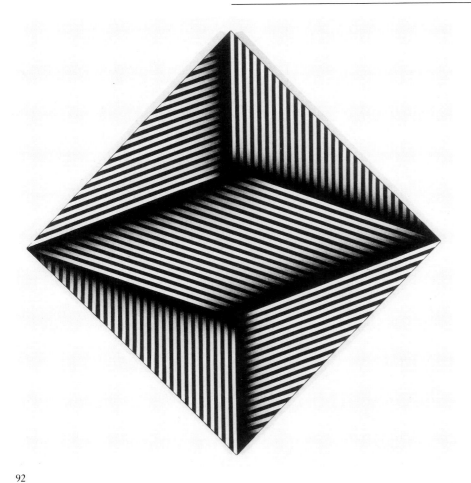

92

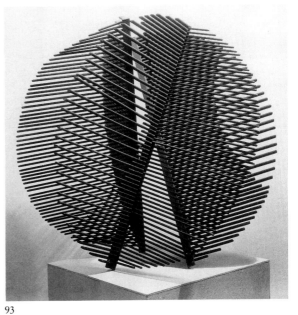

93

Alejandro Otero
91. *Color Rhythm No. 1.* 1955
    Duco on board, 78¾ x 18¼″
    Collection The Museum of Modern Art, New York.
    Inter-American Fund
    Photo: courtesy The Museum of Modern Art

Omar Rayo
92. *Sunday in the Attic.* 1966
    Acrylic on canvas, 40 x 40″
    Private collection, New York
    Photo: Tony Velez

Gego
93. *Sphere.* 1959
    Welded brass and steel, 22″ diameter
    Collection The Museum of Modern Art, New York.
    Inter-American Fund
    Photo: courtesy The Museum of Modern Art

only Colombian to partake in the optical and kinetic trends of contemporary art.[100] The effects of Omar Rayo's paintings are surprising, unexpected, and ambiguous. The artist's basic elements consist of rigorously ordered black-and-white bands. Skilled craftsmanship, symmetry, and clearly defined borders produce constructions of great severity. He creates within these bounds trompe l'oeil effects produced by a deceptive interplay of two-dimensional elements and an insistent use of spatial tensions. In creating these optical illusions Rayo resorts to shadings, to superimpositions, to doublings, and to interweavings. He has become passionately involved in these experiments, in which balance between the real and the false produces a peculiar feeling of depth (plate 92). Rayo also created prints in relief, which he made by taking impressions of objects of daily use. They are simply impressions on white paper. Along with his paintings, this is the type of work Rayo exhibited during his residence in New York.

In 1961 he had two one-man shows, one at OAS headquarters in Washington and the other at The Contemporaries gallery in New York. That same year he took part in two group shows, one at the Baltimore Museum of Art, the other at the Wiggin Gallery in Boston. Thereafter, he exhibited with increasing frequency. In 1965 he had four one-man shows; in both 1968 and 1969 he was included in ten group shows in the United States, in which he exhibited paintings, drawings, and prints.

In 1964 he was included in *Magnet: New York* at the Bonino Gallery, one of the most important Op art shows of the decade. He received a number of distinctions: in 1965 he was the recipient of an award from the Philadelphia Museum of Art; in 1967 he received a purchase prize at the National Prints Exhibition held at the State University College in Potsdam, New York; and in 1969 he won a prize at the International Print Exhibition held at the Manchester Institute of Arts and Sciences in New Hampshire. Works by Rayo are to be found not only in private collections in the United States but also in some twenty public institutions, including The Museum of Modern Art, the Art Institute of Chicago, the Metropolitan Museum of Art, the Baltimore Museum of Art, and the Smithsonian Institution in Washington, D.C.

Gego

Gego (Gertrude Goldschmidt) is a painter, sculptor, and printmaker of German origin who has lived in Venezuela since 1939. She is also an architect and has taught at the University of Caracas. She has become singularly well adjusted to the Latin American cultural environment and has played a highly original role in the development of the arts.

In 1959 she spent a year in the United States. She first occupied herself with metallic sculpture and then took up printmaking. When she returned to sculpture, she executed works of great importance, including *Sphere*, which is found in the collection of The Museum of Modern Art (plate 93).

In 1960 she appeared in three exhibitions in Manhattan: *New Names* at the Betty Parsons Gallery; *Recent Sculpture* at the David Herbert Gallery; and *Recent Acquisitions* at The Museum of Modern Art. Late in 1962 she received a fellowship from the Central University of Venezuela to research the trends of basic art courses being taught in U.S. universities. In 1964 she participated in the *World Show* at the Washington Square Galleries in New York, and in 1965 she took part in the *Responsive Eye* at The Museum of Modern Art. In 1966 she did a series of lithographs at the Tamarind Lithography Workshop in Los Angeles, and in 1970 she had a show of drawings at the Graphics Gallery in San Francisco. At the *New Painting and Sculpture* show at the Center for Inter-American Relations she was represented by one of her "environments," which constitute the most powerful and creative aspect of her œuvre.

It was in the period from 1960 to 1970 that the artist achieved full maturity, incorporating architectural space into her compositions, giving an airy lightness to her lines, experimenting with structures that make sculptures transparent, or assembling them out of reticular modules. Maturity is indeed a fitting term for this output. First, the structural system on which her major works of this decade were built was derived from her 1957 experimentation in both drawing and sculpture with networks of parallel lines. One can therefore speak of a coherent process of growth and development. Second, the term "maturity" suggests the element of nature which Marta Traba discerned. "From

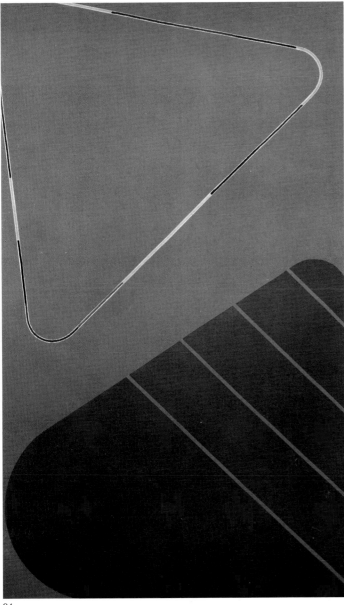

94

95

Gerd Leufert
94. *Tirina.* 1966
    Acrylic on canvas, 98½ x 58⅞″
    Museum of Art, Rhode Island School of Design,
    Providence. Nancy Sayles Day Collection of Latin
    American Art
    Photo: courtesy Museum of Art, Rhode Island
    School of Design

César Paternosto
95. *The South.* 1969
    Acrylic on canvas, 48 x 48″
    Collection the artist
    Photo: Quesada/Burke, New York

the nonfigurative viewpoint, her close identification with the organic world imparts a vivacity to her work, which is transmitted to the spectator. Its qualities of freshness, dynamism, originality, incompleteness, subtlety, and absurdity form part of the repertory of surprises which we always expect from nature."[101] This assertion leads us once again to one of the peculiar characteristics of Latin American Geometric Abstraction. Amid the rigorously ordered elements of Gego's Constructivist compositions forms take on an organic character. Tensions and contrasts give life to airy geometric structures and render areas of space effectively. Considering the mobility required of the spectator in order to experience the interrelationship of the networks, Alfred Barr spoke of the "parallactical charm" of her work.[102]

Gerd Leufert

Rarely does one find in a single individual the combination of disparate yet complementary elements that Leufert represents: an early but well-defined artistic vocation; sound professional training; a constantly evolving capacity for artistic creation; a concern for theory that inspires him to keep fully up to date on international developments in art; a surprising aptitude for teaching and generosity in passing on professional secrets to his students; a natural talent for human relations; and an unusual persistence in his endeavors.[103]

This was Gabriel Rodríguez's description of the Lithuanian artist who has been established in Venezuela since 1951. Equal praise came from Alejandro Otero, who said: "Graphic design in Venezuela falls into two periods: before and after Leufert." Leufert was closely connected to the art world of Venezuela. During the period that he served as design director of the Caracas Museum of Fine Arts, that institution issued no less than 372 publications, most of them designed by Leufert, which enhanced the museum's reputation immeasurably.

Shortly before his appointment at the museum in 1960, Leufert had been engaged in special studies at the State University of Iowa and the Pratt Institute in New York. Graphics by Leufert are to be found in the Pratt's collection as well as in The Museum of Modern Art and the Library of Congress.[104] He also took part in a number of exhibitions, including *Magnet: New York* in 1964, where he was represented by an oil painting entitled *Union Square*, and *The Emergent Decade*, where he presented an undated oil and latex painting on canvas entitled *Betijoque*.[105]

The Geometric Elementalism of the La Plata Group: César Paternosto and Alejandro Puente

César Paternosto and Alejandro Puente went to live in the United States in 1967. Both were natives of the city of La Plata, the capital of the Province of Buenos Aires, and they had been active in artistic circles there and in Buenos Aires. In the early 1960s they and other Informalist artists had formed the Grupo Sí (Yes Group).

In 1963 and 1964 Paternosto was eagerly engaged in experimentation in nontraditional uses of geometric form. Prior to departing for the United States, he exhibited in *Visión Elemental* (Elemental Vision), which took place at the National Museum of Fine Arts in Buenos Aires in September and October 1967. It gathered together a number of important geometric artists—not only Paternosto and Puente but also Gabriel Messil, César Ambrosini, Dalmiro Sirabo, Juan Antonio Sitro, and Enrique Torroja.

In the theoretical pronouncements the artists issued on the occasion of the exhibit, they stressed their opposition to Concrete Art, calling it the last bastion of a traditional type of painting in which forms are interrelated on the basis of factors of composition and balances. Their aim was to establish a new syntax based on opposition between elements rather than interconnection. They were also concerned with format, choosing to abandon the traditional frame for a shaped canvas, which at times assumed a sculptural presence.

The second show in which Paternosto participated was the *Third Córdoba Biennial* (also known as the Kaiser Biennial, since Kaiser Industries provided the financial backing), which took place in October 1966. The international jury, composed of Alfred Barr, Arnold Bode, Sam Hunter, Carlos Villanueva, and Aldo Pellegrini, awarded Paternosto first prize. The works he had presented were in keeping with the group's manifesto, but by the time he exhibited at the A. M. Sachs Gallery in New York in 1968 his style had evolved. The Sachs show was his first one-man exhibition in the United States, and the newspaper reviews it occasioned discussed his new style. John Canaday wrote in *The New York Times*:

Comment on the work of most minimal or serial sculptors boils down to a description of the geometrical patterns each has adopted as his hallmark, and the color he paints it. Mr. Paternosto can be called a sculptor, though strictly speaking his wall-size creations are shaped canvases, or "structured canvases," according to the gallery's designation. His scheme encloses a series of rectangular blocks within the embracing arms of paired magnet shapes.

The September 27, 1968, issue of *Time* magazine carried this comment:

Singing colors, good craftsmanship, and a deft hand at playing off symmetrical and asymmetrical forms make this Argentine's New York debut an important one. The works fall somewhere between painting and sculpture, minimal and serial: each is composed of at least seven individual units, some of canvas, others of wood, which are mounted on the wall to form echoing arrangements of color, pattern, and mathematical dimensions.

The *Art News* reviewer called attention to other aspects of the works:

César Paternosto from Buenos Aires shows four very large multiart canvases which he calls "Symmetrical-Asymmetrical." The strongly colored acrylic surfaces, size and shape of the individual pieces of each painting balance and unbalance, form and deform the vision. These impressive works at first seem all the same, other than obvious color differences, but the viewer is gradually aware of the particularity of the way the stresses—his symmetry-asymmetry—differ from work to work. Each painting is composed of a separated ellipse which encloses either three, four, five, or six shapes and establishes the tension of the work.

A note in *Arts Magazine* brought out still further details:

In cut-out wall reliefs which Paternosto likes to call "complex units" he starts with large horseshoe shapes that contain anywhere from three to six smaller sections within them. They are modular forms painted in bright, sunny, close-valued acrylics that vary from one unit to the next. They are deceptively simple. The slight variations in shapes and colors are the key to symmetrical-asymmetrical relations which the artist forced me to search out. The work is architectural, minimal but cheerful.

While living in New York in 1969 he entered upon another phase of activity, adopting a style he called "The Oblique Vision," which was also the name he gave to his show at the A. M. Sachs Gallery in 1970. This involved sequential interaction between lateral and frontal viewpoints: it obliges the spectator to change position and carries the pictorial image to extreme (plate 95). In *Arts Magazine* of January 1970 a reviewer commented:

The next logical step for artists to take as an extension of Color Field painting is to make the color literally spill itself off the canvas. It has been pushed to the outermost limits and driven to the edges as well, so that in effect, the only direction left is to paint around the sides. This is precisely what Paternosto does, although this "framework" is more complicated than most easel paintings.

Paternosto later worked on polyptychs composed of fragmented forms. When viewed from a predetermined distance, they seem to form a unit. His œuvre was enhanced with unexpected achievements in matters of form and color and the

96

Alejandro Puente
96. *Untitled.* 1965
Acrylic on canvas, 55⅛ x 55⅛″
Museo de Arte Contemporáneo, Buenos Aires
Photo: Pedro Roth

97

Carmen Herrera
97. *Green and Orange.* 1958
  Acrylic on canvas, 60 x 72"
  Courtesy Rastovski Gallery, New York
  Photo: Tony Velez

relationships he established between them. Paternosto's present concern is with the relationship between the Constructivist concept and ancient Inca cultures, relating to some degree of geometric form and Americanist research that was explored by Torres-García.

A Guggenheim Fellowship brought Puente to New York in 1967. Previously, like Paternosto, he had been a member of the Grupo Sí in La Plata, partaking in the general search for a new type of geometric expression. He and Paternosto had had a show entitled *New Geometry* at the Lirolay Gallery in Buenos Aires in October 1964. The catalog introduction was written by Aldo Pellegrini, one of the most brilliant and creative critics to be found in Argentina at that time:

On the national scene[106] *Puente and Paternosto are the artists who are laying a new foundation for geometric expression. They are taking a new approach, which might be given the name of Lyric Geometry.*[107] *The geometric figure ceases to be an active element; it becomes a merely passive support, providing, one might say, a neutral setting for the real protagonists of the picture: color and texture. Annulment of the dominant role played by geometric form is obtained by maximum simplification of plastic description, and by subordination to rather strict symmetry. Color then stands out as the active element, mobility being provided by the opposition of bands of diverse colors within the forms....*

Pellegrini also called attention to the importance of texture, "which Puente creates by shading the colored surfaces and eroding the outlines of forms."

But there were certain important differences between Puente's work and Paternosto's. Both at the 1967 *Elemental Vision* show and in *Beyond Geometry* at the Center for Inter-American Relations, Puente made use of L-shaped modules lined up one after another on the floor. In other words, without exactly being sculpture, the composition made a claim on real space. Color was applied to the modules without emotional or decorative intent, but in conformity with rigorous rules. For example, Puente took a hue and used it in accordance with a programmatic scale of values. In short, by the time Puente arrived in the United States there was a conceptual element to his work, exemplified by his systematic use of color (plate 96).

The first group show he appeared in after his arrival was *American Artists*, which took place at the Delaware Art Center in 1968. At that exhibition, space requirements obliged Puente to place his serial units against the wall, but in *Beyond Geometry* and in an exhibit at the Paula Cooper Gallery in New York they were lined up on the floor in accordance with the artist's original intention. Programmed color in sculpture or works projecting into the third dimension had not been previously used in the United States. In 1969 Puente took part in *Groups*, which was organized by Lucy Lippard and put on at the School of Visual Arts Gallery in Manhattan. For this show Lippard invited artists to experiment within given restrictions. Puente's contribution was atypical, since the conceptual element in his work took over. The piece consisted of a series of photographs accompanied by a text referring to the time-space relationship established in photographs.

This experiment was not altogether unrelated to his other activities, for his modular units were apt to be accompanied by sketches of measurements, details, and fragments, giving the spectator an idea of how the work was put together. At The Museum of Modern Art's 1970 *Information* show, Puente had the opportunity to carry his ideas to greater extremes. He provided a sort of illustration of the Conceptual Art theory, consisting of glass tubes of pigment, bottles of liquid color, modular elements, and a text on the grammar and syntax of color and the rules for its use.

In several newspaper articles Puente has referred to the important effect his stay in New York had on his work, particularly in terms of the opportunity it gave him to explore the relationship between Geometric Abstraction and ancient American civilizations.

A.P.—When I lived in New York I was working along a line which was known internationally as Geometric Abstraction. It was then that I realized the need to give my works a feeling of place. I felt the need to give them identity—that is why the feeling of place makes its appearance. Place implies not only physical data (topography, climate, materials) but also elements of memory (tradition, culture, history).

One of the things that inspired me in this development was my observation of the relationship between the works I was doing and the art of ancient American civilizations, in which I discovered both potential and modernity. Bidimensionality, geometry, abstraction, and construction were all to be found in the art.

When the reporter interrupted to question him further on this point, Puente's answer confirmed what has been noted above.

Q—Did the fact that you were living in New York influence that discovery? Did you share your concerns with other South American artists?
A.P.—I think that it is in an environment like that of New York that one can begin to realize the place to which one belongs. It also became clear to me that the reason we didn't dare seek inspiration in our own cultures lay in the fact that we were always looking to see what was going on in the Northern Hemisphere. It was a state of dependency. And all of a sudden several of us South American artists began to share this same idea and to try to produce something that would identify us.[108]

Lygia Clark and Brazilian Geometric Art

The Constructivist movement in Brazil has been extremely active. Ivan Serpa, Abraham Palatnik, and Mavignier, its chief adherents, established contact with Argentine Constructivist groups to promote this art. A series of events in the early 1950s— an exhibition of works by Max Bill, the establishment of the São Paulo Bienal, the appearance of the Rottura (Rapture) group in São Paulo and the Forte (Strong) group in Rio de Janeiro—inspired many artists to adopt new approaches. As Frederico de Morais has pointed out, as early as 1954 there had been a separation between São Paulo Concretism, with its emphasis on the machine and technology, and Rio Neo-Concretism, which took a more organic approach to form.

In 1959 there was a Neo-Concretist show at the Rio Museum of Modern Art, featuring paintings by Lygia Clark, Lygia Pape, and sculptures by Weissman. However, just as the Argentine groups Concrete Art Invention Association, Madi, and Perceptism —groups of exceptional importance—established no presence in the United States, so too were the activities of the Brazilian Constructivists confined to Brazil, Paris, and Zurich.

However, a few of the Brazilians at least made an appearance in the United States. The sculptor Amilcar de Castro had a show at the Kornblee Gallery in New York and received a Guggenheim Fellowship for 1968–69 and for 1970–71 (plate 99). Between 1950 and 1970 Ivan Serpa, Lygia Pape, and Abraham Palatnik had shows at OAS headquarters. Lygia Clark and Ivan Serpa were also included in the exhibition *Art of Latin America since Independence*.[109]

Lygia Clark had earlier been invited to take part in a show of works by Brazilian artists at OAS headquarters in 1962. In 1960, The Museum of Modern Art had purchased one of her works. In 1963 she had a solo exhibition in New York at the Louis Alexander Gallery, and she also participated in a group show at the art gallery of the Pepsi-Cola Company in New York. Her sculptures always called for collaboration from the viewer. She once said: "The work of art should demand direct participation from the spectator, and the latter should be immediately involved in it."[110]

Her geometric constructions are flexible; they can be rejoined and manipulated, and they are endowed with unexpected suggestions of movement. She gradually abandoned the pure formalism of her early work and, availing herself of their possibilities of transformation and movement, made surprisingly organic pieces, which were dubbed *"Bichos"* (Animals). This flexibility of form is another route unique to Latin American Constructivism.

Carmen Herrera

In November 1986 the Cuban painter Carmen Herrera had a retrospective at the Alternative Museum of New York. Judith Neaman, the curator of the exhibit, in her preface to the catalog expressed her surprise that "work of such importance is not better known in the United States."

This does not seem to have worried Carmen Herrera unduly. She has always been more concerned with the quality and inner coherence of her work than with success. She took courses at The Art Students League in New York in 1943, after which she studied architecture in Havana. There followed a period of residence in Paris from 1949 to 1952. In 1953 she settled permanently in New York. In 1956 she took part in a group show at the New York City Center and had a solo exhibition at the Galería Sudamericana. In an article published at the time in *The New York Times*, Dore Ashton expressed the opinion that she was one of the best of nonfigurative Cuban painters and commented at some length on her highly original use of color (plate 97).[111]

She had other solo exhibitions at the Trabia Gallery in New York in 1963 and at the Cisneros Gallery in New York in 1965. She also took part in a group show of Cuban painters in 1965, which Hilton Kramer reviewed:

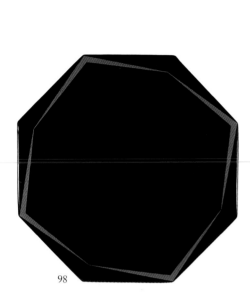

98

Within the limits of the geometrical and hard-edge modes, a painter's success often depends on a correct gauging of what personal innovations are possible within the conventions of these styles. Miss Herrera shows a canny understanding of this problem and is thus widely and expertly practiced. In the painted frames that adorn her pictures, however, her tact sometimes fails her; these frames occasionally work very well, but it is probably a mistake to adopt them as unvarying practice.[112]

From the beginning, Carmen Herrera's work has been marked by orderliness and simplicity. She started out creating optical space by using systems of adjacent bands of black and white paint. "At the time I never thought I was creating Op Art," she said. "It simply resulted from my rational ordering of black and white."[113] As her art matured, she developed a more personal handling of black and white, with greater freedom of finish and distribution of masses. During the 1960s Carmen Herrera deliberately reduced her paintings' elements to a minimum, bringing out individual colors in all their splendor.

Carmen Herrera has developed a highly personal kind of Geometric Abstraction, both in her definition of forms (which gives her works a resemblance to hard-edge painting) and in her unexpected use of soft colors, such as sky blue and lemon yellow. She has always stripped her work down to essentials, creating a precise balance between forms that are occasionally identical and organizing them so as to occupy the whole of the surface. Her economy of means is astonishing, as is the dynamic use she makes of colors—she confined herself to two colors per painting during the 1960s. Line, mass, space, and color are all orchestrated to produce tensions that are resolved with superb subtlety.

Domingo López

Domingo López, born in Puerto Rico, is the youngest of the Geometric Abstractionists mentioned in this essay. When he was only seventeen he went to the United States to study at Washington High School in New York, but he returned home to San Juan to complete his education at the University of Puerto Rico. In 1965 he again went to New York, where he was to remain for eight years. That same year he set up an art gallery known as Aspira for the Puerto Rican community and took part in two exhibits there. In the following years his activity was divided between the continental United States and his native island (plate 98).

99

In 1967 The Museum of Modern Art purchased a silk-screen print of his entitled *Phases of Time*. Reflection on time has inspired a large part of his work. In 1967 he participated in a three-man show at the Tibor de Nagy Gallery and two years later was included in a group show at the Puerto Rican Art Gallery. The Institute of Puerto Rican Culture gave him a grant to study in New York from 1969 to 1970, and at that time he took part in the group show *Latin American Graphics '70* at the Cisneros Gallery.

Constructivism and geometric art produced tremendous creativity in Latin America. Artists were interested in visual research—in part the result of a need for formal structural clarification and in part a reaction opposed to the exuberance present in the culture of some Latin American countries as a valuable way out of the picturesque art that outsiders associated with the region (plate 99).

Latin American artists started working synchronistically with the international centers where this kind of contemporary art was being worked out, searching for an equilibrium between the technology of a mass society and their positive goals. There were remarkable differences between the societies but it is important to consider that nonfigurative art cannot (because of its intrinsic characteristics) closely reflect economic and social environments, so categorizations according to country cannot easily be made.

The Latin American presence showed, on the one hand, the multiplicity of resources offered by geometric art, and, on the other hand, the way in which these resources could handle solutions independent of European proposals. The vitality and the lack of restraint in Latin American abstraction is characteristic of the countries. Latin Americans, in some instances, exhibited minor degrees of subjectivity rather than sticking to rational orthodoxy. They opened doors to the esoteric, the mystical, and the symbolic, and they looked to the art of ancient American cultures, where geometric, abstract, and Constructivist characteristics seemed to create a bridge across the centuries.

Domingo López
98. *Orange Energy*. 1969
Plexiglas, 51 x 51 x 3″
Museo de Antropología, Arte y Historia,
Universidad de Puerto Rico, Recinto de Río Piedras
Photo: John Betancourt, San Juan

99. *Amilcar de Castro and Family, New Jersey*
Photo: courtesy the artist

New York Dada and New World Surrealism

by Lowery S. Sims

Both as periodic visitors and as émigrés Latin American artists were key participants in the promulgation of Surrealism in the United States. Conversely, Surrealism was instrumental in opening up avenues of self-expression that allowed the "Latin" sensibility to become a viable part of artistic expression. Artists such as Wifredo Lam, Frida Kahlo, and Roberto Matta introduced New World cultural elements and political sensibilities into the framework of European avant-garde contextures, thereby providing other Latin American artists with paradigms to express their unique cultural situations—as well as creating their own pertinent and potent nationalistic statements. As Latin American artists continually worked in two or three locales—Latin America, the United States, and Europe—they also effected an interesting and even crucial linkage between the many-headed hydra that is contemporary art.

In the late 1930s, as the European powers marshaled their resources for war, the focus of artistic energy in modern art—which had been centered in European cities such as Paris, London, Madrid, Barcelona, and Rome—began shifting to the Americas. As intellectuals and artists who were political opponents of fascism fled to the United States, Central and South America, and the Caribbean for asylum, they brought with them the ideas, the organizations, and even the patronage to guarantee the fertilization of modernism in the Western Hemisphere, which up until this point had been regarded as the cultural backwater of Western civilization.[1]

This development had in fact been preceded by the return of Diego Rivera to Mexico in 1921 and Joaquín Torres-García to Uruguay in 1934 after extensive stays in Europe, where they had been immersed in the most advanced artistic circles of the day. Rivera had been associated with the Cubists during a twenty-year sojourn in Paris. Upon his return to Mexico he became a leading figure in the national cultural movement. He was later to influence numerous artists in the United States and Mexico through his mural work in San Francisco, Detroit, and New York.[2] Torres-García, who for over thirty years led a peripatetic existence abroad, living in Spain, France, Italy, and the United States before returning to Uruguay, was active in the modernist movement in Barcelona at the beginning of this century. During his peregrinations he had synthesized Cubism, Symbolism, and Neo-Plasticism with Amerindian and Egyptian pictographic systems to create a unique solution to the dilemma of figuration in the age of abstraction.[3]

Within their respective societies these two artists were able to achieve new pictorial languages that melded European modernism with aspects of their traditional cultures and with the peculiar "Creole" characteristics of postcolonial cultures on this side of the Atlantic.[4] The result was the advancement of a new vocabulary in modern art that had repercussions throughout the Western Hemisphere as a whole and in New York in particular. But the progression of their impact was circuitous and requires an understanding of European artists' perceptions of America as well as Latin Americans' perceptions of Europe.

Surrealism was a specific technique of intellectual investigation that sought to free the European bourgeoisie from conventional and habitual approaches to empirical reality by cultivating an interest in the noncontiguous associations provided by "chance" or subconscious thinking.[5] To this end, the writers and artists associated with the movement employed automatic activity—automatism—and conjured up the anomalies of dream imagery in their work. Freudian analysis and the dark morbidity of a quirky cult novel *Chants de Maldoror*—which was written in the nineteenth century by the Uruguayan-born Frenchman Isidore Ducasse, who wrote under the pseudonym of the Comte de Lautréamont[6]—were among the key precedents for these investigations. Surrealist painting and sculpture exploited either disjointed dream imagery (as in the work of Salvador Dali and René Magritte) or the "found" imagery of unspecific and "unguided" doodling (as in the work of Max Ernst and André Masson). In their search for an unexpected, unfettered imagery, the Surrealist artists came to appreciate other artistic expressions that manifested a different perspective on reality or had an ethos distinct from that of the average middle-class European (and American) intellectual. Thus the art of children, the insane, the intuitive or untutored, and the so-called primitive cultures of precolonial America, Africa, and Asia were admitted into the realm of "high" art.

Dadaism, the movement that preceded Surrealism, had established important intellectual and aesthetic precedents for the ideas that Surrealism promulgated after the 1920s.[7] Dada, which purported to destroy art by designating as art the detritus of everyday life—including discarded paper trash and such nonart objects as Duchamp's legendary urinal fountain—was created out of a rebellious contempt for the failures of Western civilization that were so evident on the eve of World War I. Dadaism, which itself drew on the nihilistic militancy of the Futurists and the penchant for exhibitionism that became part and parcel of the modern avant-garde posture, set the stage for Surrealism.

Interestingly, it was two artists of Latin American heritage who were the key players in Dada as it was manifested in New York City between 1913 and 1917. One was Francis Picabia, the French-born son of a Cuban father and a French mother. Picabia created mechanistic fantasy machines endowed with highly sexual nuances. Along with Marcel Duchamp, he was responsible for forming the backbone of Dada in New York and Paris. Picabia came to New York in 1913 on the occasion of the Armory Show—the first major exhibition of avant-garde art from Europe and America in the United States. There he made the acquaintance of the art dealer and photographic pioneer Alfred Stieglitz, who was one of the principal supporters and promoters of modern art in the United States.[8] The other Latin American Dadaist in New York was Marius de Zayas, a Mexican caricaturist and literary aficionado, who also worked with Stieglitz at the beginning of this century promulgating the ideas of modernism.[9] De Zayas was an important figure in the development of modernism in New York. He had arrived in the city in 1906 after his family left Mexico because of political differences with President Porfirio Díaz. De Zayas's father, Rafael, had been the poet laureate of Mexico and had published periodicals for which Marius provided cartoons, illustrations, and the caricatures that were his forte. In New York, de Zayas showed his work first in a joint exhibition at Stieglitz's gallery Photo-Secession (also known as "291" after its address on Fifth Avenue) with John Nilsen Laurik in 1909. Soon after that exhibition, de Zayas became an associate of the gallery, and by 1911 he was advising Stieglitz about modern art. At the turn of the century he had spent some time in Paris with his brother and was familiar with the major trends in art. De Zayas was especially instrumental in making the art world aware of African and Mexican pre-Columbian art. He started the Modern Gallery in 1915 and was instrumental in establishing communications with Tristan Tzara of the Dada contingent in Zurich. After closing the Modern Gallery in 1918, he opened the De Zayas Gallery, which lasted for just over two years, closing in 1921. In both of these establishments, de Zayas sought to recreate the atmosphere in Stieglitz's galleries. Buying the most advanced European art provided by his Parisian contacts, which included his brother, the dealer Paul Guillaume, and his friend Paul Haviland, de Zayas exhibited contemporary art alongside photography and African and Mexican art.

After his second gallery closed, de Zayas traveled in Europe and the United States until the outbreak of World War II. He worked on various international art projects and served as a link between European and American artists. He also took up painting seriously, working in a Cubist style that at once recalls Picasso's and Picabia's work of 1913–14. Besides being an art-world catalyst and dealer, de Zayas was also a fairly prolific writer, publishing some of the earliest appreciations of African art and modern art. He published an article on caricature in Stieglitz's *Camera Work*, and he

100

Frida Kahlo
100. *Suicide of Dorothy Hale.* 1938
   Oil on Masonite, 23 ¼ x 19″
   Phoenix Art Museum. Anonymous gift, 60/20
   Photo: courtesy Phoenix Art Museum

101

Frida Kahlo
101. *Self-Portrait with Monkey*. 1938
Oil on Masonite, 12 x 15¾″
Albright-Knox Art Gallery, Buffalo, New York.
Bequest of A. Conger Goodyear, 1966
Photo: courtesy Albright-Knox Art Gallery

was involved in the production of Stieglitz's magazine *291*, in which he published "African Negro Art: Its Influence on Modern Art." In 1913 he coauthored *A Study of the Modern Evolution of Plastic Expression* with Paul Haviland, which he published later through the Modern Gallery.

The interest expressed by de Zayas and his associates in caricature and primitive art were explored in articles and presentations that appeared in the various Surrealist periodicals published in the 1920s, 1930s, and 1940s. *La révolution surréaliste, La Surréalisme au service de la révolution, Documents, Minotaure, VVV*, and *View* reflected the preoccupations of the ever-permutating Surrealist movement. Articles on aspects of American cultures were featured: Haitian vodun, black American blues and boogey, Native American shamanism, and the innate "surrealism" of Mexican culture were all tapped for ideas. This last subject was the focus of the May 1939 issue of *Minotaure*, which chronicled André Breton's visit to Mexico, the result of which was the transplanting of Surrealism to the Americas.[10]

Breton's hosts during his visit to Mexico were Diego Rivera and his wife, Frida Kahlo, who was also a painter. When André Breton first encountered Kahlo's paintings, he was moved to enthuse:

I was witnessing here, at the other end of the earth, a spontaneous outpouring of our own questioning spirit: what irrational laws do we obey, what subjective signals allow us to establish the right direction...which symbols and myth predominate in a particular conjunction of objects of web of happenings, what meaning can be ascribed to the eye's capacity to pass from visual power to visionary power.[11]

Breton was writing as much about his overall impressions of Mexico, a country which for him encapsulated the unexpected and the marvelous: *"le merveilleux—* an impassioned fusion of wish and reality in a surreality where poetry and freedom are one."[12] The interface of the pre-Columbian legacy with the dramatic, emotional character of Spanish Catholicism, the fatalistic acceptance of the coexistence of the physical and the metaphysical, and the ornate sensibilities of both Spanish and Mexican cultures had resulted in an innate surrealism that was quite unlike the self-conscious intellectual, psychological, and artistic manipulations of the French Surrealist movement.

Two key events resulted from Breton's meeting with Rivera and Kahlo: an international exhibition of Surrealist art in Mexico City was jointly organized by Breton and the Mexican artist and critic César Moro at the Galería de Arte Mexicano;[13] and Kahlo agreed to visit Paris, where Breton organized an exhibition of her work. With Breton's imprimatur Kahlo officially became a Surrealist artist.[14] His tribute to her, quoted above, was also published as a catalog essay for Kahlo's first New York exhibition in 1938 at the Julien Levy Gallery. Although this was her first exhibition in the United States, it was not her first visit. She had traveled to San Francisco in 1930 with Rivera, who had been commissioned to paint murals for the stock exchange and for the California School of Fine Arts (now the San Francisco Institute of Art). Because of Rivera's reputation, they were immediately introduced to the art circle there. Kahlo, who was recovering from surgery, resumed painting for the first time since her student days. The next year she was in New York with her husband on the occasion of his retrospective at The Museum of Modern Art. There, they also met many of the most influential art patrons, including the legendary Alfred Barr, who later visited Kahlo's studio in Mexico.

As late as 1931 Kahlo's artwork was virtually unknown outside of her immediate circle of friends, but it was during a prolonged stay with Rivera in Detroit in 1932–33 that she began to paint in earnest as a response to her physical and psychological travails, which included a rather traumatic miscarriage and recurring problems with a spinal injury she had sustained as a teenager. In Detroit, with the encouragement of Rivera, Kahlo began to adapt her painting style, making it more like folk art, more "popular" in character. This was a fortuitous choice because the vehicle of traditional Mexican *retablos*—votive paintings that depict miracles secured through the intercession of various saints—afforded Kahlo a means to express in a rather direct and personal way the extraordinary physical and psychic pain that she had to endure

most of her life. This mannerism was also compatible with Rivera's aesthetic politics—
his conviction that Mexican art should reflect the native manifestations of the indigenous
culture, thereby asserting comradery with the populace as a whole.[15]

This antielitist, even anti-European bias was characteristic of the "Mexicanismus"
philosophy that came out of the populist revolution in 1917 and influenced Rivera to
reject self-consciously the conventions of avant-garde, quasi-abstract art, which were
associated with Europe, in favor of a figurative style that he utilized to celebrate his native
culture. Similar ideas were germinating in the conceptual formulations of other artists
in the Americas. For example, in an essay he published in 1927 entitled the "Red Man,"
Marsden Hartley, an artist associated with the Stieglitz circle, extolled the character of
Native American culture, especially its spirituality and intimate relationship with nature.
He dared to suggest that American artists look to their way of life and mode of
expression for ways to find a truly American artistic expression.[16] Hartley's strategy
was one of many by artists trying to deal with the reality of strong public resistance
to the Armory Show and subsequent manifestations of modern art in the United States.
European modernism was often equated with foreign subversion; one of the more
organized manifestations of this attitude was the Regionalist movement, which was
spawned by Thomas Hart Benton, who had abandoned his early Synchromist style to
work in a mode that celebrated the unique "Americanness" of the rural heartlands.[17]

That Surrealism would have an impact on this dialogue, in which American art
could manifest itself in conservative or radical forms, is ironic. But the Surrealists had
demonstrated a particular awareness of the political implications of appropriating the art
and culture of non-Western cultures. Unlike the Cubists, who were content to take
advantage of the formal characteristics of folk and primitive art, the Surrealists explored
the psychological bondage that European bourgeois conventions had imposed on Latin
America, the Caribbean, and Africa when they pushed the local populations into
disparaging their own indigenous cultural forms and assuming Western values. By
contrast, the Surrealists perceived the inherent values of these traditional cultures as
antidotes to the failure of Western industrial society—a failure that was vividly
demonstrated by the devastations of the two world wars.[18] This perspective also served
to reinforce the artistic purposes of Kahlo, Lam, and Matta, and through them other
Latin American artists working in the United States who were seeking to express their
modern identity but to temper it with a unique national profile.

It is against this complex scenario that Breton's enthusiasm for Kahlo's work
can be evaluated and Kahlo's actual relationship with the Surrealist movement can be
considered. Kahlo's Surrealism (and that of Lam, and to a lesser extent that of Matta)
was a reflection of innate cultural expressions more than it was a disjuncture of empirical
reality as defined by the European art movement, which evaluated "surreality" from a
rationalist's point of view. In fact, the reviewers of Kahlo's New York exhibition were
quite clear about the distinction. They noted her relationship to native Mexican art and
had this to say about her association with Surrealism, the art movement: "…this painter,
who did not know the word Surrealist till told she was one, is poignantly of her
time…she knows so well the things she tells of; and feeling strongly about them,
speaking of them with the openness that comes of conviction, her work goes beyond
the trial stage of a young artist's first show; it is definitively a beautiful achievement."[19]

From New York, Kahlo sailed to Europe for the exhibition in Paris organized
by Breton, who carried out his nativist fancies by installing her art with pre-Columbian
artifacts. Kahlo's work was seen again in the United States in 1940 when she was
included in the *Golden Gate International Exhibition* in San Francisco. At this time she
also sent her powerful self-portrait *The Two Fridas* (plate 102) to the *Twenty Centuries
of Mexican Art* exhibition at The Museum of Modern Art in New York. During the
next two years her work was seen in group shows of Mexican art at Boston's Institute
of Modern Art, the Philadelphia Museum of Art, and Peggy Guggenheim's Art of
This Century gallery. As a result of this activity Kahlo always asserted that it was in the
United States that she received her first acclaim as an artist. From about 1947 until her
death in 1954 she remained for the most part in Mexico, where she was a popular and
influential teacher of young artists.[20]

In the late 1930s Breton had also met two other artists from Latin America and

102

Frida Kahlo
102. *The Two Fridas.* 1939
Oil on canvas, 68⅛ x 68⅛″
Museo de Arte Moderno, Instituto Nacional de
Bellas Artes, Mexico City
Photo: Gerardo Suter

103

Roberto Matta
103. *Eclosion.* 1952
Oil on canvas, 29 x 40½"
Collection David and Tanya Brillembourg,
New York
Photo: courtesy C.D.S. Gallery, New York

the Caribbean who were to have an impact not only on the Surrealist group in Paris but also on the New York art world. In 1937 a young Chilean of Basque descent, Roberto Matta, abandoned his architecture studies in the studio of Le Corbusier and joined the Surrealist group in Paris. In 1938, the same year as Breton's tour of Mexico, the Cuban-born Wifredo Lam, who had been active as a Loyalist sympathizer in the Spanish Civil War, arrived in Paris with a letter of introduction to Picasso. Picasso liked the artist, who had spent fourteen years in Spain working his way out of academic painting and toward a Picasso-inspired Cubist style, and he introduced him to Breton, who immediately embraced him as a Surrealist.[21] As the impact of the war was beginning to be felt in Europe, Breton and the Surrealists fled Paris for the south of France, beyond the immediate reach of the Nazi forces. Matta managed to get to New York in 1939 on the same boat as Yves Tanguy. Lam and Breton, along with the Surrealist poet Benjamin Péret and the anthropologist Claude Lévi-Strauss, secured transatlantic passage from Marseilles to Martinique. Lam then returned to his native Cuba and Breton continued to New York, where he was reunited with members of the Surrealist group, including André Masson, Max Ernst, and Matta.[22]

The presence of the Surrealists in the United States during the war, specifically in New York City, has long been recognized as a crucial factor in the development of the New York School into an international force. Several individuals who were especially compatible with the North Americans, and certainly Matta was one, have been singled out as being particularly instrumental in this process.[23] Matta's command of English afforded him contacts with New York artists that even Breton was not able to achieve. Matta had met Gordon Onslow-Ford, an early Surrealist proselytizer in America, while they were both in Paris in the late 1930s, which also helped to ease his social passage during this period. Through the exercises in automatism that he organized in his studio in the early 1940s, Matta is credited with revolutionizing the work of such artists as Arshile Gorky, William Baziotes, Gerome Kramowski, Jackson Pollock, and Robert Motherwell (who traveled with him to Mexico in 1944). He was especially influential for Gorky at a point when the Armenian émigré was making the transition from his skillfully mimetic style to a style that merged the psychosexual aspects of Surrealism with landscape painting and metamorphic aspects of automatism with broad abstract fields of color.[24] In addition, influential dealers, critics, and curators, including Sidney Janis, Nicholas Calas, Meyer Schapiro, and James Johnson Sweeney, welcomed Matta into the avant-garde circle in New York. He had regular exhibitions at the Julien Levy Gallery and at Pierre Matisse's, and his work was included in many exhibitions of the "new" painting in America. He also exhibited in Peggy Guggenheim's Art of This Century gallery in 1942 and 1944, and was included in Breton's *Surréalisme en Peinture* published by Brentano's in New York in 1942.[25]

Matta's approach to the morphology of painting—his creation of evocative surfaces, which he achieved by wiping, thinning, and drawing with paint, was of interest to the Americans, who were trying to liberate themselves from the Cubist grid that predicated most modernist compositional structures. Although much of the early criticism of this work in New York ascribed a rather enigmatic quality to Matta's paintings, the art world as a whole seems to have been aware that his work was distinctive—even within the extensive lexicon of modernist postures—and his technique and imagery were seen as pointing clearly to the future.[26] Matta's frequent suggestions of nether worlds of chaos and creation predicted the imagery of the Abstract Expressionists during the 1940s, which in the words of Mark Rothko were intended to create "new counterparts to replace the old mythological hybrids who have lost their pertinence" (plate 107).[27]

In the early 1940s Matta's work featured horizonless spaces that evoked states of mind as well as physical locations (which might as well be cosmic as aquatic). The recurring title for these works was "inscape," with the additional qualifier "psychological morphology." William Rubin has described Matta's approach as akin to "the landscape designing itself as the work progressed."[28] His improvisational approach predicated Pollock's "drip" paintings of the late 1940s and the Abstract Expressionists' "action painting." By the mid-1940s Matta had reintroduced perspectival elements into his space with a "nervous linearity…[that is] a symbolic drama of the mind's journey into its own

105

104

Roberto Matta

104. *Studies.* 1942
Crayon, pencil on paper, 31 x 36½″
Collection Dolores Smithes, New York
Photo: Quesada/Burke, New York

Frida Kahlo

105. *How Beautiful Life Is When It Gives Us Riches.* 1943
Oil on canvas on Masonite, 15½ x 19½″
Collection Francisco and Laura Osio. Courtesy
Galería Arvil, Mexico City
Photo: Gerardo Suter

106

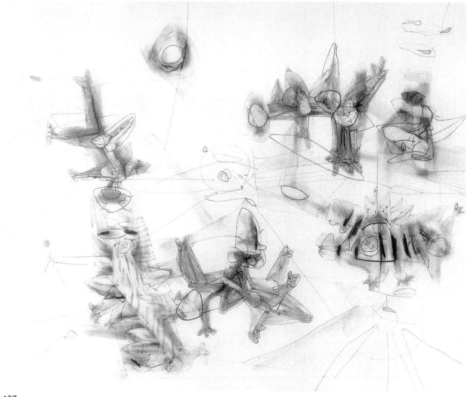

107

Roberto Matta
106. *Spherical Roof Around Our Tribe (Revolvers).* 1952
Tempera on canvas, 79⅝ x 115⅞″
Collection The Museum of Modern Art, New York.
Gift of D. and J. de Menil
Photo: courtesy The Museum of Modern Art

Roberto Matta
107. *Untitled.* 1942-44
Crayon, pencil on paper, 18¼ x 21¾″
Collection Dolores Smithes, New York
Photo: Quesada/Burke, New York

unconscious."[29] His wandering linear elements would later coalesce to define awesome, masked figures involved in horrific rituals. While these sacrificial scenes were obviously inspired by the atrocities of the war, it is not unrealistic to relate them to pre-Columbian art, in which sacrificial rituals were an important thematic component.[30] In Matta's works even the planar dimensions seem to have gone mad, and whiplike lines are accompanied by panels or planes that seem to have been lifted out of the environment and independently activated, disrupting the integrity of the architectural settings. These compositions became the prototypes for the quasi-political, quasi-cosmic paintings that Matta created for the next forty years. They influenced many artists from Latin America who were seeking to make their own peculiarly nationalistic statements within a modernist idiom.

Matta's evocation of pre-Columbian and other primitivistic mythic imagery had parallels in the imagery being explored by Jackson Pollock and Adolph Gottlieb.[31] His adroit handling of scale was also an important example for New York artists. For the new band of "myth-makers," the monumentality of Matta's easel creations in the 1940s was influential in the transition from traditional easel-oriented paintings to huge, monumental works that could be conceived on the floor or directly on the wall. Matta's vision was comparable to that of the Mexican muralists who worked in this country in the 1930s.[32] Even after Matta had left the United States in 1947, and even after he had been "expelled" from the Surrealist fold by Breton in 1948, his work continued to inspire American artists and Surrealists, both in the United States and in Europe. In 1957 The Museum of Modern Art organized a retrospective of his work, and he was also included in a massive exhibition at the museum in 1966 that surveyed Dada and Surrealism.

Because Wifredo Lam never stayed in the United States for any length of time, the nature of his interaction with the aesthetic and intellectual circles in New York in the early 1940s has often been overlooked. But his influence was felt, and like Matta he was one of the important links between Surrealism in Europe and the Americas. In the early 1940s Lam shared several goals with the New York artists of his generation. Willem de Kooning, Arshile Gorky, Jackson Pollock, and to a certain extent Robert Motherwell used Cubism as "a means for structuring the doodles from psychic automatist procedure."[33] Remnants of the Cubist grid persisted in their work even after they had experimented with the aformal technique of automatism. In *The Jungle* of 1943, Lam grappled with Cubism and Surrealism, adapting their respective vocabularies to his new and powerful imagery. Lam used this syntax to visualize his interpretations of the Cuban (originally African) religion Santería. He achieved a foreboding and primal feeling that was similar to contemporaneous works by New York artists who were trying to convey the new cosmology described by Mark Rothko as being "… of the Earth, the Damned, and the Recreated."[34] In Lam's work of the early 1940s Cubist elements in the composition were adapted to accommodate the multiplicities of realities that inhabit the physical and psychological jungle of Afro-Cuba. But the Cubist still-life iconography Lam made merged human and plant forms into a surreal world conceived in the imagination of an animistic force. On the one hand Lam's visual mimicry of Cubism may be understood as a pun at the expense of European art; on a deeper level, however, it deliberately reflects the syncretistic compositional approach that characterized the development of African culture as it survived in the Americas and the Caribbean. Like the blend of Catholic liturgy with African religions that has taken place in the Caribbean and South America—namely in Santería, vodun, and the Brazilian candomble— Lam infuses a European art form with Afro-Cuban symbolism. By utilizing a format that would be accessible to the international art world, Lam was able to engage in cultural politics and at the same time communicate with his artistic peers in Paris and New York (plates 108–114).[35]

The success of this strategy was attested to by the professional receptivity to his paintings during the 1940s in New York. His work had been seen in New York since 1939, when he had his first show at the Perls Gallery—a joint exhibition with Picasso. His 1943 exhibition at Pierre Matisse's gallery was notable not only because of the controversy engendered by his refusal to participate in an officially organized exhibition of Cuban art but also because *The Jungle* was purchased by James Johnson Sweeney for

108

109

Wifredo Lam
108. *The Kiss.* 1939
Watercolor, gouache, and pastel on canvas,
24 x 17"
Collection Deborah and David Guss, La Jolla,
California
Photo: courtesy C.D.S. Gallery, New York

Wifredo Lam
109. *Untitled.* 1941
Watercolor and ink on paper, 18⅜ x 12¼"
Collection Mrs. Edwin A. Bergman, Chicago
Photo: Michael Tropea

110

Wifredo Lam
110. *Annunciation.* 1944

Oil on canvas, 61¼ x 50¼"
Museum of Contemporary Art, Chicago. Gift of
Mr. and Mrs. E. A. Bergman
Photo: Joe Ziolkowski

111

112

Wifredo Lam
111. *Woman with Flowers.* 1942
Gouache on paper, 41¾ x 33¼"
Courtesy Pierre Matisse Gallery, New York
Photo: courtesy Pierre Matisse Gallery

Wifredo Lam
112. *Mother and Child.* 1957
Pastel on paper, 28¾ x 22⅞"
Collection Mrs. Edwin A. Bergman, Chicago
Photo: Michael Tropea

the collection of The Museum of Modern Art. Lam also was featured in a two-person exhibition with Matta at the Arts Club of Chicago in 1942. Critics took due note of his relationship to Picasso: "The symbols themselves might have been snitched from *Guernica*...Lam uses [them] in a frank and simple way as though they were the acknowledged property of all artists, and then goes on to say things of his own."[36] There were frequent references to Lam's interest in primitive art. As one critic wrote about Lam's work in 1945: "A world of fantasy appears, reflecting something of the character of Chinese painting, of primitive African art, and in the many round, otarine heads, a suggestion of the symbolic figures of the Alaskan Indians."[37] This last comment was written two years before Barnett Newman's elegy to Native American artists on the occasion of the exhibition *The Ideographic Picture* at the Betty Parsons Gallery, which was the first strong indication of white America's interest in its indigenous cultures since Marsden Hartley's own elegy in the 1920s.[38]

Lam's first visit to New York was in 1946, when he was en route to Paris from Cuba. That August his work was mentioned in a late-summer review of the previous art season. The anonymous writer used the work of Lam, Motherwell, and Gottlieb to discuss the various developments in "killing space" in contemporary art. At this time Lam also became friendly with Gorky and the mosaicist Jeanne Reynal, and he called on Jackson Pollock at his studio in East Hampton.[39] Lam continued to visit the United States periodically, especially in the 1950s. He was featured in an article in *Art News* in 1950, written by a reporter who interviewed and photographed the artist in Cuba.[40] Although Lam's actual presence in New York was scarce, his work was fairly well known. In 1959 he was made a fellow of the Graham Foundation in Chicago, a city which has had a large number of collectors of the work of Lam and Matta and Surrealism in general.[41]

In 1944 Matta created the cover design for the last issue of the Surrealist journal *VVV*, which had been published in the U.S. for the previous two years. Perhaps it was a prophetic action that summarized the role that Matta and Lam played in New York. They had transformed Cubism and Surrealism into a new art and thereby fulfilled and affirmed the Surrealists' goals of accommodating the coexistence of a "primitive" and "civilized" world order—a goal which was considered especially urgent in an era when conventional perceptions of "civilization" were being annihilated by war. In spite of their passionate admiration for, and evocation of, an integral world view, the Surrealists were conscious that they ultimately lacked the capacity to step fully into that peculiar sensibility. In Kahlo, Matta, and Lam, they found citizens of the New World who were capable of bridging the gap. By the mid-1940s, too, American artists were already moving beyond the psychological preoccupations of Surrealism and reaching for a world view that was closely related to specifically American traditions.[42] But in the 1950s and 1960s, as the work of Lam, Matta, and even Kahlo was seen more widely in Latin America—Lam and Matta in particular began traveling throughout the continent and their work was collected by museums and individuals—they came to exemplify the mode by which younger Latin American artists could be both modern artists and Latin American.

Wifredo Lam, Roberto Matta, and Frida Kahlo were notable for their peculiar relationships to the art scene in New York and Europe. There were many other Latin American artists working within the Surrealist tradition who also spent significant portions of their career in the United States. Although their peculiar contributions may not have been as well known, it is nevertheless important to chronicle their participation in the art scene of this country.

Born in Minas Gerais, Brazil, in 1900 Maria Martins belongs to the same generation as Wifredo Lam. In her early sculptural work she progressed from using terra-cotta to using marble and then bronze as her primary medium. When she was in her late thirties she left Brazil and lived in Brussels with her husband. There she worked with the Belgian sculptor Oscar Jesper. During her extended sojourn abroad she was in contact with many of the influential artistic personalities of her time. During the 1940s in New York she was acquainted with Marcel Duchamp, Yves Tanguy, Alexander Calder, and Piet Mondrian. She exhibited her work in New York throughout the decade and had a one-person show in Washington, D.C. Her work was included in an

113

Wifredo Lam
113. *Noncombustible*. 1950
Oil on canvas, 35½ x 42½"
Collection Robert H. Bergman, Chicago
Photo: Michael Tropea

114

Wifredo Lam
114. *The Eyes in the Grillwork.* 1942
Gouache on paper, 41 ½ x 33″
Courtesy Pierre Matisse Gallery, New York
Photo: courtesy Pierre Matisse Gallery

international exposition in Philadelphia in 1940 and the exhibition *Origins of Modern Sculpture* in St. Louis in 1946. The next year she participated in the *International Surrealist Exhibition* in Paris, perhaps the last great group exhibition of the Surrealist movement. At this time she was close to André Breton and Benjamin Peret. She stayed in Paris until the early 1950s when she returned to Brazil. Martin's characteristic Surrealist work features organic forms that some critics have compared to the lush, overgrown flora of the Brazilian jungle (plate 115).

After Lam, the Cuban artist who participated most actively in the art scene in the United States during the 1940s was Mario Carreño (plate 116). Carreño was a decade younger than Lam but followed the same artistic journey in many instances. After pursuing a rather turbulent career as a political illustrator, he went to Spain in 1932, where he continued to design revolutionary posters.[43] He was forced to return to Cuba in 1935, but still in search of his métier, he went to Mexico. In 1937 he left for Europe, this time going to Paris with the Dominican painter Jaime Colson, whom he had met in Mexico. He seems to have eschewed the more radical manifestations of Parisian art, choosing instead to immerse himself in a study of the Italian Renaissance paintings in the Louvre. A 1939 composition, *Harlequin*, shows the improbable juxtaposition of a flayed harlequin in the company of a nude woman who wears a veil (and would be comfortable in the company of Picasso's blocky nudes of 1906–07). It is a fascinating mélange of modernist tendencies and more traditional European art that is particularly distinguished by its "surreal" setting.

The outbreak of World War II forced Carreño to flee first to Italy, where he spent time in Florence and Naples, and then to the United States, where he settled in New York City. He had his first one-man show in New York in 1941 at the Perls Gallery, and he also exhibited at the Institute of Modern Art in Boston. A reviewer of his exhibition noted: "Carreño has looked at the School of Paris—Chirico and the classic Picasso in particular—but carved himself out something quite personal."[44] Although it is clearly the post-Surrealistic de Chirico that had influenced Carreño, it was not until three years later that critics remarked on the Surrealist association, by paradoxically noting the *absence* of Surrealist nuances in his current work.[45] Carreño's work, they noted, now shows a more "tropical color [that] makes the new excitement in his pictures… Carreño is at his best when it is bold and strong as in the Afro-Cuban series [which] gives out some of the usual harmonics of a Matisse."[46] The Afro-Cuban reference certainly brings to mind the contemporaneous work of Lam, who in addition also manifested tantalizing relationships to the work of Matisse, especially in the late 1940s.[47] In addition, the reviewer's description of the "color geometrically compartmentalized by means of heavy black outlines"[48] makes a stylistic connection between Carreño's work and that of another contemporary Cuban painter Amelia Peláez. The one aspect of the artist's work that consistently attracted attention was his use of Duco paint—a medium he had first experimented with in Cuba in the 1930s—which seems to have been of great technical interest. This same reviewer also noted the "intricate spattery surfaces of richness and brilliancy."[49]

Carreño returned to Cuba at the end of 1941 and spent the next three years working through the artistic impulses he had encountered over the last decade. He also reacquainted himself with the Cuban life and climate, painting still lifes on beaches, scenes of hurricanes, and allegorical presentations of the Antilles atoll. Some of these works show an energetic rhythm that recalls the forms of Diego Rivera and Thomas Hart Benton. The Mexican painter David Alfaro Siqueiros, who visited Havana in 1943, inspired Carreño to work once again with Duco paint. The particular viscous quality of this paint resulted in Carreño's more abstract compositions, which also featured found objects he added to achieve three-dimensional effects.

Carreño returned to New York in 1944, where he stayed until 1951. His work underwent perhaps its most dramatic transformation, evidencing a Cubistic fracturing of forms. He explored Afro-Cuban themes extensively, and his presentations of natural forms and human figures in simple, flattened patterns showed a more specific visual relationship to the work of Lam. By this time Carreño had also come to some very specific ideas about the purpose of painting. He held that painting should not only represent but also enact magic rituals, as in the art of prehistoric, African, Oceanic, and

115

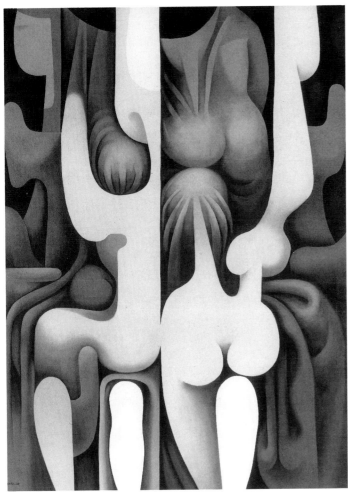

116

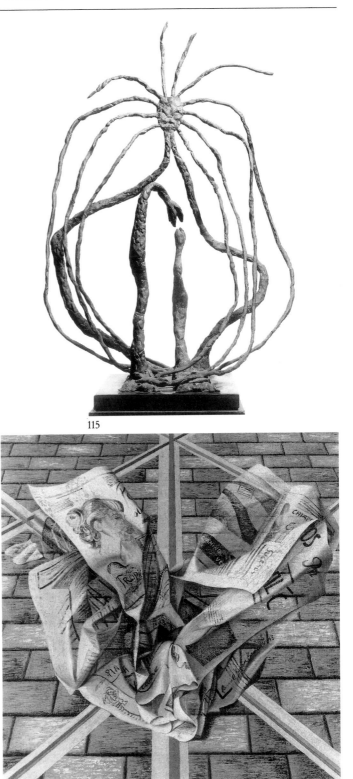

117

Maria Martins
115. *Untitled.* 1940
    Bronze, 52 x 38 x 24"
    Collection Gilberto Chateaubriand Bandeira de
    Mello, Rio de Janeiro
    Photo: Rômulo Fialdini

Mario Carreño
116. *Study for Encounter in Blue Space.* 1967
    Oil on canvas, 64 x 47⅝"
    Collection Mr. Richard Weisman, New York
    Photo: Tony Velez

Daniel Serra-Badué
117. *The Clamoring Newspaper.* 1948
    Oil on canvas, 28 x 27"
    Courtesy José Sobrino Diéguez & Angela R.
    Sobrino, New York
    Photo: Tony Velez

118

Nemesio Antúnez
118. *New York, New York 10008.* 1967
Oil on canvas, 22 x 24″
Courtesy Galerie Couturier, Stamford, Conn.
Photo: Patricia Lambert

119

120

Rodolfo Abularach
119. *Vinac.* 1970
     Pen and ink on paper, 23 x 29″
     Archer M. Huntington Art Gallery, University of
     Texas at Austin. Archer M. Huntington Museum
     Fund, 1979
     Photo: Courtesy Archer M. Huntington Art Gallery

Marcelo Grassmann
120. *Untitled.* 1962
     Etching on paper, 20⅞ x 30¾″
     The Bronx Museum of the Arts. Anonymous gift,
     1987
     Photo: Quesada/Burke, New York

Amerindian people. Yet Carreño's work seems rather conservative when viewed next to Lam's totemic evocations. It was not until the 1950s, when he moved to Chile, that he again became increasingly Surrealistic in approach, and then his work was characterized by a more mechanistic rendering of the human anatomy in tubelike forms that recall Léger's figures.

Carreño's contemporary and compatriot Daniel Serra-Badué demonstrated an affinity with the Surrealism of Salvador Dali and René Magritte (plate 117). In his still-life compositions he exploited contrasts between relatively anomalous juxtapositions of objects and painstakingly precise renderings. Serra-Badué, who has lived in New York since 1962, first came to the United States during the 1920s as a student. He attended the Art Students League, the National Academy of Design, and Pratt Institute. He also traveled to England, Ireland, and Canada. He returned to New York for two years in 1938 on a Guggenheim Fellowship, and he continued to visit New York periodically until he established permanent residence there.

In a review of his first major New York exhibition in 1957, a critic noted that the artist "attempts to create subtle Surrealist shock and poetry in the meticulous renderings and juxtaposition of objects such as walnut shells, a sewing machine or an egg-beater."[50] He faulted the artist on his "commonplace" method and "slight" sense of mystery.[51] In 1966 Jacqueline Barnitz, writing in *Arts* magazine, noted that Serra-Badué's paintings comment on "pomp, hero worship and the dehumanization of city life. Serra-Badué often combines the suspense of a Delvaux and the spiritual drama of a Chirico in the same canvas."[52] But given the prominence that Color-Field Painting and Pop art were enjoying at this time in the art world, one can readily understand how the more poetic use of objects by Serra-Badué was out of step with the consumerism of Pop art. Serra-Badué has exhibited in Europe, Cuba, and in New York at the Milch and The Contemporaries galleries. He has taught at the Brooklyn Museum Art School and at St. Peter's College in New Jersey.

Two Surrealist artists of the generation born after Carreño and Serra-Badué are the Chilean Nemesio Antúnez and the Cuban Agustín Fernández. Antúnez arrived in the United States to study architecture at Columbia University in 1943.[53] This was nine years after his compatriot Matta went to Paris to study architecture with Le Corbusier. Like Matta, Antúnez was soon lured away from his architectural studies. He studied briefly at Stanley Hayter's graphic studio, Workshop 17, and later followed Hayter to Paris in 1950. In 1953 he returned to Chile, where he set up his own graphic workshop, Taller 99, in Santiago. After serving as director of the Contemporary Art Museum at the University of Chile, he returned to the United States in 1965 as cultural attaché to the Chilean Embassy. In 1966 he executed the mural *Heart of the Andes* at the United Nations in New York. He was also known for illustrating the work of such writers as Pablo Neruda and Allen Ginsberg. He has lived in Barcelona since 1974.

On the occasion of Antúnez's first New York exhibition in 1950, reviewers noted that although the artist was best known as an engraver, his paintings showed an "exploitation of anthropomorphic landscape, places somewhere in the Inferno"[54] and he used "an almost Impressionist technique to achieve an un-Impressionist effect."[55] Antúnez later came to adapt the optical effects of Color-Field Painting and Op art while exploring illusions achieved by perspectival anomalies caused by geometric patterns. The influence of Vasarely and Riley can be seen in his work, and his involvement in Geometric Abstraction is indicative of the strong presence of this aesthetic tendency in Latin American art, a presence that dates from the 1920s and 1930s. But there are eerie spaces of undefinable mystery in his paintings that recall the more architectonic spatial dramas of Matta. Antúnez's work has a rather ascetic, geometric character, but his dramatic presentations of space are as unsettling as the violent vortexes seen in Matta's work of the mid-1940s. Forms, inevitably rectangular boxes, successively telescope out of one another while suspended in some unknown, horizonless plane of existence. The transparency of the forms gives rise to overlappings that create yet other planar configurations of varying opacity, and occasionally the whole opens up into another cosmos beyond the middle ground of the picture, presenting an almost endless expanse of space. These more astral spaces are sometimes given specific terrestrial locations, such as "underground" play areas, arenas, or city plazas populated by hundreds of minuscule figures dwarfed by the space (plate 118).

Agustín Fernández studied at The Art Students League in New York during the summers of 1949 and 1950, while pursuing his degree in art in Havana.[56] He continued his studies in Madrid, and lived there until 1968, before settling in Puerto Rico. He has exhibited in the United States over the last twenty years, most notably in New York at the Duveen Graham Gallery in 1956, the Condon Riley Gallery in 1958, and at the Bodley Gallery in 1959. Fernández's figurative art seems to have been influenced by the French Fauvists and the idiosyncrasies of Chaim Soutine in the late 1940s. By the mid-1950s Fernández had moved from a schematic Cubism to a more fragmented, biomorphic vocabulary whose morphology is suggested through titles that focus on vegetation and ovum. Reviews of his exhibition in the mid-1950s note a "tropical" character to the color, and a skeletal scaffolding to his structure.[57] By the late 1950s his work resembled the biomorphic figuration of Matta. His figures and background are almost inseparable in the whirling ambience of color and light, which one reviewer described as "lush flamboyant abstractions…which extrapolate from a calligraphic horizon. [The] nucleus of the canvas [is] a cluster of red and yellow shapes like glowing coals [that] radiate outward, fractually diminished until absorbed in the stillness of iridescent blues and greens."[58] There are also references to "primordial" worlds and correlations made between Fernández's work and that of his compatriot Wifredo Lam.[59]

Fernández's characteristic style, which evolved in the early 1960s, features ovoid forms that are suggestive of bodily organs, particularly eyes and sexual organs. The duality and ambiguity of similar forms is an iconographic punning device that has a well-established precedent in classical Surrealism. The most complete explication of it is to be found in the esoteric novelette *Story of the Eye* by Georges Bataille, an early Surrealist associate and the editor of the Surrealist magazine, *Documents*.[60] Observers have in fact cautiously mentioned René Magritte and Salvador Dali as inspirations for Fernández, one in terms of his concepts and the other for his technique. Dali used the eye as a means to demonstrate the perceptual ambiguity inherent in the transitory fleetness of seeing. Magritte's precisely rendered surfaces, which are both sensuous and tactile, influenced the precision of Fernández's depiction.[61] But Fernández's Surrealist tendencies are not as programmed as that of his two predecessors, who remained committed to the accurate portrayal of objects and figures, albeit subverting the empirical relationships set up by traditions of human interaction and etiquette. Instead Fernández's paintings provoke readings that must come out of the viewer's individual libidos and psyches, given the dearth of specifically descriptive material. It is, in fact, Odilon Redon, that ultimate Surrealist predecessor, who surfaces again and again in discussions of Fernández's work.[62] This comparison is especially apt since Fernández eventually abandoned color for a severe black-and-white palette, as did Redon. Concurrently, Fernández's images achieved a more fanciful, highly personalized eroticism that again parallels those of Redon. These compositions are characterized by a texturing, a hatching, and a scumbling of the surfaces; strong, energetic directional lines can also be observed in Redon's work.

Redon also comes to mind when contemplating the obsessive occurrence of ocular forms in the works of Rodolfo Abularach, who has lived in New York City and Central America since the 1960s (plate 119).[63] He received two grants from the Simon Guggenheim Foundation, in 1959 and 1960, and worked at the Pan American Union between 1963 and 1964 and at the Tamarind Lithography Workshop in Los Angeles in 1966. In 1960 Abularach's work was featured in a portfolio presentation in *Art in America* entitled "New Talent USA."[64] The artists, who were presented by John Canaday, art critic for *The New York Times*, were chosen by a jury that included Dorothy C. Miller, Katherine Kuh, David Campbell, William S. Lieberman, Beaumont Newhall, and Henry Russell Hitchcock. A year later, in 1961, Abularach's first gallery exhibition in New York attracted some notices. Reviewers remarked on his meticulously rendered drawings. One noted that the artist was "preoccupied with dramas of radiant whites struggling to emerge through grays and blacks….These painstaking pictures convey an intense mystical vision of cosmic order."[65] Nine years later, when he had his second New York exhibition, his characteristic eye-shaped icons had appeared. The

121

122

Chelo González Amézcua
121. *Corners of King Solomon.* May 15, 1970
Mixed media on paper, 22 x 28″
Courtesy Livia Fernandez, New York
Photo: Quesada/Burke, New York

Félix Bonilla-Norat
122. *Four Beasts, Pegasus, and Woman.* 1954
Oil on canvas, 25½ x 32″
Collection the artist
Photo: John Betancourt, San Juan

artist was quoted as being interested in the eye because "through the eye one can see the world and all its human drama, since all is an extension of the human body."[66] The reviewer conceded that while "all the drawings share a necessary similarity…each one manages a special mystery….the artist's concern is not so much the obvious subject but rather the accurate sensitivity of this organ."[67]

In fact, Abularach's disembodied eyes are thematically close to Redon's work. Redon also presented fanciful eye/suns, and head/flowers. Abularach's eyes are at once flirtatious and foreboding. With their full irises, luscious lashes, and painstaking detail, the eyes are orifices that alternately engage a sexual interest and define the surface of the canvas as the proverbial window into the space beyond the picture plane. While Magritte filled such space with other worlds, Abularach leaves it undefined. And while Magritte transposed the seen and the means of seeing, Abularach in a way returns the eye to its primordial, prophylactic function, evoking the gorgon's awful and fatal stare or the wizard's evil eye. It would not be farfetched to suggest some subliminal relationship between his eyes and the ex-voto or *milagro*, the charm offered up in thanksgiving for the accomplishment of a miracle. While Abularach has been involved in a particularly exhaustive study of the eye over the last two decades, his more recent work consists of skyscapes, in which forms suggest eyes and figures appear subliminally in the clouds.

The Brazilian Marcelo Grassmann, who now works primarily in the graphic medium, manifests in his work similar elements of fantasy and nightmares that may be said to refer to the work of Redon or even the proto-Surrealist fantasies of fifteenth- and sixteenth-century Flemish and German artists (plate 120). His animal, insect, and human forms metamorphosize into improbable and awful hybrids that are suited to our worse nightmares. These apparitions perhaps reached their apogee in the 1950s and 1960s in his "incubi" and "succubi" series.[68] Grassmann's work is known in the United States primarily due to the exhibitions of the Nancy Day Sayles collection of Latin American art, which is housed at the Rhode Island School of Design. (This collection was shown most recently in New York at the Center for Inter-American Relations in the spring of 1987.[69])

Both Matta and Lam have inspired and engendered a multitude of followers in the Latin American art community. After 1950, both of them began to have exhibitions of their work in Latin America, and they both managed to reestablish contact with their native countries, working and communicating with younger artists. Consequently, either through direct contact or by the example of their work, Matta and Lam have continued to provide artists with a means to explore figurative art without narratives. They were also instrumental in making the younger generation conscious of the emotive and even political potential of formal conceits taken not only from European and American modes but also from Amerindian and African sources. The specific stylistic modes utilized by many of these artists are not Surrealist in a traditional sense, but they may evoke the imagery and effects of Surrealism.

Rafael Colón-Morales exemplifies this dynamic. He has been working and teaching in the United States since the early 1970s and is currently curator at El Museo del Barrio in New York City. Over the last twenty years, Colón-Morales has searched for subject matter in the lore and topography of his native Puerto Rico, studying Arawak and Taino artifacts and the symbology implicit in indigenous plant and animal life. The hybrid insects, birds, horses, and humans that populate his compositions are inspired by the "Creolizing" of subject matter that characterized the work of Wifredo Lam. Like Lam, Colón-Morales explored the various meanings that can be visited upon a commonly recognized element in a different context. For example, the appearance of horses in his compositions has been perceived as a political entity, symbolizing the colonial European who introduced the animal to the New World.[70] Two fascinating predecessors can be found for these horses in the work of Picasso and Lam, in which a similar transposition of symbols can be found with two entirely different nuances. In Picasso's work, the horse took on a decidedly female identity, especially when juxtaposed with the bull or the Minotaur, which were distinctly male. In *Guernica* and other compositions the horse represented a passive force. In Colón-Morales's oeuvre, the horse, by contrast, represents the conqueror rather than the conquered. Wifredo Lam utilizes the same form as a *"femme cheval"* (horse-headed woman). But instead of

123

Carlos Raquel Rivera
123. *Fog.* 1961–65
Oil on Masonite, 48⅛ x 65⅛″
Instituto de Cultura Puertorriqueña, San Juan
Photo: Tony Velez

124

Carlos Raquel Rivera
124. *Paroxysm.* 1963
Oil on canvas, 21 ⅜ x 29 ¾″
Instituto de Cultura Puertorriqueña
Photo: John Betancourt, San Juan

being the passive, weak, even victimized symbol, she has taken back her power through a reconnection with her primal cultural roots. She is the devotee who is "ridden" and thus empowered when possessed by the orisha.[71] Thus we can see that through his evocation of a symbol shared by the Surrealist artist Wifredo Lam, who is in turn the Cubist artist influenced by Surrealism, Colón-Morales fulfilled the legacy of the first generation of Latin American artists.

Colón-Morales's older compatriot Félix Bonilla-Norat also featured the bull and horse in his allegorical compositions of the mid-1950s. Bonilla-Norat has trained artists at the serigraph workshop of the Division of Community Education in Puerto Rico and directed the Puerto Rican Artists' Cooperative. He was professor of art at the University of Puerto Rico.[72] (plate 122)

Carlos Raquel Rivera has been cited by critics as manifesting Surrealist elements in his work although his intention is not specifically Surrealist (plates 123 and 124). Rivera's foremost goals have been to manifest the Puerto Rican identity in his art and to convey political communications between artists and the general public. He has understandably worked quite a bit in graphics, but his painting has been characterized by a carefully applied pictorial surface that is expressive. The sociopolitical framework of his art has been constructed in such a way that the "elements…coexist without any apparent rational context and…frequently the juxtaposition of images creates a visual shock which we tend to associate with Surrealism."[73] But Rivera's work is true to its own program, not an outside system of ideas, and focuses mainly on the ability to convince the spectator. Rivera studied at the Edna Coll Academy of Art in San Juan. He went to New York in 1950 to study at The Art Students League with Reginald Marsh and Jon Corbino. After a brief sojourn in New York he decided to return to Puerto Rico, where he quickly became involved with the workshop of Juan Rosado and worked with Rafael Tufiño and Antonio Maldonado. His role as a charter member of the Centro de Arte Puertorriqueño influenced and formulated his artistic purpose and identity.

The Surrealists had a special feeling for the work of untutored or nonacademic artists. Indeed, their appreciation for the stylistic conventions adopted by Frida Kahlo sometimes led to more apocryphal assertions of her naiveté and simplicity that are quite unfounded. There are three Latin American artists—among others—who have pursued this particular strain of art in the United States. In the case of one artist—Pedro Friedeberg, who was a trained architect, the more folk manifestations seem to be a more self-conscious tactic—as was the case with Kahlo. In the case of Chelo González Amézcua and Manuel Ramírez, on the other hand, the stylistic characteristics are the result of their compulsive, even obsessive need to make art, which is characteristic of "true" folk or naive artists.

Pedro Friedeberg's work is characterized by a quirky, personal approach to representation that has been called "Surrealist" (plate 125). Born in Italy in 1937, he emigrated to Mexico as a child.[74] Friedeberg was trained as an architect at the Ibero-American University in Mexico, and he later studied art with the German-Mexican painter and sculptor Mathias Goeritz. Friedeberg's architectural drawings manifest a compulsively decorative quality that can be compared with González Amézcua's art, but his sense of perspective and the provenance of his decorative motifs point to his more tutored background. The illusionistic effects of his drawings seem as complex as the patterns of Escher. His playful assemblages of decorative motifs and positioning of architectural plans along the contours of such atypical shapes as butterflies rest squarely within the tradition of architectural designs for follies and the utopian idealism of late-eighteenth-century French architects such as Boullé. His sculpture, which features chairs in the shapes of hands and various multilegged hybrid creations—often with as many heads and arms—is akin to the anatomical anomalies that were favored by such Surrealists as Dali, Victor Brauner, and Hans Bellmer.

Although Friedeberg did not begin to exhibit his work until the 1960s—long after the heyday of the Surrealist movement—André Breton pronounced his compositions to be "among the most fully realized works in the Surrealist manner."[75] His gallery shows in New York City during this decade seem to have generated quite strong reactions. His architectural drawings were appreciated for their adroit exploitation of optical effects,[76] due, no doubt, to the currency of the Op art movement. His furniture

125

Pedro Friedeberg
125. *Musical Madhouses in Mesopotamia.* 1960
Ink and acrylic on board, 30 x 40″
Collection the artist
Photo: courtesy the artist

seems to have caused more controversy, and there were critical approbations against "a certain cuteness,"[77] although they were appreciated for their disconcerting and bizarre character. The designs were featured in a portfolio presentation that the critic B. H. Friedman presented in the summer 1964 issue of *Art in America*. Friedeberg's furniture fantasies were seen along with those of other artists with more Surreal and fantastic bents, such as Joann Beall [Westermann], Lee Krasner, Arman, Man Ray, Alfonso Ossorio, William Copley, Isamu Noguchi, Alexander Calder, and Harry Bertoia.[78]

Chelo González Amézcua was a self-taught artist who persisted in her aim to make art in spite of the fact that family circumstances prevented her from following her dream of studying art formally.[79] Born in Mexico, she lived her entire life in Del Rio, Texas. González Amézcua combined writing—poems and mythological tales—with the imagery of ancient Aztec personages to create works of a highly personal character. Using only ballpoint pens on paper or cardboard, she created intricate presentations of specific rulers and cultural heroes of pre-Columbian and Amerindian cultures. She herself dubbed these webs of line "filigree art," observing their closeness to the intricate metalwork used frequently in Mexico to make earrings and bracelets (plate 121).

The compulsive side of González Amézcua's art is also found in the work of Manuel Ramírez, a Mexican American laborer who lived in California. He began making art when he was hospitalized for mental disorders in 1930.[80] Like González Amézcua, Ramírez was infatuated with the memory of elegant, chivalrous, and decorative figures and episodes from his Mexican and Amerindian heritage, although his depictions were not as specifically historical as González Amézcua's. Despite the obvious difficulties in obtaining materials to make his work, Ramírez demonstrated an uncanny ability to work on a relatively large scale. He collaged bits of paper—cups, envelopes, paper bags—with a paste he concocted out of saliva and mashed potatoes. He then drew his elaborate allegories in pencil, colored pencils, and crayons; occasionally he collaged photographs from magazines onto the images. It became easier for him to continue making art once he had the support and understanding of Dr. Tarmo Pasto, a teacher of abnormal psychology who became acquainted with the artist later in his life. Ramírez died in 1960, and in 1968 the Chicago artist Jim Nutt and his wife, Gladys Nilsson, came across the works that Pasto had collected from a number of psychotic patients, including Ramírez. Their interest in Ramírez's art led them to show it to Nutt's dealer, Phyllis Kind, who has exhibited the work in her galleries in Chicago and New York over the last fifteen years. Ramírez has since received widespread notice, particularly with the recently renewed interest in the art of the so-called "outsiders."[81] In the catalog for the exhibition *Hispanic Art in the United States* at the Corcoran Gallery in Washington, D.C., Octavio Paz extolled Ramírez as an emblem of Hispanic artists and communities in the United States: "The contradictory currents that animated his life—an immersion in the self and an escape toward the outside, toward an encounter with the world...is a metaphor for the condition of the Hispanic artist."[82]

With the recent resurgence of interest in art produced by artists of a Latin American heritage—both those working in South and Central America and the Caribbean and those working in the United States—their contribution to the art world begins to be illuminated. Although they have not been recognized since the 1940s, it is clear that Latin artists have been diligent carriers of the Surrealist and the expressively figurative strain in contemporary art. This aesthetic has seen a resurgence in the 1980s. There is a full-scale embrace of Surrealism's mythological, religious, and autobiographical manifestations under the guise of "New Figuration" or "Neo-Expressionism." This has accompanied the identification of a specific Latin American market by auction houses and galleries. But while all this has helped to increase an awareness of the presence of Latin American artists working specifically within the art world in the United States, it has also posed problems for the art historian and the critic. If this survey indicates nothing else, it should indicate the inadequacy of an overall rubric such as "Latin American." Given the immense diversity of considerations that come into presenting a profile of persons of Latin American descent—birthplace, education, habitation modes, artistic interests, class and economic status, not to mention specific national identities—it is clear that generalizations about Latin Americans are foolhardy. It will be the task of future investigations to delineate the specifics of this situation with more precision and care. It will be sufficient now just to have demonstrated the consistent and crucial contributions that Latin American artists have made to international art.

The United States and Socially Concerned Latin American Art: 1920–1970

by Eva Cockcroft

The Mexican Mural Renaissance

Latin American art still provokes in the minds of many people in the United States images of marching masses and revolution. The association of Latin American art with Social Realism in general and the Mexican School in particular developed because of the profound influence the three great muralists—Rivera, Siqueiros, and Orozco—had on American artists during the years between the two world wars. It is an association that remains with us today despite intensive campaigns in the United States since the mid-1940s to destroy it and to promote instead Latin American abstraction of the so-called International Style.

The ability of the Mexican muralists, in particular Diego Rivera, to create and mold our knowledge of Latin American art was the result of several factors. It was certainly important that Rivera was accorded by modernists the prestige attached to a member of the French Cubist group. In a period when U.S. art was no less provincial than that of Latin America, Rivera's work was exhibited in New York together with works by Picasso, Braque, Picabia, Cézanne, and Van Gogh.[1] In the 1920s young artists from the United States, just like those from the nations to the south, still traveled to Europe to study the masters and to bring back the latest art fashion. In spite of the influence of the 1913 Armory Show on the eventual development of American abstraction, in the 1920s there was still little understanding or sympathy for the small and largely imitative abstract movement in the United States. Barbara Rose, a sympathetic commentator on modernism, notes in *American Art since 1900*, one of the classic texts on the subject:

Even the efforts of some artists, such as William and Marguerite Zorach and Konrad Cramer, who had a firmer grasp of Cubism because they had watched it develop in Europe, were remarkable only because they were early examples of modern painting in America, not because they were successful Cubist pictures....To be an American Cubist was by definition to be an imitator.[2]

Because Rivera was an integral part of the Cubist movement in Paris and his murals showed a secure grasp of Cubist composition, his work from the 1920s was appealing not only to his most likely constituency, North American Realists, but also to modernists.

The search for an "American" style of painting, which dominated art criticism during the 1920s and 1930s, was a symptom of the sense of inferiority felt by the U.S. art world. It was also a symptom of isolationist sentiments following World War I. On the political stage isolationism was manifested in the Red scares, tough new immigration laws, and the execution of the "foreign subversives" Sacco and Vanzetti in 1927. In the artistic arena, fewer artists experimented with modern Parisian styles. It was felt that increased industrialization and the massive migration of Americans to the cities had led to the loss of solid moral values. American Scene painters and Regionalists tried to recapture the "good old days" through nostalgic depictions of rural scenes.

Other artists, responding to the injustices of the economic depression of the 1930s, were influenced by left-wing movements and began to use art as a tool for social criticism. For these artists, the Mexican example of an avant-garde, nationalistic art at the service of social concern provided an almost irresistible model. In his book *A History of American Painting*, the art historian Matthew Baigell credits the Mexican muralists with providing the crucial inspiration: "Without the combination of an unprecedented economic depression and Mexican influence, there probably would not have been an art of social realism in this country."[3]

The historian Francis V. O'Connor has also noted the factor of timing, which was so crucial to the strength of the Mexican influence:

One of the phenomena of twentieth-century art in the Americas is that Mexico produced two such artists (Rivera and Orozco) at a time when the United States, having lost Albert Ryder in 1917, exiled Arthur Dove to his houseboat in 1920, and not yet aware of the strength of Thomas Hart Benton and Stuart Davis, possessed not one artist of comparable stature. Unlike marginal modernists of the 1920s, such as Edward Hopper, John Marin, Alfred Mauer, Charles Sheeler, and Max Weber, who were still trying to figure out what happened at the Armory Show so they could imitate it, the Mexicans were busy misreading the School of Paris, the Italian Renaissance, and their own indigenous culture within the ideological context of Marxism. That the Mexicans were influential in the United States during the 1930s is not surprising; they filled a cultural and ideological vacuum.[4]

The flamboyant personalities of these artists and the controversy and media attention their activities engendered also contributed to the immense impact they were able to have on the U.S. art scene—in spite of a certain level of disregard that North Americans have felt for Latin Americans since the days of the Alamo and the declaration of the Monroe Doctrine. From 1927 to 1934, when the anti-Communist fervor of the Calles presidency in Mexico forced the muralists to search for more liberal pastures to the north, each of the *tres grandes*, as they are now called, spent time painting in the United States. This was when people in the United States not only received a firsthand view of the new fresco painting but also were introduced to three powerful and distinctive personalities.

Diego Rivera, who had an extraordinary talent for controversy and scandal, naturally captured the lion's share of attention. Even before his arrival in the United States in 1930, Rivera's work and philosophy were quite well known in this country. From 1923 to 1925 eight articles about the Mexican movement had appeared, most of them published in art magazines.[5] Of these, three focused on Rivera, one on Orozco, and two already referred to the movement as a "renaissance." In addition, the influential art critic Walter Pach included the Mexican movement and Rivera in his book *Masters of Modern Art*, which appeared in 1923. In 1929, one year before Rivera's and Orozco's first U.S. commissions, two books on Mexican art appeared. Ernestine Evans's lavishly illustrated *The Frescos of Diego Rivera* and Anita Brenner's pathbreaking *Idols Behind Altars*, which put forth what became the standard interpretation of the Mexican movement.

Ironically, interest in the Mexican muralists and the organization of exhibitions of their work in the United States after 1927 were encouraged by improved relations between the governments of Mexico and the United States. This newfound harmony was the direct result of the conservative attitudes of the Calles presidency, the same government that had discouraged further mural work in Mexico itself. Soon after the appointment of Dwight Morrow as ambassador to Mexico in 1927, Mexico's oil concessions were returned to their foreign owners in perpetuity, the foreign debt was renegotiated, and the interests of foreign capital guaranteed. Ambassador Morrow, an astute diplomat, catered to Mexican nationalistic pride by furnishing his home with Mexican handicrafts. He also commissioned a mural by Rivera for the Palace of Cortés in Cuernavaca as a gift from the United States to Mexico, and he proposed a massive exhibition of Mexican art be organized by René d'Harnoncourt in cooperation with the Mexican government for the Metropolitan Museum of Art in New York.

Rivera arrived in San Francisco in November 1930 shortly after the opening of the Metropolitan Museum exhibition, which included a few of his paintings. To coincide with a commission he had received for a mural at the San Francisco Stock Exchange, a large retrospective of his work was mounted at the San Francisco Palace of the Legion of

126

127

Diego Rivera
126. *The Forge.* 1931
Ink on paper, 36 x 30½"
Collection Alma Elizabeth del Río, Mexico City.
Courtesy Galería Arvil, Mexico City
Photo: Crispin Vasquez

Diego Rivera
127. *Man at the Crossroads.* 1932
Pencil on paper, 24¼ x 61¾"
Collection The Museum of Modern Art, New York
Photo: courtesy The Museum of Modern Art

Honor. The San Francisco murals were well received, and a contract was soon signed for Rivera's next project, a mural in Detroit (funded by Edsel Ford). Shortly thereafter an exhibition of Rivera's work was put on display at the Detroit Institute of the Arts.

Both the San Francisco and the Detroit murals celebrated the advances of technology, science, and the worker without being specifically critical of the bourgeoisie. A minor scandal erupted on the completion of the Detroit mural when a small scene of a vaccination was accused of being antireligious. After Edsel Ford publicly stated his support for the mural, Rivera's popularity remained intact, and his next commission at Rockefeller Center was unaffected.

A relationship between Rivera and the Rockefeller family began in July 1931. The artist was offered a solo exhibition at the new Museum of Modern Art, which had been founded by Abby Aldrich Rockefeller and her friends. Rivera had the second solo exhibition at the museum (Matisse had the first). The exhibition included 8 portable fresco panels, 143 paintings, and several works on paper. It was seen by almost fifty-seven thousand people.[6] In addition to the catalog, the museum also published a portfolio of color prints reproducing a selection of Rivera's most important Mexican murals. Shortly before the exhibition opened, Mrs. Rockefeller bought for her collection a sketchbook Rivera had created after seeing the 1928 May Day parade in the Soviet Union.[7]

The Rockefeller Center mural, *Man at the Crossroads* (plate 127), commissioned by Nelson Rockefeller for his new office complex, was not very different from Rivera's other work in the United States. It eulogized the advances of science and technology and idealized the worker, who was placed in the center of the picture at the controls of a machine. However, Rivera's inclusion of a portrait of Lenin as a symbol of the future enraged the Rockefellers. When Rivera refused to remove the portrait, the mural was covered and then destroyed. It became a cause célèbre. If Rivera had been well known in the United States before 1933, after the Rockefeller Center scandal he became a household name. There were news stories, meetings, debates, articles, and even a satirical poem ridiculing Rockefeller by E. B. White.[8] After the controversy, Rivera's prospects for future commissions in this country disappeared. He took the money from the Rockefeller commission and used it to paint a Marxist version of U.S. history, entitled *Portrait of America*, at the New Workers School in New York.

Although Orozco arrived in New York in 1927, he did not receive his first mural commission in the United States until 1930, when he went to California to paint *Prometheus* at Pomona College in Claremont. In 1931, while deeply influenced by theories of dynamic symmetry (which he in fact abandoned after this project), Orozco painted a series of frescoes at the New School for Social Research.[9] Dealing with the themes of universal brotherhood and world revolution, these murals included stiffly painted portraits of Gandhi, Lenin, and Felipe Carillo Puerto. From 1932 to 1934, after a trip to Europe, Orozco worked on murals for the Dartmouth College library, his most important U.S. commission (plate 128). The theme he addressed at Dartmouth was the rise of American civilization, which included the story of Quetzalcoatl, the legendary white god who brought art and culture to the Toltec civilization of pre-Columbian Mexico. While there was some controversy about the fact that such an important commission had been given to a foreign artist, the murals were vigorously defended in the art world, and they received a great deal of acclaim. Edward Alden Jewell, in *The New York Times* of February 25, 1934, called this work "instinct with genius" and "the finest mural accomplishment to date, from any hand, in the United States."

In 1932, while Rivera was at work in Detroit and Orozco at Dartmouth, Siqueiros arrived in Los Angeles to teach fresco painting at the Chouinard School of Art. Working with a team of young artists, he painted three murals, the most important of which was *Tropical America*, created for a courtyard on Olvera Street. A rather direct criticism of U.S. imperialism, the mural showed a Mexican *peón* crucified under the spreading wings of a gigantic eagle. In making these murals, Siqueiros was already experimenting with industrial paints and spray guns. Because of the patron's objections to the subject matter, the mural was whitewashed shortly after its completion, and Siqueiros moved on to Argentina. In 1934 he visited New York for an exhibition at the Delphic Studios. He returned to New York again in 1936 to set up the Experimental

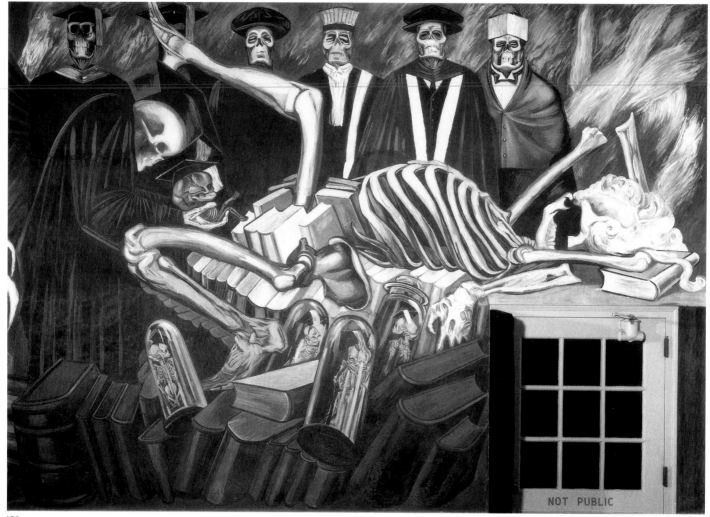

128

José Clemente Orozco
128. *The Epic of American Civilization; Gods of the
Modern World.* 1932–34
Fresco, Dartmouth College, Hanover, New
Hampshire
Courtesy the Trustees of Dartmouth College
Photo: courtesy Hood Museum of Art,
Dartmouth College

Art Workshop, where he continued to experiment with industrial materials and photography for mural painting (plate 129). Jackson Pollock, then a young artist, participated in the workshop's activities.

With the rise to power in Mexico of the populist president Lázaro Cárdenas in 1934 and renewed government support for the mural movement, Rivera, Orozco, and Siqueiros returned home to create the great murals of their mature period. Rivera was invited to paint at Bellas Artes (where he re-created the Rockefeller Center painting, *Man at the Crossroads*) and the National Palace. Orozco was commissioned to paint the interior domes of the Great Hall of the University of Guadalajara and the Hospicio Cabanas in Guadalajara, where he painted the culmination of his Prometheus imagery, *Man in Flames*. Siqueiros returned to Mexico City to paint his stirring appeal against fascism at the Electrical Workers Union building, *Portrait of the Bourgeoisie*.

Although the American fascination with the Mexican "Communist" muralists ended in 1934, their direct influence in this country was only beginning to be felt. Indeed, the Mexican mural renaissance was cited by artist George Biddle (who was to head the WPA artists program) in a 1933 letter to President Franklin Delano Roosevelt proposing a government-sponsored public art program.

The Mexican artists have produced the greatest national school of mural painting since the Italian Renaissance. Diego Rivera tells me that it was only possible because [Mexican president] Obregón allowed Mexican artists to work at plumbers' wages in order to express on the walls of the government buildings the social ideals of the Mexican revolution.

The younger artists of America are conscious as they have never been of the social revolution that our country and civilization are going through; and they would be eager to express these ideals in a permanent art form if they were given the government's cooperation.[10]

The first of the New Deal's artist programs, the PWAP (Public Works of Art Program), was begun a few months after this letter was written. Of the social muralists of the 1930s, Victor Arnautoff (the Coit Tower murals), Ben Shahn, George Biddle, Marion Greenwood, and Lucienne Bloch, among others, had worked directly with Rivera, and his influence was clearly reflected in their work. A good case for Rivera's influence on Thomas Hart Benton has been made as well.[11] Benton had already ventured into mural painting by 1930, but he was certainly familiar with Rivera's Mexican mural work, which had already been reproduced in the United States in the 1920s.

Each of the *tres grandes* exerted an important influence on later U.S. and Latin American art. Diego Rivera was most directly influential in the United States during the 1930s and 1940s, when the muralists, Social Realists, and Regionalists closely studied his example. Rivera's influence continued to be seen in the 1950s in the mural work of black American artists, including Charles White, John Biggers, and Hale Woodruff. Rivera's work was also important to William Walker, the father of the contemporary mural movement, which began in the late 1960s.[12] Orozco's expressionist style, his caricatures, drawings, and humanist statements set important precedents for the Neo-Humanist movement of the late 1950s and early 1960s, both in Mexico and the United States. The influence of Siqueiros was twofold. Initially, his use of Duco and other experimental mural painting techniques was his most significant contribution. However, with the resurgence of muralism in the United States in the late 1960s and early 1970s, especially among the Chicanos of California, Texas, and New Mexico, Siqueiros's dynamic compositions, with their spatial distortions and inverse perspectives, became an important model.

From the beginning, the Mexican movement extended beyond muralism to include the graphic arts. Indeed, the satirical engravings of José Guadalupe Posada, who popularized the use of traditional Mexican symbols like the *calavera*, or skeleton, to comment on political events, were cited as a source of inspiration by both Rivera and Orozco. Drawings and caricatures by Orozco, Siqueiros, Javier Guerrero, and others of the original group of muralists were published regularly in the newspaper *El Machete*, which was the organ of the Syndicate of Technical Workers, Painters, and Sculptors,

129

David Alfaro Siqueiros
129. *The Challenge.* 1954
Pyroxylin on Masonite, 79¼ x 69⅝"
Courtesy Galería Arvil, Mexico City
Photo: Gerardo Suter

the muralists' union.

In 1937, during the post-Cárdenas revival of muralism in Mexico, a group of artists from a second artists' union, LEAR, including Leopoldo Méndez and Alfredo Zalce, founded the Taller de Gráfica Popular (TGP). This was a cooperative print workshop that published portfolios and individual prints on revolutionary subjects in order to educate the public on social issues. As before, the lines between graphic art and muralism were quite fluid: both Méndez and Zalce were also important figures in the second generation of muralists in Mexico.

The work of Méndez and the TGP emphasized the creation of clearly legible political messages. Conventional symbols, such as the eagle, cactus, or snake, were used, and events from the Mexican Revolution and difficult moments in peasant life were frequently illustrated. The preferred medium was the linoleum print. If its clear contrasts of black and white were emphasized, it could have a very direct impact. The Museum of Modern Art bought several prints by Méndez, and his work was well received in the United States. The major impact of the TGP in this country, however, was indirect. The workshop influenced other Latin American printmakers, whose work in turn was seen in the United States, a development that was especially important during the 1950s as well as later when painting was dominated by abstraction and the graphic medium offered the only acceptable approach for the artistic expression of social content.

Another important influence of the TGP was the example of the workshop system itself: the artists collaborated to support the venture's equipment and publications. The workshop form of organization became the model for Latin American print production, and similar enterprises have been important in the development of graphic movements in Puerto Rico and Cuba and among Chicanos in the United States.

From Nationalistic Realism to Abstraction: The 1940s

The influence that the Mexican muralists had on monumental Realist painting was also important for Latin American artists. Three Latin American Realists who exhibited frequently in New York during the 1940s, Héctor Poleo of Venezuela, Mario Carreño of Cuba, and Antonio Berni of Argentina, were directly influenced by the Mexicans. The Brazilian Candido Portinari was also at least indirectly affected.[13] Carreño and Poleo both went to Mexico to study in the mid-1930s, while Berni was influenced by Siqueiros during the Mexican's stay in Argentina in 1933. These three artists, along with Portinari, were the leading figures in the second wave of Latin American Realists to be influential in the United States.

The importance the tres grandes had given to monumentality was stressed by U.S. critics who reviewed the second generation. However, attempts were made to separate this new group of Latin American artists from their politically active predecessors. For example, José Gómez Sicre, director of the Pan American Union in Washington, D.C., in his introduction to Mario Carreño's one-man show at the union in 1947, acknowledged the influence of Diego Rivera on some of Carreño's earlier work—a factor which had led Carreño to study in Mexico. "But there," Gómez Sicre claimed, Carreño had "recoiled from the impact of the intense interest in politics characteristic of the new art movement…reacted in the opposite direction and devoted himself to technical studies in which the ideologies that hitherto had been his greatest preoccupation had no part. Nevertheless, the Mexican school influenced his work, especially in the monumental sculptural quality of his figures."[14]

During this period, even the work of the Mexicans themselves began to be described as "nationalistic" rather than political. In the foreword to the 1940 Museum of Modern Art exhibition catalog Twenty Centuries of Mexican Art, the writer states: "The social and political content expressed by the Mexican mural painters was conspicuous, but equally important was their strong nationalism." The writer goes on to stress the artists' interest in ancient art and folk art.[15]

United States critics treated Portinari as the Brazilian equivalent of Rivera—but without the Mexican's dangerous politics. Writing in 1940, Robert C. Smith made this comparison abundantly clear: "Unlike the Mexicans he [Portinari] has no didactic social message to expound. But what he has observed he states with sympathy and dignity, untouched by propaganda."[16] In the mid-1930s Portinari was painting scenes of peasant labor and festivities similar in subject matter and style to Rivera's 1923–28 depictions of laborers and their fiestas in the patios of the Ministry of Education in Mexico City. Portinari's paintings of this period, like Rivera's, express the natural dignity of the worker and demonstrate his knowledge of Cubist composition. Unlike Rivera, however, Portinari did not condemn the injustice inherent in the workers' poverty or point an accusatory finger at capitalism or the rich. Portinari's painting *Coffee*, a sympathetic treatment of coffee pickers on a Brazilian plantation, won a mention at the *Pittsburgh International Exhibition* of 1935 (plate 130). In 1938, The Museum of Modern Art bought his painting *The Slum* (plate 131), and in 1940 the museum gave him a one-man exhibition, entitled *Portinari of Brazil*.

The emphasis on the artist's nationality in the title is significant. It implies that the exhibition was not only in honor of Portinari's work, it was also in honor of a representative of Brazilian art—a kind of "cultural ambassador." The emphasis on cultural exchange was made quite clear by Rockwell Kent in his introduction to a book of Portinari's work published by the University of Chicago Press in 1941. Kent described a conference sponsored by the Department of State on "Inter-American Relations in the Field of Art" in 1939 that was "actuated by the worthy hope that something in these trying times might somehow be contrived and set afoot to bring the peoples of the Western world in closer cultural sympathy."[17]

According to Kent, Portinari's paintings celebrate the Brazil the artist knew, rather than criticizing its poverty: "We see its workers and their poverty—not agonized about, just told. And told with love.... 'Blessed are the meek' would seem to be the utterance from his heart."[18] In case this art still did not seem safe enough after the controversial Marxist Mexicans, Josias Leao explicitly stated in his description of Portinari's life in the same book: "He does not discuss politics—which he believes disgusting. He thinks of the war only in terms of its possible implications on the lives and works of the painters and their freedom of expression."[19]

Although the United States had not yet entered the war against fascism in 1940, the struggle in Europe was already a major topic of debate and concern. With the fall of Poland, Holland, and Belgium and the entrance of England and France into the war by 1940, sentiment for direct U.S. involvement was rising.

The flurry of exhibitions of Latin American art during the war years was directly related to U.S. concerns about Latin American sympathy for German, Italian, and Spanish fascism and fears of an Axis infiltration of the Western Hemisphere. In spite of strong profascist sentiments in Brazil, the Vargas government was persuaded to join the Allies. Argentina, however, where the pro-Axis elements were dominant, remained neutral. Profascist sentiments in Mexico and oil-rich Venezuela were also of concern to Washington. Thus, throughout World War II a concerted effort to woo Latin American nations into hemispheric unity and defense pacts was carried out in both the economic and cultural spheres.

In 1939 Nelson Rockefeller resigned his position as president of The Museum of Modern Art's board of directors to become Roosevelt's coordinator of the Office of Inter-American Affairs. (Later he was appointed assistant secretary of state for Latin American Affairs.) During the war years, The Museum of Modern Art organized nineteen exhibitions of contemporary American painting for Rockefeller's department to tour throughout Latin America. That this was a conscious part of the war effort was made clear in a Central Press wire story in June 1941 that heralded the museum as the "latest and strangest recruit in Uncle Sam's defense line-up."[20]

From 1940 to 1945 there were eight exhibitions of Latin American art at The Museum of Modern Art alone, five of them with catalogs.[21] In 1940, in addition to the Portinari show, the museum also hosted the extensive *Twenty Centuries of Mexican Art*. In 1942 The Museum of Modern Art sponsored a "Design Competition for 21 American Republics" and a "Poster Competition from a United Hemisphere."[22] The emphasis on Brazilian art continued in 1943 with the exhibition *Brazil Constructs*, which was accompanied by a book of photographs by G.E. Kidder-Smith. A show of Cuban painting in 1944 included younger artists like Mario Carreño, René Portacarrero, Cundo Bermúdez, and Mariano Rodríguez as well as more established modernists such as Amelia Peláez.

130

131

132

Candido Portinari
130. *Coffee.* 1935
Oil on canvas, 51¼ x 76⅞"
Museu Nacional de Belas Artes, Rio de Janeiro
Photo: courtesy Museu Nacional de Belas Artes,
Rio de Janeiro

Candido Portinari
131. *The Slum.* 1933
Oil on canvas, 44⅞ x 57½"
Collection The Museum of Modern Art, New York.
Abby Aldrich Rockefeller Fund
Photo: courtesy The Museum of Modern Art

José Sabogal
132. *The Antiquarian.* 1949
Woodcut on paper, 11½ x 9⅛"
Collection Isabel Sabogal de Málaga, Lima, Peru
Photo: courtesy Isabel Sabogal de Málaga

The museum was also encouraged to purchase Latin American art during the war years. In 1943 an exhibition and catalog of the museum's Latin American collection were produced. The collection was begun in 1935 when Abby Rockefeller donated Orozco's 1928 painting *The Subway* to The Museum of Modern Art. In 1942, the Inter-American Fund provided the money for the purchase of 195 works. These, along with 29 donated works, constituted the 1943 exhibition. Although a smaller exhibition (without a catalog) of Latin American art from the museum's collection was held in 1967 in conjunction with Pan American week, no major exhibitions of modern Latin American painting and sculpture organized by The Museum of Modern Art have been held at the museum since the 1940s.[23]

The 1943 exhibition of The Museum of Modern Art's Latin American collection included two other national Realist painters, José Sabogal (plate 132) of Peru and Oswaldo Guayasamín of Ecuador, who were exhibited in the United States during the 1940s. Subsequently, they were largely ignored in this country, although each of them went on to found a national school of indigenist painting. During a trip to Ecuador in 1942, Nelson Rockefeller bought five of Guayasamín's paintings and arranged for the twenty-three-year-old artist to visit the U.S. for six months. After his visit, Guayasamín went to Mexico, where he worked with Orozco, and then on a journey throughout South America. His travels inspired a series of 103 paintings entitled *Huacaynán* (The Way of Tears) honoring the mestizo, Indian, and Negro cultures of Latin America. In his only other U.S. exhibition, paintings from *Huacaynán* were shown at the Pan American Union in 1955.

The establishment of the Pan American Union's exhibition program in Washington, D.C., in the mid-1940s marked the beginning of the ghettoization of Latin American art. Thereafter, the union became the primary avenue for Latin American art entering this country. For twenty years, its director, José Gómez Sicre was the most important tastemaker in this field. Most new young Latin American artists were introduced to this country by one-person shows at the union. The necessity for a separate showcase for Latin American art that the union represented symbolized the removal of this art from mainstream exhibition channels like The Museum of Modern Art in the postwar period. With the exception of a few international art-world giants like Wifredo Lam and Roberto Matta, who came to New York with reputations that had been made in Paris, Latin American artists are still poorly represented in exhibitions by mainstream institutions and in the permanent collections of major museums in the United States. While specialized institutions such as the Pan American Union (now the Museum of Modern Art of Latin America) and the Center for Inter-American Relations (CIR) in New York are places where Latin American art can be seen in this country, they do not reach the general public with anything like the success of the major museums and galleries.

The effects of the growing strength of the abstract movement and the corresponding decline of Social Realism in the United States were already evident in The Museum of Modern Art's Mexican exhibition of 1940. Orozco, the least "Communist" of the *tres grandes*, was invited to execute a special fresco as part of the exhibition. *"Dive Bomber"* or *Six Interchangeable Panels* was one of Orozco's few attempts at abstraction. MacKinley Helm, Orozco's biographer, saw this work as an unsuccessful attempt by an artist "aware of The Museum of Modern Art's partiality to formalist painting" to worship at the "newest of churches."[24]

The pamphlet that accompanied the mural, "Orozco Explains," gives an insight into the temper of the times. Adopting a traditional modernist stance, the artist condemned the whole idea of explanation:

The public wants explanations about a painting. What the artist had in mind when he did it. What he was thinking of…if he is glorifying or cursing. If he believes in Democracy [emphasis added].[25]

That even Orozco was willing to experiment with formalist painting is an indication of the increasing strength of the reaction against Social Realism within U.S. art circles at this time. The Mexican artist who was most strongly promoted during this period was Rufino Tamayo, whose work was seen as being both "abstract" and "Mexican" in its embodiment of the Indian spirit. Realistic depictions of Indian subjects by the Mexican Francisco Dosamantes and the Guatemalan Carlos Mérida were also popular in New York and Washington during the war years.

In spite of the growing support for abstraction among the avant-garde in the 1940s, Regionalism and mural painting continued to be important until the mid-1950s. That Portinari, like Rivera and Orozco, also painted murals made him an ideal replacement for the Mexicans in the public's mind. His heroic black figures were more controversial in Brazil (where the white elite objected to that image of their nation) than in the United States. In addition, as Smith noted in The Museum of Modern Art catalog, just as Charlot, Rivera, and Orozco painted the Indian and the mestizo, Portinari "is the foremost interpreter of that great force which is daily growing more articulate—the Negro of the Americas."[26] In 1941 he was invited to paint a series of murals for the Hispanic Foundation of the Library of Congress, a project sponsored jointly by Brazil and the United States.

In writing about Portinari's murals for the Library of Congress in 1950 (plates 133–34), the Brazilian art critic Mario Pedrosa attempted to distinguish the work of Portinari from that of the Mexicans and the School of Paris. First, he credited Picasso, whose work Portinari saw during his trip to Paris in 1928, rather than Rivera for the Cubist influence in Portinari's mural compositions, although he granted some credit to the Mexican for Portinari's Ministry of Education murals. It is the difference in aim rather than means that Pedrosa found significant: "the attainment of monumentality and massiveness of form by the Brazilian artist on the one hand, and the expression of social consciousness by the Mexican mural movement, on the other…"[27] While never subordinating "plastic expression to subject matter," Portinari, according to Pedrosa, also was part of "a daring attempt" on this continent to "restore to subject matter its artistic dignity, which had been lost in the purely analytical phases of modern art and…to reintegrate in painting, from which he had been excluded, man as a human being and as a social entity."[28]

Portinari's humanist perspective dominated his approach to his most ambitious and political mural, a nine-hundred-square-foot painting condemning the excesses of war. Entitled *War and Peace*, it was commissioned by Brazil for the General Assembly of the United Nations in New York. Ironically, considering the previous attempts to depoliticize his art, when the work was installed in 1953 *Time* magazine referred to Portinari as an "avowed communist." Its critic categorized his mural with Picasso's *War and Peace* mural for the Vallauris chapel as two "Murals from the Party." However, *Time* did quote Portinari as stating that his murals "have no party intention…they are the point of view of mankind."[29]

The canvases from the early 1940s of the Venezuelan Héctor Poleo offer another version of the monumental treatment of peasant figures. In addition to strong outlines and meticulously painted details, Poleo's work of this period is characterized by mystery and emotion that portend his later Surrealist phase. In his *Comisarios*, one of his most powerful works from the mid-1940s, a trio of mysterious figures is seen from behind, their faces hidden by sombreros and their bodies covered by shawls. They loom over a mountain village more like bandits plotting an ambush than lawmen. Another work from this period, *Andean Family*, places a group of mysteriously isolated figures before a Venezuelan mountain landscape (plate 135).

Poleo gave his peasant figures a dignity and respect far above their station in Venezuelan society. Yet during this period his work became synonymous with Venezuelan art in the United States. Poleo's paintings, like those of Portinari, Berni, and Carreño, were included in the Riverside Museum's *Latin American Exhibition* during the New York World's Fair of 1939. After an exhibition at the Seligmann Gallery in New York in 1943, Poleo moved to New York and lived there from 1944 to 1948. In 1945 his work was exhibited at the Pan American Union in Washington and included in the *Arts Fiesta of the Americas* at the Grand Central Galleries in New York. After 1945, Poleo turned from Venezuelan subject matter to Surrealism. After moving to Paris in 1959, he painted amorphous and lyrical abstractions.

Like Poleo, Mario Carreño lived intermittently in New York during the

133

134

Candido Portinari
133. *The Discovery. Sketch for "Discovery of the Americas"*
(mural at The Hispanic Foundation, The Library of
Congress, Washington, D.C.). 1941
Gouache on paper, 11⅝ x 11⅜″
Prints and Photographs Division, The Library of
Congress, Washington, D.C.
Photo: courtesy The Library of Congress

Candido Portinari
134. *Discovery of the Americas (detail)*. 1941–42
Mural, The Hispanic Foundation, The Library of
Congress, Washington, D.C.
Photo: courtesy The Library of Congress

135

Hector Poleo
135. *Andean Family.* 1944
Oil on canvas, 27 1/2 x 23"
The Museum of Modern Art of Latin America,
Organization of American States, Washington, D.C.
Photo: Angel Hurtado

136

Antonio Berni
136. *New Chicago Athletic Club.* 1937
Oil on canvas, 72¾″ x 118¼″
Collection The Museum of Modern Art, New York.
Inter-American Fund
Photo: courtesy The Museum of Modern Art,
New York

1940s. In 1941, Carreño began to show with the Perls Gallery. After a youthful phase as a Cubist antigovernment cartoonist in Havana, he became a Social Realist. Some of his early Realist work was characterized by references to classical Italian painting, especially shortly after his return from Europe in 1939. In 1943, when Siqueiros was in Havana, Carreño began to experiment with industrial paints like Duco. For several years Carreño painted brightly colored figurative compositions and Cubistic village landscapes. It was for this national Realist work that Carreño became known in New York. Alfred H. Barr, Jr., writing in The Museum of Modern Art *Bulletin*, was impressed by the artist's use of Duco in his large, monumental figure paintings like the *Cane Cutters* of 1943.[30] In 1944 Carreño was included in The Museum of Modern Art's exhibition *Cuban Painting Today*, and in 1946 he was appointed a professor of painting at the New School for Social Research.

By the early 1950s Carreño was part of a group of Cuban abstractionists that included Luis Martínez Pedro, Cundo Bermúdez, René Portacarrero, and Amelia Peláez, all of whom used the modernistic vocabulary of late Cubism (flatness, decorative lines, and abstract areas of color) but who were still distinctively "Cuban" in feeling and thus fell within the nationalist stereotype, even though their art was no longer Realist in character. Stuart Preston, writing in *The New York Times* in 1951, noted that "the highly geometricized idiom of Mario Carreño's recent work at the Perls Galleries is a far cry from his comparative naturalism of a decade ago….As a style, it translates very happily into pictorial language the staccato musical rhythms illustrated in *Cuban Musicians*."[31]

In 1951, when Carreño moved to Chile and became a Chilean citizen, his work changed from colorful Regionalism to international Surrealism. He painted images of petrified and fragmented human statues in dreamlike volcanic landscapes that expressed a kind of generalized, existential despair: "My painting is only a reflection of occurrences which sometimes converts to something Surrealistic. My figures are turned to stone by their sorrow, their suffering and by the barbaric things that are happening."[32]

Another artist who was first introduced to the United States public in the 1940s during his period as a Social Realist painter was the Argentine Antonio Berni. Born in Argentina in 1905, Berni studied and lived in Europe from 1925 to 1931, where he was influenced by the Surrealism of Salvador Dali and Giorgio de Chirico. On his return to Argentina in the 1930s he developed into a Realist painter influenced by the art of the *tres grandes*, and he worked with Siqueiros in 1933 when the Mexican was in Argentina. The Museum of Modern Art bought a Berni painting of that period, *The New Chicago Athletic Club* of 1937 (plate 136), a Realist group portrait of a boys' soccer club set against a Surrealistic Latin American landscape. Beautifully composed, the compelling painting shows a profound sense of sympathy and concern for individuality.

Berni's work was shown in the United States in the 1940s in the context of Latin American Realism and again after 1962, when he won the Venice Biennale graphics prize for his narrative series about a poor slum boy, Juanito Laguna (plate 137). He was given one-man shows at the Museum of Modern Art in Miami in 1963, at the Trenton Museum in New Jersey in 1966, and at the Huntington Hartford Gallery in New York, also in 1966. In the Juanito Laguna series, Berni began to integrate found objects into his prints, collages, and constructions, managing to combine a baroque sense of fantasy with naturalism and social commentary. He followed the Juanito Laguna series with an even more elaborate series about a fictional character, Ramona Montiel, who travels from childhood poverty to prostitution to religion. In his later work social concern is no longer approached directly; instead he uses satire and witty combinations of materials. Raphael Squirru, director of the Pan American Union's Department of Cultural Affairs, saw "the abundant, the prolific, and their aesthetic equivalent, the baroque" as a continuous and specifically Argentine quality in Berni's work in spite of the stylistic changes.[33]

Although Berni and Carreño turned from Social Realism toward various other stylistic directions after 1950, their work continued to express the social concerns which characterized their earlier period. In the case of Portinari and Berni, who continued to live in their own countries, a strong national flavor was retained as well. In spite of the long and varied careers of these artists, however, their major impact and exposure in the United States came during their Realist phases in the 1940s. Work from this period was

137

Antonio Berni

137. *Juanito Laguna Bringing Food to His Father,
a Steelworker.* 1961
Oil and collage on wood, 82¾ x 61″
Museo de Arte Moderno, Buenos Aires
Photo: Pedro Roth

collected by Nelson Rockefeller, IBM, Helena Rubinstein, and The Museum of Modern Art among others, and it was during this time, when their art fit into the prevalent U.S. view of Latin America, that they received attention in this country.

Neo-Humanism and the International Style: The 1950s and 1960s.

At the peak of the Cold War, when the globe was strictly divided between the "Free World" and the "Communist Bloc," New York replaced Paris as the cultural capital of the West. With the "triumph of American painting"[34] and the ascendancy of the New York School as the leader of modernist painting, a period of strict adherence to abstractionist standards was initiated.

While the abstract movement had been gaining in strength within elitist art circles since the early 1940s, Regionalist and figurative painters continued to receive exposure up to the mid-1950s. Indeed, conservatives in Congress still considered abstract art to be part of a communist plot rather than a national triumph. In 1952, The Museum of Modern Art's director, Alfred H. Barr, Jr., still felt compelled to defend abstract art in rhetorical articles with such titles as "Is Modern Art Communistic?" (published in *The New York Times Magazine*).[35]

The Venice Biennale of 1954, which featured Ben Shahn and Willem de Kooning, was one of the last times that both Realist and abstract painters were shown together to represent U.S. art. But the pendulum had already swung. Clement Greenberg, whose criticism was crucial to both the promotion and trajectory of modernism on its path from Abstract Expressionism to Minimalism, proclaimed the concomitant beginning of U.S. cultural dominance and abstract supremacy in 1955:

When they started out, the "abstract expressionists" had the traditional diffidence of American artists. They were very much aware of the provincial fate lurking all around them....At the Biennale in Venice in 1954, I saw how de Kooning's exhibition put to shame not only the neighboring one of Ben Shahn, but that of every other painter his age or under in the other pavilions. The general impression is still that an art of high distinction has as much chance of coming out of this country as a great wine. Literature—yes, we know that we have done some great things in that line; the English and French have told us so. Now they can begin to tell us the same about our painting.[36]

Abstract Expressionism was promoted as the artistic equivalent of "freedom"; the most courageous way to express the existential angst suffered by modern man living in the atomic age. Sartrian existentialism also generated Neo–Humanist responses among postwar artists. Violent distortions of the human body were typically used to express man's inner crisis. But, in spite of the fame of individual artists such as Francis Bacon, Leonard Baskin, and Rico Lebrun, attempts like Peter Selz's 1959 *New Images of Man* show at The Museum of Modern Art to promote figurative art as an alternative to Abstract Expressionism failed. However, for young Latin American artists forced to choose between the legacy of the *tres grandes* and abstraction, Neo-Humanism emerged during this period as the preferred style for socially concerned art.

The publicity accompanying the European exhibitions of Abstract Expressionism contrasted the "socialist realist" style of Soviet and fascist art with the "freedom" of U.S. abstraction. The position that totalitarianism and Realism go together was first argued by Clement Greenberg in his pivotal 1939 defense of modernism, "Avant Garde and Kitsch," and formed the basis of Barr's 1952 article as well. The Regionalist and Social Realist art of the 1930s was buried behind a wall of silence. It became impossible for Realist artists to get exposure, and their work already in the museums was relegated to storage. Art history textbooks ignored the period of the 1930s almost entirely, giving the Mexican mural movement a mere paragraph or two— a situation that has only begun to change with the revival of "political" and Neo-Expressionist art in the post-modern atmosphere of the early 1980s.

Together with Realism, nationalistic art also fell into disfavor. As the United States shouldered its new responsibilities as the leader of the free world, internationalism replaced isolationism as the new buzzword. However, U.S. ethnocentrism meant that "internationalism" as viewed from New York became the "American Way" and the

"New York School" became the "International Style."

Internationalism posed a problem even for abstract Latin American artists during this period. This was poignantly expressed by José Gómez Sicre in the foreword to the catalog of the *Gulf-Caribbean Art* exhibition at the Houston Museum of Fine Arts in 1956:

The case of Tamayo alone should suffice to show that something new had appeared upon the Mexican scene as early as 1928. In order to gain prominence, however, it was necessary for the artist to take up residence in New York for half of each year; and before his works could enjoy the boom that has recently raised their prices to astronomical levels, Tamayo had to win consecration in European markets....A similar case is that of Roberto Matta, who, though Chilean, has to be classed as belonging to the "Paris School" or the "School of New York" in order to be exhibited on 57th Street. Likewise the jungle visions produced by the rich tropical imagination of Wifredo Lam in his Havana studio must make their way into the Manhattan market under the aegis of French surrealism or with the sponsorship of Paris dealers.[37]

The depths to which recognition of Latin American painting in the U.S. had sunk during this period is exemplified by the organization of the Houston exhibition. The work of the Caribbean artists, many of them of the stature of Tamayo and Lam, was shown on an equal basis with a juried selection of local artists' paintings from the Gulf states. Gómez Sicre lamented the sad situation of Latin American abstractionists trying to battle the Rivera stereotype. Although he had been showing a "different" kind of Latin American art at the Pan American Union since 1946, Gómez Sicre claimed that he had "not yet dared to propose a single artist who has exhibited in Washington to any gallery in New York."[38]

The phenomenon of denationalization of foreign artists and the use of the term "International Style" may have happened at least partly because of the contribution of foreign artists to the U.S. cultural triumph. It was the massive influx of important European artists seeking refuge during the war years that provided the impetus that finally pulled U.S. art out of its provincial status. Two of the leading U.S. Abstract Expressionists were adults when they came to New York: Willem de Kooning left Holland when he was twenty-two; Hans Hofmann left Germany when he was fifty-three. As Leslie Judd Ahlander, curator of contemporary art of the Ringling Museum in Sarasota, Florida, wrote with unconscious racism in his introduction to that museum's *Latin American Horizons* show in 1976: "So international are such painters and sculptors as Matta and Lam, Soto or Marisol, that it is difficult to think of them as Latin American at all."[39] It is not surprising, therefore, that when *Time* magazine wished to praise the Uruguayan printmaker Antonio Frasconi in 1953, it referred to him as "the U.S.'s foremost woodcut artist."[40]

Because of the dominance of abstractionism in painting and sculpture, most of the socially conscious Latin American art shown in the United States in the 1950s was made by graphic artists rather than painters. In the tradition of Goya and Daumier, who had established the legitimacy of angry, biting, satirical images critical of political and social issues, social content was more acceptable in the graphic arts than it was in painting. Botero's painted grotesques, first shown in 1957, had to wait for the post–Pop art mid-1960s to be noticed, but the ban on figuration did not extend to graphic media. Frasconi, Mauricio Lasansky of Argentina, and José Luis Cuevas of Mexico, figurative artists of the Neo-Humanist school who were popular during the 1950s, are known for their drawings and prints rather than their paintings. They each spent a considerable amount of time in the United States during the 1950s, and Frasconi and Lasansky became permanent residents, another helpful requisite for recognition.

Frasconi came to the United States in 1945 and a year later had his first exhibition at the Brooklyn Museum. His work was still in the Social Realist tradition of the TGP. He exhibited twenty woodcut prints dealing with the life of the Uruguayan peasant and other social themes (plate 138). During the late 1940s and early 1950s Frasconi continued to develop and refine his technique, moving toward more subtle relationships of values and textures and introducing color into many of his prints. His

138

139

Antonio Frasconi
138. *Lettuce Worker II, Salinas Valley*. 1953
    Woodcut on paper, 24 x 19"
    Courtesy Terry Dintenfass Gallery, New York
    Photo: Mel Adelglass

Antonio Frasconi
139. *Beasts and Graves (from Ode to Lorca Series)*. 1962
    Lithograph, 30 x 22⅜"
    Courtesy Terry Dintenfass Gallery, New York
    Photo: Mel Adelglass

140

Lasar Segall
140. *Exodus.* c.1940
Oil on canvas, 52 x 54″
The Jewish Museum, New York. Gift of Messrs.
James Rosenberg and George Baker in memory of
Felix M. Warburg, JM 25-48
Photo: John Parnell

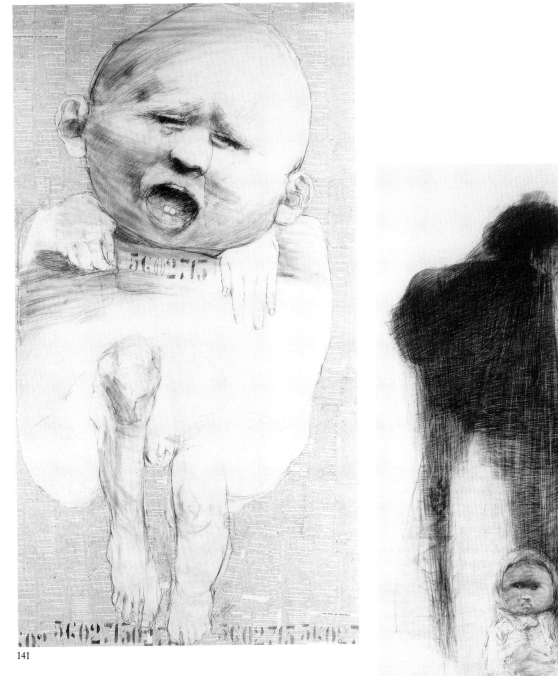

141

142

Mauricio Lasansky
141. *Drawing No. 28 (from the Nazi Drawings Series).*
1961–66
Collection Richard S. Levitt Foundation
Photo: courtesy the artist

Mauricio Lasansky
142. *Mexican Sketches No. 2.* 1963-65
Pencil, turpentine, and sanguine wash on paper
75¼ x 45″
Collection Mr. and Mrs. Harold E. Rayburn Family,
Iowa City, Iowa
Photo: Robert Weaver

work began to be considered remarkable for its sensitivity to the textures of the wood, boldness of design, exuberance, and wit.[41] In 1952 he was given a ten-year retrospective exhibition by the Cleveland Museum of Art, which included 263 prints. His first book, *Twelve Fables of Aesop*, printed in 1955 by The Museum of Modern Art, was chosen as a book of the year by the American Institute of Graphic Arts. Since 1945, his subject matter has ranged from scenes of rural Vermont and urban New York to illustrations of Whitman, Poe, Lorca, and children's books to portraits of César Chávez and Malcolm X (plate 139).

His series Ode to Lorca condemns Spanish fascism, depicting Franco as a bull with tin horns and Spain as a land of graves over which praying figures whirl on the backs of monsters. Charlotte Willard, who included his *Death of a Poet* in a survey of contemporary drawing for *Art in America* in 1964, recognized him as "one of the few artists who have not abdicated their brotherhood with man."[42]

Like Frasconi, Lasansky was first recognized for etchings on Latin American subjects and praised for mastery of technique. As the head of the prestigious printmaking department of Iowa State University, Lasansky had his greatest influence in this country as the teacher of a whole generation of younger printmakers. Repelled by fascism, Lasansky devoted five years to his masterpiece series, The Nazi Drawings, of 1966 (plate 141). This suite of thirty large drawings, almost all of them about six feet high and four feet wide, constitutes a monumental treatment of the Holocaust. In Lasansky's work the images are both individual and universal. The drawings of skull-helmeted generals, prostitutes, wailing children, and obscenely degraded victims represent the essence of fascism's evil effects on individuals and are as applicable to the Argentine military dictatorship as to Nazi Germany. As the poet Edwin Honig wrote:

Whatever we do, the drawings will continue to disturb us. And no wonder, since they constitute such an awesome rendering of our times—our worst historical experiences reduced to basic terms of manmade slaughter, innocent suffering, erotic and religious demonism, and these recorded in the simplest medium an artist can use: lead pencil, earth colors, turpentine wash, and a common commercial paper.[43]

The approach to social issues taken in these drawings is part of the Neo-Humanist ethos as it was expounded by Selden Rodman in his book *The Insiders*, published in 1960. *The Insiders* calls attention to the unspeakable degradation of the individual. According to Rodman, the insider "never depicts misery in the mass, as does the communist artist, because he conceives of evil and redemption in personal terms, soluble only through the volition of the free spirits."[44] By not pointing the finger at social forces but instead by individualizing evil, the Neo-Humanist approach was more acceptable and less threatening to the U.S. sensibility in the climate of the 1950s than the more ideological Social Realism of the 1930s and 1940s.

During the 1950s a distinction was made in the United States between Orozco and the other two *grandes*. As Rodman, who considered Orozco a precursor of the kind of thinking that influenced *The Insiders*, put it, "Orozco infrequently descends into the banalities of propaganda that occupied his colleagues."[45] Orozco's early drawings of prostitutes, his black-and-white mural at Jiquilpán, and his Guadalajara murals were often cited as examples of his humanist approach. In her book on the Mexican Neo-Humanists, *Contemporary Mexican Painting in a Time of Change*, Shifra Goldman pointed out that while "there were moments when Orozco approached Social Realism," as in his caricatures of the wealthy and the church elders in the Preparatoria murals or his image of a Zapata figure being attacked by U.S. imperialists in the Dartmouth College library murals, often "'the class enemy' is not identified and the assumption is that evil (and good) are inherent in human nature. It is this aspect, perhaps, that made Orozco so attractive to the anti-ideological young artists of the 1950s and 1960s."[46]

In 1954 José Luis Cuevas (plate 143) had his first U.S. exhibition at the Pan American Union, where he was presented as Orozco's heir. In the catalog notes, Gómez Sicre wrote:

Cuevas depicts mankind at its lowest social levels, or as seen in its irrational aspects. He

*has produced a highly emotional series of drawings, of convulsionary and hallucinatory
effect, suggestive of the eerie late manner of Goya, and of the brutal, sarcastic early
productions of Orozco.*[47]

The exhibition sold out on opening night, and Cuevas, aged only twenty-three,
achieved instant fame. One year later, Picasso bought two of his drawings from an
exhibition at the Edouard Loeb Gallery in Paris, and the first monograph about Cuevas
with texts by Jean Cassou and Philippe Soupault followed almost immediately. During
a two-month stay as an artist-in-residence at the Philadelphia School of Art, Cuevas
drew the illustrations for his first book, *The Worlds of Kafka and Cuevas.* By 1957
he had been given a one-person show in New York at the Aenlle Gallery. Dore
Ashton, writing in *The New York Times,* cited Velázquez, Goya, and pre-Columbian
artists as the forerunners for Cuevas's predilection for "satire" and the "monstrous."[48]
Cuevas defined his attitude toward social criticism in a statement accompanying
his 1960 exhibition at the David Herbert Gallery in New York:

*What I see is a sweat-stained mass of businessmen, priests, clerks, prostitutes, bank
cashiers, and pregnant women, who go their way, without realizing what they are,
seeking oblivion. I seize upon them for my themes; I make symbols of them, stripping
them of all that is transient, all that is of the here and now. I seek to render them
universal in their repulsiveness. It is for this reason that I draw zoomorphic monsters,
gluttonously obese, obscene with lust. There they stand, each and every one of them, in
the world I have striven to create after beholding the one that lies about me.*[49]

Cuevas's rise to international fame was aided by his Riveraesque flair for
controversy and publicity. In an interview with *Time* magazine on the opening night
of his 1954 exhibition he condemned the Mexican mural movement. This was a
controversial position for a Mexican to take in a foreign land, but it was in keeping
with the spirit of the 1950s and the general campaign by the United States in Latin
America against Social Realism. In Mexico, in particular, artists were divided in
an acrimonious battle in which, with the help of the Pan American Union, the Esso
competitions, and U.S. cultural policy, government support was wrested by the
abstractionists from the Mexican School by 1960.[50]
In the same way that the need for hemispheric unity during World War II
provoked increased exposure for Latin American art in the United States, the Cuban
Revolution of 1959 marked the beginning of a renewed interest in Latin America by the
U.S. art world that was manifested in a series of large museum exhibitions that
continued into the mid-1960s. These exhibitions concentrated on contemporary art and
emphasized the major centers of the International Style in Latin America, particularly
Argentina, Brazil, and Venezuela. They helped to consolidate the victory of the
International Style locally within Latin America by giving it exposure in the United
States. In 1959 the Dallas Museum of Fine Arts presented *South American Art Today*
and the Art Institute of Chicago held *U.S. Collects Latin American Art.* This was
followed by the Institute of Contemporary Art's *New Departures* in Boston in 1960, the
Walker Art Center's *New Art of Brazil* in 1962 and *New Art of Argentina* in 1964; the
Guggenheim Museum and Cornell University exhibition *The Emergent Decade* in
1965–66; the Peabody Museum's *Venezuelan Painting* in 1965; and Yale University's
Art of Latin America since Independence in 1966.
In Mexico, where the Realist school was most entrenched and the battle
against abstraction fought most fiercely, a third stylistic direction emerged that rejected
both muralism and abstraction and aligned itself with the international Neo-Humanist
movement. Three factors coincided that led to the beginning of this movement in 1960:
the publication of Rodman's book *The Insiders,* the imprisonment of Siqueiros, and the
controversial *Second Mexican Bienal,* in which the abstractionists won all the prizes. The
cofounders of the Nueva Presencia group, Arnold Belkin and Francisco Icaza, as well as
Cuevas, were among the almost one hundred Mexican artists who refused to participate
in the *Bienal* as part of an international protest against the imprisonment of Siqueiros.
Their poster-size manifesto *Nueva Presencia,* which appeared one month after the first

143

144

José Luis Cuevas
143. *The History of Crime (from the Crime Series)*
1968. Lithograph on paper, 21⅞ x 29⅞"
Art Institute of Chicago. Gift of Mr. and Mrs.
Joseph R. Shapiro, 1977
Photo: courtesy Art Institute of Chicago

Arnold Belkin
144. *The Dream.* 1964
Oil on canvas, 65 x 55"
Phoenix Art Museum
Photo: courtesy Phoenix Art Museum

group exhibition in 1961, originated as a newsletter for Siqueiros. The first issue consisted of an eleven-point program that called for an art that was "anti-decorative, anti-aesthetic, anti-intellectual. It should be raw, human, with social responsibility, eloquent, real, complete, and universal."[51] The second issue, a few months later, made clear their debt to Orozco and Rodman. The group even tried calling themselves *Interioristas*, their translation of "insiders." The second issue included a review of Rodman's book by Belkin and a statement by Cuevas, who participated in the early group exhibitions, entitled "Turning Toward a New Humanism" (*"Se orienta hacia un nuevo humanismo"*):

Man, as the most important artistic theme, must be penetrated, vivisectioned, his entrails exposed to the world to show the agony and the despair of existence today.[52]

Cuevas also cited Rodman's designation of himself as the contemporary example of an "insider" artist in Mexico. In fact, Rodman's definition of the insider could have been written precisely to fit Cuevas. According to Rodman, the insider is someone who "employs distortion, sometimes violent distortion, of the human body, to emphasize an imposed affliction or an inner crisis." He is more likely to be a sculptor or a draftsman and "if he uses color at all, it is primarily in an effort to intensify the emotion he is projecting, always as a complement to the drawing, never for its own sake." His subject is apt to be "the sick, the maimed, the rejected, the isolated."[53]

During the three years of its existence, the Nueva Presencia group had a revolving membership, but its core included Icaza, Belkin, Francisco Corzas, and Leonél Góngora. Cuevas and Rafael Coronel were both members briefly. From the beginning, Belkin and Icaza jointly provided leadership for the group and cultivated links with the United States. They established a correspondence with the leading U.S. Neo-Humanist artist Rico Lebrun in California, who came to visit them in Mexico in 1962. The work of the Nueva Presencia group was shown in the United States, but except for Cuevas's art, which was already famous, their works never entered the mainstream. The group exhibited together in the United States at the Cober Gallery in New York, the Zora Gallery in Los Angeles in 1962, and the Morse Gallery in Rollins, Florida, in 1963. That year they were also included in *Pintores Neo-Humanistas* in San Antonio and San Francisco, *Voices of Mexico* in Riverside, California, and *Art in Mexico Today* at the Zora Gallery. Belkin, Icaza, and Góngora continued to exhibit individually at the Zora Gallery and elsewhere in the United States throughout the 1960s.

Belkin, a Canadian by birth but now a Mexican citizen, came to Mexico in 1947 at age seventeen to study mural painting. He worked as an assistant to Siqueiros from 1949 to 1950. Belkin's early murals *Warsaw Ghetto Uprising* of 1959 and *We Are All Guilty* of 1961 are Orozcoesque statements about human suffering, evil, and victimization. The Bay of Pigs incident in 1961 inspired Belkin's Invasion of Cuba series, in which he attempted to use the cramped and distorted human figures compressed by the edges of the paper to make a political statement. In his Earth Beings and War and Peace series, the emphasis on victims is reduced. The classically modeled, serene figures common in Belkin's later work first appear in these drawings as a counterpoint to his more expressive figures, creating an effect of extreme tension and beauty. A prolific writer as well as a painter, Belkin was also important as an organizer and theorist within the Latin American art scene (plate 144).

Icaza's expressionism is rooted in the art of Ensor and Munch. Much of his work from the 1960s uses metamorphosed bird and animal figures to express the conflict between bestiality and spiritual transcendence that divides the individual. In 1961 he painted *Dead Spain* and *Los Juanes* as part of a series of antifascist paintings in which he attacked the alliance between the Church, the aristocracy, and the military that delivered Spain to fascism.

Although born and raised in Cartago, Colombia, Leonél Góngora has lived in the United States since 1964, when he was appointed to the faculty of the University of Massachusetts. He studied at Washington University in St. Louis and in 1959 traveled in Europe. From 1960 to 1963 Góngora lived in Mexico and was part of the Nueva Presencia group. It was in that context that his work was first presented in this country.

145

146

Fernando Botero
145. *The Pinzón Family*. 1965
Oil on canvas, 68¼ x 68¼"
Museum of Art, Rhode Island School of Design,
Providence
Photo: courtesy Museum of Art, Rhode Island
School of Design

Fernando Botero
146. *The Sleeping Bishop*. 1957
Oil on canvas, 9½ x 35"
Courtesy Mr. and Mrs. Miguel Aranguren,
Arlington, Virginia
Photo: Félix Angel

A masterful draftsman, Góngora is fixated on violence and sexuality. This may be in part a reaction to the killings and mutilation he saw as a youth during the period of civil strife in Colombia that followed the assassination of the Liberal leader Gaitán in 1948 and to the strict and hypocritical puritanism of Colombian Catholicism.

While Neo-Humanist art was a strong undercurrent in the U.S. art world during the early 1960s, it could not overcome the dominance of abstract art and gain acceptance from the major art institutions. It was not until the emergence of Pop art during the social turbulence of the mid-1960s that the ban against representational art in the major New York galleries was lifted and some kinds of Latin American figurative painting were again able to gain national prominence. Although Pop art loudly proclaimed its abstract origins, the simple fact that it reintroduced representational objects and figures into the art context opened the door to figurative painting—as long as it was witty and cool. The career of the Colombian painter Fernando Botero illustrates this change in sensibility after the mid-1960s.

Botero's work had been exhibited in the U.S. since 1957, when he first showed at the Pan American Union Gallery in Washington. He moved to New York in 1960 after winning a Guggenheim prize for Colombian artists. The Museum of Modern Art bought one of his paintings in 1961, and he had solo shows at the Gres Gallery in Washington in 1960, The Contemporaries in New York in 1962, and the Zora Gallery in Los Angeles in 1965. But, in spite of these small successes, he remained a struggling artist until after his solo exhibition at the Milwaukee Art Center in 1967. This was followed by a one-man show at the Center for Inter-American Relations (CIR) in 1969. In 1971 he was offered a contract with Marlborough-Gerson Galleries, one of the major international dealers.

The Milwaukee catalog introduced Botero as "a Latin American artist in the sense that his roots are there and in the fact that many of the things he paints and at least part of his attitude stem from the tradition of his homeland. He is unique among contemporary Latin American artists however in that he stands apart from the general international abstractionist trend recently prevalent there."[54] Stanton Catlin, in the foreword to the CIR show, placed Botero within the more general Latin American Neo-Humanist movement, but "at the bright end of a mostly dark spectrum." For Catlin, Botero's particular form of ironic wit is quintessentially Spanish American, "aimed at what is essentially a Latin quality of decadence" with roots in the opulence of colonial religion. Botero was given the usual antecedents for Latin American Neo-Humanists: Goya and Orozco. However, Catlin distinguished Botero's social criticism from that of Orozco: "The forms of social obsolescence which Orozco destroys with overt force, Botero allows to fall from their own over-ripeness or wafts away with infinite lightness."[55] With Botero, the quality of visual wit and punning was added to the new stereotype of Latin American art.

Other writers, like German Arcinegas, saw Botero's world as a giant playroom. Although Botero was painting generals, ministers of war, and dictators, Arcinegas saw them as "playthings of their own destiny, entering the scene like children who wind up toy automobiles and arm themselves with cardboard swords."[56] The implication was that Botero had stripped the rich and powerful of dignity and rendered them harmless (plate 146).

However, though Botero's painted caricatures do not scream with anger, they are not without malevolence, as seen especially in his paintings of the 1960s, which are often both funny and horrible (plate 145). Small details, such as flies hovering over bloated figures, hint at imminent decay. The scale of his overstuffed mannequins and the way they seem to be barely contained by the boundaries of the canvas provide a subtle quality of menace. As *Art International* commented after his CIR exhibition: "His art avoids the simply 'political,' becoming so only when one poses the question, 'What is responsible for this horror?' "[57]

From the first exhibition of Cuevas in the mid-1950s to the paintings and drawings of the Neo-Humanists and Botero's work in the 1960s, a new image of Latin American art as Goyaesque (when not indistinguishably international) was established. Antecedents were also found in the exquisite painterliness but subtle cruelty of Velázquez's and Goya's portraits, the distortions of Picasso's *Guernica* and the refinement of his drawings, as well as the expressive distortions found in Mexican pre-Columbian sculpture. Much was made of the Mexican (and Spanish) fascination with death, the grotesque, black humor, and mordant wit. Critics appreciated the artists' social messages only when they were unobtrusively introduced, either in the Neo-Humanist's expressive distortion of the universal individual or in the presentation's visual wit and charm.

The New Left and Revolutionary Art: 1965–1970

With the resurgence of social activism in the United States in the mid-1960s, a new attitude toward art with social content developed. The agitation over civil rights and the Vietnam War had repercussions in the art world. Artists began to organize not only around major political issues but also in opposition to the exclusionary character of the art world, which had become divided into "mainstream" and "alternative" currents. Women and ethnic artists, excluded from the mainstream, founded alternative spaces: cooperative galleries, community art centers, poster workshops, mural painting groups, and collectives of all kinds. At the same time, the government and the new National Endowment for the Arts, as part of a general effort to contain unrest that followed the assassination of Martin Luther King in 1968, began to provide a modicum of funding for these new organizations.

Along with riots, Black Power, and flower children, 1968 saw the rise of Minimalism as the latest style in mainstream art. The much-lamented gap between art and life had become an impassable canyon. Young artists, trained in the new abstract academies, began to reexamine their commitment to mainstream art. Many left traditional artmaking entirely, turning to "happenings," Performance, and Video art. Others began to explore advertising imagery and to reexamine traditional realism and muralism in a search for sources that could reintroduce content to art and make it relevant once again to a nonelite audience.

Because of the charismatic nature of its young leaders and the romantic quality of the struggle, media coverage of the Cuban Revolution in this country was extensive, and much of it sympathetic to the revolutionaries. Posters of Ché and Fidel joined those of rock stars on teenagers' walls. For the 1960s generation Ché and Fidel joined Martin Luther King, Malcolm X, Abbie Hoffman, Bobby Seale, Dylan, and Joan Baez in the galaxy of heroes. When Susan Sontag's and Dugald Stermer's book, *The Art of Revolution: Castro's Cuba: 1959–1970*, appeared, it crystallized a growing interest within the New Left in Cuban poster art and allowed it to cross over into the mainstream.

Unlike the Social Realist movement of the 1930s, which was the mainstream art of that period, protest art in the 1960s was primarily the domain of an alternative culture. Very little politically inspired art was shown in established museums or galleries. Very few articles appeared in reputable art publications. Coverage was primarily limited to general news in newspapers or alternative publications.

However, the posters from Cuba, especially those represented in the Sontag-Stermer book, provoked universal interest. Sontag emphasized the use by the Cubans of elements from U.S. modernist art: Pop, Op, and "Hard Edge" abstraction and the social freedom that this represented.

In their beauty, their stylishness, and their transcendence of either mere utility or mere propaganda, these posters give evidence of a revolutionary society that is not repressive and philistine. The posters demonstrate that Cuba has a culture which is alive, international in orientation, and relatively free of the kind of bureaucratic interference that has blighted the arts in practically every other country where a communist revolution has come to power.[58]

In addition, the fact that silk-screen poster images are by their very nature "flat" rather than modeled made this art more congenial to eyes trained in the modern aesthetic of flatness. In his article "Public Graphics in Cuba: A Very Cuban Form of Internationalist Art," art historian David Kunzle has emphasized that in spite of the Cuban appropriation of U.S. art styles, "the richly decorative patterns reminiscent of Op or psychedelic art became, in Cuban graphics, no longer 'pure' visual onslaughts and avenues of drug-related sensory escape, but expressive of moral pleasure in the ideas incarnated in the revolution, together with a kind of physical joy in its achievements."[59] The Cuban poster artists employed abstract styles to convey their message in much the same way that an earlier generation of Cubans had imbued Parisian modernism with a distinctly Cuban flavor.

Although the Cuban revolution occurred in 1959, the period of the finest poster production did not begin until 1964. Raul Martínez, one of the leading exponents of the Cuban Pop art poster, is still one of Cuba's leading painters. During the Batista period, he was part of a group of Abstract Expressionist painters who expressed their opposition to the dictatorship through the use of titles. After the revolution, Martínez's work evolved into a style influenced by Robert Rauschenberg in which real objects were added to his abstract paintings. His distinctive brand of Cuban Pop art evolved when he adopted a linear style of simplified drawing, based on naive art, to depict representative Cuban heroes and typical characters in bright and joyous compositions (plate 147).

Alfredo Rostgaard was perhaps the most inventive and eclectic of the Cuban poster artists and was responsible for many of the best-known images (plate 148). His image of a bleeding rose, designed for a festival of protest music and used as the cover image for the Sontag-Stermer book, has become almost synonymous with the idea of protest culture. In Cuba, each institution produced its own posters. The best known of the Cuban posters, most original, and richest in design were produced by the film institute, ICAIC. Artists were given free rein, without any restrictions beyond reproducing the title of the film. Political posters for international consumption were produced in offset by OSPAAL and accompanied each issue of the internationally distributed *TriContinental Magazine*. During the period of the finest poster production in the 1960s, Rostgaard was the director of the poster group at OSPAAL.

Political and educational posters for internal consumption were produced by the Commission on Revolutionary Orientation of the Communist Party. During the mid-1960s, under the directorship of Félix Beltrán, these were often quite abstract in design. Beltrán, a graduate of the School of Visual Arts in New York, often worked in a hard-edged, geometric style. His poster *Clic*, a single word on an electric blue background produced for a campaign to save electricity, is an example of this kind of clean, contemporary design.

During the brief period of radical chic when revolution became fashionable and members of the Black Panther party were invited by the very rich to exclusive cocktail parties, poster collecting had a tremendous boom. In fact, the student movement of 1968 and its aftermath produced an international revival of interest in political posters not unlike the interest generated by the Mexican revolutionary artists forty years earlier. Exhibitions of revolutionary posters became common in European museums. The Cuban posters had an important influence on the development of political posters in this country and created greater public interest in other manifestations of revolutionary culture.

Although the Puerto Rican poster movement preceded the Cuban one, it was first introduced to the U.S. audience in the late 1960s in the context of the Puerto Rican independence and Young Lord movements. To understand the development of Puerto Rican protest art and its reception in the United States it is necessary to understand the special political relationship of Puerto Rico and the United States. Conquered by the United States during the Spanish-American War, Puerto Rico was governed as a colony through acts of Congress and had an appointed governor until 1947. At that time, in response to pressure from the United Nations, Puerto Rico was given the right to elect its own governor.

The question of Puerto Rico's relationship with the United States was not resolved, however, and a period of intense activity by the Puerto Rican independence movement began in 1950. This included armed actions, namely an attack on President Truman's residence, Blair House, in November 1950, and an incident in 1954 when four nationalist guerrillas, including a woman, Lolita Lebrón, fired on the U.S. Congress. These incidents, as well as the 1936 massacre in Ponce (where nineteen people were killed when police fired on a nationalist demonstration) and the jailing and martyrdom of Independence party leader Pedro Albizu Campos, provided much of the subject

147

148

Raul Martínez
147. *Lucia.* 1968
Silk-screen on paper, 18 x 12"
Courtesy the artist, Agency ICAIC, and the
Center for Cuban Studies, New York
Photo: Tony Velez

Alfredo Rostgaard
148. *Now.* 1965
Silk-screen on paper, 29¾ x 20¼"
Courtesy the artist, Agency ICAIC, and Center for
Cuban Studies, New York
Photo: Tony Velez

149

Lorenzo Homar
149. *5to Festival de Teatro (Fifth Theater Festival)*. 1962
Silk-screen on paper, 17 x 17⅞"
Instituto de Cultura Puertorriqueña, San Juan
Photo: John Betancourt, San Juan

matter for the activist *Independentista* art that accompanied the political movement. Symbols of the Taino Indian heritage and specifically Puerto Rican traditions and religious customs were also commonly used images. Since Puerto Ricans were subject to the U.S. military draft, the anti–Vietnam War activism of the 1960s and criticism of U.S. politicians were also important.

Socially committed Puerto Rican art has taken two forms: protest art, which concentrates on attacking injustice and oppression, and nationalist art, which celebrates the Puerto Rican identity and national heritage. The kind of government-sponsored nationalist art produced in Mexico, Cuba, and the United States during the WPA period, was also initiated in Puerto Rico in 1946 as part of the "New Deal" programs of Luis Muñoz Marín and his Partido Popular Democrático (PPD) after they won the 1944 elections.

The Motion-Picture and Graphics Art Workshop was originally formed by a group of former WPA artists from the United States. Irene and Jack Delano, Edwin Rosskam, and Robert Gwathmey produced educational posters and films as part of the Muñoz government's campaign for social reforms and education. In the early years under Irene Delano, the poster workshop created sociopolitical art inspired by the work of Ben Shahn and other U.S. Social Realists for a largely rural audience. The posters used easily understood depictions of the human figure, broad areas of flat color, and line drawing as basic elements. *Defiéndalos* by Irene Delano is an example of this early style.

By 1949, when the program became the Division of Community Education, a number of Puerto Rican artists, including Julio Rosado del Valle, Lorenzo Homar, Rafael Tufiño (who had studied in Mexico with Leopoldo Méndez and Alfredo Zalce), Carlos Osorio, and Carlos Raquel Rivera, returned to the island to join the workshop. At this time, more sophisticated cultural posters for art exhibitions and films began to be produced in addition to the rural educational works. Educational books illustrated with prints made with the linoleum-print technique popularized by the Mexican TGP were also produced by the workshop.

The illustrated *Plenas* (a typical Puerto Rican song form) designed by Tufiño and Homar is one of the finest early examples of Puerto Rican prints. Like the popular broadsheets of Mexican ballads illustrated by Posada in the beginning of the twentieth century, the *Plenas* serves as both recognition and expression of a popular cultural form. The reevaluation of popular cultural forms, as opposed to the acceptance of colonial culture, has often been part of the development of revolutionary consciousness. Writing as part of the independence movement in Guinea, the African nationalist Amilcar Cabral noted the importance of culture for revolutionary struggle:

The study of the history of national liberation struggles shows that generally these struggles are preceded by an increase in expression of culture, consolidated progressively into a successful or unsuccessful attempt to affirm the cultural personality of the dominated people, as a means of negating the oppressor culture.[60]

On the other hand, the negation of the existence of an indigenous culture is one of the strongest weapons of the oppressor. According to Cabral, domination "can be maintained only by the permanent, organized repression of the cultural life of the people concerned."[61] Like most colonial powers, the United States imposed its language and values on Puerto Rico. However, since the United States ideologically opposes colonialism, having fought the Revolutionary War to escape English domination, it has tried to deny that any indigenous culture existed in Puerto Rico or that there was any repression. In such a situation, a nationalist art that simply asserts the existence of an indigenous culture becomes a revolutionary act. The U.S. denial of its colonial role in Puerto Rico may also help to explain the extreme neglect that Puerto Rican art has suffered on the mainland. There is almost no attention paid to Puerto Rican art from the island in English-language art publications and Puerto Rican art still has not received the recognition that it merits.[62]

Beginning with the *Plenas* series, the work of Rafael Tufiño has been characterized not only by Puerto Rican subject matter but also by formal qualities that are seen as typical of Puerto Rico: strong line, rich color, and spontaneity. A large

150

151

152

Antonio Martorell
151. *Scorpion Playing Card: Ace (from "Barajas Alacrán").* 1968
Silk-screen on paper, 37 x 22"
Collection the artist
Photo: John Betancourt, San Juan

Carlos Raquel Rivera
150. *The Mother Country.* 1959
Oil on panel, 33 x 48"
Collection Cooperativa de Seguros Multiples, San Juan
Photo: John Betancourt, San Juan

Myrna Báez
152. *The Judge.* 1970
Collograph on paper, 19½ x 22"
Museo de Antropología, Historia y Arte, Universidad de Puerto Rico, Recinto Río Piedras
Photo: John Betancourt, San Juan

153

painting on the *plena* theme was commissioned for a documentary on that subject in 1951. Recently, the mural-sized painting was restored and installed in the new Bellas Artes building in San Juan.[63] Much of the art produced by New York–born Puerto Rican artists, as well as by Chicano and black artists, includes nationalist subject matter.

The distinctive style of the Puerto Rican poster movement, with its emphasis on expressive letters, textures, and a highly developed silk-screen technique, is largely due to the influence of Lorenzo Homar. In 1952 Homar replaced Irene Delano as head of the Division of Community Education poster workshop, and after its formation in 1957 he began to direct the Graphics Workshop of the Institute for Puerto Rican Culture. During Homar's twenty-two-year tenure as director of Puerto Rico's major graphics workshops, he was responsible for developing the silk-screen method to its fullest potential. From ten to twenty different color runs were frequently used in the execution of a single poster. The importance of the workshop as a training ground for the next generation of Puerto Rican artists and Homar's role as a teacher cannot be overestimated. Among the artists who were trained at Homar's workshop were three leaders of the 1960s generation: José Rosa, Antonio Martorell, and Myrna Báez. Homar's own exquisitely executed posters often combine a political image or a portrait with a decorative text (plate 149).

Political commitment, exquisite technique, and a powerful wit characterize the work of Antonio Martorell. After stays in the United States and Spain, Martorell returned to Puerto Rico, where he began to work under Lorenzo Homar in the Graphic Workshop of the Institute of Puerto Rican Culture. In 1968 Martorell founded the Taller Alacrán, an independent workshop, which made political posters as well as commercial and cultural works. His posters, like those of Homar, are exquisitely executed and designed examples of silk-screen technique that combine painterly images with expressive lettering.

One of Martorell's works from the late 1960s that shows his creative and original approach to political art is *Barajas Alacrán*, a giant deck of cards printed with political symbols that satirize the "colonial" elections(plate 151). The joker is Lyndon B. Johnson represented as a Puerto Rican *jíbaro*, or cowboy. Martorell also became known as a book designer and creator of artists' books. His *Puerto Rican ABC* (created with poetry by Isabel Freyre de Matos and vocabulary by Rubén del Rosario), like Frasconi's quadrilingual children's *See and Say* book, was designed to educate children about their cultural heritage while indirectly criticizing the ethnocentric nature of U.S. education.

The work of Carlos Raquel Rivera falls more into the critical form of satirical protest than that of nationalist affirmation. His prints carry on the tradition of Leopoldo Méndez and the Mexican TGP, using strong contrasts of black-and-white and easily understood images to tell their story (plate 150). In *Colonial Elections*, the contrast between the overpowering American eagle and masses of tiny people presents a clear message, while the complex patterns and textures give the picture visual interest. His paintings are more subtle, surreal, and very richly colored. In *The Mother Country* (plate 150), like Posada, he uses the *calavera*, in this case, to criticize the pretensions of Spain.

The prints and paintings of Myrna Báez quietly criticize the pretensions and manners of Puerto Rican society by presenting carefully observed views of interiors and figures that force the viewer to see the subject in a new way (plate 152). As a printmaker, Báez has developed the technique of colorgraph printing to achieve very rich textural and color effects. Another printmaker, Carlos Irizarry, who was trained in New York, has also moved away from the traditional Puerto Rican graphic techniques to develop photo silk-screen as an expressive medium for his political graphics.

The experience of Puerto Rican and Mexican American artists born in the United States was quite distinct from that of Latin American artists growing up in their own country. They were both part of the dominant culture yet isolated from it. From their earliest days they were subjected to an all-encompassing racism in the schools, in advertising, and in television, which urged them to reject their language and culture and become American yet constantly made them aware of their "otherness."

The Chicano and Puerto Rican American art movement that began to develop after 1965 was part of the American civil rights struggle. One aspect of this struggle was

154

155

Rupert Garcia
153. *Zapata.* 1969
Silk-screen on paper, 66 x 51″
Courtesy the artist and Iannetti-Lanzone Gallery,
San Francisco
Photo: Ben Blackwell

Melesio Casas
154. *Humanscape No. 65.* 1969-70
Acrylic on canvas, 72 x 96″
Collection Ann and James Harithas, New York
Photo: Tony Hickey-Robertson

Luis Jiménez
155. *The American Dream.* 1967–69
Fiberglass and epoxy resin, 20 x 31 x 35½″
Collection the artist. Courtesy Phyllis Kind Gallery,
New York
Photo: Bruce Berman

the rejection of the melting-pot philosophy and an attempt to reassert national culture and identity. It was during this period that Chicano, Puerto Rican, and Black Studies departments were established in American universities. Before the mid-1960s artists from minority groups trained in the U.S. university system tried to succeed by deemphasizing their Latin heritage, and they worked in mainstream styles. In the climate of the late 1960s and under pressure from political activists within their community, these artists began to change. Some introduced political or nationalist content into their art while others rejected the gallery scene altogether and began to make art for the community. Most fell somewhere between these two extremes.

Two Texas artists, Melesio Casas and Luis Jiménez, had already begun to exhibit work with a Pop art sensibility by the mid-1960s. By 1970, as a result of the Chicano movement, they had converted this style into a vehicle to criticize American racism and explore Chicano values. Casas began his series of Humanscapes, paintings that used a movie-theater format to criticize media images, in 1965 (plate 154). He projected onto his screens images of blond, blue-eyed women from advertising or films, focusing on close-ups of lips, eyes, or parts of faces, that called attention to the unreality and horror of the images. By 1970 Casas began to paint specifically Chicano themes that dealt with the stereotypes of the Mexican American and other outsiders. His approach, like that of Botero, used visual puns to present a critical viewpoint. Casas also added ironic texts to his paintings: "Brownies of the Southwest" is a typical label he painted on a picture of Indians, Chicanos, and chocolate cakes. As James Harithas, director of the Contemporary Arts Museum in Houston, Texas, wrote: "Using *pachuco* logic, *barrio* humor, and a piercing intellectual approach to integrate the message content, Casas establishes a sophisticated didactic painting."[64]

Luis Jiménez also attacked racial stereotypes in his art not only through subject matter, but indirectly through a style that glorified the kitsch in Chicano artifacts and color preferences. In the catalog to his 1969 one-person show at the Graham Gallery in New York, Jiménez wrote: "Art should in some way make a person more aware, give him insight 'to where he's at' and in some way reflect what it is like to be living in these times and in this place."[65] His garishly colored fiberglass and epoxy sculptures provided a critique of the dominant culture and of the effects of racism within his own subculture (plate 155). Like Casas, Jiménez criticized the blond, blue-eyed media image of women that provided the single standard for female beauty in America and excluded all darker people: "The Mexican American or anyone who is not blond and blue-eyed is super aware of it, because he does not fit this image."[66] There is a proclamation of his Chicano identity in his assault on decorum and good taste. *American Dream* of 1968 shows a doll-like woman merged with a Volkswagen Beetle in a way that suggests sexual intercourse. This outrageous sculpture has several levels of criticism. It criticizes both the car culture and the advertising fantasy used to sell cars, and at the same time it also makes fun of the Mexican American subculture with its fixation on lovingly decorated Lo-riders.

The transformation of elements drawn from the "national" culture into their American version is also the subject matter for some of the work of New York–born Puerto Rican artist and former Young Lord Jorge Soto. In his extraordinary drawings, Soto represents the transformation of the Puerto Rican experience after migrating to New York, the change from a rural island society to a drug-infested ghetto. Soto resolved the problem of "living simultaneously in two cultures," Corinne Robins wrote in her introduction to Soto's 1979 exhibition at the Museo del Barrio, by creating a "record of the inner city of the mind, a mind that is purposely ethnic and Puerto Rican in its assimilation of diverse sources ranging from religious icons to the existing refuse of the city streets."[67]

Soto was part of Taller Boricua, a workshop founded in 1969 by a group of young New York–bred Puerto Rican art school graduates guided and inspired by two older Puerto Rican artists, Carlos Osorio and Rafael Tufiño, who had participated in the Puerto Rican poster movement. The original Taller Boricua was located in East Harlem across the street from the Young Lords party. The workshop made posters for the Puerto Rican Socialist party, Young Lords, and other community organizations; set up exhibitions in parks and on outdoor walls in the Puerto Rican community; and provided a place where young artists could develop not only their skills but also a sense of identity. Some of the artists who participated in the workshop were Carlos Osorio (who guided the group during its formative period), Marcos Dimas (one of the founders and long-time director), Nitza Tufiño, Manuel Otero, Adrián García, Rafael Colón-Morales, and Soto. During the early years of the workshop the emphasis was on rediscovering the Taino Indian heritage of Puerto Rico and integrating this knowledge into both their personal paintings and educational exhibits.

The workshop form of organization was typical of the highly nationalistic and idealistic Puerto Rican and Chicano community art movements in the late 1960s. As Shifra Goldman and Tómas Ybarra Frausto explained in their *Chicano Bibliography*, "Art was part of a whole movement to recapture a people's history and culture, albeit at times romantically, as part of the struggle for self-determination."[68] Much of the early work of the Chicano art movement took the form of street murals and posters that seemed to erupt spontaneously in many places at the same time. While artwork was produced for the farm-workers' movement and the Raza Unida party, as well as for university and community struggles, it was not until after 1970 that the institutions of the Chicano movement, community art centers, mural groups, poster workshops, and galleries were established. Sources for the early Chicano murals, which were often the work of students and self-taught artists, ranged from reproductions of Siqueiros and Cuban posters to kitsch images of Aztec warriors and the Virgin of Guadalupe taken from postcards and calendars. In 1970 many of the artists who were to emerge as leaders of the poster and mural movements were just beginning to produce art, including the poster artists Malaquías Montoya and Rupert García (plate 153), and the muralists Eduardo Carrillo, Esteban Villa, José Montoya, Michael Rios, Ray Patlán, Judy Baca, Carlos Almaraz, Victor Ochoa, and Willie Herrón.

The activist Puerto Rican and Chicano art of the late 1960s played a crucial role in the revival of directly political art. In making art that was relevant to the lives of community people rather than to an educated elite, the community artists began to bring art back to its historic function. In this sense, though sometimes unconsciously, they were returning art to the social role it played in Mexico during the mural renaissance. Their revival of muralism to a vital social art renewed interest in the art of the 1930s and has slowly begun to bring back recognition to the masters of that earlier period.

Latin American art has been crucial in the United States as an impetus and example for an art of social content. The work of the *tres grandes* has provided a model for all later nationalist mural movements, either to be followed or rejected, but never ignored. The humanist art of Frasconi, Lasansky, and the Nueva Presencia group in the 1950s and 1960s provided an alternative approach to abstraction and was a way of dealing with the existential situation during the Cold War period. Latin American graphic art movements from the Mexican TGP to the Cuban, Puerto Rican, and Chicano silk-screen poster movements have been in the forefront of these fields.

The demands of U.S. foreign policy and internal political events as well as art issues have influenced the exposure and reception of Latin American art in this country. These considerations have also influenced the specific type of art being promoted and, to a certain extent, produced. A crisis situation in one country, as in Mexico after the revolution of 1917, Cuba in 1959, and Nicaragua today, will tend to spark interest in the entire region as the United States attempts to protect its interests and exert its influence. In the cultural sphere this is manifested by cultural exchange programs, exhibitions, and commissions. National security concerns about enemy bases in our "backyard," as during World War II, have provoked greater interest and exposure of Latin American art. The social and political climate within the United States has also affected the reception given to Latin American art, especially art with social content. During periods of social upheaval, for example, as in the Depression years of the 1930s or the social movements of the 1960s, there has been greater interest in an art that deals with social as well as formal issues.

Latin American artists have been in the vanguard of the search for a committed art about society that educates without preaching and convinces without rhetoric. The problem has not been resolved, but in the context of the present revival of political art in this country, the Latin American contribution is being examined with new interest.

The Latin American Presence

by Félix Angel

Introduction

Latin Americans and the people of the United States have long had different perceptions of the Western Hemisphere. For the people of the United States, the hemisphere is geographically divided into two continents, North and South America. Culturally, "Latin America" is viewed as a single area, beginning at the Rio Grande and extending to Cape Horn. For Latin Americans, however, the hemisphere is divided into four distinct parts. First, there is North America, which includes Canada, the United States, and Mexico; next comes Central America, running from Guatemala through Panama; then there is the Caribbean, consisting of the arc of islands that runs from Cuba to Trinidad and Tobago. Some of the Caribbean territories (Cuba, Haiti, the Dominican Republic, Puerto Rico, and the French departments of Guadeloupe and Martinique) are Latin in culture; others are not. Finally, there is South America, which is commonly subdivided into the Andean countries (Venezuela, Colombia, Ecuador, Peru, and Bolivia), the Southern Cone (Chile, Argentina, Uruguay, and Paraguay), and the vast expanse of Brazil and the Guianas. The subregional divisions are as much ethnic and cultural as geographic. The Latin American, a term we are now resigned to using for convenience, finds this quadripartite breakdown a convenient means of expressing his perception of broad differences within what is for him a single continent, America, that stretches from pole to pole.

There is still another way of distinguishing the peoples of Latin America, whose current differences are a result of cultural evolution in the region since colonial times. In his short presentation in the catalog to Leopoldo Presas's 1967 exhibit at the Gallery of Modern Art in New York, the Argentine critic Rafael Squirru wrote: "Latin America is a mestizo continent, a concept that must be understood culturally more so than racially, even though racially it may also be true. One can recognize in the continent three regions with distinct cultural complexes: the Afro-Latin in the Caribbean and northern Brazil, the Indo-Latin in the Andean regions, and the Euro-Latin in the south of South America."[1]

It is not surprising therefore that Latin Americans should be disconcerted by a generalization such as "Latin American culture." The term is not without validity when it refers to the colonial cultural heritage of the majority of the countries south of the United States, but it is not applicable to the present cultures of twenty individual countries and one semiautonomous territory. Literature provides a pertinent example: one would not lump the Argentine Jorge Luis Borges together with the Colombian Gabriel García Márquez, or the Chilean José Donoso with the Peruvian Mario Vargas Llosa, although all are part of the recent Latin American literary boom. The need for similar distinctions must also be recognized in other aspects of culture, including the plastic arts.

Art history is a relatively new discipline in Latin America, and the general public has often confused criticism with the objective interpretation of works of art. Criteria for analysis have been derived almost exclusively from European standards, as if art in Latin America were the product of that tradition alone, uninfluenced by other human and spiritual forces. While Latin America is indeed part of the West, this acknowledgment should not consign it to a secondary role in the development of twentieth-century art. An informed and balanced cultural viewpoint is essential for studying Latin American art. We must not forget, for example, that for most Latin

Americans contradiction and the element of the irrational are accepted components of life: not everything has to be completely explained to be assimilated naturally into the process of living; not everything has to be completely logical to be civilized. Alternatively, the disenchantment outsiders feel when they innocently expect to find the true "Latin soul" in all artistic expressions corresponds with the parochial stereotype that has been created about Latin Americans internationally. Latin America is more than tango, carnivals, and drugs, just as the United States is more than hamburgers and Ku Klux Klansmen. Culture is a far more complex, unpredictable matter. As Squirru pointedly noted in the aforementioned introduction: "Presas, like some of his distinguished colleagues, has Spanish blood from all his ancestors. Why should he feel, then, that by placing himself in the current of Mediterranean culture he is being less authentic than if he were to record pre-Columbian influences, which in his particular case have less meaning to him than Bonnard or Picasso?"[2]

Another stereotype that also needs to be examined is the idea of the Hispanic heritage. In the United States the term *Hispanic* is used to refer to an ethnic minority. Arbitrary though the classification may be, it is important to note it and to realize that a distinction must be made between U.S. *residents* of Latin American or Spanish descent and Latin Americans who have been active in the United States or who have taken up permanent residence in this country. One can hardly consider Latin Americans a "minority," given that they come from twenty countries, a single one of which, Brazil, has more than 130 million inhabitants.

The Latin American artists who at one time or another have made an appearance in the United States number in the thousands. Information on file at the Museum of Modern Art of Latin America in Washington, D.C., indicates that more than twenty-five hundred Latin American artists have been presented either individually or collectively in the gallery at the headquarters of the Organization of American States (OAS) since its exhibition program began in the 1940s. For purposes of this essay, "presence" has been determined by the degree of professional connection between the artist and the United States. This criterion explains why many significant artists are not included below. Either their activities were focused primarily in Europe or Latin America or their appearance on the U.S. art scene took place after 1970.

Moreover, with respect to the international reception given to Latin American artists this century, it must be stressed that the term *international* should not apply exclusively to the U.S. scene. The work of Joaquín Torres-García was recognized much earlier in Spain and Latin America than in New York, but this fact of course does not mean that his work lacked international respect. Latin Americans do not consider and never did consider New York the sole place to achieve artistic prominence. They recognized New York simply as the most active place where art happened to be exhibited after 1950, just as Rome, Madrid, Berlin, or Paris were such venues in the past and are again today. The aura surrounding these international places has tended to result in art from other parts of the world being categorized as provincial.

There are indeed a number of important Latin American artists whose importance has yet to be recognized internationally. Emilio Pettoruti, Andrés de Santamaría, Armando Reverón, Amelia Peláez, Carlos Mérida, and Pedro Figari, for example are still not very well known in the United States. They developed their ideas about visual imagery within the European aesthetic tradition, but their main contribution was to take that tradition further in its evolution and to enrich it with elements of the Latin American sensibility. Mérida, for instance, introduced into the Constructivist language visual rhythms derived from pre-Columbian music. The great Mexican muralists, especially Diego Rivera, redefined Cubism, which they learned from European artists. They redirected this modernist language, applying its vocabulary to ideological art, while European artists were engaged in problems related to form per se. Simultaneously, the Mexicans paid homage not only to the Renaissance mural technique but also to the pre-Columbian tradition of decorative programs of religious art.

After World War II, when the modern ideas disseminated from Europe became the patrimony of the West, including the United States and Latin America, a new generation of Latin American artists emerged; but we cannot base their importance on whether they were accepted in New York or Europe at the time. What is good for Europe or for the United States is not always good for Latin Americans (and this applies not only to artists). This postwar generation of artists were convinced of the integrity of their culture, and they knew they had been unwillingly compromised to the whims of more technologically advanced societies. They also recognized that their governments and economy were closely monitored as a result of the restless struggle for control of the world among the superpowers. Yet cultural expression could not be so easily controlled. Latin American artists accepted the challenge of competing internationally and made their presence felt as much as they could by trying to demonstrate the independent values of their own visual expressions. In New York, however, their work was relegated to the status of a "regional expression." There were few open minds to present the artists and their accomplishments in an appropriate context. The evidence offered in this essay deceptively suggests that Latin American artists received plenty of proper and unbiased treatment in the U.S. art world, but very rarely were they exhibited together with Pollock and Motherwell, with Still or Nevelson, or for that matter exhibited with their international contemporaries at The Museum of Modern Art. By contrast, the Museum of Contemporary Art of Caracas has important works by North American contemporary artists, including Edward Kienholz, Larry Rivers, Richard Smith, Larry Bell, and George Segal, British artists Francis Bacon and John Davies, Germans Josef Albers and Richard Lindner, the Hungarian Nicolas Schöffer, as well as works by the great modern masters Picasso, Miró, Arp, Matisse, and Braque. Even modest museums in Latin America, such as the Museum of Modern Art of Bogotá or the Tertulia Museum of Modern Art in the city of Cali, offer the public a complete overview of contemporary U.S. and Latin American art. They also organize exhibits of foreign artists' works and reproduce the art in their catalogs. The same can be said about museums in São Paulo, Mexico City, and Buenos Aires.

At the educational level, interest in affairs south of the Rio Grande has been limited to the specialized field of Latin American studies. Yet it is not surprising that the most important exhibit of Latin American art in the United States in the last forty years, *Art of Latin America since Independence*, was organized by an educational institution, Yale University. At the gallery level, commercial implications prevented many art dealers from taking the risks inherent in offering art by Latin Americans. When Latin American artists competed under the same circumstances as European or U.S. artists, they got reviews and were able to sell their work, but the galleries who showed them were small in terms of financial resources and institutional relations and thus not powerful enough to last out the battle to establish new, "foreign" artists. Most of these galleries did not survive. The ones that did survive succeeded only by offering artists already recognized in Europe, such as Matta.

Moreover, despite the shower of reviews of Latin American artists that did appear in New York's and the country's periodicals, only the mural controversies were really given significant media coverage. Armando Morales, for example, one of Nicaragua's greatest painters, lived in New York for almost ten years during the 1960s at the very time a second generation of North American Abstract Expressionists was beginning to be recognized. Morales left New York having had little influence on the artistic circles, except among the small group of inter-American affairs specialists. Only today, after moving to Paris and becoming represented by one of Paris's most important galleries, which has a branch in New York, is his painting attractive to North American collectors. The United States' cultural mechanisms are very efficient in giving the public what it wants: Latin American art is simply not as palatable to the capitalist appetite. Thus, the quantitative information offered here should not be confused with the qualitative elements that make the information relevant. Yes, there were reviews, many of them. But they were not oriented to develop a consciousness about the importance of the art of Latin America. As a consequence, these reviews were like shots in the dark.

This essay will focus on Latin American practitioners of abstraction (though not Geometric Abstractionists, who are discussed in Chapter Three) between 1950 and 1970 and artists active in the figurative current from 1940 to 1970 (with the exception of the Surrealists and artists who focused on social issues, who are discussed in chapters Four and Five). Those who are emphasized here were closely involved in the U.S. art scene, developed highly personal visual styles, and related their expressions to specific aspects of their cultural evolution. They were as innovative as their North American or European counterparts, and they enriched the repertory of imagery that evolved in the West.

A Latin American Perspective

Until the late 1930s figurative art was dominant in Latin America as well as in the United States. This art had two main branches. One incorporated regional characteristics expressed in landscapes, portraits, and genre scenes. Its practitioners used variations on European styles, from Impressionism to Cubism. This art was popular in Argentina, Brazil, Venezuela, Uruguay, and Chile—countries that maintained active contact with Europe.[3] The second branch, particularly noticeable in the Andean and Central American countries, developed along sociopolitical lines and evolved into Indianism. The spirit of this movement was eloquently defined by one of its most outstanding representatives, the Ecuadorian Camilo Egas, who wanted "to paint the Indians in an attempt to show the tragedy that has become those who once were a great race, and the damage that centuries of oppression have caused them."[4] Both these approaches to figurative art were nationalistic and owed a debt to the Mexican School. There was an important difference, however, between the regionalism practiced by Latin American artists and that of the United States. U.S. artists such as Grant Wood, Thomas Hart Benton, even Jackson Pollock in his early work, were more concerned with the "scene," the "subject," or the "theme" than with ideology. They depicted reality without polemics, whereas in Latin America art served as a vehicle for focusing attention on a variety of social, political, economic, and cultural problems.

Nearly every country in the Western Hemisphere experienced a considerable inflow of people from Europe as a result of political events in the 1930s. Countries with relatively strong economies, such as Brazil and Argentina, attracted great numbers of cultured, sophisticated Europeans, including artists. Many Latin American intellectuals in Europe also found it prudent to return home. The Peruvian Ricardo Grau, who was born in Burdeos in 1907 of Peruvian parents and studied in Paris and Brussels under André Tavory, André Lhote, Othon Frieze, and Fernand Léger, was among those who left France at the end of the 1930s. Grau became director of the School of Fine Arts in Lima. Due to his influence, his pupils adopted many stylistic characteristics of the School of Paris. The Ecuadorian Manuel Rendón, like Grau, was living in Paris before he returned to the Ecuadorian city of Cuenca. The Cuban Wifredo Lam also returned from France to Havana in 1941. But by far the greatest number of émigrés made their way to the United States, particularly to New York and Chicago, due to the country's solid economy and the security of its geographical location, remote from the theaters of conflict. Outstanding among the European émigré artists were the German painters Hans Hofmann, Josef Albers, and Max Ernst, French artist Yves Tanguy, and the German architect Mies van der Rohe, as well as the Chilean Roberto Matta. Matta, like the other émigrés, brought with him ideas that were seminal in the development of modern art in the United States.

Matta left Paris for New York in October 1939. Julien Levy, a well-known gallery owner, not only gave him his first New York show in 1940 but helped him contact others in the art business. Bernard Reis, a collector of Surrealist art, became one of Matta's first patrons. Among the artist's earliest acquaintances in Manhattan was Francis Lee, whose studio was a gathering place for artists, including William Baziotes, Gerome Kamrowski, Jackson Pollock, and Robert Motherwell.

In 1966, when Matta was in Minneapolis at the invitation of the Minneapolis School of Art, he and the U.S. artist Peter Busa were interviewed by Sidney Simon. Busa, looking back on the early days of the New York School, declared that in the last stages of the WPA projects some artists had begun to experiment privately with the automatism advocated by the Surrealists. Stronger influences, however, came from artists such as Léger, the American Stuart Davis, and above all Picasso: "Picasso was God. Picasso influenced all of us."[5] Matta for his part noted the surprise he had felt on learning that U.S. artists thought the only valid art was imported from abroad. Busa pointed out that Matta "personalized Surrealism" in their eyes.

In fact, the Latin American's studio was frequented assiduously by Pollock, Busa, and others for whom Matta, with his European experience and Surrealist background, constituted the stereotype of the famous, established artist. In the interview with Simon, Busa said that while all the artists of their group were about the same age, Matta was the furthest advanced artistically: "He was the most mature of our group. Matta's work was not dogmatically Surrealist, but was on an *idea* plane, which made it more exciting."[6]

The group met periodically until the fall of 1942. In the summer of 1941 the Mattas had rented a house on Cape Cod and invited Max Ernst to stay with them. Matta recalled Ernst's experiments with dripping, saying it was the first time he had ever seen anyone make systematic use of the technique. However, Matta himself had had recourse to both dripping and accident in his paintings of 1938 and 1939. Pollock's works in a similar vein were to come much later. The issue of "scale," according to Busa, was raised only after contact with Matta.[7] Except for the Luminists, with their panoramic landscapes, U.S. painters had never really developed canvases of broad dimensions.

Early in 1943 Matta met Arshile Gorky and Willem de Kooning. Matta was working with anthropomorphic forms, and the other two artists were also introducing human elements into their work. "*Art* and not *life* were the main preoccupations of American Action Painting," according to Matta. In January 1967 Simon interviewed Robert Motherwell, who asserted that Matta was "the most energetic, enthusiastic, poetic, charming, brilliant young artist that I have ever met."[8] Motherwell did not care much for Matta's painting, but he was greatly attracted to his drawings of the late 1930s and the 1940s. In Motherwell's words, they "are among the most beautiful, if not the most beautiful work made in America at that time." According to Motherwell, Matta "converted Gorky on his own to the theory of automatism." Prior to his exhibit of collages that Peggy Guggenheim was organizing for her New York gallery, Motherwell showed his compositions to Matta, who encouraged him to do them on a larger scale: "If you can do them that well little, you can do them bigger," Motherwell recalls Matta saying. "And I did. They became the core of my first show at Peggy Guggenheim's in October 1944."[9]

Though the historic roles played by the artists who gave birth to Abstract Expressionism have not yet been fully clarified, there can be no doubt that Matta was a key figure. Despite being an *official* member of the Surrealist group—the youngest, in fact—he had always envisioned the possibility of establishing his personal superiority over the movement. Motherwell recalls that on one occasion he began to plan an exhibition in the style of the Armory Show that would give him the opportunity to demonstrate his creative supremacy. While Matta may be considered a Surrealist painter, the importance of his work far transcends that classification. Matta was as important to Action Painting as Duchamp and some Dada artists were to Conceptual Art in the 1960s. But his extreme independence led him back to Paris in 1948, at which time he was expelled from the ranks of the Surrealists. After returning to Europe, Matta lost interest in the U.S. art scene and refused to allow himself to be manipulated by Manhattan art dealers. This attitude of independence was expressed determinedly by the artist: "I feel the role of the artist is to storm Art, to hit deep the roots, like an art-quake and not art-kissing."[10]

Once the war was over, Europe entered upon a great phase of reconstruction, aided by a massive influx of U.S. capital. Latin America had escaped physical destruction, yet it had suffered from the economic impact of the wartime blockades.[11] There was some revival of the weak national economies, but postwar monopolistic concessions and regional reliance on limited types of exports did not favor the development of an independent economic infrastructure. The situation of the United States was unique. Exempt from the physical ravages of the war, it had benefited enormously not only from the demand for goods and services occasioned by the conflict but also from the technological and military advances, from the influx of talented people from Europe, and from the control of commercial transportation and means of distribution.[12] By the end of the war the United States was unquestionably master of the hemisphere's destiny.

In part due to the war-related dispersal of creative talent, artists were free to seek new forms of aesthetic expression—forms that would help to change a world that had just passed through terrible disasters. There is indeed a close relationship between the idea of a new beginning after the war and a new form of artistic expression, a phenomenon also expressed by the Surrealists in Paris after World War I. This is not the only explanation why abstract art emerged in the Americas, but it was a reason why the ideas patronized by

European artists continued developing in the New World. American societies, not concerned with physical reconstruction, were free to promote artistic research. New York, the financial capital of the United States, became the new center of fashionable culture, replacing Paris as the home of the avant-garde. With an aggressiveness encouraged by its economic resources, New York set itself up as the locus for a new generation. Latin Americans understood this fact clearly. Europe for them remained a place to learn the teachings of the past. They admired New York not only for taking the lead in renewal but also for the enormous opportunities they thought were available to them there. In time, however, the U.S. art world became impervious to the accomplishments of other countries, forgetful of the fact that it was due to their artists that it had been able to enter with such speed into a new stage of artistic development.

There were, for example, artists who questioned the validity of the abstract language and its capacity to reflect the particular situation of third world countries. Débora Arango, an artist from Medellín, Colombia, developed a furious figurativism during the early 1950s. She mocked the hypocrisy and cowardice of the leaders of Colombia's traditional political parties during the unrest that characterized this period. Thirty years later we see surprising similarities in the paintings of Berlin's artists, where chaos and its devilish symbols dominate the vocabulary of their paintings. Débora Arango was not interested in the internationalization of her work. Thus, her paintings remained unknown despite their contemporary values.

Although Abstract Expressionism dominated the North American art scene in the 1950s, mere numbers of practitioners do not constitute a balanced perspective on the art of the period.[13] For a decade, Peruvian art was basically represented by a single figure, Fernando de Szyszlo, an abstract painter in our view as important as any of his U.S. counterparts, including Mark Rothko or Robert Motherwell. It would be a mistake, however, to assume that the art of this country during this period is otherwise unimportant or that there was not any other kind of national artistic activity.

New York's aspirations to artistic hegemony via the new international movement inspired in Europe and Latin America the reaffirmation of individual national styles. In Europe this reaction was reinforced by the consciousness of the Continent's long-standing traditions. In Latin America, however, traditions needed to be defined. Latin Americans came to the conclusion that new cultural expressions should be supported in part by their Western heritage and in part by the spirit of native cultures, which in some cases went back for a thousand years or more and had coexisted with the Hispanic culture throughout the colonial period.

Latin American artists were consumed with a desire to manifest their identity in visual expressions that were consonant with modern art trends but that also incorporated peculiarly Latin American elements, quite different from the images of U.S. culture or traditional European culture. Latin Americans assigned a specific function to art: it was to constitute a link between the present, the genuine, and old values characteristic of its own cultures.

The idea of an abstract art did not reach the Americas in the guise of a formally defined doctrine.[14] Instead, the basic principles were gradually introduced and artists throughout the hemisphere transformed them in accordance with their individual aesthetic perceptions. A good example can be provided by Torres-García's workshop in Montevideo, where Uruguayan artists adhered to the philosophy of Universal Constructivism without sacrificing their individuality. In this attempt to define a form of expression distinct to Latin America, preference was given to traditional artistic techniques, such as oil painting, sculpture, and drawing. These media had the economic and social advantages of low cost that not only favored artistic activity but also made it possible for a growing public to understand that participation in the cultural process was open to more than the elite. (Although, by the end of the decade, some Latin American artists did begin making use of technology, using light effects and motion in their art. This activity was centered mainly in Paris through the Argentine Groupe de Recherche d'Art Visuel and the Venezuelan Kinetic group. They developed an ingenious system in which natural forces and the basic physical properties of color displaced the machine as its main element. This is clear in the *Solar Wing* of Alejandro Otero of the 1970s, the *Penetrables* of Jesús Soto, the Physiochromes of Carlos Cruz Díez, as well as in the luminous works of

Julio Le Parc.)

Artists of the generation that came to the fore in the 1950s, born for the most part around 1920, had different agendas from figures such as Andrés de Santamaría, Pedro Figari, Héctor Basaldua, Fidelio Ponce de León, and Amelia Peláez, who were born in the second half of the preceding century. Members of the earlier generation had sought to assert themselves as individuals, working in hostile environments that did not take well to their departures from the European models to which they were accustomed. Before the 1940s these artists found acceptance only among a small minority of the art-viewing public. The new generation however, aimed to place their activities on a par with the international art centers, but they lacked the infrastructure to make their work fashionable and the resources to promote it. In artistic terms, however, they achieved their goals.

We must also remember that the goals of Latin America's artists were often quite distinct from the objectives of the New York School. There was no point or desire for them to be considered Abstract Expressionists, a category that really applied only to artists in the United States. Contemporary art for Latin Americans in the 1940s and 1950s could be geometric, figurative, abstract, or even based on the folk tradition. Their visual language had evolved without losing sight of man and his problems. Indeed, the idea of an international movement was largely promoted by the United States. The concept afforded the opportunity to provide for its cultural achievements within the framework of the Western tradition. But international art was destined for a society conceived in abstract terms, technologically standardized in behavior and needs. Thus, many Latin Americans, particularly the figurative artists, dismissed the art of Jackson Pollock, Franz Kline, Robert Motherwell, and even Willem de Kooning, considering it rigidly attached to formulas of unemotional principles.[15] Latin American artists sought inspiration in absolute, spiritual, human values, whereas they saw the international movement as a discipline to which man had to adapt.

Predictably, Latin American artists found it difficult to gain acceptance outside their own region. Their art was viewed either as a parochial manifestation void of universal significance, or, ironically, as exhibiting too many elements foreign to preconceived ideas of Latin America. The art audience in the United States still thought Latin American art was best represented by the Mexican School, then in its last gasp, and by the Brazilians Candido Portinari and Carmen Miranda. New York newspapers' reviews of shows by Latin Americans during the 1950s and 1960s reinforced these notions. Elementary parallels with Inca and Aztec imagery were often discussed, as if the works on view fell within the realm of folk art. Reviewers also tended to make generally invidious comparisons with works by Europeans, particularly Picasso, blithely ignoring the particular context from which this art sprang.

Just as the Mexican School had counted on official patronage from the state, which in turn relied on artists for ideological cooperation in educating the masses in the precepts of the Mexican Revolution, so in the United States artists could count on backing from private enterprise, which had assumed responsibility for educating the taste of the public (which hitherto had shown a preference for European art). The argument that the Latin American avant-garde lacked the vitality of its U.S. counterpart has always been based on the premise that the region's artists were lacking in the required creative energy. This erroneous concept was developed and sustained in the United States and seemed to be confirmed as Latin America's economic, political, and social problems spiraled. Thanks in one case to geographical proximity and in the other to political union, Mexican and Puerto Rican artists enjoyed a certain access to the U.S. art scene. Mexico, moreover, still basked in the glory of its great muralists, but the rest of Latin America was at a geographic and logistical disadvantage. Moreover, Latin American artists had to display exceptional mobility, journeying between their own countries and Europe and the United States to participate in the international art world. Some wound up settling abroad. Those who took up residence in Europe found it easier to identify with the local avant-garde than those who settled in New York. The consensus was that in the United States it was difficult to break through the barriers of self-interest erected by the local establishment for its own protection.

In the 1950s the principle of artistic freedom was established in Latin America; recognition of artistic achievement from abroad, however, was not forthcoming. The situation was counterbalanced by a series of artistic events, biennials, and interregional salons that gave local artists the opportunity to exhibit their work on an equal footing with artists from other parts of the world. In countries such as Argentina, Colombia, and Mexico, there was a revival of interest in figurative art, while nonrepresentational art took on renewed vigor, attaining at times a violence of expression that could be seen as foreshadowing the repressive regimes that were to come into power when the United States tightened its grip on the region. Latin American art of that period made evident as never before that the region's artists were committed to freedom of expression and that various methods of achieving this reflected cultural differences that have to be respected and understood before any attempt is made to view its manifestations internationally.

Latin American Artists in the United States

Latin American artists made their presence felt on the U.S. art scene during the 1950s and 1960s in three ways. One group traveled to the United States using their own initiative and resources or under the auspices of foundations and institutions for the promotion of the arts, including Pan-American cooperation societies. A second group had works included in museum exhibitions that were organized to create, in a limited way, public awareness of artistic activity in Latin America. A third had works presented at commercial galleries. In the case of the first two groups, there was no conscious plan to compete with U.S. art on the international stage; rather the aim was to exhibit alongside U.S. artists and have the work judged accordingly. The Latin Americans were seen not only as foreigners but as strangers from underdeveloped countries. Not much was expected of them, and few people were willing to recognize their originality. From an institutional viewpoint there was little attempt to coordinate the artists' efforts and no effort to establish a firm regional presence. For the most part, the impression audiences must have received from the U.S. institutions that presented the artists was that Latin American art was a provincial expression suffering from a lack of coherence: it was not a pivotal force in contemporary art. The main reason for this impression was ignorance about the evolution of modern Latin American art, which today in the United States is still a story almost totally unexplored. Only in rare opportunities, such as Yale University's *Art of Latin America Since Independence*, were the historic and sociological implications of the visual imagery produced in the area investigated. U.S. curators prefer to concentrate on European and North American art. The Latin American artists who eventually were successful in the United States were introduced by the private sector, employing the same resources utilized in the promotion of U.S. artists.[16]

Institutions

In 1925 Simon Guggenheim and his wife set up the John Simon Guggenheim Memorial Foundation, named for their son, who died on April 26, 1922. The foundation was to add to the educational, literary, artistic, and scientific power of the United States and to provide better international understanding.[17]

From 1925 to 1967 the foundation awarded 6,238 fellowships in all fields to individuals from the Western Hemisphere and the Philippines. From 1950 to 1967 twenty Latin American artists received fellowships. The fellowships were renewed at least for one more year to half of the artists. (Maurico Lasansky of Argentina benefited the most from these fellowships. His was renewed five times between 1943 and 1964.) This represented a considerable increase from the period 1925–50, when only six artists from Latin America working in the visual arts received grants. The increase can be interpreted perhaps as an indirect result of U.S. interest in penetrating Latin America and establishing itself as the dominant culture. The United States could exploit economic and political connections as well as cultural ones in developing an edge in the Cold War.

On June 9, 1937, Solomon R. Guggenheim established the Solomon R. Guggenheim Foundation to promote art education and appreciation. He was also interested in collecting art, and over the years friends of the foundation donated works of art. In 1959 the foundation acquired a permanent home, the present Solomon R. Guggenheim Museum, in a building on Fifth Avenue designed by Frank Lloyd Wright. The only Latin American represented in the Guggenheim collection at that time was Wifredo Lam, whose work was given by Joseph Cantor, a well-known collector of

Cuban art. Although Lam's reputation was sufficiently established to justify his inclusion in the collection, the fact that he was the only Latin American representative was symptomatic of the lack of awareness of Latin American art. In later years other Latin American artists made their way into the museum's collection, in large part due to the personal interest of its director Thomas Messer and the help of the Neumann Foundation of Caracas, which in 1966 helped to finance *The Emergent Decade*, an exhibition of Latin American artists held at the museum.

The establishment of the Guggenheim International Award was an important undertaking of the Solomon R. Guggenheim Foundation and the Guggenheim Museum. The International Association of Art Critics, the International Council of Museums, and the International Association of Plastic Artists served as consultants for the first competition and selected the entries for the competition. The exhibition took place from March 27 to June 7, 1956. There were three levels of prizes. The top-ranked Guggenheim International Award went to the British sculptor Ben Nicholson. The Guggenheim Continental Award, a regional award to be given to a representative from one of the Latin American countries invited to participate in the event, was conferred on the Argentine Emilio Pettoruti for his 1954 work *Sea Twilight*. National awards were also given to artists from the Latin countries, including representatives of Mexico, Argentina, Chile, Brazil, Colombia, and Cuba. The Latin American presentation was solid. It included Roberto Matta, Rufino Tamayo, and Amelia Peláez. Guggenheim national awards went to the Colombian Alejandro Obregón for his *Vigil* (also known as the *Wake*) and to the Brazilian Candido Portinari for his oil on wood *Women Crying*.

The next competitive exhibition was held from October 2, 1958, to February 23, 1959. National prizes went to Enrique Zañartu of Chile for his *Composition*, to Alfredo Volpi of Brazil for his *Composition*, and to Eduardo Ramírez Villamizar of Colombia for his *Horizontal, White and Black*. Rufino Tamayo participated in the event in a special category. For reasons that are not clear, only Zañartu's work was put on display in the accompanying exhibition. The competition was held again in 1960. National-level prizes went to Fernando Botero of Colombia for his *Battle of the Arch-Devil*, to Jośe Antonio Fernández Muro of Argentina for his *Painting*, to Emilio Hermansen of Chile for his *Painting*, and to María Leontina of Brazil for a work entitled *The Episodes*. Rufino Tamayo of Mexico received a prize in the extra-national category, which apparently replaced the continental award. This category also included works by José Luis Cuevas of Mexico and Armando Morales of Nicaragua. The competition's exhibition was on display from November 1, 1960, to January 29, 1961.

The fourth competition for the Guggenheim International Award did not take place until 1964, when the exhibition was held from January 16 to March 29. There were several fundamental changes in the organization of the event. In the first place, the selection was made by the Solomon R. Guggenheim Museum, without the aid of international juries picking national representatives. The national and extra-national prizes were replaced by three awards for merit in addition to the International Award, which on this occasion went to the Italian Alberto Giacometti. For the first time all works submitted by the selected artists were exhibited. No Latin American won a prize on this occasion, although artists selected for the event included David Alfaro Siqueiros, Rufino Tamayo, Fernando de Szyszlo, the New Figuration Group from Argentina, and fifteen others from Mexico, Venezuela, Argentina, Cuba, Chile, and Peru. The total number of artists invited was eighty-two.

In 1967 the event took the form of an exhibition entitled *Sculpture from Twenty Nations*, and was held from October 20 of that year to February 4, 1968. This was a joint undertaking of the Solomon R. Guggenheim Museum, the National Gallery of Canada (Ottawa), the Art Gallery of Ontario (Toronto), and the Montreal Museum of Fine Arts. National categories of representation were eliminated, and prizes were replaced by purchase awards. Edgar Negret of Colombia was the sole Latin American included in the show of seventy-six artists. The next competition, known as the *Guggenheim International Exhibition*, was held from February 11 to April 11, 1971. Twenty artists were included in the show: Antonio Dias of Brazil was the only Latin American. The last competition was held from November 22, 1985, to February 6, 1986, and exhibited under the title *Transformation in Sculpture: Four Decades of American and European Art.* There were no prizes, and no Latin Americans were invited to participate.

A quick look at the development of the Guggenheim International Award competition shows a decreasing interest and appreciation for art by Latin Americans. It also shows patronizing and segregational criteria were adopted for the limited inclusion of Latin Americans. The existence of national and extra-national prizes and the segregation of Latin Americans from the other participants were artificial divisions not rooted in issues of quality that prevented the Latin Americans from competing on an equal footing. In the second competition only one Latin American was included in the exhibition; and in the fourth competition, when the national categories were eliminated, no Latin American won a merit prize, although Matta, Tamayo, Siqueiros, and Lam participated. In the fifth and sixth exhibitions only one Latin American made it into the show, and in the seventh there was no representation whatsoever, despite the exhibition's misleading title. The curators in effect suggested that in four decades Latin America produced no distinguished sculpture. Prizes and invitations were offered when Latin Americans could be categorized into regional groups, but when the competition was reduced in scope, the Latin Americans were the first to be eliminated.

The Organization of American States (OAS) has the longest continuous record of promoting Latin American artists of any institution headquartered in the United States, but the effectiveness of its efforts is open to question. The cultural exchange activities of the organization's General Secretariat, formerly known as the Pan-American Union, date back to 1917, the year in which an education section was established pursuant to a resolution of the Second Pan-American Scientific Congress. In 1929 the section was renamed the Office of Intellectual Cooperation, in recognition of the manifold new activities for which it had been given responsibility. Until 1948 it was charged not only with educational matters but also with following cultural developments of all kinds in Latin America. Its concerns included archaeology (principally legislating for the protection of artistic and historic monuments), the plastic arts, music, literature, university faculty and student exchanges, and treaties on intellectual cooperation between countries. Among its subdivisions was the Visual Arts Unit, which in 1946 began a systematic program of exhibitions at the organization's headquarters in Washington, D.C., with the clearly stated intention of making Latin American art better known in the United States.

Another of the General Secretariat's principal components was the Department of Cultural Affairs, which included the Division of Music and Visual Arts. The OAS initiated a permanent art collection in 1957, with a small fund for acquisitions voted by the Permanent Council the same year. The permanent collection grew through the years by donations. The most important of which was a gift of twenty works, donated by the IBM Corporation, including important pieces by Amelia Peláez of Cuba, Héctor Poleo of Venezuela, and Héctor Basaldua of Argentina. Other significant donations included a work by Joaquín Torres-García, which was a gift from Nelson Rockefeller; a painting by Pedro Figari, a gift from the National Bank of Uruguay; and a painting by Roberto Matta, a gift from the Workshop Center for the Arts of Washington, D.C. One of the first purchases made with the acquisitions fund was Alejandro Obregón's *Vigil*, which had won one of the national prizes at the Guggenheim International Award in 1956. Currently, the holdings of the Museum of Modern Art of Latin America (in which the collection is now housed) numbers about eight hundred items. It includes paintings, sculptures, drawings, prints, collages, photographs, and works in mixed media, from the thirty-one member countries of the OAS.

Since 1946 works by more than twenty-five hundred artists have been presented at OAS headquarters.[18] For many artists their appearance in Washington marked the beginning of their reputations in the United States and abroad. The staff of the Visual Arts Unit participated in many of the most important art events in Latin America, such as the São Paulo biennials, at which the OAS frequently was assigned an exhibition room of its own. Since it was the only entity in the United States that specialized in Latin American art, the OAS was often called on to serve as a consultant to institutions in the United States and abroad. Besides collaborating on important exhibitions, including *Three Thousand Years of Colombian Art* in 1960, the staff was responsible for OAS exhibits at expositions such as the New York World's Fair in 1964 and *Hemisfair '68* in San Antonio, Texas, at which works from the permanent collection were presented. In 1966 the OAS collaborated with the Smithsonian Institution on a traveling exhibit of works by five artists entitled *New Names in Latin American Art*.[19] The OAS sent several shows to the Carroll Reece Museum in Johnson City, Tennessee, among them a 1969 exhibit of forty-five artists' works entitled *Latin American Painting*. The organization also helped curate an exhibit of Latin American art that traveled the Mississippi and Ohio rivers in 1962 as part of the Festival of the Americas.

Thanks to its comfortable economic situation (it was funded by contributions received from the member countries) and its administrative flexibility, the OAS enjoyed a period of great activity during the 1950s and early 1960s. Its activities were helped too by the United States Alliance for Progress, a policy of President John F. Kennedy conceived after the Cuban Missile Crisis of 1962. Its goal was to prevent the spread of communism in Latin America by the effective participation of the United States in the economic and cultural development of the region. The Visual Arts Unit had access to funds for such publications as the *Boletín de Artes Visuales* and a series entitled "Art in Latin America Today," which published the writings of a number of Latin American critics, thereby introducing them to university, museum, and commercial gallery circles.[20]

Due in large part to the technical, economic, scientific, social, and cultural-assistance programs carried out by the OAS in their promotion of the Alliance for Progress policy, the organization became a prestigious institution in Latin America. In the visual arts field, the OAS gallery became an obligatory way station for artists on the path to international recognition. Since there were not many places in Washington showing contemporary art on a regular basis then, the newspapers usually covered the OAS exhibits. The importance of the OAS gallery, however, was more relevant to its Latin American audience than to the U.S. public. Indeed, many artists were disappointed by the way their works were received in Washington. Moreover, since most of the exhibiting artists had to return to their countries, their only contact was with the Visual Arts Unit. By the end of the 1960s the influence of the OAS gallery was declining. Washington was rapidly shedding its provincial status in the art world, and artistic activity in the city was shifting attention away from the OAS gallery. Moreover, the Alliance for Progress policy had proved to be a failure: it had come to be seen as a political tool for U.S. interests.

Since its establishment in 1929, The Museum of Modern Art in New York has taken an interest in Latin American art, due to the personal interest of the Rockefeller family and the vision of one of its directors, Alfred H. Barr, Jr. In 1931 the museum presented an exhibition of works by Diego Rivera that circulated to a number of educational institutions in the United States. From 1935 to 1940 Abby Aldrich Rockefeller presented the museum with her extensive collection of paintings, drawings, and prints by Rivera, and a painting by Orozco. These donations led to the creation of a collection of Latin American art, which grew over the course of subsequent years. The first exhibit of the collection took place at the museum in 1943. It was in part motivated by the U.S. government's "Good Neighbor" policy, which was initiated by Franklin Delano Roosevelt to soften Latin American resentment aroused by the humiliating restrictions imposed on the hemisphere by the United States during the war. In 1944 there was an exhibit of modern Cuban painters at the museum. Small-scale exhibits were staged sporadically thereafter, including *Drawings, Watercolors, and Collages* in 1959. Rodolfo Abularach and Raquel Forner were among the artists represented on that occasion. Exhibits of the museum's acquisitions also sometimes included Latin Americans: Armando Morales and Alejandro Otero were among eight Latin Americans represented in the annual exhibition for 1957. But an important exhibition of Latin American art, save for the one-person show of Roberto Matta in 1957, has not been presented at the museum since 1944. An exhibition presented with forty-two works from the permanent collection was shown in 1967, but only for two weeks (April 13–30) as a promotional event tied to Pan-American Week festivities. The limited number of works on exhibit was inadequate, especially given the pronouncements of the press bulletin issued by the museum on the occasion, in which it was stated that the holdings of examples of Latin American art consisted of 160 paintings and sculptures and 1,400 drawings and prints, as well as photographs, films, and objects. The exhibit was divided into two chronological sections, 1930–50 and 1950–67: no attempt was made to examine art before 1930.

The reluctance of The Museum of Modern Art to exhibit Latin American art either within the context of the hemisphere's art or of Western art has had a negative impact on Latin American art and on the general public that visits the museum. Prior to the remodeling of the museum in 1985, Roberto Matta, for example, one of the four or five Latin Americans whose work was consistently on exhibit, was always presented in the company of the French Surrealists and represented by one work, usually *El Vértigo de Eros*. This was not in itself inappropriate, but Matta's importance as stated in the museum was restricted incorrectly to that particular area without any suggestion of his role as an innovator in the realm of abstract painting before 1940. Wifredo Lam has always been represented in the museum by *The Jungle*, but it is located in a lobby, without any didactic references to the artist's sources in Afro-Cuban myths or to his relationship to Latin American Magic Realism.[21] No one can deny the important role The Museum of Modern Art has played in studies of twentieth-century art, in disseminating knowledge of modern art, in increasing the appreciation of it, and in molding the taste of the American public. This is particularly true of the period before 1960, after which other museums dedicated to modern art were built in New York, among them the Guggenheim and Whitney museums. The holdings of The Museum of Modern Art, however, remain unequaled and have permitted the museum to make a number of important visual statements in a highly authoritative manner. Yet its approach has tended to be exclusive and nationalistic, overemphasizing the importance of local movements like the New York School and North American Pop Art. One would expect to see the artists of the Mexican School well represented, especially since the museum owns many of their works, but these are rarely on exhibit.

Intentionally or not, the museum has obstructed the appreciation of Latin American art, a very sad reality given the institution's enormous influence in U.S. art circles. This attitude has become more pronounced over time. At the exhibit *Kinetic Art*, which opened in February 1965, seven Latin Americans were included, although Otero and Soto were not represented. In 1985, however, the show *Contrast of Form: Geometric Abstract Art, 1910–1980* included no Latin Americans whatsoever, not even Torres-García, despite the fact that this art was dominated by Europeans and Latin Americans.[22] Even the Matta retrospective of 1957 was disappointing. The artist's connections with European Surrealism were stressed, divorcing him from his South American roots.

The museum's potential in the area of Latin American art is largely unrealized. While Latin America is indeed well represented in its holdings, the works are for the most part in storage, and the U.S. public, which crowds the museum daily, has little opportunity to make their acquaintance. The position taken by the museum is but one of a number of factors contributing to the U.S. public's lack of knowledge of and enthusiasm for Latin American art. One must also take into account the nature of the art establishment in the United States and the operations of the art market. Commercial galleries, dealers, and art consultants to corporations all wield great power and often seek to increase appreciation of works they are offering for sale by getting a prestigious institution to add a given artist to its collection or at least to give a one-person show that will enhance an artist's reputation. The process is self-perpetuating. The lack of representation of Latin American artists in U.S. museums in general also makes galleries reluctant to promote the artists. The public in turn is not inclined to buy works by foreign artists who are not represented in leading institutions, since this implies that they are not worthy of serious consideration. The institutions themselves are not interested in artists that are not "successful."

In the late 1960s the art gallery of the Center for Inter-American Relations in New York, funded by the Rockefeller family, began activities aimed at making Latin American art better known. Although there has been a notable falling-off of their efforts, they continue with their charge even today. Their heyday began with the 1967 exhibition *Forerunners of American Modernism* and continued until the late 1970s. (During these last years emphasis was laid on presenting artists who were relatively young.) Among the artists included in the 1967 exhibit were Dr. Atl, Juan Blanes, Stuart Davis, Thomas Eakins, Pedro Figari, Diego Rivera, Joaquín Torres-García, and Amelia Peláez. This was a rare occasion in which North American artists were integrated with their contemporaries from Latin America. In 1968 the center exhibited *Five Latin American Artists at Work in New York* and *Beyond Geometry*, an exhibit organized by the Torcuato di Tella Institute of Buenos Aires. In 1969 one-man exhibitions by Fernando Botero of Colombia and Rómulo Macció of Argentina were held. In September 1969 there was an exhibition of works that had been presented by the Neumann Foundation of Caracas to the Solomon R. Guggenheim Museum, after *The Emergent Decade* exhibition. In 1970 Alejandro Obregón had a retrospective of works he painted between 1952 and 1970. The center's fame grew rapidly among Latin American artists, for whom exhibiting there represented an important step in the promotion of their work. It was seen as having more international appeal than the Organization of American States and its Visual Arts Unit, which was beginning to show signs of exhaustion. For the New York establishment, however, the center was seen as a public-relations institution; the art exhibits were just a colorful note in a program of activities promoting good will between the United States and Latin America.

By the end of the 1960s the Latin American intellectual and artistic community was highly politicized. The Rockefeller family's involvement in the center resulted in a boycott of its activities by a group of Latin American artists living in New York. A particular target was an ambitious project conceived by Stanton Catlin, who hoped to convince some of New York's most influential galleries to exhibit simultaneously several Latin American artists. Printed statements were sent to the galleries involved expressing the artists' disapproval of the action. The galleries withdrew their participation, and Catlin was forced to resign. A good chance for Latin American artists to be seen at commercial galleries in New York was destroyed by these passions.

During the 1950s and 1960s, other U.S. institutions were also engaged in promoting or at least investigating the development of the plastic arts in Latin America. The University of Texas at Austin had a broad program of Latin American studies, and art exhibits at the institution led to the establishment of the Twentieth-Century Latin American Collection within the Archer M. Huntington Art Gallery of the university. This collection today is one of the most comprehensive of its kind in the United States. The Corcoran Gallery of Art in Washington, D.C., also occasionally exhibited works by Latin Americans, but since the late 1970s it has specialized entirely in U.S. art. In fact, the Corcoran had never been particularly international in outlook and contemporary foreign art had been presented only in shows organized by other institutions for which the gallery lent its exhibit space, but considerable good will was demonstrated by such shows as the eclectic *Collecting for Pleasure* (1956), which included Edgar Negret; *From Latin America* (1956), organized by the Washington Institute of Contemporary Art; *The Contemporary Spirit* (1966), in which Marisol, Julio Le Parc, and Carlos Mérida were featured; *Contemporary Painting and Sculpture of Peru* (1966); and an exhibit of Uruguayan art (1967) that included most of the forerunners of modernism from that country as well as representatives of newer generations. Latin American art exhibits were relatively scarce in the 1970s. Worthy of note are a traveling exhibition of the sculptor Edgar Negret (1974) and a show of Raquel Forner's work (1976).

The Institute of Contemporary Art in Boston exhibited Latin Americans on several occasions. In 1956 it was the site of an Armando Reverón retrospective, organized by the Ministry of Education of Venezuela and sponsored by that country's Creole Petroleum Company. In 1960 the institute had a group show entitled *Latin America: New Departures,* in which Manabu Mabe, Fernando de Szyszlo, Alejandro Obregón, Alejandro Otero, Ricardo Martínez, and Armando Morales were represented by five works each, and the Argentine artists Miguel Ocampo, Clorindo Testa, Sara Grilo, José Antonio Fernández Muro, and Kasuya Sakai by single compositions. This exhibition was organized while Thomas Messer was director.

In 1960 the Walker Art Center of Minneapolis received a gift of Latin American works from Mrs. Edward R. Weir, who had bought them specifically to donate them to the Walker. It included compositions by Joaquín Roca Rey, Rodolfo Abularach, Raquel Forner, Marcelo Grassman, José Luis Cuevas, Luis Seoane, Fayga Ostrower, Libero Badi,

Luis Piza, and Héctor Basaldua. During the 1960s the Miami Museum of Modern Art began to present Latin American artists on a regular basis. In the first five years of the decade there were shows by Alberto Davila, Fernando Maza, Vicente Forte, Antonio Berni, Omar Rayo, Oswaldo Romberg, and Jorge Demirjian. In March 1962 the museum presented *New Art from Brazil.*

Latin American exhibits cropped up from time to time at other institutions around the country. A notable example was a 1964 retrospective of prints made by Antonio Frasconi. The exhibition was seen at the Baltimore Museum of Art and the National Collection of Fine Arts in Washington, D.C. Fernando Botero had a one-person exhibit at the Milwaukee Art Center in 1966; Nemesio Antúnez, who had served as cultural attaché at Chile's Permanent Mission to the United Nations for a number of years, had a retrospective at the Stanford Museum and Nature Center in Connecticut in 1969. The National Gallery of Art in Washington, D.C., was responsible for *A Century and a Half of Argentine Painting* in 1956, which included seventy artists, from Jean Phillipe Goulu (1797–1855) to artists born about 1920, such as Fernández Muro and Sara Grilo.

The Riverside Museum (no longer in existence) in Manhattan and the Brooklyn Museum had occasional exhibits in which Latin Americans participated. In 1957 the former organized an important exhibit of Puerto Rican art, sponsored by the Institute of Puerto Rican Culture. This exhibit traveled to OAS headquarters. In 1959 the Riverside Museum had a show of prints selected by the Pratt Institute of New York that included works by Antonio Frasconi, Emilio Sanchez, and Rufino Tamayo. In 1960 it joined with the Roland de Aenlle Gallery in presenting a group show of works by Fernández Muro, Grilo, de Szyszlo, Bonevardi, Abularach, and Hurtado. *The National Print Exhibition* annually held at the Brooklyn Museum several times included the work of Latin Americans.

A few Latin Americans were invited to the artist-in-residence programs of universities. Fernando de Szyszlo was at Cornell in 1962, followed by Manuel Felguérez and Ernesto Deira in 1965. In 1966 Cornell also presented a show of prints by Antonio Berni. The Argentine Kasuya Sakai was given a show at the Cleveland Institute of Art in 1963. With but few exceptions, presentations of Latin American artists at the university level came about as a result of the presence of the artist in the United States at the time.

Although there were many exhibits of Latin American art organized in the United States between 1950 and 1970, few attempted to examine in depth the quality of the work being done below the Rio Grande. U.S. art circles viewed—and continue to view—Latin America as an area of secondary importance in the plastic arts. According to Grace Glueck, New York circles in the 1950s found Latin American art "extravagant" and too fantastic, elements unappealing to North Americans.[23] New York in particular was infatuated with its own artistic tendencies and became increasingly ignorant of other movements and manifestations. This position was in contradistinction to Latin America, whose artists and intellectuals have been receptive to outside influences since the independence movements began.

For most of the postwar period the United States was unaffected by the mass emigrations from Cuba and Central America, which, added to an increasing inflow of Mexicans and Puerto Ricans, have created a significant Hispanic minority and new political, social, and cultural tensions in U.S. society—as well as new cause to examine things Latin American. Most of the exhibitions organized in connection with Pan-American celebrations and industrial fairs, including the modest exhibition at The Museum of Modern Art in 1967, were of minor significance and fell beyond the purview of the art establishment. They had mere curiosity value. Latin American artists were hampered by another disadvantage in the United States, namely the lack of critical and historical reference material in English that could have served to educate the public about their work. This was one of the factors motivating the OAS Visual Arts Unit to produce material in English, but the organization's range was very limited. Even today the alarming paucity of such material is a serious obstacle to the art history of the countries to the south. The majority of exhibits did not engender documentation of importance, demonstrating the lack of scholarly investigation in these superficial surveys. Most of the exhibition catalogs mentioned in this section contained no more than a short presentation, which was often quite unrelated to the art. The texts ran into generalizations that exaggerated characteristics common to all Latin American countries. Only artists who attracted the attention of commercial galleries could hope for informative publications issued by the backers.

There was, and still is, very little interest in art promotion at the government level. Occasionally, private enterprise came to the rescue, but this often provoked criticism because of the political agenda of such enterprises. The exhibit *Three Thousand Years of Colombian Art,* which first opened in Miami in 1960, was financed by the International Petroleum Company. This exhibit went to Europe, where it was seen in Stockholm and Rome, among other cities. But before it left the United States the show suffered from several changes, especially in the contemporary section. Another example of private-sector support was the *New Art of Argentina* exhibit, held at the Walker Art Center in Minneapolis in 1964. Organized with the cooperation of the Torcuato di Tella Institute of Buenos Aires, it traveled to the Akron Art Institute, the Atlanta Art Association, and the Art Gallery of the University of Texas at Austin. This exhibit covered the current trends in Argentine art. It also left a catalog of documentary value, with some interesting ideas about Argentina (which provoked questions by Jorge Romero Brest, one of the leading critics of Buenos Aires). *The Esso Salon of Young Artists* was patronized by the Standard Oil Company in 1965. The final phase of this was staged in Washington, D.C.

One of the first group shows to bring Latin American and U.S. artists together was the *Gulf-Caribbean Art* exhibition held at the Houston Museum of Fine Arts in April 1956. The show had financial backing from Brown and Root, Inc. It presented artists from five U.S. states bordering on the Gulf of Mexico together with artists from Colombia, Cuba, the Dominican Republic, El Salvador, Guatemala, Haiti, Honduras, Jamaica, Mexico, Venezuela, Nicaragua, Panama, Puerto Rico, Suriname, and Trinidad and Tobago. At the request of the museum authorities, the OAS Visual Arts Unit had assumed responsibility for selecting the artists outside the United States. The frequent choice of the OAS Visual Arts Unit as an adviser in the selection of artists became a double-edged sword for Latin American artists. The bureaucratic structure of the unit—as opposed to a sophisticated curatorial body—and its poor financial health made it a badly managed, limited office.

After closing in Houston, the show traveled to the Dallas Museum of Fine Arts, the Institute of Contemporary Art in Boston, the Carnegie Institute of Pittsburgh, and other institutions. There were five purchase prizes and five lesser prizes, equally divided between U.S. and Latin American artists. One of the purchase prizes went to the Colombian Alejandro Obregón for his *Cattle Crossing the Magdalena River* and another to the Cuban Cundo Bermúdez for his *Havana Sextet.* Oswaldo Vigas of Venezuela, Carlos Mérida of Guatemala, and Armando Morales of Nicaragua were among the winners of the lesser prizes. The competition was a major event for Latin Americans, but for North Americans it was a regional competition for Southeast and Southwest artists. Latin Americans who participated in this exhibition received more recognition in their own countries than in the United States.

For many years the triennial *Pittsburgh International Exhibition,* organized by the local Carnegie Institute, was considered one of the most important shows of its kind in the United States. On the occasion of its forty-first exhibition in 1958, a considerable number of Latin Americans were invited to participate for the first time. Their work was exhibited separately, and none of them received a prize. In the following years Latin Americans always participated in the competition. The 1964 event gathered art from thirty-five countries throughout the world, including ten Latin American countries. The representative of Nicaragua, Armando Morales, won the J. L. Hudson Purchase Prize for his *Winter.* The system of prizes that had been in force at the *Pittsburgh International* since 1896 was abolished in 1970. A different criterion was adopted in organizing the show, placing stress on novelty—in contemporary art. The number of invited artists was reduced to one-third of the number in previous exhibitions. Participating in the 1970 exhibition were Lam, Marisol, Matta, Le Parc, and Alicia Peñalba. In addition to the general exhibition, there was a special show of eleven "masters," in which no Latin Americans were included.

In Chicago the most important exhibit of the last thirty-five years in which Latin American artists figured prominently was the 1959 show *The United States Collects Pan-American Art,* organized by the Art Institute. It was the institute's contribution to the Festival of the Americas held in Chicago that year. The exhibition included Canadians, but no U.S. artists. The show was dominated by Rivera, Siqueiros, Orozco, Tamayo, Lam, and Matta, who were responsible for 39 of the 105 canvases on display.[24] The same year, in October, the Dallas Museum of Fine Arts put on an exhibit entitled *South American Art Today.* Every country south of Panama was represented. The OAS Visual Arts Unit again acted as consultant in the selection process. The exhibition received considerable publicity. Some of the artworks were purchased for the museum's collection, although some have since been deaccessioned. But despite the prestige of the institutions involved, these exhibitions were just "special events" related to a particular celebration and in no way reflected a trend toward investigating Latin America's visual evolution. The museums' interest in the subject seemed to end with the closing of the exhibits.

Nineteen sixty-five to nineteen sixty-six was a very important period for Latin American artists. Several significant exhibitions were developed. *The Esso Salon of Young Artists* was conceived and financed by the Standard Oil Company (now Exxon Corporation) as a contribution to the seventy-fifth-anniversary celebrations of the inter-American system. It was curated by the OAS Visual Arts Unit. There were fifty-nine participants, all less than forty years of age, representing all of the member countries of the Organization of American States, except the United States. (Puerto Rico, however, was represented by Luis Hernández Cruz, Olga Albizu, and Tomás Batista.) The artists were selected on the basis of regional competitions held in Latin America and the Caribbean and sponsored by the respective subsidiaries of the Esso Standard Oil Company in each country. At each competition several purchase prizes were awarded, which entitled the recipient to compete at the final event held in Washington, D.C. The regional salons received excellent coverage, and the final exhibit was announced in national magazines. The international jury was composed of Alfred H. Barr, Jr., Thomas Messer, and Gustave Von Groschwitz, then director of the Carnegie Institute. The ultimate winners were Rogelio Polesello of Argentina in painting and Hermann Guggiari of Paraguay in sculpture. Honorable mentions in painting went to Fernando de Szyszlo, Fernando Botero, Ernesto Cristiani, and Mortes Merisier. Honorable mentions in sculpture were awarded to Tomás Batista of Puerto Rico and Alberto Guzman of Peru. The collection, which had become the property of the sponsoring corporation was donated in 1970 to the Lowe Art Museum of the University of Miami, in Coral Gables, Florida. The catalog of this exhibit, however, contained only the biographies of the artists and their pictures and a few pages of introductory remarks praising the initiative of the sponsor. It did not give any synthesis of the process developed in the regional salons, nor did it survey the national movements.

In contrast to the short-term project of the *Esso Salon,* Cornell University officially dedicated the academic year 1965–66 to Latin America and commissioned the Solomon R. Guggenheim Museum to organize an art exhibit as part of the program of lectures and other cultural events directed toward increasing public awareness of the problems and achievements of the region. The exhibition was entitled *The Emergent Decade: Latin American Painters and Paintings of the 1960s.* It included some eighty paintings by fifty-five artists representing eight countries. Though limited in coverage, it constituted a solid selection, representative of the best in contemporary Latin American painting. The catalog issued to accompany the show was a work of documentary importance, for in it were compiled the views and opinions of many Latin American art critics. It was probably the first opportunity they had to make their presence felt through a publication of that kind. Even today it continues to constitute a valuable reference work for the analysis of the work of many of the artists included in the show. The exhibit was first presented at the Fine Arts Museum in Caracas, the point of assembly for the collection, and from May 20 to June 19 it was on view at the Guggenheim Museum in New York City. The show traveled afterward to other institutions in the United States.

The most ambitious and complete exhibition of Latin American art held in the

United States to date was conceived, however, by Yale University and presented at the art gallery on its campus in New Haven, Connecticut, in January 1966. Although it was limited to works of a two-dimensional nature, the extensiveness of the collection (the catalog numbers 395 items), the focus given to the presentation, and the comprehensive catalog made the exhibit a model of academic seriousness. The display was divided into five periods, beginning in 1765, and an attempt was made to present works in a Latin American context, duly noting significant cultural influences. Emphasis was placed on the idea that while certain features were derived from the colonial past common to the area as a whole, division into independent republics had produced regional differences in plastic expression. Following the Yale venue, the exhibit traveled to the University of Texas at Austin, which had collaborated in the organization of the show, then to the Fine Arts Museum of San Francisco, the Contemporary Art Museum of La Jolla, California, and finally the Isaac Delgado Museum in New Orleans.

Commercial Galleries

The only sphere in which Latin American artists appeared shoulder to shoulder with other artists was in the commercial galleries. Some galleries made a real commitment to the artists and promoted them alongside North American artists. Artists such as Tamayo, Marisol, Botero, and Emilio Sanchez were able to present their work regularly. There were striking geographical contrasts between commercial gallery presentations during the decades considered here. In the Southwest and Far West, the artists featured were almost exclusively Mexicans; in the East, more particularly New York, the artists came from other parts of Latin America and the Caribbean. The Midwestern galleries struck a balance between the two. Outside the principal urban centers, however, Latin Americans were conspicuous only by their absence.

During the 1950s galleries seemed to take little account of national origin, judging by the freedom with which artists of various nationalities were included together in group shows. In the 1960s galleries seemed to concentrate on particular artists who, by reason of long-term residence in New York or Europe, had come to acquire the "international" image considered necessary to acceptance and success. One contributing factor may have been a gradual falling-off in interest on the part of private institutions, an attitude that had a particularly strong impact in the major centers.

The number of commercial galleries that at one time or another presented Latin American artists was considerable. For purposes of this study mention can be made only of those that did so more or less on a regular basis or whose prestige was such that an exhibition of a given artist constituted an open declaration of support. Two New York galleries were particularly committed to Latin American artists during the 1950s: the Galería Sudamericana, owned and operated by Armando Zegri, and the Roland de Aenlle Gallery. Both opened in the early 1950s and dealt almost exclusively with Latin American art. Other galleries in New York active with Latin Americans as well as with North Americans were the David Herbert Gallery, which opened in 1959 and specialized in sculpture, including work by Edgar Negret. The Contemporaries, Knoedler Gallery, Berta Shaefer Gallery, Baronet Gallery, Peridot Gallery, Moskin Gallery and Weyhe Gallery, among others, presented artists selected in this essay. In Washington D.C., Gres Gallery was inaugurated in 1957 with a joint show of works by Jack Youngerman and Edgar Negret. Gallery 4 of Detroit and Main Street Gallery presented Latin American artists from time to time.

At the beginning of the 1960s New York galleries continued their activities, but save for the Galería Sudamericana (now named Zegri Gallery) none of them specialized in Latin American art. The Roland de Aenlle Gallery closed. Other galleries opened briefly, such as the Cisneros Gallery. Still others, including The World House Gallery, Feigen Gallery, Catherine Viviano Gallery, Albert Landry Gallery, Cober Gallery, Staempfli Gallery, Marlborough Gallery, Rose Fried Gallery, Tibor de Nagy Gallery, and Sidney Janis Gallery, selected Latin American artists on a tentative basis, testing their acceptance by the public.

Of particular importance for the commercial promotion of the most important exponents of Latin American art was the appearance in New York of the Galería Bonino. It opened its doors in October 1962, initially using the name Andrews-Morris Gallery, with a group show in which Tamayo, Obregón, Mabe, de Szyszlo, Otero, Morales, Cuevas, and Fernández Muro represented Latin America. Among the U.S. and Canadian artists in the same exhibition were Calder, de Kooning, Motherwell, Kline, and Johns. The Galería Bonino had branches in Rio de Janeiro, Buenos Aires, and London. Owing to the seriousness of its artistic and commercial purposes, it was a mark of prestige in the 1960s to be a member of the gallery's stable. Bonino was largely responsible for the systematic introduction into New York of the best in current Argentine art, from the end of the abstract trend through New Figuration and Generative Art. In 1964 the gallery presented, under the auspices of the Inter-American Foundation of New York, the exhibit entitled *Magnet: New York*, which gathered together a number of artists previously mentioned.

However, the proportion of the establishments selling Latin American art among the privately owned gallery population in New York was very small. The galleries that specialized in Latin American art barely survived one decade of continuous enterprise; many rapidly turned to selling U.S. and European art and just kept one or two Latin American artists—usually ones who were already residents of New York City. Marisol and Botero, both residents of New York, and Tamayo and Matta, who lived in New York for many years, were the most well-known artists. But even some artists living in New York at the time, such as Maria Luisa Pacheco, had difficulty obtaining recognition for their work. By contrast, Latin American artists well known in Europe, such as Soto, Otero, Fontana, Le Parc, and Bravo, to name just a few, awakened little interest in U.S. circles despite the innovative character of their work and their unconventional techniques.

There was also a division between those artists being promoted by the commercial galleries and others presented at institutions. The cost involved in transporting large and heavy artworks from Latin America perhaps obstructed galleries from importing this work. There was more variety of techniques presented at the commercial gallery level, especially in drawings, watercolors, and graphics, which were small scale and more suitable for selling than the grander paintings favored by institutions.

Part I: The Abstract Spirit: 1950–1970

The two main trends in U.S. art from 1950 to 1970 were Abstract Expressionism and Pop art. Abstraction manifested itself not only in Abstract Expressionism, but also in Action Painting, and Color-Field Painting. Two main currents were also to be observed in Latin American art of the period, but they were quite different from those of the United States.[1] One was abstraction, which had two major subcurrents: Geometric Abstraction[2] and Lyric Abstraction.[3] The other current was figurative art, which developed along a variety of lines and included subject matter from political topics to new forms of expressionism.

An examination of the compositions Latin American abstract artists executed in this period verifies that they were working quite independently of their U.S. counterparts. They were not uninformed, however, and one reason for their independence was the fear that their art would reflect some sort of "cultural penetration" by the United States. During the 1950s Latin American artists were very sensitive to their responsibility to update artistic expression. There was an enthusiastic adherence to Geometrical Abstraction and to Kinetic art, particularly in Venezuela and Argentina, which was an artistic response to the needs of these increasingly industrialized societies. Like better living conditions and social justice, abstract art was seen as the appropriate modern solution. In some countries, however, when abstract art seemed about to impose itself, artists turned to figuration as a counterbalance.

It is often difficult to draw clear dividing lines between the two main currents and their various tendencies. The artistic freedom achieved in the early 1950s meant that it was no longer necessary to develop a personal style within the precise boundaries of a given movement. In the case of artists such as Eduardo Ramírez Villamizar (Lyric Geometry), Jesús Rafael Soto (Kinetic art), Eduardo Mac Entyre (Generative Art), and Manabu Mabe (Lyric Abstraction), it is relatively easy to analyze their compositions and establish their stylistic differences. However, in the case of the Colombian Alejandro

Obregón, whose work is basically figurative but whose compositions are made up in part of abstract elements, it is more difficult to categorize his art. This blend of different visual languages was certainly not new. Cubism, of course, had already pioneered these possibilities. But the artists extended their search not only by experimenting with different forms and planes but also by redefining the role of color. They were committed to creating a type of art that was going to evoke—not represent— the tragedies and joys of both our psychological and physical worlds. The compromises made between the artists' perception of the present, their reevaluation of the past, and their need to link their art to specific aspects of their own culture—as well as to update the visual repertoire of images and to create an art different from those of other cultures—represent another kind of "engagement" that began with the early modern traditions of Mexican Muralism, Indianism, and other regional movements. This complex dynamic was unique to Latin American practitioners of abstract art.

The search for a form of visual expression based on abstract elements was generally undertaken with a view to conveying emotional experience without resorting to any kind of story telling. Abstraction as a new idiom of plastic expression made its way to the Americas from Europe, not as a clearly defined language, but as a set of principles. In several cases its principles were brought to the Western Hemisphere by Latin Americans who, as members of the pre–World War II European avant-garde (Diego Rivera, Carlos Mérida, Torres-García, Wifredo Lam, Emilio Pettoruti, among others), had contributed to its evolution. Just as abstract art was able to develop in the United States in a fashion peculiar to that country, so it did in Latin America's countries.

In the United States, as Matta pointed out, after the popularity of Social Realism and Regionalism—influenced by the Mexican School—waned, artists became concerned primarily with art itself as a creative exercise with laws of its own, disconnected from life.[4] Pollock left behind his early bucolic realism, studied Picasso's images, and began using the theories of accident and automatism patronized by the Surrealists. He understood that painting as matter had a power of its own. In Latin America, however, art and life were more closely bonded. Since pre-Columbian times art had been a tool to advance messages, be they mythical, religious, or political.

The abstract spirit had three main lines of development in Latin America. Some artists drew on ideas derived from pre-Columbian cultures, from the colonial period, or even from contemporary society, not only renewing the visual value of stylistic motifs but inventing new languages with them. Carlos Mérida of Guatemala, María Luisa Pacheco of Bolivia, Fernando de Szyszlo of Peru, and Enrique Tábara of Ecuador were practitioners of this tendency. For others, the abstract principle served as a point of departure for the creation of a poetic, at times romantic, visual universe. Angel Hurtado of Venezuela, Luis Hernández Cruz of Puerto Rico, and José Antonio Fernández Muro and Sara Grilo of Argentina, worked in this vein. A third path was taken by artists in whose work the appearances of reality take abstract form, for example the New Figuration group of Argentina, as well as individuals such as Armando Morales of Nicaragua.

Carlos Mérida
In a 1950 article entitled "Self-Portrait,"[5] Mérida (plate 157) divided his work into two phases:

...that of my initiation, from 1915 to 1925, and that of my transformation, from 1929 until the present. The new period represented a new concept of painting dominated by a breadth of poetry and eagerness to arrive at lyric fact. Forms and elements no longer have literal meaning. All this has confirmed my trend toward abstract form. There can be no liberation from nature, no liberation from concrete fact until that fact is transformed into a plastic organism.

The date of the article is important, for it confirms the early existence of a new approach to painting on the part of Latin American artists, an approach that resulted from changes wrought by the shattering events of the previous decade as well as from the general dissemination of ideas by the pre–World War II European avant-garde.

156

157

Carlos Mérida
157. *Skies over Texas.* 1943
    Gouache on paper, 23½ x 19″
    Phoenix Art Museum. Gift of Mr. and Mrs. Burton
    Tremaine
    Photo: courtesy Phoenix Art Museum

Roberto Matta
156. *Years of Fear.* 1941
    Oil on canvas, 44 x 56″
    Solomon R. Guggenheim Museum, New York
    Photo: David Heald

Mérida played a leading role in the formulation and assimilation of those ideas in Latin America. He had first gone to Europe in 1912 and had been closely associated with the Parisian avant-garde. In addition to having an "eagerness to arrive at lyric fact," he always sought inspiration in "the Mayan world of ancient myths and ancient gods." "The sources on which I draw are American," Mérida said, "and this in essence is what distinguishes my effort from other modes of expression which might seem similar."[6]

Indeed, neither his years in Europe nor those in the United States, which he first visited in 1917, changed Mérida's perception of his heritage; on the contrary, his experience abroad merely served to sharpen his consciousness and aroused a desire to create work consistent with his heritage.[7] As he said on returning from his first trip to Europe in 1914: "The spectacle of the brilliant raiment of our aborigines, their unction-filled ritual dances, the marvelous landscapes to be seen in Guatemala, the age-old plastic expressions we have inherited from our ancestors—the builders of Palenque and Quiriguá—made me deeply aware that I was being unfaithful to my tradition and to my race in failing to heed the inner voices that called to me so insistently."[8]

Mérida's philosophy was exceptional. Although he was of the same generation as the Mexican mural painters and at one time actively participated in the movement they led, his ideas about painting and the function of art developed quite differently from those of the muralists.[9] By 1937, when Siqueiros was experimenting with new materials and their effects and Jackson Pollock was still painting landscapes in the style of Orozco, Mérida's work was nonobjective, almost Minimalist, but nevertheless responsive to the needs of Latin American society. Together with Tamayo and Matta, Mérida was one among the pioneers of modern Latin American art who continued to be active until the 1980s. These three artists constituted a bridge between the forerunners of Latin American modernism and the artists of the 1950s and thereafter. All three remained faithful to the "voices deep within" that insisted on the need for them to preserve a relationship between the cultural characteristics of the peoples from which they sprang and present-day artistic expression. Mérida's varied and prolific oeuvre developed in several phases, one of which is associated with his research into the rhythms and musical structure of the pre-Columbian melodies. These works are visual equivalents to the harmonious syncopation and austere simplicity of pre-Hispanic music. (Music was a field Mérida would have explored in its own right had he not suffered from hearing problems during his childhood.)

In 1951 Mérida had an exhibit in the gallery at OAS headquarters in Washington, D.C. From that year until 1970, when he exhibited at the Museum of Modern Art in Mexico City, Mérida was tirelessly active in Guatemala (where he received several decorations), Europe, and the United States. He exhibited among other places in San Antonio, Texas, in 1962; in the Phoenix Art Museum in 1965; and in the Martha Jackson Gallery in New York in 1966.[10]

María Luisa Pacheco

In 1951 the Bolivian María Luisa Pacheco went to Spain on a grant from the Spanish Ministry of Foreign Affairs. In Madrid she studied with the painter Daniel Vásquez Días. On returning to La Paz in April 1952 she continued painting figurative works, notably socially concerned images. Her figures were not presented naturalistically, however; they were interpreted as planar structures. These were her first experiments in abstraction, or at least her first images whose relationships to reality were hard to establish. In 1956 Pacheco moved to New York, which was to remain her residence until her death in 1982. By 1959 all figurative elements had been eliminated from her work. While her paintings have usually been interpreted and promoted as attempts to describe the Bolivian landscape in an unconventional manner, in fact she aimed to create paintings based purely on forms, colors, and textures that were evocative of the geography of her native environment. There is a similarity between her interest in the structure of the pictorial surface and the work of such contemporaries as Richard Diebenkorn. But her approach is powerfully austere and earthy (plate 159). Reviewing her works, the Venezuelan critic Roberto Guevara observed:

It would be easy to point out resemblances to the harsh, barren landscape of the South

American cordilleras; the works exude a similar feeling of immense, overwhelming isolation. But they also have an immediate plastic purpose, which can and should be judged on its own merits. This purpose is not concerned with perspective, geography, biographical detail or other aspects of graspable reality. It relates to the domain of spontaneous, personal creation—a domain in which elements of reality, while retaining their power of evocation or suggestion, at the same time function as the components of a structure which exists solely on canvas.[11]

Thus, while some of her paintings, especially those done in the five years preceding her death, might suggest landscapes with mountains, this was not the artist's primary intention.

Pacheco exhibited constantly in various galleries in Manhattan and elsewhere and took part in important group exhibitions. Some paintings were acquired by leading museums, but she lacked the support of a powerful commercial gallery in New York that might have given her real standing in the United States. The result was that her work was never accorded the acclaim it deserved. By contrast, she exercised considerable influence in Latin America, particularly in her native Bolivia. Her painting possessed some characteristics that might be termed "national" (namely the allusions to the Bolivian landscape).

Fernando de Szyszlo

The conflict between deriving artistic inspiration from the pre-Columbian civilization of Peru and the unavoidable reality of four hundred years of Spanish rule is an important theme in the work of Fernando de Szyszlo. Unlike Mérida, de Szyszlo belongs to the generation of the 1950s that looked to Europe not to validate his right to be an artist but as a place to learn more about his heritage as part of a process of self-definition. De Szyszlo first studied architecture but then enrolled in the art school of the Catholic University in Lima in 1944. In 1946 he exhibited for the first time in Peru's annual national salon. His first experiments in abstract art date from that year. His interests led him to establish relations with a group of Lima intellectuals that met under the name of "Espacio" (Space). This group was composed of painters and architects who sought renewal in their disciplines, confronting the Indianism that had controlled the arts for almost twenty years.[12] He exhibited his paintings in Lima in 1947 and 1948, and in 1949 he went to Europe. He exhibited in Paris and published a portfolio of lithographs entitled *Tribute to Vallejo* (*Homenaje a Vallejo*), honoring the celebrated Peruvian poet. In 1950 he returned to Lima and took up residence there. By that time his work was thoroughly abstract. It reflected the sense of abstract design characteristic of pre-Incan art, but it departed from the Indianism that was then thoroughly entrenched in the art of Peru, indeed of all the Andean countries. De Szyszlo made his first trip to the United States in 1953, and his first exhibit there was presented at OAS headquarters. He has experimented extensively with elements derived from his country's Indian cultures, the signs and geometric devices invented by the pre-Hispanic peoples and employed by them in reliefs, painted decorations, vessels, jewelry, and textiles. From textiles, in particular, he derived his refined color combinations, and their complex knottings suggested to him textural values that he incorporated into his work with telling visual effect. His compositions are full of mysterious suggestions, evocative of the rich cultural tradition he inherited. De Szyszlo recognizes the importance of his contact with European art, but he has gleaned most of his inspiration from pre-Columbian art: "To think that we were trying to do abstract art with the help of the discoveries of the European artists, when some centuries ago Peruvian artists were producing a highly developed, obviously autonomous, powerful art. That [thought] was very explosive...."[13]

In the 1970s de Szyszlo began to develop artworks that, although not figurative, contained elements suggestive of reality. In the two decades of concern here, however, de Szyszlo's work was essentially abstract. Certain themes were present in his work, particularly the subject of death. At times the shapes most favored by him recall objects used in sacrifices, like the sharp blades of knives, ceremonial tables, or tombs where strange forms wrapped in exquisite and dense bands of color evoke bodies covered with sacred gowns and tapestries. Sometimes this theme was presented more abstractly. Marta Traba has noted in this regard: "Everywhere in de Szyszlo's work there is evidence of a clear intent to provide a creative response to the tremendous problem posed for both ancient and moderns by man's reduction to nothingness at the moment of death. All of his compositions [reflect] a struggle to recreate a primitive world, which, thanks to the depth of its roots, survives its inevitable destruction…the dynamism produced by violently aggressive shifts of color reflects that never-ending cycle of earthly renewal which is interpreted as a creative force or response."[14]

Beginning with his trip to the United States in 1953, de Szyszlo entered into a period of intense activity. After a short sojourn in Florence and a visit to Lima, he returned to the United States to work as a consultant in the OAS Visual Arts Unit from 1957 to 1960. The death of his father occasioned another trip to Peru. Soon thereafter, however, he was again exhibiting in the United States, where his work was gradually acquired by various institutions, including The Museum of Modern Art and the Solomon R. Guggenheim Museum, as representative examples of Latin American art. In 1961 he was included in the show *Latin America: New Departures*, organized by Boston's Institute of Contemporary Art, and throughout the 1960s his work appeared in the most important group exhibitions held in the United States. In 1962 he was artist-in-residence at Cornell University in Ithaca, New York (plate 160); in 1966 he was a visiting lecturer at Yale University in New Haven, Connecticut.

Even though he was frequently absent from Peru between 1950 and 1970, when he settled down in Lima permanently, de Szyszlo had a strong influence on the young artists in Peru, particularly from 1950 to 1965. This dynamic was not unusual. María Luisa Pacheco of Bolivia or Alejandro Obregón of Colombia also enjoyed considerable prestige at home—due in part to the fame that came from representing the country not only in the United States but in international events, such as the São Paulo Bienal. Young artists in Latin America were inspired to follow his example, but they transformed pre-Columbian influences into their own images or turned to a different sort of figuration.

Enrique Tábara

In Ecuador abstract art developed in the port city of Guayaquil. By contrast, Quito, the capital, was the citadel of "modernized" Indianist figuration perpetuated by Eduardo Kingman and his follower Oswaldo Guayasamín. It was in Guayaquil in 1954 that Tábara began to create his first fully abstract paintings. In 1955 Tábara moved to Barcelona and participated in the Hispanic-American Biennial held there. In Spain he made contact with Informalism,[15] but he borrowed from it only textural qualities, which he adapted to works composed of pre-Columbian signlike motifs. The influence Tábara exerted from Barcelona on Ecuadorian art, especially in Guayaquil, was remarkable. In a noticeable change of direction, a whole group of young artists took up textural art. Artists such as Aníbal Villacis, Gilberto Almeida, and Estuardo Maldonado quickly took up the trend, although they were later to travel their own roads (Maldonado, for example, switched later to Constructivist art, then to geometrically patterned canvases).

Spanish Informalism led Tábara to a type of painting in which the use of texture skirted on decoration. By 1959 he recognized that texture is basically an effect and that its meaning for painting lies in the mystery with which it can imbue a composition. For Tábara, Informalism in the Spanish manner was too "dry," too concerned with formal issues. He took inspiration instead from native Indian forms, which he reinterpreted quite freely. The textures he borrowed give an inviting, tactile quality to his visual structures. Tábara continued living in Europe until the early 1960s, when he returned to Ecuador for good. He participated in important events in the United States and came to be recognized in Latin America as the most innovative and original representative of Ecuadorian art. The sporadic nature of Tábara's participation in shows held in the United States in a period when Abstract Expressionism was at its peak and Pop art was just starting to make its appearance on the New York scene may explain why his originality was little appreciated in the United States. Indeed his work was overshadowed by that of Tapiés and other Spaniards. Today, the primitive, magical atmosphere of his canvases can be viewed as the work of an artist who gave vent—in simplified sign language—to the inner feelings of a race still in the process of trying to

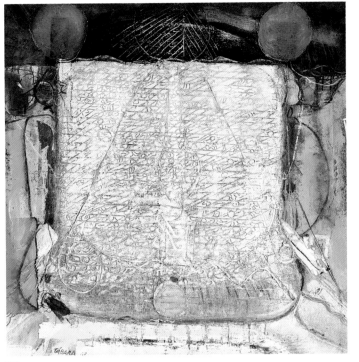

158

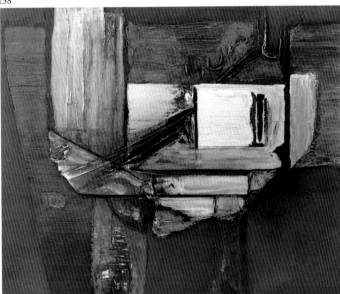

159

160

Enrique Tabara
158. *The Region of the Shiris.* 1967
Oil on canvas, 43 ⅜ x 43 ¼"
Archer M. Huntington Art Gallery, University of
Texas at Austin. Gift of John and Barbara Duncan,
1971
Photo: courtesy Archer M. Huntington Art Gallery

Maria Luisa Pacheco
159. *Petrous.* 1965
Oil and collage on canvas, 50 x 59⅞"
Albert and Vera List Visual Arts Center,
Massachusetts Institute of Technology, Cambridge
Photo: David Hewitt

Fernando de Szyszlo
160. *Untitled.* 1962
Oil on canvas, 52 x 36"
Herbert F. Johnson Museum of Art, Cornell
University, Ithaca, New York. Membership Purchase
Fund
Photo: Emil Ghinger

assimilate the cultural heritage of the Occident and to fuse it with the legacy of age-old native traditions (plate 158).

Armando Morales

Between 1956, the year in which he participated in the *Gulf-Caribbean Art* exhibition, and 1967, when he had a show of recent works at the Fine Arts Museum of Caracas (an exhibition which was presented the following year at the Palace of Fine Arts in Mexico City), Armando Morales experimented with abstraction and then figuration. Observing the paintings Morales created in the late 1960s, the Venezuelan critic Roberto Guevara noted: "These most recent works, dating from 1967, show what appears to be increased emphasis on figuration. Objects are clearly shaded, though lovingly enveloped by a dense fog. This development is in marked contrast with the absolute landscapes of five years ago, when broad planes, distinguished by relief, incisions, and contrasts, gave expression to the artist's visions in almost exclusively abstract terms."[16] Even in his most abstract paintings, Morales remained a figurative artist, concerned with landscape (beaches, forests, the sea, rivers, the sky) and with the human figure, standing out in solitary relief against the landscape. Morales's abstract journey went from the symbolic figuration of the 1950s to works embodying a carefully mediated mode of viewing reality. The latter are paintings of great formal austerity, employing a sophisticated palette limited to grays and other neutral tones; the images are totally divorced from traditional representation. The art is the visual representation of a feeling that has been converted into form and color. The result is abstraction, for the idea of reality has been reduced to an abstract concept. The sole remaining reference to the source of inspiration is the title (plate 161).

Morales had his first exhibit in the United States at the Angeleski Gallery in New York in 1962, two years after he had moved to New York to study at Pratt Institute. Morales remained in New York until the end of the decade, when he moved to Costa Rica and then to Paris, where he now resides. During his stay in the United States, he participated in a number of art contests both in this country and abroad, and he won some significant prizes. After 1969 he returned to figurative art. He continues, however, to practice his characteristic use of glazes, polish, and superimposed brush strokes, but he has broadened the range of his palette.

The prestige Morales enjoys today in Paris and in the United States is very different from the relatively cold reception that he had in New York during the 1960s. It is true that he was included in almost every important show of Latin American art held in the United States during the 1950s and 1960s, but like many of his fellow Latins, particularly those living in New York at the time, his work was viewed as a conservative form of abstraction, and abstraction was gradually going out of fashion. New York's art world never embraced European abstraction. There was no interest in assimilating carefully crafted painting, and most artists were by now opposed to the traditional concepts of painting.

Manabu Mabe

The most significant one-man exhibition of Manabu Mabe's work to be presented in the United States did not occur until 1970, when the Houston Museum of Fine Arts exhibited thirty-eight large-format paintings, nearly all dating from 1969, that represented Mabe at the zenith of his career. These compositions combined the tropical, baroque exuberance of Brazilian civilization with the "mystery, symbolism, and aura of the Orient," in the words of the exhibition's curator, Mary Hancock Buxton.[17]

Yet Mabe's work was hardly unknown in the United States before the Houston exhibit. In 1955 he had turned to painting abstract works marked by a lyricism that has characterized his art ever since. In 1957 and 1958 Mabe was a prizewinner at national salons in Brazil; he received the Braun Prize at the *First Biennial of Youth* in Paris; he won the first national prize for painting at the *Fifth São Paulo Bienal*; and his 1959 oil-on-masonite painting *Shakuhun* was awarded a purchase prize at the *South American Art Today* show held at the Dallas Museum of Fine Arts that same year. *Time* magazine devoted an article to him in a November 1959 issue. At the *Thirtieth Venice Biennale* (1960) he was awarded the Fiat Prize, and in 1962 he received first prize at the *First American Biennial of Art* in Córdoba, Argentina. He had a one-man show at the Time-Life building in New York in 1960, followed by others in Trieste, Venice, and Paris, and in 1962 he had an exhibit at OAS headquarters in Washington, D.C. That same year he was included in *New Art from Brazil*, a show that traveled to the Walker Art Center in Minneapolis, the City Art Museum of St. Louis, the San Francisco Museum of Art, and the Colorado Springs Fine Art Center. Marta Traba wrote of Mabe (plate 162):

The titles this artist gives to his works—Agony, Solemn Pact, The Afternoon's Illusion— make clear Mabe's aim of evoking not merely vague states of soul or mind but moments crucial to life and death. His strong contrasts of light and shade, his splashes of white, his spectacular graphic marks, his bold blobs of color and drips of pigment may well derive their dramatically emotional character from his intent.... The whole of his work being pervaded by an almost desperate preciseness in rendering imprecision. Despite its notoriously theatrical effects, it maintains an intimate bond with the eloquent silence of the Japanese current in Brazilian art.[18]

Mabe, as Traba implied, was not the only individual of oriental descent active in Brazil's cultural scene. Brazil, like the United States, has drawn large numbers of immigrants both from Europe and from the Far East. São Paulo currently has the largest Japanese population of any city outside Japan, and it has long been the center of an art movement based in part on the oriental traditions of calligraphy and textural treatment of the pictorial surface. A group known as SEIBI (São Paulo Association of Japanese Artists) had its first show as early as 1938. Members of the group include Mabe, Tomie Ohtake, Kazuo Wakabayashi, Yutaka Toyota, Tikashi Fukushima, Iomoo Handa, Flavio Shiro, and Masumi Tschimoto.

In recognition of the importance of the oriental contribution to Latin American art, a show was presented at OAS headquarters in Washington in 1961 entitled *Japanese Artists of the Americas*. It included Arturo Kubotta of Peru, Manabu Mabe of Brazil, Luis Nishizawa of Mexico, Kenso Okada of the United States, and Kasuya Sakai of Argentina. In 1965 a similar exhibition was presented at the same institution, this time limited to the Brazilian members of SEIBI. An observation in the catalog to the first exhibition bears repetition:

The Japanese who have come to the New World have enriched artistic production here by their highly refined plastic sensitivity. Their open form of composition, the asymmetrical organization of their paintings, the calligraphic quality of their brush stroke, their sense of space are invaluable contributions to contemporary Latin American art. Their art, following dictates of no single school of cultural tradition, is representative, in its freedom of expression, of the essential liberty of the peoples of the Western Hemisphere and clear evidence of the universal quality of the civilization which here has come into being.[19]

Most of the members of SEIBI were introduced to the United States either through group shows of contemporary Brazilian art or through individual exhibits in the gallery at OAS headquarters. Tomie Ohtake had a solo show in 1968; Yutaka Toyota in 1972; and Tikashi Fukushima in 1972.

Kasuya Sakai
Kasuya Sakai, an Argentine artist of Japanese descent, was born in Buenos Aires in 1927, but he was educated in Japan and lived there until 1951, when he returned to his birthplace. His first exhibit in Argentina was in 1952. In 1958 he won the gold medal at the Brussels World's Fair, and in 1962 he was one of the artists presented at the Argentine pavilion in the *Thirty-first Venice Biennale*. In 1963 he moved to New York and that same year had one-man shows at the Martin Schweig Gallery in St. Louis and the Cleveland Museum of Art. Through the rest of the decade he was included in the most important exhibits of Argentine art sent to the United States and Europe. His 1964 work *The Little Theater*, a mixed-media acrylic that appeared in the *New Art from*

161

162

Armando Morales
161. *Seascape.* 1964
    Oil on canvas, 50 x 40⅛"
    Art Museum, Princeton University, New Jersey
    Photo: courtesy Art Museum, Princeton University

Manabu Mabe
162. *Melancholy Metropolis.* 1969
    Oil on canvas, 72⅞ x 78¾"
    Walker Art Center, Minneapolis. Gift of the T.B.
    Walker Foundation, 1963
    Photo: courtesy Walker Art Center

Argentina show, is representative of the artist's style at that time. It combines abstract informalism with elements drawn from the Italian *Arte Povera*, achieving effects similar to Robert Rauschenberg's collages—although in Sakai's work there are obvious formalistic formulas that closely follow trends in Argentine abstract painting.

Armando Villegas

Armando Villegas, a Peruvian by birth, went to Colombia early in the 1950s and studied at the fine arts school in the capital until 1953, when he had a one-man show at the Central Art Galleries in Bogotá. He soon acquired a national reputation. He was included in the Colombian section of the *Gulf-Caribbean Art* exhibition in 1956, in several São Paulo biennials, and in a number of Colombian group exhibitions that circulated abroad, including *Three Thousand Years of Colombian Art* in 1960. In his presentation of Villegas's exhibition at the Galería El Callejón in 1955, Gabriel García Márquez, then a writer on the staff of the Bogotá daily *El Espectador,* wrote:

I have the satisfying impression that I am witnessing the beginnings of an astonishing career in painting. The most demanding of critics will find in these compositions evidence of this new artistic personality. It seems to me that in these paintings Armando Villegas is trying to present through forms and colors a new and highly personal concept of reality…a living, dynamic reality, the elements of which he learned or inherited from the Peruvian underclass. It is from their hieratically conceived figures and magnificent use of color that his first experiments in figuration seems to spring.[20]

The compositions presented by Villegas on that occasion offered a type of Constructivism in which an intricate system of symbols or figures articulated the surface, as in early works by Torres-García. This art has parallels in work by other abstract artists from countries with strong pre-Columbian traditions, such as the Mexican Vicente Rojo. Although artists like de Szyszlo, Tabara, Villegas, and Rojo knew about one another, and it is possible to talk about a "movement," they were not grouped or organized in the way European movements traditionally were. This movement within the realm of Latin American abstraction was more the result of a convergence of independent artists' concepts that flourished simultaneously and shared a common motivation. The artists used geometric simplifications and abstract designs drawn from the indigenous civilizations of the Americas, producing, in Marta Traba's words, "a semifigurative painting that aspired to establish itself on the basis of the ancient geometro-magic tradition characteristic of pre-Columbian crafts."[21]

Villegas had his first one-man show in the United States in 1958 at OAS headquarters. An oil-on-canvas painting entitled *Alambrico*, which was included in that exhibit, exemplifies Villegas's development of a formal repertoire rooted in the ancient visual imagery of his pre-Hispanic predecessors and also can be related to some degree to the African magical imagery of Wifredo Lam. Thereafter Villegas's art went through a number of phases, from abstractions based on patches of color in 1959 to an emphasis on texture, evidenced in his 1962 exhibit at the Luis Angel Arango Library in Bogotá, to fantastic figuration, featuring imaginary warriors, in the late 1960s. While his different styles have been viewed by some critics as a sign of inconsistency, it has not hindered him from producing interesting works in each of these periods (plate 165).

David Manzur

An artist regarded as one of the most promising young talents during the 1950s is David Manzur, who first came to the United States from Colombia in 1956. He enrolled at The Art Students League in New York, where his teachers included Arnold Blanch and Doris Lee. By 1958 he was back home in Bogotá, rapidly developing a formidable reputation. In 1961 he had a one-man show at OAS headquarters and received a Guggenheim Fellowship, which was later renewed for another year. In 1962 he established residence in New York. With a 1964 fellowship from the OAS he was able to study at the Pratt Institute. The subjects of the works he made while at Pratt, abstractions based on images of the moon, the planets, outer space, and unidentified flying objects, were inspired by a course in astronomy he had taken.

163

Until his 1961 trip to the United States, Manzur's work had been significantly influenced by the work of Obregón. This was readily evident in the paintings he exhibited at OAS headquarters in 1961. Those works, however, marked the culmination of that phase of his development. Little by little, Manzur began to show an interest in Constructivism, and by the late 1960s he was producing three-dimensional compositions made up of heterogeneous objects and colored thread. One of them won a prize at the *Second Medellín Biennial*. During the 1960s Manzur had a number of one-man shows in the United States, including one at the Obelisk Gallery in Washington, D.C., in 1962. He was also included in various group shows, such as *Magnet: New York* at the Bonino Gallery in New York.

Over the last three decades Manzur's work has undergone considerable development, from Lyric Abstraction to Constructivism to figuration. Manzur has defended his explorations:

In the course of my evolution as an artist I have felt the pull of forces quite different from one another. Mere confrontation with the mystery of all surrounds me, intuitions of mine which are later confirmed by science, the need to engage in denunciation, the simple effects of sights, sounds, and feelings, all these have a constant impact on my work and undoubtedly have led me to give different expression to the same content.[22]

Sergio Castillo and Raul Valdivieso

Among the Latin American sculptors active in the United States during the 1960s were two Chileans whose work differed widely in character. Sergio Castillo had his first one-man show in the United States in 1958 at the Galería Sudamericana in New York. He had a second exhibit there in 1962, and in the same year exhibited his art for the first time in the gallery at OAS headquarters. In 1965 he showed at the Zegri Gallery (formerly Galería Sudamericana), and in 1967 his work again appeared at the OAS, this time in a show of outdoor sculpture—the first time OAS had ever presented art in its garden. Perhaps for this reason alone the exhibit received unusually wide coverage in the local press: *The Evening Star*, *The Washington Post*, and the Washington *Daily News* reviewed the show—although not altogether favorably. The artist's last show of the decade took place in 1969, once again at the Zegri Gallery. Group exhibitions in which Castillo participated included the *Esso Salon of Young Artists* (1965) and *Five Contemporary Latin American Sculptors* at the Baltimore Museum of Art (1968). Castillo's activity was by no means confined to the United States; he was extremely busy in Latin America and Europe as well, and continues to be so to this day. His sculptures of the period were made of scrap metal, usually steel, and reflected his interest in choreographing forms in space (plate 163).

Raul Valdivieso initiated his international career in London, having been granted a fellowship by the British Council in 1958. He then went on to Paris, where he attended free courses at the Grande Chaumière. In 1961 he set up a studio in Madrid and exhibited there and in Brussels in 1963. In February 1964 he was presented at OAS headquarters in Washington. The review published in *The Washington Post* said that the compositions "recall forms in nature, but they are highly abstracted....Some works skirt the edge of repulsiveness, but it is the fear of the unknown and strange that repels, rather than the forms themselves. Always masculine, often erotic, the work has great power."[23]

The organic nature of Valdivieso's work also aroused controversy. There was a scathing article in *The Sunday Star*: "Much contemporary sculpture is called abortive, but the term applies with rare accuracy to Mr. Valdivieso's bronzes. Many of them specifically and all of them generally remind you of those poor infants whose mothers had taken the wrong drugs in pregnancy."[24] Nevertheless the show excited considerable public curiosity and most of the works were sold.

Valdivieso was included in the 1966 traveling exhibit *New Names in Latin American Art*, organized by the Smithsonian Institution. Among the other artists in the show were Rogelio Polesello of Argentina, Enrique Castro-Cid of Chile, and Omar Rayo of Colombia. In 1966 Valdivieso had a show at the Museum of the University of Puerto Rico in San Juan, and in 1967 he showed at the *Pittsburgh International Exhibition*. Now living in Spain, the artist continues to create works of a totemic,

164

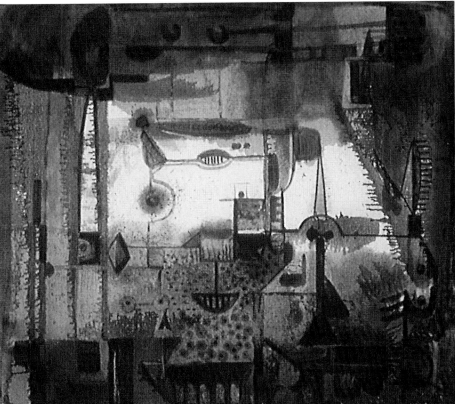

165

Raul Valdivieso
164. *The Feathered Serpent.* 1963
Bronze, 19 x 44 x 8″
Museum of Modern Art of Latin America,
Organization of American States, Washington, D.C.
Photo: Angel Hurtado

Sergio Castillo
163. *Totem.* n.d.
Steel, 57½ x 11¾ x 8⅝″
Museum of Modern Art of Latin America,
Organization of American States, Washington, D.C.
Photo: Angel Hurtado

Armando Villegas
165. *Electric Panorama.* 1958
Oil on canvas, 43½ x 49¾″
Museum of Modern Art of Latin America,
Organization of American States, Washington, D.C.
Photo: Angel Hurtado

167

166

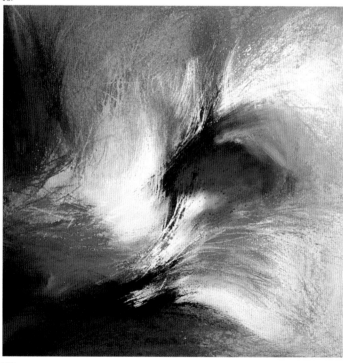

168

Sarah Grilo
167. *Black, Ocre.* 1961
Oil on canvas, 45 1/2 x 45 1/2"
Museo de Arte Contemporáneo, Buenos Aires
Photo: Pedro Roth

José Antonio Fernández Muro
166. *Violet Line.* 1961
Oil on canvas, 51 1/4 x 37 3/4"
Museo de Arte Contemporáneo, Buenos Aires
Photo: Pedro Roth

Miguel Ocampo
168. *Author of White.* 1963
Oil on canvas, 51 x 51"
Courtesy Bonino Gallery, New York
Photo: Quesada/Burke, New York

magical character in which the abstract spirit predominates—notwithstanding an occasional inclusion of organic forms (plate 164).

Humberto Jaime Sánchez and Angel Hurtado

A fellowship from the Venezuelan government permitted Humberto Jaime Sánchez to study in Europe from 1954 to 1957, chiefly in Rome and Paris. In November 1957 the artist had his first one-man show in the United States at OAS headquarters. The following year he had individual exhibits at the Gres Gallery in Washington, D.C., and the Roland de Aenlle Gallery in New York. He had previously participated in the *Gulf-Caribbean Art* exhibition in Houston and had been included in a 1954 show featuring six Venezuelan artists organized by the Smithsonian Institution in collaboration with the OAS Visual Arts Unit. By that time Sánchez's paintings were entirely abstract and his compositional structures were defined by the interpenetration of chromatic areas.

The Venezuelans Mateo Manaure and Alejandro Otero had introduced elements of nonobjective art to Venezuela as early as the late 1940s. Other artists, such as Pascual Navarro in Paris, were working within a style related to the thick impastos of Dubuffet's figurative informalism. They used aggressive brush strokes and colors and strong contours to define forms. By the early 1950s there was a vibrant abstract movement in the country, divided between those who were inclined toward Geometric Abstraction and the illusionistic effects of color and those who concentrated on the plastic effects of matter on the surface of the canvas. Jaime Sánchez's work of this period may be assigned to the latter category. He maintained a certain structural order, however. Beginning in the early 1960s, his work showed a predilection for broad, graciously articulated impastos in which color played a very important role. The mechanical rigidity of Kinetic art, a movement led by the Venezuelans Soto, Cruz Díez, and Otero and the Argentines García Rossi and Le Parc, galvanized the Venezuelan art scene, and a violent, almost gestural abstraction was a counterforce adopted by some artists who opposed Geometric Abstraction. Gradually, however, Jaime Sánchez returned to the lyricism of his work of the 1950s.

The attraction France held for Venezuelan artists was particularly evident in the 1950s, when a large number of artists seemed to lose interest in the New York scene and went to Paris instead. Angel Hurtado arrived at the French capital in 1954 and stayed until 1959, when he returned to Caracas. A second sojourn in Paris lasted from 1964 to 1970. On leaving Paris he went to Washington D.C., to direct the audiovisual program of the OAS Visual Arts Unit; he has remained there ever since.

Hurtado has always been noteworthy for the poetic spirit that imbued his abstract compositions. In 1957, on the occasion of the *Fourth São Paulo Bienal*, two of his works, *Day* and *Night*, were bought by Alfred H. Barr, Jr., for The Museum of Modern Art.[25] In 1959 he was invited to exhibit in the gallery at OAS headquarters. This was his first one-man show in the United States. His second took place that same year at the Roland de Aenlle Gallery in New York. These were his only individual appearances during the period 1950–1970, but he was a frequent participant in group shows, among them the *Gulf-Caribbean Art* exhibition and *South American Art Today*. Hurtado has never departed from abstraction, though his work has undergone subtle developments over the course of thirty-five years. During the 1950s he stressed the disposition of surface elements; in the 1960s texture acquired special importance, and he used it with more determination than Jaime Sánchez did. Hurtado's work projected a more intense lyricism than Jaime Sánchez's painting, as well as a more pronounced inclination toward solutions inspired by French Tachism. In the 1970s he rendered forms more softly by using glazes and transparent coatings. At all times color has played a major role in his painting, giving his creations halos of mystery.

José Antonio Fernández Muro and Sara Grilo

After leaving his native Spain in 1938, José Antonio Fernández Muro traveled to Buenos Aires and shortly thereafter took out Argentine citizenship. His first one-man show in the United States took place in 1957 at OAS headquarters while the artist was touring the United States and Europe on a travel grant from UNESCO to study museology. At the time of the show his style was not fully defined, but following that exhibit he was to be in all the important Latin American or Argentine shows held outside his adopted country.

Fernández Muro started out as a figurative painter, but contact with Argentine art and more especially with the Geometric Abstractionists of that country led him to adopt that style, as evidenced in the works he exhibited in Washington. The organic character of the geometric compositions of that period hints at fundamental changes to come. Beginning in the 1960s forms became areas, which, though geometrically defined, were saved from mathematical coldness by the incorporation of textures (plate 166). The compositions have a mysteriously poetic quality, heightened by the artist's use of very dark colors. On arriving in New York in 1962, which was to become his home for several years, Fernández Muro began to work in relief, using metallic surfaces as his medium. In the introduction he wrote for the catalog of Fernández Muro's 1963 show at the Andrews-Morris Gallery, Cleve Gray noted:

The lyricism in Fernández Muro's painting is new, the control is not....He limits his color with severity; he composes his forms into monolithic shapes; he organizes his overall design on an axis which has the architecture of both man-made geometry and nature's forms. His technique, based upon small, stencilled black dots glazed over by layers of color, leaves no room for capricious brush strokes. In short, he has found a personal way of controlling an expression which might otherwise become over-sensitive or precious.[26]

Tangential Red, in the Solomon R. Guggenheim Museum, is representative of the artist's best work, as is *The Gunshot in the Back*, a work he made in New York City that won a prize at the *First Medellín Biennial* in 1968.

One of the reasons for Fernández Muro's move to New York was the fact that his wife, Sara Grilo, had been awarded a Guggenheim Fellowship. The couple resided in New York until 1970, when they left for Europe. (They returned to Buenos Aires in the late 1970s.) While their careers have parallels in terms of professional activities, their work expresses their decided differences in personality and visual interests. Grilo exhibited in Washington, D.C., along with her husband, in 1957. At that time she was working in a Constructivist style but using delicate color harmonies imbued with a certain air of romance. Although Fernández Muro was then pursuing a somewhat similar aesthetic, their work was by no means the same. In the 1960s Grilo freed herself completely from geometry. The works she presented at a 1961 show for the branch of Galería Bonino in Buenos Aires exhibited her interest in the use of pictorial "accidents," similar to the experiments the Mexican artists were trying at the end of the 1930s (plate 167). This period of her work was well documented in shows she held at the Obelisk Gallery in Washington, D.C., in 1963, and at the Bianchini Gallery in New York in November 1963. A show in 1967 at the Byron Gallery in New York presented evidence of a new and original phase of her endeavor, initiated in 1964. A good example is provided by *Charge*, a work included in the *Magnet: New York* show. Incorporated into the surface are graffiti symbols and other scribblings. She anticipated by a decade the systematic use of graffiti generated by the street artists of New York. Her work was joyful and amusing, but handled with a highly refined plastic sensibility. Like her husband, Grilo received a prize at the *First Medellín Biennial* for her *Methuselah's Birthday*, a work made in New York and thoroughly characteristic of her style at the time.

Miguel Ocampo

Miguel Ocampo was born in Buenos Aires in 1922 and lived there until 1948 when he received his degree in architecture and left for Paris. There he studied with a number of artists, among them André Lhote. He returned to Buenos Aires in 1950, having developed a figurative style typical of the School of Paris. His first exhibit in the United States took place at the Roland de Aenlle Gallery in 1958, at which time he was serving as cultural attaché to the Argentine embassy in Rome. From 1961 to 1966 he held a similar post at the embassy in Paris. In 1969 he began a period of residence in New York. Ocampo was represented in most of the exhibits of Argentine art that circulated abroad or that were organized in the United States. His one-man show of 1958 hinted at his later developments, more clearly defined in the late 1960s (plate 168). In his exhibit at

OAS headquarters in 1970 his painting was characterized by broad planes of color that fused into one another. The planes are organized into zones of color; however, their occasional interpenetration suggests volume. Soft colors applied in overlapping layers of tiny dots—an effect achieved by the use of an airbrush—cause the surfaces to vibrate. The breakdown of color into tones creates an illusion of the dissolution of form. This is the style in which Ocampo has done his best work (inviting comparisons with the painting of the Russian-born Jules Olitski).

Lucio Fontana

Lucio Fontana is an artist with a thoroughly transatlantic background. Indeed, both Italy and Argentina claim him as their artist. Born in Rosario, Argentina, in 1899, he was taken by his parents to Italy in 1905. After serving in the army during World War I, he went back to Argentina in 1921, only to return to Italy in 1927 to study sculpture with Adolfo Wildt. In 1934 Fontana, Fausto Melotti, Atanasio Soldati, and Luigi Veronesi founded the Abstraction-Création group in Milan as an expression of their common commitment to modern art. In 1936 Fontana moved to Paris, where he met Joan Miró, Tristan Tzara, and Constantin Brancusi. The outbreak of World War II led to his return to Argentina in 1939. In 1946 he joined with Jorge Romero Brest (who later became one of the leading art critics during the 1960s in Buenos Aires), Emilio Pettoruti, Atillio Rossi, Mario Soldi, and Jorge Larco to establish the Altamira Academy, a place where artists and intellectuals sympathetic to modern visual theories congregated. Nineteen forty-six saw the publication in Buenos Aires of the "White Manifesto," a statement of the Argentine plastic avant-garde that Fontana influenced but did not sign. In 1947 he returned once again to Milan. The following year he published two *"Manifesti Spaziali"* (Spatial Manifestos): "All his manifestos accord a primary role to space as expression of an art with contemporary implications. Fontana wanted to exceed the illusionistic space that had dominated painting since the Renaissance, that moved overwhelmingly into the foreground during the Baroque period and that preoccupied the Futurists as a dynamic process."[27] Other manifestos followed in 1950, 1951, and 1952. The sixth and last came out in 1953. In 1949 he began to create his first works based on perforations of the canvas (plate 169). His first one-man show in the United States took place at the Martha Jackson and David Anderson galleries in New York in 1961. By that time he had already received considerable acclaim in Europe: in 1951 he had executed a neon-tubing arabesque 270 meters long for the Palace of Fine Arts in Milan, the site of the *Ninth Milan Triennial*; in 1954 he was assigned a special room at the *Twenty-Seventh Venice Biennale*; and in 1958, at the *Twenty-Ninth Venice Biennale*, he exhibited his first *Atesse* (Expectations), consisting of slashed canvases. In 1966 the Walker Art Center of Minneapolis honored him with a retrospective. However, Hilton Kramer, the reviewer for *The New York Times*, was not complimentary:

Mr. Fontana's pictorial signature is the razor slash he performs to perfection. It is just austere enough to seem meaningful, just violent enough to seem spirited, while the results keep comfortably within the boundaries of impeccable taste. It is another one of those "daring" ideas that turn into something chic before they can menace a single one of our estethic assumptions.[28]

The review could have destroyed Fontana had he been a younger, more insecure artist. Indeed, it was not the first attack on his work. In 1961 Brian O'Doherty, writing for the same paper on the occasion of Fontana's exhibit at the Martha Jackson Gallery, had said:

We hear a lot nowadays about painters attacking the canvas. Mr. Fontana attacks the canvas so energetically that he goes right through it. Apart from the multiple puncture method, his repertoire also includes slits and slashes. I can only say that Mr. Fontana's work leads me to imagine what one might expect in cinema decoration in ten years' time, a sort of cinema-foyer, neotasteless grotesque.[29]

In the same year of his show at the Walker Art Center, Fontana, representing

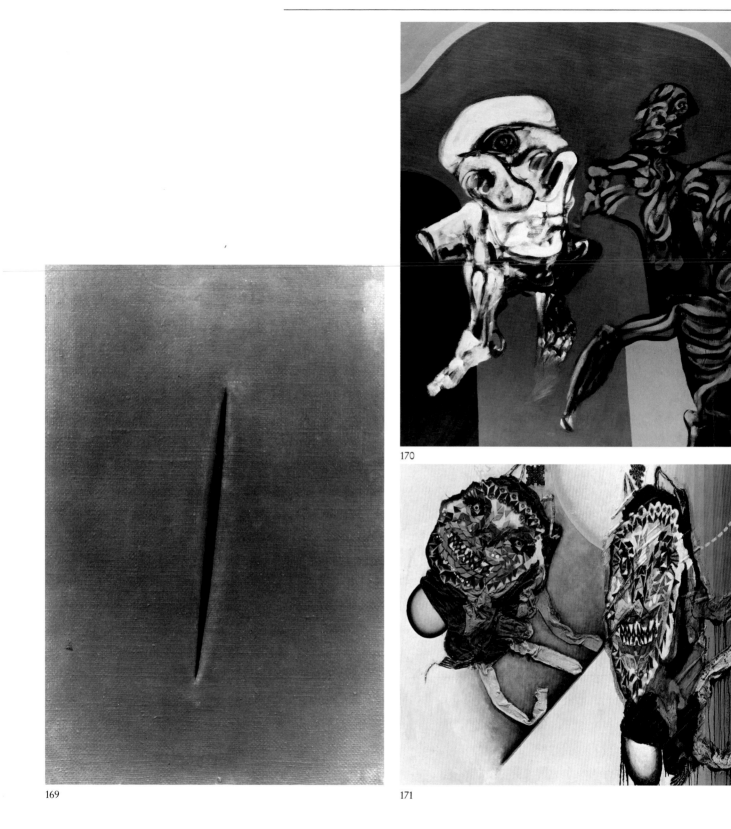

169

170

171

172

Jorge de la Vega

171. *Anamorphic Conflict No. 1 (The Measurement).* 1964
     Oil and collage on canvas, 63¾ x 76¾"
     Solomon R. Guggenheim Museum, New York.
     Purchased with funds contributed by Fundación
     Neumann, Caracas, Venezuela
     Photo: Robert E. Mates

Jorge de la Vega

172. *Mountain Dance.* 1963
     Oil on canvas, 77 x 51"
     Courtesy Bonino Gallery, New York
     Photo: Manu Sassoonian

Italy, received one of the grand prizes at the *Thirty-Third Venice Biennale* (another went to Julio Le Parc, representing Argentina). The Walker Art Center show traveled to the Museum of the University of Texas at Austin, the Marlborough-Gerson Gallery in New York, and the Torcuato di Tella Institute in Buenos Aires.

Lucio Fontana died in 1968. In 1977 the Solomon R. Guggenheim Museum organized the show *Lucio Fontana, 1899–1968: A Retrospective.* The guest curator for this exhibition was Erika Billeter, associate director and curator for modern art at the Zurich Kunsthaus. In her introductory essay to the catalog of the show, she wrote:

Lucio Fontana in 1948 challenges the history of painting. With one bold stroke he pierces the canvas and tears it to shreds. Through this action he declares before the entire world that the canvas is no longer a pictorial vehicle and asserts that easel painting, a constant in art heretofore, is called into question. Implied in this gesture is both the termination of a five-hundred-year evolution in Western painting and new beginning, for destruction carries innovation in its wake. A new pictorial beauty grows with Fontana out of the act of destruction. The punctured painting becomes a work of art in its own right, and the pierced canvas affords possibilities for a new formulation of easel painting.[30]

The Argentine New Figuration Painters: Ernesto Deira, Romulo Macció, Luis Felipe Noé, and Jorge de la Vega.

It is sometimes difficult to draw a dividing line between abstract and figurative art. Nowhere is this more evident than in the early works of the Argentine group known as New Figuration. The most interesting examples of their work were executed between 1961 and 1965. They borrowed from the figure in the same way a figurative artist borrows visual elements from the real world to express his ideas, but they expressed the figure on the canvas with emphatic gestures and distortions. The resulting images were sometimes unrecognizable as human figures, and the violent brush strokes developed into graffitilike abstract painting (as in Deira's work) or into textured, informalistic compositions and "collages" (as in de la Vega's paintings). Many Argentine writers would agree with Guillermo E. Magrassi that New Figuration was "the most original and significant movement in Argentine plastic arts of the twentieth century."[31]

After 1965 the New Figuration group disbanded, and its members developed personal styles within the figurative tradition. The leading members of the group were Ernesto Deira, Jorge de la Vega, Rómulo Macció, and Luis Felipe Noé, all natives of the Argentine capital. In 1961 the Peuser Gallery presented the first important exhibit of the new group, an exhibit entitled *Another Figuration.* Until this exhibition, postwar Argentine art had developed a strong tradition of Geometric Abstraction, and artists like Berni were unfashionable. Two years before, for example, the Generative Art group had made its appearance and gained almost immediate acceptance by the advanced circles of Buenos Aires and Latin America. New Figuration, along with other Latin American groups like the Nueva Presencia of Mexico, and certain European groups such as CoBrA prefigured the neo-expressionism of German Savage Painting, Italian Trans-avant-garde, and North American Bad Painting of the 1980s. (The current Argentine figurative movement known as New Image stems directly from New Figuration.)

One of the chief preoccupations of the New Figuration group was the existential condition of man. "The man of today finds no shelter in his image," said Luis Felipe Noé in the catalog to the *Another Figuration* show. "He is in a permanent existential relationship with his fellow men and with things. I believe that this element of relationship is fundamental to 'the other figuration.' Things do not devour one another; they are fused with one another." The group was officially dissolved in 1965, but its members usually received joint invitations to participate in important exhibitions abroad. In 1965 Rómulo Macció went off to Europe and de la Vega to the United States, where he had been invited to serve as artist-in-residence at Cornell University. Deira and Fernando de Szyszlo had received similar invitations previously. In 1962 de la Vega, Deira, Noé, and Macció had all been in Paris for a short time, returning home the following year.

Many critics consider Jorge de la Vega the most interesting artist of the group (plates 171 and 172). Jorge Romero Brest said that de la Vega was "the most imaginative of the four."[32] He had an exhibition at OAS headquarters in June 1963, his first in the United States. Some of the titles of the compositions presented on that occasion (such as *Nude, Two Heads, Cat in the Mirror*), indicated the figurative nature of his work, while others (such as *Sound of the Ocean, Forms of Respiration*, and *One Day, the Adventure*) reflected the artist's varied interests. But only with a great deal of imagination can the viewer relate the works to scenes in the real world. The paintings are extremely rich in pictorial effect and often enhanced by the addition of collage. It is impossible to know how de la Vega's work might have developed after the gestural violence that characterized his best production. In 1967, after a two-year stay in the United States, his work was almost exclusively in black and white. Although the choice of colors suggested a return to more traditional figuration, the paintings continued to reflect his iconoclastic intentions.

Ernesto Deira began to paint in 1954, four years after graduating from law school. At the time he joined the New Figuration group his work shared the gestural violence common to that of his colleagues. However, it also possessed the individual qualities that mark his oeuvre: violent contrasts of color, elongated brush strokes, drawinglike graphisms, nervous calligraphy, and morbid "figures." His preferred paint was industrial enamel. The brilliance of its colors reinforced the strident character of his images. Deira applied enamel paint as a background surface for his canvases, which were intentionally modest in proportions, and on top of the enamel he used oils directly from the can or applied acrylics directly from the tube. Sometimes he took a large canvas he had already painted, cut it into pieces and made several paintings out of it. He began to use this process in 1962, after a trip he made to Europe on a fellowship from the Argentine National Endowment for the Arts. At that time he also began to use acrylics. (Deira's technical eclecticism during this period has presented problems for conservators—physical durability of art works was not a major concern of the New Figuration group.) In general, the compositions of the 1960s show Deira's preference for broad planes interrupted by dark-toned graphic signs and dribbles, the intricacies of which produce faces and figures that are hard to make out. Drawing was a technique Deira exploited with highly expressive results. His charcoal drawings of the 1960s are no less expressive than his paintings, which depend on color and accident for effect. The malleability of the charcoal medium permitted Deira to shade, distort, and "dirty" with his hand the lines he had drawn, producing an overall softness that was a constant of his style even in his last paintings, when his colors took on a phosphorescent aura (plate 170).

In the 1960s the Bonino Gallery in New York was one of the most active galleries in Latin American art. In 1966 Romulo Macció, another member of the New Figuration group, was presented there. (He had exhibited in December 1963 at the Galería Bonino in Buenos Aires.) Macció made use of abstract effects to make the overall effect more dramatic. On the occasion of his second New York exhibition, entitled *Fictions*, which was held at the Center for Inter-American Relations in February 1969, the artist wrote in a preface to the catalog: "I realized that painting for me is practice for the adventuresome play of Free-Imagination in order to create spaces and images, imaginary in height and width. For this reason *Fictions* seemed more on the mark."[33]

In the same catalog, the critics Aldo Pellegrini and Damián Bayón analyzed the visual and conceptual components of Macció's art (plates 173 and 174). Bayón asserted:

Macció's work possesses a sense of design, which is not exactly that of composition....He sketches closely, or scribbles, fills in large spaces with opaque painting, superimposing figures—real, dreamed—on which he delightedly draws an enormous face, enlarged to the size of a school poster hung in front of the blackboard....It is the context that plays at being infantile so that the horror may be yet more awesome...in Macció we find an implicit criticism, an accusation....Macció explains clearly and in cold blood what is happening to him—which is a great deal—and to us, in this world of sordid and marvelous abysses through which we move simultaneously like dreamlike walkers on a tightrope.[34]

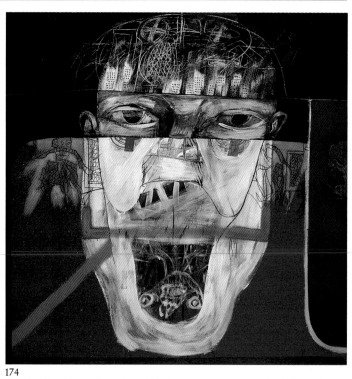

174

173

175

Rómulo Macció
173. *The President on the Balcony.* 1963
Oil and enamel on canvas, 59 x 59"
Museo de Arte Contemporáneo, Buenos Aires
Photo: Pedro Roth

Rómulo Macció
174. *To Live Without a Guarantee.* 1963
Oil on canvas, 72 x 72"
Collection Akira and Louis Shorenstein, New York
Photo: Quesada/Burke, New York

Luis Felipe Noé
175. *When the Sun Hits the Fatherland.* 1963
Oil, photograph, and plaster on canvas, 80 x 80"
Courtesy Bonino Gallery, New York
Photo: Quesada/Burke, New York

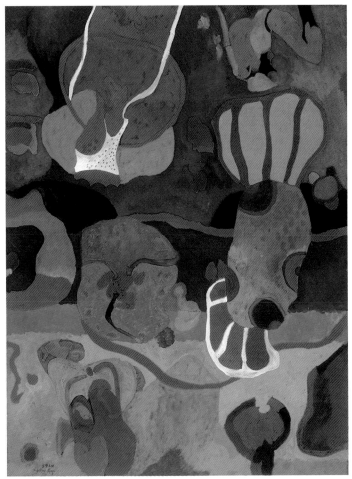

176

177

Gunther Gerzso
177. *Water Mansion.* 1965
Oil on canvas, 31⅞ x 39⅞″
Archer M. Huntington Art Gallery, University of
Texas at Austin. Gift of John and Barbara Duncan,
1971
Photo: George Holmes, Archer M. Huntington Art
Gallery

Luis López-Loza
176. *Children's Dream.* 1965
Oil on canvas, 51 x 38¼″
Collection Ernst Rohner
Photo: Quesada/Burke, New York

179

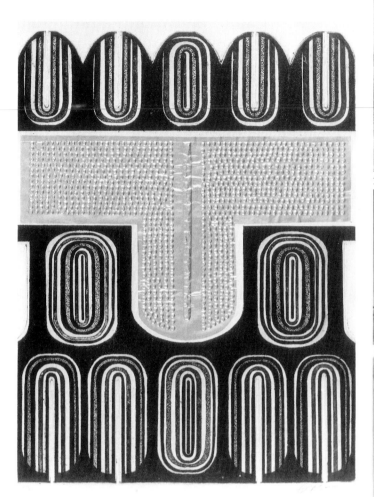

178

180

Marcos Irizarry
178. *Hummingbird Portfolio.* 1970
   Relief etching on paper, 25½ x 19½"
   Museo de Antropología, Arte y Historia,
   Universidad de Puerto Rico, Recinto de Río Piedras
   Photo: John Betancourt, San Juan

Luis Hernández Cruz
179. *Subsoil.* n.d.
   Oil on canvas, 59¾ x 69⅛"
   Lowe Art Museum, University of Miami. Gift, Esso
   Inter-America, Inc.
   Photo: Roland I. Unruh

Jaime Romano
180. *Mythic Landscape.* 1969
   Acrylic on canvas, 60¼ x 48¼"
   Museo de Arte de Ponce, Puerto Rico
   Photo: John Betancourt, San Juan

Throughout the 1960s strong design was the common denominator in Macció's production. Otherwise his work of the decade can be divided into two streams. During the first period his images hold the disorderly energy typical of New Figuration; during the second, the surface became more refined, accidental pictorial elements are "cleaned up," and a more traditional concern for craftmanship is evidenced. Pellegrini observed: "Macció arrives at an authentic simplification rather than the elimination of specific details. But in contrast to what happens in other tendencies that aim for the same result, it is simplification without coldness."[35] In the 1970s Macció turned to Neo-Expressionism.

Luis Felipe Noé was perhaps the most introspective member of the New Figuration group (plate 175). Jorge Gluzberg wrote in this regard: "Anxiety, a passion for existence, and an ever-changing rhythmic vitality distinguish the work of Luis Felipe Noé, who uses forms, ranges of color, and spaces as arms in a struggle with life and with death."[36]

Noé is self-taught. He first became involved with art as a critic writing for the Buenos Aires paper *El Mundo*. He had his first exhibit in the Argentine capital in 1959. In 1965 a Guggenheim Fellowship took him to New York, where he had his first U.S. show at the Bonino Gallery the following year. Previously he, like other members of the New Figuration group, had participated in a majority of the Argentine exhibits that were sent abroad, and he had a show of "oil-assemblies" at the Buenos Aires Museum of Modern Art. These works were a clear reflection of his ideas regarding the relationship between man and his environment, a relationship Noé found basically chaotic, for chaos reigned in the exhibit. The whole gallery was filled with large fragmented canvases on which the frames, some of which were painted, were arbitrarily nailed against the stretchers. These "paintings" gave the impression of being environmental works, a field Noé was involved with.[37] Shortly after his return to Buenos Aires, Noé let it be understood that his interest in art had weakened; that he had turned from objects to "environments," and from there to a state of great dissatisfaction.[38] In fact, Noé ceased all his artistic activity in 1970, only to start up again in 1985.

Abstraction in Mexico and Puerto Rico

As the chapters on Mexico and Puerto Rico (Chapters I and II) address the particular situations regarding the struggles between figurative and abstract artists in these two countries, this essay will only survey briefly the work of artists who reinforced the acceptance of the abstract spirit as a valid visual language in these two countries.

Gunther Gerzso, Luis López-Loza, and Rufino Tamayo

After studying set design in the United States, Gunther Gerzso established contact with the Surrealist artists who had sought refuge in Mexico during World War II. His acquaintances included Remedios Varo, Leonora Carrington, Benjamin Peret, and Wolfgang Paalen. In 1962 Gerzso turned to pre-Columbian forms for inspiration. His first one-man show in the United States was at the Phoenix Art Museum in 1970. A year earlier he had begun to use an architectural drafting machine to produce works of a new character. Since his abstract beginnings in the early 1950s, Gerzso's work has maintained formal unity. At certain points he has incorporated textures into his canvases, but the results are not as effective as his use of color to reinforce the two-dimensional character of the planes into which he breaks up a painting's surface. That effect is premeditatedly metaphysical and designed to produce a "harmonious imbalance" (plate 177).

Another Mexican who has practiced abstraction since the early 1950s is Luis López-Loza. His compositions (plate 176) present biomorphic forms within a color field. Color is of primary importance to the overall image. López-Loza is a good example of the generation that followed the great muralists, a generation that has sought to bring new life to artistic expression in Mexico. In this connection, special mention should be made of Rufino Tamayo. Although he is a figurative painter in the sense that his forms usually relate to the visible world, his innovative use of color, form, and texture contributed notably to the development of abstraction, a term originally applied in Mexico to all that departed from traditionally "Mexican" art (plates 181 and 182).

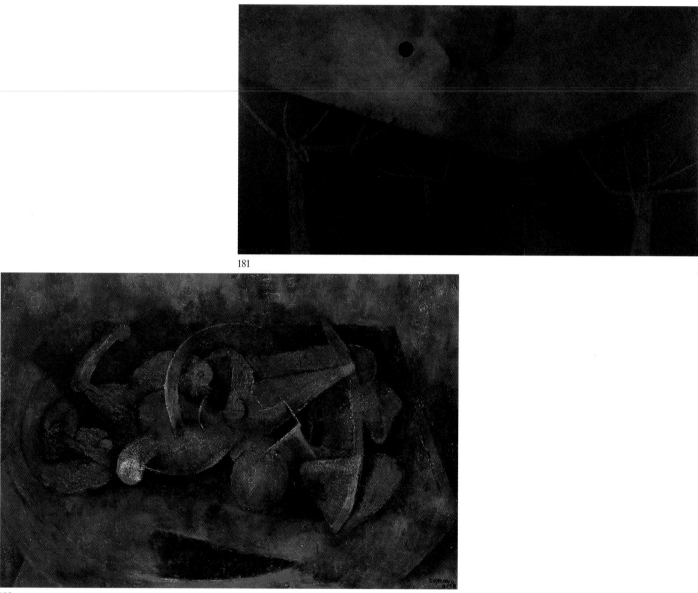

181

182

Rufino Tamayo
181. *Infinite Road.* 1949
Oil on canvas, 29 x 55″
Collection Elva Podesta de Holm. Courtesy Galería
Arvil, Mexico City
Photo: courtesy Galería Arvil

Rufino Tamayo
182. *Insomnia.* 1958
Oil on canvas, 38½ x 57″
Collection Francisco and Laura Osio. Courtesy
Galería Arvil, Mexico City
Photo: Gerardo Suter

Julio Rosado del Valle and Olga Albizu

The principal representative of abstract art in Puerto Rico is Julio Rosado del Valle. He started as a figurative painter, but about 1955 he began to turn to abstraction. The transition was slow—as can be seen in the painting *Carnival Devil*, a composition dating from 1955 in which the devil mask used in the island's popular parades served as inspiration for the warm, artist's organic abstraction. He has led a rather solitary artistic existence, for it was not until the 1960s that activity in abstraction took root in the island. The work done by Rosado del Valle between 1955 and 1967 represents the most interesting phase of his career. His use of color was generally austere. Neutral tones were applied in carefully controlled impasto onto canvas or wood. The large-scale compositions in particular are unusually rich in pictorial effects (plate 61).

By contrast with Rosado del Valle, Olga Albizu typifies the case of the Puerto Rican artist who has been absorbed into the Manhattan mainstream. In New York she made contact with Hans Hofmann, who had a great influence on her work, particularly noticeable in the thick impasto application of color.

Luis Hernández Cruz and Jaime Romano

The outstanding figure in Puerto Rican abstract art during the 1960s was probably Luis Hernández Cruz. Hernández Cruz's abstractions were marked by a high degree of lyricism, an element totally absent from Albizu's art. This is readily apparent in a comparision between Albizu's *Growth* and Hernández Cruz's *Subsoil*, the works by which they were represented at the *Esso Salon of Young Artists* in 1965 and which are now the property of the Lowe Art Museum in Coral Gables, Florida (plates 66 and 179).

With Hernández Cruz, abstraction took a poetic turn in Puerto Rico, a phenomenon that occurred rather generally in Latin America at that time. The poetic element often took the form of allusions to myth and ancestral heritage. By contrast with the nationalist tendency of the 1950s and the art engagé of that period in which figuration and story-telling went hand in hand, the artists of the 1960s assumed more independent, personal stances. Abstraction became a viable alternative to inspiration derived from the landscape or culture of Puerto Rico.

Jaime Romano's career began in the 1960s in San Juan. His colors were lyrical and achieved "an atmosphere of mist," in the words of the critic Mari Carmen Ramírez (plate 180).

Part II: Reality and Figuration

During the 1920s and 1930s figurative painting in the Americas drew inspiration from two main sources: the Mexican School and Surrealism. By the early 1940s, however, these sources were for the most part exhausted, although the influence of the Mexican School persisted in a few countries, where it served to call attention to problems of a political or social nature. Surrealism in the European manner had had considerable impact in countries such as Argentina and Chile, which boasted large European populations, but it could not prosper throughout Latin America as a whole, perhaps because the element of the irrational has always been taken for granted in Latin America, in contradistinction to the highly organized societies of Europe. Likewise in the New World, Surrealism or, better said, the element of the fantastic, was shocking in the United States, the model of a technological, functional society in which individual behavior is regulated by the demands of society; whereas in Latin America centuries-old traditions of magic practices and mythic beliefs had long been syncretized with the Catholic faith. In Latin America, Surrealism was explored as a way to express the complexities and contradictions of reality, dispossessed of metaphysical speculation. This rechanneling of Surrealist principles can be observed in the early works of Raquel Forner, Roberto Aizemberg, and Antonio Berni of Argentina.

The advent of nonobjective art forced artists who wished to continue painting with images derived from the real world to realize that the time had come for a reevaluation of the concept of the figure. A mere change in style would not suffice. Artists could no longer reject Cubism and other speculative experimentation and opt for conventional language as a vehicle for the promotion of political ideas. Originality was not possible if that course was taken. Artists of the 1940s who sought to keep figuration alive independently came to the same conclusion: it was reality itself that had to be analyzed, and from its peculiarities inspiration was to be drawn. By 1950 there was an appreciable difference between analyses made in Latin America and those made in other parts of the world. (Compare, for example, the works of the British artist Francis Bacon and the Mexican José Luis Cuevas.)

Freedom to focus on a particular aspect of reality—a freedom that Latin American artists availed themselves of in abundance—did not prevent many from questioning the very nature of reality. Raquel Forner, for one, took a futuristic approach, speculating on the transitory nature of human existence and the possible existence of other worlds. The fascination with the unknown and the desire to understand the universe was an old pre-Columbian disquietude. The Mexican José Luis Cuevas began an introspective exploration of the deformities and debilities that humans suffer. Alejandro Obregón found drama in landscapes, sometimes the tragic scenarios of violence. Social and political establishments were irreverently exploited by Fernando Botero, Marisol Escobar, and Enrique Grau for purposes of humor and satire. The folk tradition, rich in imagination, was reinterpreted with sophisticated language by Pedro Figari and renewed by Amelia Peláez and Rufino Tamayo. In each case, the results were artistically valid and universally evocative. By maintaining a firm stand against the avalanche of abstract art and the flood of "isms" that overwhelmed the Western world, these artists were able to create a wonderfully varied gallery of works quite different from figurative art with a social message. Their art was inspired by the simplest and most basic aspects of daily existence. Figuration in Latin America thus became a stable counterproposal to abstract and geometric imagery as well as to the ephemeral trends developed in the technological societies of the Western world.

Raquel Forner

When Raquel Forner had her first individual exhibit in the United States at OAS headquarters in Washington, D.C., in 1957, she was already well known at home and abroad. She had won a number of awards and had represented Argentina at such significant events as the 1935 *Pittsburgh International Exhibition.* As late as 1955 her work was strongly imbued with the spirit of European Surrealism, which she knew from her studies and sojourns in Paris. Her subject matter, however, was often about violence and was not completely divorced from reality (such as a series she made about the Spanish Civil War).

Beginning in 1956, Forner started to abandon narratives and became increasingly interested in purely plastic matters. Her expressionistic treatment of the human figure, which she had maintained for two decades, was replaced by more painterly concerns, which put emphasis on the richness of surfaces created by heavy impastos of oil. But her style was so personal that it is difficult to relate these paintings with those of Jean Dubuffet or the Spanish Informalists. Cosmic visions, stars, and moons invaded her canvases. There were still figures to be seen, but they seemed to have come from an unexplored universe, where all might be possible. In 1957 The Museum of Modern Art purchased her *Moons,* a painting in tempera belonging to her Space series. Forner also created a series of Astrobeings, which at first glance seem like abstractions. Her 1961 *Black Astrobeings* is representative of one of her most interesting periods, in which she gave new meaning to the use of oil, not just formally but also as a painterly equivalent to the fantastic personages of science-fiction films. The thick impastos she used in the late 1950s and early 1960s were moderated by 1965, and the figure once more became readily perceptible in her compositions, particularly in the series of Astronauts she began in 1965. Forner's work of this period can be identified to some extent with a group of Argentine artists who practiced a particularly violent type of figuration, perhaps as a reaction against the elegant sophistication of the country's Lyric Abstraction and the mathematical coldness of Geometric Abstraction. Forner participated in most of the significant exhibitions of Latin American art held in the United States, including *South American Art Today* in Dallas. Today she is still very active, not only in Buenos Aires but in Canada and Europe as well (plate 184).[1]

Antonio Berni

Antonio Berni was a figure of peculiar importance in Argentine art. In 1925 he traveled to Europe on a scholarship from the Rosario Jockey Club. In 1926 he studied at the Grande Chaumière for several months, receiving instruction from André Lhote and Othon Friesz. In 1928 he made contact with the Surrealists, who were to exercise a significant influence on his work. Returning to Argentina in 1930, Berni encountered great difficulties promoting his new style of painting. In 1932 he had a show of Surrealist pictures at the gallery of the Friends of Art in Buenos Aires, but by the following year he had taken up a style he termed "New Realism." His subjects were usually blue-collar workers and the environments in which they lived—people from humble neighborhoods who amused themselves with simple activities. It was the beginning of his most important paintings, and a style he continued to develop until the end of the 1960s. Berni is of Italian descent, and in his work one can perceive the bold descriptions of reality portrayed in Italian films of the postwar era. In 1934 he worked with Siqueiros, who was then in Buenos Aires, and in 1939 he and his fellow countryman Lino Eneas Spillimbergo were charged with executing murals for the Argentine pavilion at the New York World's Fair. In 1935 he was appointed to a professorship at the National School of Fine Arts in Buenos Aires, a post he held until 1946.

It was only in the mid-1950s that Berni's work began to appear abroad on a regular basis. He exhibited in Europe, where compositions of his were included in a traveling exhibit that toured Bucharest, Warsaw, Prague, and Moscow. In 1958 he began to make use of collage and assemblage techniques, methods to which he had resorted in his Surrealist work of the early 1930s. In 1960 he created two characters, Juanito Laguna and Ramona Montiel, fictitious representatives of the unfavored segments of the *populacho*, for whom life is a game with nothing to lose but with lots of possible gains. Ramona is sometimes a prostitute, a "femme fatale," the smart lover of a general, or, if it is necessary, the mistress of the entire armed forces. Juanito is at once a pathetic and abandoned child, a pickpocket, and the scum of the city wards. These two characters were to be the centerpiece of Berni's work for more than a decade. The resulting imagery is unique in the art of the hemisphere during those years, and the only comparable approach is the Italian Arte Povera (although that tendency was basically conceptual). The critical intention of the compositions is rendered clear by Berni's use of junk material, which he gathered in the crowded shantytowns of the Buenos Aires slums. Berni assembled the figures with screws, pieces of wood, empty cans flattened by cars— anything that was discarded. Not without coincidence his endeavor was paralleled by the resurgence of industry in Buenos Aires. Berni included his two personages in his paintings, collages, and prints. In his prints he built up the plates with three-dimensional objects. After an assemblage was passed through a press, the resulting intricate and ornate effects were somehow similar to pre-Columbian reliefs and had a distinctly Latin feeling, imbued of course with daring, avant-garde qualities. Prints such as these won the international prize for engraving at the Venice Biennale in 1962. Thereafter, Berni's work began to appear frequently in exhibitions in the United States, such as *New Art of Argentina* at the Walker Art Center in Minneapolis. Berni had a one-man show at the Miami Museum of Modern Art in 1963 and a retrospective at the New Jersey State Museum in Trenton in 1966.

Berni's compositions executed after 1960 coincide with the resurgence of figuration and the appearance of Generative Art in Argentina. He remained independent, not only from the local scene but also from the international one. Some critics sought to link his work to Pop art, owing to his use of scrap materials in collages (an approach Robert Rauschenberg also used) and the social message implicit in his work; but in Berni's creations the plastic purpose as well as the message are quite different. He questions not just the artifice of modern society but also the myth of industrialization, which was falsely promoted as a solution for economic prosperity in the third world. Berni's pictorial means reflect this philosophy. The rotten elements he used to compose his works criticized the "bourgeois" mentality of the ruling groups and its strong attraction to salon painting. His interest in conveying such social statements began in the mid-1930s. In terms of technique, too, his art is in fact a reaction against the formal

183

184

185

Rufino Tamayo
183. *White Horse*. 1934
Gouache on paper, 12¼ x 15"
Courtesy Galería Arvil, Mexico City
Photo: Gerardo Suter

Raquel Forner
184. *Black Astrobeings*. 1961
Oil on canvas, 47 x 47"
Museum of Modern Art of Latin America,
Organization of American States, Washington, D.C.
Photo: Angel Hurtado

Emilio Sanchez
185. *Cottage on San Andres Island*. 1969
Oil on canvas, 54 x 38"
Private collection, New York City
Photo: Quesada/Burke, New York

188

186

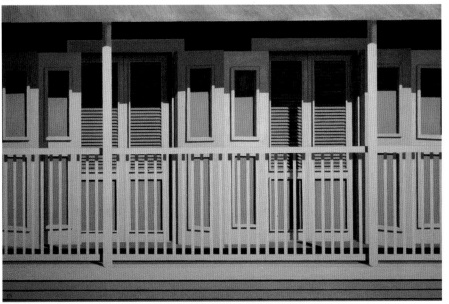

187

Emilio Sanchez
187. *Green and White Cottage.* 1969
Oil on canvas, 49 x 72″
Collection the artist
Photo: David Cunningham

Alejandro Obregón
188. *The Wake.* 1956
Oil on canvas, 59 x 72″
Museum of Modern Art of Latin America,
Organization of American States, Washington, D.C.
Purchase Fund, 1957
Photo: Angel Hurtado

Alejandro Obregón
186. *Cattle Crossing the Magdalena.* 1955
Oil on canvas, 62½ x 49⅝″
Museum of Fine Arts, Houston. Gift of Brown and
Root
Photo: Allen Mewbourn

approaches of the Pop movement. Berni's intaglios have an almost baroque, exuberant charm, and his textural richness is unique.

Alirio Rodríguez

The paintings of the Venezuelan Alirio Rodríguez have been inspired in part by the urge to transcend traditional spatial concepts. For many years the achievements of his work were underplayed even in his native country, perhaps due to certain pictorial similarities between his art and that of Francis Bacon. His first one-man show in the United States took place in 1969 at OAS headquarters in Washington, D.C. That same year he exhibited in group shows at the Zegri Gallery in New York, the University of Alabama, the Art Museum of Tulsa, Oklahoma, and the Newland Gallery in Los Angeles. He became particularly active in the United States in the 1970s. Rodríguez is viewed today as one of the principal artists in the revival of figuration in Latin America. His figures seem to penetrate new dimensions. They are often suspended in space, about to dissolve under the pressure of otherworldly forces and self-released energy. They make an existential statement, relating man to the universe rather than to earth.

Emilio Sánchez

The Cuban Emilio Sánchez has found inspiration in the most commonplace themes, and at the same time he has engaged in bold experiments with colors. He first appeared on the New York scene in 1949 with a show of watercolors at the Luyber Gallery. His interest in architectural subjects, particularly the humble Victorian dwellings to be found in the islands of the Caribbean, was already apparent at that time. Like James Rosenquist, who utilized the commercial images of billboards as a point of departure for his whimsical compositions, Sánchez transformed images of houses into simplified structures of light and shade, void of literal resemblances to reality. The color schemes retain the paintings' allusions to popular Caribbean taste. *Arts* magazine said of his 1956 show at Peridot Gallery: "The pastel watercolors are very pale, looking almost as if the color had been bleached by a strong sun.…The neo-Gothic houses are placed flat-footedly down in the center of the picture, acquiring almost a Surreal intensity" (plates 185 and 187).[2]

Sánchez took up permanent residence in New York in 1952 and had a number of exhibits there during the period covered by this study, including shows at the Feragil Gallery (1951, 1953), Galería Sudamericana (1958, 1968), and The Contemporaries (1966). He has maintained the same style for the past three decades. His palette and his treatment of spatial environments continues to identify his art with the Caribbean.

Alejandro Obregón

The exuberance of the tropics, the overwhelming grandeur of the Colombian landscape, and the drama of everyday life have found a romantic and dramatic interpreter in Alejandro Obregón. After serving briefly as director of the School of Fine Arts in Bogotá, Obregón went to France in 1949 for five years. By 1956 he was internationally renowned as one of the leaders of Colombian painting. At the *Gulf-Caribbean Art* exhibition held at the Houston Museum of Fine Arts he won first prize for his *Cattle Crossing the Magdalena* (plate 186). With *The Wake* (also known as *Vigil* and *The Dead Student*), a work inspired by massacres of students during the dictatorship of General Gustavo Rojas Pinilla (1953–1957), Obregón won the prize for Colombia in the 1957 Guggenheim competition (plate 188). The structure of his compositions is determined by planes of color, producing at first glance a geometric effect that erroneously has been thought to have been derived directly from Cubism.[3] But it is color that is his most important element, and it has increasingly acquired the main role in his art. Forms are defined by loose brush strokes, which present an imposing array of broad areas rich in pictorial effects and a sense of three-dimensionality quite different from the flattened and two-dimensional surfaces of Matisse's paintings.

The subjects in Obregón's paintings are nearly all drawn from the flora, fauna, geography, and history of Colombia. Like Paul Gauguin's work in Tahiti, however, it is Obregón's vigorous plastic reinterpretation that saves his art from classification as a regional expression. As the 1960s advanced, Obregón's work was executed more freely, but he remained committed to his selected themes, consciously avoiding completely abstract solutions. The critic Marta Traba has compared the gestural periods of Obregón's painting with the work of artists such as Clyfford Still and Adja Yunkers: "Obregón's break with space with Rauschenberg's and Dine's incorporation into a lyric space...of ordinary objects that 'place' the painting, [bring art] down to the level of everyday reality, thereby impeding flights of emotion."[4]

In 1962 Obregón won the prize given at the *Fourteenth National Colombian Salon* with a work entitled *Violence.* The subject was not a new one for Obregón, who used it in *The Wake* and in his 1948 *Massacre of April the Tenth,* a work inspired by the riots that swept Bogotá after the assassination of the leader of the Liberal Party, Jorge Eliécer Gaitán. Other series he painted up to 1970 bear such names as Barracudas (1963), Cold River (1965), Icaruses (1967), Landscapes for Angels (1968), and Magic Spells (1969). The titles suggest the artist's interests: the snow-crowned volcanos of the Colombian cordillera where the Andean condor, one of the symbols of Colombian independence and the country's national bird, flies alone and undisturbed; the rain forest of the Colombian jungle, filled with exotic legends and the generous rivers that carry its magnificent and colorful aquatic fauna, but which sometimes are also the settings of human dramas when, for example, floods erase villages without compassion. This is the natural stage for Obregón, who settled many years ago in the walled city of Cartagena, called "The Heroic City," on the Caribbean coast, to be close to the mangrove swamps and lagoons, and to the sea and the sky of the country he has loved so much. His rich, baroque compositions have been compared by several critics, Marta Traba among them, with the fanciful narratives of Colombian writer Gabriel García Márquez.

From the time of the Houston exhibition until the retrospective with which he was honored at Center for Inter-American Relations in New York in 1970, Obregón was one of the most active figures on the international scene, representing Colombia at all the important Latin American shows held in the United States during those years. His works were acquired by some of the leading museums of South America, Europe, and the United States. He continues to be a highly prolific artist.

Enrique Grau

During the 1960s, Enrique Grau, along with Botero, Obregón, and the Geometric Abstractionists Edgar Negret and Eduardo Ramírez Villamizar were considered the masters of contemporary Colombian art. They are contemporaries, each except Botero born about 1920. (Botero was born in 1932, but the ten years' difference was quickly erased due to his aggressive appearance on the art scene and the sudden positive response his work received from art critics.) As a generation that assumed artistic renewal as a serious challenge, the Colombian group is comparable to Venezuela's Kinetic movement (Soto, Otero, and Cruz Díez) and the Argentine Generative Art and New Figuration movements.

For Grau, reality is found in absurdly trite situations that are rich in black humor. His style became well defined after 1960. In the 1950s he was influenced by Obregón. After a short sojourn in Florence in 1955 he adopted geometric solutions to figures and objects. In his series *Breakfast in Florence* there is usually a figure, sometimes two, dressed in Roman tunics and standing by a table with utensils on it. Through a window in the background, the traditional campanile of a city can be seen. In this series, the ambiguous situations created by the assorted objects and eras and the imprecise purpose of the figure hint at Grau's later moments of humor.

About 1960 Grau's portrayal of the figure underwent radical changes. His style became more naturalistic, exuding, in the words of one critic, a "carnal vitality...[with his] ornaments, cheap costume jewelry, plastic flowers, moth-eaten feather boas.... Commonness is for Grau the definitive characteristic of the world in which we live, and it is this quality which he seeks to bring out in his works."[5] The results are humorously absurd, and, unlike Obregón, Grau shows contempt for romanticism. He also began to place increasing emphasis on painterly craftsmanship. He continued, however, to cultivate the note of ambiguity that had characterized his subjects for some time. The refinement of his technique has been impressive, but the exaggeration and ridicule with which the artist treats his subjects, his mockery of innocence, and his stress on unusual situations is disturbing. The contrast of form and substance mirrors the paradoxes

189

190

191

Santiago Cárdenas
189. *Seventh Avenue Supermarket.* 1965–66
Oil on canvas, 70⅞ x 48¼"
Museo del Minuto de Dios, Bogotá, Colombia
Photo: Jaime Ardila, Camilo Lleras

Enrique Grau
190. *Boy with Umbrella.* 1964
Oil on canvas, 40 x 44"
Museum of Modern Art of Latin America,
Organization of American States, Washington, D.C.
Photo: Angel Hurtado

Marisol Escobar
191. *Charles de Gaulle.* 1965
Painted wood, 107¼ x 86¼ x 31⅞"
National Museum of American Art, Smithsonian
Institution, Washington, D.C. Gift of Mr. and Mrs.
David K. Anderson. Martha Jackson Memorial
Collection
Photo: courtesy National Museum of American Art,
Smithsonian Institution

193

192

194

Fernando Botero
193. *The Young Boy from Vallecas (after Velazquez).* 1959
Oil on canvas, 52⅝ x 56⅜″
Baltimore Museum of Art. Gift of Geoffrey Gates
Photo: courtesy Baltimore Museum of Art

Fernando Botero
192. *Santa Rosa de Lima (after Vásquez).* 1966
Oil on linen, 49⅝ x 53⅝″
Archer M. Huntington Art Gallery, University of
Texas at Austin. Gift of John and Barbara Duncan,
1971
Photo: courtesy Archer M. Huntington Art Gallery

Fernando Botero
194. *Rubens's Wife.* 1963
Oil on canvas, 72⅛ x 70⅛″
Solomon R. Guggenheim Museum, New York.
Purchased with funds contributed by Fundación
Neumann, Caracas, Venezuela, 1966
Photo: Robert E. Mates

Grau finds between social convention and actual human behavior. The element of the irrational often appears reflected in amusing and whimsical combinations of humans and objects. Grau surrounds figures with arbitrary elements to make his pictures' meanings become absurd. His work was particularly significant during the 1960s, when Hyper-Realism was beginning to emerge and great attention was paid to the traditional values of painting. But Grau was not interested in the simple and detailed representation of reality per se (plate 190).

From 1940 to 1943 Grau studied in New York on a grant from the Colombian government. In 1950 he exhibited in a show at the New School for Social Research along with his compatriots Eduardo Ramírez Villamizar and Edgar Negret. His first one-man show in the United States took place in 1957 at OAS headquarters in Washington, D.C. By that time, Grau enjoyed a reputation as one of the leaders of Colombian painting. He was more frequently in shows held in the United States during the 1950s than the 1960s, but he was always presented as one of the leading figures in contemporary Colombian art. His compositions appeared at the 1964 *Pittsburgh International Exhibition,* at the *South American Art Today* show in Dallas, and in the exhibit *Three Thousand Years of Colombian Art.* In the 1960s he was also included in group shows in Manchester, New Hampshire; at Brandeis University in Massachusetts; in a Latin American show organized by the OAS Visual Arts Unit for presentation at the Carrol Reece Museum in Johnson City, Tennessee, and at the University of Oklahoma.

Marisol Escobar and Fernando Botero

Latin American artists have frequently resorted to humor, irony, and satire—even artists who are not Expressionists or Realists per se. Good examples are furnished by two figures of international renown: Marisol Escobar and Fernando Botero (plates 191–194).

After attending the École des Beaux-Arts in Paris, Marisol went to New York for further study at The Art Students League (1950) and the New School for Social Research (1951-54). Simultaneously she attended a school maintained by Hans Hoffman. Her work at first was identified with Pop art, but the originality she displayed soon made it clear that she really had little in common with that movement. As one critic noted: "Though her art is highly sophisticated, the influence on her early work includes pre-Columbian Mochica pottery, early American folk art, and Mexican boxes with pictures inside. The playful early sculptures she was making from about 1953 include roughly carved wooden figures, sometimes placed behind glass in boxes. But in her mature work she has made use of such primitive, folklike approaches to create sculptural tableaux satirizing social and political attitudes."[6]

Marisol has had about ten solo shows in New York. Among the places at which she has exhibited are the Leo Castelli Gallery (1958), the Stable Gallery (1962, 1964), and the Sidney Janis Gallery (1966, 1967, 1975, 1978). She has also had shows at the Estudio Actual in Caracas (1974) and the Hanover Gallery in London (1967). In 1963 she was included in *Americans 1963* at The Museum of Modern Art. Works by her are to be found in that institution, the Whitney Museum, and the Albright-Knox Gallery in Buffalo. On the occasion of her first individual show at the Leo Castelli Gallery in 1958, *Picture* magazine wrote: "Marisol, a young sculptress from Venezuela, is showing at the Castelli Gallery. Experimental and impressively vital, she seems nonetheless to stem from the great traditions of South American sculpture, native as well as colonial and European baroque."[7]

Fernando Botero's works resemble Marisol's in the monumental quality both painters impart to the figure. Like Marisol, Botero engages in humorous criticism of the establishment, but their work is otherwise quite different. For example, Marisol includes in her sculptures blocks of wood on which she sketches faces, articles of clothing, or other aspects of the figure in question, or she may amplify pieces with masks; whereas Botero has always shown great respect for conventional artistic techniques. In his youth he traveled to Mexico, Spain, France, and Italy, spending a great deal of time in Florence studying the Renaissance masters. Until 1966 he divided his activities between Colombia, Europe, and the United States. He received a number of prizes in Colombia and was included in many exhibits in the United States. His first one-man show in the United States was at OAS headquarters in Washington, D.C., in 1957. In 1960, after winning the

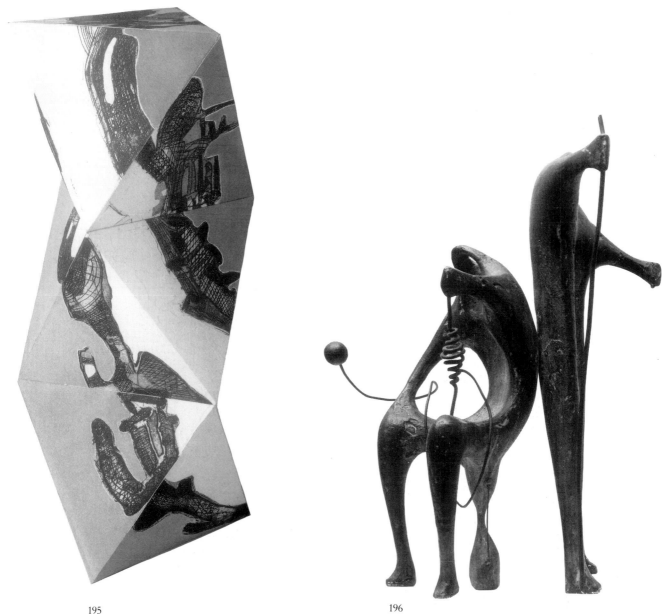

195

196

Juan Gómez-Quiroz
195. *Spiral.* 1968
    Folded intaglio on paper, 32 x 12 x 24″
    Collection the artist
    Photo: courtesy the artist

Joaquín Roca Rey
196. *Study for an Unknown Political Prisoner.* 1957
    Bronze, 13 x 9 x 10″
    Museum of Modern Art of Latin America,
    Organization of American States, Washington, D.C.
    Photo: Angel Hurtado

prize for Colombia in that year's Guggenheim competition, he moved to New York, where he was based until 1973. (He now resides in Paris.) His *Mona Lisa at the Age of Twelve* was purchased by The Museum of Modern Art in 1961. This was one of a series of compositions inspired by Leonardo's portrait. At about the same time he created several series derived from Renaissance works, including a work "after" Velázquez's *Niño de Vallecas* and a version of *La Camera degli Sposi*, a homage to Mantegna. The first of these won him the first prize at the *Eleventh National Colombian Salon* (1958); the second, executed in 1961, is now in the Hirshhorn Museum in Washington, D.C.

Until 1963 Botero exaggerated the volume of his figures, making use of short brush strokes and much cross-hatching; thereafter he began to use gentler strokes. Volumes became still more pronounced, but were softened by shading. During the next years his mastery of oil techniques became increasingly evident. This was a confirmation of his admiration for the great artists of the past. In 1969 the Center for Inter-American Relations in New York honored him with a show, and shortly afterward the Marlborough Gallery became his sole agent. Botero is one of the few Latin American artists that has received this kind of commercial and artistic recognition in the United States.

Botero's bloated figures and the monolithic, sacerdotal air that surrounds them, particularly in compositions of his earlier years, suggest the influence of the great pre-Columbian stone figures at San Agustín in the artist's native country. The attraction he feels for the scenes and events of his youth is reflected in his picturesque gallery of military leaders, politicians, and social climbers. Despite the bizarre appearance of his figures, Botero has stated many times in different interviews that his main visual interest is the sensuality he can achieve in handling form.[8]

Botero, Marisol, Frasconi,[9] and a few other Latin American artists belong in a special class of Latin American artists. They have long been highly successful, established figures in the United States, but they are hardly considered Hispanic or Latin American artists. It would seem that success, rather than an artist's intrinsic contribution, can cause political, sociological, and racial differences to disappear. Indeed, an article published in a Washington paper commented with unintentional irony on the participation of Marisol and Frasconi in the *Thirty-fourth Venice Biennale:* "The entire Uruguayan exhibit was devoted to the work of an artist we consider American chiefly because he has lived and worked in Norwalk, Connecticut, for so many years, Antonio Frasconi, the woodcut man." The reviewer continued: "The talk around the Venice art world all summer has centered on Marisol, the beautiful Venezuelan sculptor, whom, like Frasconi, we consider American and who provided the entire exhibition for Venezuela....Her exhibition attracted more comment than any from the professionals and fashionables. The betting in Venice has been that if the judges do...agree upon a grand prize, it will probably go to Marisol."[10]

Santiago Cárdenas

Santiago Cárdenas received his high-school and art education in the United States. He obtained a bachelor's degree from the Rhode Island School of Design in 1960 and attended Yale University in 1962, where Jack Tworkov, Al Held, Neil Welliver, and Alex Katz were his teachers. Among his classmates were Richard Serra, Chuck Close, Nancy Graves, and Jennifer Bartlett. From 1960 to 1962 he did a tour of duty in the U.S. armed forces, serving in West Germany in order to keep his resident status in the United States. In 1965 he returned to Colombia and has lived in Bogotá ever since.

When Cárdenas made his professional appearance on the Colombian art scene, his work reflected the influence of his teacher Alex Katz in the preference he revealed for the almost two-dimensional representation of people and objects of daily use. His paintings were classified at first as Pop art. The objects chosen were not ones that normally figure in paintings: electric plugs, ironing boards, clothes hangers, umbrellas, overcoats. They were reproduced with fidelity, and little by little they became more realistic, to the point of being almost ultrarealist. This served to emphasize the artist's basic idea of the relationship between objects and the beholder: "Everyday objects have not been overused in art, whereas less common ones, such as flower vases and the

197

Rafael Tufiño
197. *The Bottle.* 1963
Oil on Masonite, 48 x 36″
Museo de Arte de Ponce, Puerto Rico. Fundación
Luis A. Ferré
Photo: John Betancourt, San Juan

198

199

Leonél Góngora
198. *Stop!* 1966
Oil and collage on canvas, 65 x 78″
Collection Vita Girogi, New York
Photo: Tony Velez

Manuel Hernández Acevedo
199. *The Chapel.* 1950
Oil on panel, 23 x 14″
Instituto de Cultura Puertorriqueña, San Juan
Photo: John Betancourt, San Juan

human body, have.…The point to my painting is that what you see is an object, not a picture." Writing of Cárdenas, the critic German Rubiano Caballero said: "Cárdenas's pictures can never be viewed as attempts at photographic reproduction of reality. They are admirable both as painted surfaces void of tricks and stridency and as works of art from which we can receive lessons in moderation and, should we so desire, learn to correct our embittered vision of the world."[11] The way Cárdenas isolates his subjects and places them within the surface of the canvas or paper, in conjunction with his skillful draftsmanship, sometimes produces an almost mystical effect. Indeed José María Galván wrote in the Madrid periodical *Triunfo* that for Cárdenas painting was a secondary matter: "A secondary matter, but one of which he has a thorough mastery. It is precisely this mastery which permits him to engage in dialogue with phantoms. Indeed, as a painter Cárdenas is endowed with everything required for the kind of 'realism' he practices" (plate 189).[12]

Antonio Enrique Amaral

Like many other artists from Latin America, the Brazilian Antonio Enrique Amaral had his first one-man show in the United States at OAS headquarters in Washington, D.C., in 1959. Previously he had studied at the Pratt Institute in New York under Siko Munakat and Antonio Frasconi, from whom he learned the technique of printmaking. Amaral is primarily a painter, however. For two decades he concentrated on painting gigantic fruits enlarged to heroic scale and endowed with great powers of suggestion. Amaral once declared, with a great dose of humor, that for him the banana was the symbol of Brazil. Magnified, these traditional still-life subjects are transformed into organic fetishes filled with mysterious fascination. Amaral became more active in the United States in the 1970s, and his thematic repertory was enlarged to include flowers and other elements of the vegetable kingdom. Later he introduced metallic objects, such as gigantic forks and knives that penetrated the fruits. Amaral said in a television interview that his intention was to express the conflict felt between the machine and the organic power of matter, between technology and nature.[13]

Figuration in Mexico and Puerto Rico

In Puerto Rico figurative art has continuously sought to bring out regional characteristics that distinguish the island's culture from that of the mainland United States. From the turn of the century through the 1970s, this marked inclination toward picturesque regionalism *(costumbrismo)* has been an artistic reflection of the ambiguous status of the Puerto Rican people. Indeed, the dominant form of Puerto Rican figurative art during the 1950s was a politically charged *art engagé*. Landscape painting, including urban scenes, is another important genre within this tendency, but attention has also been given to portraiture and to the representation of the various types of people that make up the population of the island. A classic example is provided by *Goyita*, a work of Rafael Tufiño, which is a portrait of his mother. In the painting, Tufiño makes a pictorial statement about the strong "mulatto" women of the island. In the 1950s the works of Manuel Hernández Acevedo marked a break with descriptive figuration. Although based on representation, they reveal an interest in the formal and plastic aspects of painting. This is even more evident in the work of Francisco Rodón, whose work represents a further development in figuration. Rodón used traditional subject matter, especially portraits of famous people (among them the former governor Luis Muñoz Marín, the writer Jorge Luis Borges, the ballerina Alicia Alonso, and the critic Marta Traba), and transformed the likenesses into kaleidoscopes of small geometric shapes of different colors. Interest in figuration was heightened in Puerto Rico during the 1960s in reaction to the appearance of abstract art in the island, which was seen as a mainland export (plates 197 and 199).

In Mexico, the dominant influence of the Mexican School extended into the 1940s. Raul Anguiano and Julio Castellanos, among others, represented this tradition into the 1940s and 1950s. Two figures of particular interest are Jean Charlot and Miguel Covarrubias. Charlot sought to "modernize" pre-Columbian models of the human figure in his work. Covarrubias did important work in illustration and caricature in the United States.

201

200

202

Amelia Peláez
200. *Hibiscus.* 1943
Oil on canvas, 45½ x 35″
Museum of Modern Art of Latin America,
Organization of American States, Washington, D.C.
Gift of IBM Corporation
Photo: Angel Hurtado

Pedro Figari
201. *Candombe.* 1920-30
Oil on board, 15¾ x 19½″
Courtesy C.D.S. Gallery, New York
Photo: courtesy C.D.S. Gallery

Jacobo Borges
202. *Without Shades.* 1965
Oil on wood, 54⅝ x 54⅝″
Collection Clara Diament Sujo, New York
Photo: Oscar Monsalve

One of the most vigorous personalities in Mexican art from the 1950s is José Luis Cuevas, who is in part responsible for the contemporary recognition of the importance of drawing (one could count in this small group the American Leonard Baskin) in the Americas. Usually drawing has been considered of secondary significance, particularly in Mexico, where mural painting has reigned supreme. Cuevas has also contributed greatly to the development of a type of expressionistic figuration that is concerned with portraying aspects of the human personality and soul. Like other important Latin American artists during the 1950s, Cuevas not only strongly rejected abstract painting but questioned the importance of this tendency. He even mocked its results in a series of monochromatic paintings he executed during the mid-1950s to demonstrate its superficiality. Oddly enough, the paintings resembled gigantic fragments of drawings.[14]

Cuevas's work helped to develop in Mexico a new generation of figurative artists, who formed different groups and published their own manifestos but who reunited to practice a type of figurative art that was not going to please the traditional aesthetic values of the public, not even those accustomed to the great era of the Mexican School. Leonel Góngora is one of these artists. He was born in Colombia, but his early professional years were spent in Mexico City. There he took part in the Nueva Presencia and Neo-Humanist movements. He had more than seven exhibitions in 1963 and 1964 alone. After being away from Colombia for twelve years, Góngora returned to exhibit at the Museum of Modern Art of Bogotá, where his crude and erotic manner of depicting the human body had a great impact on other artists. His evolution was noted by Walter Engel: "In the particular case of Góngora, he was first impelled toward figurative expressionism by close contact with German Expressionists. After studying at the School of Fine Arts in Bogotá, he went to Washington University in St. Louis where he had Max Beckmann as a teacher."[15]

According to Engel, Góngora also drew inspiration from the works of Goya and Rembrandt and from literature about psychopathic and psychoanalytic subjects that take delight in "revealing the secret life, the intimate passions, and the inclinations deeply hidden or submerged in the subconscious which may evidence themselves only in dreams."[16] From 1954, when he was a student in St. Louis, up to 1970, by which time he was professor of drawing at the University of Massachusetts in Amherst, Góngora had fifteen one-man shows in the United States. He also participated in numerous group exhibitions, nearly always being identified as a Mexican artist. Among these exhibitions were *Neo-Humanist Painters*, seen in San Antonio, Texas, in 1963 and *Mexico: The New Generation*, a traveling show presented in Portland, Houston, Austin, Fort Worth, and San Diego in 1967. His work was exhibited at the Mexican Pavilion at *Expo 67* in Montreal. He had significant one-man shows at the Cober Gallery in New York in 1965, 1966, 1967, and 1968. Góngora's art has always centered on the female figure, which he portrays undergoing all sorts of metamorphoses as the prey of unbridled male passion. The expressionistic violence of his style anticipates by two decades the works of the European Trans-Avant-Garde of the late 1970s and 1980s (plate 198).

Pedro Figari, Amelia Peláez, and Rufino Tamayo
In closing this section devoted to reality and figuration, mention must be made of three artists whose contribution to the development of contemporary art have been widely recognized. Two of them, Amelia Peláez and Pedro Figari, took no active part in the art life of the United States, although their work figured in important exhibitions here. The third, Rufino Tamayo, has been an extremely prominent figure on the art scene not only in the United States but worldwide. Tamayo had his first U.S. show in 1926 at the Weyhe Gallery in New York. In 1935 he moved to New York and lived there for fifteen years. He was not only completely unaffected by the various fashions that succeeded one another there, but he also managed to win full acceptance for his personal and innovative adaptation of Magic Realism, an approach to art which the Mexican imagination has always found to be a singularly appropriate vehicle for expression. The metaphysical effect of Mark Rothko's color harmonies can be found in Tamayo's early paintings, but Tamayo's application of such color effects to figurative solutions is unique.

Figari spent a number of years in Europe, particularly in Paris. He belonged to the Post-Impressionist group the Intimists, whose outstanding representatives were Bonnard and Vuillard. In a recent publication his work was summarized:

His astonishing artistic career did not begin till 1921, when he had his first exhibit in Buenos Aires. Figari moved in 1925 to Paris, where he remained for nine years. In the seventeen years following his first exhibit he turned out some three thousand paintings on cardboard, covering a wide range of subjects drawn from his native country: social topics, landscapes, interiors of colonial patios, folk dances of African origin, Blacks, country women, horses, gauchos. As an assembly they constitute a sort of visual chronicle of Uruguayan life and tradition, part historic, part fanciful, narrated with a freedom that is derived from French Post-Impressionism [plate 201].[17]

Amelia Peláez has been described as one of the artists who "brought Cuban art into the twentieth century."[18] She was in many group exhibitions in the United States beginning in 1939, when her work appeared at the *Latin American Exhibition of Fine and Applied Art* held at the Riverside Museum in New York. In 1941 she had her only individual exhibit in the United States at the Galería Norte. It is appropriate to note that during the 1930s, when Mexican artists were still controlled by the ideas advocated by the great muralists, Cuban artists such as Peláez were more concerned with the development of figurative images that did not necessarily carry any particular ideology, except the freedom of a more formalistic visual theory. They were motivated by the freedom inspired by the variety of artistic concepts in the early twentieth-century European movements. In the U.S. we see this in the work of several artists, Stuart Davis among them. But while Davis seemed to respect the strict geometric and structural order patronized by Cubists and Constructivists, Peláez's work is vested with a baroque nature of her own that reflects the exuberant Caribbean environment. Among the institutions in the United States at which her work has been seen are the San Francisco Museum of Modern Art (1942, 1945), the Brooklyn Museum (1943, 1949), The Museum of Modern Art in New York (1943, 1944), the Institute of Modern Art in Boston (1947), OAS headquarters (1946, 1947, 1952, 1959), and the Art Institute of Chicago (1959).

Amelia Peláez's painting is replete with allusions to her native Cuba. The intricate networks that usually lace together her colors recall the cane-bottomed chairs of the Caribbean, Victorian fanlights, and patterned curtains. Amelia Peláez had a notable influence on Cuban artists, mainly by virtue of the way she structured compositions, in which the elements are sometimes aggressively decorative. An exceptionally fine example of her work is her 1943 *The Hibiscus* in the Museum of Modern Art of Latin America (plate 200).

The practice of figurative art unattached to academic European models as a means to apprehend and define reality is a tradition in Latin America that encompasses the evolution of artistic expression since independence was won from Spain. Its manifestations have taken different routes depending on the changes that the countries have gone through and the personal interpretations of artists. Between 1950 and 1970 the persistence of an important group of Latin American artists practicing figurative expression and resisting the more publicized trends and fashions created an important body of work that not only represents a visual answer to the problems, joys, and aspirations of the people and lands they are part of, but is also a statement of cultural independence from the overwhelming power of the technologically oriented cultures and their pretensions of uniformity. The artists felt it was their historical responsibility to transmit this message to future generations of Latin Americans.

203

204

Jacobo Borges
203. *Something Has Broken.* 1965
    Oil on canvas, 54⅝ x 54⅝"
    Solomon R. Guggenheim Museum, New York. Gift
    of Mr. and Mrs. Cedric H. Marks, 1971
    Photo: Robert E. Mates

Antonio Segui
204. *My Mother, The Car.* 1963
    Oil on canvas, 43 x 32½"
    Courtesy C.D.S. Gallery, New York
    Photo: Pollitzer, Strong & Meyer

"Magnet—New York": Conceptual, Performance, Environmental, and Installation Art by Latin American Artists in New York

by Carla Stellweg

In 1964 John Canaday wrote in *The New York Times*: "It is not exactly an invasion but there is at least a strong Latin American infiltration into the international strongholds so largely cornered by New York galleries. The exhibition currently at the Bonino Gallery arranged by the Inter-American Foundation for the Arts might have been called *Target: New York*, in which case the comment would be in order that a sound hit, although not a bull's-eye, has been scored. But the exhibition is more tactfully called *Magnet: New York* since all twenty-eight artists represented have been lured from their homelands to reside in this wonderful and terrible city."[1] In the next paragraph he addressed the artists not as residents but as "visitors" who are welcome, clearly illustrating the ambivalent attitudes of U.S. critics in the evaluation of Latin American artists: should these artists be viewed as part of the establishment or should they be seen as outsiders and "in transit" visitors?

These artists, being internationalists themselves, were already outsiders in their own countries. Prior to coming to the United States, they had made it their business to be very up-to-date and had thereby broken with the ethnocentrism that continued to prevail in their homelands. The art history and traditions they wanted to be a part of were far beyond their places of birth and natural roots. They brought with them to the United States this condition of artistic exile and searching, and it granted them the possibility to continue confronting conventional mediums and to acquire their own place among the innovative modes prevalent in New York during the 1960s.

To the degree that they were all faced with the same rules, Latin American or Caribbean artists who came to New York to develop careers within what from today's vantage point are movements called Conceptual Art, Performance, Environmental Art, and Installation Art, were little different from those who came from Europe, Japan, or elsewhere. The motives and means by which each artist made the move to New York varied, just as each work of art revealed individual responses to given circumstances. This dynamic ameliorates the idea of a Latin American Conceptual group or movement per se. While the artists' backgrounds have few aspects in common, in general they do share a solid university training, and they all rejected the strictly academic approaches to artmaking prevalent in Latin American art schools. In addition, their intellectual information extended beyond the boundaries of Latin American or Caribbean cultures. Most were bilingual or trilingual, and they incorporated several intellectual discourses into their work. By contrast, the New York art establishment applied measures of appreciation to artists who came from a world they knew little or nothing about. Major art institutions in the United States had exhibited pre-Columbian art and examples of the Mexican muralists, but by and large Latin American art was *terra incognita*. On an academic level there were very few Latin American scholars and hardly any courses available for Americans who wished to study Latin American art. Latin American culture was the domain of the departments of Romance languages, and even there it is noteworthy that the Latin American literary boom had not yet begun. Gabriel García Márquez's *One Hundred Years of Solitude*, published in Spanish in 1967, was not available in English until 1970.

Contrary to the sparse knowledge of things Latin American in the United States, Latin American intellectuals had access to plenty of information about cultural and artistic developments in the United States. North American films, books, magazines, and a series of traveling exhibitions organized by the United States Information Agency promoted U.S. culture. A Latin American intellectual's familiarity with U.S. culture served as an incentive to explore new artistic horizons. By the 1960s it became a real possibility for artists to leave their homelands in pursuit of the international scene that New York promised. A long list of art organizations actively promoted the international standards of New York in Latin America and served as springboards to get to the United States. Under the directorship of Jorge Romero Brest, the Torcuato di Tella Institute in Buenos Aires invited many critics and curators from the United States and Europe to view and select local artists for shows and grants. There was also El Eco, an experimental space created in 1953 by Mathias Goeritz in Mexico City. Under Goeritz's umbrella of "Emotional Architecture," artists of all disciplines were invited to break with functional and formal precedents. Music, film, dance, poetry, and performance were created by such international artists as Luis Buñuel, Henry Moore, and Walter Nicks, as well as by Rufino Tamayo and Carlos Mérida. The protests of the prevailing Social Realist Mexican School, headed by Diego Rivera, doomed El Eco's future, but the experiment inspired many Latin American artists to seek out arenas beyond their national borders.

Under the sophisticated guidance of Francisco Matarazzo, the São Paulo Bienal became one of the most effective platforms for younger Latin American artists looking for new options and hoping to communicate with experimental ideas from abroad. There they were given firsthand experience of the work of Andy Warhol, Roy Lichtenstein, Jasper Johns, and the experiments of young Minimalists, including Sol LeWitt and Carl Andre, in addition to Conceptual works by Joseph Kosuth, Bruce Nauman, and others, and special exhibitions of major international figures such as Francis Bacon, Jackson Pollock, and Joseph Beuys.

In the early 1960s John F. Kennedy's Alliance for Progress and human rights concerns produced the idea of a United States, concerned and liberal, in favor of Latin American civil rights. But it was also the time of the nuclear missile crisis and the Bay of Pigs in Cuba. It can be assumed that a Latin American artist coming to the United States carried with him a complicated baggage of information and started with at least an ambivalent perspective.

In 1977, thinking back on the days before he left for New York City with a Guggenheim grant in 1961, the Uruguayan artist Luis Camnitzer wrote:

It was a time that Montevideo was infested with fascist groups who would kidnap leftists, preferably Jewish, and tattoo swastikas into their skin with razor blades. Well-intentioned friends gave me some weapons to defend myself with; since I didn't know how to use them, it only increased the weight of my carrying case. New York seemed fascinating: the center of the empire. The measuring stick for success was set by the empire and not in the colonies. Even refusal or rebellion are determined and qualified by the central office of the empire. [2]

Some U.S. critics supported these assumptions of cultural imperialism. In April 1967 Sam Hunter wrote: "In Buenos Aires, a thriving and sophisticated art center, the avant-garde di Tella Institute and its gifted impresario, Romero Brest, have been decisive in promoting an awareness of rapidly accelerating artistic changes during the sixties. The criteria of global art, based in fact on the going styles of New York, have been established as the framework for local expressions." He further observed: "It is in abstraction that the South Americans excel and make their most significant contribution." [3] Lawrence Alloway had an equally paternalistic, if less generous, point of view. In a text about the 1965 international scene in Latin America he referred to the abstract art he had seen: "The thick surface of 'matter painting' as practiced in Spain by Antoní Tapiés and others, is repeated in numerous turgid, sandy, and sluggish slabs in Latin America. In a new way, matter painting is the new form of colonialism, the analogue in mud of the Baroque architecture of Hispanic domination." [4]

Despite their aesthetic disagreements, both critics found that whatever was being produced in Latin America corresponded to a dominated and colonial expression of the

205

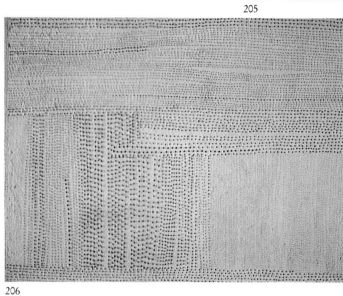

206

207

Jaime Davidovich
205. *Adhesive Video-Tape Project.* 1970
Adhesive tape, ink, and photo on paper, 30 x 40″
Collection the artist
Photo: courtesy the artist

Mathias Goeritz
206. *Message XIX.* 1959
Wood, plaster, nails, and paint, 39¾ x 48 x 2⅝″
Collection Atlantic Richfield Company, California
Photo: courtesy Atlantic Richfield Company

Mathias Goeritz
207. *Red Realizations.* 1959–61
Painted wood
Photo: courtesy Art in Public Places, Dade County,
Florida

international artistic movements. However, the Latin Americans who were Conceptual artists constituted a very sophisticated group, ready to take on the empire. Back home they were already in the forefront of art, and they were ready to show that they lived in a contemporary world. Their deliberately hostile attitude to convention enabled them, once in New York, to advance their ideas.

Mathias Goeritz was the first important representative of Latin America's commitment to the new international styles. To those Latin Americans who followed in his footsteps, he was an artist who had moved beyond his regional boundaries and made an international impression. Born in Danzig in 1919, Goeritz studied in Berlin and obtained a doctorate in philosophy by the outbreak of World War II. In the 1930s he traveled extensively throughout Europe, meeting Käthe Kollwitz, Karl Schmidt-Rotluff, László Moholy-Nagy, and various members of the Bauhaus, Dada, and Surrealist groups.[5] In 1939 he fled Germany for North Africa, then moved to Spain, where he founded the Altamira School, a loose-knit artists' and critics' organization that produced manifestos, a magazine, and exhibitions promoting the ideas of the avant-garde in the wake of the war's destruction. The group's romantic and hopeful purpose, stated by Goeritz in a manifesto, was to bring about "the spiritual metamorphosis of mankind. A new brotherhood of men will be born, one for whom life and art will not be contradictory."[6] The Dau Al Set group in Barcelona as well as the Grupo Pórtico from Zaragoza also adhered to these principles, so Goeritz began collaborating with their members, including Joan Miró, Antonio Saura, Manuel Millares, Modest Cuixart, and other prominent Spanish artists and critics.

In 1948 Goeritz left Spain for Mexico, where he was invited to teach at the new architecture school of the University of Guadalajara. The chance to leave Europe for the New World seemed an appropriate challenge to the pioneering spirit Goeritz had already developed by then. He has remained in Mexico ever since.

Many of Goeritz's friends and colleagues left Europe for the United States, and invariably they invited him to visit New York. Herbert Bayer and Moholy-Nagy continued to communicate with Goeritz from the United States. Goeritz's first major exhibition in New York was in 1960 at the Carstairs Gallery. The proposals and drawings he showed there, although apparently Minimalist in style, were an example of his theory of Emotional Architecture.

While in New York, in an extended Conceptual gesture, Goeritz decided to launch a protest during the performance of Jean Tinguely's self-destructive sculpture *Homage to New York* at The Museum of Modern Art. This was the first time that a Latin American artist confronted the international avant-garde of New York. Outside the museum Goeritz handed out a leaflet that called for a halt to Tinguely's type of art: "PLEASE STOP the aesthetic so-called profound jokes! STOP boring us with another sample of egocentric folk art! All this is becoming pure vanity!" it exclaimed. The leaflet emphatically begged for the return of spiritual and emotional qualities in art, ending with: "Be consequent, honor the tradition of Hugo Ball! Go forward and be decisive, the most difficult step of Huelsenbeck's NEW MAN: from Dada–to faith!"[7]

Seven years older than Tinguely, Goeritz had experienced the mechanized self-destruction of Europe. Thereafter he believed in art that promoted and elicited belief, if only the belief in believing. He advocated emotionally charged art that went beyond rationalizations, that eliminated the contradictions between life and art, whereas Tinguely's proposition suggested life is in perpetual change, its permanence untrue. When Goeritz wrote "it is not true that what we need is to accept instability. That is again the easy way. We need static values,"[8] he emphasized his hope for a meaningful and greater art, one that would address the spiritual needs of man.[9] These inclinations in Goeritz's work were not seen by several critics, including Gregory Battcock, who simply noted: "In 1960 the Mexican sculptor-architect Mathias Goeritz exhibited at the Carstairs Gallery in New York City proposals and drawings for huge structures of a grand architectural scale—works that apparently approximated the flat and sculptural style that has come to be known as Minimal Art."[10]

Goeritz never presumed to be an early Minimal artist; his work was conceptually connected to deeper emotional expressions. Sibyl Moholy-Nagy, in referring to Goeritz's vision as it was exemplified in the *Five Towers*, built in 1957 at the entrance to Ciudad Satélite in Mexico City, spoke of the "Obelisks of Luxor, the spires of a cathedral, the towers of a Lombard stronghold, the forest of chimneys in a great production center, or the skyscrapers that announce America to the seafarer. No one lives in these towers and no one can climb up inside them. They are wasteful, prideful, beautifully durable exclamation marks of human ambition."[11]

Parallel to creating the El Eco and the *Five Towers*, Mathias Goeritz produced a series entitled Messages with subtitles from the names of books of the Bible. Although these works looked abstract, they were almost like small chapels, explicitly designed to evoke spiritual sensations in the spectator. Each and every installation of his work, whether outdoors or indoors, was meant to convey his conviction that art was not just to be viewed but to be experienced in a profound manner, as though in communion with values higher than materialism (plates 206 and 207). It is on this level that his work influenced artists from all over the world, particularly those who had begun to question the meaning of dematerialized art. Luis Camnitzer recalls today: "Goeritz was a very influential figure that we had all heard of and admired. Aside from his work, he was an inspiration in terms of the attitudes towards artmaking."[12] And Liliana Porter remembers, "Mathias Goeritz had been my teacher in Mexico City and his teachings had already made an impact on me before coming to New York."[13]

Much younger than Mathias Goeritz, these artists tended to work toward building a sense of community among Latin Americans in New York, whereas Goeritz had caught the attention of the art world by his isolated actions. Porter remarked: "With Camnitzer and the Argentine Installation artist Luis Felipe Noé, we went to exhibitions and visited the museums together, and we learned a lot from the interchange. Noé was waiting for an exhibition at the Bonino Gallery, and at that point it was extremely important that you showed your ideas first, before anyone else beat you to it."[14] (Although Noé stopped producing art for several years, in order to write a book, Porter considers today that "he also was a key figure in our development."[15])

Jaime Davidovich, from Argentina, found the cultural climate in his country stifling, reiterative, and "derivative of the main abstract art theories from Europe and the United States."[16] Already teaching in Buenos Aires at the age of twenty-three, he first saw the work of modern artists he had studied and read about during a visit to the São Paulo Bienal. He decided that the prospect of becoming part of yet "another Argentinian young, or not-so-young, art movement based on European or North American abstract art models, wasn't for me."[17] A grant awarded to him by Romero Brest of the Torcuato di Tella Institute enabled him to leave Argentina for the United States for a year. He then decided to stay beyond that first year, learn English, and adjust to the new environment. Davidovich spent much of his time in New York viewing the original art he had not seen while studying in Argentina: "I was actually amazed when I first saw a Mondrian painting at the Modern, that one could see the brush strokes. I had always thought the paintings were flat, without any texture or any surface qualities. It was surprising to have a tactile contact with the original pieces of art."[18]

Davidovich brought with him the notion to break and challenge the boundaries of conventional painting. In Argentina he had created paintings that were conceptually related to the idea of vacuums and emptiness, symbolic not only of the Pampas landscape but also of the Argentine cultural and political void. He named these works *Pizarrones Negros* (Blackboards) and exhibited them next to works by Alberto Greco and Zulema Damianovich, Argentine artists who at the time exchanged ideas with several of the future Conceptual artists from Latin America.

It was not until several years later, when Davidovich moved to Ohio, that he began to take his works off the stretchers and to tape the canvases directly to the wall of a given space, assimilating and extending artworks into the environment (plate 205). The critic John Matturri wrote: "From the tape mountings emerged Davidovich's interest in the use of adhesive tape as a media in its own right."[19] Referring back to this period in Davidovich's career, Roger A. Welchans described the presentation of the *Carroll Wall Project* at John Carroll University in Cleveland: "Davidovich, a native of Argentina, has shed the 'furniture' of painting— the frames, stretchers, and supports— and moved the remaining aesthetic elements, the textures and compositional concerns, out into the environment."[20] Reviewing a show of six "New York" artists, Michael

Sundell wrote: "Jaime Davidovich, Athena Tacha, Craig Lucas, Karen Eubel, Joe Breidel, and John Pearson vary considerably in maturity, talent, and preoccupation. But all the work is generally in the new international style of the late 1960s—the style which the finicky or precise subdivide with labels like 'conceptual,' 'process,' 'systemic,' and 'arte povera.' Thus all six move in that mainstream of contemporary art which usually flows so thinly through the Western Reserve."[21]

Even though Davidovich did not yet form part of the "mainstream," his work at that time already pointed to his later visibility within New York's parameters of highly regarded Conceptual Art. He was also invited to Canada to participate in a symposium, "Education through the Arts," organized by Herbert Read, with whom he had corresponded from Argentina. At the symposium he was introduced to video and television and has since made these media an integral part of his work, culminating in the first Soho cable program, "Artists Television Network," in the early 1970s. His early underground video work gained the respect of all major artists working with that medium. With the technology available to him in the United States, Davidovich was able to develop a body of work that confronted mass culture, examined popular heroes, and documented the creative thoughts of other artists, such as Laurie Anderson. He thereby became one of the active participants in the New York avant-garde.

Another Argentine artist, Marta Minujín, went to Paris in 1962 on a French government award, which enabled her to continue in directions she had tentatively tested in Buenos Aires. She associated with the Nouveau Réaliste French artists, who manipulated found objects so as to bring a "new reality" to their audience. Minujín won the Torcuato di Tella Institute's First National Prize on her return to Argentina in 1964. Two years later, armed with a Guggenheim Foundation grant, she arrived in New York. Minujín's first exhibit to gain attention in New York had been an environmental happening, staged in Buenos Aires at the di Tella Institute in 1966. Before her arrival in New York, Barnard L. Collier had reviewed the happening in *The New York Times*: "A vocal and vivacious group of young Argentine artists is led, it seems, by a slim 24-year-old girl named Marta Minujín, who is supposed to go to New York on a Guggenheim Fellowship and who has set up sixty television sets with a chair before each. For nearly two and a half hours Miss Minujín, in a silvery jumpsuit, and her companions did various things before closed-circuit television cameras while the people grew restless."[22] Of this work, which explored new ideas of self-interaction, the video artist and critic Douglas Davis said: "The Argentine intermedia artist Marta Minujín invited sixty well-known celebrities to a theater, filmed them, and asked them to return one week later, where they were barraged with playback information about themselves on sixty television sets and sixty radios. Miss Minujín called the event *Simultaneity in Simultaneity*."[23]

Evidence that Minujín's cultural antennae were sharply tuned could be seen in all her technological communication experiments. Upon her arrival in New York, she installed an environment, complete with sensory experiences—smells, sights, and sounds. It was called *El Batacazo* (The Long Shot). Of this work, Grace Glueck wrote in *The New York Times*: "*El Batacazo* is meant to be toured by a gallery visitor alone, while viewers watch him through transparent panels. He climbs a slippery staircase that leads him past the rabbits (twitchy but caged) and brooks no turning back. Then, to reach an upper platform, he plows through the rugby players. From there he toboggans down a slide to land on the face of the amorous nude. And then the final angst: an odyssey through a tunnel of flies (active, but entrapped in plastic panels)."[24] Marta Minujín, very impressed by the ideas of Marshall McLuhan, particularly those expressed in *Understanding the Media*, was generally regarded to be doing a Latin version of Pop art or a "hot" Pop art.

Jacqueline Barnitz associated Minujín's work also with the New Realism: "It is no accident that the Latin Americans refer to their new realism as the art of things (like the French *art des objets*) rather than Pop art. Pop art speaks of 'things,' the things that surround us, whereas the 'art of things' paradoxically speaks of people. It employs objects in order to create an image of man. In this sense it is not very different from Goya's commentary on war and reason, or from the Mexican muralists' social criticism. But in keeping with an age of industry and mass production, contemporary artists have recourse to more strident means in order to be heard."[25] And heard she was, in more than one way. Marta Minujín, perhaps keener than many other Latin American artists to grasp the trend, the latest ideas, the generally fashionable, caught on to the celebrity aspect of the art world. Moving around New York on roller skates, she was highly visible, both socially and intellectually. *Newsweek*, reporting on *El Batacazo*, even lauded Minujín's environmental work:

The precise blend of disturbance and delight in a happening is hard to achieve, but last week New York's Bianchini Gallery presented a near bull's-eye. Painting and sculpture are through, proclaims Marta Minujín, the red-haired, kitten-eyed, 29-year-old Argentine sprite who conjured this elegant and exuberant labyrinth.[26]

In 1969 several aspects of Minujín's social awareness and multimedia, McLuhanesque concerns were combined in an Environmental work entitled *Minucode*, of which John Perreault noted: "Marta—blond, Argentine, outgoing, and familiar to everyone on the 'art scene'—is presenting her latest Conceptual, multimedia complexity: *Minucode*. Will this be followed by *Minutype, Minumobiles, Minuplanes, Minumix*?"[27]

Part of the fascination with the new technological materials were the attempts to make them an extension of the central nervous system, as suggested by Marshall McLuhan. Marta Minujín revealed this best in her *Minuphone* of 1967. The *Minuphone* looked like an ordinary phone booth of the 1960s, except that it did not behave like one. When a number was dialed, a series of events occurred: the walls changed colors, smoke enveloped the user, lights flickered, a television set showed the user the expressions on his face, sirens went off, and wind came blasting from behind the screen. In *Look* magazine, William Zinsser wrote: "Well, if it is a function of art to tell us something about our lives—to reveal truth, if necessary, by exaggerating it—I had three minutes' worth of art from Miss Minujín. By assaulting my various senses, by turning me on with a series of processes that were far more psychedelic than rational, she made me see the telephone booth for what it is: an intimate part of my daily environment."[28] Minujín had hopes that the *Minuphone* would be mass-produced and installed all across the United States.

Although her media-oriented ideas were already crystallizing in Argentina, her reaction to the U.S. technological society, to the possibility of global communication, allowed her to become very quickly an American technological creation. By choosing the most debated issues of the times and presenting these in media spectacles, Marta Minujín became, more than any other Latin American artist, a media celebrity not unlike Andy Warhol. She adapted to United States culture and became an outright proponent of the American dream (plates 209 and 210).

Like Marta Minujín, Rafael Montañez-Ortiz was also extremely effective in his employment of the media. In addition, both artists had unique interpretations of Dada's dictums. Among the Latin Americans, it seems that the work of these two best addressed the disruption of established order and the utilization of shock. Rafael Montañez-Ortiz (Ralph Ortiz), born in New York City of Puerto Rican, Mexican, and American Indian ancestors, was to be the first truly *Hispanic* artist to acquire a significant reputation. He considers himself first an American, regardless of whether he chooses to work with Latin American subject matter or not. In 1963 he independently developed the mattress and piano-destruction pieces that made him a principal exponent of the Destruction in Art movement. The same year, he was included in an exhibition of contemporary sculptors with Mark Di Suvero, Rosalyn Drexler, and others. One reviewer stated: "Ralph Ortiz's smashed and gutted open-out couches and chairs were notable." Another commented: "Ralph Ortiz slices davenports and lays out the halves side by side, showing the stuffing, springs and supporting tape. He composes the sections somewhat, by placing one end at the top of one half and the other end at the bottom of the second half."[29] However, Ortiz was really showing decomposition rather than trying to "compose" what had been destroyed. It is no surprise that his work caught the attention of Richard Huelsenbeck, one of the founders of Dada, who wrote: "When I think about Ralph Ortiz it comes to mind that he does not do entire things. He is fascinated by things that are not or are not yet. When Ralph Ortiz wants to show

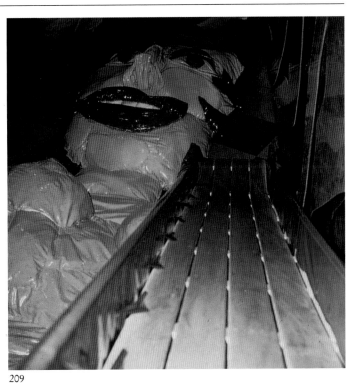

209

208

210

Rafael Montañez-Ortiz
208. *Archaeological Find 3.* 1961
    Burnt mattress, 74⅞ x 41 x 4¼"
    Collection The Museum of Modern Art, New York.
    Gift of Constance Kane
    Photo: courtesy The Museum of Modern Art

Marta Minujín
209. *Installation of "The Long Shot."* 1966, Buenos Aires
    and New York
    Photo: courtesy the artist

Marta Minujín
210. *Minucode.* 1969
    Photo: courtesy the artist

291

us a mattress he does not show a mattress but an object that is torn by undefinable forces as they work in time."[30]

Ortiz is primarily interested in using art as a strategy to provoke deep emotional and radical changes (plate 208). He once took a used mattress, carried it to the ocean at Coney Island, quickly set it afire with lighter fluid, soaked it in the sea, and for a week, while it dried in the sun, he tore the material every day or spilled acid on it. Crowds gathered to watch and cops asked what he was doing. Ortiz explained it was an art project. Through this type of "disassembly," Ortiz attracted the attention of the art world and effected the inclusion of his work in the collections of the Whitney Museum of American Art and The Museum of Modern Art. James Thrall Soby, then chairman of the acquisition committee of The Museum of Modern Art, justified purchasing the mattress: "A rather difficult object to live with, it is indeed a powerful and horrifying image; but at the same time an object capable of moving the viewer after he has recovered from the first shock of revulsion, and I think our visitors will find it so."[31]

By 1965 Ortiz began formalizing the performance aspects of his destructive events. Contrary to our acceptance of physical decay or planned obsolescence in everyday life, when these concepts are incorporated into art, the result almost always provokes controversy. In his manifesto for the Destruction in Art Symposium in London, in 1966, Ortiz noted: "Our tragic dilemma is that because of our limited psychological evolution we have, unwittingly, instituted our biological and physical limitations. We have instituted for the ultimate destruction of our species."[32] Edward Lucie-Smith, then art critic for the London *Times*, declared: "Surrounded by a world in which violence reigns, I find it hard to assume that in the sphere of art, sweet reason must nevertheless continue to prevail. If people complain that breaking up a chair in the name of art shows a certain lack of dignity, I am inclined to wonder what's so dignified about a race riot."[33]

In another work of 1966 Ortiz confronted the ideas of regression and evolution: "Every performance piece had its own narrative, a Dada-Surrealist narrative, sounds that related to communication preceding language, the irrational preverbal sounds."[34] Expanding on the issue of art and psychology, he wrote to Kristine Kiles in 1982: "It is because the dream is our primal authenticating link to the magic of our mind, body, and spirit, to all our processes of imagination that I perceive it to be the key to all our processes of art. Any and all research that illumines behavior illumines art."[35] Art also illuminated behavior. In his book *Primal Scream*, behavioralist Arthur Janov acknowledged that the invention of the process he used with his patients originated from Ortiz's *Self-Destruction* performance. He credited the artwork with inspiring his use of a popular and accepted therapeutic treatment.[36]

Ortiz received a doctorate from Columbia University's Teachers College. Aside from agitating during the 1960s for the improvement of the New York Puerto Rican cultural conditions, he has not been disposed to teach about or romanticize his Latin heritage: "Ethnocentric concerns continue to blend high art into the limitations of folk culture. I am committed to viewing my profession from a perspective that will permit me a historically relevant contribution. I don't deny folk art's integrity or its place in art history. I never wanted to be folk Hispanic or a folksy anybody but have looked beyond my limitations, whether imposed on me or by me. This is why education is meaningful so that art at the larger world level of problem solving becomes like any other profession. Nuclear physics also evolve beyond naive and primitive notions. This led me to investigate the area of destruction in art, the unmaking of made things. My art from the late 1950s and 1960s is not just the result of exploring my own roots but rather based on questioning diverse historical and aesthetic contexts."[37] From 1968 till the end of the decade Ortiz continued to be a leading exponent of Destruction in Art principles and was a prominent and visible presence in the media. Next to artists such as Yoko Ono, John Hendricks, Wolf Vostell, Les Levine, and others, he actively staged Performance rituals at various locations throughout the United States, was on radio programs, and even had an appearance on the Johnny Carson show.

In terms of Latin American art, Ortiz's experiments remain among the most influential examples that art can make an impact beyond conventional, commercial standards—that it can affect people's lives. In contrast to Ortiz's experiments, in which the individual learned through the processes of the irrational and emotional, was the work that brought Julio Le Parc to the forefront in New York. He studied prevailing mass culture and the electronic communication that our society seems to have successfully promoted. Like most Kinetic artists, he followed much of the earlier movements that addressed the democratization of the arts, such as Futurism, the Bauhaus, or De Stijl. Le Parc's first show in New York was in 1962, when he exhibited as a member of the collective Groupe de Recherche d'Art Visuel–GRAV. This group was formed in 1960, in Paris, and its founding act was signed by the artists Demarco, García Miranda, García Rossi, Le Parc, Molnar, Morellet, Moyano, Servanes, Sobrino, Stein, and Yvaral. In its founding charter GRAV stated its purpose was to emphasize team effort, its members were to exhibit anonymously in joint exhibitions, and spectators were to be inspired to participate in the art. The members stated that they would leave their individual activities and by means of organized investigation into one another's work establish a solid theoretical and practical aesthetic from this collective experience. In 1964–65, after holding a Labyrinth (exhibition) in Europe, GRAV and Le Parc created two Labyrinths at The Contemporaries gallery in New York (plate 213). Reflecting on the group's work, Douglas Davis wrote: "No one became more skilled at *l'instabilité* than Le Parc, who emerged as GRAV's central force. His kinetic-light murals and small constructions used bland and repetitive forms, allowing the play of light and shade across their surfaces to create a continually shifting impression upon the eye."[38] In Kinetic art, *l'instabilité* refers to the disappearance of permanent forms, putting the spectator in front of all sorts of projections, constantly moving and blinking lights, and shadows that slide across mirrored surfaces in order to induce multiple sensorial responses. In *Kunst Licht Kunst*, a key exhibition of Kinetic art held in Amsterdam, GRAV issued a statement: "It is not the purpose of the group to create a super-spectacle, but by producing an unexpected situation, to influence directly the public's behavior and to substitute for the work of art and the spectacle an evolving situation that calls for the active participation of the spectator."[39]

László Moholy-Nagy had written in the 1920s that light would bring forth a new form of visual art. After he came to the United States in 1937, he became the promulgator for future generations of Kinetic artists, including Le Parc. Having been born to a working-class family in Argentina, Le Parc shared the goals outlined by Moholy-Nagy and his fellow Bauhaus associates of creating art directed at the masses. His ideology is present throughout the collective writings of GRAV, including the manifesto published with the second Labyrinth in New York: "A spectator conscious of his power and tired of so many errors and mystifications will be able to make his revolution in art and follow the signs: Handle and Cooperate."[40]

Today, Le Parc states: "In New York GRAV helped to point to the existence of a new tendency in direct opposition to Pop art, which was emerging in those years. This was achieved in a failed, coopted exhibition, *The Responsive Eye*, at MOMA. We were in touch with Ellsworth Kelly, Jack Youngerman, and Donald Judd, who then acted as a critic. New York City was less exclusive. Now I believe that our presence was erased, to the extent of denying its existence. An art, or artists' relationship toward today's pretended superiority of North American art cannot be but one of opposition."[41]

However, objections were voiced publicly about Kinetic art's failure to produce the real participation of the spectator, who instead was generally assaulted by technological devices. In addition there was the problem of the cooption of its ideas by facile commercial ventures. *Newsweek*, reporting on *The Responsive Eye* show, alluded to this drawback as well: "Perhaps, since such art is meant to be impersonal and neutral, its real future is functional. At the Newark Museum, some of the liveliest Op pieces currently on view are most functional indeed, warm comforting quilts in splendid, radiant colors and intricate geometric patterns, made by little old New England ladies a full century ago."[42]

Despite these objections, Julio Le Parc continued working toward a community-oriented art that would transcend the proverbial individualism allotted to high art practitioners in our society. "Creativity, like anything else in society, should be concerning everyone and not be relegated to a small group, whether in its creative aspects, its value system aspects or its social inclusion," he stated recently.[43]

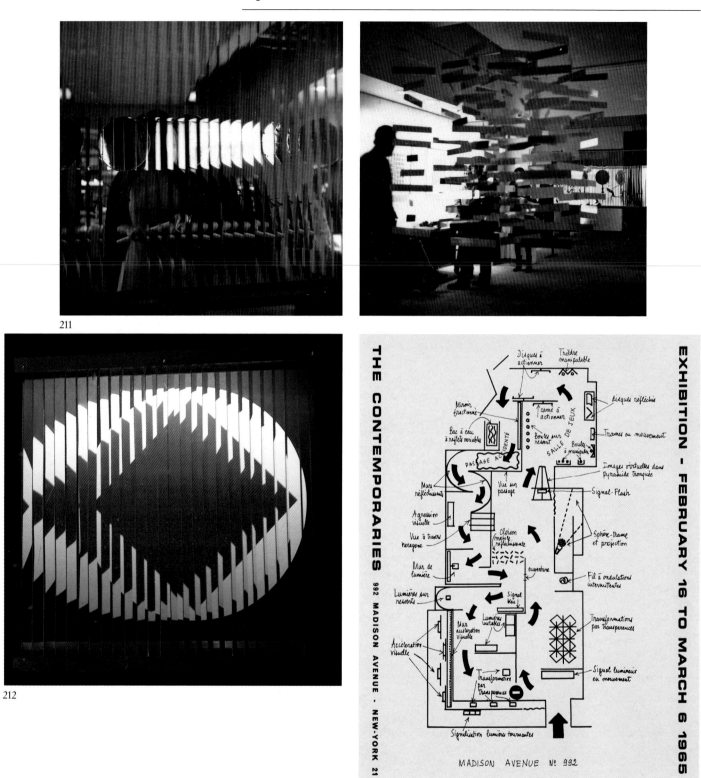

EXHIBITION · FEBRUARY 16 TO MARCH 6 1965

MADISON AVENUE Nº 992

211

212

213

Julio Le Parc
211. *Installation Views.* March 11–April 1, 1967, Howard
    Wise Gallery, New York
    Photo: courtesy the artist

Julio Le Parc
212. *Virtual Forms for Displacement of the Spectator
    with Changeable Themes.* 1966
    Wood, metal, and light, 51 x 40 x 20"
    Collection the artist
    Photo: courtesy the artist

**Groupe de Recherche d'Art Visuel de Paris (Garcia
Rossi, Le Parc, Morellet, Sobrino, Stein, Yvaral)**
213. *Exhibition Brochure for Labyrinthe 3, New York.*
    February 16–March 6, 1965, The Contemporaries,
    New York
    Collection Julio Le Parc, Paris
    Photo: Tony Velez

Le Parc's attitude regarding the purpose of art stems from a long Latin American tradition that began with tentative examples after the Latin American independence movements and culminated in the Mexican Revolution and its subsequent popular muralist movement. Moreover, during the 1960s, most Latin American artists were informed about how the Cuban Revolution dealt with the issue of the artist's freedom and his commitment to the society he lived in. Inspired by the social pronouncements of early twentieth-century artists, such as those of the Constructivists, many Latin American artists were influenced to incorporate social objectives into their art. Therefore, aside from Le Parc's prominence within the international Kinetic movement, his example as an artist with a social conscience continued to exercise influence over future generations of Latin American artists who considered art a vehicle for social change (plates 211 and 212).

Whereas the Latin American Environmental artists in Europe were aiming to control technology, New York artists, including those who came from Latin America, did not concern themselves with control. Some even considered it anathema, and in general their use of machines and technology was more experimental. They followed in the footsteps of the happenings, in which artists were willing to grant part of the creative process to other elements.[44]

Even though many Latin American artists were drawn to Paris, where their Latin American colleagues, such as Le Parc and Soto, had gained a strong reputation, Enrique Castro-Cid chose to go to New York in 1962. Born and raised in Santiago, Chile, he left his country at the age of nineteen and first went to Mexico, motivated by a desire to find new sources with which to challenge the European-oriented education he received in Chile. Today he recalls that he thought the French art scene seemed devoid of the energy he sensed existed in New York. Shortly after his arrival he was introduced to John Chamberlain and Willem de Kooning. He remembers that "with this group of artists I went abruptly from a kind of Chilean *joie de vivre* into a New York artistic violence," experiencing culture shock on all levels. "From the weak and boring French philosophical rhetoric, I began to focus on ideas coming out of Wittgenstein or D'Arcy Thompson, specifically geometry and mathematics."[45]

His first robots, shown at the Richard Feigen Gallery in 1965, were a response to the technology he confronted in the United States: "The early robots are interesting for their painful sterility: no longer the clanking metallic beasts of the 1920s, these are more akin to humans divested of their corporeal form, mere brains placed in bell jars with appropriate electrodes inserted, sending commands to mechanical limbs," wrote the art historian Jack Burnham.[46]

His next exhibition at the Richard Feigen Gallery was in 1966. Entitled *Compressed Air Sculptures*, it included whimsical and magical mechanical sculptures and was reviewed in *Time* magazine by Peter Sims: "Castro-Cid made toylike, motor-driven robots. They jousted like a 21st-century Punch-and-Judy show, chasing tiny balls with spinning hoops in an electronic version of Alexander Calder's 1926 *Circus*. His latest works avoid the clanking humdrum of much Kinetic art. Magically, when someone approaches his *Sensitive Sphere*, a multicolored ball bounces into the air. In a variation, an 8mm film is projected onto an airborne ball, playfully contorting and distorting the tiny images of human figures. Another work presents the appearance of a bouncing ball inside a shaped screen by means of rear-view projection."[47] Of these robots (plate 214), Burnam wrote: "Castro-Cid's energies have gravitated toward a mode of sculpture which could be termed 'cybernetic games.' They simulate the precise, instantaneous technology of a computer system in which playfulness is merely an aspect of some greater hidden function." Touching on the deeper, ethical approach to the use of technology already present in the work of Castro-Cid, he added: "In terms of their psychic complexity these works appear to be trivial, but as a means of introducing ideas for reshaping the world, they transcend the single-purpose machines of Kinetic art and move beyond the limitations of scientific Constructivism."[48]

Castro-Cid's environmental installations developed as visualizations of the concepts set forth by Norbert Wiener in *The Human Use of Human Beings— Cybernetics and Society*. Wiener's ideas influenced many artists working with technology at that time. Alongside Nam June Paik, Castro-Cid was a leading exponent of machine-operated works invested with human qualities. At the forefront of the avant-garde, he received acclaim from art historians and the general press alike.

Another artist from Chile, Juan Downey, traveled first to Barcelona and Paris before going to New York in 1965. In Paris, Downey had studied printmaking in the atelier of the American Stanley Hayter. "There wasn't any specific reason for leaving Chile other than that I knew that to make art I had to move to a cultural center, one where art is marketed. When I came to New York, I found a city full of fantasy where everyone was ready to play, which is something I did not experience in Paris," he recalls today.[49] Downey had read the Futurists and was greatly impressed by Marinetti's claim that museums would become obsolete, superseded by forms of technological beauty. "In Paris I was painting machines, with a consciousness of trying to represent movement and energy. Then when I got here in 1965, I immediately understood that that kind of representation wasn't necessary. That I could directly manipulate electricity and use light."[50] After creating a series of light sculptures, Downey very quickly moved on to create interactive environments, and by 1966 he exhibited an electronic sculpture installation at the Judson Memorial Church Gallery. Douglas Davis commmented on the exhibition: "At the opening of Juan Downey's show at the Judson Gallery in New York the crowds were so large that none of the machines, which in each case depend upon an interval of passivity, functioned. Neither did the system, which reduced itself to a hum in the presence of the crowded bodies. This failure made him very happy."[51] Earlier that year, Billy Klüver and Robert Rauschenberg, founders of Experiments in Art and Technology (E.A.T.), a movement that brought artists into contact with technology, organized "Nine Evenings: Theater and Engineering," also at the Judson Memorial Church Gallery in New York. During these evenings Robert Whitman, Yvonne Rainer, Lucinda Childs, John Cage, and other artists presented large, technologically oriented works. The Judson show was therefore a timely opportunity for Downey, instantly putting him in touch with some of New York's most prominent artists. The interchange between these artists continued to be mutually influential in the following years.

Anti-art, a term invented by Marcel Duchamp, was—besides all its connotations—foremost defined as art that opposed using art as a commodity, the object cultus. As such, a majority of Conceptual, Performance, Environmental and Installation artists created anti-art and regarded Marcel Duchamp as their prophet. Juan Downey, however, was closer to the sensibility of Francis Picabia. Shortly after his first visit to New York in 1913, to visit the Armory Show, Picabia switched his aesthetic allegiance from Cubism to machine-oriented Dadaism. His wife, Gabrielle Buffet-Picabia, remarked: "Picabia found in anti-painting a formula of black humor which gave him free reign to express his rancor against men and events, an inexhaustible vein of plastic and poetic sarcasm."[52] Downey has said that Picabia influenced him in "an anarchic sense, in the way that he constantly subverted his own career."

Downey's early electronic sculpture environments also were part of his flirtation with Dada. *Nostalgic Item*, an electronic sculpture Downey exhibited in 1967 at the Martha Jackson Gallery, contained two slide projectors and tape recorders with prerecorded lists of famous classical paintings and photographs of his family. The projectors were activated by the viewer through an electronic eye, while the exterior finish was soft and furry. "This work was about memory and about the things that I loved enormously," recounts Downey today.[53]

In 1968 Downey had an exhibition of his electronic sculptures at the Corcoran Gallery of Art in Washington, D.C., in which he showed a variety of pieces that again addressed issues of audience participation through interactivity. The works were created with the collaboration of an engineer, Fred Pitts. In spite of this they did not have an engineered or manufactured look; they had instead the quality of found objects seen in early 1920s machine art. One of the most enigmatic pieces was appropriately named *Invisible Energy*. The notion that whatever is imagined by the mind does not stay still and does not present itself as a single static image only is clearly evident in this work. It is also the only work in the Corcoran exhibition that could not be operated by the viewer. Its actions were controlled by arbitrary radiowaves it picked up from a ten-mile radius (police broadcasts, ham radios, taxicabs), which activated two semicircular, moon-shaped wedges into a rocking motion. The intention behind Downey's

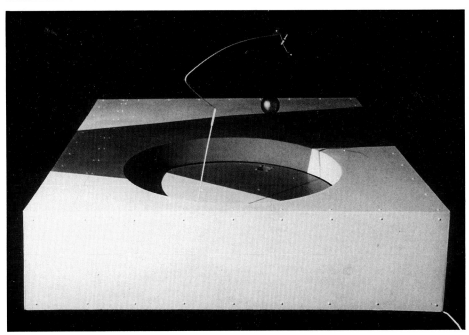

214

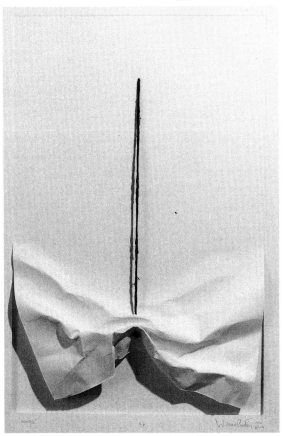

215

Enrique Castro-Cid
214. *Set No. 1.* 1965
    Motorized wood construction, 60 x 72 x 12″
    Collection the artist
    Photo: Nelson Morris, *Time* magazine

Liliana Porter
215. *Untitled.* 1970
    Wrinkled paper, string, and embossing on paper,
    20 x 13″
    Collection the artist
    Photo: courtesy the artist

216

Luis Camnitzer
216. *Leftovers.* 1970
Paint, gauze, plastic, and cardboard (80 boxes),
80 x 127 x 8″
Yeshiva University Museum, New York
Photo: Tony Velez

environments was to comment on mass communication by actively engaging viewers. In the accompanying text to the show, James Harithas wrote about a novel the artist created for the exhibition: "This novel by Juan Downey illustrates in another medium the artist's concept of audience participation. It consists of several dialogues, each of which Downey, as one of the participants, keeps alive by a preconceived pattern of yes-no answers. The sparse nature of these replies places the whole burden of communication on the other participant."[54] This exercise in the various levels and forms of communication between people—the subjectivity of information as it is perceived and transformed—was manifested throughout Downey's work. In his 1970 exhibition at the Howard Wise Gallery in New York, he was asked to do a performance piece. Instead, he decided to create what he called a "Pollution Robot"—a large, eight-foot-tall box that concealed him from the gallery's visitors. In this container on wheels, he was able to move around, pursue the audience (spotted through a two-way mirror), and blow hot air on them. They, in turn, could ask questions, answered by Downey in an automated robotic manner. "Perception is a two-way phenomenon," he said. "The mirror is ultimately an invitation to everyone to see themselves."[55] As Anne Hoy has observed: "Videotape's capabilities in surveillance, feedback, and delay also intrigued him. He first used the medium in installations with voice-activated components, and in 1968 created a high-tech electronic environment, complete with walkie-talkies and AV equipment for viewers, at an event called 'Communication' at the Smithsonian Institution in Washington, D.C."[56]

By the end of the 1960s, however, the Vietnam War had spiraled into grotesque proportions, opening up a debate on the benefits of technology. Technology was associated with large corporations that were implicated with the military-industrial complex. These considerations were part of the reexamination of the relationship of art and technology that influenced artists like Juan Downey. He moved on to do several ecology-oriented pieces and then switched to television. Television was to become the tool with which he could treat issues of communication even more effectively.

Thinking of himself as an outsider, Juan Downey nevertheless considers New York to be his city, "a city of outsiders, a sort of hospital with an open-door situation like nowhere else in the world." He concluded that "my art is about nomadism, about leaving, going away, and taking off."[57] Like other Conceptual artists, Downey felt New York was indeed the place to come to and where his work would be free to develop into any direction his mind chose. Downey's later work exemplifies this freedom and has inspired numerous other New York arrivals from Latin America.

Luis Camnitzer, who grew up in Uruguay as the child of immigrant parents, also faced the problems of being an outsider from a very early age. In architecture and art school in Montevideo he studied his own process of assimilation and became active in the student movement. "We abolished the 'national artist' diploma and created popular fairs, moved into the poor neighborhoods and our school became like a community. The courses we designed went beyond the Bauhaus, Montessori, or any other dream about what a school could be."[58]

When he arrived in New York in 1962 he was an outsider used to examining cultural mechanisms. He continued to question the complexities of the structures behind artmaking and those that operated its distribution and effectiveness. Camnitzer shared his apartment with Luis Felipe Noé, who was concerned with "assuming chaos" and was already an active anti-art practitioner:

New York helped to accelerate the process, and I started to make a work in which I opposed fragments, playing with the stretchers. These, starting from the wall, extended in various directions and continued onto the floor; parts were empty stretcher bars, parts were just canvas without stretchers, with cut-out shapes. Soon, after having gone back to Buenos Aires and then returned to New York, I came to realize that my proposal of assuming opposites was really an expression of me against myself, which was at that time considered to be taboo. One was supposed to prescind the "self."[59]

This tendency to replace the "artist" with the "art worker" had its impact on Luis Camnitzer as well:

*One thing was that esthetics was a by-product, the packaging, but not a departure point
for art. I tried to ignore composition as such, to limit myself to certain propositions that
could "flexibilize" the viewer in such a way that the artist was an intermediary between
reality and the consumer was eliminated—to reverse the consumer into creator, which
I guess was a common idea at that time. So I began to use language to describe certain
visual situations. It was also part of my rejection of expensive materials that added to
a "poor esthetic," one that was less authoritarian.*[60]

This is a mirror. You are a written sentence was one of his first strictly language
works. Messages made of self-adhesive tape were placed directly on the walls as well as
on small metal boxes shown at the Marian Goodman Gallery (Multiples, Inc.), in New
York in 1966. These self-adhesive stickers were then sent into the world by mail. Mail
art was another vehicle with which to confront the status of art as private property.
Although most technologically based art also emphasized art's social responsibility, it
usually required an intense assault on the viewer's senses. By contrast, Camnitzer's work
had more of an affinity with the social projections of the European Arte Povera group.
His was generally an art about content and context rather than about its means and
ways of representation.

In 1968 Camnitzer decided to make *Living-Comedor*, a type of family room in
Latin America, by employing the words that described the space and what was in it
directly on a floor and four walls. The installation was created in a museum in Caracas,
and the public maneuvered carefully around the "table" while walking on the "rug": "I
discovered that when logic is taken to the extreme it leads to something quite magical.
To inhabit an architectural drawing resulted in something more moving than to inhabit
the architecture itself."[61]

Sections of the *Living-Comedor* were installed at the I.C.A. in Philadelphia in
1969 and at the Dwan Gallery in New York in 1970. This work revealed with precision
the patterns of behavior that guide the viewer, something the philosophical questions
of much Conceptual Art of the 1960s constantly confronted. Allowing for the viewer's
freedom and letting the words generate a response were premises of Camnitzer's
experimental art: "A newspaper headline is the perfect example of the viewer becoming
the producer of the results. He creates his own images and does not consume those
of the person who did the headline."[62] Language and linguistics were also vehicles with
which to bridge the gap between art and didactics. Teaching, or the means with which
a person acquires knowledge, are central issues in Camnitzer's career. He has not only
taught and written extensively on education but also on the mechanisms of culture.
Thinking that the Tupamaros, the Uruguayan guerrilla fighters of the 1960s, could be
utilized in his art, he began incorporating oppression into his subject matter. He set up
an installation in the Museo de Bellas Artes in Santiago with a floor plan of a massacre
that had occurred in Puerto Montt in 1969. At the Paula Cooper Gallery in New York
in 1970 he created an inventory of the armaments used for repression in Latin
America, to which he added a wall of boxes wrapped in bloodstained gauze. Each box
was stenciled with the word "leftover" and had a Roman numeral on it to indicate
the identity of the victims. The look of the installation emphasized the artist's intentions.
As Camnitzer himself has insisted: "Technical virtuosity is about convincing the viewer
that the work is the perfect incarnation of the intention, even when it is really only
an approximation shaped by an accumulation of mistakes that are more or less wisely
administered" (plate 216).[63]

His participation in the New York Graphic Workshop is another expression
of the socially oriented artmaking concerns he has maintained. But today he views
printmaking not as an alternative to the private appropriation of art but more
as a medium that promotes the possibility for an anonymous group of stockholders
to acquire a piece of his work. By contrast with other North American and European
Conceptual artists, such as Joseph Kosuth, Robert Morris, Hans Haacke, and Joseph
Beuys, Camnitzer did not pursue a career through the gallery and dealer system. His
influence was then and now through organizing group endeavors, curating marginal,
noncommercial exhibitions, and publishing in a variety of magazines in the United
States, Europe, and Latin America. Together with José Guillermo Castillo and Liliana

Porter, he was the cofounder of the New York Graphic Workshop, which was to become a springboard for many socially oriented art activities in the following years.

Liliana Porter, born in Argentina, began art school at the age of twelve and went to Mexico City when she was sixteen. There she studied with Mathias Goeritz and the Colombian printmaker Guillermo Silva Santamaría at the Universidad Iberoamericana in Mexico City. At the age of seventeen she exhibited at the Mexican avant-garde Galería Proteo. In 1964, on her way to Paris, she stopped over in New York and, after visiting the Metropolitan Museum of Art, decided to stay in America. Then she continued her studies at Pratt Institute and shortly thereafter was invited to participate in group shows like *Magnet: New York*, at the Bonino Gallery. This first exhibition gained her a mention by John Canaday in *The New York Times*.[64]

Used to working within the limited facilities of Latin America, Porter thrived in New York, where she was introduced to a vast amount of technical equipment. Porter has remarked of those days: "It was like being a kid walking into F.A.O. Schwartz."[65] These possibilities made her create an enormous amount of work, and this intense activity was coupled with exhibitions, including one at the Van Bovenkamp Gallery in 1964, that led to the creation of the New York Graphic Workshop. There she found a platform from which to rethink the graphic medium on artistic and social levels. The teamwork that developed between Porter, Camnitzer, and Castillo enriched her work enormously: "We gave a lot of consideration to the political and moral aspects of artmaking, and through prints there was this idea we were working toward mass culture. Painting was reactionary. While this seemed intellectually coherent, my interest was always more toward the poetics of printmaking."[66] Her work took on Minimalist forms when she saw that incredibly complicated printing techniques could be replaced with more simple approaches to content and means: "I thought there would be more impact and magic in showing the absence of whatever I chose to work with rather than its presence, or the presence of many things. Somehow this was the beginning, and I started to make shadows of the subjects I was focusing on."[67] These shadows, such as the shadow of a glass and an olive, eventually were shown together at an exhibition at the Torcuato di Tella Institute in 1969. Shadows of a typical opening crowd, painted directly on the museum's walls, interacted with the real crowd. Porter explained: "People do not relate to a shadow as though it is an object but read it as the absence of a person, which is a mystical experience."[68] In 1967 the New York Graphic Workshop published a series Porter created using the motif of a man's silhouette under the general heading of *Retratos de Nadie* (Portraits of Nobody).

In 1968 she executed a book entitled *Wrinkle*, with ten photo-etchings showing a page getting progressively more wrinkled. At this time she also explored new media: "embroidered prints," silk screen, plastic prints, Xerox, and offset. By 1970 she reached an almost total reduction of subject matter, just printing the relief of a printing plate with the bottom part of the paper slightly wrinkled (plate 215). In this work it is evident that the notion of fusing reality with illusion had acquired a very personal and unique format. Gregory Battcock observed: "What Porter does is construct an event that is only partially real. Certain factors that distinguish the real from the illusive are offered in illusory form; therein lies the paradox. For example, a piece of string is attached to a screw that, alas, is not real but is a silk-screened photograph. Or, we find a nail protruding from a tear in the canvas surface. The tear is quite real, the nail is not. One is not quite sure sometimes, what is real and what is not, and therein lies Porter's proposition."[69]

Together with José Guillermo Castillo and Luis Camnitzer, Porter participated in a series of events that addressed the political issues of the times. When she exhibited in a group show at New York University's Loeb Center, Luis Camnitzer, acting as curator, wrote: "Porter and Castillo are both members of the New York Graphic Workshop, which believes in the production of FANDSOS, that is, Free Assemblable Non-functional Disposable Serial Objects. Essentially the ethical concern of mass-produced art is to eliminate the high cost and pompous ritual that separate art from the public."[70] Of that period Porter remembers: "Luis seemed more religiously political than José Guillermo, who approached mass production from design; as for myself, I saw it as a mystical thing, the idea that something is born, happens, and then dies. Which is

Rafael Ferrer
217. *Untitled.* 1970 (reconstructed 1988)
  Water, glass, tarpaulins, neon, drums, and monitors,
  Courtesy the artist
  Photo: courtesy the artist

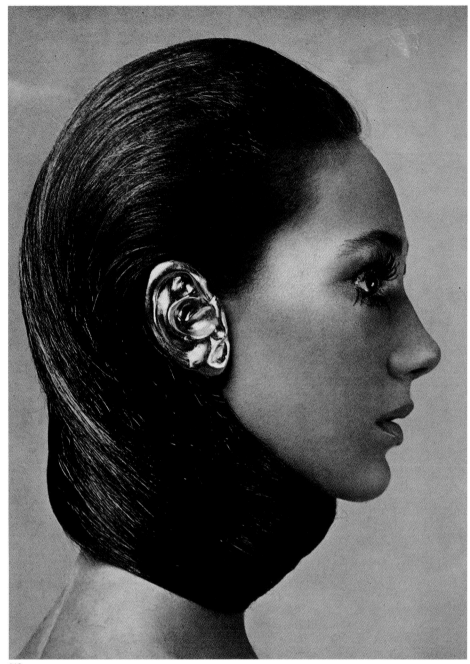

219

218

Nicolas Uriburu
218. *International Coloration (The East River, New York)*. 1970
Colored photograph and map documentation
Collection the artist
Photo: courtesy the artist

Eduardo Costa
219. *Fashion Fiction No. 1*. 1966
(Reproduced in *Vogue*, February 1968)
Photo: Richard Avedon. Copyright 1968 Richard Avedon, Inc.

why I chose to do *To be wrinkled and thrown away* for the *Information* show at MOMA in 1970."[71]

In 1970 the New York Graphic Workshop disbanded: José Guillermo Castillo returned to Venezuela, and Porter and Camnitzer became increasingly more active in political art. The Center for Inter-American Relations in New York became a target of artists' hostility since it had several board members that most Latin American artists in New York seemed to distrust.[72] Several boycotts were organized by large numbers of Latin American artists and their American colleagues. These first actions inspired the artists to organize. In a letter sent by Luis Camnitzer to John Perreault at *The Village Voice*, the group specified their objectives: "To create a center for Latin American cultural dissemination on a nonofficial level; to report on repression of culture in Latin American countries; to take actions against institutions that misrepresent or ineptly represent Latin American culture; to create special services for Latin American artists."[73]

First grouped under the name Museo Latinoamericano, the artists began to disagree and soon divided, so that a new group developed which called itself Museo para la Independencia Cultural Latinoamericana. This latter group then produced the *Counter Biennial*, an artist's book against participation at the São Paulo Bienal (because it was supported by the Brazilian dictatorship). In this publication artists from Latin America, including Julio Le Parc, Mathias Goeritz, José Luis Cuevas, Luis Felipe Noé, and Gordon Matta-Clark, utilized one page each for their contribution, which could be either visual, literary, or both. In addition to a call to abstain from participating in these type of international art shows in Latin America, the book also promoted a consciousness about the military repressions in South America. An attempt was made to distribute the book commercially; however, it really circulated by word of mouth and in an underground fashion. Soon thereafter it became clear that aside from basic political disagreements, a lot of artists were in no position to protest and confront the establishment, either because their immigration documents were insufficient or because of financial and personal pressures. Nevertheless, for over a year the group called attention not just to Latin American artists but to Latin America in general. They distributed information to the press, university teachers, and the general public. For everyone involved it was to be an eye-opening education on the lack of information and communication about Latin America and an introduction to the distinct components within Latin America. By the group's zenith, Rafael Ferrer, Leandro Katz, Eduardo Costa, Helio Oiticica, Rubens Gerchman, and Lygia Clark had already become known in New York.

Rafael Ferrer occupies a special place within the anti-art and Conceptual movements. Due to his early involvement with Surrealism through his teacher E. F. Granell in Puerto Rico in the 1950s, he approached artmaking organically, much in the way that the Latin American and Hispanic world treated Surrealism (as opposed to the objective analytical process North American Conceptual artists favored). In 1968 Ferrer deposited autumn leaves in the elevator of the building where the Fischbach and Tibor de Nagy galleries were located, then dropped twenty-one bushels of leaves in front of Leo Castelli's East Seventy-seventh Street gallery, after which he drove on to Castelli's Upper West Side warehouse. There he filled three landings of the staircase with more leaves.

Marcia Tucker, a curator of the Whitney Biennial in 1969, remembered:

My first contact with Ferrer's work was extraordinarily disconcerting. At the opening of Castelli's uptown warehouse in 1968, the entire hallway and staircase were densely covered with autumn leaves, pungent, musty, crackling underfoot. No one knew how they got there, why they were there, whether the leaves were "art" or not. The only certainty was that they were not there by accident or design of nature—at least not in December, in New York, indoors. They remained a mystery. In 1969 Ferrer appeared with some photographs. It was only then that I discovered who had been responsible for the leaves.[74]

Ferrer remembers mostly that in New York, "I could do anything I wanted," an idea he proceeded to put into practice.[75] For the Whitney Biennial Ferrer installed two and a half tons of ice blocks on the ramp of the museum and inside he deposited a huge haystack, kept in place by steel bars. He smeared grease on the walls and the ceiling so that more hay was stuck to those surfaces. Ferrer commented: "Life can't be resolved in terms of clean spaces, light, cubes and control; life is messy and full of problems that can't be resolved. Life is open."[76]

Many critics hinted at the use of time in these early works. For the Western world time implies a cycle, with its implicit meaning of order. But in Latin America time is perceived as a simultaneous function of life and death, where one can only act in the small instances in between. In an interview with Stephen Prokopoff, Ferrer stated: "I really have never been interested in pursuing an attachment to something as a way of sustaining a style. Grease is a terrific material and it revealed all kinds of unsuspected things to me, but they were related to particular places, to limitations of time and space. For those reasons my use of it was strategic rather than stylistic."[77] In keeping with his idea, he also employed peat moss, corrugated metal, sheets of glass, tents, branches, even neon, constantly challenging himself to create layers of meanings regardless of the medium.

Much of the critical response to his early work was haunted by the critics' current partiality to Minimalist or cool approaches to art. Peter Schjeldahl observed: "We are faced here with an art movement that is destined to rise and fall leaving less *objets d'art* of a familiar order in its wake than even Dada."[78] Hilton Kramer wrote:

You may also need a pair of boots. For to get to the main section of the exhibition which is housed on the Whitney's fourth floor, you are obliged to traverse an improvised moat of melting ice and heaps of dead leaves at the very entrance of the building; this free memento of a messy December thaw, the work of Rafael Ferrer—is not surprisingly called "Ice." It is that kind of show. Materials you see. Procedures. And no illusion.[79]

No one grasped the underlying meaning of working with materials that exist as physical and visual examples of two extremes. Ice and grease are chaotic, formless, and liquid when warm, but ordered, defined, and contained when cold. To traverse this image is naturally upsetting, something Ferrer's paradoxical work of those times strived for (plate 217).[80]

Rafael Ferrer, along with Richard Serra, Keith Sonnier, Robert Morris, and Walter de Maria, stands out as an influential artist who changed the face of the 1960s art scene. With these pioneers of the so-called Anti-Form movement, Ferrer was testing the conventional notions of sculpture to their limits.[81]

The Argentine Leandro Katz was active as a poet, editor, founder of small presses, and organizer of poetry performances in Peru, Ecuador, Colombia, Costa Rica, and Mexico. In 1966 he came to New York. He recounts today: "There was no particular intention when I left Argentina. It wasn't like going into voluntary exile even though it turned out to be very much like that. It had to do with the desire to meet some of the artists I had already translated, like Ferlinghetti and Ginsberg. Once in New York I became involved with the St. Marks Church group."[82]

Just as the Conceptual artists turned to language, many poets and writers had begun to use language for its visual qualities, crossing over into Performance works and artist's books, which were generally visualizations of poetic conceptions. Many exhibitions, largely under the umbrella of Concrete Poetry, gave examples of the idea that the word is a picture, in fact a topography, a vast visual landscape. In 1968 Leandro Katz realized that he too had moved away from syntactical uses of language into a more Conceptual way of writing:

I wanted to become more visual. Whether that came from migrating to a new language, the dichotomy of the language in which you thought and the new language, or whether it came as a result of a personal wish to move into further means of expression, is not so important. What was important was that I started to do scrolls and began also to explore film.[83]

Katz had read some of the early texts by Roland Barthes relating language to an

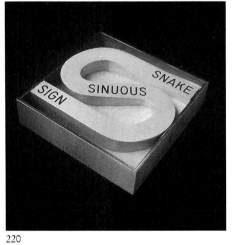

220

221

Rubens Gerchman

220. *Snake, Sinuous, Sign.* 1969
Stainless steel and sand, 70 x 70 x 12″
Collection Fundaçao José e Paulina Nemirovsky
Photo: courtesy the artist

Rubens Gerchman

221. *Americamerica (Homage to R.O. de Andrade).* 1969
Stainless steel and sand, 39⅜ x 39⅜ x 27½″
Museu de Arte de São Paulo
Photo: courtesy the artist

Leandro Katz

222. *Word Column.* 1970
Paper, typewriter, and table
Collection the artist
Photo: courtesy the artist

222

architectural formation of the mind and named his scrolls of accumulated writing Word Columns (plate 222). On these, a subconscious flow of words were typed, and no attempt was made to rationalize or create an order. Soon it became clear that the project was infinite, and Katz decided to give the work some parameters by choosing the arbitrary number of twenty-one columns. In a sense this numerical choice suggested endless columns: two plus one being three, it evoked the triangle, a symbol for infinity. After that he began to see the columns as Conceptual sculptures, imaginary monuments that could be placed in different sites all over the world. As he reflected: "I would choose the name of a town in Bolivia, name the scroll after that town and place it somewhere in Canada, like in a mining wasteland town called Cobalt. After that I took photographs and sent out postcards of the *Column* all over the world."[84] Many Conceptual artists were at that time putting themselves through rigorous exercises, reducing the aesthetic choices to a minimum. Leandro Katz shared this approach with other artists, including Hanne Darboven and On Kawara. While the work had a meditative and spiritual quality, it also made a pronounced and culturally relevant comment, which is a goal Katz has continuously pursued in his work.[85] As with many Latin American artists, Katz has consistently examined his roots, showing Latin American cultural forms in an ample visual language that combines contemporary modes, such as photography, with archaeological motifs in a unique format. Aside from Katz's artistic contributions, his role as a curator and publisher, as well as a teacher, has made him a prominent figure in the intellectual and cultural community of New York.[86]

Eduardo Costa, who was also from Argentina, was another artist-writer who moved from text to visuals. For Costa, language was first sounds and forms, before it could be put to some rational use. When he developed this idea into an artwork, *Tape Poems*, he found a collaborator in John Perreault, a poet-critic who participated in much of the anti-art of those times. The idea of *Tape Poems* was to recuperate the richness of oral language, the tone of voice, and its clues to the age, sex, and social status of those speaking. These elements, according to Costa, get lost in the written language. Five hundred copies of *Tape Poems*, created specifically for tape, were published with an introduction that stated, among other things, "Tape recordings have become snapshots. But there is a difference between photo documentation and sound documentation. In a photograph the materiality is not the same as the materiality of the object represented. For instance, a photo of a person is not flesh but paper. But when we play a tape we have sound as in the original phonic language."[87]

In 1968, shortly after arriving in New York, Costa gained attention with his unusual concept of art jewelry, or "wearable" art. He molded and casted gold ears, gold strands of hair, gold fingers, and gold breasts to people, as anatomical extensions of their bodies (plate 219). At the height of the miniskirt and the radical statements of the sexual revolution, his innovation was immediately embraced by the art-oriented fashion world. *Vogue* "dressed" Marisa Berenson in Costa's creation, adding additional status to the concept. Lawrence Alloway commented: "Costa's jewels are a commentary on anatomy. He treats adornment as a kind of fiction."[88]

In 1969, incorporating fashion into the visual arts, Costa, together with John Perreault and Hannah Weiner, organized the *Fashion Show Poetry Event* at the Center for Inter-American Relations in New York. Alan D'Archangelo, Les Levine, Claes Oldenburg, and Enrique Castro-Cid, among others, exhibited a wide variety of "wearable art." The media instantly applauded these "wearable" fictions. As one reviewer commented: "*The Fashion Show Poetry Event* could have been just another disintegration into more irrelevancy. But get this—it wasn't. It went slamming across all right, only to prove once again that the artists and poets are already into fashion's creative lunar orbit while most pro designers are still grounded."[89] Although Costa's gold ears and breasts could have been mass-produced, they remained art objects, collected by museums and individuals.

Expanding on the idea of "useful" art, Leandro Katz pointed out that the relationship a Latin American artist has toward the object is very different from that cultivated in the United States, where it is formulated by the materialistic aspects of a society obsessed with consumption. Since Latin America's history is unresolved and not yet stabilized, the artist approaches the object with a sense of trying to define an identity: the object is thus converted into a subject. Costa's "wearable and useful" art definitely emphasized this distinction between object and subject.[90]

Vito Acconci, Anne Waldman, Scott Burton, Bernadette Mayer, Marjorie Strider, and many others took part in a saturation of innovations on the edges of "art." Eduardo Costa led the way with his "useful" art of translating street signs from English to Spanish and vice versa. These Streetworks were to be an integral part of what Lucy Lippard designated "dematerialized art." This art intended to undermine New York's capacity to market any kind of innovation that was simply a formal innovation rather than an ideological one. In general, however, most activities surrounding the "dematerialization" of art insisted on works that liberated the spectator's own creative processes.

Rubens Gerchman, a Brazilian artist, also incorporated text and writing into a series of works that confronted issues of importance to Brazil's "black" society. Some critics regarded Gerchman as a Pop artist. To decide for himself whether he fit into that category, Gerchman moved to New York in 1968, where he found his work had few connections with Pop art but did have affinities with certain popular expressions, such as the murals of Chicano and Puerto Rican artists. In New York, he developed themes he had already explored in Brazil. For the *Fashion Show Poetry Event*, he created portable shelters for people to inhabit; he also developed large sculptural words. His explorations into language as a source of imagery were influenced by the writings of Claude Lévi-Strauss. Gerchman later created "pocket stuff," small boxes that created simple written messages and were intended to be mass-produced. Gerchman returned to Brazil in 1973, having been an important contact for newly arrived Latin American artists in New York. However, by contrast with Gerchman, most Latin American Conceptual artists favored anti-art methods or uncritical forms of mass communication (plates 220 and 221).

Antonio Dias, who was from Brazil but went into exile in Europe in 1966, made Conceptual works about dematerialization. Having communicated from Europe with Luis Camnitzer, Liliana Porter, and several other Latin American artists in New York, he went to New York in 1970. That same year he was included in group shows at the Kiko Gallery in Houston, the Felix Landau Gallery in Los Angeles, and the Bonino Gallery in New York. Edward Fry, then organizing the *Sixth Guggenheim International Exhibition*, selected several of his 1960s works—those that best represented Dias's Conceptual approach. Mentioning the culturally oppressive climate of Brazil, Fry stated: "Antonio Dias, who works in Milan, has in recent works demonstrated his awareness of the necessity for a post-formalistic aesthetic in painting and has emerged as an important investigator of the linguistic structure underlying visual imagery."[91] *Newsweek* selected Dias, Joseph Kosuth, and Jiro Takamatsu as "radical exponents of the communication of ideas rather than physical suggestions."[92] Later Dias lived in New York with the help of a Guggenheim Foundation award, and he has always kept in close touch with his New York colleagues. But he qualifies his presence here as being "a discreet one." Keeping in touch with artists and critics, however, was enough for his inclusion in major contemporary shows, including the *Guggenheim International Exhibition*.[93]

Nicolás Uriburu left Argentina for Paris on a French government grant in 1965. For the Venice Biennale in 1968, at the height of the student protests, he colored the Grand Canal in fluorescent green. His gesture suggested a desire to reconstruct the universe according to a scheme based on emotion and harmony rather than urbanistic theory. "Venice is an eternal city, and they say no one can change it, but you can change Venice in a day, without damage, or cost, by art. I used about sixty pounds of nontoxic dye," the artist commented.[94]

By 1969 artists everywhere had moved outdoors, making natural energy a substance of art. Ecology became a household word. Global communication was imminent. Christo, Richard Long, Robert Smithson, and Joseph Beuys were shaping what was called Earth Art and Land Art. Important exhibitions revealed the aesthetic shift both in Europe and the United States. Uriburu's goals were more humanistic than intellectual. Coming from South America, a continent known for its great rivers, he wanted "to raise an alarm against pollution!"[95] His first U.S. series, begun in New York in 1970, was appropriately entitled "Antagonism Between Nature and Civilization" and was shown at the Bonino Gallery in New York. The real piece was created outdoors, on the East River in New York (plate 218). Uriburu, dressed in a chartreuse green shirt, had invited about fifty people to the Heliport base from which he took off on a tugboat, with half a dozen barrels of dye to be poured into the river. *The New York Times* reported: "The rusty powder foamed white, then turned green. Streaks of green quickly twisted into serpentine lines, then spread out into a system of three large blobs. The blobs coalesced into roundish shapes, roughly 175 feet by 50 feet."[96] John Perreault reported: "A helicopter hovered above filming everything and followed the green stain for a while as it made its way out to sea. On shore we were given a handbill titled 'Green New York—Intercontinental Project of Waters Environment.' In the next two months Uriburu will also color the Seine, the canals of Venice, and the Riachuelo River in Argentina. I myself enjoyed the spectacle and the ambiance of the whole thing and thought the stain as it swirled down the river surprisingly beautiful. It was the best watercolor I've seen in a long time."[97] Uriburu's concern for the abuse of nature has persisted over the years. He has made works in Europe and South America and sometimes collaborated with other artists, including Joseph Beuys, with whom he planted trees at Documenta in Kassel.

By 1969 Lygia Clark and Helio Oiticica, both from Brazil, were also known in New York. John Perreault wrote: "Lygia Clark...a very important artist, virtually unknown in this country...has been a pioneer in manipulatory sculpture and in 'Poor Art.' She is now almost totally concerned with touch...Helio Oiticica, who is temporarily in England, makes clothing and capes with inside pockets that contain various powders for you to touch while you are walking around. He has also done various street festival art works. Brazil is a dictatorship so neither artist can get any support from the government."[98]

Dore Ashton, who met Oiticica in Brazil through the art historian Mario Pedroza, recalls: "He took me dancing to the *favelas* where he was well known. He used to design carnival costumes for the denizens of these poorest neighborhoods, and they respected him. When he came to New York, he took a very small and uncomfortable loft near my home...and it was an extraordinary 'happening' in itself. Or perhaps a 'site-specific' sculpture. The only thing that might be compared to that loft was Schwitters's Merzbau. Helio divided the space in horizontal planes. All around the walls and hanging from the ceiling were boxes, sometimes those plastic milk containers, and in them little organizations of odd matters. You had to make your way through this animated maze, and the feeling of no up and no down was intense. Helio was a *perpetuum mobile* of invention."[99]

Regarding his presence in New York, the writer and critic Ted Castle said: "I saw him as being a classical exile. He absolutely adored Brazil but not being able to operate there, because of the regime, he left. He was always planning for his return. Perhaps this accounts for him not having done much publicly in New York. His element was largely language. He loved to write in Portuguese, and he was a brilliant thinker. As anti-artist, affected by Baudelaire, he was a proposer of creative activities, making his work his life, like the *Babylonests* he created where he lived."[100]

After being involved in the Brazilian Neo-Concrete movement, Oiticica independently began to work on what can be called today forerunners of the Anti-Form sculptural breakthroughs in America. His *Nucleos* was a type of "Mondrian dissolved into space, recycled by the tropics," as the Brazilian art historian Federico Morais put it. He developed his Environmental works into a more intensely sensorial series called *Penetrables*, which were labyrinths with myriad colors and materials that the viewer could inhabit and interact with. In 1963 the boxlike structures entitled *Bólides* came into being. These were incandescent containers one could touch, smell, feel, and become one with. In 1969, Guy Brett, the British art historian and curator of Oiticica's Whitechapel Gallery exhibition in London, observed that with these works, "Instead of merely looking at color, you plunge your hands into it, you weigh it, you put it around your body and clothe yourself in it."[101] In 1964 Oiticica had begun to visit the Mangueira, a shantytown, and after what the Brazilian art historian and curator Mario

223

224

225

Cildo Meireles
224. *Insertions in Ideological Circuits: Coca-Cola Project.*
1970
Coca-Cola bottles and adhesive stickers
Collection the artist
Photo: Pedro Oswaldo Cruz

Helio Oiticica
225. *Installation of "Nests."* 1970. *Information,*
July 2–September 20, 1970, The Museum of
Modern Art, New York
Photo: courtesy Projecto HO, Rio de Janeiro

223. *(left to right) Iva de Freitas, Amilcar de Castro,
Helio Oiticica, Rubens Gerchman, and Roberto
de Lamonica.*
Photograph reproduced in "Our Men in New York,"
Manchete magazine, Brazil, 1970
Photo: courtesy Rubens Gerchman

Pedroza called "his painful initiation," he created the *Parangolés.*[102] These capes, tents, and banners or flags—no precise translation or explanation exists—were a unique and metaphorical means for transgression. The user became the work; inside this second skin he shared the collective myth of the samba. Oiticica's influence extended beyond his exhibitions, leaving a lasting impression on artists and critics in South America, Europe, and New York. In addition, a sequel of younger Brazilian artists that later ventured to New York also learned by his example (plate 225).

One of these artists was Cildo Meireles, who met Kynaston McShine during his visit to Brazil in 1969 and was invited to participate in the *Information* show at The Museum of Modern Art. He created a work entitled *Insertions into Ideological Circuits* (plate 224). This work, composed of two projects, inverted the idea of the "ready-made" by creating an art that acted in concert with the industrial complex and utilized its support system. *Coca-Cola* consisted of returning empty bottles to circulation after information and critical opinions had been attached to the bottles by way of silk-screen stickers. The texts were invisible when the bottles were empty, but as they were refilled in the factory, the information became legible. Meireles hoped the consumer of Coca-Cola would become part of an "ideological" circuit. By "circuit" he meant the cyclical repetition of information transmitted through various vehicles. The work also resembled the age-old practice of bottles being thrown into the ocean with messages to be picked up by someone at the other end of the world.

Of the artists discussed above, Luis Camnitzer, José Guillermo Castillo, Liliana Porter, Rafael Ferrer, Marta Minujin, and Helio Oiticica were included in the *Information* show. Remarkably, of the ninety-six participating artists, twenty-one were from Latin America (and many of the twenty-one were not U.S. residents). In the catalog, too, a significant number of images came from Latin American sources: the film section, for example, included work by David Lamelas, Paulo Roberto Matina, Jorge Sirito de Vives, Alfonso Sanchez, Rafael Colón-Morales, Alfonso Pagan-Cruz, Luis Vale, and Edgar Sanchez. The *Information* show was also an exceptional event in itself. The museum became a transmitter of raw materials, presenting art to the public without a critical guide. The variety of media and the unabashedly messy quality of many of the presentations made viewing the exhibition a new experience, similar to a festive event or a Latin American fiesta. The exhibition was intended to be a demonstration of the unrestricted motivations that propelled artists in the 1960s. Freedom, as presented by the borderless transmission of information (an idea influenced by Marshall McLuhan's concept of a global village), was particularly meaningful for Latin American artists in the United States. These artists made global communication and nomadic information the centerpieces of their work.

Selected Biographies

Biographies of artists are given when available and cover only selected events in their careers in the United States between 1920 and 1970. Significant group exhibitions only are listed with the exhibition's complete title and only the sponsoring museum's name is given.

Abularach, Rodolfo. b. 1933, Guatemala City. Studied at Escuela de Ingeniería, Universidad de Guatemala, 1951. Visited Pasadena, Calif., 1953; Mexico City, 1954. Worked as draftsman, Museo Nacional de Belles Artes, Guatemala, 1956–57. Received scholarships from Museo Nacional de Belles Artes, Guatemala, 1958; John Simon Guggenheim Memorial Fellowship, 1949; Pan American Union, Washington, D.C., 1962, 1964; Tamarind Lithography Workshop, Los Angeles, 1964. Solo exhibitions: Pan American Union Washington, D.C.,1959; David Herbert Gallery, N.Y.C., 1961; Galería Colibrí, San Juan, 1970; Graham Gallery, N.Y.C., 1970. Group Exhibitions: *Pan American Exhibition*, Milwaukee Art Center, 1957; *The United States Collects Latin American Art*, Art Institute of Chicago, 1959; The Museum of Modern Art, N.Y.C., 1960, 1961, 1962, 1963, 1964, 1965, 1969, 1970; American Federation of the Arts, Washington, D.C., 1960; David Herbert Gallery, N.Y.C., 1961, 1962; Fleming Museum, University of Vermont, Burlington, 1962; St. Paul Art Center, Minn., 1963; Pennsylvania Academy of the Fine Arts, Philadelphia, 1963; Pratt Institute, N.Y.C.,1964, 1965; Associated American Artists, N.Y.C., 1964; Modern Art Institute, Washington, D.C., 1964; Bonino Gallery, N.Y.C., 1964; The Jewish Museum, N.Y.C., 1964; Washington Square Gallery, N.Y.C., 1964; World's Fair, Queens, N.Y., 1964; IBM Galleries, N.Y.C., 1965; The Brooklyn Museum, N.Y., 1966, 1970; *Art of Latin America since Independence*, Yale University, New Haven, and University of Texas, Austin, 1966; Zegri Gallery, N.Y.C., 1969; Dulin Gallery, Knoxville, Tenn., 1970; San Francisco Museum of Art, 1970; Pyramid Gallery, Washington, D.C., 1970. Collections: Chase Manhattan Bank, N.Y.C.; High Art Museum, Atlanta; Metropolitan Museum of Art, N.Y.C; Milwaukee Art Center; The Museum of Modern Art, N.Y.C.; Museum of Modern Art of Latin America, Washington, D.C.; New York Public Library, N.Y.C.; New York University, N.Y.C.; R.C.A. Corporation, N.Y.C.; University of Massachusetts, Amherst; Universidad de Puerto Rico, San Juan; Walker Art Center, Minneapolis.

Albizu, Olga. b. 1924, Ponce, P.R. Resided in U.S. since 1956. Studied at Universidad de Puerto Rico under Spanish painter Estebán Vicente (B.A., 1948). Received Universidad de Puerto Rico scholarship for graduate studies under Hans Hoffman at The Art Students League, N.Y.C., 1948–51. Also studied at Academie de la Grande Chaumière, Paris, and Accademia di Belle Arte, Florence, 1951. Solo exhibitions: Panoras Gallery, N.Y.C., 1956; Ateneo Puertorriqueño, San Juan, 1957, 1958, 1961; Roland de Aenlle Gallery, N.Y.C., 1959, 1960; Pan American Union, Washington, D.C., 1960; Galería Santiago, San Juan, 1969. Group exhibitions: New York City Center, 1956; Riverside Museum, N.Y.C., 1957, 1959; Instituto de Cultura Puertorriqueña, San Juan, 1957, 1962; Stable Gallery, N.Y.C., 1957; *Thirty Latin American Artists*, Riverside Museum, N.Y.C.,1960; Casa de Arte, San Juan, 1962, 1963; RCA Pavilion, World's Fair, Queens, N.Y., 1964; Pan American Union, Washington, D.C., 1966. Artwork appeared on record covers for RCA and other companies. Collections: Ateneo Puertorriqueño, San Juan; Instituto de Cultura Puertorriqueña, San Juan; Museo de Arte de Ponce, P.R.; Museum of Modern Art of Latin America, Washington, D.C.; Universidad de Puerto Rico, San Juan.

Alfaro Siqueiros, David. 1896–1974. b. Chihuahua, Mexico. Studied at La Esmeralda, Mexico City, 1911–13. Studied in Europe on Mexican government scholarship, 1919–22. Edited two issues of Spanish magazine *Vida Americana*, 1921. Organized "Syndicate of Technical Workers, Painters and Sculptors" in Mexico, 1923, and workers' unions in Guadalajara, 1925–30. Jailed for political activities, 1930; exiled from Mexico, 1932. Painted three murals at the Chouinard School of Art, Los Angeles (*Workers' Meeting*); Plaza Art Center, Los Angeles (*Tropical America*); and Dudley Moore residence, Santa Monica (*Portrait of Mexico*), 1932. Traveled to Uruguay, Argentina, and Mexico, 1933–34. Organized Siqueiros Experimental Art Workshop, N.Y.C., 1936. Served in Spanish Republican Army, 1937–39. Returned permanently to Mexico, 1939. Solo exhibitions: Jede Zeitlin Bookshop, Los Angeles, 1932; Stendahl Ambassador Galleries, Los Angeles, 1932; Pierre Matisse Gallery, N.Y.C., 1940; A.C.A. Gallery, N.Y.C., 1962; New Center Art Gallery, N.Y.C., 1964; Center for Inter-American Relations, N.Y.C., 1967; Marion Koogler McNay Art Institute, San Antonio, 1968. Group exhibitions: *Art of Latin America since Independence*, Yale University, New Haven, and University of Texas, Austin, 1966; *Latin American Art: 1931–1966*, The Museum of Modern Art, N.Y.C., 1967. Collections: The Museum of Modern Art, N.Y.C.; Rhode Island School of Design, Providence.

Alpuy, Julio. b. 1919, Tacuarembó, Uruguay. Resided in U.S. since 1961. Studied at Taller Torres-García, Montevideo, 1939–50. Traveled and studied in Europe, 1951–53; in Latin America, 1956. Awarded New School for Social Research fellowships, 1963, 1965. Solo exhibitions: J. Walter Thompson Company, N.Y.C., 1964; University of Massachusetts, Amherst, 1969; Zegri Gallery, N.Y.C., 1969. Group exhibitions: Washington Gallery, N.Y.C., 1964; *Magnet: New York*, Bonino Gallery, N.Y.C., 1964; Hofstra University, Hempstead, N.Y., 1965; Center for Inter-American Relations, Washington, D.C., 1968; Marymount College, Tarrytown, N.Y., 1970. Collections: J. Walter Thompson Company, N.Y.C.; New Jersey State Museum, Trenton; University of Texas, Austin.

Anguiano, Raul. b. 1915, Jalisco, Mexico. Studied at the Escuela Libre de Pintura, Guadalajara, Mexico, 1930; mural technique in Mexico City, c. 1930s. Joined Taller de Gráfica Popular, 1938. Traveled to Cuba and U.S., 1939–41; studied at The Art Students League, N.Y.C., 1940–41. Appointed guest professor, Trinity University, San Antonio, Texas, 1966. Solo exhibitions: San Francisco Museum of Art, 1953; Gallery of the Mexican consul general, Washington, D.C., 1966. Illustrated *Rural Mexico*, by Nathan L. Whetten (1953), and *On the Watch*, by Adolfo López Mateos (1970). Group exhibitions: *Golden Gate International Exposition*, San Francisco, 1940; Institute of Modern Art, Boston, 1940; Art Institute of Chicago, 1940; *Twenty Centuries of Mexican Art*, The Museum of Modern Art, N.Y.C., 1940; Cincinnati Art Museum, 1958. Collections: Colorado Springs Fine Arts Center; Museum of Fine Arts, Boston; The Museum of Modern Art, N.Y.C.

Antúnez, Nemesio. b. 1918, Santiago. Visited France (on invitation of French government), Italy, and Switzerland, 1936. Studied architecture at Universidad Católica de Santiago, 1937–1943; and Columbia University, N.Y.C.

(M.S.,1945). Traveled throughout Latin America, 1946. Awarded scholarship to study with S.W. Hayter of Atelier 17, N.Y.C., 1947. Lived in Paris, 1950–53. Founded Taller 99 (artists' collective), Santiago, 1954. Director, Museum of Contemporary Art, Universidad de Chile, Santiago, 1961–64; cultural attaché, Chilean embassy, N.Y.C., 1964–69; director, National Museum of Fine Arts, Santiago, 1969–73. Solo exhibitions: Norlyst Gallery, N.Y.C., 1945; Bodley Gallery, N.Y.C., 1950, 1966. Group exhibitions: Galerie Couturier, Stamford, Conn, 1965; *Art of Latin America since Independence*, Yale University, New Haven, and University of Texas, Austin, 1966; Bodley Gallery, N.Y.C., 1966. Collections: Cincinnati Art Museum; Library of Congress, Washington, D.C; Metropolitan Museum of Art, N.Y.C.; The Museum of Modern Art, N.Y.C.; New York Public Library, N.Y.C.; Rhode Island School of Design, Providence.

Baca, Judith Francisca. b. 1946, Los Angeles. Studied at California State University, Northridge, (B.A., 1969; M.A., 1979); Taller Siqueiros, Cuernavaca, Mexico, 1977. Professor of fine art, University of California, Irvine, 1981 to the present. Cofounder and artistic director of Social and Public Arts Resource Center (SPARC), Venice, Calif., 1981; founder, Los Angeles Citywide Mural Project, 1974. Painted murals at Alemany High School, Los Angeles, 1969, (*Untitled*); Hollenbeck Park, Los Angeles, (*Mi Abuelita*), 1970.

Báez, Myrna. b. 1931, Santurce, P.R. Studied science at Universidad de Puerto Rico, 1951; art at Academia de San Fernando, Madrid 1957; Taller de Artes Graficas, Instituto de Cultura Puertorriqueña, San Juan, c. 1960. Studied graphic techniques at Pratt Institute, N.Y.C., 1969–70. Awarded prize for entry in *Pratt Graphics Center Exhibition*, 1970. Solo exhibitions: Instituto de Cultura Puertorriqueña, San Juan, 1962; Galería Colibrí, San Juan, 1966. Group exhibitions: Riverside Museum, N.Y.C., 1961; Universidad de Puerto Rico, San Juan, 1962, 1968; Instituto de Cultura Puertorriqueña, San Juan, 1965; Galería Sudamericana, N.Y.C., 1966, 1967, 1968, 1969, 1970. Collections: Fort Lauderdale Museum, Fla.; Instituto de Cultura Puertorriqueña, San Juan; Metropolitan Museum of Art, N.Y.C.; Museo de Arte de Ponce, P.R.; The Museum of Modern Art, N.Y.C.; Universidad de Puerto Rico, San Juan.

Belkin, Arnold. b. 1930, Calgary, Canada. Resided in Mexico, 1947–68; in U.S., 1968 to present. Assistant to David Alfaro Siqueiros, 1949–50; Coedited magazine *Nueva Presencia* with Francisco Icaza, Mexico City, 1961.Visiting professor of painting, Pratt Institute, N.Y.C.,1967. Solo exhibitions: Cober Gallery, N.Y.C., 1962; Zora's Gallery, Los Angeles, 1962, 1963, 1964; Phoenix Art Museum, 1967; Ankrum Gallery, Los Angeles, 1967; Berman-Medalie Gallery, Boston, 1968. Group exhibitions: Zora's Gallery, Los Angeles, 1963; Riverside Museum, N.Y.C., 1963; San Antonio Art Museum, 1963; Solomon R. Guggenheim Museum, N.Y.C., 1964; Phoenix Art Museum, 1964; Galaxy Gallery, Phoenix, 1964; Simon Patrick Gallery, Los Angeles, 1966; *Hemisfair*, San Antonio, 1968. Collections: Citibank, Chicago; Dayton Art Museum; Des Moines Art Museum; Grinnell College, Iowa; Los Angeles County Museum; Massachusetts Institute of Technology, Cambridge; Museo de Arte de Ponce, P.R.; Phoenix Art Museum; University of Texas, Austin.

Berni, Antonio. 1905–1981. b. Rosario, Argentina. Studied art in Rosario. Painted in the Pampas, 1921. Visited Spain, France, Italy, Belgium, and Holland and studied in Paris under Orthon Friesz and André Lhote, 1925–30. Founded New Realism movement in Argentina (political organization of painters), 1932. Worked with David Alfaro Siqueiros, Buenos Aires, 1934. With Eneas Spillimbergo, executed murals for Argentine Pavilion, World's Fair, N.Y.C., 1939. Taught at Escuela Nacional de Bellas Artes, Buenos Aires, 1935–46. Asked by Comision Nacional de Cultura to study pre-Columbian art and paint Latin American themes, 1941. Traveled to Mexico, Peru, and U.S., c. 1940s. Solo exhibitions: Miami Museum of Modern Art, 1963–64; New Jersey State Museum, Trenton, 1966. Group exhibitions: *Golden Gate Exposition*, San Francisco, 1939; *Latin American Exhibition of Fine Arts*, Riverside Museum, N.Y.C., 1940; San Francisco Museum of Art, 1942; *New Art of Argentina*, Walker Art Center, Minneapolis, 1965; *Art of Latin America since Independence*, Yale University, New Haven, and University of Texas, Austin, 1966; Collections: The Museum of Modern Art, N.Y.C.; Museum of Modern Art of Latin America, Washington, D.C.; University of Texas, Austin.

Bonevardi, Marcelo. b. 1929, Buenos Aires. Resided in N.Y.C. since 1958. Studied architecture at Universidad Nacional de Córdoba, Argentina. Traveled to Italy, 1950. Taught in school of architecture, Universidad Nacional de Córdoba, 1956–58. Awarded John Simon Guggenheim Memorial Fellowship, 1959; and New School for Social Research fellowships, 1963–65. Solo exhibitions: Gallery 4, Detroit, 1959; Roland de Aenlle Gallery, N.Y.C., 1960; Pan American Union, Washington, D.C., 1960; Latow Gallery, N.Y.C., 1961; Bonino Gallery, N.Y.C., 1965, 1967, 1969; Arts Club of Chicago, 1968. Group exhibitions: Birmingham Museum of Art, Ala.; Chautauqua Art Association, N.Y.; *Thirty Latin American Artists*, Riverside Museum, N.Y.C., 1960; The Museum of Modern Art, N.Y.C.; Washington Gallery of Art and Corcoran Rental Gallery, Washington, D.C., 1963; Institute of Contemporary Arts, Washington, D.C., 1964; Washington Square Gallery, N.Y., 1964; *Magnet: New York*, Bonino Gallery, N.Y.C., 1964; *Selections from the Nancy Sayles Day Collection*, Museum of Art, Rhode Island School of Design, Providence, 1965; The Museum of Modern Art, N.Y.C., 1965; Bonino Gallery, N.Y.C., 1965, 1966; Hood Museum of Art, Dartmouth College, Hanover, N.H., 1966; Santa Barbara Museum of Art, Calif., 1966. Collections: Albright-Knox Art Gallery, Buffalo, N.Y.; Atlantic Richfield Co., N.Y.C.; The Brooklyn Museum, N.Y.; Chase Manhattan Bank, N.Y.C.; Solomon R. Guggenheim Museum, N.Y.C.; The Museum of Modern Art, N.Y.C.; Owens-Corning Fiberglass Corp., Toledo, Ohio; Philadelphia Museum of Art; Rhode Island School of Design, Providence; J. Walter Thompson, Co., N.Y.C.; United Nations, N.Y.C.; University of Southern Illinois, Carbondale; University of Texas, Austin; Window South, Palo Alto, Calif.

Bonilla-Norat, Félix. b. 1912, Cayey, P.R. Studied at Instituto Politécnico de San Germán, Puerto Rico, Childe-Walker School of Fine Arts, Boston, Ernst Thurn School of Fine Arts, Gloucester, Mass., 1931–35. Received Puerto Rican government scholarship to study at Academia de San Fernando, Madrid, and Accademia San Marco, Florence, 1936–39. Opened atelier, N.Y.C., 1940. Established serigraphy workshop, N.Y.C., 1946. Taught serigraphic techniques in Division of Community Education, San Juan, 1949. Taught in art department, Universidad de Puerto Rico, 1956. Founding member of the Borinquen 12 group (artist's co-operative active in Puerto Rico, 1967–69). Solo exhibitions: La Mansión, Santurce, P.R. Group exhibitions: A.C.A. Gallery, N.Y.C.,1947; Riverside Museum, N.Y.C., 1956.

Borges, Jacobo. b. 1931, Caracas. Studied at Escuela de Artes Plásticas y Aplicadas Cristóbal Rojas, Caracas, 1949–51. Traveled to Paris on a scholarship and studied at Salon des Jeunes Artistes of Musée de l'Art Moderne de la Ville de Paris, 1952–56. Studied at the Taller Libre de Arte, Caracas, 1957. Group exhibitions: Solomon R. Guggenheim Museum, N.Y.C., 1964; University of California at Oakland, 1965; American Federation of the Arts, Washington, D.C., 1965; Pan American Union, Washington, D.C., 1965; *The Emergent Decade*, Solomon R. Guggenheim Museum, N.Y.C., and Cornell University, Ithaca, N.Y., 1965; *Art of Latin America since Independence*, Yale University, New Haven, and University of Texas, Austin 1966. Collections: CDS Gallery, N.Y.C.; Solomon R. Guggenheim Museum, N.Y.C.

Botero, Fernando. b. 1932, Medellín, Colombia. Resides in N.Y.C. and Paris. Studied at Academia de San Fernando, Madrid, 1952; fresco techniques at Accademia San Marco; art history under Roberto Longhi at Universita degli Studi, Florence, 1953–54. Moved to Mexico, 1956. Appointed professor of painting at Escuela de Bellas Artes, Universidad Nacional de Colombia, Bogotá, 1958. Moved to N.Y.C. and awarded John Simon Guggenheim Memorial Fellowship, 1960. Solo exhibitions: Pan American Union, Washington, D.C., 1957; Tannia Gres Gallery, Washington, D.C., 1960, 1962; The Contemporaries, 1962; Zora's Gallery, Los Angeles, 1965; Milwaukee Art Center, 1967; Center for Inter-American Relations, N.Y.C., 1969. Group exhibitions: *Gulf-Caribbean Art*, Museum of Fine Arts, Houston, 1956; *South American Art Today*, Dallas Museum of Fine Arts, 1959; OAS Headquarters, Washington, D.C., 1960; *Magnet: New York*, Bonino Gallery, N.Y.C., 1964; *The Emergent Decade*, Solomon R. Guggenheim Museum, N.Y.C., and Cornell University, Ithaca, N.Y., 1965; *Contemporary Art of Latin America*, Institute of Contemporary Arts, Washington, D.C., 1965; *Art of Latin America since Independence*, Yale University, New Haven and University of Texas, Austin, 1966; *Latin American Art: 1931–1966*, The Museum of Modern Art , N.Y.C., 1967; The Museum of Modern Art, N.Y.C., 1969. Collections: Baltimore Museum of Art; Solomon R. Guggenheim Museum, N.Y.C.; Hirshhorn Museum and Sculpture Garden, Washington, D.C.; Milwaukee Art Center; Museo de Arte de Ponce, P.R.; The Museum of Modern Art, N.Y.C.; Museum of Modern Art of Latin America, Washington, D.C.; New York University, N.Y.C.; Pennsylvania State University, State College; Rhode Island School of Design, Providence; University of Texas, Austin.

Brizzi, Ary. b. 1930, Buenos Aires. Studied at Escuela Nacional de Bellas Artes Manuel Belgrano and Escuela Superior de Bellas Artes Ernesto de la Cárcova, Buenos Aires. Appointed professor of painting at Escuela Nacional de Bellas Artes Prilidiano Pueyrredon and researcher at Centro de Investicaciones de Comunicación Masiva, Arte y Tecnología de la Ciudad de Buenos Aires, 1951. Visited U.S. on government invitation, 1965. Solo exhibitions: Pan American Union, Washington, D.C., 1970. Group exhibitions: Pepsi-Cola Gallery, N.Y.C., 1964; Esso Salon of Young Artists, N.Y.C., 1965; Center for Inter-American Relations, N.Y.C., 1968, 1970; Bonino Gallery, N.Y.C., 1969; *Latin American Painting*, Philbrook Art Center, Tulsa, Okla. and City Museum of Art, University of Oklahoma, Norman, 1969. Collections: Albright-Knox Art Gallery, Buffalo, N.Y.; Bank of Boston Galleries; Esso Collection, Coral Gables, Fla.; IBM Collection, N.Y.C.; The Museum of Modern Art, N.Y.C.; Museum of Modern Art of Latin America, Washington, D.C.

Camnitzer, Luis. b. 1937, Lubec, Germany. Family emigrated to Uruguay, 1939. Resided in U.S. since 1962. Studied sculpture and architecture at Universidad de la República Oriental del Uruguay, Montevideo, c. 1950s; printmaking and sculpture on German government scholarship at Akademie der Bildenden Künste, Munich, 1957. Awarded John Simon Guggenheim Memorial Fellowship, 1964; Memorial Foundation for Jewish Culture Fellowship, 1965, 1966; University of Pennsylvania Fellowship, 1968. Taught at Pratt Institute, N.Y.C., 1966; Fairleigh Dickinson University, Madison, N.J., 1965–68; State University of New York, Old Westbury, since 1969. Solo exhibitions: Galería Sudamericana, N.Y.C., 1963; Van Bovenkamp Gallery, N.Y.C., 1964; Marion Goodman Gallery, N.Y.C., 1966; Institute of Contemporary Arts, Washington, D.C., 1969; Dwan Gallery, N.Y.C., 1970; Paula Cooper Gallery, N.Y.C., 1970. Group exhibitions: *Magnet: New York*, Bonino Gallery, N.Y.C., 1964; The Jewish Museum, N.Y.C., 1964; Van Bovenkamp Gallery, N.Y.C., 1965; University of New Mexico, Albuquerque, 1966; Pratt Institute, N.Y.C., 1968; New Jersey State Museum, Trenton, 1968; Cincinnati Art Museum, 1968; Smithsonian Institution, Washington, D.C., 1968. Collections: Fairleigh Dickinson University, Madison, N.J.; The Jewish Museum, N.Y.C.; Metropolitan Museum of Art, N.Y.C; The Museum of Modern Art, N.Y.C.; New Jersey State Museum, Trenton; New York Public Library, N.Y.C.; Whitney Museum of American Art, N.Y.C.; Yeshiva University, N.Y.C.

Cárdenas Arroyo, Santiago. b. 1937, Bogotá. Studied painting under Robert Hamilton and Gordon Peers at Rhode Island School of Design (B.F.A., 1960). Served in the U.S. Armed Forces, 1960–62. Studied painting under Alex Katz, Al Held, Jack Tworkov, and Neil Welliver at Yale University (M.F.A., 1964). Taught painting at Universidad de los Andes, Universidad Jorge Tadeo Lozano, and Universidad Nacional de Colombia, Bogotá, beginning in 1965. Appointed director of fine arts, Universidad Nacional de Colombia, 1972. Group exhibitions: Galería Angell, Providence, 1960; Brown University, Providence, 1960; Yale University, New Haven, 1964; Renssaleer Polytechnic Institute, Troy, N.Y., 1965. Collections: Chase Manhattan Bank, N.Y.C.; The Museum of Modern Art, N.Y.C.

Carreño, Mario. b. 1913, Havana. Joined Grupo Minorista, (group of avant-garde artists), 1927. Printer and illustrator for magazines *Revista de Havana* and *Diario de la Marina*, 1927. Traveled to Spain, 1932; Mexico, 1936. Lived in Paris, 1937–39; Italy, 1939; N.Y.C., 1940. Returned to Havana, 1941. Taught painting at New School for Social Research, N.Y.C., 1944–57. Moved permanently to Chile, 1957. Solo exhibitions: Perls Gallery, N.Y.C., 1941, 1944, 1945, 1951; Institute of Modern Art, Boston,1943; San Francisco Museum of Art, 1943–44; New School for Social Research, N.Y.C., 1950. Group exhibitions: *The Latin American Collection of The Museum of Modern Art*, N.Y.C., 1943; Pan American Union, Washington, D.C., 1946, 1952; Morse Gallery, N.Y.C., 1947; *Pittsburgh International Exhibition*, Carnegie Institute, 1951, 1953, 1956, 1957; *The United States Collects Latin American Art*, Art Institute of Chicago, 1959; *Art of Latin American since Independence*, Yale University, New Haven, and University of Texas, Austin, 1966. Collections: Carroll Reese Museum, Nashville; The Museum of Modern Art, N.Y.C.; The Museum of Modern Art of Latin America, Washington, D.C.; San Francisco Museum of Modern Art.

Carrillo, Eduardo. b. 1937, Santa Monica, Calif. Studied at Los Angeles City College, 1955–56; University of California, Los Angeles, (B.A., 1962, M.A., 1964); Círculo de Bellas Artes, Madrid, 1960–61. Founded Centro de Arte Regional, Baja California, Mexico, 1966. Taught at San Fernando State College, 1969–70; Sacramento State College, since 1970. Created mural at Chicano Library, University of California, Los Angeles, with Ramsés Norlego, Saul Solache, Sergio Hernández, 1970. Solo exhibitions: Ceejee Gallery, Los Angeles, 1962. Group exhibitions: Museum of Fine Arts, Houston, 1963; Hayward Gallery, Sacramento, 1966.

Casas, Melesio. b. 1929, El Paso, Texas. Studied at Texas Western College (B.A.,1956); University of the Americas, Mexico City, (M.A.,1958). Taught at University of Texas at El Paso and the department of art, San Antonio College. Solo exhibitions: YWCA, El Paso, 1961; Mexican consulate, San Antonio, 1963, 1968; Trinity University, San Antonio, 1967; Texas Lutheran College, Seguin, Texas, 1967. Group exhibitions: Maude Sullivan Gallery, El Paso, 1959; El Paso Museum of Art, 1960; Mexican Consulate, San Antonio, 1962; Witte Memorial Museum, San Antonio, 1962, 1963, 1966, 1967; El Paso Museum of Art, 1962, 1963, 1964, 1965; North Star Gallery, San Antonio, 1963, 1964, 1965, 1966; Two Twenty Two Gallery, El Paso, 1964; Men of Art Guild, San Antonio, 1963, 1964, 1965; San Antonio Public Library, 1964; Oklahoma Art Center, Oklahoma City, 1969.

Castellanos, Julio. 1905–1947, b. Mexico City. Studied at La Esmeralda, Mexico City, 1918. Traveled to U.S., 1920.

Studied at workshop of Manuel Rodríguez Lozano, Mexico City, 1921–24. Traveled to Buenos Aires, France, and Spain, 1924–25. Created set designs for the ballet, N.Y.C., 1946. Group exhibitions: *Pan-American Exhibition*, Baltimore Museum of Art, 1931; College Art Association traveling exhibition, 1934; *Art of Latin America since Independence*, Yale University, New Haven, and University of Texas, Austin, 1966. Collections: Museum of Fine Arts, Boston; The Museum of Modern Art, N.Y.C.; Philadelphia Museum of Art.

Castillo, Sergio. b. 1925, Santiago. Studied at École des Beaux-Arts and Academie Julien, Paris, 1948–52; Escuela de Bellas Artes, Universidad de Chile, Santiago, 1952–56. Appointed visiting professor at University of California, Berkeley, 1969. Completed public works for Chilean Airlines, N.Y.C.; Chilean embassy gardens, Washington, D.C.; town of Sausalito, Calif. Solo exhibitions: Galería Sudamericana, N.Y.C., 1958, 1962; Zegri Gallery, N.Y.C. 1965, 1969; Pan American Union, Washington, D.C., 1962, 1967. Group exhibitions: Esso Salon of Young Artists, N.Y.C., 1965; IBM Gallery, N.Y.C., 1965; Zegri Gallery, N.Y.C., 1966; San Francisco Museum of Art, 1966; Baltimore Museum of Art, 1968; J.P. Speed Museum, Louisville, 1969. Collections: Esso Collection, Coral Gables, Fla.; Museum of Modern Art of Latin America, Washington, D.C.

Castro-Cid, Enrique. b.1937, Santiago. Studied art at Escuela de Bellas Artes, Universidad de Chile, Santiago, 1957–59. Resided in U.S. since c.1962. Awarded OAS Fellowship, 1962; John Simon Guggenheim Memorial Fellowship, 1964; William Copley Award, 1966. Taught art at New School for Social Research, N.Y.C., 1962; University of Illinois, Urbana, 1968; School of Visual Arts, N.Y.C., 1970. Solo exhibitions: Feigen-Palmer Gallery, Los Angeles, 1963; Richard Feigen Gallery, N.Y.C., 1963, 1964, 1965, 1966, 1968, 1969; University of Illinois, Urbana, 1968. Group exhibitions: Pan American Union, Washington, D.C., 1961; Byron Gallery, N.Y.C., 1964, 1965; *Pittsburgh International*, Carnegie Institute, 1964; Institute of Contemporary Arts, Washington, D.C., 1964; University of Illinois, Champaign, 1965, 1967; Kornblee Gallery, N.Y.C., 1965; American Federation of Arts, N.Y.C., 1966; *Art of Latin America since Independence*, Yale University, New Haven, and University of Texas, Austin, 1966; Sidney Janis Gallery, N.Y.C., 1966; Architectural League of N.Y.C., 1966; The Jewish Museum, N.Y.C., 1966; Smithsonian Institution, Washington, D.C. ,1966; Herron Museum of Art, Indianapolis, 1968; Isaac Delgado Museum, of Art, New Orleans, 1968; The Museum of Modern Art, N.Y.C., 1969; The Brooklyn Museum, N.Y., 1970. Collections: Solomon R. Guggenheim Museum, N.Y.C.; Lowe Art Museum, Miami; The Museum of Modern Art, N.Y.C.; Museum of Modern Art of Latin America, Washington, D.C.; Phoenix Art Museum.

Charlot, Jean. 1898–1979. b. Paris; Mexican citizen. Studied drawing and painting, Paris, 1915–21. Traveled to Mexico to work on the National Preparatory School murals as assistant to Diego Rivera, 1922–23. Art director, Mexico's English-language magazine *Mexican Folkways*, 1925–27. Visited N.Y.C. and Washington, D.C., 1929. Taught at Student's Art Association and Columbia University, N.Y.C., 1930; University of Georgia, Athens, 1931; University of Hawaii, Honolulu, 1947. Appointed director of School of Fine Arts, Colorado Springs Fine Arts Center, 1947. Painted murals in the McDonough (Ga.) post office and University of Georgia, Athens, 1944; The First National Bank, Waikiki and Honolulu Branches, 1951–52; Tempe, Arizona, 1952; University of Hawaii, Honolulu, 1953. Authored *The Mexican Mural Renaissance: 1920–1925* (Yale University Press, 1953). Exhibitions: Smith College, Northampton, Mass.,1936; Stendhal Galleries, Los Angeles, 1938; Associated American Artists, N.Y.C., 1951; Honolulu Academy of Arts, 1966. Collections: Baltimore Museum of Art; Museum of Fine Arts, Boston; Cleveland Museum of Art; Fine Arts Gallery, San Diego; The Museum of Modern Art, N.Y.C.; Phillips Collection, Washington, D.C.

Chavez, Eduardo. b.1917, Wagonmound, New Mexico. Studied at the Colorado Springs Fine Arts Center. Painted murals commissioned by Works Progress Administration

(WPA/FAP) for post offices of Glenwood Springs, Colo., 1937; Geneva, Nebr., c.1938; The Center, Texas, 1941; West High School, Denver, Colo., 1939; Recreation Hall, Fort Warren, Wyo.,1943. Taught at The Art Students League, N.Y.C., 1954, 1955–58; Colorado College, Colorado Springs, 1959; Syracuse University, N.Y., 1960–61; Dutchess Community College, Poughkeepsie, N.Y., 1963. Appointed artist in residence, Huntington Fine Arts Gallery, W.Va., 1967; Ogden Utah City School System, 1968. Awarded Louis Comfort Tiffany Award, 1948; Pepsi-Cola Prize for American Painting, 1947; Hermine Kleinert Award, 1952; Childe Hassam Purchase Award, 1952. Solo exhibitions: Denver Art Museum, 1937; Associated American Artists, N.Y.C., 1948, 1949; Ganso Gallery, N.Y.C., 1950–54; Museum of New Mexico, Santa Fe, 1954; American Museum of Natural History, N.Y.C., 1955; Alexander Rabow Gallery, San Francisco, 1955; John Heller Gallery, N.Y.C., 1956, 1960; Anne Werbe Gallery, Detroit, 1957; New York State College for Teachers, Albany, 1960; Lowe Art Center, Syracuse University, N.Y., 1961; Art Collector's Place, N.Y.C., 1965. Collections: Columbus Museum of Art; Grand Rapids Museum of Art; Hirshhorn Museum and Sculpture Garden, Washington, D.C.; Library of Congress, Washington, D.C.; The Museum of Modern Art, N.Y.C.; Museum of New Mexico, Santa Fe; Newark Museum of Art, N.J.; University of Minnesota, Minneapolis.

Chávez Morado, José. b. 1909, Guanajuato, Mexico. Studied painting at Chouinard School of Art, Los Angeles, 1930; printmaking and painting at La Esmeralda, Mexico City, 1931. Taught drawing in elementary and secondary schools in Mexico, 1933–37. Joined LEAR (League of Revolutionary Writers and Artists), founded in 1933 by Luis Arenal, Xavier Guerrer, Leopoldo Méndez, and others. Member of the Taller de Gráfica Popular, 1938–41. Exhibitions: San Antonio Museum of Art, 1959. Collections: Colorado Springs Fine Arts Center; Museum of Fine Arts, Boston; Philadelphia Museum of Art.

Clark, Lygia. 1920–1988. b. Belo Horizonte, Brazil. Studied under Robert Burle Marx, in Rio de Janeiro and under Fernand Léger and Arpad Szenes, in Paris, 1950–52. Member of the Neo-Concrete movement. Taught at the Sorbonne, Paris, 1970–75. Solo exhibitions: Louise Alexander Gallery, N.Y.C., 1963. Ten-year retrospective mounted at the Venice Biennale, 1968. Group exhibitions: The Museum of Modern Art, N.Y.C., 1960; Pan American Union, Washington, D.C., 1962; Pepsi-Cola Gallery, N.Y.C., 1963; *Art of Latin America since Independence*, Yale University, New Haven, and University of Texas, Austin, 1966. Collection: The Museum of Modern Art, N.Y.C.

Colón-Morales, Rafael. b. 1941, Trujillo Alto, P.R. Resided in N.Y.C. since 1970. Received scholarship to study art at the Universidad de Puerto Rico, (B.F.A., 1964). Studied at American University, Washington, D.C., 1965–1966. Granted scholarship to study at Academia de San Fernando, Madrid, 1966–67. Member, Borinquen 12 group (artist's cooperative active in Puerto Rico), 1967–69. Emigrated to N.Y.C., 1970. Instructor, Universidad de Puerto Rico, Rio Piedras, 1968–70; Brooklyn Community College, N.Y., 1972–76; State University of New York, Albany, 1972–76; School of Art, El Museo del Barrio, N.Y.C., 1978–81. Appointed curator, El Museo del Barrio, N.Y.C., 1984. Solo exhibitions: Ateneo Puertorriqueño, San Juan, 1962; Universidad de Puerto Rico, San Juan, 1963; First Federal Gallery, N.Y.C., 1964; Instituto de Cultura Puertorriqueña, San Juan, 1965; Galería Santiago, San Juan, 1968; Colegio Regional de Avecibo, 1969. Group exhibitions: Universidad de Puerto Rico, 1961. Collections: Ateneo Puertorriqueño, San Juan; El Museo del Barrio, N.Y.C.; Instituto de Cultura Puertorriqueña, San Juan; Museo de Arte de Ponce, P.R.; Museum of Modern Art of Latin America, Washington, D.C.; Universidad de Puerto Rico, San Juan.

Costa, Eduardo. b. 1940, Buenos Aires. Studied at the Universidad Nacional de Buenos Aires, 1965. Appointed literacy advisor to Center for Inter-American Relations, N.Y.C., 1968. Taught at City University of New York, N.Y.C., 1969–71. Produced intermedia collaboration with John Perreault, 1969, N.Y.C. Participated in live and taped

events at the Poetry Center, N.Y.C., Yale University and WRVR Radio, N.Y.C., 1966–69; Center for Inter-American Relations, N.Y.C., (*Fashion Show Poetry Event*), 1969; Hunter College, N.Y.C., (*Theater Absences*), 1969; Wadsworth Atheneum, Hartford, Conn., (Scott Burton's *4 Theater Pieces*), 1970. Collection: Metropolitan Museum of Art, N.Y.C.

Covarrubias, Miguel. 1904–57. b. Mexico City. Moved to N.Y.C., 1923. Illustrator for *Vanity Fair*, *Fortune*, and *Harper's Bazaar*, 1923. Published *Negro Drawings*, 1929; *The Prince of Wales and Other Famous Americans*, 1926; *The Eagle, the Jaguar, and the Serpent*, 1937. Traveled to Bali on a John Simon Guggenheim Memorial Fellowship, 1937. Curated modern section of *Twenty Centuries of Mexican Art*, The Museum of Modern Art, N.Y.C., 1940. Painted murals for the World's Fair, San Francisco, 1940; Museum of Natural History, N.Y.C., c. 1950. Group exhibitions: *Art of Latin America since Independence*, Yale University, New Haven, and University of Texas, Austin, 1966. Collections: Cleveland Museum of Art; Museum of Fine Arts, Boston; The Museum of Modern Art, N.Y.C.; Philadelphia Museum of Art; Seattle Art Museum.

Cravo, Mário Junior. b.1923, Salvador, Brazil. Studied sculpture under Humberto Cozzo, Rio de Janeiro, 1946; under Ivan Mestrovic at Syracuse University, N.Y., 1947–49. Solo exhibitions: Norlyst Gallery, N.Y.C., 1949; *Contemporary Art of Latin America*, Institute of Contemporary Arts, Washington, D.C., 1965; Brazilian Embassy, Washington, D.C., 1965. Group exhibitions: *Art of Latin America since Independence*, Yale University, New Haven, and University of Texas, Austin, 1966. Collections: The Museum of Modern Art, N.Y.C.; Walker Art Center, Minneapolis.

Cruz-Diez, Carlos. b.1923, Caracas. Resided in France since 1960. Studied at the Escuela de Artes Plásticas y Aplicadas Cristóbal Rojas, Caracas, 1939–46. Artistic director, McCann-Erickson Publicity Agency, N.Y.C., 1946–51. Founded workshop for graphics and industrial design, Caracas, 1957. Taught at Escuela de Bellas Artes, Caracas, and the Universidad Central de Venezuela, Caracas, 1958–60. Group exhibitions: *Pittsburgh International*, Carnegie Institute, 1961; *The Responsive Eye*, The Museum of Modern Art, N.Y.C., 1965; *Latin American Art: 1931–1966*, The Museum of Modern Art , N.Y.C., 1967. Collections: Hirshhorn Museum and Sculpture Garden, Washington, D.C.; Museum of Contemporary Art, Chicago; The Museum of Modern Art, N.Y.C.; Museum of Modern Art of Latin America, Washington, D.C.; Rhode Island School of Design, Providence.

Cuevas, José Luis. b. 1932, Mexico City. Studied at La Esmeralda, Mexico City, 1944. Invited by the Ford Foundation to work at the Tamarind Lithography Workshop, Los Angeles, 1965. Published lithographs in *Cuevas-Chareton*, 1966. Visiting artist, Philadelphia Museum School of Art, 1957–58; San Jose State College School of Art, 1969–70. Solo exhibitions: Pan American Union, Washington, D.C., 1954; Roland de Aenlle Gallery, N.Y.C., 1957, 1959; Grass Gallery, Washington, D.C., 1957; David Herbert Gallery, 1960, 1962; Silvan Simons Gallery, 1960, 1962, 1964, 1966; Philadelphia Museum of Art, 1960; Fort Worth Art Center, 1960; Santa Barbara Museum, 1961; University of Texas, Austin, 1961; Occidental College, Los Angeles, 1962; Andrew Morris Gallery, N.Y.C., 1963; Grace Borgenicht Gallery, N.Y.C., 1965, 1967; Munson-Williams-Proctor Institute, Utica, N.Y., 1965. Group exhibitions: *Gulf-Caribbean Art*, Museum of Fine Arts, Houston, 1956; *Pittsburgh International*, Carnegie Institute, 1959; The Museum of Modern Art, 1960; *The Emergent Decade*, Solomon R. Guggenheim Museum, and Cornell University, Ithaca, N.Y., 1965; *Art of Latin America since Independence*, Yale University, New Haven, and University of Texas, Austin, 1966; Center for Inter-American Relations, N.Y.C., 1969; Delaware Art Center, Wilmington, 1969. Collections: Art Institute of Chicago; The Brooklyn Museum, N.Y.; Dallas Museum of Art; Milwaukee Art Center; The Museum of Modern Art, N.Y.C.; Museum of Modern Art of Latin America, Washington, D.C.; Philadelphia Museum of Art; Phillips Collection, Washington, D.C.; Santa Barbara Museum; Walker Art Center, Minneapolis.

da Motta e Silva, Djanira. b. 1914, São Paulo. Self-taught painter. Visited U.S., 1945–46. Solo exhibitions: New School for Social Research, 1945; Pan American Union, 1946; Solomon R. Guggenheim Museum, N.Y.C., 1958.

Davidovich, Jaime. b. 1937, Buenos Aires. Resided in U.S. since 1963; U.S. citizen since 1968. Studied at Escuela Nacional de Bellas Artes, Buenos Aires, 1954–58; Universidad de la República Oriental del Uruguay, Montevideo, (M.F.A., 1961); School of Visual Arts, N.Y.C., 1963. Argentine representative in the International Congress of Plastic Arts, United Nations, N.Y.C., 1965; Argentine representative to the U. S. for the Art Center of the Instituto Torcuato di Tella, of Buenos Aires. Solo exhibitions: Art Institute, Canton, Ohio, 1963; Spectrum Gallery, N.Y.C., 1965, 1966, 1967, 1968. Collections: Akron Art Institute; Dayton Art Institute; Everson Museum of Art, Syracuse, N.Y.

de Castro, Amilcar. b. 1920, Minas Gerais, Brazil. Studied design and painting at Escola Parque, Belo Horizonte, Brazil, 1948–50. Moved to Rio de Janeiro, and joined Neo-Concrete movement, 1952. Designed newspaper *Jornal do Brasil* and with Ferreira Gullar published Neo-Concrete manifesto. Awarded John Simon Guggenheim Memorial Fellowship, 1965, 1968, 1970. Lived in New Jersey, 1968–71. Exhibitions: Kornblee Gallery, N.Y.C., 1969; New York University, N.Y.C., 1969. Collections: Kornblee Gallery, N.Y.C.; Palm Beach Museum, Fla.

Deira, Ernesto. b. 1928, Buenos Aires. Studied law at Universidad Nacional de Buenos Aires (J.D., 1950); painting under Leopoldo Torres Aguero and Leonardo Presas in Buenos Aires, 1954–61. Traveled to Europe, 1953. Awarded scholarship from Argentine National Fund for the Arts to travel in Europe, 1962. Received Fullbright Fellowship, 1967. Appointed guest professor of painting, Cornell University, Ithaca, N.Y., 1969. Solo exhibitions: Pan American Union, Washington, D.C., 1964. Group exhibitions: *The Emergent Decade*, Solomon R. Guggenheim Museum, N.Y.C., and Cornell University, Ithaca, N.Y., 1965; *New Art of Argentina*, Walker Art Center, Minneapolis, 1964; Museum of Art, Rhode Island School of Design, Providence, 1965; San Francisco Museum of Art, 1966; *Art of Latin America since Independence*, Yale University, New Haven, and University of Texas, Austin, 1966; La Jolla Museum of Art, Calif., 1966; Delaware Art Center, Wilmington, 1968. Collections: Esso Collection, Coral Gables, Fla.; Solomon R. Guggenheim Museum, N.Y.C.; The Museum of Modern Art, N.Y.C.; Rhode Island School of Design, Providence; Museum of Modern Art of Latin America, Washington, D.C.

Delano, Irene. 1919–1982. b. Detroit. Studied at Pennsylvania Academy of the Fine Arts, Philadelphia, 1933–37. Assisted Anton Refregier in mural for World's Fair, N.Y.C., 1939. Visited Puerto Rico with her husband Jack Delano (Farm Security Administration photographer), 1946. Returned to Puerto Rico to establish Motion-Picture and Graphic Arts Workshop of Commission of Public Recreation, 1946 (Workshop became part of the Division of Community Education of Department of Education of Puerto Rico, 1949). Director, Division of Community Education, 1949–52. With Félix Bonilla-Norat trained Puerto Rican artists in serigraphic techniques, 1949–52. Independent designer, San Juan, 1952–70. Editor, *Que Pasa* magazine, 1970–82. Awarded American Institute of Graphic Arts prize, 1948. Collections: American Institute of Graphic Arts, N.Y.C.; Brooklyn Art Books, N.Y.; Division of Community Education, San Juan; UNESCO, N.Y.C.

de la Vega, Jorge Luis. 1930–1971, b. Buenos Aires. Studied architecture at Universidad Nacional de Buenos Aires. Received National Fund for the Arts Fellowship, 1962. Visited France, Belgium, Germany, Italy, the Netherlands, Spain, Switzerland, and England, 1962. Lived in U.S., 1965–67. Solo exhibitions: Pan American Union, Washington, D.C., 1963. Group exhibitions: Pan American Union, Washington, D.C., 1962; *Pittsburgh International*, Carnegie Institute, 1964; *New Art of Argentina*, Walker Art Center, Minneapolis, 1964; *The Emergent Decade*, Solomon R. Guggenheim Museum, N.Y.C., and Cornell University, Ithaca, N.Y., 1965; *Art of Latin America since Independence*, Yale University, New Haven, and University of Texas, Austin, 1966. Collections: Solomon R. Guggenheim Museum, N.Y.C.; The Museum of Modern Art, N.Y.C.; Museum of Modern Art of Latin America, Washington, D.C.; Oakland Museum, Calif.; Rhode Island School of Design, Providence.

Delgado, Osiris. b. 1920, Humacao, P.R. Studied at Universita degli Studi, Florence, 1937–39; under Maurice de Vlaminck in Paris, 1939; under Manuel Benedeto at Academia de San Fernando, Madrid, 1940; under Yasuo Kuniyoshi at The Art Students League, N.Y.C., 1941. Studied at Universidad de Puerto Rico (B.A., 1951); Universidad Centrale de Madrid (Ph.d., 1961). Director of fine arts department, Universidad de Puerto Rico, 1957–64. Director of Museo de Antropología, Historia y Arte, Universidad de Puerto Rico, 1964–75. Collections: Colegio de Agricultura y Artes Mecánicas, Mayaguez, P.R.; Museo de Antropología Historia y Arte, San Juan; Museo de Arte de Ponce, P.R.

de Szyszlo, Fernando. b. 1925, Lima. Studied at Escuela de Arte, Universidad Católica, Lima, 1944–46. Visited U.S., 1953. Lived in Paris and Florence, 1949–55. Taught at Escuela de Arte, Universidad Católica, Lima, 1957–76. Consultant to Visual Arts Division, Pan American Union, Washington, D.C., 1957–60. Artist-in-residence, Cornell University, Ithaca, N.Y.,1962; Yale University, New Haven, 1966. Solo exhibitions: Pan American Union, Washington, D.C., 1953; Cornell University, Ithaca, N.Y., 1962. Group exhibitions: *Pittsburgh International*, Carnegie Institute, 1958; *The United States Collects Latin American Art*, Art Institute of Chicago, 1959; *Latin America: New Departures*, Institute of Contemporary Art, Boston, 1961; Solomon R, Guggenheim Museum, N.Y.C., 1963; *The Emergent Decade*, Solomon R. Guggenheim Museum, N.Y.C, and Cornell University, Ithaca, N.Y., 1965; *Art of Latin America since Independence*, Yale University, New Haven, and University of Texas, Austin, 1966. Collections: Cornell University, Ithaca, N.Y.; Dallas Museum of Fine Arts; Solomon R. Guggenheim Museum, N.Y.C.; Museo de Arte de Ponce, P.R.; The Museum of Modern Art, N.Y.C.; Museum of Modern Art of Latin America, Washington, D.C.; University of Texas, Austin.

Dias, Antonio. b. 1944, Paraiba, Brazil. Resided in Milan since 1968. Lived and worked in Rio de Janeiro, 1960–66. Received painting scholarship to study in Paris, 1966–67. Visited N.Y.C., 1970. Awarded John Simon Guggenheim Memorial Fellowship, 1971. Group exhibitions: Kiko Galleries, Houston, 1966, 1970; Felix Landau Gallery, Los Angeles, 1970; Dezon-Zacks Gallery, Chicago, 1970; Bonino Gallery, N.Y.C., 1970; Solomon R. Guggenheim Museum, N.Y.C., 1970. Collections: The Museum of Modern Art, N.Y.C.; Window South, Palo Alto, Calif.

Dosamantes, Francisco. b. 1911, Mexico City. Studied at La Esmeralda, Mexico City. Joined *30-30* (painter's collective), Mexico City, 1928. Worked as a printmaker in Emilio Amero's lithography workshop at La Esmeralda, c.1930. Member of LEAR (League of Revolutionary Painters and Sculptors), 1934–38. Lived in N.Y.C., 1940s. Solo exhibition: A.C.A. Gallery, N.Y.C., 1946. Group exhibitions: International Exposition of N.Y.C., 1940; Philadelphia Arts Alliance, 1948; Pan American Union, Washington, D.C., 1948; *Art of Latin America since Independence*, Yale University, New Haven, and University of Texas, Austin, 1966. Collections: Art Institute of Chicago; Library of Congress, Washington, D.C.; Los Angeles County Museum of Art; Metropolitan Museum of Art, N.Y.C.; Museum of Fine Arts, Boston; The Museum of Modern Art, N.Y.C.; New York Public Library, N.Y.C.; Philadelphia Museum of Art; San Francisco Museum of Modern Art.

Downey, Juan. b. 1940, Santiago. Resided in U.S. since 1965. Studied architecture at the Universidad Católica de Santiago, Chile (B.A., 1964); engraving at Nemesio Antúnez's workshop, Santiago, 1957–61; under S.W. Hayter, in Paris, 1963–65; Pratt Institute, N.Y.C., 1965–69. Presently, professor of architecture, Pratt Institute, N.Y.C. Awarded John Simon Guggenheim Memorial Fellowship, 1971, 1976. Solo exhibitions: Pan American Union, Washington, D.C., 1965; Judson Memorial Church Gallery, N.Y.C., 1966; Howard Wise Gallery, N.Y.C., 1970. Group exhibitions: Martha Jackson Gallery, N.Y.C., 1967; The Brooklyn Museum, N.Y., 1968; Corcoran Gallery of Art, Washington, D.C., 1969. Collections: The Art Museum, Princeton University, N.J.; Associated American Artists, N.Y.C.; Cape May Art Center, N.J.; Museum of Modern Art of Latin America, Washington, D.C.

Felguérez, Manuel. b. 1928, Zacatecas, Mexico. Studied at Academia de San Carlos and La Esmeralda, Mexico City, 1948; under Osip Zadkine in Paris, 1949. Visiting artist at Cornell University, Ithaca, N.Y., 1966. Solo exhibitions: Bertha Shaeffer Gallery, N.Y.C., 1959, 1960; Pan American Union, Washington, D.C., 1960. Group exhibitions: *Gulf-Caribbean Art*, Houston Museum of Fine Arts, 1956; The Brooklyn Museum, N.Y., 1958; World's Fair, Seattle, 1962; Gallery of Fine Arts, San Diego, 1966; The Portland Art Museum, 1966; University of Nebraska, Lincoln, 1966; University of Texas, Austin, 1966; *Hemisfair*, San Antonio, 1968.

Fernández, Agustin. b. 1928, Havana. Resided in U.S. since 1972. Studied at Academia de San Alejandro, Havana (B.A., 1950); under George Grosz and Yasuo Kuniyoshi at The Art Students League, N.Y.C., 1949–50; philosophy at the Universidad de Habana, 1950–52. Traveled to Europe, 1952. Studied at the Academia de San Fernando, Madrid, 1953. Awarded Cuban Government travel scholarship, 1959. Lived in France, 1959–68; San Juan, P.R., 1968–72. Solo exhibitions: Pan American Union, Washington, D.C., 1954; Duveen Graham Gallery, N.Y.C., 1956; Condon Riley Gallery, N.Y.C., 1958; Bodley Gallery, N.Y.C., 1959. Group exhibitions: *The United States Collects Latin American Art*, Art Institute of Chicago, 1959; *Latin American Art: 1931–1966*, The Museum of Modern Art, N.Y.C., 1967. Collections: The Detroit Institute of Arts; Library of Congress, Washington, D.C.; The Museum of Modern Art, N.Y.C.; New York Public Library, N.Y.C.; Yale University, New Haven.

Fernández Muro, José Antonio. b. 1920, Madrid. Moved to Argentina, 1938. Lived in Madrid and Paris, 1948–50. Traveled in Europe and United States on a UNESCO fellowship, 1957–58. Awarded John Simon Guggenheim Memorial Fellowship, 1960. Resided in U.S., 1962–70. Solo exhibitions: Pan American Union, Washington, D.C., 1957; Andrew Morris Gallery, N.Y.C., 1963; Bonino Gallery, N.Y.C., 1965, 1967. Group exhibitions: J. L. Hudson Gallery, Detroit, 1958; *Pittsburgh International*, Carnegie Institute, 1958; *The United States Collects Latin American Art*, Art Institute of Chicago, 1959; *South American Art Today*, Dallas Museum of Fine Arts, 1959; Solomon R. Guggenheim Museum, N.Y.C., 1960; *Latin America: New Departures*, Institute of Contemporary Art, Boston, 1961; Oakland Art Museum, 1964; *Magnet: New York*, Bonino Gallery, N.Y.C., 1964; University of Illinois, Urbana, 1965; *The Emergent Decade*, Solomon R. Guggenheim Museum, N.Y.C. and Cornell University, Ithaca, N.Y., 1965; *Art of Latin America since Independence*, Yale University, New Haven, and University of Texas, Austin, 1966; Herron Museum of Art, Indianapolis, 1966; New School for Social Research, N.Y.C., 1966; *Latin American Art: 1931–1966*, The Museum of Modern Art, N.Y.C., 1967. Collections: Dallas Museum of Fine Arts; The Ford Foundation, N.Y.C.; Solomon R. Guggenheim Museum, N.Y.C.; Massachusetts Institute of Technology, Cambridge, Mass.; The Museum of Modern Art, N.Y.C.; Museum of Modern Art of Latin America, Washington, D.C.; Oakland Art Museum, Calif.

Ferrer, Rafael. b. 1933, San Juan, P.R. Resided in U.S. since 1966. Studied music at Syracuse University, N.Y., 1951; under Eugenio Fernández Granell at Universidad de Puerto Rico, 1953. Returned to Puerto Rico, 1960. Solo exhibitions: Universidad de Puerto Rico, Mayagüez, 1964; Pan American Union, Washington, D.C., 1966; Leo Castelli

Gallery, N.Y.C., 1968, 1970; Eastern Connecticut State College, Hartford, 1969; Philadelphia Museum of Art, 1970; University of Hartford, Conn., 1970. Group exhibitions: Universidad de Puerto Rico, 1961, 1964; Pennsylvania Academy of the Fine Arts, Philadelphia, 1967; Martha Jackson Gallery, N.Y.C., 1967; University of Pennsylvania, Philadelphia, 1968; Universidad de Puerto Rico, Mayagüez, 1968, 1969; Whitney Museum of American Art, 1969, 1970; *Information*, The Museum of Modern Art, N.Y.C., 1970; Finch College of Art, N.Y.C., 1970; Oberlin College, Ohio, 1970; Contemporary Arts Center, Cincinnati, 1970. Collections: Albright-Knox Art Gallery, Buffalo, N.Y.; Chase Manhattan Bank, N.Y.C.; El Museo del Barrio, N.Y.C.; Indianapolis Museum of Art; Madison Art Center, Wis.; Metropolitan Museum of Art, N.Y.C.; University of North Carolina, Chapel Hill; Museo de Arte de Ponce, P.R.; Museum of Contemporary Art, Chicago; The Museum of Modern Art, N.Y.C.; New York State Facilities Corporation, N.Y.C.; Pasadena Museum of Art, Calif.; Philadelphia Museum; Prudential Insurance Company of America, Newark, N.J.; Universidad de Puerto Rico, San Juan; Vassar College Art Gallery, Poughkeepsie, N.Y.; Virginia Museum of Fine Arts, Richmond; Whitney Museum of American Art, N.Y.C.

Figari, Pedro. 1861–1938. b. Montevideo. Founded Sociedad Amigos del Arte, Buenos Aires. Traveled in Europe as diplomatic representative of Uruguay. Lived in Paris, 1925–34. Solo exhibitions: Knoedler Gallery, N.Y.C., 1946; Council for Inter-American Cooperation, N.Y.C., and Organization of American States, Washington, D.C. (posthumous retrospective), 1946. Group exhibitions: *Olympic Exhibition*, Los Angeles, 1932; Pan-American Fair, N.Y.C., 1942; *The Latin American Collection of the Museum of Modern Art*, N.Y.C., 1943; San Francisco Museum of Art, 1945; Knoedler Gallery, N.Y.C.; Pan American Union, Washington, D.C.; Vassar College, Poughkeepsie, N.Y.; Baltimore Museum of Art; Detroit Institute of Arts; Walker Art Center, Minneapolis; Nelson Gallery of Art, Kansas City, Mo.; Seattle Art Museum; Pasadena Museum; and Isaac Delgado Museum, New Orleans, 1946–48; *Art of Latin America since Independence*, Yale University, New Haven, and University of Texas, Austin, 1966. Collections: CDS Gallery, N.Y.C.; Museum of Fine Arts, Houston; Mary Anne Martin Fine Art, N.Y.C.; The Museum of Modern Art, N.Y.C.; Museum of Modern Art of Latin America, Washington, D.C.; National Cowboy Hall of Fame, Oklahoma City.

Fonseca, Gonzalo. b.1922, Montevideo. Resided in N.Y.C. since 1957. Studied architecture at Universidad de la República Oriental del Uruguay, 1939–41. Studied painting under Joaquín Torres-García, Montevideo, 1942–49. Traveled to Middle East, 1950–52. Lived in Paris, 1952–57. Designed sculptural projects for New School for Social Research, N.Y.C., 1959–61; Reston, Va., 1963–64; PS 46, N.Y.C.; Bronx, N.Y.,1968; Alza Laboratory, Palo Alto, Calif., 1970. Solo exhibitions: Portland Art Museum, 1962–63. Collection: The Brooklyn Museum, N.Y.

Fontana, Lucio. 1899–1968. b. Rosario de Santa Fe, Argentina. Family moved to Milan, 1905. Attended Instituto Tecnico Carlo Catteneo, Milan, 1914–15. Returned to Rosario de Santa Fe to work as sculptor in father's studio, 1922–24. Studied sculpture under Adolfo Wildt at Accademia di Brera, Milan, 1928. Lived in Milan, 1928–34; Paris, 1934–36. Joined the Abstraction-Création group, 1934. Returned to Argentina, 1939–47. With Jorge Romero Brest, established Academia Altamira, Buenos Aires, 1946. Author of first and third Spatialist manifestos, Milan, 1947, 1950. Awarded International Grand Prize for Painting, Venice Biennale, 1966. Solo exhibitions: Martha Jackson Gallery, N.Y.C., 1961, 1970; Wadsworth Atheneum, Hartford, Conn., 1961; Walker Art Center, Minneapolis, 1966; Marlborough Gallery, N.Y.C., 1968; Solomon R. Guggenheim Museum, N.Y.C. (posthumous retrospective), 1977. Group exhibitions: The Museum of Modern Art, N.Y.C., 1949; *Latin American Art: 1931–1966*, The Museum of Modern Art , N.Y.C., 1967. Collections: Aquavella Galleries, N.Y.C.; Solomon R. Guggenheim Museum, N.Y.C.; Hirshhorn Museum and Sculpture Garden, Washington, D.C.; The Museum of Modern Art, N.Y.C.; Washington University, St. Louis, Mo.

Forner, Raquel. b. 1902, Buenos Aires. Studied painting at Academia Nacional de Bellas Artes, Buenos Aires; under Emile Othon Friesz, Paris, 1929–30. Founded Cursos Libres de Arte Plastíco (first private academy of modern art in Argentina) with Alfredo Guttero, Pedro Dominguez, and Neira and Alfred Bigatti, 1932. Solo exhibitions: Pan American Union, Washington, D.C. 1957; Roland de Aenlle Gallery, N.Y.C.,1958. Group exhibitions: *Pittsburgh International*, Carnegie Institute, 1935, 1958, 1964, 1967; National Gallery of Art, Washington, D.C., 1958; International Arts Festival, N.Y.C., 1958; *South American Art Today*, Dallas Museum of Fine Arts, 1959; Widger Gallery of Modern Art, Washington, D.C., 1961; Duke University, Durham, N.C., 1963; *Art of Latin America since Independence*, Yale University, New Haven, and University of Texas, Austin, 1966. Collections: The Bronx Museum of the Arts, N.Y.; Dallas Museum of Fine Arts; The Museum of Modern Art, N.Y.C.; Museum of Modern Art of Latin America, Washington, D.C.; Walker Art Center, Minneapolis.

Frasconi, Antonio. b. 1919, Buenos Aires. Moved to Montevideo during childhood. Resided in U.S. since 1946. Attended Circulo de Bellas Artes, Montevideo, and architecture school. Worked as political cartoonist and graphic illustrator since 1938. Studied at The Art Students League, N.Y.C., 1945. Moved to Santa Barbara, Calif., 1946. Received scholarship from New School for Social Research to study mural painting, 1946. Illustrated *Aesop's Fables* (The Museum of Modern Art, N.Y.C.,1955). Received scholarship to study lithography at the Tamarind Workshop, Calif., 1962. Designed a U.S. postage stamp, 1963. Solo exhibitions: Santa Barbara, Calif., 1946; The Brooklyn Museum, N.Y., 1946, 1964; Cleveland Museum of Art, 1952 (retrospective exhibition; traveled to 20 North American cities); Baltimore Museum of Art, 1963. Group exhibitions: *Art of Latin America since Independence*, Yale University, New Haven, and University of Texas, Austin, 1966. Metropolitan Museum of Art, N.Y.C.

Friedeberg, Pedro. b. 1937, Florence, Italy. Family moved to Mexico, 1940. Studied at the Art Institute of Boston, 1953–54; architecture under Mathias Goeritz, Universidad Iberoamericana, Mexico City, 1958–61. Cofounded Los Hartos group with Mathias Goeritz and José Luis Cuevas, 1961. Solo exhibitions: Carstairs Gallery, N.Y.C., 1962; Pan American Union, Washington, D.C., 1963; Byron Gallery, N.Y.C., 1964, 1966, 1969; Kiko Gallery, Houston, 1968. Group exhibitions: Museum of Contemporary Crafts, N.Y.C.,1964; *Hemisfair*, San Antonio, 1968.

García, Antonio. b. 1901, Monterrey, Mexico. Family moved to San Diego, Texas, c.1911. Studied at Art Institute of Chicago, 1927–30. Taught art at Del Mar College, Corpus Christi, Tex., c. 1950–70. Illustrator of books and magazines. Painted murals under the auspices of WPA/FAP at La Bahia Mission, Goliad, Texas; Sacred Heart Church and Minor Seminary, Corpus Christi, Texas; San Diego (Texas) High School, c.1930; National Scapular Center, Aylesford, Ill.; Sacred Heart Church, Corpus Christi (*Virgin de Guadalupe*), 1946–47. Exhibitions: *Texas Centennial Celebration*, Corpus Christi, 1936.

García, Rupert. b. 1944, French Camp, Calif. Studied at Stockton College, Calif., (A.A., 1962); painting and printmaking, San Francisco State University (B.A., 1968; M.A., 1970); art history, University of California, Berkeley, (M.A., 1981). Taught at San Francisco State University, San Francisco Art Institute, and University of California, Berkeley, 1969–86. Received California Arts Council artist-in-residence grant, 1986; San Francisco Arts Commission Award, 1986. Solo exhibitions: Oakland Museum, Calif., 1970; Artes 6, San Francisco, 1970. Group exhibitions: San Francisco Museum of Art, 1970; Oakland Museum, Calif., 1970. Collections: University of California, Berkeley; Galerie de la Raza, San Francisco; University of Minnesota, Minneapolis; National Museum of American Art, Washington, D.C.; Oakland Museum, Calif.; San Francisco Museum of Modern Art; Sonoma State University, Calif.

Gego. b. 1912, Hamburg, Germany. Daughter of Venezuelan immigrants. Studied architecture at Universität Stuttgart, c. 1932. Associate professor, Universidad Central de Venezuela, Caracas, 1958–67. Taught sculpture, at Escuela de Artes Plásticas y Aplicadas Cristóbal Rojas, Caracas, and Universidad Central de Venezuela, Caracas. Visited U.S. on travel grant, 1958–59. Taught at Instituto de Diseño, Caracas since 1964. Awarded Tamarind Lithography Workshop grant, Los Angeles, 1966. Solo exhibitions: Center for Inter-American Relations, N.Y.C., 1969. Group exhibitions: David Herbert Gallery, N.Y.C., 1960; Betty Parsons Gallery, N.Y.C., 1960; The Museum of Modern Art, N.Y.C., 1960; St. Paul Art Center, Minn., 1963; Washington Square Gallery, N.Y.C., 1964; *The Responsive Eye*, The Museum of Modern Art, N.Y.C., 1965; *Art of Latin America since Independence*, Yale University, New Haven, and University of Texas, Austin, 1966; *Latin American Art: 1931–1966*, The Museum of Modern Art, N.Y.C., 1967; Whitney Museum of American Art, N.Y.C., 1969; Graphics Gallery, San Francisco, 1970. Collections: Amon Carter Museum, Fort Worth, Tex.; Art Institute of Chicago; Braniff Airlines, Dallas; California State University, San Luis Obispo; Greenwald Graphic Art Collection, Los Angeles; University of Iowa, Ames; La Jolla Museum of Art, Calif.; Library of Congress, Washington, D.C.; New York Public Library, N.Y.C.; Pasedena Museum, Calif.; San Diego Museum, Calif.; University of Texas, Austin.

Geiger, Anna Bella. b. 1933, Rio de Janeiro. Studied etching under Fayga Ostrower and art history under Hannah Levy at Metropolitan Museum of Art, N.Y.C., 1953–55. Lived in N.Y.C., c.1968. Solo exhibitions: European Gallery, N.Y.C., 1963; Columbia University, N.Y.C., 1968. Collections: Franklin Furnace Archive, N.Y.C.; The Museum of Modern Art, N.Y.C.; New York Public Library, N.Y.C.

Gerchman, Rubens. b. 1942, Rio de Janeiro. Studied at Liceu de Artes e Ofícios, Rio de Janeiro, 1958; Escola Nacional de Belas Artes, Rio de Janeiro, 1961. Graphic artist for various magazines and newspapers, Rio de Janeiro, 1958–66. Visited the U.S., 1965. Lived in N.Y.C., 1968–73. Awarded John Simon Guggenheim Memorial Fellowship, 1978. Made films: *Hermetic Triumph* and *Environvision*. Solo exhibition: Brazilian Trade Bureau, N.Y.C., 1968. Group exhibitions: *Fashion Show Poetry Event*, Center for Inter-American Relations, N.Y.C., 1969. Collection: Heller Gallery, N.Y.C.

Gerzso, Gunther. b. 1915, Mexico City. Studied in Mexico and Switzerland, 1925–31. Designed theater sets and costumes, Mexico, 1931–34. Lived in U.S., 1936–42. Studied theater design and cinematography at Cleveland Playhouse, Ohio; appointed staff set designer of playhouse, 1936. Began painting, 1939. Art director for Mexican, American, and French film directors, including Luis Buñuel, John Ford, and Yves Allegret, Mexico, 1942–65. Solo exhibitions: Phoenix Art Museum, 1970. Group exhibitions: Cleveland Museum of Art, 1939; *Pittsburgh International*, Carnegie Institute, 1952; *Gulf-Caribbean Art*, Museum of Fine Arts, Houston, 1956; University of Michigan, Ann Arbor, 1959; Fort Worth Art Center, 1959; Birmingham Museum of Art, Ala., 1965; Phoenix Art Museum, 1965; *Art of Latin America since Independence*, Yale University, New Haven, and University of Texas, Austin, 1966. Collections: Agency for the Performing Arts, N.Y.C.; Art of the Americas Collection, N.Y.C.; The Museum of Modern Art, N.Y.C.; Museum of Modern Art of Latin America, Washington, D.C.; University of Texas, Austin.

Goeritz, Mathias. b. 1919, Danzig, Poland. Studied philosophy in Berlin. Began painting, 1934; sculpture, 1947. Traveled to Spanish Morocco, c. 1939. Lived in Spain, 1942–49. Emigrated to Mexico, 1948. Founder of four art galleries in Guadalajara and Jalisco. Constructed experimental museum El Eco with Carlos Mérida and Rufino Tamayo, Mexico City, 1953. Wrote *Please Stop*, manifesto that inspired founding of Los Hartos (artist's group) by Pedro Friedeberg and José Luis Cuevas, 1960. Solo exhibitions: Carstairs Gallery, N.Y.C., 1956, 1960, 1962. Group exhibitions: *Gulf-Caribbean Art*, Museum of Fine Arts, Houston, 1956; The Brooklyn Museum, N.Y., 1959; Martha Jackson Gallery, N.Y.C., 1960; University of Illinois, Urbana, 1961; The Museum of Modern Art, N.Y.C., 1961; *Pittsburgh International*, Carnegie Institute, 1961–62. Collections: University of Arizona, Tucson; Lannan Foundation, Palm Beach, Fla.; F. Olsen Foundation, Guilford, Conn.

Gómez-Quiroz, Juan. b. 1939, Santiago. Resided in N.Y.C. since 1962. Studied at Universidad de Chile, Santiago, 1961–62. Awarded Fullbright Fellowship to study at Rhode Island School of Design, Providence, 1962–63, and Yale University, New Haven, 1963–64; Pan-American Fellowship to study at Pratt Graphic Arts Center, N.Y.C., 1964–65; John Simon Guggenheim Memorial Fellowship, 1966. Taught at University of California, Santa Barbara, 1967; New York Community College, 1969–70; New York University, 1969–76; Summit Art Center, N.J., 1972–77. Director, New York University Photo-Etching Workshop, N.Y.C., 1972–73. Solo exhibitions: Kie Kor Gallery, New Haven, Conn., 1964; Ledesma Gallery, N.Y.C., 1964; Alonzo Gallery, N.Y.C., 1968, 1970. Group exhibitions: Associated American Artists, N.Y.C., 1962; Weyhe Gallery, N.Y.C., 1963; Amel Gallery, N.Y.C., 1964, 1965; *Magnet: New York*, Bonino Gallery, 1964; The Brooklyn Museum, N.Y., 1964, 1966, 1968; The Museum of Modern Art, N.Y.C., 1965; New York Public Library, N.Y.C., 1966; Hartford Art Foundation, Conn., 1966; *Art of Latin America since Independence*, Yale University, New Haven, and University of Texas, Austin, 1966; University Gallery, Santa Barbara, Calif., 1967; Couturier Galerie, Stamford, Conn., 1967; Britton Gallery, San Francisco, 1968; Munson Gallery, New Haven, 1968; Potsdam College, N.Y., 1969. Collections: The Brooklyn Museum, N.Y.; Cincinnati Art Museum; Center for Inter-American Relations, N.Y.C.; Chase Manhattan Bank, N.Y.C.; Cornell University, Ithaca, N.Y.; Everson Museum of Art, Syracuse, N.Y.; Solomon R. Guggenheim Museum, N.Y.C.; Instituto de Cultura Puertorriqueña, San Juan; Library of Congress, Washington, D.C.; Massachusetts Institute of Technology, Cambridge, Mass.; Metropolitan Museum of Art, N.Y.C.; Museum of Fine Arts, Boston; The Museum of Modern Art, N.Y.C.; New York Public Library, N.Y.C.; New York University, N.Y.C.

Góngora, Leonél. b. 1932, Valle de Cauca, Colombia. Resided in U.S. since 1964. Studied at Escuela de Bellas Artes, Universidad Nacional de Colombia, Bogotá; under Max Beckmann at Washington University, St. Louis. c. 1950s. Lived in Italy, 1959; Mexico City, 1960–63. Taught painting at University of Massachusetts, Amherst, 1970. Member of Nueva Presencia group. Solo exhibitions: International Institute, St. Louis, 1955; Peoples Art Center, St. Louis, 1955; Ryder Gallery, Los Angeles, 1962; Pan American Union, Washington, D.C., 1962; Zora's Gallery, Los Angeles, 1963, 1964; Cober Gallery, N.Y.C., 1963, 1964, 1965, 1966, 1967, 1968; Ohio State University, Columbus, 1968; Boris Mirski Gallery, Boston, 1969; Arizona State University, Tucson, 1970. Group exhibitions: University of St. Louis, 1954; City Art Museum, St. Louis, 1954; Cober Gallery, N.Y.C., 1962; Zora's Gallery, 1962, 1963; Rollins College, Fla., 1963; Hofstra University, Hempstead, N.Y., 1965; Portland Art Museum, Oreg., Museum of Contemporary Art, Houston, University of Texas, Austin, Fort Worth Art Center, and University of San Diego, 1967; Arizona State University, Tucson, 1968; Collections: Arizona State University, Tucson; Museum of Fine Arts, Houston; University of Massachusetts, Amherst; Minnesota Museum of Art, St. Paul; The Museum of Modern Art, N.Y.C.; Museum of Modern Art of Latin America, Washington, D.C.; New Jersey State Museum, Trenton; Phoenix Art Museum; Smith College, Northampton, Mass.; Washington University, St. Louis.

González Amézcua, Consuelo "Chelo." 1903–1975. b. Villa Acuna, Mexico. Family moved to Del Rio, Texas, 1913. Largely unknown outside Del Rio until first solo exhibition: Marion Koogler McNay Art Museum, San Antonio, 1968.

Grassmann, Marcello. b. 1925, São Paulo. Studied at Liceu de Artes e Ofícios do São Paulo, 1943–49. Moved to Rio de Janeiro, 1949. Solo exhibitions: Dallas Museum of Fine Arts, 1959; Pan American Union, Washington, D.C., 1960; Brazilian Cultural Institute, Washington, D.C., 1964; University of Chicago, 1966. Group exhibitions: Pan American Union, Washington, D.C., 1959; *Art of Latin America since Independence*, Yale University, New Haven, and University of Texas, Austin, 1966. Collections: Metropolitan Museum of Art, N.Y.C.; Dallas Museum of Fine Arts; Museum of Modern Art of Latin America, Washington, D.C.; Rhode Island School of Design, Providence; Walker Art Center, Minneapolis.

Grau, Enrique. b. 1920, Cartagena, Colombia. Awarded scholarship by Colombian government to study in U.S., 1940. Studied under Harry Sternberg and George Grosz at The Art Students League, N.Y.C., 1940–43. Taught at Escuela de Bellas Artes, Universidad Nacional de Colombia, Bogotá, 1951–52, 1957–61. Visited Mexico, 1953. Studied mural painting at Accademia San Marco, Florence, 1955–56. Films made: *La Langosta Azul, blanco y negro*, 1964; *Maria*, 1965. Solo exhibitions: Pan American Union, 1957, 1964; Roland de Aenlle Gallery, N.Y.C., 1957. Group exhibitions: Argent Gallery, N.Y.C., 1943; American Institute of Decorators, N.Y.C., 1943; Brooks Memorial Gallery, Memphis, Tenn., 1943; A.C.A. Gallery, N.Y.C., 1943; New School for Social Research, N.Y.C., 1950; *Gulf-Caribbean Art*, Museum of Fine Arts, Houston, 1956; *Pan-American Exhibition*, Milwaukee Art Center, 1957; *Pittsburgh International*, Carnegie Institute, 1958, 1964; *South American Art Today*, Dallas Museum of Fine Arts, 1959; Solomon R. Guggenheim Museum, N.Y.C., 1960; American Institute, Washington, D.C., 1965; *Art of Latin America since Independence*, Yale University, New Haven, and University of Texas, Austin, 1966; *Latin American Painting*, University of Oklahoma, Norman, 1969. Collection: Museum of Modern Art of Latin America, Washington, D.C.

Grilo, Sarah. b. 1921, Buenos Aires. Lived in Madrid and Paris, 1948–50; Traveled to U.S., 1957–58; Lived in N.Y.C., 1962–70. Awarded John Simon Guggenheim Memorial Fellowship, 1962. Solo exhibitions: OAS headquarters, Washington, D.C., 1957; Obelisk Gallery, Washington, D.C., 1963; Bianchini Gallery, N.Y.C., 1963; Byron Gallery, N.Y.C., 1967. Group exhibitions: National Gallery of Art, Washington, D.C., 1956; *The United States Collects Latin American Art*, Art Institute of Chicago, 1959; *South American Art Today*, Dallas Museum of Fine Arts, 1959; Institute of Contemporary Art, Boston, 1959; *Latin America: New Departures*, Institute of Contemporary Art, Boston, 1961; *Painters Residing in the U.S. from Latin America*, Institute of Contemporary Arts, Washington, D.C., 1964; *Magnet: New York*, Bonino Gallery, N.Y.C., 1964; *New Art of Argentina*, Walker Art Center, Minneapolis, 1965; *The Emergent Decade*, Solomon R. Guggenheim Museum, N.Y.C., and Cornell University, Ithaca, N.Y., 1965; *Art of Latin America since Independence*, Yale University, New Haven, and University of Texas, Austin, 1966. Collection: The Museum of Modern Art of Latin America, Washington, D.C.

Guayasimín, Oswaldo. b. 1919, Quito, Ecuador. Studied painting and sculpture under Pedro Leon Donoso at Escuela de Bellas Artes, Quito, 1940. Invited by U.S. Department of State to visit U.S., 1943. Studied fresco painting with José Clemente Orozco in Mexico, 1943. Solo exhibitions: Mortimer Brandt Gallery, N.Y.C., 1952; Duveen-Graham Gallery, N.Y.C., 1952; Pan American Union, Washington, D.C., 1955. Group exhibitions: *The Latin American Collection of The Museum of Modern Art*, N.Y.C., 1943; Art Institute of Chicago, 1944; *Pittsburgh International*, Carnegie Institute, 1955; *South American Art Today*, Dallas Museum of Fine Arts, 1959; *Art of Latin America since Independence*, Yale University, New Haven, and University of Texas, Austin, 1966; Philbrook Art Center, Tulsa, Okla., 1969; Center for Inter-American Relations, N.Y.C., 1970. Collections: Art Institute of Chicago; The Museum of Modern Art, N.Y.C.; Museum of Modern Art of Latin America, Washington, D.C.; San Francisco Museum of Modern Art.

Guerrero Galván, Jesús. b. 1910, Tonalá, Jalisco, Mexico. Studied art in San Antonio, Texas. Moved to Mexico City, 1925. Taught art in elementary schools, 1925–38. Professor of painting and figure drawing at La Esmeralda, Mexico City, 1939–42. Appointed artist-in-residence and painted murals at University of New Mexico, Albuquerque, 1942. Solo exhibitions: La Quinta Gallery, Albuquerque; Art League of New Mexico, Albuquerque, 1942; Julien Levy Gallery, N.Y.C., 1943; Mexican Art Gallery, San Antonio, 1959. Group exhibitions: World's Fair, N.Y.C., 1939; *Twenty Centuries of Mexican Art*, The Museum of Modern Art, N.Y.C., 1940. Collections: Colorado Springs Fine Arts Center; The Museum of Modern Art, N.Y.C.; Philadelphia Museum of Art.

Hernández Acevedo, Manuel. b. 1921, Aguas Buenas, P.R. Shoemaker by trade. Studied silkscreen under Irene Delano at Graphic Arts Workshop, San Juan, 1947. Exhibitions: Universidad de Puerto Rico, 1955; Riverside Museum, N.Y.C., 1957; Instituto de Cultura Puertorriqueña, San Juan, 1960. Collections: Ateneo Puertorriqueño, San Juan; Instituto de Cultura Puertorriqueña, San Juan; Museo de Arte de Ponce, P.R.; Universidad de Puerto Rico, San Juan.

Hernández Cruz, Luis. b. 1936, San Juan. Studied under Cristóbal Ruiz, Fernández Granel, and Damián Bayón at Universidad de Puerto Rico (B.A., 1958); under Ben Summerford and Robert Gates at American University, Washington, D.C., (M.A., 1959). Taught art at Escuela Superíor Gabriella Mistral, Rio Piedras, P.R., 1960; Universidad de Puerto Rico, 1961–63. Director of fine arts section, Ateneo Puertorriqueño, San Juan, 1966–71. Professor of fine arts, Universidad de Puerto Rico, 1968. Awards: First Prize, Instituto de Cultura Puertorriqueña Urban Landscape Competition, 1963; First Prize, ESSO Inter-American Competition, 1964. Solo exhibitions: Instituto de Cultura Puertorriqueña, San Juan, 1967. Group exhibitions: IBM Gallery, N.Y.C., 1966; Tibor de Nagy Gallery, N.Y.C., 1967; Pan American Union, Washington, D.C. Collections: American University, Washington, D.C.; Chase Manhattan Bank, N.Y.C. and San Juan; Circulo de Bellas Artes, San Juan; El Museo del Barrio, N.Y.C.; Esso Collection, San Juan; EXXON Corporation, Miami; Instituto de Cultura Puertorriqueña, San Juan; Kidder Peabody & Co., N.Y.C.; Library of Congress, Washington, D.C.; Lincoln Hospital, The Bronx, N.Y.; Lowe Art Museum, Coral Gables, Fla.; Metropolitan Museum Art Center, Coral Gables, Fla.; The Museum of Modern Art, N.Y.C.; Museum of Modern Art of Latin America, Washington, D.C.; Museo de Arte de Ponce, P.R.; Universidad de Puerto Rico, Rio Piedras; R.J. Reynolds Tobacco Company, P.R.

Herrera, Carmen. b. 1915, Havana. Resided in U.S. since 1954. Studied art and art history at Academia de San Alejandro, Havana, 1948–52; Marymount College, Paris, 1952–53; architecture at Universidad de Havana, 1953. Moved to N.Y.C. and studied at The Art Students League, 1954. Solo exhibitions: Galería Sudamericana, N.Y.C., 1956; Trabia Gallery, N.Y.C., 1963; Cisneros Gallery, N.Y.C., 1965. Group exhibitions: City Center, N.Y.C., 1956; Cisneros Gallery, N.Y.C., 1965; State University of New York, Syracuse, 1967, 1969; Center for Inter-American Relations, N.Y.C., 1968. Collections: Cintas Foundation, N.Y.C.; Cornell University Medical Center, N.Y.C.; Rusk Institute of Rehabilitation, N.Y.C.

Homar, Lorenzo. b. 1913, San Juan. Family emigrated to N.Y.C., 1928. Studied at The Art Students League, N.Y.C., 1931. Worked as design apprentice at Cartier (jewelers), 1937–40. Studied at Pratt Graphics Art Center, N.Y.C., 1940. Drafted by U.S. army, 1940; published combat drawings and caricatures in *Yank*, *Infantry Journal*, *Bell Syndicated*, and *El Mundo* (San Juan, P.R.), 1941–45. Studied under Arthur Osver and Rufino Tamayo at The Brooklyn Museum Art School, N.Y., 1945. Returned to Puerto Rico, 1950. Joined Ateneo Puertorriqueño and worked in Division of Community Education as designer and book illustrator, 1951. Director of Graphic Arts Department of Division of Community Education, 1952–57. Awarded John Simon Guggenheim Memorial Fellowship, 1956. Directed Graphics Arts Workshop of Instituto de Cultura Puertorriqueña, San Juan, 1957–73. Solo exhibitions: The Brooklyn Museum, N.Y., 1946; Ateneo Puertorriqueño, San Juan, 1950; Instituto de Cultura Puertorriqueña, San Juan, 1960; Universidad de Puerto Rico, San Juan, 1960. Collections: American Institute of Graphic Arts, N.Y.C.; Ateneo Puertorriqueño, San Juan; El Museo del Barrio, N.Y.C.; Instituto de Cultura Puertorriqueño, San Juan; The Museum of Modern Art, N.Y.C.; Museum of Modern Art of Latin America, Washington, D.C.; Museo de Arte de Ponce, P.R.; Princeton University Library, N.J.; Universidad de Puerto Rico, San Juan.

Hurtado, Angel. b. 1927, Tocuyo, Lara, Venezuela. Resided in Arlington, Va., since c.1960. Studied at Escuela de Artes Plásticas y Aplicadas Cristóbal Rojas, Caracas. Lived in Paris, 1954–59; 1964–1970. Director of photography on four short art films. Worked at Organization of American States, Washington, D.C., 1959 to the present. Solo exhibitions: Pan American Union, Washington, D.C., 1959; Roland de Aenlle Gallery, N.Y.C., 1959. Group exhibitions: *Gulf-Caribbean Art*, Museum of Fine Arts, Houston, 1956; *South American Art Today*, Dallas Museum of Fine Arts, 1959; *The United States Collects Latin American Art*, Art Institute of Chicago, 1959. Collection: Museum of Modern Art of Latin America, Washington, D.C.

Icaza, Francisco. b.1930. Son of a Mexican diplomat, traveled throughout Europe, Asia, and the Middle East for first 22 years. Studied in several European universities. Cofounder with Arnold Belkin of magazine, *Nueva Presencia*, Mexico City, 1961. Solo exhibitions: Long Beach Museum of Art, Calif., 1968; Arizona State University, Tucson, 1968. Group exhibitions: Solomon R. Guggenheim Museum, N.Y.C., 1964; La Jolla Museum of Art, Calif., 1966; Phoenix Art Museum, 1967.

Irizarry, Carlos. b. 1938, Santa Isabel, P.R. Emigrated to N.Y.C., c. 1948. Studied at School of Art and Design, N.Y.C.; joined atelier Friends of Puerto Rico; organized exhibitions of Puerto Rican artists in N.Y.C., c.1950s. Lived in Puerto Rico, 1963–68. Opened Galería 63, San Juan, 1963. Returned to N.Y.C., 1969. Solo exhibitions: Caravan House, N.Y.C., 1963; Tibor de Nagy Gallery, N.Y.C., 1967. Group exhibitions: *Latin American Art: 1931–1966*, The Museum of Modern Art, N.Y.C., 1967; *Biennial of Latin American Graphics*, San Juan, 1970. Collections: Ateneo Puertorriqueño, San Juan; Instituto de Cultura Puertorriqueña, San Juan; The Museum of Modern Art, N.Y.C.; Museum of Contemporary Hispanic Art, N.Y.C.; Museo de Arte de Ponce; Universidad de Puerto Rico, San Juan.

Irizarry, Marcos. b. 1936, Mayagüez, P.R. Studied under Cristóbal Ruiz at Universidad de Puerto Rico, 1952–54; Escuela Vocacional Miguel Such de Río Piedras, 1952–54. Moved to Spain and studied at Academia de San Fernando, Madrid, 1958. Solo exhibitions: Instituto de Cultura Puertorriqueña, San Juan, 1965; Universidad de Puerto Rico, San Juan, 1967; Universidad de Puerto Rico, Rio Piedras, 1967, 1968; Galería Colibrí, San Juan, 1967, 1968. Group exhibitions: Galería Colibrí, San Juan, 1964, 1966; Pioneer Museum, Calif., 1964; Crocker Art Gallery, Sacramento, 1965; Rogue Art Gallery, Calif., 1965; Mills Art Gallery, Calif., 1965; Portland State University, Oreg., 1965; Galería Sudamericana, N.Y.C., 1966; Pratt Institute, N.Y.C., 1966. Collections: El Museo del Barrio, N.Y.C.; Esso Collection, Coral Gables, Fla.; Instituto de Cultura Puertorriqueña, San Juan; The Museum of Modern Art, N.Y.C.; Universidad de Puerto Rico, Rio Piedras; Museo de Arte de Ponce, P.R.

Jaime Sánchez, Humberto. b. 1930, San Cristóbal, Venezuela. Studied painting at Escuela de Artes Plasticas y Aplicadas Cristóbal Rojas, Caracas, 1954. Lived in Europe, 1954–57. Awarded scholarship to study at École des Beaux-Arts, Paris, 1956. Traveled to U.S., 1957–58. Solo exhibitions: OAS, Washington, D.C., 1957; Gres Gallery, N.Y.C., Washington, D.C., 1958; Roland de Aenlle Gallery, N.Y.C., 1958. Group exhibitions: Smithsonian Institution, Washington, D.C., 1955; *Gulf-Caribbean Art*, Museum of Fine Arts Houston, 1956; Pittsburgh International, Carnegie Institute, 1958; *The U.S. Collects Pan American Art*, Art Institute of Chicago, 1959; South American Art Today, Dallas Museum of Fine Arts, 1959; *The Emergent Decade*, Solomon R. Guggenheim Museum, N.Y.C., and Cornell University, Ithaca, N.Y., 1965. Collections: Cleveland Institute of Art; Museum of Fine Arts, Houston; The Museum of Modern Art, N.Y.C.; Museum of Modern Art of Latin America, Washington, D.C.; Rockefeller Collection, N.Y.C.

Jiménez, Luis. b. 1940, El Paso, Texas. Studied architecture and art at University of Texas, Austin (B.A.,1964). Received National University of Mexico scholarship and traveled to Mexico, 1964. Moved to N.Y.C., 1964. Solo exhibitions: Graham Gallery, N.Y.C., 1968, 1970. Group exhibitions: Brandeis University, Waltham, Mass., 1968; UNESCO, Washington, D.C., 1968; Graham Gallery, N.Y.C., 1969; Dillard Paper Company, Greensboro, N.Y., 1969; David Stuart Gallery, New Orleans, La., 1969; Whitney Museum of American Art, N.Y.C., 1969; St. Edwards University, Austin, 1970. Collections: Albuquerque Museum; Art Institute of Chicago; Denver Art Museum; Long Beach Museum, Calif.; Metropolitan Museum of Art, N.Y.C.; National Collection of Fine Art, Washington, D.C.; National Museum of American Art, Washington, D.C.; New Orleans Museum of Art; Phoenix Art Museum; The Plains Art Museum, Moorehead, Minn.; Roswell Museum and Art Center, N. Mex.; Sheldon Memorial Gallery, Lincoln, Neb.; Witte Memorial Museum, San Antonio.

Kahlo, Frida. 1907–1954. b. Coyoacán, Mexico. Studied at Escuela Nacional Preparatoria, Mexico City, 1923; drawing under Fernando Fernández, Mexico City, 1925. Suffered serious injury in accident in 1926. Met Diego Rivera, 1923; married Rivera, 1929. Joined Mexican Communist party, 1928. Traveled to San Francisco, Detroit, New York, with Rivera, 1930–34. Traveled to N.Y.C. and Europe, 1938–39. Appointed professor of painting, La Esmeralda, Mexico City, 1940. Exhibitions: Julien Levy Gallery, N.Y.C., 1938; Golden Gate International Exhibition, San Francisco, 1940; The Museum of Modern Art, N.Y.C., 1940; Philadelphia Museum of Art, 1941–42; Institute of Modern Art, Boston, 1941–42; Art of This Century, N.Y.C., 1942. Collections: Albright-Knox Art Gallery, Buffalo, N.Y.; The Museum of Modern Art, N.Y.C.; Phoenix Art Museum; San Francisco Museum; Window South, Palo Alto, Calif.

Katz, Leandro. b. 1938, Buenos Aires. Resided in U.S. since 1966. Studied at Universidad Nacional de Buenos Aires, (B.A., 1960). Lived in Peru, Ecuador, Mexico, 1961–65. Solo exhibitions: Betzalel Gallery, San Francisco, 1964; Galería Sudamericana, N.Y.C., 1965; Washington Square Gallery, N.Y.C., 1965; Center for Cybernetic Research, Detroit, 1967; Museum of Contemporary Crafts, Smithsonian Institution, Washington, D.C.; Allen Memorial Art Museum, Oberlin College, Ohio, and Iowa State University, Ames, 1968–69. Performances: Folklore Center, N.Y.C., 1966; taped performance with Eduardo Costa and John Perreault, Yale University, New Haven, 1966; *Lightworks for a Night Garden*, Masque Theater, N.Y.C., 1969; *Lightworks for Grand Tarot*, Gotham Art Theater, N.Y.C.,1969. Created radio pieces broadcast on WRVR, N.Y.C., 1966–70. Coeditor of TVRT Press, N.Y.C., 1970. Taught at School of Visual Arts, N.Y.C., since 1970. Awarded a John Simon Guggenheim Memorial Fellowship, 1979, for work in film and video.

Lam, Wifredo (Wifredo Oscar de la Concepción Lam y Castillo). 1902–1982, b. Sagua la Grande, Cuba. Moved to Havana, 1916. Studied at Academia de San Alejandro, Havana, 1918–20. Studied under Fernández Alvarez de Sotomayor, Curator of Prado, and at Academia Libre de la Alhambra, Madrid, 1923. Lived in Spain, 1923–37. Joined the Surrealist movement, Paris, 1938. Traveled to France, Martinique, St. Thomas and Havana, 1940–41. Lived in Paris, N.Y.C., and Havana, 1946–52. Settled permanently in Paris, 1952. Appointed member of the Graham Foundation of Advanced Study in the Fine Arts, Chicago, Ill., 1959. Received John Simon Guggenheim Memorial Fellowship, 1964. Solo exhibitions: Pierre Matisse Gallery, N.Y.C., 1943, 1944, 1945, 1948, 1950; Notre Dame University, South Bend, Ind., 1961; New York University, N.Y.C., 1961; Gimpel Gallery, N.Y.C., 1970. Group exhibitions: Perls Gallery, N.Y.C., 1939; Art Institute of Chicago, 1941; French Relief Societies, Inc., N.Y.C., 1942; Arts Club of Chicago, 1942; The Museum of Modern Art, N.Y.C., 1947, 1969; Hugo Gallery, N.Y.C., 1947; Sidney Janis Gallery, N.Y.C., 1950; *Pittsburgh International*, Carnegie Institute, 1959, 1970; Solomon R. Guggenheim Museum, 1959; National Gallery of Art, Washington, D.C., 1963–64; *Art of Latin America since Independence*, Yale University, New Haven, and University of Texas, Austin, 1966; *Dada, Surrealism and Their Heritage*, The Museum of Modern Art, N.Y.C., Museum of Fine Arts, Boston; The National Gallery of Art, Washington, D.C., The Museum of Fine Arts, Chicago, San Francisco Art Institute, 1968. Collections: The Museum of Modern Art, N.Y.C.; Museum of Modern Art of Latin America, Washington, D.C.; Solomon R. Guggenheim Museum, N.Y.C.; Rhode Island School of Design, Providence.

Lamonica, Roberto de. b. 1933, Mato Grosso, Brazil. Studied at Liceu de Artes e Ofícios do São Paulo. Traveled to China, USSR, and Europe, 1957. First Brazilian artist to win a John Simon Guggenheim Memorial Fellowship, 1965. Solo exhibitions: Pan American Union, Washington, D.C., 1961. Group exhibitions: *Art of Latin America since Independence*, Yale University, New Haven, and University of Texas, Austin, 1966. Collections: Library of Congress, Washington, D.C.; Walker Art Center, Minneapolis.

Lasansky, Mauricio. b. 1914, Buenos Aires. Became U.S. citizen, 1952. Studied painting, sculpture, and engraving at Escuela Superior de Bellas Artes Ernesto de la Cárcova, Buenos Aires, 1933. Appointed director of Escuela Libre de Bellas Artes, Villa Maria, Córdoba, 1936; director, Taller Manualidadas, Córdoba, Argentina, 1939. Traveled in the U.S., 1943–45. Taught graphic arts at Iowa State University, Ames, 1945. Appointed Virgil M. Hancher Distinguished Professor of Art, University of Iowa, 1967. Awarded John Simon Guggenheim Memorial Fellowship, 1943–45, 1953; Honorary Doctor of Arts, Iowa Wesleyan University, 1959; Honorary Doctor of Fine Arts, Pacific Lutheran University, Tacoma, Wash., 1969. Solo exhibitions: San Francisco Museum of Art, 1945, 1950; Art Institute of Chicago, 1947, 1960; American Federation of the Arts, Washington, D.C., 1960 (retrospective); The Brooklyn Museum, N.Y., 1961; Philadelphia Museum of Art, 1966. Group exhibitions: Art Institute of Chicago, 1936; Walker Art Center, Minneapolis, 1949; Metropolitan Museum of Art, N.Y.C., 1952; Institute of Contemporary Art, Boston, 1959; *Art of Latin America since Independence*, Yale University, New Haven, and University of Texas, Austin, 1966; *Latin American Art: 1931–1966*, The Museum of Modern Art, N.Y.C., 1967. Collections: Art Institute of Chicago; The Brooklyn Museum, N.Y.; IBM Collection, N.Y.C.; Joslyn Art Museum, Omaha, Neb.; Library of Congress, Washington, D.C.; The Museum of Modern Art, N.Y.C.; Museum of Modern Art of Latin America, Washington, D.C.; National Gallery of Art, Washington, D.C.; New York Public Library, N.Y.C.; Pennsylvania Academy of the Fine Arts, Philadelphia; Philadelphia Museum of Art; Walker Art Center, Minneapolis.

Lee, Wesley Duke. b. 1931, São Paulo. Studied at Museu do Arte de São Paulo; graphic arts at Parsons School of Design, N.Y.C., 1952–55; design and painting under Karl Plattner, São Paulo, 1955–58; engraving under Johnny Friedlaender, Paris, 1958. Joined international movement Phrases, 1964. Group exhibitions: Solomon R. Guggenheim Museum, N.Y.C., 1965; *Art of Latin America since Independence*, Yale University, New Haven, and University of Texas, Austin,1966; *The Emergent Decade*, Solomon R. Guggenheim Museum, N.Y.C., and Cornell University, Ithaca, N.Y., 1965; *Art and Technology*, Los Angeles County

Museum, 1969. Collections: University of Massachusetts, Amherst; Philadelphia Museum of Art.

Le Parc, Julio. b. 1928, Mendoza, Argentina. Studied at Escuela Nacional de Bellas Artes Prilidiano Pueyrredón, Buenos Aires. Joined Arts-Concrete movement and Spatialists. Received scholarship to study in Paris, 1958. Joined Kinetic Tendency, movement founded by Victor Vasarely. Cofounded Groupe de Recherche d'Art Visuel (GRAV), artists interested in creation of Kinetic environments, 1960. Solo exhibitions: The Contemporaries, N.Y.C., 1964–65; Howard Wise Gallery, N.Y.C., 1966, 1967. Group exhibitions: *Pittsburgh International*, Carnegie Institute, 1961; Museum of Fine Arts, Houston, 1963; Howard Wise Gallery, N.Y.C., 1964, 1968; *New Art of Argentina*, Walker Art Center, Minneapolis, 1964; The Museum of Modern Art and Akron Art Institute, Ohio, 1965; *Latin American Art: 1931–1966*, The Museum of Modern Art, N.Y.C., 1967; *Art of Latin America since Independence*, Yale University, New Haven, and University of Texas, Austin, 1966; Howard Wise Gallery, N.Y.C., 1968. Collections: Albright-Knox Art Gallery, Buffalo, N.Y.; The Museum of Modern Art; N.Y.C.; New Jersey State Museum, Trenton; Walker Art Center, Minneapolis.

Leufert, Gerd. b. 1914, Memel, Lithuania. Studied at the Akademie der Bildenden Künste, Munich, on scholarship from the state of Bavaria, 1947–48; Pratt Institute, N.Y.C.; Iowa State University, Ames. Moved to Venezuela, 1950. Received art research scholarship from U.S. Department of State, 1959–60. Appointed director of Graphic Arts, Escuela de Bellas Artes, and professor of architecture, Universidad Central de Venezuela, Caracas. Currently curator at the Museo de Bellas Artes, Caracas. Solo exhibitions: San Francisco Museum of Art, 1954; Landau Gallery, Los Angeles, 1954. Group exhibitions: *Magnet: New York*, Bonino Gallery, N.Y.C., 1964; *The Emergent Decade*, Solomon R. Guggenheim Museum, N.Y.C., and Cornell University, Ithaca, N.Y., 1965. *Art of Latin America since Independence*, Yale University, New Haven, and University of Texas, Austin, 1966. Collections: Chase Manhattan Bank, N.Y.C.; Library of Congress, Washington, D.C.; The Museum of Modern Art, N.Y.C.; University of Iowa, Iowa City; New York Public Library, N.Y.C.; Pratt Graphic Center, N.Y.C.

López, Domingo. b. 1942, Gurabo, P.R. Studied art in Puerto Rico and in N.Y.C., 1959. Lived in N.Y.C., 1965–73. Worked with Friends of Puerto Rico, and founded ASPIRA, organizations that sponsor Puerto Rican and Hispanic artists in N.Y.C., 1965. Awarded Instituto de Cultura Puertorriqueña grant for study in N.Y.C., 1969. Solo exhibitions: Universidad de Puerto Rico, Rio Piedras, 1964; Galería 63, San Juan, 1967. Group exhibitions: Galería APRAG, N.Y.C., 1966; Tibor de Nagy Gallery, N.Y.C., 1967; Universidad de Puerto Rico, Rio Piedras, 1967; Cisneros Gallery, N.Y.C., 1970.

López-Loza, Luis. b. 1939, Guadalajara, Mexico. Resided in N.Y.C. since 1963. Studied at La Esmeralda, 1954–58; Centro de Estudios Avanzados de las Artes Gráficas, Mexico City, 1958–62. Solo exhibitions: San Antonio Public Library, 1963; Long Island University, 1963; Southampton College, Long Island University, 1965; Galería Berman, Boston, 1970. Group exhibitions: The Jewish Museum, N.Y.C., 1964; Martha Jackson Gallery, N.Y.C., 1965; San Diego Museum, 1966; Portland Art Museum, 1966; University of Nebraska, Lincoln, 1966; University of Texas, Austin, 1966; Pratt Institute, N.Y.C., 1968; New Jersey State Museum, Trenton, 1970; Misrachi Gallery, N.Y.C., 1970; Center for Inter-American Relations, 1970. Collections: Martha Jackson Gallery, N.Y.C.; The Museum of Modern Art, N.Y.C.; Pratt Institute, N.Y.C.; San Antonio Public Library; State University of New York, Stonybrook; University of Texas, Austin; Yale University, New Haven.

Mabe, Manabu. b. 1924, Kumamoto, Japan. Moved to Brazil, 1934. Farmer by profession. Began painting in 1943. Received Purchase Award, Dallas Museum of Fine Arts, 1959. *Time* proclaims 1959 "Year of Manabu Mabe." Visited U.S., 1961–62. Created mural for OAS General Secretariat

Building in Washington, D.C., 1962. Solo exhibitions: Time/Life Building, N.Y.C., 1961; Pan American Union, Washington, D.C., 1962; Catherine Viviano Gallery, N.Y.C., 1968, 1970; Houston Museum of Fine Arts, 1970. Group exhibitions: *South American Art Today*, Dallas Museum of Fine Arts, 1959, 1966; *Pittsburgh International*, Carnegie Institute, 1961; Walker Art Center, Minneapolis, City Art Museum, St. Louis, Colorado Springs Fine Arts Center, and San Francisco Museum of Art, 1962; *Art of Latin America since Independence*, Yale University, New Haven, and University of Texas, Austin, 1966. Collections: Dallas Museum of Fine Arts; Institute of Contemporary Art, Boston; Lowe Art Museum, Coral Gables, Fla.; Museum of Modern Art of Latin America, Washington, D.C.; Walker Art Center, Minneapolis.

Macció, Rómulo. b. 1931, Buenos Aires. Worked in publishing, graphic design, theater decoration, Buenos Aires, 1945. Awarded John Simon Guggenheim Memorial Fellowship, 1964. Awarded De Rider Award, 1959; Instituto Torcuato di Tella First International Prize, 1961, 1963. Solo exhibitions: Bonino Gallery, N.Y.C., 1965; Center for Inter-American Relations, 1969. Group exhibitions: Pan American Union, Washington, D.C., 1961; Organization of American States, Washington, D.C., 1962; *New Art of Argentina*, Walker Art Center, Minneapolis, 1964; Solomon R. Guggenheim Museum, N.Y.C., 1964; *Art of Latin America since Independence*, Yale University, New Haven, and University of Texas, Austin, 1966; Bonino Gallery, N.Y.C., 1966. Collections: Aldrich Museum of Contemporary Art, Ridgefield, Conn.; Hirshhorn Museum and Sculpture Garden, Washington, D.C.; Rhode Island School of Design, Providence; Walker Art Center, Minneapolis.

Mac Entyre, Eduardo. b. 1929, Buenos Aires. Self-taught. Cofounder, Arte Alternativo group, 1959. Awarded UNESCO Prize, 1961. Traveled to U.S., 1967; and on Argentine government scholarship, 1968. Solo exhibitions: Pan American Union, Washington, D.C.,1968; Bonino Gallery, N.Y.C., 1970. Group exhibitions: *New Art of Argentina*, Walker Art Center, Minneapolis, 1964; Akron Art Institute, Ohio, 1964; Atlanta Art Association, Ga., 1964; University of Texas, Austin, 1964; *20 South American Artists*, Oakland Museum, Calif., 1964; Solomon R. Guggenheim Museum, N.Y.C., 1964; *The Emergent Decade*, Solomon R. Guggenheim Museum, N.Y.C., and Cornell University; Ithaca, N.Y., 1965; *Art of Latin America since Independence*, Yale University, New Haven, and University of Texas, Austin, 1966; *Latin American Art: 1931–1966*, The Museum of Modern Art, N.Y.C., 1967; Pan American Union, Washington, D.C., 1966; *Pittsburgh International*, Carnegie Institute, 1967; *Hemisfair*, San Antonio, 1968; Center for Inter-American Relations, N.Y.C., 1968; Bonino Gallery, N.Y.C., 1968; Flint Institute of Arts, Mich., 1968; Kent State University, Ohio, 1968, 1970; *Latin American Painting*, Oklahoma Art Center, University of Oklahoma, Norman, 1969; Philbrook Art Center, Tulsa, Ok., 1969. Collections: Albright-Knox Art Gallery, Buffalo, N.Y.; Bonino Gallery, N.Y.C.; Chase Manhattan Bank, N.Y.C.; Fine Arts Gallery of San Diego; Fogg Art Museum, Cambridge, Mass.; Solomon R. Guggenheim Museum, N.Y.C.; I.B.M. Corporation, N.Y.C.; Kennedy Center for the Performing Arts, Washington, D.C.; The Museum of Modern Art, N.Y.C.; Museum of Modern Art of Latin America, Washington, D.C.; Philadelphia Art Museum; Rockefeller University, N.Y.C.; University of Texas, Austin.

Maldonado, Juan. b. 1941, Santurce, P.R. Traveled to Italy, France, Austria while in the U.S. armed forces, 1960–65. Studied in Vicenza, Italy, in collaboration with the Universitá di Perugia, 1966. Instructor, Society of Friends of Puerto Rico, N.Y.C., 1969–71; P.S. 25, Bronx, N.Y., 1971–73; Pratt Institute, N.Y.C., 1973. Artist-in-residence, The Bronx Museum of the Arts, N.Y., 1983–86. Solo exhibitions: Hotel St. George, San Juan, 1970. Group exhibitions: Fiesta Folklorica, N.Y.C., 1969, 1970; Taller Boricua, N.Y.C., 1969; Suffolk County College, Selden, N.Y., 1970.

Manzur, David. b. 1929, Neira, Colombia. Studied at Escuela de Bellas Artes, Universidad Nacional de Colombia,

Bogotá, 1951–56; The Art Students League, N.Y.C., c. 1961; Pratt Institute, N.Y.C.,1963–64. Awarded John Simon Guggenheim Memorial Fellowship, 1961–1962; Pan American Award, 1964–65. Solo exhibitions: Pan American Union, Washington, D.C., 1961, 1964; Obelisk Gallery, Washington, D.C.,1962; Galerie Royal Athena II, N.Y.C., 1963; Galerie Green-Rose, N.Y.C., 1964. Group exhibitions: Bonino Gallery, N.Y.C., 1964; Art Institute of Chicago, 1965; *Contemporary Art of Latin America*, Institute of Contemporary Arts, Washington, D.C., 1965. Collections: Cleveland Museum of Art; Library of Congress, Washington, D.C.; Museum of Modern Art of Latin America, Washington, D.C.; University of Oklahoma, Norman; Pratt Institute, N.Y.C.

Marin, Augusto. b. 1921, Santurce, P.R. Studied under Reginald Marsh, Harry Sternberg and Ivan Olinsky, The Art Students League, N.Y.C.; County Art Institute of Los Angeles.

Marisol (Marisol Escobar). b. 1930, Paris. Raised in Caracas; resided in N.Y.C. since 1960. Studied under Howard Warshaw, Jepson School, Los Angeles, 1946–49; École des Beaux-Arts and Academie Julien, Paris, 1949–50; under Yasuo Kuniyoshi at The Art Students League, N.Y.C., 1950; under Hans Hofmann and at the New School for Social Research, N.Y.C., 1951–54. Worked with sculptor Bill King, N.Y.C., 1953. Moved to Rome, 1957. Performed in Andy Warhol's films *The Kiss* (1963) and *The 13 Most Beautiful Women* (1964). Solo exhibitions: Leo Castelli Gallery, N.Y.C., 1958; Stable Gallery, N.Y.C., 1962, 1964; The Art Club of Chicago, 1965; Sidney Janis Gallery, N.Y.C., 1966, 1967; Moore College of Art, Philadelphia, 1970. Group exhibitions: Stable Gallery, N.Y.C., 1954, 1955, 1956, 1957; *Pittsburgh International*, Carnegie Institute, 1959, 1967; *The United States Collects Latin American Art*, Art Institute of Chicago, 1959; Dallas Museum of Fine Arts, 1961; The Museum of Modern Art, N.Y.C., 1961, 1963; American Federation of Arts, N.Y.C., 1962; Sidney Janis Gallery, N.Y.C., 1965; *Latin American Art*, The Museum of Modern Art, N.Y.C., 1966–67; Whitney Museum of American Art, N.Y.C., 1966, 1967; Los Angeles County Museum of Art, 1967; The Museum of Modern Art, N.Y.C., 1968. Collections: Albright-Knox Art Gallery, Buffalo, N.Y.; Arts Club of Chicago; Hawaiian Statuary Hall, Honolulu; The Museum of Modern Art, N.Y.C.; National Museum of American Art, Washington, D.C.; Whitney Museum of American Art, N.Y.C.; Worcester Art Museum, Mass.

Martínez, Raul. b. 1927, Diego de Avila, Cuba. Family moved to Havana, 1940. Studied at Escuela Anexa a San Alejandro and at Instituto de Segunda Enseñanza de la Habana, 1941–48. Founded Nuestro Tiempo group, 1951. Studied at Chicago Institute of Design, 1952–53. Returned to Cuba, 1953. Joined the group Los Once, 1954. Worked in a publicity agency. Appointed director, *Lunes de Revolución* (periodical), 1960. Taught in school of architecture, Universidad de Habana, 1961–65. Worked for Instituto Cubano del Libro designing posters and book illustrations, 1967. Exhibitions: Galería Sudamericana, N.Y.C., 1955.

Martins, Maria. (Maria de Lourdes Alves Martins Pereira de Souza). 1900–1973. b. Minas Gerais, Brazil. Traveled to Ecuador, 1926. Studied music and painting in Paris, c. 1930. Traveled to Japan. Studied sculpture in Belgium under Oscar Jesper, 1939. Joined Surrealist movement, c. 1940. Moved to U.S., c. 1942. Organized first São Paulo Bienial, 1951. Cofounded Fundação do Museu de Arte Moderna do Rio de Janeiro. Awarded prizes in the second and third São Paulo Bienials, 1953, 1955. Solo exhibitions: Corcoran Art Gallery, Washington, D.C., 1941; Valentine Gallery, N.Y.C., 1942, 1943, 1944, 1946. Group exhibitions: *Pittsburgh International*, Carnegie Institute, 1940; *Latin American Exhibition of Fine Arts*, Riverside Museum, N.Y.C., 1940; Bucholz Gallery, N.Y.C., 1942; Dayton Museum, 1944; City Art of Saint Louis, 1946. Collections: Metropolitan Museum of Art, N.Y.C.; Philadelphia Museum of Art.

Martorell, Antonio. b. 1939, Santurce, P.R. Studied in Spain under Julio Martín Caro, 1961. Member of Taller de

Artes Graficás, Instituto de Cultura Puertorriqueña, 1962–65. Founded Taller Alacrán, (Scorpion Workshop), a print collective, San Juan, 1968. Created satirical graphic works for popular audiences. Solo exhibitions: New York Art Director's Club, 1964; Galería Colibrí, San Juan, 1968. Group exhibitions: Galería Colibrí, San Juan, 1964; Randolph Gallery, Houston, 1965; Galerie San Juan, 1968, 1969, 1970. Collections: American Institute of Graphic Arts, N.Y.C.; Art Institute of Chicago; Ateneo Puertorriqueño, San Juan; Casa del Libro, San Juan; Casa Roig, San Juan; Chase Manhattan Bank, N.Y.C.; El Museo del Barrio, N.Y.C.; Huntington Art Gallery, Austin; Instituto de Cultura Puertorriqueña, San Juan; Inter-American University, San Juan; Library of Congress, Washington, D.C.; Metropolitan Museum of Art, N.Y.C.; The Museum of Modern Art, N.Y.C.; Museo de Arte de Ponce, P.R.; Princeton University Library, N.J.; Universidad de Puerto Rico, Río Piedras; Rochester Polytechnic Institute, N.Y.

Matta (Roberto Sebastian Antonio Matta Echaurren). b. 1911, Santiago. Resided in Rome since 1948. Studied at Collegio del Sagrado Corazon; architecture at Universidad Católica de Santiago, Chile, 1929. Traveled in Europe, 1933. Assistant to Le Corbusier in Paris, 1934–37. Traveled to Soviet Union, Finland, and Britain, 1936–37; Mexico, 1944; Cuba, 1963; Cuba and South America, 1966–68. Joined Surrealist movement, Paris, 1938. Lived in U.S., 1939–47. Lived in Paris, 1954–58. Solo exhibitions: Julien Levy Gallery, N.Y.C., 1940 (regular showings); Pierre Matisse Gallery, N.Y.C., 1941–48 (regular showings); Art of This Century, N.Y.C., 1942, 1944; Hugo Gallery, N.Y.C., 1947; William Copley Gallery, Beverley Hills, Calif., 1948; Sidney Janis Gallery, N.Y.C., 1950 (regular showings); Allan Frumkin Gallery, N.Y.C., 1952; Pan American Union, Washington, D.C., 1955; The Museum of Modern Art, N.Y.C., 1957 (retrospective); Walker Art Center, Minneapolis, 1967. Group exhibitions: Pierre Matisse Gallery, N.Y.C.,1942; *First Papers of Surrealism*, French Relief Societies Inc., N.Y.C., 1942; Arts Club of Chicago, 1942; *The Emergent Decade*, Solomon R. Guggenheim Museum, N.Y.C., and Cornell University, Ithaca, N.Y., 1964; *Dada, Surrealism and Their Heritage*, The Museum of Modern Art, N.Y.C., 1968. Collections: Art Institute of Chicago; Baltimore Museum of Art; University of Chicago; Alan Frumkin Gallery, N.Y.C.; Solomon R. Guggenheim Museum, N.Y.C.; Maxwell Davidson Gallery, N.Y.C.; The Museum of Modern Art, N.Y.C.; Museum of Modern Art of Latin America, Washington, D.C.; Pierre Matisse Gallery, N.Y.C.; San Francisco Museum of Modern Art; Williams College, Williamstown, Mass.

Medellín, Octavio. b. 1907, Matehuala, Mexico. Moved to San Antonio, Tex., 1920. Studied painting under José Arpa and drawing under Xavier Gonzalez at San Antonio School of Art, 1921–28; Art Institute of Chicago, 1928. Traveled in rural Mexico, 1929–31; Yucatan, 1938. Taught sculpture at Villita Art Gallery and Witte Memorial Museum, San Antonio, c.1930; North Texas State College, Denton, 1938–42; and Southern Methodist University, Dallas, 1945–66. Illustrated *Xtol*, a book chronicling his travels in Mexico (Dallas Museum of Fine Arts, 1962). Established art school in Dallas, 1969. Exhibitions: Art Institute of Chicago, 1928; The Museum of Modern Art, N.Y.C., 1942. Collections: Frank L. Paxton Company, Fort Worth, Tex. Papers and art studies included in Syracuse University Library, Collection of Manuscripts of Sculptors.

Meireles, Cildo. b. 1948, Rio de Janeiro. Studied at Escola Nacional de Belas Artes, and in engraving workshop at the Museu do Arte Moderno, Rio de Janeiro. Lived in N.Y.C., 1971–73. Group exhibition: *Information*, The Museum of Modern Art, N.Y.C., 1970.

Méndez, Leopoldo. 1902–1969. b. Mexico City. Studied at La Esmeralda, Mexico City, 1917–20. Continued studies at open-air school organized by Alfredo Ramos Martínez, Chimalistac, Mexico. Joined the Stridentist Group, 1921. Traveled to the U.S., 1930. Illustrated Heinrich Heine's *The Gods in Exile*, (N.Y.C.: Haldeman-Julius, 1931). Appointed director of Ministry of Public Education, Mexico, 1932. Cofounded LEAR (*League of Revolutionary Writers and Artists*), 1933. Cofounded Taller de Gráfica Popular with Pablo O'Higgins, Luis Arenal, and Alfredo Zalce, Mexico City, 1937. Received John Simon Guggenheim Memorial Fellowship, 1939. Group exhibitions: Jeke Zeitlan Bookshop, Los Angeles, 1930; Art Institute, Milwaukee, 1930; San Francisco Museum of Art, 1934, 1944, 1945; *Art of Latin America since Independence*, Yale University, New Haven, and University of Texas, Austin, 1966. Collections: Art Institute of Chicago; Colorado Springs Fine Arts Center; Fine Arts Gallery, San Diego; Museum of Fine Arts, Boston; The Museum of Modern Art, N.Y.C.; Worcester Art Museum, Mass.

Mérida, Carlos. 1891–1984. b. Guatemala City. Studied art in Guatemala, 1902–05; under Kees Van Dongen in Paris, 1912–14. Lived in U.S., 1917–19. Moved to Mexico, 1919. Assistant to Diego Rivera on mural project at Simón Bolívar Amphitheater of Escuela Nacional Preparatoria, Mexico City, 1922. Lived in Paris in 1927–29. Visiting professor of art at North Texas Teachers College, Denton, 1941–42. Designed mosaic mural for San Antonio Convention Center, 1968. Solo exhibitions: Valentine-Dudensing Gallery, N.Y.C., 1926; The Delphic Studios, N.Y.C., 1930; John Becker Galleries, N.Y.C., 1930, 1932; Katherine Kuh Gallery, Chicago, 1935; Stendhal Gallery, Los Angeles, 1936; Stanley Rose Gallery, 1940; Pan American Union, Washington, D.C., 1951–52; Passedoit Gallery, N.Y.C., 1957; Marion Koogler McNay Art Museum, San Antonio, 1962; Gallery of Modern Art, Scottsdale, Ariz., 1964; Martha Jackson Gallery, 1966. Group exhibitions: World's Fair, Queens, N.Y., 1964; *Art of Latin America since Independence*, Yale University, New Haven, and University of Texas, Austin, 1966; *Latin American Art: 1931–1966*, The Museum of Modern Art, N.Y.C., 1967. Collections: Museum of Fine Arts, Boston; Cleveland Museum of Art; The Museum of Modern Art, N.Y.C.; Phoenix Art Museum; San Francisco Museum of Modern Art; Seattle Art Museum.

Minujín, Marta. b. 1943, Buenos Aires. Studied at Escuela Nacional de Bellas Artes, Buenos Aires, 1953–59; Escuela Superior de Bellas Artes, Buenos Aires, 1960–62. Postgraduate studies in Paris. Awarded French Embassy scholarship, 1962; John Simon Guggenheim Memorial Fellowship, 1966; Fairfield Foundation Grant, 1967; Center for Inter-American Relations Grant, 1968. Lived in U.S., 1965–69; 1970–74. Appointed guest artist at Corcoran School of Art, Washington, D.C., 1972–73. Solo exhibitions: Bianchini Gallery, N.Y.C., 1966; Howard Wise Gallery, N.Y.C., 1968; Center for Inter-American Relations, N.Y.C.,1968. Group exhibitions: *Art of Latin America since Independence*, Yale University, New Haven, and University of Texas, Austin, 1966. Produced the following Happenings: *Three Country Happening*, with Allan Kaprow and Wolf Vostell, 1966; *Minuphone*, Howard Wise Gallery, N.Y., 1967; *Minucode*, Center for Inter-American Relations, N.Y.C., 1968; *Golden Gate Park Happening*, San Francisco, 1969. Collections: Chase Manhattan Bank, N.Y.C.; United Nations, N.Y.C.

Montañez-Ortiz, Rafael (Ralph Ortiz). b. 1934, New York City. Studied at High School of Art and Design, N.Y.C.; The Brooklyn Museum Art School; Pratt Institute, N.Y.C., (B.S., M.F.A., 1964); Columbia University Teacher's College, N.Y.C., (Ph.D., 1967). Taught at New York University, 1968; adjunct professor at Hostos Community College, The Bronx, N.Y., 1970. Received John Hay Whitney Fellowship, 1965–66. Performed "Piano Destruction Concert" for BBC television, 1966. Solo exhibitions: Artists' Gallery, N.Y.C., 1960; Barrett's Candy Store, Provincetown, Mass., 1965; Fordham University, The Bronx, N.Y., 1967. Group exhibitions: School of the Museum of Fine Arts, Boston, 1962; Bolles Gallery, N.Y.C., 1962; Hackley Art Gallery, Muskegon, Mich., 1963; Tucson Art Center, 1963; Washington University, St. Louis, 1963; Cornell University, Ithaca, N.Y., 1963; University of Indiana, Bloomington, 1963; Isaac Delgado Museum of Art, New Orleans, 1963; University of Oregon, Eugene, 1964; Park Palace Gallery, N.Y.C., 1964; Welfare Island, N.Y.C., 1964; San Francisco State College, 1964; University of Southern Florida, Tampa, 1964; Detroit Institute of Arts,

1964: The Chrysler Museum, Provincetown, Mass., 1965, 1966; The Museum of Modern Art, N.Y.C., 1965; *Latin American Art: 1931–1966*, The Museum of Modern Art, N.Y.C., 1967; Whitney Museum of American Art, N.Y.C., 1965. *Destruction Arts Symposium*, N.Y.C., 1968. Collections: Chrysler Museum of Fine Art, Richmond, Va.; El Museo del Barrio, N.Y.C.; Everson Museum, Syracuse, N.Y.; The Museum of Modern Art, N.Y.C.; Whitney Museum of American Art, N.Y.C.

Montoya, José. b. Albuquerque, New Mexico. Studied at Oakland School of Arts and Crafts. With Esteban Villa, Malaquias Montoya, René Yañez, and Manuel Hernández founded Mexican American Liberation Art Front (M.A.L.A.F.), San Francisco, 1970, an organization dedicated to creating new art symbols for the Chicano movement, as well as organizing exhibitions and workshops.

Montoya, Malaquias. b. Albuquerque, New Mexico. Studied at Reedely College, San Jose State City College and University of California, Berkeley.

Morales, Armando. b. 1927, Granada, Nicaragua. Resided in Paris since 1982. Visited U.S. on American Council of Education grant, 1957. Studied at Pratt Institute, N.Y.C., 1960. Lived in U.S., 1960–72. Moved to Costa Rica, 1972. Awarded John Simon Guggenheim Memorial Fellowship, 1960; OAS Fellowship, 1962. Traveled to Canada, Panama, France, and Spain, 1963; to Germany, England, Spain, Italy, South America, and Mexico,1965–67. Taught at The Cooper Union, N.Y.C., 1972–73. Solo exhibitions: Angeleski Gallery, N.Y.C., 1962; OAS Headquarters, Washington, D.C., 1962; Lee Ault and Company, N.Y.C., 1963; Bonino Gallery, N.Y.C., 1964, 1966, 1968. Group exhibitions: *Gulf-Caribbean Art*, Museum of Fine Arts, Houston, 1956; The Museum of Modern Art, New York, 1957; *Pittsburgh International*, Carnegie Institute, 1958, 1964, 1968; *Latin America: New Departures*, Institute of Contemporary Art, Boston, 1961; Pan American Union, Washington, D.C., 1963; Solomon R. Guggenheim Museum, N.Y.C., 1963, 1969; *Magnet: New York*, Bonino Gallery, N.Y.C., 1964; *The Emergent Decade*, Solomon R. Guggenheim Museum, N.Y.C., and Cornell University, Ithaca, N.Y., 1965; *Art of Latin America since Independence*, Yale University, New Haven and University of Texas, Austin, 1966; Rhode Island School of Design, Providence, 1966; New School for Social Research, N.Y.C., 1966; Pennsylvania Academy of the Fine Arts, Philadelphia, 1967; Center for Inter-American Relations, N.Y.C., 1970. Collections: Chase Manhattan Bank Collection, N.Y.C.; Cincinnati Art Museum; Detroit Institute of Arts; Esso Collection, Coral Gables, Fla.; The Solomon R. Guggenheim Museum, N.Y.C.; Institute of Contemporary Art, Boston; Museum of Fine Arts, Houston; The Museum of Modern Art, N.Y.C.; Museum of Modern Art of Latin America, Washington, D.C.; Philadelphia Museum of Art; Philbrook Art Center, Tulsa, Okla.; Princeton University, N.J.; Rhode Island School of Design, Providence; University of Texas, Austin.

Morales, José. b. 1947, New York. Studied at High School of Art and Design, N.Y.C.; The Art Students League, N.Y.C.; Academia de Peña, Madrid; École de Beaux-Arts, Paris, 1961–68. Lived in Sweden, 1968–73. Group exhibition: Bronx Community College, N.Y., 1967. Collections: Albuquerque Museum; El Museo del Barrio, N.Y.C.; San Antonio Museum of Art.

Muñoz-Bachs, Eduardo. b. 1937, Valencia, Spain. Moved to Cuba, 1941. Designed posters for ICAIC (Instituto Cubano de Arte e Industria Cinematografica) featured in over 140 international exhibitions, 1960–70. Collections: Center For Cuban Studies, N.Y.C.

Negret, Edgar. b. 1920, Popayan, Colombia. Studied at Escuela de Bellas Artes, Universidad Nacional de Colombia, Bogotá, 1938. Traveled to France and Spain, 1948–54. Lived in N.Y.C., 1955–63. Solo exhibitions: Peridot Gallery, N.Y.C., 1950; Pan American Union, Washington, D.C., 1956; David Herbert Gallery, N.Y.C., 1959; Graham Gallery, N.Y.C., 1965, 1966; Galerie Simone Stern, New Orleans, 1968. Group exhibitions: New School for Social Research,

N.Y.C., 1950, 1960; Peridot Gallery, N.Y.C., 1951; University of Nebraska, Lincoln, 1951; The Museum of Modern Art, N.Y.C., 1955; Institute of Contemporary Arts, Washington, D.C., 1956; *Gulf-Caribbean Art*, Museum of Fine Arts, Houston, 1956; *Pittsburgh International*, Carnegie Institute, 1956; Corcoran Gallery of Art, Washington, D.C., 1956; Riverside Museum, N.Y.C.; 1957; Camino Gallery, N.Y.C., 1957; Yale University, New Haven, 1957; *South American Art Today,* Dallas Museum of Fine Arts, 1959; Lowe Art Gallery, Coral Gables, Fla., 1960; David Herbert Gallery, N.Y.C., 1961; The Museum of Modern Art, N.Y.C., 1961; *Latin American Art: 1931-1966*, The Museum of Modern Art, N.Y.C., 1967; Barone Gallery, N.Y.C., 1961; Pepsi-Cola Art Gallery, N.Y.C., 1964; Daniel Gallery, N.Y.C.,1964; Pan American Union, 1966; Solomon R. Guggenheim Museum, N.Y.C. ,1969. Collections: Solomon R. Guggenheim Museum, N.Y.C.; The Museum of Modern Art, N.Y.C.; Museum of Modern Art of Latin America, Washington, D.C.; University of Nebraska, Lincoln; Rhode Island University, Providence.

Neri, Manuel. b. 1930, Sanger, California. Studied ceramics in Los Angeles, 1949–50; sculpture at San Francisco State College, 1950–51; University of California, Berkeley, 1952; Bray Foundation, Helena, Mo., 1953. Traveled to Mexico,1955. Studied at California College of Arts and Crafts, Oakland, 1955–57; California School of Fine Arts, (now the San Francisco Art Institute), 1957–59. Taught at California School of Fine Arts, San Francisco, 1959; University of California, Davis, 1964–69. Solo exhibitions: Stempfil Gallery, N.Y.C., 1962; Contemporary Art Museum, Houston, 1962; Primus Stuart Gallery, Los Angeles, 1962, 1963; Judd Gallery, Portland, Oreg., 1968; Reed College, Portland, Oreg., 1969; Louisiana State University, Baton Rouge, 1969. Group exhibitions: Six Galleries, San Francisco, 1955, 1957; San Francisco Museum of Art, 1959, 1965, 1968; Stempfil Gallery, N.Y.C., 1961; California Palace of Legion of Honor, San Francisco, 1962; Stanford University, Calif., 1962, 1963; San Francisco Art Institute, 1963, 1970; Oakland Museum, Calif., 1963; David Stuart Gallery, Los Angeles, 1963; University of California, Berkeley, 1967, 1970; Portland Art Museum, Oreg., 1968; Jason Adler Gallery, San Francisco, 1969; University of California, Davis, 1970; Whitney Museum of American Art, N.Y.C., 1970. Collections: Bank of Dallas; Crocker Art Museum, Sacramento, Calif.; Honolulu Academy of Arts; Lannan Foundation, Palm Beach, Fla.; Mexican Museum, San Francisco; Oakland Museum, Calif.; San Francisco Museum of Modern Art; Seattle Art Museum.

Noé, Luis Felipe. b. 1933, Buenos Aires. Studied at Taller de Horacio Butler, Buenos Aires, 1950–52; law at Universidad Nacional, Buenos Aires, 1955–57. Wrote art reviews for *El Mundo*, Buenos Aires, 1956. Received French government scholarship, 1961–62; Instituto Torcuato di Tella Foundation award, 1963; John Simon Guggenheim Memorial Fellowship, 1965. Solo exhibition: Bonino Gallery, N.Y.C., 1966. Group exhibitions: Pan American Union, Washington, D.C., 1962; Institute of Contemporary Arts, Washington, D.C., 1964; Fairleigh Dickinson University, Madison, N.J., 1964; *The Emergent Decade*, Solomon R. Guggenheim Museum, N.Y.C., and Cornell University, Ithaca, N.Y., 1965. Collections: Solomon R. Guggenheim Museum, N.Y.C.; Metropolitan Museum of Art, N.Y.C.; University of Rhode Island, Providence.

Obregón, Alejandro. b. 1920, Barcelona, Spain. Moved to Colombia during childhood. Studied in Spain, France, and at Museum of Fine Arts, Boston, 1937–41. Lived in France, 1949–54. Director, Movimento Nacional de Artes, Bogotá, 1955. Awarded First Prize, *Gulf-Caribbean Art*, Museum of Fine Arts, Houston; Guggenheim International Prize, 1957. Solo exhibitions: Pan American Union, Washington, D.C., 1955; Center for Inter-American Relations, N.Y.C., (retrospective), 1970. Group exhibitions: Pan American Union, Washington, D.C., 1955; *Pittsburgh International*, Carnegie Institute, 1955; *Gulf-Caribbean Art*, Museum of Fine Arts, Houston, 1956; *South American Art Today*, Dallas Museum of Fine Arts, 1959; *Latin America: New Departures*, Institute of Contemporary Art, Boston, 1961; University of Miami, 1966; *The Emergent Decade*, Solomon R. Guggenheim Museum, N.Y.C., and Cornell University, Ithaca, N.Y., 1965; *Art of Latin America since Independence*, Yale University, New Haven, and University of Texas, Austin, 1966. Collections: Dallas Museum of Fine Arts; Solomon R. Guggenheim Museum, N.Y.C.; The Museum of Modern Art, N.Y.C.; Museum of Modern Art of Latin America, Washington, D.C.

Ocampo, Miguel. b. 1922, Buenos Aires. Studied architecture at Universidad Nacional, Buenos Aires. Lived in Paris, 1948–50. Cultural attaché to Argentine embassy, Rome, 1956–59, and Paris, 1961–66. Solo exhibitions: Roland de Aenlle Gallery, N.Y.C., 1958; Pan American Union, Washington, D.C., 1970. Group exhibitions: National Gallery of Art, Washington, D.C., 1955; *South American Art Today*, Dallas Museum of Fine Arts, 1959; Art Institute of Chicago, 1959; *New Art of Argentina*, Walker Art Center, Minneapolis, 1964; *Latin America: New Departures*, Institute of Contemporary Art, Boston, 1961; Center for Inter-American Relations, N.Y.C., 1970. Collections: Albright-Knox Art Gallery, Buffalo, N.Y.; The Museum of Modern Art, N.Y.C; Museum of Modern Art of Latin America, Washington, D.C.; University of Texas, Austin.

Oiticica, Helio. 1937–1980. b. Rio de Janeiro. Studied under painter Ivan Serpa at Museu do Arte Moderna, Rio de Janeiro, 1954. Member of Frente Group, 1955–59; Neo-Concrete movement, Rio de Janeiro, 1959. Danced with the Mangueira Samba School, Rio de Janeiro, 1963–75. Dancer and performer, N.Y.C., c. 1968. Exhibitions: *Information*, The Museum of Modern Art, N.Y.C., 1970.

Orellana, Gaston. b. 1933, Valparaíso, Chile. Resides in Italy. Studied at Accademia della Brera, Milan; Smithsonian Institution, Washington, D.C. Taught at Universidad de Madrid; Instituto Torcuato di Tella, Buenos Aires; Pan American Union, Washington, D.C. Moved to Europe, 1967. Solo exhibitions: Pan American Union, Washington, D.C., 1966; Bienville Gallery, New Orleans, 1967. Group exhibitions: World's Fair, Queens, N.Y., 1964. Collection: Hirshhorn Museum and Sculpture Garden, Washington, D.C.; Metropolitan Museum of Art, N.Y.C.; Museum of Modern Art of Latin America, Washington, D.C.; New Orleans Fine Art Museum; New York Public Library, N.Y.C.

Orozco, José Clemente. 1883–1949. b. Jalisco, Mexico. Family moved to Guadalajara, 1885; Mexico City, 1890. Studied at Escuela de Agricultura de San Jacinto, 1899–1904; Academia de San Carlos, Mexico City, 1908–14. Published caricatures and architectural drawings in local newspapers, 1911. Illustrator for *La Vanguardia Mundial*, (official newspaper of Venustiano Carranzza Constitutionalist Army), Mexico City, 1915. Visited San Francisco and New York, 1917–19. Returned to Mexico and painted his first murals in the Escuela Nacional Preparatoria, Mexico City, 1922. Member of Sindicato de obreros técnicos, pintores y escultores, 1923–24. Lived in N.Y.C., 1927–34. Painted murals at Pomona College, Claremont Calif., 1930, and New School for Social Research, N.Y.C., 1930. Traveled to Europe, 1932. Painted murals at Dartmouth College, Hannover, N.H., 1934; The Museum of Modern Art, N.Y.C., 1945–46. Visited U.S., 1945–46. Solo exhibitions: The Art Students League, N.Y.C., 1929; Delphic Studios, N.Y.C., 1930; Museum Exposition Park, Los Angeles, 1930; Downtown Gallery, N.Y.C., 1931; Grace Horne Galleries, 1931; Wisconsin Union, Madison, 1931; Civic Auditorium, La Porte, Ind., 1934; Arts Club of Chicago, 1934; *Twenty Centuries of Mexican Art*, The Museum of Modern Art, N.Y.C., 1940; *The Latin American Collection of the Museum of Modern Art*, The Museum of Modern Art, N.Y.C., 1943; Pan American Union, Washington, D.C., 1952; Institute of Contemporary Art, Boston (retrospective exhibition), 1953; The Museum of Modern Art, N.Y.C, 1961, 1967; *Art of Latin America since Independence*, Yale University, New Haven, and University of Texas, Austin, 1966. Collections: Baltimore Museum of Art; Museum of Fine Arts, Boston; Fogg Art Museum, Cambridge, Mass.; Museum of Fine Arts, Houston; Metropolitan Museum of Art, N.Y.C.; The Museum of Modern Art, N.Y.C.; Museum of Modern Art of Latin America, Washington, D.C.; Philadelphia Museum of Art; San Francisco Museum of Modern Art.

Osorio, Carlos. 1927–1984. b. Caguas, P.R. Traveled to Japan, 1951. Studied at School of Cartoonists and Illustrators (now School of Visual Arts), N.Y.C., 1953–54. Designed posters and illustrated books for Division of Community Education, San Juan, 1956–64. Lived in U.S., 1964–80. Joined Taller Boricua (organization founded in N.Y.C. to promote Hispanic artists), 1969. Founding member of El Museo del Barrio, N.Y.C., 1969. Returned to Puerto Rico, 1980–84. Solo exhibitions: Campeche Gallery, San Juan, P.R., 1956–59; Instituto de Cultura Puertorriqueña, San Juan, 1964; Universidad de Puerto Rico, San Juan, 1965. Group exhibitions: Pintadera Gallery, San Juan, 1959. Collections: El Museo del Barrio, N.Y.C.; Brooklyn College, N.Y.; Columbia University, N.Y.C.; Instituto de Cultura Puertorriqueña, San Juan; Kutztown University, Pa..; Lincoln Hospital, The Bronx, N.Y.; Metropolitan Museum of Art, N.Y.C.; Museo de Arte de Ponce, P.R.; Rutgers University, New Brunswick, N.J.; Taller Boricua, N.Y.C.

Otero, Alejandro. b. 1921, El Manteco, Venezuela. Studied at Escuela de Artes Plásticas y Aplicadas Cristóbal Rojas, Caracas, 1939–45. Traveled to France on Venezuelan government scholarship, 1945–52. Traveled to U.S., 1948. Appointed coordinator of the Museo de Bellas Artes, Caracas, 1952. Returned to Paris, 1960. Currently lives in Caracas. Awarded John Simon Guggenheim Memorial Fellowship, 1971. Solo exhibitions: Pan American Union, Washington, D.C., 1948. Group exhibitions: *Latin American Exhibition of Fine Arts*, Riverside Museum, N.Y.C., 1939–40; Pan American Union, Washington, D.C., 1948, 1953; *Pittsburgh International*, Carnegie Institute, 1955, 1958; The Museum of Modern Art, New York, 1957; *South American Art Today*, Dallas Museum of Fine Arts, 1959; *The United States Collects Latin American Art*, Art Institute of Chicago, 1959; David Herbert Gallery, N.Y.C., 1960; OAS Headquarters, Washington, D.C., 1960; *Latin America: New Departures*, Institute of Contemporary Art, Boston, 1961; Solomon R. Guggenheim Museum, N.Y.C., 1964; *Art of Latin America since Independence*, Yale University, New Haven, and University of Texas, Austin, 1966; *Latin American Art: 1931-1966*, The Museum of Modern Art, N.Y.C., 1967. Collections: University of Arizona, Tucson; Dallas Museum of Fine Arts; The Museum of Modern Art, N.Y.C.; Museum of Modern Art of Latin America, Washington, D.C.; National Air and Space Museum, Washington, D.C.

Pacheco, Maria Luisa. 1919–1982. b. La Paz, Bolivia. Studied under Cecilio Guzman Derojas and Jorge de la Reza at Academia de Bellas Artes, La Paz, 1934. Illustrator for newspaper *La Razon*, La Paz, 1948–50. Taught at Escuela de Bellas Artes, La Paz, 1950–51; Academia de San Fernando, Madrid, 1951–52; and under Daniel Vasquez Diaz in Madrid, 1952. Traveled in Africa, 1952. Lived in N.Y.C., 1956–82. Illustrator for *Life* magazine, c.1956. Awarded John Simon Guggenheim Memorial Fellowship, 1957, 1959, 1960. Worked as textile designer, N.Y.C., 1959. Solo exhibitions: Galería Sudamericana, N.Y.C., 1956, 1958; Pan American Union, Washington, D.C., 1957; Rose Fried Gallery, N.Y.C., 1962; Bertha Shaefer Gallery, N.Y.C., 1965, 1967; Zegri Gallery, N.Y.C., 1968. Group exhibitions: United Nations Headquarters, N.Y.C., 1958; Dallas Museum of Fine Arts, 1958; Roland de Aenlle Gallery, N.Y.C., 1958; Bodley Gallery, N.Y.C., 1958; Pan American Union, Washington, D.C., 1959; *South American Art Today*, Dallas Museum of Fine Arts, 1959; *The United States Collects Latin American Art*, Art Institute of Chicago, 1960; Museum of Art, Birmingham, Ala., 1960; International Avant-Garde, Newport, Rhode Island, 1961; Joslyn Art Museum, Omaha, Nebr., 1962; University of Illinois, Urbana, 1963; Institute of Contemporary Arts, Washington, D.C., 1963; Bertha Schaefer Gallery, N.Y.C., 1963; *Magnet: New York*, Bonino Gallery, N.Y.C., 1965; *The Emergent Decade*, Solomon R. Guggenheim Museum, N.Y.C., and Cornell University, Ithaca, N.Y.; *Art of Latin America since Independence*, Yale University, New Haven, and University of Texas, Austin, 1966; Pennsylvania Academy of the Fine Arts, Philadelphia, 1967; State University of New York, Stony Brook, N.Y., 1968; Hellen Newland Gallery of Art, Los Angeles, 1969; *Latin American Paintings*, Philbrook Art Center, Tulsa, Ok., 1969; *Latin American Paintings from the John and Barbara Duncan Collection*, Center for Inter-American

Relations, N.Y.C., 1970. Collections: Dallas Museum of Fine Arts; IBM Corporation, Washington, D.C.; Solomon R. Guggenheim Museum, N.Y.C.; Massachusetts Institute of Technology, Cambridge, Mass.; Museum of Modern Art of Latin America, Washington, D.C.; Mobil Oil Laboratories, Princeton, N.J.; New York Savings Bank, N.Y.C.; University of Texas, Austin.

Paternosto, César. b. 1931, La Plata, Argentina. Resided in N.Y.C. since 1967. Studied law at Universidad Nacional de Buenos Aires, 1951–58. Studied painting under Jorge R. Mieri and at the Escuela de Bellas Artes, Universidad Nacional de Buenos Aires, 1957–61. Received John Simon Guggenheim Memorial Fellowship, 1972. Solo exhibitions: A.M. Sachs Gallery, N.Y.C., 1968, 1970. Group exhibitions: *Art of Latin America since Independence*, Yale University, New Haven, and University of Texas, Austin, 1966; *Latin American Art: 1931–1966*, The Museum of Modern Art, N.Y.C., 1967; *Contemporary Latin American Artists*, Delaware Art Center, Wilmington, 1968; Center for Inter-American Relations, N.Y.C., 1968; Ringling Museum, Sarasota, Fla., 1970. Collections: Albright-Knox Art Gallery, Buffalo, N.Y.; Solomon R. Guggenheim Museum, N.Y.C.; Hirshhorn Museum and Sculpture Garden, Washington, D.C.; McCrory Corporation, N.Y.C.; The Museum of Modern Art, N.Y.C.

Amelia Peláez. 1897–1968. b. Santa Clara, Cuba. Family moved to Havana, 1915. Studied under Leopold Romañach at Academia de San Alejandro, Havana, 1916–24; The Art Student's League, N.Y.C., 1924; Academie de la Grande Chaumière, L'École des Beaux-Arts, L'École de Louvre, and under Russian artist Alexandra Exter, Paris, 1927–34. Traveled to Spain, Germany, Italy, Czechoslovakia, and Hungary, 1927–34. Solo exhibitions: Galleria Norte, N.Y.C., 1941. Group exhibitions: *Latin American Exhibition of Fine Arts*, Riverside Museum, N.Y.C., 1939–40; San Francisco Museum of Art, 1942, 1945; The Brooklyn Museum, N.Y., 1943, 1949; The Museum of Modern Art, N.Y.C., 1943, 1944; Institute of Modern Art, Boston, 1947; Pan American Union, Washington, D.C., 1946, 1947, 1952, 1959; Institute of Contemporary Art, Boston, 1952; American Federation of the Arts, Washington, D.C., 1956–57; *The United States Collects Latin American Art*, Art Institute of Chicago,1959; *Latin American Art: 1931–1966*, The Museum of Modern Art, N.Y.C., 1967. Collections: Museum of Modern Art of Latin America, Washington, D.C.

Peñalba, Alicia. b. 1918, Buenos Aires. Studied at Escuela Superior de Bellas Artes, Buenos Aires. Traveled to Paris on a French government grant; studied sculpture under Osip Zadkine and at Academie de la Grande Chaumière, Paris, 1948. Solo exhibitions: Otto Gerson Gallery, N.Y.C., 1960; Fine Arts Associates Gallery, N.Y.C., 1960; Devorah Sherman Gallery, Chicago, 1962; Bonino Gallery, N.Y.C., 1966; Phillips Collection, Washington, D.C., 1966. Group exhibitions: Solomon R. Guggenheim Museum, N.Y.C., 1958, 1962; Fine Arts Associates Gallery, N.Y.C., 1959; Cleveland Museum of Art, 1960; Currier Gallery of Art, Manchester, Vt.; *Pittsburgh International*, Carnegie Institute, 1964, 1967, 1970; Aldrich Museum of Contemporary Art, Ridgefield, Conn., 1964; Phillips Collection, Washington, D.C., 1966. Collections: Albright-Knox Art Gallery, Buffalo; Carnegie Institute, Pittsburgh; Cleveland Museum of Art; Dallas Museum of Fine Arts; Isaac Delgado Museum of Art, New Orleans; Phillips Collection, Washington, D.C.

Pettoruti, Emilio. 1882–1971. b. La Plata, Argentina. Granted scholarship by Province of Buenos Aires for European study, 1913. Studied in Europe, 1913–24. Joined Futurist movement, Milan, 1913. Returned to Argentina, 1924. On invitation of Committee of Inter-American Artists, traveled to the U.S., 1942. Awarded John Simon Guggenheim Memorial Fellowship, 1956. Solo exhibitions: San Francisco Museum of Art, 1942; National Academy of Design, N.Y.C., 1943; City Art Museum, Saint Louis, 1943; Nelson Gallery, Kansas City, 1943; Hatfield Galleries, Los Angeles, 1943; Portland Art Museum, 1944; Seattle Art Museum, 1944; San Francisco Museum of Art, 1944; Pan American Union, Washington, D.C., 1947. Group exhibitions: San Francisco Museum of Art, 1941; Pan American Union, Washington, D.C., 1955; Western College for Women, Oxford, Ohio, 1955; Solomon R. Guggenheim Museum, N.Y.C., 1957; *Pittsburgh International*, Carnegie Institute, 1959; *South American Art Today*, Dallas Museum of Fine Arts, 1959; Chalette Gallery, N.Y.C., 1960; Contemporary Art Center, Cincinnati, 1960; Art Club of Chicago, 1960; Walker Art Center, Minneapolis, 1961; *Art of Latin America since Independence*, Yale University, New Haven, and University of Texas, Austin, 1966; Center for Inter-American Relations, N.Y.C., 1967. Collections: Museum of Modern Art of Latin America, Washington, D.C.; San Francisco Museum of Modern Art.

Poleo, Hector. b. 1918, Caracas. Studied at Escuela de Artes Plásticas y Aplicadas Cristóbal Rojas, Caracas, 1930–37. Studied mural painting in Mexico, 1938–40. Traveled to U.S., Colombia, and Ecuador, 1938–40. Lived in N.Y.C., 1944–48. Awarded John Simon Guggenheim Memorial Fellowship, 1947. Traveled to Europe, 1948–52. Lived in Venezuela, 1952–58. Moved permanently to Paris, 1959. Solo exhibitions: Pan American Union, Washington, D.C., 1945; San Francisco Museum of Art, 1945, 1966; Seligmann Gallery, N.Y.C., 1943, 1945, 1948; Denver Art Museum, 1946; Library of Congress, Washington, D.C., 1948. Group exhibitions: *Latin American Exhibition of Fine Arts*, Riverside Museum, 1939–40; John Herron Art Institute, Indianapolis, 1945; Grand Central Art Galleries, N.Y.C., 1945; Knoedler Gallery, N.Y.C., 1947; International Festival of Art, N.Y.C., 1950, 1960; Peabody Art Museum, Nashville, 1965; *Art of Latin America since Independence*, Yale University, New Haven, and University of Texas, Austin, 1966; La Jolla Museum of Art, Calif., 1966; Isaac Delgado Museum of Art, New Orleans, 1966; Arts Center, Forth Worth, Tex., 1966; *Biennial of Latin American Engraving*, San Juan, P.R., 1970. Collections: Art Institute of Chicago; IBM Corporation, N.Y.C.; John Herron Art Institute, Indianapolis; The Museum of Modern Art, N.Y.C.; Museum of Modern Art of Latin America, Washington, D.C.; San Francisco Museum of Modern Art.

Polesello, Rogelio. b. 1939, Buenos Aires. Studied at Escuela Nacional de Bellas Artes, Buenos Aires. Awarded First Prize, Esso Salon of Young Artists from Latin America, Washington, D.C., 1965. Solo exhibitions: Pan American Union, Washington, D.C., 1961; Janie C. Lee Gallery, Dallas, 1968. Group exhibitions: University of Nebraska Art Gallery, 1959; *South American Art Today*, Dallas Museum of Fine Arts, 1959; Pan American Union, Washington, D.C., 1960; *New Art of Argentina*, Walker Art Center, Minneapolis, 1964; American University, Washington, D.C., 1964; Pan American Union, Washington, D.C., and IBM Gallery, N.Y.C., 1965; *Artists of Latin America*, Smithsonian Institution, Washington, D.C., 1965; *The Emergent Decade*, Solomon R. Guggenheim Museum, N.Y.C. and Cornell University, Ithaca, N.Y., 1966; *Latin American Art, 1931–1966*, The Museum of Modern Art, N.Y.C., 1966; *Art of Latin America since Independence*, Yale University, New Haven, and University of Texas, Austin, 1966; The Museum of Modern Art, N.Y.C., 1967; *Pittsburgh International*, Carnegie Institute, 1967; Center for Inter-American Relations, N.Y.C., 1968; Bonino Gallery, N.Y.C., 1968; Flint Institute of Arts, Mich., 1968; *Latin American Works Acquired by The Museum of Modern Art*, N.Y.C., 1969; The Museum of Modern Art, N.Y.C., 1969; Center for Inter-American Relations, N.Y.C., 1970. Collections: Albright-Knox Art Gallery, Buffalo; Chase Manhattan Bank, N.Y.C.; Flint Institute of Arts, Mich.; Florida State Museum, Gainesville; Solomon R. Guggenheim Museum, N.Y.C.; Lowe Art Museum, Coral Gables, Fla.; The Museum of Modern Art, N.Y.C.; Museum of Modern Art of Latin America, Washington, D.C.; Pan American Union, Washington, D.C.; Rhode Island School of Design, Providence; University of Texas, Austin.

Porter, Liliana. b. 1941, Buenos Aires. Resided in N.Y.C. since 1964. Studied at Escuela Nacional de Bellas Artes, Buenos Aires, 1953; under Mathias Goeritz at Universidad Iberoamericana, Mexico City, 1958–64. Appointed artist-in-residence, University of Pennsylvania, Philadelphia, 1968. Awarded First Prize, *First Latin American Print Biennial*, San Juan, P.R.; John Simon Guggenheim Memorial Fellowship, 1980. Exhibitions: *Magnet: New York*, Bonino Gallery, N.Y.C., 1964; New York University, N.Y.C., 1968; Paula Cooper Gallery, N.Y.C., 1969; *Information*, The Museum of Modern Art, N.Y.C., 1970. Collections: Chase Manhattan Bank, N.Y.C.; Hunter Museum of Art, Chattanooga, Tenn.; Mellon Bank, Pittsburgh; The Museum of Modern Art, N.Y.C.; New York Public Library, N.Y.C.; Phillip Morris Collection, N.Y.C.; RCA Corporation, N.Y.C.; University of Texas, Austin.

Portinari, Candido. 1903–1962. b. São Paulo. Studied at Escola Nacional de Belas Artes, Rio de Janeiro, 1918; figure drawing under Lucilio de Albuquerque and painting under Amoedo and Batista da Costa, Rio de Janeiro, 1921. Awarded scholarship for travel to France, Great Britain, and Italy, 1928. Lived in Paris, 1929–31. Taught at Universide do Distrito Federal, Rio de Janeiro, 1936–39. Traveled to U.S., 1940. Painted murals at Library of Congress, Washington, D.C., 1941–42; and United Nations, N.Y.C., 1952–56. Illustrated several books for Paris publishing house Gallimard. Awarded Legion of Honor medal, 1946; Guggenheim National First Prize, 1957; Hallmark Art Award, 1957. Solo exhibitions: Pan American Union, Washington, D.C., 1940, 1947, 1950; Wildenstein Gallery, N.Y.C., 1959. Group exhibitions: *Pittsburgh International*, Carnegie Institute, 1935; Brazilian pavilion, World's Fair, N.Y.C., 1939; *Latin American Exhibition of Fine Arts*, Riverside Museum, N.Y.C., 1939–40; The Museum of Modern Art, N.Y.C., 1940; Pan American Union, Washington, D.C., 1947, 1949, 1953; *The United States Collects Latin American Art*, Art Institute of Chicago, 1959; *South American Art Today*, Dallas Museum of Fine Arts, 1959; *Art of Latin America since Independence*, Yale University, New Haven, and University of Texas, Austin, 1966; *Latin American Art: 1931–1966*, The Museum of Modern Art, N.Y.C., 1967. Collections: Carnegie Institute, Pittsburgh; The Jewish Museum, N.Y.C; Library of Congress, Washington, D.C.; The Museum of Modern Art, N.Y.C.; Museum of Modern Art of Latin America, Washington, D.C.

Pou, Miguel. 1880–1968. b. Ponce, P.R. Studied under Pedro Clausells, Luis Desangles, Santiago Meana, and at Instituto Provincial en Ponce (B.A. 1898). Traveled frequently in U.S., 1901–07. Studied education at Normal School, Hyannis, Mass., 1906. Taught in public education system, P.R., 1900–10; founded Miguel Pou Academy, P.R., 1910. Studied at The Art Students League, N.Y.C., 1919–20; Pennsylvania Academy of the Fine Arts, Philadelphia, 1935. Traveled to N.Y.C., 1944. Solo exhibitions: Instituto de Cultura Puertorriqueña (retrospective exhibition), San Juan, 1957. Group exhibitions: *International Exposition*, Buffalo, N.Y., 1901; Charleston, S.C., 1902; Independents Salon, N.Y.C., 1926; Aristas Gallery, N.Y.C., 1926; *National Exposition of Art*, N.Y.C., 1938. Collections: Ateneo Puertorriqueño, San Juan; IBM Corporation, N.Y.C.; Instituto de Cultura Puertorriqueña, San Juan; Museo de Arte de Ponce, P.R.; Universidad de Puerto Rico, San Juan.

Puente, Alejandro b. 1933, La Plata, Argentina. Studied art under Héctor Carter at Escuela de Bellas Artes La Plata, 1960. Founded Grupo Si, 1960. Awarded John Simon Guggenheim Memorial Fellowship, 1967. Lived in N.Y.C., 1967–71. Teaches painting at Escuela Superior de la Cordova de Buenos Aires. Group exhibitions: *Latin American Artists*, Delaware Art Center, Wilmington, 1968; Center for Inter-American Relations, N.Y.C., 1968; Paula Cooper Gallery, N.Y.C., 1969; *Information*, The Museum of Modern Art, N.Y.C., 1970. Collections: Center for Inter-American Relations, N.Y.C.; Chase Manhattan Bank, N.Y.C.; The Museum of Modern Art, N.Y.C.

Quesada, Eugenio. b. 1927, Wickenburg, Arizona. Studied at Mesa Community College and Arizona State University (B.A.). Taught at Santa Paula High School, Calif., 1954; Glendale Community College, Ariz., 1972; Arizona State University, 1972 to the present. Group exhibitions: San Francisco, California, 1969; Tempe, Arizona, 1970; Phoenix, Arizona, 1970.

Biographies

Ramírez Villamizar, Eduardo. b. 1923, Pamplona, Colombia. Studied architecture at Universidad Nacional de Colombia, Bogotá, 1940–43; sculpture at Escuela de Bellas Artes, Bogotá, 1944–45. Taught at Escuela de Bellas Artes, Universidad Nacional de Colombia, Bogotá; New York University, N.Y.C., 1960. Traveled to U.S. and Europe, 1950, 1952, 1954. Lived in N.Y.C., 1967–73. Awarded John Simon Guggenheim Memorial Fellowship, 1958. Solo exhibitions: Pan American Union, Washington, D.C., 1954; Roland de Aenlle Gallery, N.Y.C., 1956; David Herbert Gallery, N.Y.C., 1960; Center for Inter-American Relations, N.Y.C., 1968. Group exhibitions: New School for Social Research, N.Y.C., 1949; *Gulf-Caribbean Art*, Museum of Fine Arts, Houston, 1957; Corcoran Gallery, Washington, D.C., 1957; *Pittsburgh International*, Carnegie Institute, 1958, 1961, 1966; *South American Art Today*, Dallas Museum of Fine Arts, 1959; University of Miami, 1960; David Herbert Gallery, N.Y.C., 1961; Pan American Union, Washington, D.C., 1962; The Museum of Modern Art, N.Y.C., 1962; American Federation of the Arts, Washington, D.C., 1964 (traveled); *Art of Latin American since Independence*, Yale University, New Haven, and University of Texas, Austin, 1966; *Latin American Art: 1931–1966*, The Museum of Modern Art, N.Y.C., 1967; J. P. Speed Art Museum, Louisville, Ky., 1968. Collections: American Bank and Trust Company, N.Y.C., The Museum of Modern Art, N.Y.C., Museum of Modern Art of Latin America, Washington, D.C.

Raquel Rivera, Carlos. b. 1923, Río Prieto, P.R. Studied at Edna Coll Academy, San Juan, 1948–50; under Reginald Marsh and John Corbino at The Art Students League, N.Y.C., 1950. Joined Signs Workshop, Centro de Arte Puertorriqueño, P.R. Worked with Division of Community Education, P.R., until 1955. Solo exhibitions: Galería Colibrí, San Juan, 1964. Group exhibitions: Riverside Museum, N.Y.C., 1957; Instituto de Cultura Puertorriqueña, San Juan, 1961; Museo de Arte de Ponce, 1964; Collections: Ateneo Puertorriqueño, San Juan; El Museo del Barrio, N.Y.C.; Instituto de Cultura Puertorriqueña, San Juan; Museo de Arte de Ponce, P.R.; Universidad de Puerto Rico, San Juan.

Rayo, Omar. b. 1928, Roldanillo, Colombia. Received OAS fellowship to study at the Universidad Iberoamericana, Mexico City, 1959–60. Lived in N.Y.C., 1960–75. Awarded Philadelphia Museum of Art Prize, 1965; Acquisition Prize, National Print Exhibition, Potsdam, N.Y., 1967. Solo exhibitions: Pan American Union, Washington, D.C., 1961, 1964; The Contemporaries, N.Y.C., 1961, 1962, 1965; Miami Museum of Modern Art, 1963; Devorah Sherman Gallery, Chicago, 1965; Flair House Gallery, Cincinnati, 1965; Association of American Artists, N.Y.C., 1965, 1968; University of Oklahoma, Norman, 1967; Philadelphia Art Alliance, 1968; Richard Feigen Graphics, N.Y.C., 1969; Casa del Arte, San Juan, 1970; Galería Colibrí, San Juan, 1970; Lunn Gallery, Washington, D.C., 1970; Jack Misrachi Gallery, N.Y.C., 1970; Van Straaten Gallery, Chicago, 1970. Group exhibitions: Baltimore Museum of Art, 1961; Wiggin Gallery, Boston, 1961; The Print Club of Philadelphia, 1962,1964, 1967, 1968; The Brooklyn Museum, N.Y., 1962, 1964, 1968; Museum of Fine Arts, Boston, 1962; Library of Congress, Washington, D.C., 1963, 1969; Institute of Contemporary Arts, Washington, D.C., 1964; The Contemporaries, N.Y.C., 1964, 1965, 1967; The Museum of Modern Art, N.Y.C., 1964, 1966, 1968; A.A.A. Gallery, N.Y.C., 1964; *Magnet: New York*, Bonino Gallery, N.Y.C., 1964; De Cordova Museum, Lincoln, Mass., 1965; Smithsonian Institution, Washington, D.C., 1966; Whitney Museum of American Art, N.Y.C., 1966; *Art of Latin America since Independence*, Yale University, New Haven, and University of Texas, Austin, 1966; Institute of Contemporary Art, Boston, 1967; Dulin Gallery of Art, Knoxville, Tenn., 1967, 1968; Devorah Sherman Gallery, Chicago, 1967; Universidad de Puerto Rico, 1967; State University College, Potsdam, N.Y., 1968, 1970; Museum of Contemporary Art, Chicago, 1968; New York University, 1968; Zegri Gallery, N.Y.C., 1969, 1970; Graham Gallery, N.Y.C., 1969; *Latin American Paintings and Drawings from the Collection of John and Barbara Duncan*, Center For Inter-American Relations, N.Y.C., 1970; The Jewish Museum, N.Y.C., 1970. Collections: Art Institute of Chicago; Baltimore Museum of Art; Boston Public Library; The Brooklyn Museum, N.Y.; Chase Manhattan Bank, N.Y.C.; Library of Congress, Washington, D.C.; The Museum of Modern Art, N.Y.C.; Museum of Modern Art of Latin America, Washington, D.C.; New York Public Library, N.Y.C.; Philadelphia Museum of Art; Smithsonian Institution, Washington, D.C.

Rivera, Diego. 1886–1957. b. Guanajuato, Mexico. Moved to Mexico City, 1889. Studied at Academia de San Carlos, Mexico City, 1896–1902. Traveled to Spain, 1907; France, Belgium, Holland, England, 1908–09; Italy, 1920–21. Lived in Paris, 1911–20. Met Frida Kahlo, 1923; married Kahlo, 1929. Painted murals at U.S. Stock Exchange Luncheon Club, San Francisco, 1930–31 (*Allegory of California*); California School of Fine Arts, 1931 (*The Making of a Fresco*); Sterne Home, Calif., 1931; Detroit Institute of Arts, 1932–33 (*Man and Machine*); Rockefeller Center, N.Y.C., 1933 (*Man at the Crossroads*); The New Worker's School, N.Y.C., 1933 (*Portrait of America*); Golden Gate International Exposition, installed at San Francisco City College, 1940. Solo exhibitions: Worcester Art Museum, Mass., 1927; Weyhe Gallery, N.Y.C., 1928; California Palace of the Legion of Honor, San Francisco, 1930; Detroit Institute of Arts, 1931; The Museum of Modern Art, N.Y.C., 1931; Society of Arts and Crafts, Detroit, 1932; San Francisco Museum of Art, 1940; International Ladies Garment Workers Union, N.Y.C., 1942; Hackley Art Gallery, Muskegon, Mich.,1943; Museum of Fine Arts, Houston, 1951. Group exhibitions: Modern Gallery, N.Y.C., 1916; Société Anonyme, N.Y.C., 1921; Los Angeles Museum, 1925; Cleveland Museum of Art, 1927; The Art Center, N.Y.C., 1928; American Federation for the Arts, N.Y.C., 1930; College Art Association, N.Y.C., 1933; Art Institute of Chicago, 1934, 1946, 1959; Alger House, Detroit, 1936, 1938; Detroit Institute of the Arts, 1937, 1938, 1949; *Latin American Exhibition of Fine Arts*, Riverside Museum, N.Y.C., 1940; *Twenty Centuries of Mexican Art*, The Museum of Modern Art, N.Y.C., 1940; Institute of Modern Art, Boston, 1941; The Museum of Modern Art, N.Y.C., 1942, 1943, 1944; Fogg Museum of Art, Cambridge, Mass., 1942, 1948; Philadelphia Museum of Art, 1943; Worcester Art Museum, Mass., 1944; San Francisco Museum of Art, 1945; Grand Central Art Galleries, 1946; Dallas Museum of Fine Arts, 1948; Bucholtz Gallery, N.Y.C., 1948; University of Michigan, Ann Arbor, 1958; Los Angeles County Museum of Art, 1963, 1970; Rockefeller University, N.Y.C., 1965; Meadows Museum, Southern Methodist University, Dallas, 1966; *Art of Latin America since Independence*, Yale University, New Haven, and University of Texas, Austin, 1966; Fine Arts Gallery, San Diego, 1966; *Latin American Art: 1931–1966*, The Museum of Modern Art, N.Y.C., 1967; Isaac Delgado Museum of Art, New Orleans, 1968; Metropolitan Museum of Art, N.Y.C., 1970; Santa Barbara Museum of Art, 1970. Collections: Amherst College, Mass.; Art Institute of Chicago; Baltimore Museum of Art; The Brooklyn Museum, N.Y.; Cleveland Museum of Art; Colorado Springs Fine Arts Center; Columbus Museum of Art, Ohio; Des Moines Art Center, Iowa; Detroit Institute of Arts; Fogg Art Museum, Cambridge, Mass.; Hood Museum, Dartmouth College, Hannover, N.H.; Honolulu Academy of Art; IBM Corporation, N.Y.C.; Los Angeles County Museum of Art; Meadows Museum, Southern Methodist University, Dallas; Milwaukee Art Museum; Minneapolis Institute of Arts; Museum of Fine Arts, Houston; The Museum of Modern Art, N.Y.C.; Philadelphia Museum of Art; Phoenix Art Museum; San Antonio Museum of Art; San Diego Museum of Art; San Francisco Museum of Modern Art; Seattle Art Museum; Smith College Museum, Northampton, Mass.; St. Louis Museum; University of Texas, Austin; Vassar College Gallery of Art, Poughkeepsie, N.Y.; Worcester Art Museum, Mass.

Rivera-Rosa, Rafael. b. 1942, Comerío, P.R. Lived in N.Y.C., 1946–59. Studied under Lorenzo Homar at the Instituto de Cultura Puertorriqueña, San Juan, c. 1958; under Domingo García at the Taller de Artes Gráficas y Galería Campeche, San Juan, 1959. Organized the Taller Bija, (artist's collective that concentrated on political graphic art), San Juan, 1970. Collections: Ateneo Puertorriqueño, San Juan; El Museo del Barrio, N.Y.C.; Instituto de Cultura Puertorriqueña, San Juan; Museo de Arte de Ponce, P.R.; Universidad de Puerto Rico, San Juan.

Roca Rey, Joaquín. b. 1923, Lima. Studied at Escuela Nacional de Bellas Artes, Lima, and in ateliers of the Spanish sculptors Macho and Oteiza, c. 1943–48. Traveled in Europe, 1948–52; U. S., 1950. Solo exhibitions: Pan American Union, Washington, D.C, 1959; Philadelphia Museum of Art, 1966. Group exhibitions: *South American Art Today*, Dallas Museum of Fine Arts, 1966. Collections: Museum of Modern Art of Latin America, Washington, D.C.; Walker Art Center, Minneapolis.

Rodón, Francisco. b. 1934, San Sebastián, P.R. Moved to San Juan, 1949. Traveled to Central America and Mexico on scholarship, 1952–53. Studied at Academie Julien, Paris, 1953; Traveled to Spain, 1954. Studied at La Esmeralda, Mexico City, 1955; The Art Students League, N.Y.C., 1958; graphics under Lorenzo Homar at Instituto de Cultura Puertorriqueña, San Juan, 1959. Taught at Universidad de Puerto Rico, Rio Piedras, 1963. Resident painter, Universidad de Puerto Rico, Rio Piedras, 1968. Solo exhibitions: Instituto de Cultura Puertorriqueña, San Juan, 1961; Universidad de Puerto Rico, Rio Piedras, 1963, 1967, 1970; Group exhibitions: Ateneo Puertorriqueño, 1960; Universidad de Puerto Rico, San Juan, 1961, 1968; Instituto de Cultura Puertorriqueña, San Juan, 1965. Collections: Art Institute of Chicago; Ateneo Puertorriqueño, San Juan; Container Corporation of America, Chicago; Esso Collection, P.R.; Fogg Art Museum, Cambridge, Mass.; Instituto de Cultura Puertorriqueña, San Juan; Interamerican University, San Germán, P.R.; Lincoln Hospital Collection, The Bronx, N.Y.; Metropolitan Museum of Art, N.Y.C.; Metropolitan Museum of Art & Art Center, Coral Gables, Fla.; El Museo del Barrio, N.Y.C.; The Museum of Modern Art, N.Y.C.; Museo de Arte de Ponce, P.R.; Universidad de Puerto Rico, San Juan; Universidad de Puerto Rico, Rio Piedras.

Romano, Jaime. b. 1942, San Juan, P.R. Studied Humanities at Universidad de Puerto Rico (B.A., 1966); art at American University, Washington, D.C. (M.F.A. 1969). Member of Forma Universitaria, P.R., 1966–67. Lived in Washington, D.C., and N.Y.C., 1973–84. Awarded first prize for drawing, Ateneo Puertorriqueño, 1968. Solo exhibitions: Universidad de Puerto Rico, Rio Piedras, 1967; Watkins Art Gallery, Washington, D.C, 1968. Group exhibitions: San Juan Bienal, 1970. Collections: Ateneo Puertorriqueño, San Juan; Chase Manhattan Bank, N.Y.C.; Citibank N.A., N.Y.C.; Library of Congress, Washington, D.C.; Metropolitan Museum of Art, N.Y.C.; Pratt Institute, N.Y.C.

Rosado del Valle, Julio. b. 1922, Cataño, P.R. Studied under Spanish painter Cristóbal Ruiz at Universidad de Puerto Rico; at New School for Social Research, N.Y.C., and under Mario Carreño and Camilo Egas, N.Y.C., 1946. Traveled to Paris and Florence, 1946–49. Studied at the Accademia San Marco, Florence, 1947–48. Traveled to N.Y.C., 1957–58. Illustrator and poster designer for Division of Community Education, San Juan, 1949. Awarded Gold Medal, Architectural League of New York, 1955; John Simon Guggenheim Memorial Fellowship, 1957. Resident painter, Universidad de Puerto Rico, 1955. Solo exhibitions: Universidad de Puerto Rico, 1946, 1954, 1966; Instituto de Cultura Puertorriqueña, San Juan, 1959, 1963; Pan American Union, 1965. Group exhibitions: Philadelphia Museum of Art, 1955; *Gulf-Caribbean Art*, Museum of Fine Arts, Houston, 1956; Riverside Museum, N.Y.C., 1957; Pan American Union, Washington, D.C., 1957; Library of Congress, Washington, D.C., 1963; Friends of Puerto Rico, N.Y.C., 1965; Universidad de Puerto Rico, Rio Piedras, 1965, 1966, 1969; Museo de Arte de Ponce, P.R., 1967, 1970. Collections: Ateneo Puertorriqueño, San Juan; El Museo del Barrio, N.Y.C.; Instituto de Cultura Puertorriqueña, San Juan; Museo de Arte de Ponce, P.R.; Museum of Modern Art of Latin America, Washington, D.C.; Universidad de Puerto Rico, San Juan.

Rostgaard, Alfredo. b. 1943, Guantánamo, Cuba. Designed posters for ICAIC (Instituto Cubano de Arte e

Industria Cinematográfica) featured in over 140 international exhibitions, 1963 to the present. Collections: Center For Cuban Studies, N.Y.C.

Ruiz, Antonio. 1897–1964. b. Texcoco, Mexico. Studied at La Esmeralda, Mexico City, 1916; studied set and film design, Universal Films, Hollywood, Calif., 1926–29. Taught drawing in elementary schools, Calif., 1923–26; set design at Universidad Nacional de Mexico, Mexico City, 1938. Director, La Esmeralda, Mexico City, 1942–54. Founded first Taller de Modelos Tecnícos de la Escuela Avanzada de Ingeniería y Arquitectura, Mexico City, 1932. Painted four murals for The Pacific House, San Francisco, 1940. Solo exhibitions: Art Center, N.Y.C., 1928. Group exhibitions: University of Minnesota, Minneapolis, 1937; *Golden Gate International Exposition*, San Francisco, 1940; The Museum of Modern Art, N.Y.C., 1940; Institute of Contemporary Art, Boston, 1940; Philadelphia Museum of Art, 1943; *The Latin American Collection at The Museum of Modern Art*, N.Y.C , 1943; *Art of Latin America since Independence*, Yale University, New Haven, and University of Texas, Austin, 1966. Collections: The Museum of Modern Art, N.Y.C.; Philadelphia Museum of Art.

Sabogal, José. 1888–1956. b. Lima. Studied in Europe and North Africa, 1909–11; Escuela Nacional de Bellas Artes Manuel Belgrano, Buenos Aires, 1912–18; Mexico, 1922–25. Illustrated *Fire on the Andes* by Carleton Beals, 1934. Taught at Escuela Nacional de Bellas Artes, Lima, 1920–33. Director, Escuela Nacional de Bellas Artes, Lima, 1933–43. Traveled to U.S. invited by U.S. Department of State, 1942–43. Group exhibitions: Universidad de Puerto Rico, Rio Piedras, 1938; *Golden Gate International Exposition*, San Francisco, 1940; *The Latin American Collection of the Museum of Modern Art*, N.Y.C., 1943; Pan American Union, Washington, D.C., 1947; *Art of Latin America since Independence*, Yale University, New Haven, and University of Texas, Austin, 1966. Collections: Museum of Modern Art of Latin America, Washington, D.C.

Sakai, Kazuya. b. 1927, Buenos Aires. Resided in Japan until 1951; Buenos Aires, 1951–63; New York, 1963–66; Mexico since 1966. Studied at University of Tokyo. Taught at Escuela Nacional de Bellas Artes Manuel Belgrano, Buenos Aires; Universidad Nacional de Tucuman, Colegio de Mexico; Universidad Autónoma de México. Solo exhibitions: Martin Schweig Gallery, St. Louis, Mo., 1963; Cleveland Institute of Art, 1963. Group exhibitions: Pan American Union, Washington, D.C., 1959; *South American Art Today*, Dallas Museum of Fine Arts, 1959; *Latin America: New Departures*, Institute of Contemporary Art, Boston, 1961; Time-Life Building, N.Y.C., 1961; Museum of Art, University of Michigan, 1961; Des Moines Art Center, Iowa, 1961; University of Texas, Austin, 1961; Pan American Union, Washington, 1961; Widger Gallery, Washington, D.C., 1961; Pan American Union, Washington, D.C., 1962; *Magnet: New York*, Bonino Gallery, N.Y.C., 1964; *New Art of Argentina*, Walker Art Center, Minneapolis, 1964; Institute of Contemporary Arts, Washington, D.C., 1964; *The Emergent Decade*, Solomon R. Guggenheim Museum, N.Y.C., and Cornell University, Ithaca, N.Y., 1965; Dallas Museum of Fine Arts, 1966; Krannert Art Museum, Ill., 1966; De Cordova Museum of Art, Fla., 1966; Bonino Gallery, N.Y.C., 1969, 1970. Collections: University of Texas, Austin.

Sánchez, Emilio. b. 1921, Camaguay, Cuba. Resided in N.Y.C. since 1952. Studied at University of Virginia; The Art Students League, N.Y.C.; Columbia University, N.Y.C., 1943. Traveled throughout Europe and West Indies, 1946. Awarded Pennsylvania Academy of the Fine Arts Eyre Medal, 1969; New Jersey State Print Annual David Kaplan Purchase Award, 1970. Solo exhibitions: Joseph Luyber Gallery, N.Y.C., 1949; Ferargil Gallery, N.Y.C., 1951, 1953; Mint Museum, N.C., 1955; Tucker Gallery, Miami, Fla., 1955; Peridot Gallery, N.Y.C., 1956; Galería Sudamericana, N.Y.C., 1958, 1968; Philadelphia Print Club, 1958; The Contemporaries, N.Y.C., 1966; Association of American Artists, N.Y.C., 1966; Louisiana Gallery, Houston, 1967; Bienville Gallery, New Orleans, 1970. Group exhibitions: Pan Am Building, N.Y.C., 1965; Metropolitan Museum of Art, N.Y.C., 1966; Free Library of Philadelphia, 1966; The Brooklyn Museum, N.Y.,1968. Collections: Albright-Knox Art Gallery, Buffalo, N.Y.; The Brooklyn Museum, N.Y.; Free Library of Philadelphia; Metropolitan Museum of Art, N.Y.C.; The Museum of Modern Art, N.Y.C.; Walker Art Center, Minneapolis.

Sanín, Fanny. b. Bogotá. Became U.S. citizen, 1967. Studied at Universidad de los Andes, Bogotá, (degree, 1960); University of Illinois, Urbana, 1962; Chelsea School of Art, London, 1966. Lived in Mexico, 1963–66. Moved to N.Y.C., 1971. Solo exhibitions: Pan American Union, Washington, D.C., 1969; Museum of Modern Art of Bogotá, 1986 (retrospective). Collections: Everson Museum of Art, Syracuse, N.Y.; Museum of Contemporary Hispanic Art, N.Y.C.; The Museum of Modern Art, N.Y.C.; Window South, Palo Alto, Calif.

Segall, Lasar. 1891–1957. b. Vilna, Lithuania. Studied at Akademie der Bildenden Künste, Berlin, 1906–09. Lived in Dresden and participated in the German Expressionist movement, 1910–23. Moved to São Paulo, 1923. Founded SPAM (Sociedad Pró-Art Moderna; society for Modern Art). Solo exhibitions: Neumann Willard Gallery, N.Y.C., 1940; Associated American Artists N.Y.C., 1948; Pan American Union, Washington, D.C., 1948. Collections: The Jewish Museum, N.Y.C.; The Museum of Modern Art, N.Y.C.; Museum of Modern Art of Latin America, Washington, D.C.

Segui, Antonio. b. 1934, Córdoba, Argentina. Studied law and painting in Argentina, 1950; painting and sculpture in Paris, 1952. Moved to Paris, 1963. Exhibitions: San Francisco Museum of Modern Art, 1961; Institute of Contemporary Art, Boston, 1962; *Pittsburgh International*, Carnegie Institute, 1964; *New Art of Argentina*, Walker Art Center, Minneapolis, 1964; Lefebre Gallery, N.Y.C., c.1965; *Latin American Art: 1931–1966*, The Museum of Modern Art, N.Y.C., 1967; The Museum of Modern Art, N.Y.C., 1968; Delaware Art Center, Wilmington, 1968; *Latin American Print Biennial*, San Juan, 1970. Collections: Lefebre Gallery, N.Y.C.

Serra-Badué, Daniel. b. 1914, Santiago, Cuba. Resided in N.Y.C., since 1962. Studied at the studio of José Simont; The Art Students League, N.Y.C., 1926 (youngest artist ever to study at the League); Pratt Institute; under Borrell-Nicolau and Luis Muntane at Escuela de Bellas Artes, Barcelona, 1932–36; National Academy of Design; Columbia University, N.Y.C., 1938–40. Awarded John Simon Guggenheim Memorial Fellowship, 1938, 1939 (first recipient); Walter Lippincott Prize, Pennsylvania Academy of the Fine Arts, Philadelphia, 1941; Oscar B. Cintas Foundation Fellowship, 1963, 1964. Assistant Director, Ministry of Education, Havana, 1959–60. Taught at Columbia University, N.Y.C., The Brooklyn Museum Art School, St. Joseph's College for Women, Kansas City, and St. Peter's College, Jersey City, N.J. Solo exhibitions: Karl Freund Gallery, N.Y.C., 1939; Milch Galleries, N.Y.C., 1940; Whyte Galleries, Washington, D.C., 1941; The Contemporaries, N.Y.C., 1957; Galería Sudamericana, N.Y.C., 1961, 1965; State University, New Paltz, N.Y., 1961; C.W. Post College, Long Island, N.Y., 1966; Group exhibitions: Art Institute of Chicago, 1938; World's Fair, N.Y.C., 1939; Whitney Museum of American Art, N.Y.C., 1940; *Pittsburgh International*, Carnegie Institute, 1941; Galería Sudamericana, N.Y.C., 1957; Columbia University, N.Y.C., 1962; Cisneros Gallery, N.Y.C., 1967. Collections: Metropolitan Museum of Art, N.Y.C.; New York Public Library, N.Y.C.

Silva, Rufino. b. 1919, Humacao, P.R. Studied at Universidad de Puerto Rico, Rio Piedras, 1938; Art Institute of Chicago on scholarship from government of Puerto Rico, 1938–42. Taught at Layton School of Art, Milwaukee, 1946–47. Studied at Academie de la Grande Chaumière, Paris, and at Stamperia Nazionale, Rome, on a scholarship from Art Institute of Chicago,1947–51. Awarded the World's Fair Prize for Painting, N.Y.C., 1939; Clusman Prize for Painting, 1956. Appointed instructor, Art Institute of Chicago, 1952. Solo exhibitions: Art Institute of Chicago, 1952; Open Studio, Milwaukee, 1952; Ricardo Restaurant Gallery, Chicago, 1952; Hyde Park Art Center, Chicago, 1960; Paul Theobald Bookshop Gallery, Chicago, 1961; Instituto de Cultura Puertorriqueña, San Juan, 1963, 1967; Illinois Institute of Technology, Chicago, 1967; University of Wisconsin, Madison, 1968; Loyola University, Chicago, 1969; Elmherst College, Ill., 1970. Group exhibitions: World's Fair, Queens, N.Y., 1939; Art Institute of Chicago, 1939, 1940, 1945, 1946,1947, 1955, 1956, 1962, 1966; Pan American Council, Chicago, 1940; San Francisco Museum of Art, 1943; Art Circle, Chicago, 1947; Sun-Times Building, Chicago, 1960; Old Town Art Center, Chicago, 1960; Rockford College Gallery, Ill.,1960; Chicago Arts Festival, 1965; Loyola University, Chicago, 1970; *San Juan Biennial of Latin American Graphics*, 1970. Collections: Art Institute of Chicago.

Soto, Jesús Rafael. b. 1923, Ciudad Bolívar, Venezuela. Studied at Escuela de Artes Plásticas y Aplicadas Cristóbal Rojas, Caracas, 1942–47. Director, Escuela de Bellas Artes, Maracaibo, 1947–50. Resided in Paris since 1950. Awarded Apollonio Prize, *First Latin American Biennial of Drawing*, San Juan; Chevalier de l'Ordre des Arts et des Lettres, presented by French government. Solo exhibitions: Kootz Gallery,1965, 1966: Marlborough-Gerson Gallery, N.Y.C., 1969. Group exhibitions: Martha Jackson Gallery, 1959; Albright-Knox Art Gallery, Buffalo, N.Y., 1965; *The Emergent Decade*, Solomon R. Guggenheim Museum, N.Y.C., and Cornell University, Ithaca, N.Y., 1965; *Art of Latin America since Independence*, Yale University, New Haven, and University of Texas, Austin, 1966; *Pittsburgh International*, Carnegie Institute, 1967; Irving B. Harris Gallery, Chicago,1970. Collections: Albright-Knox Art Gallery, Buffalo; Larry Aldrich Museum, Ridgefield, Conn.; Solomon R. Guggenheim Museum, N.Y.C.; Hirshhorn Museum and Sculpture Garden, Washington, D.C.; The Museum of Modern Art, N.Y.C.; University of Nebraska, Lincoln.

Soto, Jorge. b. 1947, New York. Exhibited widely in New York and Puerto Rico after 1970. Member, Taller Boricua, N.Y.C. Collections: Boricua College, N.Y.C.; El Museo del Barrio, N.Y.C.; Solomon R. Guggenheim Museum, N.Y.C.; Hunter College, N.Y.C.; Museum of Contemporary Hispanic Art, N.Y.C.

Tábara, Enrique. b. 1930, Guayaquil, Ecuador. Studied painting at Escuela de Bellas Artes, Guayaquil; Barcelona; Switzerland, 1955–64. Traveled to U.S., 1964. Founded VAN (Ecuadorian artists' movement against indigenism), 1968. Solo exhibitions: Pan American Union, 1964; Universidad de Puerto Rico, Rio Piedras, 1966. Group exhibitions: Pan American Union, Washington, D.C., 1966; *Art of Latin America since Independence*, Yale University, New Haven, and University of Texas, Austin, 1966; Center for Inter-American Relations, N.Y.C., 1967. Collections: The Museum of Modern Art, N.Y.C.; The Museum of Modern Art of Latin America, Washington, D.C.; Museo de Arte de Ponce, P.R.

Tamayo, Rufino. b. 1899, Oaxaca, Mexico. Moved to Mexico City, 1911. Studied at La Esmeralda, Mexico City, 1915–17; Academia de San Carlos, Mexico City, 1917–21. Appointed department head, Ethnographic drawing, Museo Nacional de Arqueologia de la Ciudad de Mexico, Mexico City, 1921. Taught art in Mexico City elementary schools, 1926; La Esmeralda, 1928. Traveled to N.Y.C., 1926. Lived in U.S., 1936–51. Appointed director, Department of Fine Arts, Ministry of Education, Mexico City, 1932. Delegate to Art Congress, N.Y.C., 1936. Taught at Dalton School, N.Y.C., and Tamayo Workshop, Brooklyn Museum Art School, 1936–51. Painted murals for the Hillyer Art Library, Smith College, Northampton, Massachusetts, 1943; Dallas Museum of Fine Arts, 1953; Bank of the Southwest, Houston, 1955; Universidad de Puerto Rico, San Juan, c. 1958. Lived in Paris, 1949–55. Returned to Mexico, 1955. Received John Simon Guggenheim Memorial Fellowship, 1960. Elected to Institute of Academy of Arts and Letters of the United States, 1961. Awarded Ford Foundation Fellowship to work at Tamarind Lithography Workshop,

Los Angeles, 1964. Solo exhibitions: Weyhe Gallery, N.Y.C., 1926; Art Center, N.Y.C., 1927; Julien Levy Gallery, N.Y.C., 1931, 1937; Howard Putzel Gallery, San Francisco,1937; Catherine Kuhn Gallery, Chicago, 1938; Valentine Gallery, N.Y.C., 1939, 1940, 1942, 1946, 1947; Pierre Matisse Gallery, N.Y.C, 1947; Knoedler Gallery, 1950, 1951, 1954, 1956, 1959, 1962. Group exhibitions: Pan American Union, Washington, D.C., 1952; Santa Barbara Museum of Art, Calif., 1954; San Francisco Museum of Art, 1954; *Gulf-Caribbean Art*, Museum of Fine Arts, Houston, 1956; *Art of Latin America since Independence*, Yale University, New Haven, and University of Texas, Austin, 1966; *Latin American Art: 1931-1966*, The Museum of Modern Art, N.Y.C., 1967; Phoenix Art Museum, 1968. Collections: Albright-Knox Art Gallery, Buffalo, N.Y.; American Museum of Natural History, Washington, D.C.; Art Institute of Chicago; The Brooklyn Museum, N.Y.; Cincinnati Art Museum; Cleveland Museum; Dallas Museum of Fine Arts; Fogg Art Museum, Cambridge, Mass.; IBM Corporation, Armonk, N.Y.; University of Illinois, Urbana; Marlborough Gallery, N.Y.C.; Metropolitan Museum of Art, N.Y.C.; Milwaukee Art Center; The Museum of Modern Art, N.Y.C.; Museum of Modern Art of Latin America, Washington, D.C.; Neuberger Museum, Purchase, N.Y.; Perls Galleries, N.Y.C.; Phillips Collection, Washington, D.C.; Phoenix Art Museum; Universidad de Puerto Rico, San Juan; Smith College, Northampton, Mass.; University of Texas, Austin; Washington University, St. Louis.

Toral, Mario. b. 1934, Santiago. Resided in N.Y.C. since 1973. Studied painting in Argentina and Uruguay; drawing at École des Beaux-Arts, Paris, 1958-63. Returned to Chile, 1963. Solo exhibition: Galería Sudamericana, N.Y.C., 1963. Group exhibitions: *Art of Latin America since Independence*, Yale University, New Haven, and University of Texas, Austin, 1966. Awarded John Simon Guggenheim Memorial Fellowship, 1975. Collections: The Brooklyn Museum, N.Y.; The Museum of Modern Art, N.Y.C.; Museum of Modern Art of Latin America, Washington, D.C.; Window South, Palo Alto, Calif.

Torres, Augusto. b. 1913, Tarrasa, Spain. Resided in Montevideo, Uruguay since 1980. Studied under Amadee Ozenfant, and worked as studio assistant to Julio Gonzalez, Paris, 1930. Moved to Montevideo, and studied under his father, Joaquín Torres-García, 1934. Taught at Taller Torres-García, Montevideo, 1944. Awarded New School For Social Research scholarship, 1960. Traveled to N.Y.C., and organized exhibition of Taller Torres-García participants with Gonzalo Fonseca, N.Y.C., 1961-62. Lived in Spain, 1974-80. Group exhibitions: Pan American Union, Washington, D.C., 1942, 1950; New School for Social Research, N.Y.C., 1960.

Torres-García, Joaquín. 1874-1949. b. Montevideo. Moved to Barcelona, 1892. Studied at Academia de Bellas Artes, and Academia Baixas, Barcelona, 1894. Joined Cercle Artistic de Sant Luc (an association of Catholic painters), 1894. Worked with Antonio Gaudí on the design of Church of the Sagrada Familia, and on stained glass windows for Cathedral of Palma, 1903-07. Taught at Escola Mont d'Or, 1903-07. Visited Brussels, 1909; Italy and Switzerland, 1912. Lived in N.Y.C., 1920-22; Italy, 1922-26; Paris, 1926-34. Cofounded with Michel Seuphor review *Cercle et Carré*, and helped organize *First International Exhibition of Constructivist and Abstract Art*, Paris, 1930. Traveled to Spain, 1933. Founded Asociación de Arte Constructivo (Association of Constructivist), Montevideo, 1935. Published first issue of magazine *Círculo y Cuadrado*, (based on the French *Cercle et Carré*), Montevideo, 1936. Founded Taller Torres-García, Montevideo, 1944. Authored numerous books, including *Notes sobre art* (Gerona, 1913), *Universalismo Constructivo*, (Buenos Aires, 1944), and *La recuperacion del objeto*, (Montevideo, 1952). Solo exhibitions: Pan American Union, Washington, D.C., 1961; Rose Fried Gallery, N.Y.C., 1960, 1965; Royal Marks Gallery, N.Y.C., 1969; Solomon R. Guggenheim Museum, N.Y.C., and Rhode Island School of Design, Providence, 1970. Group exhibitions: Whitney Studio Club (now the Whitney Museum of American Art), 1921; Museum of

Living Art, N.Y.C., 1933; New York University, N.Y.C., 1943; Philadelphia Museum of Art, (permanent installation), 1943; *The Latin American Collection of The Museum of Modern Art*, The Museum of Modern Art, N.Y.C., 1943; Pan American Union, Washington, D.C., 1950, 1955; *The United States Collects Latin American Art*, Art Institute of Chicago, 1959; *The Emergent Decade*, Solomon R. Guggenheim Museum, N.Y.C., and Cornell University, Ithaca, N.Y., 1965; *Art of Latin America since Independence*, Yale University, New Haven, and University of Texas, Austin, 1966; *Latin American Art: 1931-1966*, The Museum of Modern Art, N.Y.C., 1967; Center for Inter-American Relations, N.Y.C., 1967, 1970. Collections: Albright-Knox Art Gallery, Buffalo, N.Y.; CDS Gallery, N.Y.C.; Solomon R. Guggenheim Museum, N.Y.C.; Sidney Janis Gallery, N.Y.C.; The Museum of Modern Art, N.Y.C.; Rhode Island School of Design, Providence; Yale University, New Haven.

Tufiño, Rafael. b. 1922, Brooklyn, N.Y. Studied under Alejandro Sanchez Felipe, Puerto de Tierra, P.R.; and under José Chavez-Morado, at Academia de San Carlos, Mexico City. Cofounder of Centro de Arte Puertorriqueño. Director, Division of Community Education, San Juan. Received painting award, Ateneo Puertorriqueño, 1952, 1957; John Simon Guggenheim Memorial Fellowship, 1966. Collections: Ateneo Puertorriqueño, San Juan; El Museo del Barrio, N.Y.C.; Instituto de Cultura Puertorriqueña, San Juan; Library of Congress, Washington, D.C.; Museum of Contemporary Hispanic Art, N.Y.C.; The Museum of Modern Art, N.Y.C.; Museo de Arte de Ponce, P.R.; Universidad de Puerto Rico, San Juan.

Uriburu, Nicolas. b. 1937, Arquitecto, Argentina. Performed *International Coloration* at many sites, including Grand Canal–Venice, Rio de la Plata–Buenos Aires, River Seine–Paris, and East River–Manhattan, 1970. Solo exhibition: Bonino Gallery, N.Y.C., 1970. Group exhibitions: *The Emergent Decade*, Solomon R. Guggenheim Museum, N.Y.C., and Cornell University, Ithaca, N.Y., 1965; Modern Art Gallery, Scottsdale, Ariz., 1966.

Valdivieso, Raul. b. 1931, Santiago. Resides in Madrid. Studied at Escuela de Bellas Artes, Universidad de Chile, Santiago. Traveled to London on a British government scholarship, 1958. Studied at La Grand Chaumière, Paris; and in Madrid and Brussels. Solo exhibitions: Pan American Union, Washington, D.C., 1964; Universidad de Puerto Rico, Rio Piedras, 1966. Group exhibitions: Smithsonian Institution, Washington, D.C., 1966; Corcoran Gallery of Art, Washington, D.C., 1967; Pan American Union, Washington, D.C., 1966, 1967, 1968; *Pittsburgh International*, Carnegie Institute, 1967. Collections: Museum of Modern Art of Latin America, Washington, D.C.; Philadelphia Museum of Art.

Vidal, Miguel Angel. b. 1928, Buenos Aires. Studied at Academia Nacional de Bellas Artes, Buenos Aires. Appointed Professor of Visual Arts, Academia Nacional de Bellas Artes, Buenos Aires, 1952. Designed books for Academia de Bellas Artes, Buenos Aires, 1966-68. Group exhibitions: *New Art of Argentina*, Walker Art Center, Minneapolis, 1964; Center for Inter-American Relations, 1968; Bonino Gallery, N.Y.C., 1968; Flint Institute of Arts, Michigan, 1969; Albright-Knox Art Gallery, Buffalo, N.Y., 1970. Collections: Albright-Knox Art Gallery, Buffalo, N.Y.; The Solomon R. Guggenheim Museum, N.Y.C.; IBM Collection, N.Y.C.; The Museum of Modern Art, N.Y.C.; Museum of Modern Art of Latin America, Washington, D.C.; University of Texas, Austin.; Westinghouse Corporation, N.Y.C.

Villarini, Pedro. b. 1933, Hato Ray, P.R. Resided in N.Y.C. since 1947. Solo exhibitions: Broadway Theater Production, N.Y.C., 1958; Aspira, N.Y.C., 1967; Campeche Gallery, San Juan, 1969; P.S. 185, N.Y.C., 1969. Group exhibitions: John Marino Gallery, N.Y.C., 1956; Riverside Museum, N.Y.C., 1957; Ateneo Puertorriqueño, San Juan, 1960; Society of Friends of Puerto Rico, N.Y.C., 1960; Galan Art Gallery, N.Y.C., 1960; Grand Street Settlement, N.Y.C., 1960; Fiesta Folklorica Puertorriqueño, N.Y.C., 1960; Caravan House Gallery, N.Y.C., 1963; Galería Hoy

and Friends of Puerto Rico, N.Y.C., 1964; Brooklyn College, N.Y., 1964; Brotherhood Action Center, N.Y.C., 1965; Association for Puerto Rican Hispanic Culture, N.Y.C., 1966; Columbia University, N.Y.C., 1966; Hunter College, N.Y.C., 1966; Art and Artifact Gallery, N.Y.C., 1966; Fashion Institute of Technology, N.Y.C., 1970; West Side Artists, N.Y.C., 1970; Instituto de Cultura Puertorriqueña, San Juan, 1970. Collections: Ateneo Puertorriqueño, San Juan; El Museo del Barrio, N.Y.C.; Museo de Arte de Ponce, P.R.

Villegas, Armando. b. 1928, Pomabamba, Ancash, Peru. Studied at Escuela Nacional de Bellas Artes, Lima, 1945-51; and at Escuela de Bellas Artes, Universidad Nacional de Colombia, Bogotá, 1952-53. Solo exhibitions: Pan American Union, Washington, D.C., 1958. Group exhibitions: *Gulf-Caribbean Art*, Museum of Fine Arts, Houston, 1956; Solomon R. Guggenheim Museum, N.Y.C., 1956, 1957; *The United States Collects Latin American Art*, Art Institute of Chicago, 1959; *South American Art Today*, Dallas Museum of Fine Arts, 1959; University of Miami, and Pan American Union, Washington, D.C., 1960-62. Collections: Art Institute of Chicago; Museum of Modern Art of Latin America, Washington, D.C.; University of Texas, Austin.

Wakabayashi, Kazuo. b. 1931, Kobe, Japan. Studied at Niki-Kai School of Fine Arts, Tokyo, 1947-50. Moved to São Paulo, Brazil, 1961. Solo exhibitions: Pan American Union, Washington, D.C., 1969. Group exhibitions: *Nippon-Brazilian Painting Today*, Washington, D.C., 1965; Rockefeller Center, N.Y.C., 1965; Amel Gallery, N.Y.C., 1966. Collections: Brazilian-American Cultural Institute, Washington, D.C.; Chase Manhattan Bank, N.Y.C.; Museum of Modern Art of Latin American, Washington, D.C.

Zañartu, Enrique. b. 1921, Paris (of Chilean parents). Moved to Santiago, 1938. Resided in Paris since 1949. Lived in N.Y.C., 1944-47; Cuba, 1947-59. Director, Atelier 17, N.Y.C., 1944-49. Taught printmaking at Akademie der Bildenden Künste, Stuttgart, 1964-65. Book illustrator, Paris, 1955-85. Solo exhibitions: Pan American Union, Washington, D.C., 1956, 1959. Group exhibitions: *Pittsburgh International*, Carnegie Institute, 1958; Solomon R. Guggenheim Museum, 1958; *The United States Collects Latin American Art*, Art Institute of Chicago, 1959. Collections: Art Institute of Chicago; Dallas Museum of Fine Arts; The Museum of Modern Art, N.Y.C.; New York Public Library, N.Y.C.; Northwestern University, Ill.; Washington University, St. Louis; Rhode Island School of Design, Providence.

Notes

Mexican and Mexican American Artists

1. Bernard S. Myers, *Mexican Painting in Our Time* (New York: Oxford U. Press, 1956), p.12. The Centro Artistico was founded by Dr. Atl and commissioned to decorate the Simon Bolívar Amphitheater in the National Preparatory School in 1910. The revolution put a stop to the project. **2.** Jean Charlot, *The Mexican Mural Renaissance: 1920–1925*, (New Haven: Yale U. Press, 1962), pp.70 and 82. Sources consulted for this section include Anita Brenner, *Idols Behind Altars* (Boston: Little, Brown, 1929); and Justino Fernández, *Arte Moderno y Contemporáneo de Mexico* (Mexico City: UNAM, 1952). **3.** Charlot, op. cit., p.46. **4.** Ibid., pp.70–71. See also Brenner, op. cit., pp.232–34 for a discussion of Mérida's work. **5.** Brenner, op. cit., pp.241–42, and Charlot, op. cit., pp.72–73. **6.** Fernández, op. cit., pp.388–89. **7.** Charlot, op. cit., p.72. **8.** Ibid., p.73. **9.** Ibid., p.99. Vasconcelos commissioned Montenegro to paint a mural in the former church of San Pedro y San Pablo, Mexico City, 1921. The work, *The Dance of the Hours*, was painted in oils. **10.** See Charlot, op. cit. **11.** Ibid., pp.241–51, and Brenner, op. cit., pp.254–59. **12.** Charlot, op. cit., pp.243–44. **13.** For references to a "Mexican Renaissance," see José Juan Tablada, "Mexican Painting Today," *International Studio*, January 1923, p.276; Ernest Gruening, "The Mexican Mural Renaissance," *Century Magazine*, February 1924; and Brenner, "A Mexican Renascence," *Arts*, September 1925, pp.127–50. **14.** See for example René d'Harnoncourt, *Mexican Arts* (see note 4, Notes to the Appendix). **15.** See Charlot, op. cit., pp.168–71 and 257–60. **16.** Classical references were used by Rivera in his mural *Creation* (1922–23) and by Orozco in his mural *Maternity* (1923). **17.** Charlot, op. cit., p.175. **18.** Ibid., p.154. **19.** Ibid., p.300. **20.** Ibid., pp.301–302. **21.** Orozco painted murals with Revolution themes in Orizaba, Veracruz (1926); Rivera painted references to the Revolution in Mexico City (1923–24, 1928 and 1929) and Cuernavaca (1929–30). **22.** Rivera used the Descent from the Cross motif in *Liberation of the Peon* and the Crucifixion motif in *Leaving the Mine*, both in the Court of Labor of the Ministry of Education (1923). Orozco used the latter for *The Barricade* (1926) in the National Preparatory School. **23.** Rivera used the Conquest theme in the Palace of Cortés and the National Palace murals (1929–30), and a pre-Columbian theme in the latter. Orozco used both themes at Dartmouth College (1932–33). **24.** Rivera painted the image of Zapata in a number of murals in Mexico from 1926 to 1931. **25.** For example, Orozco painted *The Caudillo Zapata* and another version of *The Barricade* (both 1930) in the U.S. Rivera painted a portable panel, based on his painting of Zapata in the Palace of Cortés, in New York (1931) and a lithograph of the same subject (1932). **26.** See James S. Plaut, "Mexican Maximum: Exhibition Organized by Institute of Modern Art, Boston," *Art News*, December 15, 1941, pp.1–11, and Dorothy Grafly, "Deeply National Art of Old Mexico Presented in Philadelphia," *The Art Digest*, April 15, 1943, p.8. **27.** See David Alfaro Siqueiros, "Rivera's Counter-Revolutionary Road," *New Masses*, May 29, 1934. **28.** See Raquel Tibol, *Diego Rivera: Arte y Política* (Mexico City: Imprenta Mundial, 1935), pp.111–25. **29.** See Siqueiros *No hay más ruta que la nuestra* (Mexico City: Secretaría de Educación Pública, 1945). A turning point in favor of the formalists occurred when the Mexican government invited Tamayo to submit works for a major survey of Mexican art exhibited in Paris in 1952 and invited him to paint two murals in the Palace of Fine Arts, Mexico City. See Flora Lewis, "Mexican Counter-Revolt," *New York Times Magazine*, October 12, 1952; Gladys Harrison, "Gallery Gazer," *Time-Herald* (Washington, D.C.), October 26, 1952; and Emily Grenauer, "Art and Artists: Liberation of Mexican Mural Art Hailed as Tamayo Completes Mural," *New York Herald Tribune*, October 5, 1952. **30.** See note 4, Notes to the Appendix. **31.** *Twenty Centuries of Mexican Art*, The Museum of Modern Art, New York, 1940. **32.** For example: *Philadelphia Arts Alliance Exhibition* (1939) and *From Marketplace to Museum* (1946) at the Grand Central Galleries. **33.** *Masterworks of Mexican Art: From Pre-Columbian Times to the Present*, Los Angeles County Museum of Art (1963–64), focused on the Mexican School as well as earlier art. **34.** See Orlando Suárez, *Inventario del Muralismo Mexicano* (Mexico City: UNAM 1972), p.384. **35.** See Shifra Goldman, *Contemporary Mexican Painting in a Time of Change* (Austin: U. Texas Press, 1981), pp.35–38. **36.** Ibid., p.39. **37.** See Suárez, op. cit., p.226; and Dore Ashton, *Yes, But...: A Critical Study of Philip Guston* (New York: Viking, 1976), pp.30–32. **38.** *Mexican Life* and *Mexican Folkways*, English-language magazines published in Mexico, were not distributed widely in the U.S. **39.** Tablada, op. cit., pp.267–76. **40.** Tablada, "Diego Rivera, Mexican Painter," *Arts*, October 1923, pp.221–33; and "José Clemente Orozco, the Mexican Goya," *International Studio*, March 1924, pp.492–500. **41.** Tablada, "The Arts in Modern Mexico," *Parnassus*, February 1929, pp.8–9. **42.** Brenner, "An Artist from the Maya Country, Carlos Mérida," *International Studio*, April 1926, pp.85–87; "A Mexican Rebel," *Arts*, October 1927, pp.201–209; and "A Mexican Renascence," op. cit.,pp.127–50. **43.** Brenner, "Idols," op. cit., pp.260–87. **44.** Walter Pach, *Masters of Modern Art* (New York: Ayer, 1972), pp.95, 99–100, and 113. **45.** Pach, "An Exhibition of Art Work by Mexican School Children, and Jean Charlot," *Art Center Bulletin*, April 1926, pp.244–46; and "The Evolution of Diego Rivera," *Creative Art*, January 1929, pp.21–39. **46.** Gruening, op. cit.; Eileen Dwyer, "The Mexican Modern Movement," *Studio*, October 1927, pp.262–66. **47.** Rafaél Vera de Córdova, "Art in Mexico," *The Art Digest*, December 15, 1926, p.10. **48.** Bertram Wolfe, "Art and Revolution in Mexico," *Nation*, August 27, 1924, pp.207–208. **49.** See Frederick W. Leighton, "Rivera's Mural Paintings," *International Studio*, February 1924, pp.378–81; Ernestine Evans, "If I Should Go Back to Mexico," *Century*, February 1926, pp.455–61; "Frescoes Glorify Mexican Indian Life," *New York Times Magazine*, September 26, 1926, pp.12–21; and John Dos Passos, "Diego Rivera's Murals," *New Masses*, March 1927. **50.** Evans, op. cit. **51.** Emily S. Hamblen, "Notes on Orozco's Murals," *Creative Art*, January 1929, p.46. **52.** Rivera, "The Guild Spirit in Mexican Art; as told to Katherine Anne Porter," *Graphic Survey*, May 1, 1924, pp.174–78; and "From a Mexican Painter's Notebook," *Arts*, January 1925, pp.21–23. **53.** Rivera, "The Revolution in Painting," *Creative Art*, January 1929, pp. 17–18 and 23–30; Orozco, "New World, Races and New Art," *Creative Art*, January 1929, pp.44–46. **54.** See note 47 for information on this exhibition. **55.** Flynn Paine organized the Art Center Galleries exhibition (1928). D'Harnoncourt organized the Metropolitan Museum of Art exhibition (1930–31). **56.** Helm, Clifford, and Leeper organized exhibitions at the Boston Institute of Modern Art (1940), the Philadelphia Museum of Art (1943), and the Pasadena Institute of Art exhibition (1953), respectively. **57.** See note 31 and note 4 in Notes to the Appendix. **58.** See Delmari Romero Keith, *Historia y Testimonios: Galería de Arte Mexicano* (Mexico City: Galería de Arte Mexicano, 1986). See note 32 and the Appendix for more information on exhibitions organized by Inés Amor. **59.** Charlot, "Twenty Centuries of Mexican Art," *Magazine of Art*, July 1940, pp.398–405. **60.** Plaut, op. cit., pp.1–11. **61.** Jules Langsner, "Art of Mexico at the Pasadena Art Institute," *Art News*, May 1953, p.49. **62.** See Bertram Wolfe, *The Fabulous Life of Diego Rivera* (New York: Stein and Day, 1963); and Goldman, "Siqueiros and Three Early Murals in Los Angeles," *Art Journal*, Summer 1974, pp.321–27. **63.** "Seeing Red," *The Art Digest*, October 15, 1930, p.8. **64.** Wolfe, op. cit., pp.284–87. **65.** Ibid., pp.291–93; see also "Diego Rivera Paints a Novel Theme for San Francisco Art School," *The Art Digest*, September 1, 1931, pp.3–4. **66.** "Will Detroit, Like Mohammed II, Whitewash Its Murals?" *The Art Digest*, April 1, 1933, pp.5–6 and p.30; see also "Rivera Squall," *The Art Digest*, April 15, 1933, p.6. **67.** Wolfe, op. cit., p.310. **68.** See, for example, "Rockefeller Boards up Rivera Fresco," *Art News*, May 13, 1933, pp.3–4; "Artists Quit Show in Rivera Protest," *The New York Times*, February 14, 1934, p.17, and "Art Society Quits Show in Protest," February 15, 1934, p.17. **69.** Goldman, op. cit., pp.321–27. **70.** Teresa del Conde, *J.C. Orozco: Antología Crítica* (Mexico City: UNAM, 1982), p.10. **71.** "Dartmouth Indicted," *The Art Digest*, July 7, 1933, p.12. **72.** "Orozco's American Epic at Dartmouth Starts Controversy," *The Art Digest*, September 1, 1934, pp.5–6. **73.** "Mr. Watts' Attack on Orozco's Murals Stirs a Hornet's Nest," *The Art Digest*, October 1, 1934, pp.6 and 21–22. **74.** "Watts Writes in Defiance; Mumford in Appreciation of Orozco," *The Art Digest*, October 15, 1934, pp.8, 10, and 19. **75.** Myers, op. cit., pp.89–92. **76.** Ibid., pp.100–103 and 106–114. **77.** See notes 52 and 53 for articles by Rivera. **78.** See Francis O'Connor, "An Iconographic Interpretation of Diego Rivera's *Detroit Industry Murals*," in *Diego Rivera: A Retrospective* (Detroit: Detroit Institute of Arts, 1986), p.215. **79.** Laurance Hurlburt, "The Siqueiros Experimental Workshop: New York, 1936," *Art Journal*, Spring 1976, pp.237–46. **80.** See Charlot, "Orozco's Stylistic Evolution," *Art Journal*, Winter 1949–1950, pp.148–57. **81.** The lithographs are related to the "Revolution" panels Orozco painted in the National Preparatory School in 1926. *Rear Guard*, in particular, is based on a panel on the third floor of the school. **82.** See Jacqueline Barnitz, *Latin American Artists in the U.S. Before 1950* (New York: Center for Inter-American Relations, 1981), p.16. **83.** Frederick A. Sweet, "The Leader Zapata," *Bulletin of the Art Institute of Chicago*, November 1941, pp.90–91. See also John Hutton, "'If I am to die tomorrow'—Roots and Meanings of Orozco's *Zapata Entering a Peasant's Hut*," *The Art Institute of Chicago Museum Studies*, Fall 1984, pp.38–51. **84.** See Sidney Tillim, "Studies for the Dartmouth Murals at The Museum of Modern Art," *Arts*, January 1962, pp.30–31. **85.** Orozco represented Quetzalcoatl (a pre-Columbian deity as well as legendary historical figure) as a white man, accepting the views of many nineteenth- and twentieth-century writers who refused to believe an Indian could have achieved such feats. This attitude led them to look for Old World sources to understand the civilizations of the New World. **86.** The historical figure born in Tula in the tenth century and named Ce Acatl Topiltzin (Prince One Reed) became identified with the cult of Quetzalcoatl. At Dartmouth, Orozco focused on the Prince's expulsion from Tula in the Dartmouth mural panel following a dispute with a rival group. Orozco shows him pointing east, vowing to return someday to reclaim his kingdom. The prophecy was fulfilled, or so the Indians thought, when Hernán Cortés arrived from the east in a year identified by the Aztecs as Ce Acatl or One Reed (1519). **87.** See Ralph Flint, "Rivera Frescos Seen at Museum of Modern Art," *Art*

News, December 26, 1931, pp.5–7. **88.** Rivera was barred from completing the Rockefeller Center mural on May 9, 1933. **89.** See Myers, op. cit., pp.117 and 144. **90.** Hurlburt, op. cit., pp.237–46. **91.** *Ethnography* was originally titled *The Mask* according to MacKinley Helm, op. cit., p.95. **92.** Myers, op. cit., pp.136–43. **93.** Suárez, op. cit., pp.262–63. **94.** George Raphael Small, *Ramos Martínez: His Life and His Art*, edited by Jerald Slattum (Westlake Village, Calif.: F. & J. Publishing Company, 1975). **95.** See the Appendix and Artists' Biographies for more information. **96.** Suárez, op. cit., p.212. **97.** Ibid., pp.120–21; see also Lamar Dodd, *Charlot Murals in Georgia* (Athens: U. Georgia Press, 1945). **98.** See Brenner, op. cit., pp.145–46. **99.** Suárez, op. cit., p.286. **100.** Ibid., p.287; according to Suárez, Ruiz painted four panels at Pacific House; according to a press release from the *Golden Gate International Exposition* (October 8, 1938), Ruiz aided "Covarrubias in the completion of the eight pictorially illuminated maps" for the exposition's Pacific House. **101.** *Julio Castellanos* (Mexico City: Banco Nacional de México 1962). **102.** Suárez, op. cit., p.196. **103.** Ibid., p.195. **104.** Among the portfolios of prints produced by the Taller de Gráfica Popular are *25 Grabados de Leopoldo Méndez* (1943), *Estampas de la Revolución Mexicana* (1947), and *450 años de lucha: homenaje al pueblo mexicano* (1960). **105.** Suárez, op. cit., p.121. **106.** Ibid., p.164. **107.** Ibid., p.64. **108.** Ibid., pp.129–31. **109.** Miguel Covarrubias, *The Prince of Wales and Other Famous Americans* (New York: Knopf, 1925) and *Negro Drawings* (New York: Knopf, 1927). **110.** Orozco, *José Clemente Orozco, An Autobiography*, Robert C. Stephenson, transl., (Austin: U. Texas Press 1962), pp.72 and 124. **111.** See notes 63–74 for more information. **112.** Hurlburt, op. cit., pp.237–46. **113.** O'Connor, ed., *The New Deal Art Projects: An Anthology of Memoirs* (Washington, D.C.: 1972), p.210. See also Matthew Baigell and Julia Williams, eds., *Artists Against War and Fascism: Papers of the First American Artists' Congress* (New Brunswick: Rutgers U. Press 1986). **114.** George Biddle, *An American Artist's Story*, (Boston: Little, Brown, 1939), p.268. **115.** See O'Connor, op. cit., pp.11–49. See also O'Connor, "New Deal Murals in New York," *Artforum*, November 1968, pp.41–49; and Richard D. McKinzie, *The New Deal for Artists* (Princeton: Princeton U. Press, 1973). **116.** Ashton, op. cit., pp.26 and 30. **117.** O'Connor, *Jackson Pollock* (New York: The Museum of Modern Art, 1967), p.14. **118.** O'Connor, *The New Deal Art Projects*, op. cit., p.128. **119.** See O'Connor, "The Influence of Diego Rivera on the Art of the United States During the 1930s and After," in *Diego Rivera: A Retrospective*, op. cit., pp.157–83. **120.** O'Connor, *The New Deal Art Projects*, op. cit., p.128. **121.** Ibid., pp.78–113. **122.** Ibid., pp.318–19. **123.** Suárez, op. cit., p.226. **124.** Ibid., pp.226–28. **125.** Ibid., p.227. **126.** Ibid., p.323. **127.** McKinzie, op. cit., p.178. **128.** Ashton, op. cit., pp.31–32. **129.** Ibid., p.31. See also Robert Storr, *Phillip Guston* (New York: Abbeville Press, 1986), p.13. **130.** See Sam Hunter, *Modern American Painting and Sculpture* (New York: Dell, 1963), p.139; and Barbara Rose, *American Art since 1900* (New York: Praeger, 1968), p.153. **131.** See Quirarte, *Mexican American Artists* (Austin: U. Texas Press, 1973) and *A History and Appreciation of Chicano Art* (San Antonio: Research Center for the Arts and Humanities, 1984), pp.163–68. **132.** Quirarte, *Mexican American Artists*, op. cit. **133.** Ibid., p.43. **134.** Octavio Medellín, interview with the author, 1970. **135.** See Quirarte, *Mexican American Artists*, op. cit., p.45. **136.** Ibid., pp.58–62, and *A History and Appreciation of Chicano Art*, pp. 165–68. **137.** Quirarte, *Mexican American Artists*, pp.78–80. **138.** Suárez, op. cit., p.300. **139.** Jorge Montaño, "Rufino Tamayo: Leader of a New Mexican School of Painting," *Mexican Life*, November 1929, pp.23–27. **140.** See note 29. **141.** Suárez, op. cit., p.300. **142.** James B. Lynch, Jr., *Rufino Tamayo: Fifty Years of His Paintings* (Washington, D.C.: Phillips Collection, 1978), p.18. **143.** Suárez, op. cit., p.202. See also *A Salute to Carlos Mérida* (Austin: University Museum, 1977). **144.** *A Salute to Carlos Mérida*, p.11. **145.** Suárez, op. cit., p.202. **146.** Hayden Herrera, *Frida: A Biography of Frida Kahlo* (New York: Harper and Row, Publishers, 1983), pp.228–32. **147.** The inscription on the painting reads: "Here you see us, me Frida Kahlo, with my beloved husband Diego Rivera. I painted these portraits in the beautiful city of San Francisco for our friend Mr. Albert Bender, and it was in the month of April in the year 1931." **148.** Herrera, op. cit., p.150. **149.** Ibid., pp.173–75. **150.** For reviews of Friedeberg's 1963 exhibition, see Leslie Judd Ahlander, "Gallery Notes: Latin Artists show at Pan American Union," *The Washington Post*, October 6, 1963; and "Pan American," *The Sunday Star* (Washington, D.C.), October 13, 1963. **151.** Barnitz, *Young Mexicans* (New York: Center for Inter-American Relations, 1970). **152.** Biographical information from the Archives of the Museum of Modern Art of Latin America. **153.** See note 29. **154.** Goldman, op. cit., p.33. **155.** Ibid., pp.35–38. **156.** Archives of the Museum of Modern Art of Latin American and Federico Morais, *Mathias Goeritz* (Mexico City: UNAM, 1982). **157.** See Gregory Battcock, *Minimal Art: A Critical Anthology* (New York: Dutton 1968), pp.19–20 and 25. See also Jack Burnham, *Beyond Modern Sculpture* (New York: George Braziller, 1968), p.122. **158.** "First Exhibition in New York at Carstairs Gallery," *Art News*, November 1956, p.8; V. Raynor, "Exhibition at Byron Gallery," *Art News*, March 1964, p.64. **159.** Morais, op. cit., pp.30–45. **160.** Ibid., p.34. **161.** Burnham, op. cit., p.122. **162.** Morais, op. cit., pp.34 and 37. **163.** Ibid., p.48. **164.** Battcock, op. cit., pp.19–20 and 25. **165.** *Gunther Gerzso: Paintings and Graphics Reviewed* (Austin: Michener Galleries, U. Texas, 1976). **166.** Archive of the Museum of Modern Art of Latin America. **167.** Barnitz, op. cit., p.31. **168.** Ibid. **169.** Goldman, *Contemporary Mexican Painting*, pp.37–38. **170.** Ibid., pp.46–64. **171.** Ibid., pp.42–45. Selden Rodman, *The Insiders: Rejection and Rediscovery of Man in the Arts of Our Time* (Baton Rouge: Louisiana State U. Press, 1960). **172.** Ibid., pp.35–36. **173.** Suárez, *Inventario*, p.80. **174.** Ibid., p.181. **175.** José Luis Cuevas, *Cuevas por Cuevas* (Mexico City: Ediciones Era, 1965), p.217. **176.** José Gómez Sicre, "A Backward Glance at Cuevas," *José Luis Cuevas* (Washington D.C.: Museum of Modern Art of Latin America, 1978). **177.** For books on the works of individual artists, among them Rivera, Orozco, and Tamayo, see the Bibliography. For contemporary articles see: "Mexican Volcano," *Time*, August 19, 1946, and November 10, 1947, pp.58–60; Jo Gibbs, "Diego Rivera's Mexican Retrospective," *The Art Digest*, April 1, 1950, p.23. For Tamayo's work see "Painter's Year," *Time*, March 8, 1954; and "The Talented Tamayo," *Newsweek*, November 23, 1959. **178.** Although Tamayo received attention in the art magazines in the early 1930s, it was not until the late 1930s that lengthy reviews of his work appeared. See: "Rufino Tamayo: New Works," *Art News*, February 11, 1939, p.13; "Tamayo: Glowing Color & Discreet Distortion," March 16, 1940, p.15; "Tamayo: More Strength, New Fury," February 15, 1942, p.27; "Tamayo: Ancient & Modern Savagery," November 15, 1943; "Rufino Tamayo at the Height of his Powers," January 1, 1946; Henry McBride, "Tamayo: Exhibition of Recent Paintings at Knoedler's," May 1950, p.46. "Tamayo of Mexico in New Paintings," *The Art Digest*, November 15, 1943, p.6; Ben Wolf, "Tamayo of Mexico Exhibits Massive Forms," January 15, 1946, p.9; Margaret Breuning, "Rufino Tamayo Deserts the Archaic Past," February 15, 1947, p.10; Breuning, "Tamayo Commands," December 15, 1947, p.17; Judith Kaye Reed, "Tamayo: Power of Palette and Vision," May 1, 1950, p.14; Breuning, "Tamayo: Color Is Light and Light Is Color," December 1, 1951, p.16; Sam Hunter, "Tamayo: Fire and Ice," March 15, 1954, pp.17 and 32–33. **179.** Hunter, "Tamayo: Fire and Ice," p.17. **180.** *Art News*, January 1957, p.22. **181.** "Knoedler's and New Art Center Galleries," *Art News*, December 1959, p.18. **182.** "Rufino Tamayo," *Arts Magazine*, Summer 1969, p.64. **183.** "Tamayo: More Strength, New Fury," *The Art News*, p.27. **184.** McBride, "Exhibition of Recent Paintings at Knoedler's," *Art News*, p.46. See also McBride "Escapism: One Artist Who Definitely Gets Away from This Period," *The New York Sun*, November 12, 1943, and "A Success Story," *Art News*, December 1951. **185.** "Reviews and Previews: Rufino Tamayo," *Art News*, September 1962, p.10. **186.** George Dennison, "Drawings at the Herbert Gallery," *Arts*, April 1960, pp.49–50. **187.** Jules Langsner, "Show of Drawings in Los Angeles," *Art News*, September 1960, p.51. **188.** "Show at Borgenicht Gallery," *Arts*, April 1967, p.62. Mexican American and Chicano Artists **189.** Quirarte, *Chicano Art*, op. cit., p.28. **190.** "The Chicanos Turn to Paint," *The Sacramento Bee*, June 7, 1970. **191.** Ibid. Among the artists who exhibited their work in Sacramento were Vincent Rascón, Francisco Compli, and Villa. **192.** See Quirarte, *Chicano Art*, op. cit., for more information on the Chicano muralists. **193.** Quirarte, *Mexican American Artists*, op. cit., pp.87–92 and 115–20. **194.** The literature on the Tujunga Wash mural, Los Angeles, painted by Judy Baca, provides an example of the coverage of Chicano muralists in the 1980s: *Life*, December 1980, pp.87–90; C. Rickey, "The Writing on the Wall," *Art in America*, May 1981, pp.54–57; and E.K. Mills, "The Great Wall of Los Angeles," *Ms.*, October 1981, pp.66–69 and 102.

Notes to the Appendix

1. Anita Brenner, "The Mexican Primitives," *Nation*, February 1928, pp.129–30. **2.** Orozco, op. cit., p.37. The letter to Charlot is dated February 23, 1928. **3.** "New York Sees Mexico's Revolutionary Art," *The Art Digest*, January 15, 1928, pp.1–2. **4.** René d'Harnoncourt, *Mexican Art: Catalogue of an Exhibition, 1930–1931*, Portland, Maine, 1930. **5.** Articles appeared in most of the publications of the museums where the exhibition was shown: d'Harnoncourt, "Loan Exhibition of Mexican Arts," *Metropolitan Museum Bulletin*, October 1930, pp.210–17; A.W. Karnaghan, "Exhibition of Mexican Art," *Boston Museum Bulletin*, December 1930, pp.113–16; "Mexican Art Exhibition," *Cleveland Museum Bulletin*, February 1931, pp.28–30; E.A. Jewell, "Exhibition of Mexican Arts," *Milwaukee Institute Bulletin*, May 1931, pp.1–5; and "Exhibition of Mexican Arts," *Chicago Art Institute Bulletin*, December 1931, p.126. Notices, articles, and reviews appeared in art periodicals, including *Art News*, *American Magazine of Art*, *Arts*, *International Studio*, and *The San Antonio Express*. **6.** Ralph Flint, "Metropolitan Holds Big Show of Mexican Art," *Art News*, October 18, 1930, p.3. **7.** "Philadelphia: A Mexican Exhibition," *Art News*, November 14, 1939, p.14. **8.** "Art of Mexico, Land of Social Protest at San Francisco," *The Art Digest*, March 15, 1939, p.45. **9.** *Twenty Centuries of Mexican Art* (New York: The Museum of Modern Art, 1940). **10.** Charlot, "20 Centuries of Mexican Art," *Magazine of Art*, July 1940, pp.398–405. **11.** Jeannette Lowe, "Bimillennial View of Mexican Art: A Brilliant Survey at MOMA," *Art News*, May 25, 1940, pp.6–8. **12.** Helm, *Modern Mexican Painters* (New York: Harper Brothers, 1941). **13.** Plaut, op. cit., pp.1–11. **14.** Henry Clifford, "Mexico Scene from Philadelphia," *Art News*, April 15, 1943, pp.14–17. **15.** Grafly, "Deeply National Art of Old Mexico Presented in Philadelphia," p.8. **16.** "Mexican Painting Today: Exhibition at Philadelphia Museum of Art," *Magazine of Art*, May 1943, pp.168–71. **17.** "Mexicans of the Moment at Kleeman's and Knoedler's," *Art News*, November 15, 1945, p.23. **18.** "Mexico's Ancients and Moderns Mingle in Exhibit at Grand Central Art Galleries," *Art News*, May 1946, p.53. **19.** Judith Kaye Reed, "Mexican Art—From Marketplace to Museum," *The Art Digest*, May 15, 1946, p.22. **20.** Jules Langsner, "Art of Mexico at the Pasadena Art Institute," *Art News*, May 1953, p.49. **21.** "Mexican Painting in the Pasadena Art Institute," *The Art Digest*, April 1, 1953, p.12. **22.** Henry J. Seldis, "Masterworks from Mexico," *Art in America*, October 1963, pp.86–91. **23.** Rosalind G. Wholden, "Ceremony: Hallowed and Pragmatic," *Arts*, January 1964, pp.60–63. **24.** Peter Yates, "Thirty-Five Hundred Years of Mexican Vision," *Arts & Architecture*, February 1964, pp.4–5 and 21–25.

The Special Case of Puerto Rico

1. This struggle is discussed at length in Gordon Lewis, *Puerto Rico: Freedom and Power in the Caribbean* (New York: Harper Torchbooks, 1968), pp.53–54. **2.** Fernando Picó calls the process "*la cañaveralización de Puerto Rico*" (the "sugar-caning" of Puerto Rico) in *Historia General de Puerto Rico* (San Juan: Ediciones Huracán, 1986), p.221. **3.** The most complete account of the sugar industry is José A. Herrero's *La mitología del azúcar* (San Juan: Centro de Estudios de la Realidad Puertorriqueña), mimeographed, undated. **4.** Angel Quintero Rivera, "La clase obrera y el proceso político en Puerto Rico," *Revista de Ciencias Sociales* (P.R.), March–June 1974, pp.145–200. **5.** Gervasio García and Angel Quintero Rivera, *Desafío y solidaridad, Breve historia del movimiento obrero puertorriqueño* (San Juan: Editorial Huracán, 1982). **6.** See Thomas Matthews, *Puerto Rican Politics and the New Deal* (Gainesville: U.

Florida Press, 1960), pp.154–58. **7.** See *Las Artes Plásticas, La Gran Enciclopedia de Puerto Rico*, Vol. 8 (Madrid: Ediciones "R," 1976). **8.** See the catalog of an exhibit organized by the Museo de Arte de Ponce, *Francisco Oller, un Realista del Impresionismo* (Ponce, 1983). See also the special number of *Horizontes, Revista de la Universidad Catolica de Puerto Rico*, April 1985, in which the papers presented at the international symposium "Francisco Oller and His Times" were published. **9.** César Andreu, ed., *Memorias de Bernardo Vega* (San Juan: Ediciones Huracán, 1977) constitutes an extraordinary account of the life of the tobacco workers of Puerto Rico. **10.** Quoted in Osiris Delgado, "*Evaluación, Ideas y Estilo*," in *Exposición Homenaje Ramón Frade* (San Juan: Liga de Estudiantes de Arte, 1985). **11.** See Muna Lee de Muñoz Marin, "Art Exhibitions in the University of Puerto Rico," *University of Puerto Rico Bulletin*, December 1937, p.3. **12.** These shows were nonetheless reported in the U.S.: "By the Caribbean," *Art Digest*, November 1934, p.24; "Dehner Paints Puerto Rico's Squalor," *Art Digest*, March 1936, p.11; and "Puerto Rico," *Magazine of Art*, January 1942, p.21. **13.** See Ana Valdejulli de Pou, *Miguel Pou: su vida y su obra* (Barcelona, 1968). **14.** This is the term used to describe people who live in the hill country of Puerto Rico. **15.** Pou, p.167. **16.** In *El pais de cuatro pisos* (Río Piedras: Ediciones Huracán, 1982), José Luis González discusses the problems of race denial in Puerto Rico. **17.** See Sidney Mintz, "The Cultural History of a Puerto Rican Sugar Plantation 1873–1949," *Hispanic American Historical Review*, Vol. 33, No. 3, 1953, and Rivera, op. cit. **18.** The most complete discussion of these reforms is to be found in Matthews, op. cit. **19.** See Manuel Maldonado Denis, *Puerto Rico: una interpretación histórico-social* (Mexico City, 1969). **20.** See *Las Artes Plásticas*, op. cit., p.185. **21.** See Haydée Venegas, "*Francisco Oller, maestro*," in *Horizontes*, op. cit. **22.** Rafael Colón-Morales, "*Aspectos del arte puertorriqueño en Nueva York*" (Unpublished ms., 1976). **23.** Luis R. Cancel, *Images of Villarini* (New York: El Museo del Barrio, 1981). **24.** See Colón-Morales, op. cit., and Peter Bloch, *Painting and Sculpture of the Puerto Ricans* (New York: Plus Ultra Educational Publishers, 1978). **25.** See *Eloy Blanco* (New York: Henry Street Settlement, The Bronx Museum of the Arts and El Museo del Barrio, 1978). **26.** Ibid. **27.** Ibid. **28.** See Benítez, "Lorenzo Homar y el arte contemporáneo de Puerto Rico" in *Exposición retrospectiva de Lorenzo Homar* (Ponce: Museo de Arte de Ponce, 1978). **29.** Héctor Campos Parsi, *La música en Puerto Rico, La Gran Enciclopedia de Puerto Rico*, Vol. 7, op. cit. **30.** Teresa Tió, "*Texto y contexto del cartel puertorriqueño*," in *El cartel en Puerto Rico 1945–1985* (Río Piedras: Museum of U. Puerto Rico, 1985). **31.** See Benítez, *Irene y Jack Delano* (Río Piedras: Museum of U. Puerto Rico, 1983). **32.** WPA artists had already used the process for posters. **33.** One poster is reproduced in Tió, op. cit. **34.** See Tió, op. cit. The catalog reproduces two examples of joint works: *Peligro* (Danger) and *Los Peloteros* (The Ball Players). **35.** Benítez, "*Tres décadas de gráfica puertorriqueña*," *El Sol, Revista de la Asociación de Maestros de Puerto Rico*, Río Piedras, 1984. **36.** See also Pico, op. cit. **37.** Luis Muñoz Marín, *La historia del Partido Popular Democrático* (San Juan, 1984). **38.** José Trías Monge, *Historia constitucional de Puerto Rico* (Río Piedras: U. Puerto Rico, 1983), pp.270–310. **39.** In *Historia del movimiento libertador* (Río Piedras: U. Puerto Rico, 1958), Ramón Medina Morales recounts in detail the nationalist uprisings in Puerto Rico. **40.** José A. Torres Martinó, "*El Centro de Arte Puertorriqueño*," in *Pintura y gráfica de los años 50* (San Juan: Hermandad de Artistas Gráficos de Puerto Rico, 1985). **41.** Quoted at greater length in Benítez, op. cit., pp.29–30. **42.** Antonio Martorell, "*Fue la década*," in *Pintura y gráfica de los años 50*, op. cit. **43.** See Benítez, op. cit., and "Qué es el arte puertorriqueño?" *El Reportero*, February 1979. **44.** In *Diario de Sesiones, Procedimientos y Debates de la Asemblea Legislativa*, May 18, 1955, pp.19–25, Arturo Morales Carrion compiles, and replies to, some of the criticisms in the Foreword to his *Ojeda al proceso histórico y otros ensayos* (Mexico City: Editorial Cordillera, 1963). **45.** L.H., *Art News*, January 1957, p.21. In the *New Yorker* (January 26, 1957, pp.74–75), Robert M. Coates is struck by the use of bright colors, although in truth paintings of those years tend to be somber. The critic for *The New York Times* (January 10, 1957) like other reviewers stressed the great importance of graphics. **46.** *The New York Times*, December 19, 1956. **47.** J.R.M. "In the Galleries," *Arts*, December 1959. **48.** Pedro Villarini, interview with the author, New York, October 11, 1985. **49.** Colón-Morales, op. cit., and Cancel, op. cit., note this aspect of Villarini's work, which Cancel characterizes as "evasive." **50.** In 1952 he had one-man shows at the Print Gallery of the Art Institute of Chicago, the Open Studio, Milwaukee, and the Ricardo Restaurant Gallery, Chicago. **51.** In "Resisting the Gentle Rape," *Chicago Sunday Sun-Times*, Michael Miner quotes the artist. **52.** See *Las Artes Plásticas*, op. cit., and the *Catalogo General Primera Bienal de San Juan del Grabado Latinoamericano* (San Juan: Instituto de Cultura Puertorriqueña, 1970), p.80. He continued to take part in subsequent biennials. **53.** Compiled in *Aquí en la lucha: Caricaturas de Lorenzo Homar* (San Juan, Cuadernos de *La Escalera*, 1970). **54.** Discussed in Benítez's "Qué es el arte puertorriqueño?," op. cit. See also *Jaime Suárez 1975–1985* (Ponce: Museo de Arte de Ponce, 1985). **55.** Rafael Rivera García, "Controversial Art," *The Island Times*, June 1, 1961. Three years later the same artist picketed Ferrer's exhibit of sculpture at the University of Puerto Rico in protest against the acquisition of the work *Birmingham*. See Alba Raquel Rivera, "Profesor protesta UPR compre escultura en acero de Ferrer," *El Mundo* (San Juan), February 8, 1964. **56.** Rafael Ferrer "Autobiography," in *Deseo: An Adventure: Rafael Ferrer* (Cincinnati: Contemporary Arts Center, 1973). **57.** See *Revista de Arte/The Art Review* (Mayaguez, Universidad de Puerto Rico en Mayaguez), June 1969 and subsequent numbers. The magazine provides clear evidence of the intention of the rector, José Enrique Arraras, to commission avant-garde artists and to exhibit local and international artists. **58.** See *Las Artes Plásticas*, op. cit., for a list of the members. **59.** In *Propuesta polémica sobre arte puertorriqueño* (San Juan: Ediciones Librería Internacional, 1971), Marta Traba criticizes the avant-garde art of Irizarry and other members of the "way-out group," classing it as caricature. **60.** U.S. art critic Jay Jacobs, in *The Art Gallery Magazine* (Puerto Rico issue), December 1967, nicknames the quartet of Ferrer, Hernández Cruz, Irizarry, and Lopez "the way-out group." **61.** In reviewing the show *Art Heritage of Puerto Rico* in 1973, "X.R." criticized Rosado for entitling his work *Hueso* (Bone), saying that by the mere act of giving it a name he indicated that it was not a work of "pure" artistic creation. **62.** See *Myrna Báez, diez años de gráfica y pintura (1971–1981)* (New York: El Museo del Barrio, 1981). **63.** Marta Traba, op. cit., calls it a "hand-to-hand struggle with the angel." **64.** See Benítez, "Viendo pintar a Francisco Rodón," in *Personajes de Rodón (1971–1983)* (Río Piedras: Museo de la Universidad de Puerto Rico, 1983). **65.** The show at the Panoras Gallery was reviewed in the *New York Times*, December 19, 1956. The exhibit at the Roland de Aenlle Gallery was covered in *Arts*, December 1959, by "J.R.M." *Art News*, December 1959, also carried a short review. **66.** In *Olga Albízu* (Washington, D.C.: Pan American Union, 1966), Gómez Sicre compares the relationship between bossa nova and the artist's painting, stressing the impact Albízu's record jackets had. **67.** There are no written sources of information on these activities, but from personal interviews, the author confirms the importance of the institution. **68.** Some of the written papers presented in London—Ortiz's among others—were published in *Studio International*, December 1966. Charlotte Willard reviewed *The Life and Death of Henry Penny* in "Violence in Art," *Art in America*, January–February 1969, pp.36–44. **69.** Ortiz's consistent use of Aztec mythology led to the mistaken classification of him as a Chicano artist. See Jacinto Quirarte, *Mexican American Artists* (Austin: U. Texas Press, 1973), pp.99–101. **70.** See Ortiz, "Culture and the People," *Art in America*, May 1971, p.27. **71.** Ortiz also participated in the Art Strike against Racism, Sexism, and War. In 1970 he and other artists interrupted a meeting of the American Association of Museums in New York to make radical statements on the subject of discrimination against minorities. See Grace Glueck, "Art Group Disrupts Museum Parley," *New York Times*, January 1970, p.34. **72.** Rafael Ferrer, "Autobiography" in *Deseo*, op. cit., p.52. **73.** "City Artist Shows N.Y. How to Have Cool Show," *Daily News*, New York, December 5, 1969. **74.** Ferrer, op. cit., pp.53–54. **75.** See Peter Schjedahl, "The Audacity of Rafael Ferrer," *The Village Voice*, New York, December 5, 1969. **76.** "An Interview: Rafael Ferrer and Stephen Prokopoff," in *Rafael Ferrer: Enclosures* (Philadelphia: Institute of Contemporary Art, 1971). **77.** Colón-Morales, op. cit. **78.** See *Jorge Soto: Works on Paper* (New York: El Museo del Barrio, 1979). Soto studied art at a number of institutions, among them The Art Students League. Like Blanco, he had great difficulty in making the transition from Spanish to English at school. For a time he scarcely ever spoke, resorting to drawing as a means of communication. This became an obsession with him and led to his developing exceptional skill as a draftsman. (Personal interview with Jorge Soto, June 11, 1980.) **79.** Personal interview with José Morales, October 13, 1985. Morales recounted how his teachers tried to steer him toward vocational school. His experience recalls the wall of prejudice Malcolm X encountered. See *José Morales: Paintings and Drawings* (New York: El Museo del Barrio, 1979).

Constructivism and Geometric Abstraction

1. John Stringer, "Reflections on the Present Selection," in *Aqui—27 Latin American Artists Living and Working in the United States* (Los Angeles: Fisher Gallery, UCLA). **2.** Frederico de Morais, "*A Vocacao Construtiva da Arte Latino-Americana (mas o Caos Permanece)*," in *America Latina—Geometria Sensivel*, edited by Roberto Pontual (Rio de Janeiro: Jornal do Brasil, 1987). **3.** Marta Traba, *Dos Decadas Vulnerables en las Artes Plásticas Latinoamericanas 1950–1970* (Mexico City: Siglo XXI Editores, 1973). **4.** De Morais, op. cit. The reference is to Brazil, but the idea can be applied to Latin America in general. **5.** Ibid. **6.** Dore Ashton, Christmas, 1949, p.122. **7.** Quoted by Mario H. Gradowszyk in *Joaquín Torres-García* (Buenos Aires: Ediciones de Arte Gaglianone, 1985), p.24. **8.** In an article in *Revista de la Universidad Catalana*, May 1904, he stated artistic form should never be a mere copy of reality. **9.** See "*Notes sobre Art*," "*Dialogs*," and "*El Descubrimiento de Si Mismo*," in which he insists on the difference between real painting—which stresses form and color—and storytelling paintings. **10.** See also, *Torres-García* (Buenos Aires: Museo Nacional de Bellas Artes, 1974); Barbara Duncan, "Joaquín Torres-García 1874–1949," in *Chronology and Catalogue of the Family Collection* (Austin: Archer M. Huntington Art Gallery, 1974); Mario H. Gradwoszyk, *Joaquín Torres-García* (Buenos Aires: Ediciones de Arte Gaglianone, 1985); *Torres-García 1874–1949* (Ottawa: National Gallery of Canada, 1970); *Torres-García: Grid-Pattern-Sign, Paris-Montevideo 1924–1944* (London: Hayward Gallery, 1986). **11.** Gradowszyk, op. cit., p.24. **12.** Duncan, op. cit., p.24. **13.** Margit Rowell, "Order and Symbol: The European and American Sources of Torres-García's Constructivism," in *Torres-García: Grid-Pattern-Sign*, op. cit. **14.** Société Anonyme was the characteristically provocative name Man Ray gave the association he formed with Katherine Dreier and Marcel Duchamp for the opening in 1920 of the first museum of modern art in New York. **15.** *Joaquín Torres-García: Centenario de Su Nacimiento 1874—28 Julio 1974* (Montevideo: Biblioteca Nacional, 1974). **16.** His toys were exhibited at the Dalmau Gallery in 1918. On this occasion he produced writings on toys and pedagogy. Duncan, op. cit., p.27. **17.** Nelly Perazzo, *El Arte Concreto en la Argentina* (Buenos Aires: Ediciones de Arte Gaglianone, 1983). **18.** Michel Seuphor, *Pintura Abstracta* (Buenos Aires: Ediciones de Arte Kaelusz, 1964). Compare with Gradowszyk, op. cit., p.39. **19.** In it he speaks of the artist's mission to create an order representing a bridge between the individual and the universal. **20.** Rowell, op. cit. **21.** Gladys C. Fabre, *Abstraction-Creation 1931–36* (Paris: Musée d'Art Moderne de la Ville de Paris, 1978). **22.** Duncan, op. cit. **23.** Torres-García, *Raison et Nature-Theorie* (Paris: Editions Iman, 1932 and 1974). **24.** Ibid. **25.** See Note 5 and Gonzalo Fonseca, "Torres-García's Symbols Within Squares," *Art News*, March 1960. **26.** Gradowszyk, op. cit. **27.** To cite a recent example, *Primitivism* (New York: The Museum of Modern Art, 1984). **28.** Organized by Lincoln Kirstein for The Museum of Modern Art, New York. **29.** Thomas B. Hess, "Reviews and Previews: Joaquín Torres-García," *Art News*, April 1950, p.45 (cited by Duncan, op. cit., note 84). Duncan also refers to articles in which the Janis exhibition is reviewed by Margaret Breuning

(*Art Digest*, April 1950). **30.** A. Chanin, *Sunday Compass*, April 9, 1950; and Emily Genauer *New York Herald Tribune*, April 1950. **31.** Adlow, "Artist Who Sought a Universal Picture Language," *Christian Science Monitor*, April 22, 1950. **32.** See note 15. **33.** John Baker, "Joaquín Torres-García," *Arts*, May 1969, pp.10–20. **34.** John Canaday also reviewed this exhibit in *The New York Times*, op. cit. **35.** The exhibition was at the Center for Inter-American Relations, September 19–November 12, 1967. **36.** Robert Pincus Witten, "Torres-García," *Artforum*, Summer 1969. **37.** Barbara Rose, *American Art since 1900* (New York: Praeger, 1972). **38.** Thomas Hess, *New York Magazine*, December 4, 1972; H.H. Arnason, *History of Modern Art* (New York: Harry N. Abrams, 1968). **39.** Joaquín Torres-García, "*Pettoruti, el Pionero de la Nueva Plástica*," *El Debate* (Montevideo), February 11, 1940. **40.** He was appointed director in November 1930 and dismissed for political reasons in February 1947. **41.** The exhibition was at the San Francisco Museum of Art from September 22 to October 11, 1942. It traveled to the National Academy of Design, New York; City Art Museum of St. Louis; William Rockhill Nelson Gallery of Art, Kansas City; Dalzell Hatfield Galleries, Los Angeles; Portland Museum of Art; and Seattle Art Museum. **42.** See Córdoba Iturburu, *Pettoruti* (Buenos Aires: Academia Nacional de Bellas Artes, 1980). **43.** *Quarterly Bulletin*, San Francisco Museum of Art, Vol. III, No. 2, 1944, pp.26–47. **44.** Romero Brest also stresses "his severity, which at times causes his work to be mistaken for geometric art, and his singular capacity for abstraction." **45.** Acquired by the San Francisco Museum of Art, the Seattle Art Museum, the Portland Art Museum, and The Museum of Modern Art. **46.** Pettoruti, op. cit., p.290. **47.** This work was later sold for $190,000 at a Sotheby Parke Bernet auction of Latin American art in fall 1980. **48.** Stanton Catlin, *Forerunners of American Modernism, 1860–1930* (New York: Center for Inter-American Relations, 1967). **49.** Perazzo, op. cit. **50.** See Juan Acha, "*El Geometrismo Reciente y Latinoamerica*," in *El Geometrismo Mexicano* (Mexico City: Universidad Nacional Autónoma de México, 1977). **51.** See Jacqueline Barnitz, *Latin American Artists in the U.S. 1950–1970* (New York: Godwin-Ternbach Museum, Queens College, 1983). **52.** In "*Crítica Norteamericana y Vanguardias Argentinas 1960–80*," *Arte Sur*, No. 1, 1984, Nilda Durante points out that it is not clear whether Messer is speaking of non-specialist viewers or of art critics. **53.** See artist's biography in this book. **54.** In 1948 the Pan American Union, which had been the secretariat of the Union of American Republics, became the General Secretariat of the Organization of American States. **55.** For a complete list of exhibitions and articles see *Edgar Negret: 1945–1978* (Bogotá: Garces Velásquez Gallery). **56.** Nelly Perazzo, "El Escultor Edgar Negret," *Vigencia* (Buenos Aires), September 1977. **57.** Barnitz, op. cit. **58.** Eduardo Serrano, *Un Lustro Visual* (Bogotá: Ediciones Tercer Mundo, 1976). **59.** A detailed list of his exhibitions can be found in *El Espacio en Forma—Eduardo Ramírez Villamizar—Exposición Retrospectiva* 1945–85 (Bogotá: Biblioteca Luis Angel, 1985). **60.** Traba, *Seis Artistas Contemporáneos Colombianos* (Bogotá: Alberto Barco, 1963). **61.** Camile Caleron, "*Ramirez Villamizar: Escultura y Abstracción*," in Traba, op. cit. **62.** Félix Angel, Introduction to *Five Colombian Masters* (Washington, D.C.: Museum of Modern Art of Latin America, 1985). **63.** Howard Device, "Show by Artists of Seven Nations," *The New York Times*, February 16, 1958. **64.** Alicia Peñalba, *Alicia Peñalba* (Lausanne: Alice Paoli Gallery, 1967). **65.** A note on this exhibit appeared in the *Cleveland Museum of Art Bulletin*, October 1960. **66.** For a review, see Harold Rosenberg, "Art in Orbit," *Art News*, October 1961, p.20. **67.** Alicia Peñalba, op. cit. **68.** A note on this exhibition appeared in "The Home Forum," *The Christian Science Monitor*, May 3, 1966. **69.** See Damian Bayon, "From the River Plate to the Seine," *Americas* (Washington, D.C.) August 1967. **70.** Gradowszyk, op. cit. **71.** Ibid. **72.** See first section of this essay. **73.** Julio Alpuy and Ronald Christ, *In The World and Workshop of Julio Alpuy* (New York: Center for Inter-American Relations, 1972). **74.** Michael Brenson, "Fonseca's Archaeological Sculpture,"—*The New York Times*, May 2, 1986. **75.** Barnitz, op. cit. **76.** Exhibited at the Philbrook Art Center, Tulsa, Oklahoma; the Oklahoma Art Center, Oklahoma City; and the University of Oklahoma, Norman. **77.** Ibid. **78.** Perazzo, *Ary Brizzi* (Buenos Aires: Fundacion San Telmo, 1986). **79.** This exhibit traveled afterwards to the Akron Art Institute, the Atlanta Art Association, and the Museum of Art at the University of Texas at Austin. **80.** See note 33. **81.** *The Emergent Decade, An Exhibition of Contemporary Latin American Painting*, cosponsored by Cornell University and the Solomon R. Guggenheim Museum. Exhibited at the Andrew D. White Museum, Cornell University; Dallas Museum of Fine Arts; National Gallery of Canada, Ottawa; Solomon R. Guggenheim Museum, New York; Krannert Art Museum, University of Illinois, Champaign; De Cordova Museum, Lincoln, Massachusetts; and John and Mable Ringling Museum of Art, Sarasota, Florida. **82.** A complete list of Polesello's exhibitions can be found in Ricardo Paulosa, *Rogelio Polesello* (Buenos Aires: Ediciones Gaglianone, 1984). **83.** In connection with Julio Llinas and the group known as "Phases." **84.** Eduardo Mac Entyre, interview with the author, Buenos Aires 1970. **85.** Romulado Brughetti, "Las Vanguardias Argentinas en el Arte. El Arte Genético y Geométrico, *La Nación* (Buenos Aires), April 16, 1978. **86.** See note 33. **87.** See note 82. **88.** op. cit. **89.** Claude Louis Renard, "Dialogue with Soto," in *Soto: A Retrospective Exhibition* (New York: Solomon R. Guggenheim Museum, 1970). **90.** Gloria Garnevali, interview with Carlos Cruz-Diez, *Carlos Cruz-Diez* (Caracas: Caracas Museum of Fine Arts, 1981). **91.** For further collections see artist's biography in this book. **92.** Ashton, op. cit. **93.** Ibid. **94.** Damian Bayon, *Adventura Plástica de Hispanoamerica* (Mexico City: F.C.E., 1974), p.201. **95.** Jorge Alberto Manrique, "Varios Geometristas Mexicanos en America Latina," in *Geometría Sensival*, edited by Roberto Pontual (Rio de Janeiro: Ed. Jornal do Brasil, 1978). Manrique is not unaware of the geometric aspects of the work of Orozco, Rivera and Siqueiros. However, he asserts "the success achieved by the Mexican School and the official support which it enjoyed inhibited receptiveness to, and contact and interchange with other tendencies." pp.79–80. **96.** Xavier Moyssen, interview with Gerzso, in *El Geometrísmo Mexicano* (Mexico City: Universidad Nacional Autónoma de Mexico, 1977). **97.** Luis Cardoza y Aragon, "Gunther Gerszo," in *São Paulo Bienal*, 1965. **98.** See note 33. **99.** Juan Acha, *Alejandro Otero* (Caracas: Caracas Museum of Contemporary Art, 1985). **100.** Marta Traba, *Dos Décadas Vulnerables*, op. cit., p.108. **101.** Marta Traba, *Gego* (Bogotá: Luis Angel Arango Library, 1967): "One would not suspect that her identification with nature dates back to 1939, and that ever since there has been room in her work for her inquiring eye." **102.** Quoted by Hanni Ossott, *Gego* (Caracas: Caracas Museum of Contemporary Art, 1977). **103.** Gabriel Rodríguez, *Gerd Leufert Disenador* (Caracas: Caracas Museum of Fine Arts, 1976). **104.** Information taken from the *Enciclopedia del Arte en América*, Vol. IV (Buenos Aires: Bibliográfica Omeba, 1960). **105.** See note 82. **106.** This reference is to Argentina. **107.** The term *Geometria Sensival* (here translated as Lyric Geometry) appeared in Brazil as the title of a book for which Roberto Pontual served as editor (see note 2). In his preface, Pontual writes: "The term which I shall apply to this bridge (the bridge between Torres-García's oeuvre and recent works by many Latin American Constructivists) is not altogether new, since the Argentine critics Damian Bayon and Aldo Pellegrini had used it previously; the only claim to novelty which can be made for my use of the term lies in applying it to a body of about 200 paintings, drawings, and objects created over a period of fifty years by artists ranging from Torres-García to young artists of today. And also, in giving the term 'Lyric Abstraction' a breadth and precision which the occasion seems to warrant." **108.** Interview with Augandro Puente, *La Nación* (Buenos Aires), May 25, 1986. **109.** See note 33. **110.** Gilbert Chase, *Contemporary Art in Latin America: Painting, Graphic Art, Sculpture, Architecture* (New York: The Free Press, 1970). **111.** Dore Ashton, "Carmen Herrera," *The New York Times*, 1956. There was also an article by Emily Genauer in *The Herald Tribune* at the same time. **112.** Hilton Kramer, "Cuban Painters at Cisneros Gallery," *The New York Times*, December 9, 1965. **113.** Quoted by Judith Neaman in *Carmen Herrera—A Retrospective 1951–1984* (New York: The Alternative Museum, 1985).

New York Dada

1. See Dore Ashton, *The New York School: A Cultural Reckoning* (New York: Viking, 1973); Irving Sandler, *The Triumph of American Painting: A History of Abstract Expressionism* (New York: Praeger, 1970); and William Rubin, *Dada and Surrealist Art* (New York: Harry N. Abrams, 1968). **2.** Ramón Favela, *Diego Rivera: The Cubist Years* (Phoenix: Museum of Art, 1984). **3.** Daniel Robbins, *Joaquín Torres-García; 1874–1949* (Providence: Museum of Art, Rhode Island School of Design, 1970). **4.** See Roger Bastide, *The African Religions: Towards a Sociology of Interpenetrations of Civilizations* (Baltimore: Johns Hopkins U. Press, 1978). **5.** André Breton, *Manifestos of Surrealism* (Ann Arbor: U. Michigan Press, 1969). **6.** Isidore Ducasse, *Oeuvres Complètes* (Paris: Librairie Générale Française, 1963). **7.** See Rubin, op. cit. **8.** Jean-Hubert Martin and Helene Seckel, *Francis Picabia* (Paris: Centre Georges Pompidou, 1976). **9.** This information is derived from *Marius de Zayas: Conjurer of Souls* by Douglas Hyland (Lawrence: Spencer Museum of Art, U. Kansas, 1981). **10.** André Breton, "*Souvenir du Méxique*," *Minotaure*, May 1939. **11.** Quoted in Hayden Herrera, *Frida: A Biography of Frida Kahlo* (New York: Harper and Row 1983), p.228. **12.** See Breton, op. cit. **13.** *International Exhibition of Surrealism* (Mexico City: Galería de Arte Mexicano, 1939). **14.** See Herrera, op. cit. **15.** Michael Newman, "The Ribbon Around the Bomb," *Art in America*, April 1983, pp.160–69. **16.** Marsden Hartley, "The Red Man," in *Adventures in the Arts* (New York: Boni and Liveright, 1921), pp.13–29. **17.** See Barbara Rose, *American Art since 1900: A Critical History* (New York: Praeger, 1967). **18.** Henry-Claude Clousseau, "*L'Origine et l'écart: d'un art à l'autre*," in *Paris/Paris: 1937–1957* (Paris: Centre Georges Pompidou, 1981), p.162. **19.** W.P., *Art News*, November 12, 1938, p.13. **20.** Herrera, op. cit. **21.** Max Pol-Fouchet, *Wifredo Lam* (Barcelona: Ediciones Poligrafa, 1975). **22.** William Rubin, *Dada, Surrealism and Their Heritage* (New York: The Museum of Modern Art, 1968). **23.** See Ashton, op. cit., and Sandler, op. cit., and Sidney Simon, "Concerning the Beginnings of the New York School: 1939–1943," *Art International*, Summer 1967, pp.17–23. **24.** Dawn Ades, *Dada and Surrealism Reviewed* (London: Westerham Press, 1978), p.388. **25.** André Breton, *Le Surréalisme et la Peinture* (New York: Brentanos, 1945). **26.** R.F., "Matta, Furious Scientist," *Art News*, April 15, 1942, p.13. **27.** Sandler, op. cit., p.67. **28.** Rubin, op. cit., p.166. **29.** Ibid. **30.** This has also received some exposure within French Surrealist circles, hence a receptivity to this thematic exploration on the part of Matta. See Roger Hervé, "Human Sacrifice of Central America," *Documents* (1930), pp.205–13. **31.** There is also the matter of Torres-García's influence on Gottlieb in the presentation of disjointed symbolic material within boxlike grids, but the possibility of direct attribution still needs to be explicated further. Comparisons and the dating relationships make this attribution of influence plausible. **32.** See Rubin, op. cit. **33.** Robert Hobbs, Robert Carlton, and Gail Levin, *Abstract Expressionism: The Formative Years* (Ithaca: Herbert F. Johnson Museum of Art, Cornell University, 1978), p.18. **34.** Sandler, op. cit. **35.** Lowery S. Sims, "Wifredo Lam and Roberto Matta: Surrealism in the New World," in *In the Mind's Eye: Dada and Surrealism*, edited by Terry Ann R. Neff (Chicago: Museum of Contemporary Art, 1985), pp.91–103. **36.** *The Arts Digest*, December 1, 1942. **37.** Margarete Breuning, "Lam's Magical Incantations and Rituals," *The Arts Journal*, December 1, 1945. **38.** See Rose, op. cit., p.145. **39.** "A Way to Kill Space," *Newsweek*, August 12, 1946, pp.106–108. **40.** Geri Trotta, "Wifredo Lam Paints a Picture," *Art News*, September 1950, pp.43–44. **41.** See Mary Jane Jacob, "Chicago: 'The City of Surrealism,'" in *In The Mind's Eye*, op. cit., pp.9–17. **42.** See Rubin, op. cit. **43.** José Gómez Sicre, *Carreño*. (Washington, D.C.: Pan American Union, 1947). **44.** R.F., *Art News*, March 15–31, 1941, p.43. **45.** *Art News*, April 1, 1944, p.24. **46.** Ibid. **47.** Adelaida de Juan, "*Una Silla en la jungla*," *Sobre Wifredo Lam*, pp.117–28. **48.** *Art News*, April 1, 1944, p.24. **49.** Ibid. **50.** I.H.S., *Art News*, Summer 1957, p.74. **51.** Ibid. **52.** Jacqueline Barnitz, *Arts*, January 1966, p.55. **53.** *Nemesio Antúnez: Obra Pictorica* (Mexico City: Galerias del Papacio de Bellas Artes, 1967). **54.** R.T., *Art News*, Summer 1950, p.49. **55.** Ibid. **56.** R.C. Kennedy and

Joseph A. Nocak, eds., *Agustín Fernández* (New York: Rapoport, 1973), n.p. **57.** F.P., *Art News*, November 1955, p.52. **58.** *Art News*, December 1958, p.60. **59.** *Arts*, October 1955, p.55. **60.** Georges Bataille, "*L'Histoire de l'oeil.*" **61.** Kennedy, op. cit. **62.** Ibid. **63.** See H. Gloria, "*Ojos de Formás Eróticas*," *El Pais*, April 28, 1974; and Oscar Gómez Palacio, "*Abularach, Oculista del Arte*," *Telex*, May 27, 1985. **64.** John Canaday, "New Talent: USA," *Art in America*, Spring 1960, p.37. **65.** I.H.S., *Art News*, May 1961, p.20. **66.** R.C., *Arts*, September 1970, p.61. **67.** Ibid. **68.** Roberto Pontual, *Brazilian Contemporary Art* (Rio de Janeiro: Ediciones Jornal do Brasil, 1976), p.415; and *Marcelo Grassman of Brazil: Drawings and Prints* (Washington, D.C.: Pan American Union, 1960). **69.** See also *Rhode Island School of Design Bulletin*, May 1968, pp.11–12. **70.** Gladys Pena, *Rafael Colón-Morales: Children of Darkness* (New York: El Museo del Barrio, 1983). **71.** Sims, "*Wifredo Lam: surrealismo del Nuevo Mundo*," in *Sobre Wifredo Lam*, op. cit., pp.99–116. **72.** See *Pintura y Gráfica de los Anos 50* (San Juan: El Arsenal de La Puntilla, 1985). **73.** Marimar Benítez, "The Significant Image/Observations on Some of Carlos Raquel Rivera's Work," in *Carlos Raquel Rivera: "Con su permiso..."* (New York: El Museo del Barrio, 1980), p.11. 74. *Pedro Friedeberg of Mexico* (Washington, D.C.: Pan American Union, 1963). **75.** Ibid. **76.** Jacqueline Barnitz, *Art News*, December 1969, p.12. **77.** J.H.B., *Art News*, Summer 1964, p.22. **78.** B.H. Friedman, "Useful Objects by Artists," *Art in America*, December 1964, p.55. **79.** Jacinto Quirarte, *Mexican American Artists*, pp.44–49. **80.** John Beardsley and Jane Livingston, *Hispanic Art in the United States* (Houston: Museum of Fine Arts, 1987), pp.223–24. **81.** See *Outsiders: Art Beyond the Norms* (New York: Rosa Esman Gallery, 1986). **82.** Beardsley, op. cit., p.35.

U.S. and Socially Concerned Latin American Art
1. Exhibition at the Modern Gallery: *Paintings by Cézanne, Van Gogh, Picasso, Picabia, Braque, and Rivera*. New York, February 12–March 4, 1916. **2.** Barbara Rose, *American Art since 1900: A Critical History* (New York: Praeger, 1972), p.86. **3.** Matthew Baigell, *A History of American Painting* (New York: Praeger, 1971), p.229. **4.** Francis V. O'Connor, "The influence of Diego Rivera on the Art of the United States during the 1930s and After," in *Diego Rivera* (New York: W. W. Norton, 1986), p.159. **5.** An excellent survey of the U.S. literature on the Mexican muralists appears in Chapter I of this book. **6.** Laurance P. Hurlburt, "Diego Rivera (1886–1957): A Chronology of His Art, Life, and Times," in *Diego Rivera*, op. cit., p.79. **7.** The Rivera sketchbook was donated to the museum and exhibited with a collection of Soviet posters as "recent acquisitions" in 1943. **8.** The best account of the Rockefeller mural experience is Lucienne Bloch's "On Location with Diego Rivera," *Art in America*, February 1986, pp.102–123. **9.** Orozco describes his experience with the Hambridge theory in José Clemente Orozco, *An Autobiography* (Austin: U. Texas Press, 1962), pp.145–49. **10.** George Biddle, *An American Artist's Story* (Boston: Little, Brown, 1939), p.268. **11.** O'Connor, op. cit., pp.159–66. **12.** The influence of each of the *tres grandes* on the contemporary U.S. mural movement is fully discussed in Eva Cockcroft, John Weber, and James Cockcroft, *Towards a People's Art: The Contemporary Mural Movement* (New York: E. P. Dutton, 1977). **13.** The Mexican example was also important for artists such as José Sabogal, who visited Mexico in 1922 before initiating the Indigenist movement in Peru. **14.** José Gomez Sicre, *Carreño* (Washington, D.C.: Pan American Union, 1947), p.2. **15.** *Twenty Centuries of Mexican Art* (New York: MOMA, 1940), p.1. **16.** Robert C. Smith, "The Art of Candido Portinari," in *Portinari of Brazil* (New York: MOMA, 1940), p.12. **17.** Rockwell Kent, *Portinari, His Life and Art* (Chicago: U. Chicago Press, 1941), p.5. **18.** Ibid., p.7. **19.** Josias Leao, Ibid., p.4. **20.** For a more complete discussion of MOMA's participation in the war effort see Eva Cockcroft, "Abstract Expressionism: Weapon of the Cold War," *Artforum*, May 1974, pp.39–41. **21.** The shows without catalogs were *Mexican Costumes by Carlos Mérida*, 1942; *Recent Acquisitions*, 1943; *Design Competition*, 1942. **22.** The catalog comments: "On the whole the greater professional skill and method appeared in the posters from the U.S.; but greater fecundity of imagination was to be found in those from Latin America, even in certain contributions of avowed amateurs and child artists." *United Hemisphere Poster Competition* (New York: MOMA, 1942). **23.** See also Chapter One and Biographies. **24.** MacKinley Helm, *Man of Fire: J.C. Orozco* (New York: Harcourt, Brace, 1953), p.85. **25.** J. C. Orozco, "Orozco Explains," *The Bulletin of The Museum of Modern Art*, August 1940, p.2. **26.** Smith, op. cit., pp.10–12. **27.** Pedrosa, p.56. **28.** Ibid., p.56. **29.** *Time*, June 1, 1953. **30.** Alfred H. Barr, "Modern Cuban Painting," *Bulletin of The Museum of Modern Art*, 1944. **31.** Preston Stuart, "Carreño's Paintings," *The New York Times*, January 29, 1951. **32.** Malú Sierra, Introduction to *Carreño* (Caracas: Museo de Bellas Artes, 1957). **33.** Rafael Squirru, "Antonio Berni," *Americas*, October 1965, p.21. **34.** Sandler's book is *Triumph of American Painting* (New York: Praeger, 1970). **35.** Barr, "Is Modern Art Communistic," *The New York Times*, 1952. **36.** Clement Greenberg, "American Type Painting," in *Art and Culture* (Boston: Beacon Press, 1965), p.229. **37.** Gómez Sicre, Introduction to *Gulf-Caribbean Art* (Houston: Museum of Fine Arts, 1956), p.3. **38.** Ibid., pp.3–4. **39.** *Latin American Horizons* (Sarasota: Ringling Brothers Museum, 1976). **40.** *Time*, June 15, 1953, p.72. **41.** See Leona E. Prasse, Foreword to *The Work of Antonio Frasconi* (Cleveland: Cleveland Museum of Art, 1952), pp.5–7. **42.** Charlotte Willard, "Drawing Today," *Art in America*, October 1964, p.63. **43.** Edwin Honig, "The Nazi Drawings of Mauricio Lasansky," in *The Nazi Drawings* (Philadelphia: Philadelphia Museum of Art, 1966), p.2. **44.** Selden Rodman, *The Insiders: Rejection and Rediscovery of Man in the Arts of Our Time* (New Orleans: Louisiana State U. Press, 1960), p.63. **45.** Ibid., p.73. **46.** Shifra Goldman, *Contemporary Mexican Paintings in a Time of Change* (Austin: U. Texas Press, 1981), p.14. **47.** Gómez Sicre, Catalog Note to *José Luis Cuevas, Drawings* (Washington, D.C.: Pan American Union, 1954). **48.** Cited in *José Luis Cuevas* (New York: David Herbert Gallery, 1960). **49.** Ibid. **50.** For a full account see Goldman, op. cit., and Chapter 1. **51.** Translation in Goldman, p.48. **52.** Translated by the author. **53.** Rodman, p.63. **54.** Tracy Atkinson, Foreword to *Fernando Botero: Recent Works* (Milwaukee: Milwaukee Arts Center, 1967), p.1. **55.** Stanton L. Catlin, Foreword to *Fernando Botero* (New York: Center for International Relations, 1969), p.1. **56.** German Arciniegas, *Fernando Botero* (New York: Harry N. Abrams, 1980), p.34. **57.** *Art International*, May 20, 1969, p.38. **58.** Susan Sontag, Introduction to *The Art of Revolution: Castro's Cuba: 1959–1970* (New York: McGraw-Hill, 1970), p.17. **59.** David Kunzle, "Public Graphics in Cuba," *Latin American Perspectives*, No. 7 (1975), p.95. **60.** Amilcar Cabral, "National Liberation and Culture," in *Return to the Source* (New York: Monthly Review Press, 1973), p.43. **61.** Ibid., p.39. **62.** Artists such as Rafael Ferrer who are part of the mainstream and live and work in the U.S. are treated like other international artists. **63.** For a complete account of this mural see Goldman, "The Puerto Rican *Pleña* as Mural," *Community Murals Magazine* (P.R.), Spring 1987, pp.11–13. **64.** James Harithas, *Mel Casas, Humanscapes* (Houston: Contemporary Arts Museum, 1976), p.1. **65.** *Luis Jiménez* (New York: Graham Gallery, 1969), p.4. **66.** Quoted in Jacinto Quirarte, *Mexican American Artists* (Austin: U. Texas Press, 1973), p.120. **67.** Corinne Robins, "The Drawings of Jorge Soto Sanchez," *Jorge Soto Sanchez* (New York: Museo del Barrio, 1979), p.1. **68.** Goldman and Tomás Ybarra-Fausto, *Arte Chicano* (Berkeley: U. California Chicano Studies Library, 1985), p.32.

Latin American Presence
1. Rafael Squirru, *Leopoldo Presas* (New York: Gallery of Modern Art, 1967). **2.** Ibid. **3.** Most countries awarded government fellowships to outstanding graduates of official academies for study abroad, usually in Europe. Many other individuals traveled to Europe on their own to study, either at the great academies or in private studios. This dynamic was common for individuals from the Atlantic and Caribbean countries and permitted Latin American artists to remain acquainted with European developments. **4.** Indianism, *Indigenismo*, is usually defined as a figurative tendency that explored Indian culture and its roots as a subject, considering it to be the authentic incarnation of the American spirit. Indianism developed under the auspices of the Mexican School in countries with large Indian populations. See *Camilo Egas* (Quito: Ecuadoran Central Bank, 1960). **5.** "Concerning the Beginnings of the New York School: 1939–1943," Peter Busa and Roberto Matta in an interview with Sidney Simon, December 1966. Archives of the Museum of Modern Art of Latin America, file of Roberto Matta. **6.** Ibid. **7.** Ibid. **8.** "Concerning the Beginnings of the New York School: 1939–1943," Robert Motherwell, interview with Sidney Simon, January 1967. Archives of the Museum of Modern Art of Latin America, file of Roberto Matta. **9.** Ibid. **10.** "Roberto Matta—Paintings and Drawings" (La Jolla: Tasende Gallery, 1980). **11.** Acting under pressure from the United States, the ministers of foreign affairs of American countries held a meeting in Panama from September 23 to October 3, 1939, after which the hemisphere was declared to be under isolation, surrounded by a neutrality belt. Only U.S. vessels could take on agricultural products and other raw materials, setting their own prices. **12.** At the Meeting of Consultation of Ministers of Foreign Affairs held in Rio de Janeiro in January 1942 the Hispanic American countries, once again acting under heavy pressure from the United States, broke relations with the Axis countries. **13.** See Chapter Three for details on the use of Argentine geometric art. **14.** Maria Elvira Iriarte advances this idea in *"Primeras etapas de la Abstracción en Colombia," Arte en Colombia* (Bogotá), Vol.23. **15.** In Colombia, for example, one can note the resistance to abstract painting during the 1950s. The three most prestigious painters, Obregón, Grau, and Botero were figurative artists. This resistance did not apply to sculpture, perhaps because of the abstract tradition in pre-Columbian jewelry. **16.** See note 13 above. **17.** *Directory of Fellows, 1925–1967* (New York: John Simon Guggenheim Foundation, 1968). **18.** In 1988 the museum will publish a list, compiled by Annick Casciero, of all such exhibitions held from 1946 to 1985. **19.** Featured artists were Víctor Chab, Omar Rayo, Carlos Poveda, Enrique Castro-Cid, and Raúl Valdivieso. **20.** The *Boletín de Artes Visuales* was issued from 1956 to 1973. The "Art in Latin America Today" series includes monographs on Colombia by Marta Traba, Brazil by Luiz de Almeida Cunha, Peru by Juan W. Acha, Bolivia by Dagoberto Villaroel Claure, Chile by Antonio R. Romera, Venezuela by Clara Diament de Sujo, Argentina by Manuel Mújica Lainez, Guatemala by Lionel Méndez Dávila, and Paraguay by Miguel Angel Fernández. **21.** See also Alvaro Medina "*Cartas de Nueva York*," *Arte en Colombia* (Bogotá), Vol.32. **22.** See Germán Rubiano Caballero, "*Ignorancia y Mala Fé*," *Arte en Colombia* (Bogotá), Vol.33. **23.** Grace Glueck, interview with Danielle Caillet, 1987. **24.** The museum commissioned collector Joseph Randall Shapiro to select pictures.

Part I. The Abstract Spirit
1. These classifications are very general and should be complemented by details of artistic movements or trends in individual countries. **2.** Further subdivided into Lyric Geometry, Op art, and Kinetic art. The Brazilian critic Roberto Pontual invented the term *Geometria Sensivel*, in English it is translated as Lyric Geometry. **3.** Colombian critic Marta Traba coined the term *Abstracción Sensivel* in her book *Arte de América Latina y el Caribe en su Contexto Cultural*, published by the Organization of American States. In excerpts from the text published in English for *Selections from the Permanent Collection* (Washington, D.C.: OAS, 1985), the term was rendered as Lyric Abstraction. **4.** See note 4 above. **5.** Reproduced in Luis Luján Munóz, *Carlos Mérida, Precursor del Arte Contemporáneo Latinoamericano* (Guatemala City: Serviprensa Centroamericana, 1985). **6.** Ibid. **7.** In 1914 Mérida returned to Quetzaltenango, the city from which his family had moved in 1907. He went to the United States thereafter, and then to Mexico. **8.** Munóz, op. cit. **9.** In 1921 he worked with Rivera, Charlot, and Guerrero on the encaustic mural in the Simon Bolívar Amphitheater of the National Preparatory School. In 1923 he decorated the children's library in the Secretariat of Public Education. That same year he joined the Syndicate of Technical Workers, Painters, and Sculptors. **10.** The muralists exerted great influence throughout the hemisphere, serving as a model to many, and at the same time they distinguished themselves by the aggressiveness with which they combated European formalism, returning wholeheartedly to figurative expres-

sion. **11.** Roberto Guevara: "*María Luisa Pacheco: Materia y Representación*," *El Nacional*, Caracas, October 14, 1968; and see *Tribute to María Luisa Pacheco 1919–1982* (Washington, D.C.: Museum of Modern Art of Latin America, 1986). **12.** See also artist's biography and Chapter One. **13.** Reproduced in *The Emergent Decade: Latin American Painters and Paintings of the 1960s* (Ithaca: Cornell U. Press, 1985). **14.** From the artist's file in the archives of the Museum of Modern Art of Latin America, Washington, D.C. **15.** Informalism was an abstract movement developed in Europe. Jean Dubuffet can be considered the first figurative informalist, using pictorial matter in heavy impastos to achieve a texture on the surface of the canvas which subdued the figure. In Spain Informalism was primarly abstract. One of its more important representatives was Antonio Tapíes. Along with the French movement Tachism, Informalism was the European equivalent to Abstract Expressionism. **16.** Roberto Guevara, Introduction to *Armando Morales* (Mexico City: Palace of Fine Arts, 1968). **17.** The exhibition was held from January 22 to March 29, 1969. **18.** Traba, op. cit. **19.** *Japanese Artists of the Americas* (Washington, D.C.: OAS, 1961). **20.** Gabriel García Márquez, "*Inaugurada Anoche Exposición Neo-Impresionista*," *El Espectador* (Bogotá), February 22, 1955. **21.** Traba, in *Armando Villegas* (Bogotá: National Library, 1959). **22.** David Manzur, letter to the editor, *Zumbambico* (Medellin), Vol.2, 1975. **23.** Leslie Judd Ahlander, "Art in Washington," *The Washington Post*, February 23, 1964. **24.** Frank Getlein, "Art," *The Sunday Star*, February 23, 1964. **25.** Apparently these works disappeared in a fire. There is a clipping in the artist's file at the Museum of Modern Art of Latin America in which a photograph taken in the house of Nelson Rockefeller, according to the caption, shows him with the two Hurtado paintings. **26.** The Andrews-Morris Gallery later became Bonino Gallery. **27.** Erika Billeter, "Between Tradition and Avant-Garde," in *Lucio Fontana 1899–1968: A Retrospective* (New York: Solomon R. Guggenheim Museum, 1977). **28.** Reproduced in the artist's file, Museum of Modern Art of Latin America, Washington, D.C. **29.** Ibid. **30.** Billeter, op. cit. **31.** Guillermo E. Magrassi, *De la Vega, Pintores Argentinos del Siglo XX* (Buenos Aires: Centro Editorial de América Latina, n.d.). **32.** Jorge Romero Brest, "Jorge de la Vega," *La Gaceta* (Tucumán), August 31, 1980. **33.** *Rómulo Maccío, Fictions* (New York: Center for Inter-American Relations, 1969). **34.** Ibid. **35.** Ibid. **36.** Jorge Gluzberg, *Luis Felipe Noé*. **37.** One of his environments was presented at the Riverside Museum, New York, February 24–March 22, 1967, in the exhibition *Environments/Permutations*. **38.** *Visión* carried a note in its February 18, 1966, issue containing this outburst by Noé: "Long live chaos, for it is the only thing that is truly alive!"

Part II: Reality and Figuration
1. It is interesting to compare her work with Héctor Poleo's, to note the expressionistic vein in Forner's approach. Neither artist's approach is related to the world of the subconscious, from which the European Surrealists drew their inspiration. **2.** R.V., "Emilio Sánchez," *Arts*, May 1959. **3.** Nicols Coleman, "Clichés and Olés," *The Washington Post*, May 2, 1985. **4.** Traba, *Eco* (Bogotá), March 1978. **5.** Galaor Carbonell, *El Realismo en la Obra de Enrique Grau* (Bogotá: Galería San Diego, 1977). **6.** Lavinia Learmont, *Contemporary Artists* (New York: St. Martin's, 1983). **7.** Artist's file, Museum of Modern Art of Latin America. **8.** See for example, "Interview with Michel Lancelot," in *Botero* (Caracas: Caracas Museum of Contemporary Art, 1976); and Margaret Moorman, "A Gift for Being Different," *Art News*, February 1986. **9.** For further information on Frasconi see Chapter Five. **10.** "Venice: Personal Discoveries," artist's file, Museum of Modern Art of Latin America. **11.** Caballero, "Cárdenas," *El Tiempo* (Bogotá), August 13, 1972. **12.** Galván, "Cárdenas," *Triunfo* (Madrid), April 1978. **13.** Antonio Enrique Amaral, interview with Indianapolis T.V., June 1982. **14.** See also Chapter Five. **15.** Walter Engel, "El Interiorismo," *El Espectador* (Bogotá), September 20, 1964. **16.** Ibid. **17.** Traba, *Selections from the Permanent Collection*, op. cit. **18.** Ibid.

"Magnet: New York"
1. John Canaday, "Art: A Hit Scored for 28 Painters from Latin America," *The New York Times*, September 23, 1964. **2.** Luis Camnitzer (Havana: Casa de Las Américas, 1983), pp.2-3. Written in June 1977. **3.** Sam Hunter, "São Paulo Bienal," *Art in America*, March/April 1967, p.84. **4.** Lawrence Alloway, "Latin Art," *Art in America*, June 1965, p.64. **5.** Olivia Zuniga, *Mathias Goeritz* (Mexico City: Editorial Intercontinental, 1963), pp.11-13. **6.** Ibid. **7.** From an unpublished printout obtained from Goeritz at The Museum of Modern Art, N.Y.C. **8.** Ibid. **9.** Ibid. **10.** Gregory Battcock, ed., *Minimal Art: A Critical Anthology* (New York: E.P. Dutton, 1968), p.19. **11.** Sibyl Moholy-Nagy, *Matrix of Man* (New York: Praeger, 1968), p.303. **12.** Camnitzer, conversation with the author, September 1987. **13.** Liliana Porter, taped conversation with the author, June 1987. **14.** Ibid. **15.** Ibid. **16.** Jaime Davidovich, taped statement, June 1987. **17.** Ibid. **18.** Ibid. **19.** John Matturri, *Jaime Davidovich*, unpublished doctoral dissertation. **20.** Roger Welchans, *Carroll Wall Project* (Cleveland: Fine Arts Gallery, John Carroll U., 1971). **21.** Michael Sundell, "Fixity and Transience at Akron," *Cleveland Art*, December 1972. **22.** Barnard L. Collier, "Aperture Happening," *The New York Times*, October 29, 1966. **23.** Douglas Davis, *Art and the Future* (New York: Praeger, 1973), p.194. **24.** Grace Glueck, "Inner Experience," *The New York Times*, February 6, 1966. **25.** Jacqueline Barnitz, "Latin Answer to Pop," *Arts*, June 1966, pp.20-24. **26.** "Latin Labyrinth," *Newsweek*, February 12, 1966, p.10. **27.** John Perreault, "Minujin and Mr. T," *The Village Voice*, June 6, 1968. **28.** William Zunsser, "Total Weapon," *Look*, November 14, 1967, p.24. **29.** O.J., "Ralph Ortiz," *Art News*, Summer 1963, p.10. **30.** Richard Huelsenbeck, unpublished text written for the artist's use, October 28, 1982. **31.** James Thrall Soby to Constance Levene, February 21, 1963 (The Museum of Modern Art, N.Y.C.). **32.** Ralph Ortiz, *Destructivism, Second Manifesto* (London: privately published, 1966). **33.** Edward Lucie-Smith, "Things Seen," *The Times*, September 13, 1966. **34.** Ortiz, taped conversation with the author, May 1987. **35. 36.** Arthur Janov, *Primal Scream* (New York: G.P. Putnam, 1970). **37.** Ortiz to the author, June 1987. **38.** Davis, op. cit., p.132. **39.** *Kunst Licht Kunst* (Eindhoven: Van Abbe Museum, 1966). **40.** GRAV, *Stop Art* (Paris: Denise René Editions, 1965). **41.** Le Parc to the author, September 1987. **42.** "Op: Adventure Without Danger," *Newsweek*, March 1, 1965, p.83. **43.** Julio Le Parc, "*La valoración: arma clave para la penetración cultural*," *Guadalimar* (Madrid), September 1981. **44.** Allan Kaprow, "Untitled": Manifestos, Great Bear Pamphlets (New York: Something Else Press, 1966) pp.21-23. **45.** Castro Cid, conversation with the author, July 1987. **46.** Jack Burnham, *Beyond Modern Sculpture* (New York: George Braziller, 1967), pp.349-50. **47.** Peter Sims, "Sculpture," *Time*, March 4, 1966, p.10. **48.** Burnham, op. cit., p.350. **49.** Downey, conversation with the author, June 1987. **50.** Downey, op. cit. **51.** *Juan Downey* (Washington D.C.: Smithsonian Institution, 1968). **52.** Gabrielle Buffet-Picabia, *Aires Abstraites* (Geneva: Cramer, 1957), p.35. **53.** Downey, op. cit. **54.** James Harithas, *Downey— Electronic Sculpture* (Washington, D.C.: Corcoran Gallery of Art, 1969). **55.** Anne Hoy, *The Thinking Eye* (New York: International Center of Photography, 1987). **56.** Ibid. **57.** Downey interview, op. cit. **58.** Camnitzer, op. cit. **59.** Camnitzer to the author, August 1987. **60.** *Luis Camnitzer* (Montevideo: Museo Nacional de Artes Plasticas, 1986), p.9. **61.** Ibid., pp.11-12. **62.** Camnitzer, conversation with the author, September 1987. **63.** Ibid. **64.** Canaday, op. cit. **65.** Porter, taped conversation with the author, June 1987. **66.** Ibid. **67.** Ibid. **68.** Ibid. **69.** Gregory Battcock, *Why Art?* (New York: E.P. Dutton, 1977), p.99. **70.** *Art in Editions* (New York: Pratt Center for Contemporary Printmaking, 1968), p.7. **71.** Porter interview, op. cit. **72.** *Counter Biennial—Contra Bienal* (New York: Micla, 1971). **73.** John Perreault, "Reviews," *The Village Voice*, December 4, 1969, p.63. **74.** Marcia Tucker, "Rafael Ferrer," in *Whitney Museum of American Art Biennial* (New York: Whitney Museum, 1972). **75.** *Deseo, An Adventure, Rafael Ferrer* (Cincinnati: Contemporary Art Center, 1973), p.53. **76.** Ibid. **77.** *Rafael Ferrer* (Philadelphia: Institute of Contemporary Art, U. Pennsylvania), p.6. **78.** Peter Schjeldahl, "New York Letter," *Art International*, September 1969. **79.** Hilton Kramer, "The Melting Ice, etc.," *The New York Times*, May 29, 1969. **80.** See Chapter Two of this book. **81.** Kim Levin, "A Different Drummer," *Art News*, September 1969, pp.48-51. **82.** Leandro Katz, taped conversation with the author, June 1987. **83.** Ibid. **84.** Ibid. **85.** Dore Ashton, *American Art since 1945* (New York: Oxford U. Press, 1982), pp.193-94. **86.** John Hanhardt, *The New Filmmakers Series 2: Leandro Katz* (New York: Whitney Museum, 1982). **87.** Eduardo Costa and John Perreault, eds., "Tape Poems," stereophonic tape, N.Y.C., 1969. **88.** Lawrence Alloway, "Fashion Fictional," *Vogue*, February 1, 1968, pp.170-71. **89.** Blair Sabol, "Outside Fashion," *The Village Voice*, January 23, 1969, p.12. **90.** Perreault, "Free Art," *The Village Voice*, May 1, 1969, p.14. **91.** Edward Fry, ed., *The Sixth Guggenheim International Exhibition* (New York: Solomon R. Guggenheim Museum, 1971), p.33. **92.** Douglas Davis, "The Last International?," *Newsweek*, February 22, 1971, p.64. **93.** Antonio Dias to the author, August 1987. **94.** "East River Painting Is on It," *The New York Times*, May 27, 1970. **95.** Nicolas Uriburu, unpublished text, 1981. **96.** "East River Painting Is on It," op. cit. **97.** Perreault, "Art," *The Village Voice*, June 4, 1970, p.19. **98.** Perreault, "Reviews," *The Village Voice*, December 4, 1969, p.63. **99.** Helio Oiticica to the author, July 1987. **100.** Ted Castle, conversation with the author, July 1987. **101.** Frederico de Morais, "*Pequeno Roteiro Cronologico Dan Invencoes de Helio Oiticica*" (São Paolo: Galeria de Arte, 1986). **102.** Guy Brett, *Helio Oiticica* (London: Whitechapel Art Gallery, 1969), p. 25. See also Oiticica, *Aspiro ao Grande Laberinto* (Rio de Janeiro: Projeto H.O., 1986).

Bibliography

Mexican and Mexican American Artists

Barker, V. "Mexico in N.Y." *Arts*, October 1930, pp. 16–18.

Barnitz, Jacqueline. *Latin American Artists in the U.S. Before 1950*. New York: Center for Inter-American Relations, 1981.

———. *Young Mexicans*. New York: Center for Inter-American Relations, 1970.

Brenner, Anita. "A Mexican Rebel." *Arts*, October 1927, pp. 201–209.

———. "A Mexican Renascence." *Arts*, September 1925, pp. 127–50.

———. "An Artist from the Maya Country, Carlos Mérida." *International Studio*, April 1926, pp. 85–87.

———. *Idols Behind Altars*. Boston: Beacon Press, 1929.

———. "The Mexican Primitives." *Nation*, February 1928, pp. 129–30.

Charlot, Jean. "20 Centuries of Mexican Art." *Magazine of Art*, July 1940, pp. 398–405.

———. "Orozco's Stylistic Evolution." *College Art Journal* 9 (1949), pp. 148–57.

———. *The Mexican Mural Renaissance: 1920–1925*. New Haven: Yale University Press, 1962.

"Chicanos Turn to Paint." *The Sacramento Bee*, June 7, 1970.

Covarrubias, Miguel. *Negro Drawings*. New York: Alfred A. Knopf, 1927.

———. *The Prince of Wales and Other Famous Americans*. New York: Alfred A. Knopf, 1925.

Cuevas, José Luis. *Cuevas por Cuevas*. Mexico City: Ediciones Era, 1965.

Dos Passos, John. "Diego Rivera's Murals." *New Masses*, March 1927.

Dodd, Lamar. *Charlot Murals in Georgia*. Athens: University of Georgia, 1945.

Dwyer, Eileen. "The Mexican Modern Movement." *Studio*, October 1927, pp. 262–66.

Evans, Ernestine. "Frescoes Glorify Mexican Indian Life." *New York Times Magazine*, September 26, 1926, pp. 12–21.

———. *The Frescoes of Diego Rivera*. New York: Harcourt Brace, 1929.

———. "If I Should go Back to Mexico." *Century*, February 1926, pp. 455–61.

Fernández, Justino. *Arte Moderno y Contemporáneo de México*. Mexico City: Universidad Nacional Autonóma de México (UNAM), 1952.

Flint, Ralph. "Frescoes by Rivera Seen at Museum of Modern Art." *The Art News*, December 26, 1931, pp. 5 and 7.

———. "Metropolitan Holds Big Show of Mexican Art." *The Art News*, October 18, 1930, p. 3.

Getlein, Frank. "Pan American." *The Sunday Star*. Washington, D.C. October 13, 1963.

Gibbs, Jo. "Diego Rivera's Mexican Retrospective." *The Art Digest*, April 1, 1950, p. 23.

Goldman, Shifra. *Contemporary Mexican Painting in a Time of Change*. Austin: University of Texas Press, 1981.

———. "Siqueiros and Three Early Murals in Los Angeles." *Art Journal* 33 (Summer 1974), pp. 321–27.

Goldwater, Robert J. *Rufino Tamayo*. New York: Quadrangle Press, 1947.

Gómez Sicre, José. *José Luis Cuevas*. Washington D.C.: Museum of Modern Art of Latin America, 1978.

Grafly, Dorothy. "Deeply National Art of Old Mexico Presented in Philadelphia." *The Art Digest*, April 15, 1943, p. 8.

Grenauer, Emily. "Art and Artists: Liberation of Mexican Mural Art Hailed as Tamayo Completes Mural." *New York Herald Tribune*, October 5, 1952.

Gruening, Ernest. "The Mexican Mural Renaissance." *Century Magazine*, February 1924.

Gunther Gerzso: Paintings and Graphics Reviewed. Austin: University of Texas, Michener Galleries, 1976.

Hamblen, Emily S. "Notes on Orozco's Murals." *Creative Art*, January 1929, p. 46.

Harnoncourt, Rene d'. "Exposition of Mexican Art, Metropolitan Museum." *International Studio*, October 1930, pp. 50–51.

———. "Loan Exhibition of Mexican Arts, *Metropolitan Museum Bulletin* 25 (October 1930), pp. 210–17.

———. "Loan Exhibition of Mexican Arts." *American Magazine of Art*, January 1931, pp. 5–22.

Harrison, Gladys. "Gallery Gazer." *Time–Herald* (Washington D.C.), October 26, 1952.

Helm, MacKinley. *Man of Fire: José Clemente Orozco*. New York: Harcourt Brace, 1953.

———. *Modern Mexican Painters*. New York: Harper Bros., 1941.

Herrera, Hayden. *Frida, A Biography of Frida Kahlo*. New York: Harper and Row, 1983.

Hunter, Sam. *Modern American Painting and Sculpture*. New York: Dell Publishing Co., 1963, p. 139.

———. "Tamayo: Fire and Ice." *The Art Digest*, March 15, 1954, pp. 17 and 32–33.

Hurlburt, Laurance "The Siqueiros Experimental Workshop: New York, 1936." *Art Journal* 35 (Spring 1976), pp. 237–46.

Jewell, E.A. "Exhibition of Mexican Arts Circulated by the American Federation of Art." *Milwaukee Institute Bulletin* 4 (May 1931), pp. 1–5.

José Clemente Orozco, An Autobiography. Translated by Robert C. Stephenson. Austin: University of Texas Press, 1962.

Julio Castellanos. Mexico City: Banco Nacional de México, 1982.

Langsner, Jules. "Art of Mexico at the Pasadena Art Institute." *The Art News*, May 1953, p. 49.

———. "Show of Drawings in Los Angeles." *The Art News*, September 1960, p. 51.

Leighton, Frederick W. "Rivera's Mural Paintings." *International Studio*, February 1924, pp. 378–81.

Lewis, Flora. "Mexican Counter-Revolt." *New York Times Magazine*, October 12, 1952.

Lowe, Jeannette. "Bimillenial View of Mexican Art: A Brilliant Survey at MoMA." *The Art News*, May 25, 1940, pp. 6–8.

Lynch, Jr., James B. *Rufino Tamayo: Fifty Years of his Paintings*. Washington, D.C.: The Phillips Collection, 1978.

Mechlin, L. "Mexican Exhibition." *American Magazine of Art*, January 1931, pp. 2–4.

"Mexican Art Exhibition, Cleveland Museum of Art." *Cleveland Museum Bulletin* 18 (February 1931), pp. 28–30.

"Mexican Art to be Circulated in the U.S. During 1930–1931." *The Art News*, May 31, 1930, p. 5.

"Mexican Exhibit Pictures Mexico as the Natives See it." *San Antonio Express*, August 16, 1931.

"Mexican Painting Today: Exhibition at Philadelphia Museum of Art." *Magazine of Art*, May 1943, pp. 168–71.

"Mexican Volcano." *Time*, August 19, 1946.

"Mexico's Ancients and Moderns Mingle in Exhibits at Grand Central Galleries." *The Art News*, May 1946, p. 53.

Montano, Jorge. "Rufino Tamayo: Leader of a New Mexican School of Painting." *Mexican Life*, November 1929, pp. 23–27.

Morais, Federico. *Mathias Goeritz*. Mexico City: Universidad Nacional Autonóma de México (UNAM), 1982.

"Mr. Watts Attack on Orozco's Murals Stirs a Hornet's Nest." *The Art Digest*, October 1, 1934, pp. 6 and 21–22.

Myers, Bernard S. *Mexican Painting in Our Time*. New York: Oxford University Press, 1956.

McBride, Henry. "A Success Story." *The Art News*, December 1951, p. 54.

————. "Escapism: One Artist Who Definitely Gets Away from This Period." *The New York Sun*, November 12, 1943.

O'Connor, Francis V. "An Iconographic Interpretation of Diego Rivera's *Detroit Industry* Murals in Terms of Their Orientation to the Cardinal Points of the Compass." *Diego Rivera: A Retrospective*. Detroit: Detroit Institute of Arts, 1986, pp. 215–33.

O'Connor, Francis V. *Jackson Pollock*. New York: The Museum of Modern Art, 1967.

————. "The Influence of Diego Rivera on the Art of the United States During the 1930s and After." In *Diego Rivera: A Retrospective*. Detroit: Detroit Institute of Arts, 1986, pp. 157–83.

————. "New Deal Murals in New York." *Artforum*, November 1968, pp. 41–49.

————, ed. *The New Deal Art Projects: An Anthology of Memoirs*, Washington, D.C., 1972.

Orozco, José Clemente. "A New World, New Races, and New Art." *Creative Art*, January 1929, pp. 45–46.

————. *The Artist in New York: Letters to Jean Charlot and Unpublished Writings, 1925–1929*. Foreword and notes by Jean Charlot. Austin: University of Texas Press, 1974.

"Orozco's American Epic at Dartmouth Starts a Controversy." *The Art Digest*, September 1934, pp. 5–6.

Pach, Walter. "An Exhibition of Art by Mexican Schoolchildren and Jean Charlot." *Art Center Bulletin*, April 1926, pp. 244–46.

————. "The Evolution of Diego Rivera." *Creative Art*, January 1929, pp. 21–39.

"Paint and Pistols." *Time*, November 10, 1947, pp. 58–60.

"Philadelphia: A Mexican Exhibition." *The Art News*, November 14, 1939, p. 14.

Plaut, James S. "Mexican Maximum: Exhibition Organized by Institute of Modern Art, Boston." *The Art News*, December 15, 1941, pp. 1011.

Quirarte, Jacinto. *A History and Appreciation of Chicano Art*. San Antonio: Research Center for the Arts and Humanities, 1984.

————. *Mexican American Artists*. Austin: University of Texas Press, 1973.

Raynor, V. "Exhibition at Byron Gallery." *The Art News*, March 1964, p. 64.

Reed, Alma. *José Clemente Orozco*. New York: Delphic Studios, 1932.

Reed, Judith Kaye. "Mexican Art—From Marketplace to Museum." *The Art Digest*, May 15, 1946, p. 22.

————. "Tamayo: Power of Palette and Vision." *The Art Digest*, May 1, 1950, p. 14.

"Rivera Affair." *The Art Digest*, April 1, 1933, p. 30.

"Rivera Squall." *The Art Digest*, April 15, 1933, p. 6.

Rivera, Diego. *Raíces Políticas y Motivos Personales de la Controversia Siqueiros—Rivera. Stalinismo vs. Bolchevismo Leninista*. Mexico City: Imprenta Mundial, December 1935.

————. "From a Mexican Painter's Notebook." *Arts*, January 1925, pp. 21–23.

————. "The Guild Spirit in Mexican Art; as told to Katharine Anne Porter." *Graphic Survey*, May 1, 1924, pp. 174–78.

————. "The Revolution in Painting." *Creative Art*, January 1929, pp. 27–28.

"Rockefeller Boards up Rivera Fresco Because Artist Will Not Substitute Face of Unknown Man for Lenin." *The Art News*, May 13, 1933, pp. 3–4.

Rodman, Selden. *The Insiders: Rejection and Rediscovery of Man in The Arts of Our Time*. Baton Rouge: Louisiana State University, 1960.

Romero Keith, Delmari. *Historia y Testimonios: Galería de Arte Moderno*, Mexico City: Galería de Arte Moderno, 1986.

Rose, Barbara. *American Art since 1900: A Critical History*. New York: Praeger, 1968.

"Rufino Tamayo." *The Art News*. January 1957, p. 22.

"Rufino Tamayo at the Height of his Powers." *The Art News*, January 1, 1946, p. 18.

Schmeckebier, Laurance E. *Modern Mexican Art*. Minneapolis: University of Minnesota Press, 1939.

Seldis, Henry J. "Masterworks from Mexico." *Art in America*, October 1963, pp. 86–91.

Siqueiros, David Alfaro. *No hay mas ruta que la nuestra*. Mexico City: Secretaría de Educación Pública, 1945.

————. "Rivera's Counter-Revolutionary Road." *New Masses*, May 29, 1934.

Small, George Raphael. *Ramos Martínez: His Life and His Art*. Edited by Jerald Slattum. Westlake Village, California: F. and J. Publishing Co., 1975.

Suárez, Orlando S. *Inventario del Muralismo Mexicano*. Mexico City: Universidad Nacional Autonóma de México (UNAM), 1972.

Sweet, Frederick A. "The Leader Zapata." *Bulletin of the Art Institute of Chicago*, November 1941, pp. 90–91.

Tablada, José Juan. "Diego Rivera, Mexican Painter." *Arts*, October 1923, pp. 221–33.

————. "José Clemente Orozco, The Mexican Goya." *International Studio*, March 1924, pp. 492–500.

————. "Mexican Painting Today." *International Studio*, January 1923, pp. 267–76.

"The Talented Tamayo." *Newsweek*, November 23, 1959.

Taller de Gráfica Popular. *25 Grabados de Leopoldo Méndez*. Mexico City, 1943.

————. *Estampas de la Revolución Mexicana*. Mexico City, 1947.

_____. *450 años de lucha: homenaje al pueblo mexicano.* Mexico City, 1960.

Tibol, Raquel, ed. *Diego Rivera: Arte y Política.* Mexico City: Editorial Grijalbo, 1979.

Tillim, Sidney. "Studies for the Dartmouth Murals at The Museum of Modern Art." *Arts,* January 1962, pp. 30–31.

Twenty Centuries of Mexican Art/Veinte Siglos de Arte Moderno. New York: The Museum of Modern Art, 1940.

Vera de Cordova, Rafael. "Art in Mexico." *The Art Digest,* December 15, 1926, p. 10.

"Watts Writes in Defiance; Mumford in Appreciation of Orozco." *The Art Digest,* October 15, 1934, pp. 8, 10, and 19.

Wholden, Rosalind B. "Ceremony: Hollowed and Pragmatic." *Arts,* January 1964, pp. 60–63.

Wolf, Ben. "Tamayo of Mexico Exhibits Massive Forms." *The Art Digest,* January 15, 1946, p. 9.

Wolfe, Bertram. "Art and Revolution in Mexico." *Nation,* August 27, 1924, pp. 207-08.

_____. *Diego Rivera, His Life and Times.* New York: Alfred A. Knopf, 1939.

_____. *The Fabulous Life of Diego Rivera.* New York: Stein and Day, 1963.

Yates, Peter. "Thirty-Five Hundred Years of Mexican Vision." *Arts and Architecture,* February 1964, pp. 4–5 and 21–25.

The Special Case of Puerto Rico

"An Interview: Rafael Ferrer and Stephen Prokopoff." In *Rafael Ferrer Enclosures.* Philadelphia: Institute of Contemporary Art, 1971.

Aquí en la lucha; Caricaturas de Lorenzo Homar. San Juan: Cuadernos de *La Escalera,* 1970.

Benítez, Marimar. "Lorenzo Homar y el arte contemporáneo de Puerto Rico." In *Exposición retrospectiva de Lorenzo Homar,* Ponce, P.R.: Museo de Arte, 1978.

_____. "Viendo pintar a Francisco Rodon." In *Personajes de Rodon (1971–1983),* Río Piedras: U. Puerto Rico, 1983.

_____. "¿Que es el arte puertorriqueño?" *El Reportero,* San Juan, February 25, 1984.

Bloch, Peter. *Painting and Sculpture of the Puerto Ricans.* New York: Plus Ultra Educational Publishers, 1978.

_____. "By the Caribbean." *Art Digest,* November 1984.

Cancel, Luis R. "Introducing Pedro Villarini." In El Museo del Barrio: *Images of Villarini,* New York, 1981.

"City Artist Shows N.Y. How to Have Cool Show" *Daily News,* December 5, 1969.

Coates, Robert M. "Stirrings in Puerto Rico." *The New Yorker,* January 26, 1957, p. 74.

Colón Morales, Rafael. "Aspectos del arte puertorriqueño en Nueva York." Unpublished manuscript, 1976.

"Dehner paints Puerto Rico's squalor." *Art Digest,* March 1936.

Delgado, Osiris. *Las Artes Plásticas, Volúmen 8. La Gran Enciclopedia de Puerto Rico.* Madrid: Ediciones "R," 1976.

"Evaluación, Ideas y Estilo." In *Exposición Homenaje Ramón Frade.* San Juan: UPR, 1985.

El Museo del Barrio. *Bridge Between Islands: Retrospective Works by Six Puerto Rican Artists in New York.* (Henry Street Settlement, The Bronx Museum of the Arts, El Museo del Barrio), 1978.

_____. *Jorge Soto Sánchez: Works on Paper 1974–1979.* New York, 1979.

_____. *José Morales, Paintings and Drawings.* New York, 1979.

_____. *Myrna Báez: diez años de gráfica y pintura 1971–1981.* New York, 1982.

_____. *Eloy Blanco: "Faces and Figures." A Retrospective.* New York, 1983.

Ferrer, Rafael. "Autobiography." In *Deseo: An Adventure: Rafael Ferrer,* Cincinnati: Contemporary Arts Center, 1973.

Gómez Sicre, José. *Olga Albizu of Puerto Rico.* Washington, D.C.: Pan American Union, 1966.

Instituto de Cultura Puertorriqueña. *Catálogo General Primera Bienal de San Juan del Grabado Latinoamericano.* San Juan, 1970.

Lee de Muñoz Marín, Muna. "Art Exhibitions in the University of Puerto Rico." *University of Puerto Rico Bulletin,* December 1937.

Martorell, Antonio. "Fue la década." In *Hermandad de Artistas Gráficos de Puerto Rico: Pintura y gráfica de los años 50,* San Juan, 1985.

Museo de Arte de Ponce. *Francisco Oller, un Realista del Impresionismo.* Ponce, P.R. 1983.

Museo de la Universidad de Puerto Rico. *Irene y Jack Délano en Puerto Rico.* Río Piedras, 1983.

"Puerto Rican Art Show." *The New York Times,* January 7, 1957, p. 27.

"Puerto Rico Chapter of the American Artists Professional League Incorporates." *Art Digest,* November 1939.

Rivera, Alba Raquel. "Profesor protesta UPR compre escultura en acero de Ferrer." *El Mundo,* February 1964.

Rivera García, Rafael. "Controversial Art." *The Island Times,* June 1, 1961.

Schjedahl, Peter. "The Audacity of Rafael Ferrer." *The Village Voice,* December 25, 1970.

Tió, Teresa. "Texto y contexto del cartel puertorriqueño." In *El cartel en Puerto Rico 1946–1985.* Río Piedras: UPR, 1985.

Torres Martinó, José A. "El Centro de Arte Puertorriqueño." In *Hermandad de Artistas Gráficos de Puerto Rico: Pintura y gráfica de los años 50.* San Juan, 1985.

_____. "Juan Antonio Rosado," In *Exposición Homenaje Juan A. Rosado.* San Juan, 1986.

Traba, Marta. *Propuesta polémica sobre arte puertorriqueño.* San Juan: Ediciones Librería Internacional, 1971.

Venegas, Haydee. "Francisco Oller, Maestro." *Horizontes, Revista de la Universidad Católica de Puerto Rico,* April 1985, pp. 101–106.

Von Meier, Kurt. "Violence, Art and the American Way." *Arts Canada.* April 1968.

Willard, Charlotte. "Violence in Art." *Art in America,* January–February 1969, pp. 36–44.

Constructivism

Acha, Juan. "*El Geometrismo Reciente y Latinoamérica.*" In *El Geometrismo Mexicano.* Mexico City: Universidad Nacional Autónoma de México, 1977.

_____. *Otero.* Caracas: Museum of Contemporary Art, 1985.

Angel, Félix. "Five Colombian Masters." Washington, D.C.: Museum of Modern Art of Latin America, 1985.

Barnitz, Jacqueline. *Latin American Artists in the U.S. 1950–1970.* New York: Godwin–Ternbach Museum at Queens College, 1983.

Bayón, Damián. *Aventura Plástica de Hispanoamérica.* Mexico City: F.C.E., 1974.

Carnevali, Gloria. *La Obra Cinética Cruz-Diez.* Caracas: Museum of Fine Arts.

Catlin, Stanton. *Forerunners of American Modernism.* New York: Center for Inter-American Relations, 1967.

Chase, Gilbert. *Contemporary Art in Latin America: Painting, Graphic Art, Sculpture, Architecture.* New York: The Free Press, 1970.

Christ, Ronald. "*In the World and Workshop of Julio Alpuy.*" New York: Center for Inter-American Relations, 1972.

Duncan, Barbara. "Joaquín Torres-García 1874–1949." In *Chronology and Catalogue of the Family Collection*, Austin: Archer M. Huntington Gallery, 1974.

Gradowczyck, Mario H. "Joaquín Torres–García." Buenos Aires: Ediciones de Arte Gaglianone, 1985.

Guevara, Roberto. *Omar Rayo*, Buenos Aires: Museum of Modern Art, 1971.

Iturburu, Córdoba. *Pettoruti*. Buenos Aires: Academia Nacional de Bellas Artes, 1980.

Kalemberg, Angel. *Joaquín Torres-García: Centenario de Su Nacimiento 1874–28 de julio–1974*. Montevideo: Biblioteca Nacional, 1974.

Alicia Paoli Gallery. *Alicia Peñalba*. Lausanne, 1967.

Pau-Llosa, Ricardo. *Polesello*. Buenos Aires: Ediciones Gaglianone, 1984.

Perazzo, Nelly. *Brizzi Retrospective*. Buenos Aires: Fundación San Telmo, 1986.

Perazzo, Nelly. *El Arte Concreto en la Argentina*. Buenos Aires: Ediciones de Arte Gaglianone, 1983.

Pettoruti, Emilio. *Un Pintor ante el Espejo*, Buenos Aires, Solar/Hachette, 1968.

Robbins, Daniel. *J. Torres–García 1874–1949*. Ottawa and New York: National Gallery of Canada, Ottawa; the Solomon R. Guggenheim Museum, New York; and the Rhode Island School of Design, Providence, 1970.

Rowell, Marget. *Torres-García: Grid-Pattern-Sign, Paris-Montevideo 1924–1944*. London: Hayward Gallery, 1970.

Serrano, Eduardo. *Un Lustro Visual*. Bogotá: Ediciones Tercer Mundo, 1976.

Stringer, John. "Reflections on the Present Selection, Aquí–27 Latin American Artists Living and Working in the United States." Los Angeles: University of Southern California, n.d.

Traba, Marta. *Sculptures by Gego*. Bogotá: Biblioteca Luis Angel Arango, 1967.

New York Dada

Beardsley, John, and Livingston, Jane. *Hispanic Art in the United States*. With an essay by Octavio Paz. Houston: Museum of Fine Arts, 1987.

Breton, André. *Manifestos of Surrealism*. Translated by Richard Seaver and Helen Rhone. Ann Arbor: University of Michigan Press, 1969.

———. "Souvenir du Méxique." *Minotaure*, May 1939.

———. *Le Surréalisme et la Peinture*. New York: Brentanos, Inc. 1945.

Centre Georges Pompidou. *Matta*. Paris, 1985.

Galería de Arte Mexicano. *International Exhibition of Surrealism*. Mexico City, 1939.

Herrera, Hayden. *Frida: A Biography of Frida Kahlo*. New York: Harper and Row, 1983.

Hyland, Douglas. *Marius de Zayas: Conjurer of Souls*. Lawrence: Spencer Museum of Art, University of Kansas, 1981.

Larrea, Juan. *El Surrealismo Entre Viejo y Nuevo Mundo*. Mexico City: Ediciones Cuadernos Americanos, 1944.

Pol-Fouchet, Max. *Wifredo Lam*. Barcelona: Ediciones Poligrafa, 1975.

Pontual, Roberto. *Brazilian Contemporary Art*. Translated by John Knox and Florence Eleanor Irvin. Rio de Janeiro: Ediciones Jornal do Brasil, 1976.

Prampolini, Ida Rodriguez. *El surrealismo y el arte fantástico de México*. Mexico City: Universidad National Autonóma de México (UNAM), 1969.

Rubin, William. *Dada and Surrealist Art*. New York: Harry N. Abrams, 1968.

———. *Dada, Surrealism and Their Heritage*. New York: The Museum of Modern Art, 1968.

Sims, Lowery Stokes. "Wifredo Lam and Roberto Matta: Surrealism in the New World." In *In The Mind's Eye; Dada and Surrealism*. Edited by Terry Ann R. Neff. Chicago: Museum of Contemporary Art, 1985.

The U.S. and Socially Concerned Latin American Art

General References

Africa Information Service, ed. *Return to the Source: Selected Speeches by Amilcar Cabral*. New York: Monthly Review Press, 1973.

Baigell, Matthew. *A History of American Painting*. New York: Praeger, 1971.

Cancel, Luis. *The Spirit of Independence*. New York: Cayman Gallery, 1976.

Catlin, Stanton. *Art of Latin America since Independence*. New Haven: Yale University Press, 1966.

Center for Inter-American Relations. *Looking South: Latin American Art in New York Collections*. New York, 1972.

Charlot, Jean. *Art from the Mayans to Disney*. New York: Sheed and Ward, 1939.

———. *The Mexican Mural Renaissance, 1920–25*. New Haven: Yale University Press, 1962.

Chase, Gilbert. *Contemporary Art in Latin America*. New York: The Free Press, 1970.

Cockcroft, Eva. "Abstract Expressionism: Weapon of the Cold War." *Artforum*, June 1974, pp. 39–41.

———. *Cuban Poster Art: A Retrospective 1961–1982*. New York: Center for Cuban Studies, 1983.

Cockcroft, Eva, Weber, John, and Cockcroft, James. *Towards A Peoples Art: The Contemporary Mural Movement*. New York: E.P. Dutton, 1977.

Dallas Museum of Fine Arts. *Gulf-Caribbean Art Exhibition*. Dallas, 1956.

Fondo Del Sol, *Ancient Roots/New Visions–Raíces Antiguas/Visiones Nuevas*. Tucson: Tucson Museum of Art, 1977.

Goldman, Shifra. *Contemporary Mexican Painting in a Time of Change*. Austin: University of Texas Press, 1981.

Goldman, Shifra and Ybarra-Frausto, Tomás. *Arte Chicano: A Comprehensive Annotated Bibliography of Chicano Art, 1965–1981*. Berkeley: Chicano Studies Library of University of California, Berkeley, 1985.

Kunzle, David. "Public Graphics in Cuba: A Very Cuban Form of Internationalist Art." *Latin American Perspectives*, no. 7, 1973, pp. 89–110.

Lucy Lippard, ed. "Out of Sight, Out of Mind (II) Asian and Hispanic Artists." *Upfront*, Fall 1984, pp.17–21.

The Museum of Modern Art. *Modern Cuban Painters*. New York, 1943.

Portner, Leslie Judd. "Cuban Modern Paintings." *Pan American Union*, 1950, pp. 67–69.

Ringling Museum. *Latin American Horizons*. Sarasota, Fla., 1976.

Rodriguez, Antonio. *A History of Mexican Mural Painting*. New York: G.P. Putnam and Sons, 1969.

Smith, Robert C. "Latin American Painting Comes into its Own." *Pan American Union*, September 1943.

Sotheby Parke Bernet, Inc. *Modern Mexican Paintings, Drawings, Sculpture and Prints: Public Auction*. New York, May 26, 1977.

Stermer, Dugald, and Sontag, Susan. *The Art of Revolution, Castro's Cuba: 1959–1970*. New York: McGraw Hill, 1970.

Stringer, John. "Art on the Road . . . Latin American Exhibitions Abroad." *Arte*, Spring 1987.

Wolfe, Clair. "Masterworks of Mexican Art: Modern." *Artforum*, December 1963, p. 36.

Bibliography

1940 Latin American Exhibition of Fine Arts: Brazil, Ecuador, Mexico, Venezuela. New York: Riverside Museum, 1940.

Individual Artists

Museo del La Universidad de Puerto Rico. *Myrna Báez.* San Juan, 1976.

El Museo del Barrio. *Myrna Báez, diez años de gráfica y pintura.* New York, 1981.

Museo del Palacio de Bellas Artes. *Arnold Belkin: Batallas Históricas: Trabajos en proceso.* Mexico City, 1977.

Ragon, Michel. "Antonio Berni and the Adventures of Ramona Montiel." In *Berni.* Paris: Galerie du Passeur, 1963.

Squirru, Rafael. "Antonio Berni." *Americas,* October 1965, pp. 20–29.

Museo de Arte Moderno. *Antonio Berni.* Rio de Janeiro, 1968.

Vinals, José. *Berni, Palabra e Imagen.* Buenos Aires: Imagen Galería de Arte, 1976.

Galería Rubbers. *Antonio Berni, Grabados y Tacos.* Buenos Aires, 1964.

New Jersey State Museum. *Antonio Berni.* Trenton, 1966.

Bonino Gallery. *Antonio Berni.* New York, 1977.

Arciniegas, German. *Fernando Botero.* New York: Harry N. Abrams, 1977.

Center for Inter-American Relations Art Gallery. *Fernando Botero.* New York, 1969.

The Contemporaries. *Botero.* New York, 1962.

Hunter, Sam. *Fernando Botero.* New York: Marlboro Gallery, 1975.

Milwaukee Art Center. *Fernando Botero, Recent Works.* Milwaukee, 1967.

Traba, Marta. *Fernando Botero.* Recinto De Río Piedras: University of Puerto Rico, 1970.

Traba, Marta, and Díaz, Hernán. *Seis Artistas Contemporáneos Colombianos.* Bogotá: Edición de Antares, 1963. (Botero, Obregón, Ramírez, Grau, Weidemann, Negret.)

Carreño, Mario. "The Ideas of Art." *Tiger's Eye* (Westport, Conn.), December 1947, pp. 42–47.

Pan American Union, *Carreño,* Washington, D.C., 1947.

Perls Gallery. *Mario Carreño.* New York, 1941.

Houston Museum of Contemporary Art. *Mel Casas: Humanscapes.* Houston, 1976.

Borgenicht Gallery. *Recent Drawings: José Luis Cuevas.* New York, 1965.

David Herbert Gallery. *José Luis Cuevas.* New York, 1960.

Pan American Union. *José Luis Cuevas, Drawings.* Washington, D.C., 1954.

Traba, Marta. *José Luis Cuevas.* Bogotá: Biblioteca Luis Angel Arango del Banco de la República, 1964.

Cayman Gallery. *Woodcuts and Relief Casts by Antonio Frasconi.* New York, 1977.

The Print Club of Cleveland and the Cleveland Museum. *The Work of Antonio Frasconi.* Cleveland, 1952.

Eichenberg, Fritz. "Frasconi: Artist, Printmaker." *Artists Proof.* vol. 6, no. 9, 1966, pp. 4–45.

Galloway, John. "Frasconi at Pan American." *Right Angle,* April 1949.

Favela, Ramon. *Rupert Garcia: A Survey Exhibition.* San Francisco: The Mexican Museum, 1986.

Covarrubias, Juan. *Léonel Góngora, la opera pintada.* Bogotá: Museo de Arte Moderno, 1977.

Cober Gallery. *Góngora, 65.* New York, 1965.

Camon Aznar, José. *Oswaldo Guayasamin.* Barcelona: Poligrafa, 1973.

Pan American Union. *Oswaldo Guayasamin of Ecuador.* Washington D.C., 1955.

Tibol, Raquel. *Libros y Oleos del pintor Francisco Icaza: obras de 1971 a 1978.* Mexico, D.F.: Museo de Arte Moderno, 1979.

Alternative Museum. *Luis Jiménez: Sculpture and Works on Paper.* New York, 1984.

Dallas Museum of Art. *Luis Jiménez.* Dallas, 1985.

Graham Gallery. *Luis Jiménez.* New York, 1969.

The Philadelphia Museum of Art, *The Nazi Drawings of Mauricio Lasansky.* Philadelphia, 1966.

Velásquez Chávez, Agustín. *Contemporary Mexican Artists.* New York: Covici Friede, 1937.

Elger, Frank. *Héctor Poleo.* New York: Acquavella Galleries, 1967.

———, *Héctor Poleo: A Retrospective Exhibition,* New York: Center for Inter-American Relations, 1974.

Honig, Edwin. "Portinari's New World Murals." *Quarterly Review.* Spring 1943.

Rockwell, Kent. *Portinari, His Life and Art.* Chicago: University of Chicago Press, 1940.

Pedrosa, Mario. "Portinari: From Brodowski to the Library of Congress." In *Art in Latin America.* Washington: Pan American Union, 1950.

Smith, Robert C. "The Art of Candido Portinari." *Bulletin of The Museum of Modern Art,* October 1940.

El Museo del Barrio, *"Con Su Permiso . . . " Carlos Raquel Rivera.* New York, 1980.

El Museo del Barrio. *The Graphic Work of José Rosa.* New York, 1981.

El Museo del Barrio. *Jorge Soto Sánchez, Works on Paper 1974–79.* New York, 1979.

The Latin American Presence

Angel, Félix. *Tribute to Maria Luisa Pacheco of Bolivia, 1919-1982.* Washington, D.C.: Museum of Modern Art of Latin America, Organization of American States, 1986.

Boulton, Alfredo. *Historia de la Pintura en Venezuela.* Caracas: Colección Libros de Arte, 1972.

Caballero, German Rubiano. *La Escultura en America Latina, Siglo XX.* Bogotá: Universidad Nacional de Colombia, 1986.

Caballero, German Rubiano. *Enrique Grau.* Bogotá: Centro Colombo Americano, 1983.

Castedo, Leopoldo. *A History of Latin American Art and Architecture—From Pre-Columbian Times to the Present.* New York: Praeger, 1969.

Claure, Rigoberto Villarroel. *Art in Latin America Today: Bolivia.* Washington, D.C.: Pan American Union, 1963.

Davila, Lionel Méndez. *Art in Latin America Today: Guatemala.* Washington, D.C.: Pan American Union, 1966.

Elespuru, Juan Manuel Ugarte. *Pintura y Escultura en el Perú Contemporáneo.* Lima: Editorial Universitaria S.A., 1970.

Iturburu, Córdoba. *La Pintura Argentina del Siglo XX.* Buenos Aires: Editorial Atlántida, 1958.

Kirstein, Lincoln. *The Latin American Collection of The Museum of Modern Art.* New York: The Museum of Modern Art, 1943.

McCabe, Cynthia Jaffee. *Fernando Botero.* Washington, D.C.: Hirshhorn Museum and Sculpture Garden, 1979.

Melcherts, Enrique. *Introducción a la Escultura Chilena.* Valparaíso, Chile: Ferrand e Hijos Ltda., 1982.

Miller, Jeannette. *Historia de la Pintura Dominicana.* Santo Domingo, República Dominicana: Banco de Reservas de la República Dominicana, n.d.

Mobil, José A. *Historia del Arte Guatemalteco.* Guatemala City: Editorial Serviprensa Centroamericana, 1985.

Muñoz, Luis Luján. *Carlos Mérida Precursor del Arte Contemporáneo Latinoamericano.* Guatemala City: Cuadernos de la Tradición Guatemalteca, 1985.

Serrano, Eduardo. *Cien Años de Arte Colombiano, 1886-1986.* Bogotá: Museo de Arte Moderno de Bogotá, 1986.

Squirru, Rafael. *Arte de América: 25 años de Crítica.* Buenos Aires: Ediciones Gaglianone, 1979.

Traba, Marta. *Art in Latin America Today: Colombia.* Washington, D.C.: Organization of American States, 1959.

———. *Historia Abierta del Arte Colombiano.* Cali, Colombia: Ediciones del Museo de Arte La Tertulia, Museo de Arte Moderno La Tertulia, 1974.

———. *Dos Decadas Vulnerables en las Artes Plásticas Latinoamericanas 1950-1970.* Mexico City: Siglo XXI Editores Mexico D.F., 1973.

———, et al. *Museum of Modern Art of Latin America—Selections from the Permanent Collection.* Washington, D.C.: Organization of American States, 1985.

Wolfschoon, Erik. *Las Manifestaciones Artísticas en Panamá.* Panama City: Biblioteca de la Cultura Panameña, 1983.

Magnet: New York

Arte Brasileira Contemporânea. *Lygia Clark.* Rio de Janeiro: Edição FUNARTE, 1980.

Ashton, Dore. *American Art since 1945.* Oxford: Oxford University Press, 1982.

Battcock, Gregory. *Minimal Art.* New York: E.P. Dutton, 1968.

Bonino Gallery. *Magnet: New York: A Selection of Painting by Latin American Artists Living in New York.* New York, 1964.

Camnitzer, Luis, and Peraza, Nilda. *The Latin American Graphic Arts Biennial.* New York: Museum of Contemporary Hispanic Art, 1986.

Fashion Institute of Technology. *Fashion and Surrealism.* New York: Rizzoli, 1988.

Galería Colibrí. *Liliana Porter.* San Juan, 1974.

Davis, Douglas. *Art and the Future.* New York: Fredench Praeger, 1973.

Glusberg, Jorge. *Marta Minujín.* Buenos Aires: Ediciones de Arte Gaglianone, 1986.

———. *Art in Argentina.* Milan: Giancarlo Politi Editore, 1986.

Hansen, Al. *Happenings: A Primer of Time and Space in Art.* New York: 1965.

Kubovy, Michael . *Aspects of Perception: The Visual Artist as Avant-Garde Psychologist of Perception.* Rhinecliff, New York: Bard College, 1983.

Museu de Artes Plásticas. *Luis Camnitzer.* Montevideo, 1988.

Museo de Arte Moderna do Rio de Janeiro. *Rubens Gerchman.* Rio de Janeiro: Gráficos Brunner, 1974.

Museum of Contemporary Art. *Six Sculptors: Extended Structures.* Chicago, 1971.

The Museum of Modern Art. *Information.* New York, 1970.

Oiticica, Helio. *Grande Labyrinthe.* Rio de Janeiro: Projecto HO, 1986.

Pontual, Roberto. *Entre Dois Seculos: Arte Brasileira do Século XX na Coleção Gilberto Chateaubriand.* Rio de Janeiro: Editora JB, 1987.

Projecto HO. *Hélio Oiticica.* Rio de Janeiro, 1986.

Zuñiga, Olivia. *Mathias Goeritz.* Mexico City: Editorial Intercontinental, 1963.

List of Illustrations

Luis Jiménez
Man on Fire, 1969–70. p.66; *The American Dream*, 1967–69. p.219

Frida Kahlo
Self-Portrait on the Borderline Between Mexico and the United States, 1932. p.58; *Suicide of Dorothy Hale*, 1938. p.154; *Self-Portrait with Monkey*, 1938. p.155; *The Two Fridas*, 1939. p.158; *How Beautiful Life Is When It Gives Us Riches*, 1943. p.161

Leandro Katz
Word Column, 1970. p.306

Wifredo Lam
The Kiss, 1939. p.164; *Untitled*, 1941. p.164; *Annunciation*, 1944. p.165; *Woman with Flowers*, 1942. p.166; *Mother and Child*, 1942. p.166; *Noncombustible*, 1950. p.168; *The Eyes in the Grillwork*, 1942. p.169

Mauricio Lasansky
Drawing No. 28 (from the Nazi Series), 1961–1966. p.205; *Mexican Sketches No. 2*, 1963–65. p.205

Julio Le Parc
Howard Wise Gallery. Installation, 1967. p.294; *Virtual Forms for Displacement of the Spectator with Changeable Themes*, 1966. p.294

Gerd Leufert
Tirina, 1966. p.143

Domingo López
Orange Energy, 1969. p.150

Luis López-Loza
Children's Dream, 1965. p.261

Manabu Mabe
Melancholy Metropolis, 1969. p.248

Rómulo Macció
The President on the Balcony, 1963. p.260; *To Live Without a Guarantee*, 1963. p.260

Eduardo Mac Entyre
Discontinuous Vertical on Red, 1969. p.131

Marisol
Charles de Gaulle, 1965. p.272

Raul Martínez
Lucia, 1968. p.214

María Martins
Untitled, 1940. p.171

Antonio Martorell
Scorpion Playing Card (Barajas Alacrán), 1968. p.217

Roberto Matta
Eclosion, 1952. p.159; *Studies*, 1942. p.161; *Spherical Roof Around Our Tribe (Revolvers)*, 1952. p.162; *Untitled*, 1942–44. p.162; *Years of Fear*, 1941. p.241

Octavio Medellín
The Hanged, c.1942. p.48

Cildo Meireles
Insertions in Ideological Circuits: Coca-Cola Project, 1970. p.310

Leopoldo Méndez
Vision, 1945. p.41

Carlos Mérida
The Blue Apple, 1962. p.56; *Skies over Texas*, 1943. p.241

Marta Minujín
The Long Shot, 1966. p.291; *Minucode*, 1969. p.291

Rafael Montañez-Ortiz
Henny Penny Piano Destruction, 1967. p.102; *Archaeological Find No.3*, 1961. p.291

Armando Morales
Seascape, 1964. p.248

Edward Negret
The Bridge (Homage to Paul Foster), 1968. p.123

Manuel Neri
Figure, 1958. p.66

Luis Felipe Noé
When the Sun Hits the Fatherland, 1963. p.260

Alejandro Obregón
Cattle Crossing the Magdalena, 1955. p.269; *The Wake*, 1956. p.269

Miguel Ocampo
Author of White, 1963. p.252

Helio Oiticica
Nests, 1970. p.310

José Clemente Orozco
The Beggars, c. 1940. p.21; *The Epic of American Civilization: The Machine*, 1932–34. p.28; *The Requiem*, 1928. p.28; *Vaudeville in Harlem*, 1928. p.30; *Rear Guard*, 1929. p.30; *Los Muertos (Skyscrapers)*, 1931. p.32; *Coney Island*, n.d. p.33; *New York Factory: Williamsburg*, 1928; p.33; *The Martyrdom of St. Stephen*, 1943. p.36; *The Epic of American Civilization: Gods of the Modern World*, 1932–34. p.188

Carlos Osorio
Coast, 1970. p.102

Alejandro Otero
Color Rhythm No. 1, 1955. p.140

Maria Luisa Pacheco
Petrous, 1965. p.245

César Paternosto
The South, 1969. p.143

Amelia Peláez
Hibiscus, 1943. p.280

Alicia Peñalba
The Sparkler, 1957. p.122

Emilio Pettoruti
Coparmonica, 1937. p.117

Héctor Poleo
Andean Family, 1944. p.197

Rogelio Polesello
Phase A, 1965. p.130

Liliana Porter
Untitled, 1970. p.297

Candido Portinari
Prospecting. Sketch for "Discovery of the Americas," 1941. p.2; *Coffee*, 1935. p.193; *The Slum*, 1933. p.193; *The Discovery. Sketch for "Discovery of the Americas,"* 1941. p.196; *Discovery of the Americas* (mural at the Hispanic Foundation, The Library of Congress, Washington, D.C.), 1941–42. p.196

Miguel Pou
Ciquí, 1938. p.75

Alejandro Puente
Untitled, 1965. p.146

Lenders to the Exhibition

Albright-Knox Art Gallery, Buffalo, New York
The Aldrich Museum of Contemporary Art
The Art Institute of Chicago
Atlantic Richfield Company, Los Angeles
The Baltimore Museum of Art
The Brooklyn Museum
Center for Cuban Studies, New York
The Chase Manhattan Bank, N.A.
CIBA-GEIGY Corporation
The Cleveland Museum of Art
Cooperativa de Segueros Multiples, San Juan
Dallas Museum of Art
Solomon R. Guggenheim Museum, New York
Hirshhorn Museum and Sculpture Garden, Smithsonian
    Institution
Archer M. Huntington Art Gallery, University of Texas at
    Austin
Instituto de Cultura Puertorriqueña, San Juan
Instituto Nacional de Bellas Artes, Mexico City
The Jewish Museum, New York
Herbert F. Johnson Museum of Art, Cornell University,
    Ithaca, New York
The Library of Congress, Washington, D.C.
Lowe Art Museum, University of Miami
Massachusetts Institute of Technology
The Minneapolis Institute of Arts
Museo Carillo Gil, Mexico City
Museo de Antropología, Historia y Arte, Universidad de
    Puerto Rico, Recinto de Río Piedras
Museo de Arte Contemporáneo, Buenos Aires
Museo de Arte de Ponce
Museo de Arte Moderno, INBA, Mexico City
Museo de Arte Moderno, Buenos Aires
El Museo del Barrio, New York
Museo del Minuto de Dios, Bogotá
Museu de Arte de São Paulo
Museu Naçional de Belas Artes, Rio de Janeiro
Museum of Contemporary Art, Chicago
The Museum of Fine Arts, Houston
The Museum of Modern Art, New York
Museum of Modern Art of Latin America, Organization of
    American States
Fundação José e Paulina Nemirovsky, São Paulo
New Jersey State Museum, Trenton
Philadelphia Museum of Art
The Phillips Collection, Washington, D.C.
Phoenix Art Museum
Projecto Ho, Rio de Janeiro
The Art Museum, Princeton University
Museum of Art, Rhode Island School of Design
San Francisco Museum of Modern Art
Smith, Kline & French, Colección de Carteles
    Puertorriqueños, San Juan
Torres-García Estate
Walker Art Center, Minneapolis
Yale University Art Gallery
Yeshiva University Museum
Galería Arvil, Mexico City
Bonino Gallery, New York
CDS Gallery, New York
Couturier Galerie, Stanford, Conn.
Charles Cowles Gallery, San Francisco
Galerías Cristóbal, Mexico City
Terry Dintenfass Gallery, New York
Phyllis Kind Gallery, New York
Pierre Matisse Gallery, New York
Rastovski Gallery, New York

Julio Alpuy
Mr. & Mrs. Miguel Aranguren
Claudia Thompson Balaguer
Mrs. Edwin A. Bergman
Robert H. Bergman
Tony Berlant
Maurice Bidermann
Félix Bonilla-Norat
David and Tanya Brillembourg
Luis R. Cancel
Enrique Castro-Cid
Gilberto Chateaubriand
Eduardo Chavez
Arsenio Comas
Eduardo Costa
Carlos Cruz-Diez
Jaime Davidovich
Alma Elizabeth del Rio
Juan Downey
Rafael Ferrer
Livia Fernández
Donna and Earle Florence
Elizabeth Fonseca
Pedro Friedeberg
Antonio E. García
Vita Giorgi
Juan Gómez-Quiroz
Debora and David Guss
Ann and James Harithas
Luis Jiménez
Leandro Katz
Julio Le Parc
Antonio Martorell
Dug McIntyre
Cildo Meireles
Marta Minujín
Francisco and Laura Osio
Tola Osorio
César Paternosto
Liliana Porter
Mr. and Mrs. Harold E. Rayburn
Omar Rayo
Mr. and Mrs. Manuel Reyero
Ernst Rohner
Isabel Sabogal de Málaga
Emilio Sánchez
Akira and Louis Shorenstein
Rufino Silva
Dolores Smithies
José Sobrino Díeguez and Angela R. Sobrino
Jesús Rafael Soto
Mr. and Mrs. Eric Steinfeldt
Clara Diament Sujo
Cecilia de Torres
Nicolas Uriburu
Richard Weisman
Enrique Zañartu
Joaquín Zendejas and Family

The Bronx Museum of the Arts